Royce's Sailing Illustrated

The Best of All Sailing Worlds

Patrick M. Royce

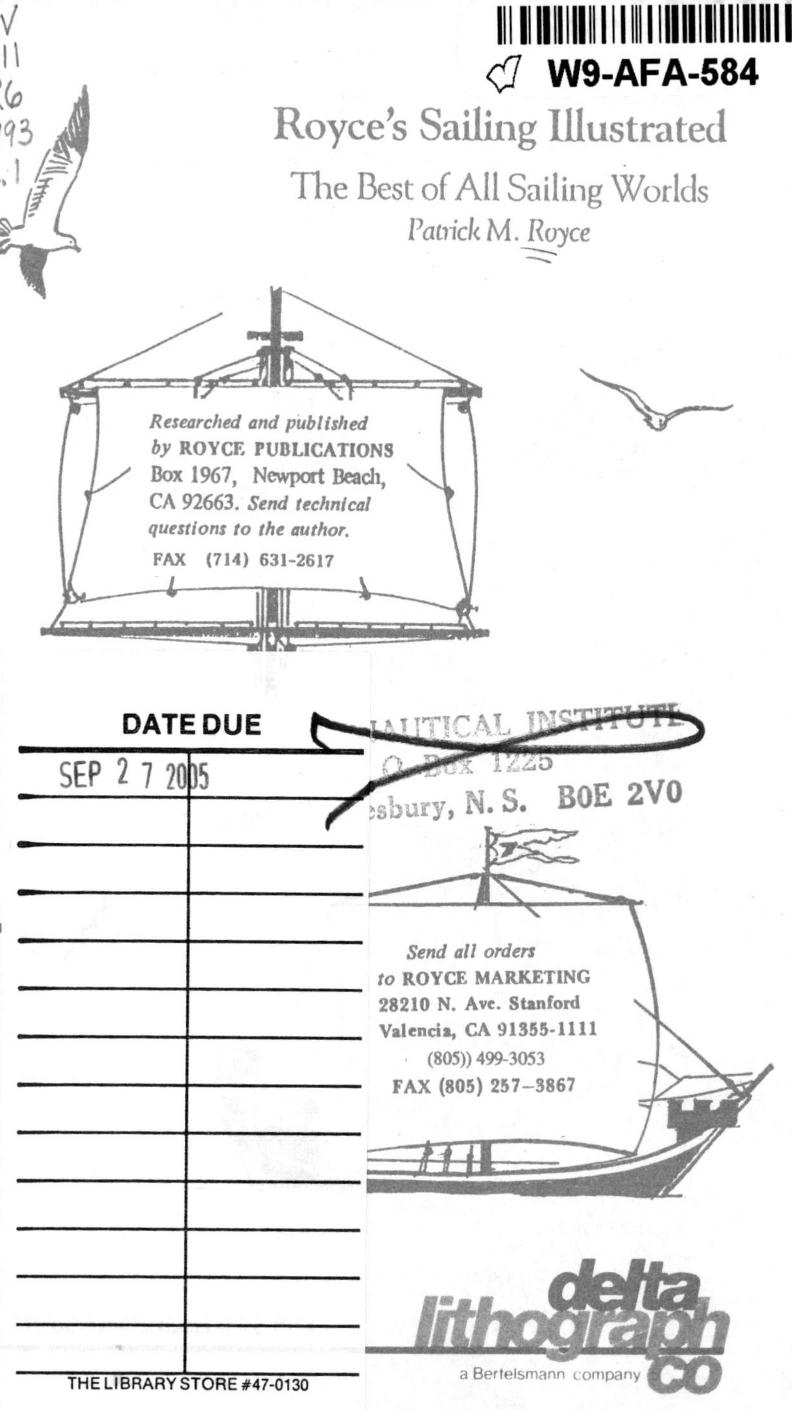

delta lithograph co
a Bertelsmann company

Snipe

Penguin

Int'l 14

Finn

Lightning

Flying Dutchman

Star

Soling

One Ten

5.5

5.5 meter

Naples Sabot

El Toro

CSK Catamaran

Hobie Cat

Thistle

Comet

Coronado 15

Pacific Cat

Kite

Laser

Windmill

Hampton

Flattie, Geary 18

Downeast 38

Newporter

Columbia Challenger

Peanut

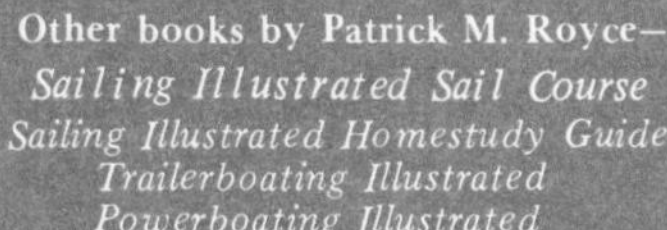
Other books by Patrick M. Royce–

Sailing Illustrated Sail Course
Sailing Illustrated Homestudy Guide
Trailerboating Illustrated
Powerboating Illustrated

SB

Shore Bird

Raven

Researched, Written, and Illustrated by Patrick M. Royce

Bird

National One-Design

Printed by Delta Lithograph Valencia, CA

ISBN 0-911284-00-1

Thunderbird

Lido 14

Sunfish
Fireball
Highlander
6
6 meter
12
12 meter
FJ
Flying Junior
Rhodes 19
Interlake
Shamrock
Sprite
Flying 15
Dyer Dhow
Turnabout
OK Dink
Catalina 22
Windrose
Tanzier 22
CCC
Cape Cod Cat
Mathilda
V
Venture
Wood Pussy
B 21
Balboa 21
B 23
Balboa 23
P
W W Potter
SJ 21
San Juan 21
M
Mariner
-R-B-
Rhodes Bantam
T
Tempest
Tech Dinghy
M
Montgomery
5 5
Five-O-Five
Bullseye (either)
Vixen
Y
Yingling
F
Force 5
Bear
Outlaw
Buckeye
Scorpion
W
Wanderer
Pelican
Scout
A
Albacore
W
Wayfarer
Hp
Hornpipe
Ck
Celebrity

C

Tornado Cat | Pioneer | Westsail | Maverick | Explorer

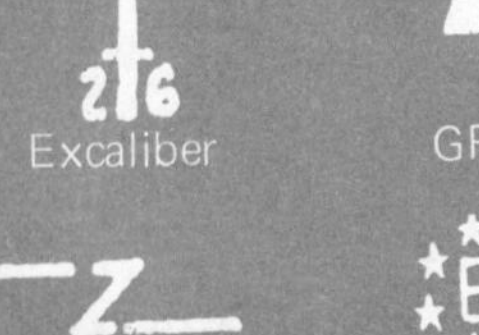

Excaliber | GP 14 | Inland Cat | Samuri | Seminole

Zephyr | Ensign | Ariel | Beetle Cat | Alberg 35

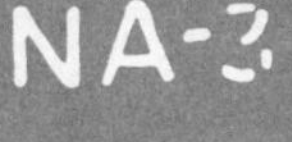

20′ Manui Kai | Etchells 22 | Naval Academy | cb Mercury | Electra

Four Twenty | Four Seventy | Folkboat, Firefly | Jolly Boat | Omega

Shark Cat | Rhodes 33 | Rebel | Rainbow | Dolphin

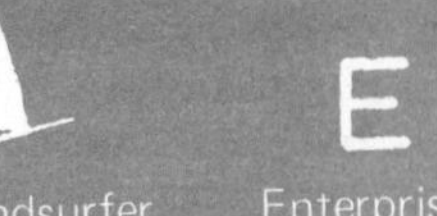

Signet-twin keel | Shields | 12′6″ Signet | Windsurfer | Enterprise

Malibu Outrigger | Cascade | Kings Cruiser | Snowbird S Class Spencer | Wildcat

D Swiftsure | Ghost | Melody | Fish | Lion

Cottontail

Butterfly

Moth, Skimmer

Day Sailer

Javelin

Jet 14

Sailing Illustrated is dedicated to my first mate Hilda, pal, and wife of 48 years marriage.

Mobjack

Flying Scott

Y Flyer, Yankee

Nipper

Arrow

Catfish

Kettenburg Series

Cal Series

Columbia Series

Islander Series

Holiday Series

Pearson Series

Vaurien

Pilot

Luder 16

Polar Bear
'Tail to Wind'

Tartan 27

Commander

Imperial
twin keel

Alacrity
twin keel

Kestral

Rawson Series

Hinkley Series

Pacific Class

Narrasketuck

Indian

Lapworth 36

Lehman
Interclub

Town Class

Whistler

Humbug

E

Personalize your copy of ***Sailing Illustrated.***

NAME *phone*

address *zip*

Welcome to the sport of sailing—
where scientific technologies
and art overlap in varying degrees.

HI!

Memories of a sailing reporter for almost forty years, seem endless from the sublime to the ridiculous, and in between. An idea that continually returns to help new sailors, was our first 20' sailboat, page 6. It decided after three weeks sailing from its Staten Island home port, the time came to humorously show who was the real boss. It wasn't a treasured memory with so many mistakes lumped into a few minutes in a nor'easter.

The next day my mate asked what I was thinking. "A Chinese proverb— an illustration is worth a thousand words, but what does that mean?" She grinned, "Why don't you *draw the sailing book* you were trying to find in bookstores and libraries?" We had ELEVEN sailing books in our small Brooklyn apartment, in a strange foreign language I could not understand as none had illustrations. So began the story of our new kind of illustrated sailing book... so the author wouldn't drown at an early age.

- The 1960's were the golden age of the new sailing world with fiberglass hulls, synthetic sails and rope. Most of this early development grew all around us in Newport Beach. For the first time many people with enough money in the bank could buy a minimum maintenance sailboat. And it was fun to teach full day sailing lessons to new sailors. one from as far away as Baharin in the Persian Gulf. What a learning experience for my growing book. With over 1600 full-day students, anything that could go wrong did, such as being port tacked by a big whale in our harbor jetty.

- *The 1970s were times of rapid local change.* While 90% of fiberglass sailboats had been built in Southern California with all our slips and anchorages full, all kinds of mergers and buy outs developed with boatbuilders moving nationwide. Confusion was everywhere as builders were trying to find what made a good cruising sailboat... sailboat prices skyrocketed as fiberglass and resins made from oil, were part of the petrochemical business.

- The 1980s were not pleasant for sailing as blisters began developing on most sailboat lines, with the pox randomly choosing its next victim on the assembly line without predictability. New sailboat prices took a major leap again as new fiberglass (composite) technologies moved in with endless new restrictive regulations for boatbuilders, especially in California.

- The 1990s entered with many small to major boatbuilders closing their doors. New sailors are facing a completely different sailing world with plusses and minuses. Our economy is way down. Instead of buying new sailboats, many are looking for new owners with a few years of water under their keel.Some are plush with installations added for the owner, to those in which the owner did few things right... with your best friend a good marine surveyor.

Our **100 page Sail Course** will help to systematically take you thru the complexities of sailing to understand the kind of sailboat that best fits your personality, while you pick up many new sailing skills on dry land, to avoid most of the hazards trying to learn these skills on the water underway

Newport Beach, California

Happy Sailing,

PAT M. ROYCE

How many popular one-design dinghies can you recognize?

We list a variety of one-design racing classifications and handicapping *(formula)* methods for your analysis–

- **One-design** sailboats are made to the same design specifications with owners joining their class association for racing and comradship.The **strict one-design classes** *(minimum evolution)* such as Laser allow no modifications to sail,rigging and hull shape.**Open one-design classes** *(controlled evolution)* provide self-improvement standards that will var from class to class.

- **Development one-design classes** *(controlled flexibility)* provide a greater rule flexibility.The Flying Dutchman Class has elastic deck and equipmen rules,with strict hull and mast rules.The International 14 rules are close to that of meter boat rules,as hull design changes can also be involved.

- **Olympic classes for 1984** were the Finn,Flying Dutchman 470,Soling, Star,and Tornado Cat.The **IYRU** *(International Yacht Racing Union)* which presides over international sailboat racing,has the responsibility for choosing racing classes for the next International Olympics.Letters on the sails in addition to numbers,indicate the owner's country,such as– *US–United States,MX–Mexico, K–United Kingdom.* We were pleased to find a wonderful 1911 design back in the 1984 Olympics...the Star.

- **Meter sailboats** are found in various meter sizes.They are designed to a mathematical formula with each meter craft different within the rules to hopefully produce a better performer...see page 259.

- **Handicap rating** is a theoretical,mathematical rated length/seconds per mile of a given rating.The purpose is to provide a method for various kinds,sizes,and lengths of sailboats to compete on a hopefully equal basis

- **OOAK Series** refer to *YACHTING'S One-of-a-Kind-Races*,so one-desi and other kinds of sailboats are able to compete with each other ever three years in five divisions.

- **Portsmouth Handicap** is the yardstick used for competition between one design classes that is parallel to OOAK one-design handicapping methods see page 258.

- **PHRF** *(Performance Handicap Rating Formula)* system is based on pa performance.It is a local handicap number which is represented in seconds-per mile of time allowance.

- **IOR** *(International Offshore Rule)* is vaguely similar to meter formula thinking with several modifications since its adoption.Length, beam, bulk,and sail areas are major factors involved...without weighing the hulls,see pages 76-81,and 259.

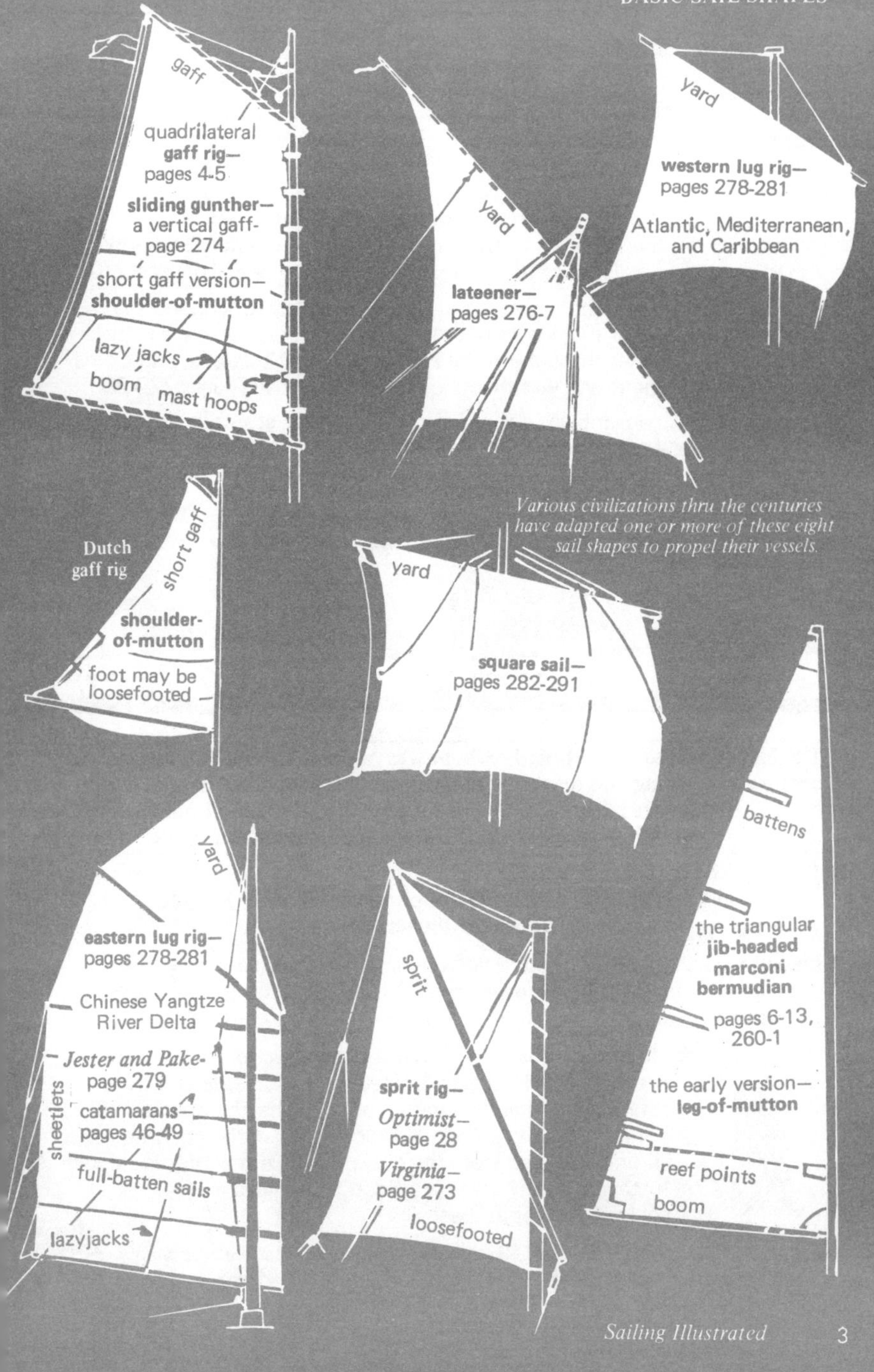

gaff
quadrilateral
gaff rig—
pages 4-5
sliding gunther—
a vertical gaff-
page 274
short gaff version—
shoulder-of-mutton
lazy jacks
boom
mast hoops

yard
lateener—
pages 276-7

yard
western lug rig—
pages 278-281
Atlantic, Mediterranean,
and Caribbean

Dutch
gaff rig
short gaff
shoulder-
of-mutton
foot may be
loosefooted

Various civilizations thru the centuries have adapted one or more of these eight sail shapes to propel their vessels.

yard
square sail—
pages 282-291

battens
the triangular
jib-headed
marconi
bermudian
pages 6-13,
260-1
the early version—
leg-of-mutton
reef points
boom

yard
eastern lug rig—
pages 278-281
Chinese Yangtze
River Delta
Jester and Pake-
page 279
catamarans-
pages 46-49
sheetlets
full-batten sails
lazyjacks

sprit
sprit rig—
Optimist—
page 28
Virginia—
page 273
loosefooted

the gaff rig

Commercial coastwise vessels preferred the quadrilateral or gaff rig to the square rig. The gaff rig became our standard fore and aft rig up to the marconi rig.

- **East coast.** Gaff-rigged schooners with or without topsails were ideal for coastal trading and fishing. Most of the wind was on the ocean's surface and often abeam. The shorter masts with minimum staying was ideal for economy of operation with minimum crews. Traditional gaff sails were laced to the gaff and boom, then secured to the mast with wooden hoops. The only 7 masted schooner, ***Thomas W. Lawson,*** required a crew of 16, page 270.
- **West coast.** 1850 saw the beginning of 3, 4, and 5 masted schooners and barkentines. Many of them with booms barely high enough to clear their cargo, carried lumber throughout the Pacific as far as Australia, and China where Oregon pine to 90' was first choice for junk masts, pages 278-280.
- **Scandalizing.** An advantage of the gaff rig in a sudden storm, is to release the peak halyard which reduces the sail area considerably. Scandalizing, page 148, is a temporary emergency measure to reduce excess wind pressure.

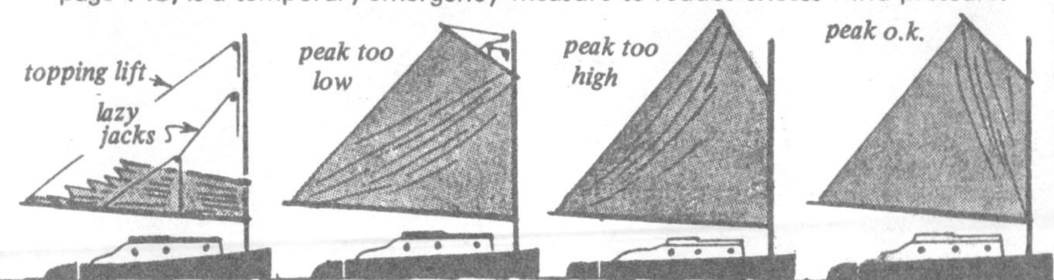

The New England **centerboard catboat** was popular around the turn of the century for fishing and oystering in shallow coastal waters. The mainsheet cockpit fitting was released, with the topping lift taking the boom out of the cockpit, providing an ideal area for handling lines, nets, or drags.

- **Fishing.** The gaff-rigged catboat was slower than other rigs. This was seldom a factor in the late 1800's, as other fishermen in the area going to market were also using similar gaff-rigged catboats.
- **Pleasure.** The long boom, round bottom, and barnyard rudder with a lot of weather helm downwind seems to limit it to a few hardy owners, while others prefer the simpler, easy to balance and reef marconi rig.
- **Modern catboat?** 1982 saw the introduction of the new Freedom 25 fin-keel catboat. It had an unstayed, fully-rotating, free-standing mast, and a full-batten mainsail, plus a spinnaker. It was designed for single-handed operation with all lines handled from the cockpit. Since the mast is stepped further forward than on a sloop, it provides more cockpit and cabin space.

Also read—**Gaff Rig** by John Leather, and **Catboats** by Stan Grayson-Int'l Marine Pub. Co., Camden, ME 04843.

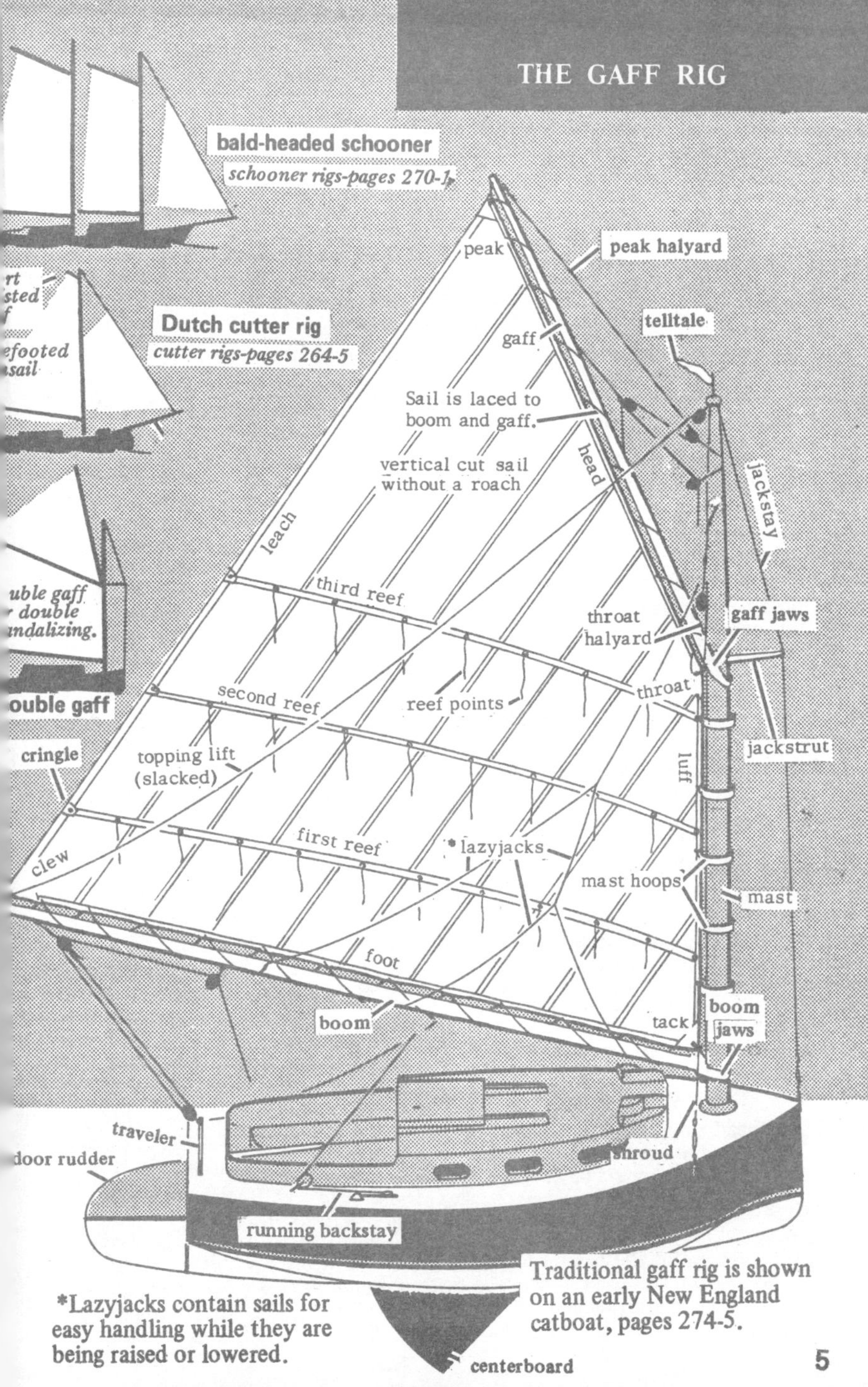

*Lazyjacks contain sails for easy handling while they are being raised or lowered.

Traditional gaff rig is shown on an early New England catboat, pages 274-5.

our 1949 sailboat

Our first sailboat bought in Staten Island taught us many lessons useful forty years later. Our first exposure to sailing on the north side of Long Island was hot and miserable with no wind. The south or ocean side however always had a breeze to move our 20′ sailboat. It proved to be the reason for the popularity of the tall inland sailing rigs in that area and the Chesapeake Bay, while the shorter gaff rig had been successful on the ocean.

- **Gaff rig ocean breezes.** The shorter gaff rigs on commercial vessels could use the undisturbed wind flow close to the ocean surface. A much taller mast was required on the Long Island Sound as useful wind was considerably above the water surface after passing over the land.

Heat thermal updrafts. They are caused by the sun's rays heating the land surface during the day, plus heat emissions from autos and manufacturing plants, plus disturbances from high hills.

- **Land breeze.** When most heat sources disappear and the land temperature is reduced, the ocean breeze stops, page 211. Around midnight when the land temperature drops below that of the ocean, a land breeze starts flowing oceanward. This seems on the average to last longer on the east coast, while disappearing earlier on the west coast as the westerlies move in.
- **The tall rig.** The triangular mainsail and jib commonly used in recreational sailing is called the **marconi** or **jib-headed rig,** called the **bermudian rig** by our British friends. As some tall early rigs were overstayed resembling Marconi wireless towers (Marconi didn't like sailing) the dubious nickname remains.
- **Today's sailing** may average 50% or more of the time upwind for short tacks with frequent tack changes. The marconi rig is excellent for this type of sailing due to its operation simplicity that eliminates the peak halyard and the running backstays required for the gaff rig. Running backstays are still standard equipment for 10 and 12 meter racers, many IOR and ULDB rigs.
- **Fractional-sloop rig.** Smaller sailboats including dinghies to smaller cabin sloops require the taller fractional sloop rig for coastal areas,inland lakes and rivers where the useful wind flow may be several feet above the water. Excellent examples we prefer for teaching are the Lido 14 and the early Lightning at right using the fractional rig with minimum rigging adjustments.
- **Three basic sloop rigs** are shown for comparison at right. ***If all hulls are identical, carrying the same total sail areas...*** the gaff-rigged sloop will have the shortest mast, with the fractional sloop rig, the tallest mast. The best compromise between for ocean cruising is the masthead sloop.
- **Masthead sloop rig.** We prefer it for ocean use on cabin sailboats 24′ and larger. It is a more basic rig, and is able to carry a larger jib for light breezes close to the water surface.
- **Coastwise cargo sailing schooners.** They successfully operated for many decades on both coasts under gaff rig with gaff tops' ls or yankees above and throughout the Pacific to Australia before steam took over. The evolution of sail design, our unique heritage since colonial days is a very fascinating history that is still underway.

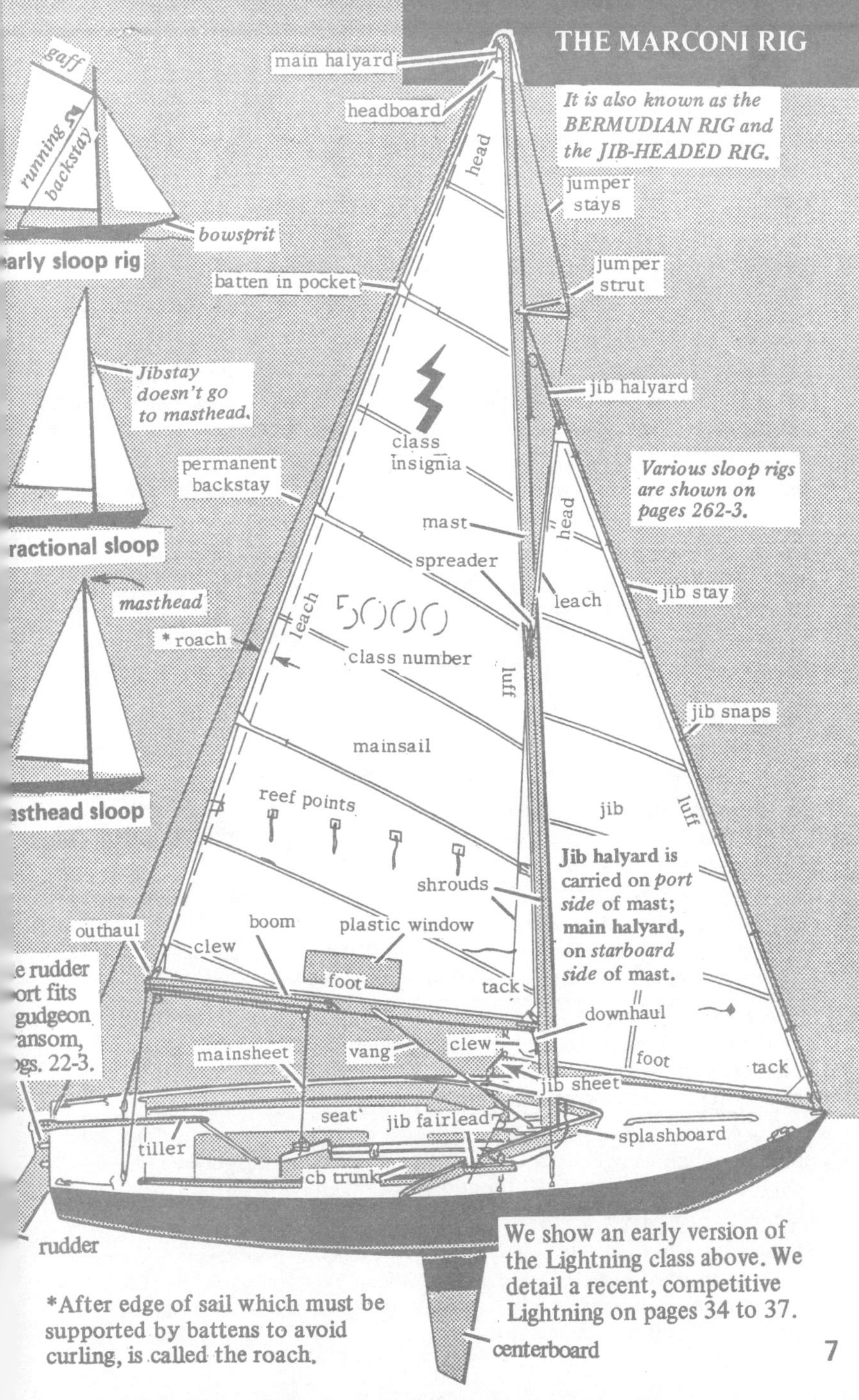

We show an early version of the Lightning class above. We detail a recent, competitive Lightning on pages 34 to 37.

*After edge of sail which must be supported by battens to avoid curling, is called the roach.

Silhouettes of various sail rigs above indicate the variety of sail designs in the U. S. today, the oldest the 1938 gaff-rig yawl *Iris.* It is interesting to find they were all successful for the purpose for which they were designed.

At right we define the basic sail rigs commonly seen today with page references for additional information.

We provide most exposure to monohulls in our book. We also include the Hobie 14 and 16 trampoline catamarans, the rigid-deck Pacific Cat catamaran, and the *Patty Cat II* catamaran 46' long with an excellent racing and cruising career of 25 years.

- **Catboat.** It has one sail regardless of size, also called the **Una rig** after *Una,* the first British catboat, not to be confused with "cat" for catamaran.
- **One mast.** The most common type seen today is the **sloop** carrying a jib and mainsail. Early sloops to 1950 without bowsprits were called **knockabouts.** I didn't like the term when preparing our first edition feeling a sloop Is a better term with or without a bowsprit, and the timing was right.
- **Sloop vs cutter.** When the jibstay or headstay goes to masthead or top of the mast it becomes a **masthead-sloop rig,** becoming a **fractional-sloop rig** if the jibstay coming from the bow doesn't go all the way to masthead. The basic *cutter rig* has one mast usually with two jibs or headsails, with the mast stepped further aft than on a sloop. For variables see page 262.
- **Two-masted** fore and aft rigged sailboats are recognized in the distance by the size relationship of their sails...then closer by the location of the **rudder post** having a tiller, wheel, or hydraulic steering.

The **yawl** has a small sail located aft of the rudder post, while the **ketch** has the rudder post aft of both masts, the after mast somewhat shorter than the forward mast. The **schooner** has two or more masts of equal height, or the after mast is taller. The schooner *Thomas W. Lawson* carried seven masts.

Aspect ratio–*the ratio of spread to chord of an airfoil or waterfoil.* The term is used by sailors to analyze sails, daggerboards, centerboards, and keels. We compare three sailboats with identical hulls and same total sail areas.with different **airfoil drive area** aspect ratios.

- **Low-aspect ratio short rigs.** Older cruising rigs tend to carry shorter masts and longer booms which are sufficient with winds on the surface of the ocean.This type of vessel can function upwind and downwind with this rig without using a spinnaker.
- **High-aspect ratio tall rigs.** IOR and ULDB single-purpose racers, pages 76 to 81, favor maximum length drive areas for upwind racing. The short-footed mainsail becomes a disadvantage for downwind sailing requiring a spinnaker for normal operation.

If 2, 3, 4, have identical hulls with same total sail area...
1
catboat
pgs.5-275
2
fractional sloop
pgs.6-7
Jibstay doesn't go to masthead.
3
masthead sloop
pgs.7-263
Jibstay goes to masthead.
4
cutter
pg. 265
It usually has two jibs.
yawl
main
pg.267
jib
5
rudder post between masts.
6
ketch
mizzen
main
pg.269
jib
rudder post aft both masts,fwd mast taller.
7
schooner
main
fores'l
pg.271
both masts same height, or after mast is taller
8
main
gaff
fors'l
jib
standard schooner rig
9
fisherman
main
stays'l
jib
staysail schooner
10
pgs.282–9
traditional rigs
If hulls 11, 12, and 13 are identical with same total sail area....
longest upwind drive area
11
low aspect ratio
12
medium aspect ratio
13
high aspect ratio

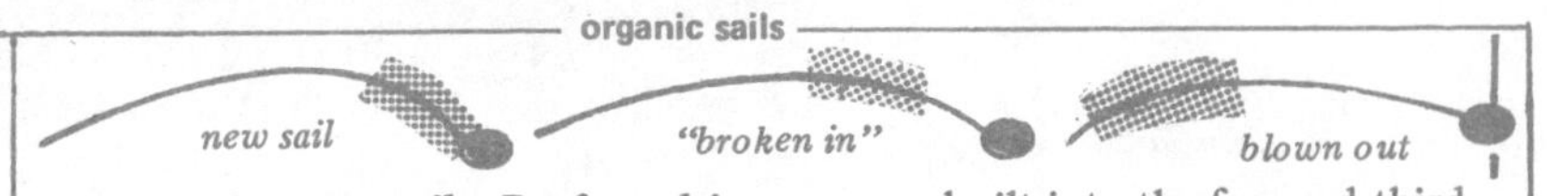

Canvas and cotton sails. *Draft or drive area* was built into the forward third of the sails up to 1960. After a few hours easy use the draft moved somewhat aft as shown with the sail *broken in.* After sufficient use, or raising a mainsail without a topping lift to support the heavy boom...the draft moved aft ending the mainsails useful upwind sailing ability.

- **Dacron sails.** Stronger, lighter, and more stable polyester fibers then began taking the lead thru the following years without a "break-in" period. Since the cloth was synthetic instead of organic canvas and cotton, damage from mildew ceased. The enemies of Dacron became chafe, and age-hardening due to the ultraviolet rays of the sun.
- **Mylar and Kevlar.** Testing began in the 1970's to find better ways to minimize sail-cloth stretch. Mylar, a plastic film with equal strength in all directions, found its main function was to form a laminated sandwich with Dacron. The laminated sail cloth gave excellent strength to weight ratio for light and medium air ***white gennies...***and the furling jib.
- **Mustard-colored Kevlar sails.** In the early days they were expensive with a short life, very brittle tending to break even when used in a laminated sandwich with other cloth.With tremendous sums spent on 12 meter cloth research, check sail magazines for the latest Kevlar information.
- **Warp-oriented sails.** Complex jigsaw panel cuts were developed in the early 1980's. They permitted sailmakers to lay out panels so that the forces are taken up by the warp, the strongest direction of the weave, see right, rather than with the bias or weakest direction of the weave.
- **Radial-cut sails.** The next step was to realign the warp threads of each panel, with the maximum strength warp fabric cloth designed to carry the greatest loads radiating from the clew, the tack, and the head.The combination of panel arrangement and sail cutting, produces sails that keep their shape longer and better than vertical or crosscut Dacron sails.
- **Cad-cam sailmaking** ***(computer–aided design, computer aided manufacturing).*** Some lofts use the computer in all phases of sailmaking. The computer helps to design the sails, then instructs cutting machines to cut the sails with precision. This improves the sailmakers output, and creates the ability to produce exact sail shapes for one-design competition.

We provide a short history of the art and science of sailmaking which has improved continuously in the past three decades with more complexity each year. Sails are lighter, stronger, more versatile and easier to handle for large apparent wind ranges than sails 2 to 3 years ago.

- **Sails today and tomorrow.** While the variables are considerable among endless numbers of sailmakers...the sails may be initially more expensive. Yet when compared to the longer expected life of new cloth materials and the puzzling array of jigsaw sail cuts, the cost may be similar to that of older sails having a shorter life expectancy. If you are interested in Chinese sail technology, turn to page 278.

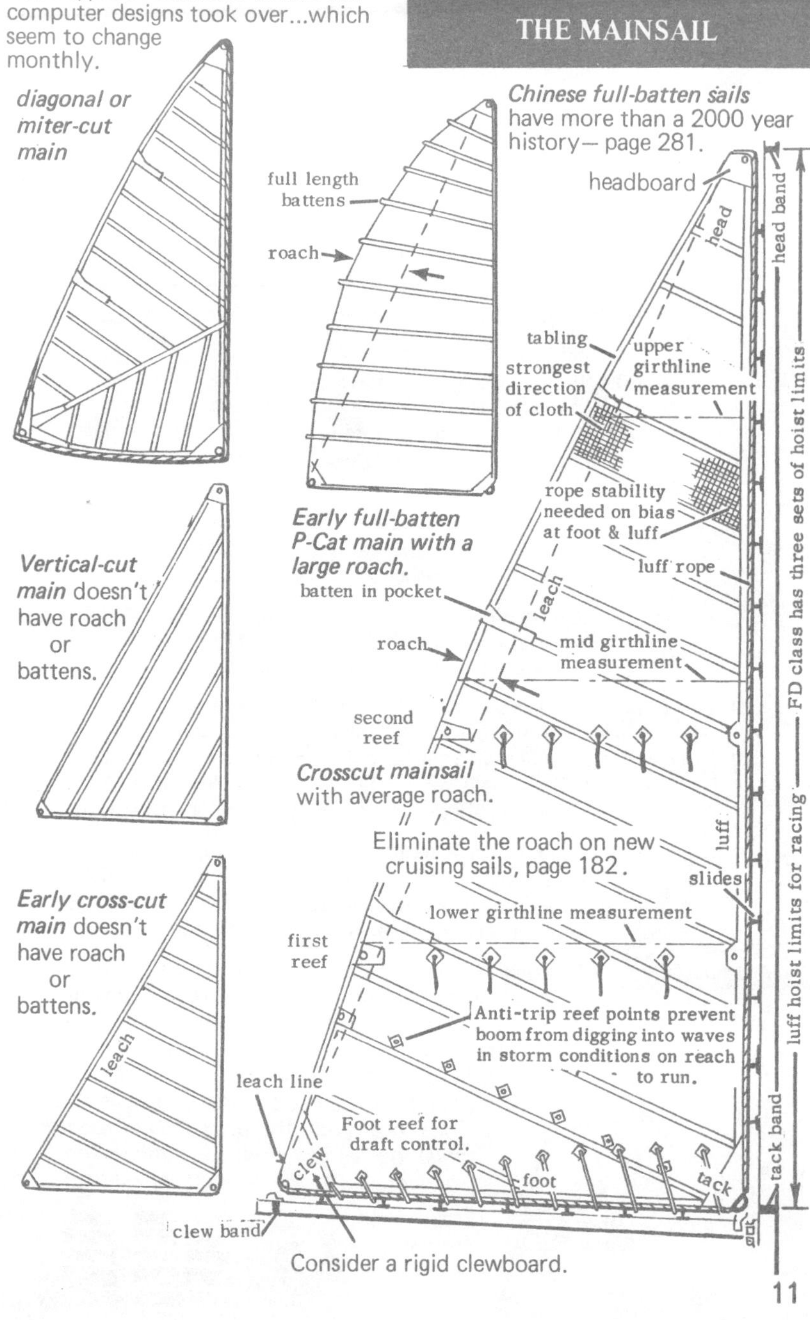
Basic types of mainsails before the computer designs took over...which seem to change monthly.
diagonal or miter-cut main
full length battens
roach
Chinese full-batten sails have more than a 2000 year history— page 281.
headboard
head
head band
tabling
upper girthline measurement
strongest direction of cloth
rope stability needed on bias at foot & luff
luff rope
Early full-batten P-Cat main with a large roach.
batten in pocket
leach
roach
mid girthline measurement
second reef
Vertical-cut main doesn't have roach or battens.
Crosscut mainsail with average roach.
Eliminate the roach on new cruising sails, page 182.
luff
slides
lower girthline measurement
first reef
Early cross-cut main doesn't have roach or battens.
leach
Anti-trip reef points prevent boom from digging into waves in storm conditions on reach to run.
leach line
Foot reef for draft control.
clew
foot
tack
clew band
Consider a rigid clewboard.
FD class has three sets of hoist limits
luff hoist limits for racing
tack band

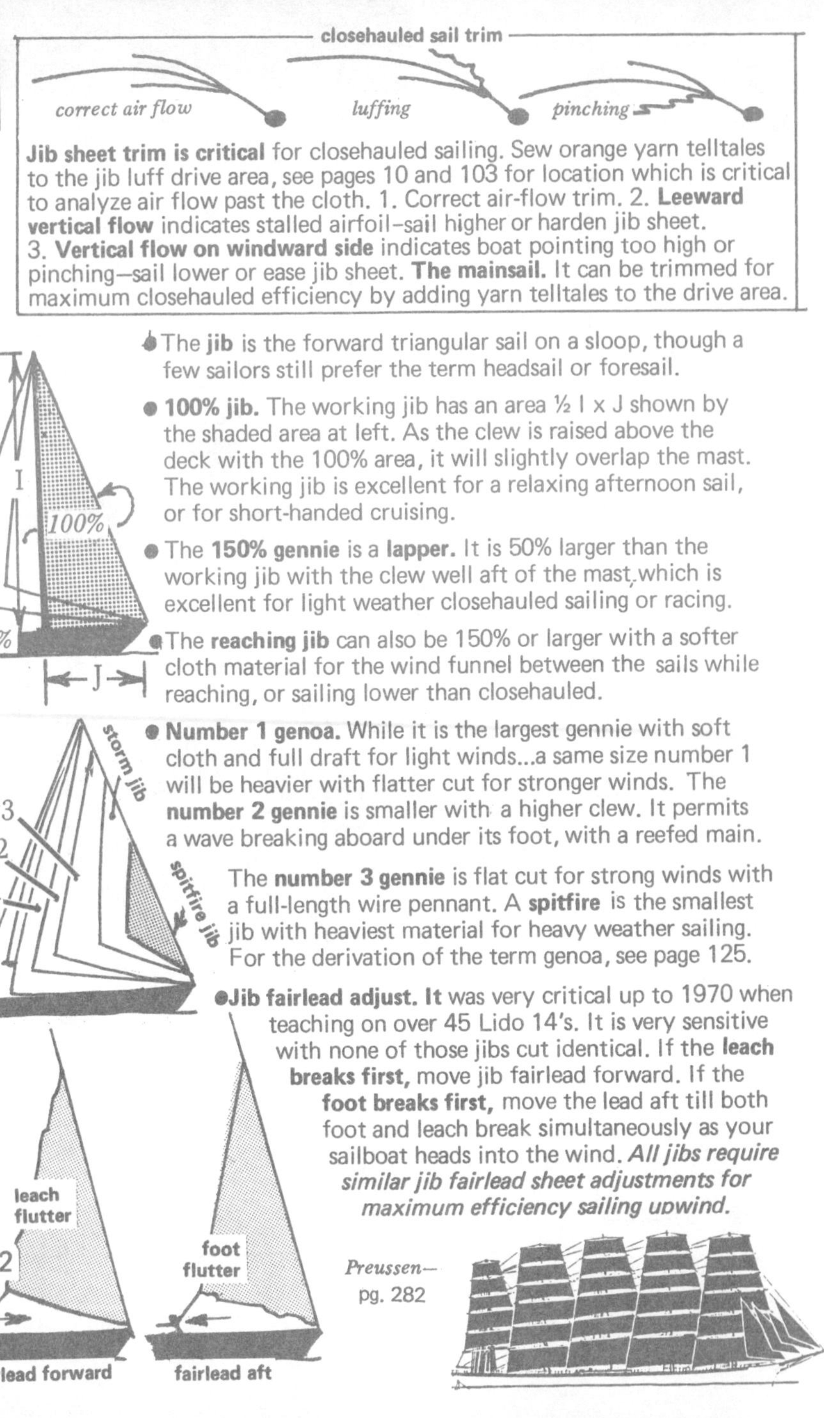

Jib sheet trim is critical for closehauled sailing. Sew orange yarn telltales to the jib luff drive area, see pages 10 and 103 for location which is critical to analyze air flow past the cloth. 1. Correct air-flow trim. 2. **Leeward vertical flow** indicates stalled airfoil–sail higher or harden jib sheet. 3. **Vertical flow on windward side** indicates boat pointing too high or pinching—sail lower or ease jib sheet. **The mainsail.** It can be trimmed for maximum closehauled efficiency by adding yarn telltales to the drive area.

- The **jib** is the forward triangular sail on a sloop, though a few sailors still prefer the term headsail or foresail.
- **100% jib.** The working jib has an area ½ I x J shown by the shaded area at left. As the clew is raised above the deck with the 100% area, it will slightly overlap the mast. The working jib is excellent for a relaxing afternoon sail, or for short-handed cruising.
- The **150% gennie** is a **lapper.** It is 50% larger than the working jib with the clew well aft of the mast, which is excellent for light weather closehauled sailing or racing.
- The **reaching jib** can also be 150% or larger with a softer cloth material for the wind funnel between the sails while reaching, or sailing lower than closehauled.
- **Number 1 genoa.** While it is the largest gennie with soft cloth and full draft for light winds...a same size number 1 will be heavier with flatter cut for stronger winds. The **number 2 gennie** is smaller with a higher clew. It permits a wave breaking aboard under its foot, with a reefed main.

The **number 3 gennie** is flat cut for strong winds with a full-length wire pennant. A **spitfire** is the smallest jib with heaviest material for heavy weather sailing. For the derivation of the term genoa, see page 125.

- **Jib fairlead adjust. It** was very critical up to 1970 when teaching on over 45 Lido 14's. It is very sensitive with none of those jibs cut identical. If the **leach breaks first,** move jib fairlead forward. If the **foot breaks first,** move the lead aft till both foot and leach break simultaneously as your sailboat heads into the wind. ***All jibs require similar jib fairlead sheet adjustments for maximum efficiency sailing upwind.***

Preussen—
pg. 282

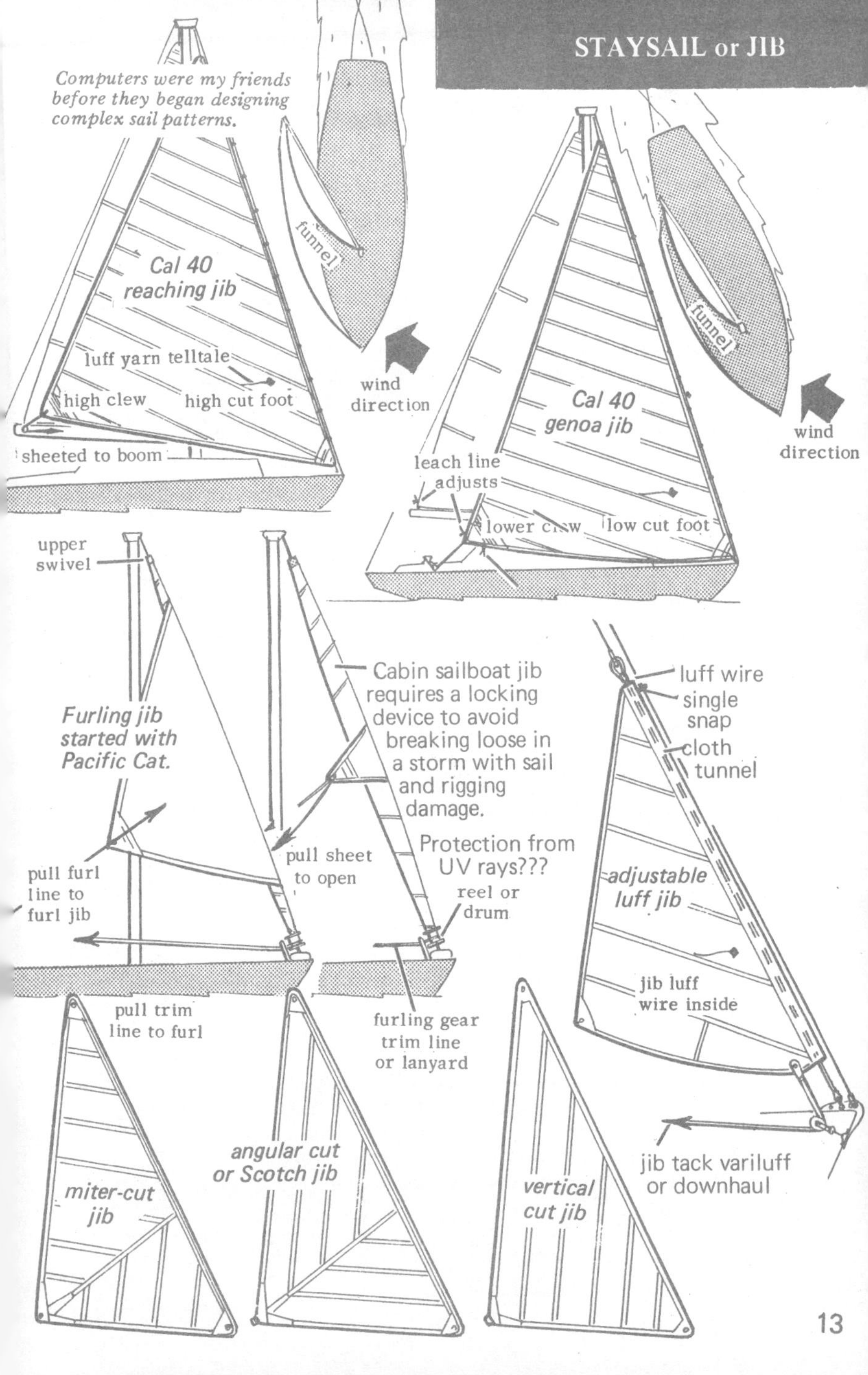
Computers were my friends before they began designing complex sail patterns.
Cal 40 reaching jib
funnel
luff yarn telltale
high clew
high cut foot
sheeted to boom
wind direction
Cal 40 genoa jib
funnel
wind direction
leach line adjusts
lower clew
low cut foot
upper swivel
Furling jib started with Pacific Cat.
pull furl line to furl jib
pull sheet to open
Cabin sailboat jib requires a locking device to avoid breaking loose in a storm with sail and rigging damage.
Protection from UV rays???
reel or drum
pull trim line to furl
furling gear trim line or lanyard
luff wire
single snap
cloth tunnel
adjustable luff jib
jib luff wire inside
jib tack variluff or downhaul
miter-cut jib
angular cut or Scotch jib
vertical cut jib

carvel-planked hull

clinker-built hull

- **Cargo ballast.** Commercial sailing vessels even before the days of the Phoenicians depended on cargo as internal ballast for weight stability affecting hull trim and performance. The heavier goods in outgoing cargo were placed on the bottom, and lighter cargo went on top. ***Dunnage*** was placed on the top layer consisting of boards, wooden blocks, canvas, etc., to prevent the cargo from shifting in heavy weather. Cargo sailing vessels on Manhattan's East River were often tied between pilings when unloading. Capsizing at the dock otherwise might occur as the empty cargo sailing vessels could become top heavy.
- **In ballast.** If cargo wasn't available on the return trip, gravel, large stones, iron, or lead was required for ballast to prevent an upset. It couldn't be stowed too high, nor too far aft or forward as the vessel had to float at its correct depth underway without the ballast shifting in heavy weather.
- **Warship ballast.** They required internal ballast with rectangular iron pigs up to 300 lbs. each. These were laid fore and aft next to the keelson to provide weight stability...with ***H.M.S. Victory,*** pg. 286, having a permanent list to starboard.
- **External keel ballast.** It is used today for our sailing to provide weight stability or upset resistance. The newcomer may find a keel sailboat somewhat tippy at the dock as it has little ***initial stability*** in an upright position. The more a keel sailboat heels underway, the greater becomes the ***ultimate stability*** force of the keel to counteract and resist further heel angle.
- **Wine-glass section.** Majority of ocean racing and cruising sailboat hulls have smooth surfaces called ***carvel planking*** if made of wood, page 73, to make minimum fuss as they go thru the water. A keel hull with a hard chine will pound more. On the other side of the issue is the 60' ***Ragtime*** with an excellent west coast racing record... it has a hard chine hull.

  A wooden ***clinker-built hull*** may be useful for dinghies, but seems questionable for cabin sailboats. Resistance developing from the overlapping planks going thru the water increases the drag, which limits upper hull speed. When leaks develop between the planks and caulking is used...the leaks may increase as the caulking swells, which is the purpose of caulking.
- **Keel shapes AND personalities.** We show 13 types on page 19, each having its own individual characteristics. What we found later in our research after assembling them into the full sequence showing how they relate to each other, was to realize they had distinct personalities. This becomes a major factor when buying a keel sailboat which will be ideal if it fits your personality. The choice can be disastrous if, for example, a competitive ULDB personality buys a replica of ***Spray.*** We found only 2 of 5 sailing students had bought the right boat for their personality the first time, improving to 4 out of 5 on their second sailboat.

LEVERAGE STABILITY

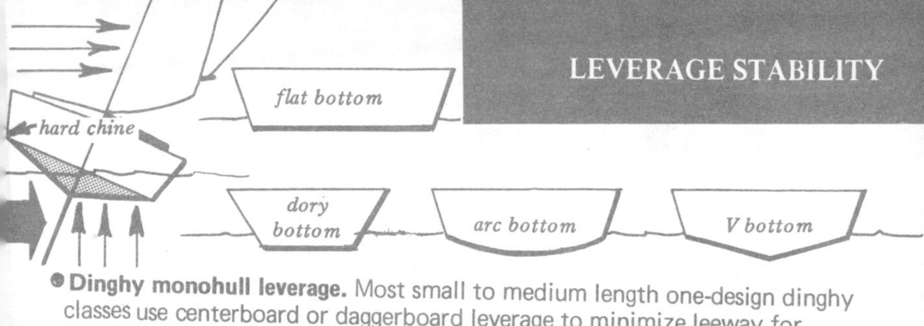

- **Dinghy monohull leverage.** Most small to medium length one-design dinghy classes use centerboard or daggerboard leverage to minimize leeway for upwind sailing.
- **Hard-chine hull leverage.** Most small to medium-length dinghies prefer the hard chine for stability. Arc or V-bottom hulls will have more initial resistance or stability to heel than a wine-glass hull. These hard-chine hull shapes also reduce rolling tendencies for racing downwind than dinghies with round bottoms. Hard chine dinghy hulls provide more resistance to upset when climbing aboard at the dock.
- **Board boat stability is neutralized** when dinghy heel passes 40 to 50 degrees. It reaches a point at which the dinghy rapidly becomes more stable in an upset position. Install an **inclinometer** with clearly marked heel limits as a warning to release the main sheet...to avoid that ***big splash.***
- **High initial multihull leverage stability**—1960-1975 time frame. Wide beam to length ratio provides tremendous initial resistance to capsize. It provides an additional advantage to keep multihull weight to a minimum.
- **Large catamarans.** It was fun cruising and racing on the Rudy Choy designed ***Patty Cat II, Allez Cat, Antigony, Seasmoke,*** and others. Their high initial stability with assymetrical hulls, and minimum underwater parasitic drag on long, lean displacement hulls, permitted better use of the available wind pressure than do similar length monohulls and trimarans. ***Patty Cat II*** page 83,easily reached and held 20 knots several times I was aboard.
- Some backyard built **early trimarans** seemed accidents looking for places to happen due to questionable promotion methods...without documented records by panels of impartial judges. A 1966 Hawaiian Multihull Transpac provided our challenge with the Ensenada Race a warmup...only the new 39'5" ***Tri Star*** appeared. I spent nine full days aboard during the Ensenada Race preparing it for the Transpac, the trimaran research I was looking for. Page 128 describes how this tri slightly outpointed and outfooted similar length monohulls...becoming a downwind powerhouse in a good wind.

▲ Well designed, adequately built monohulls, catamarans, AND trimarans **are equally efficient concepts in different worlds.** The responsibility then becomes that of the owner to understand the craft he chooses, so he can operate it efficiently to the best of its potentials.

outrigger catamaran trimaran

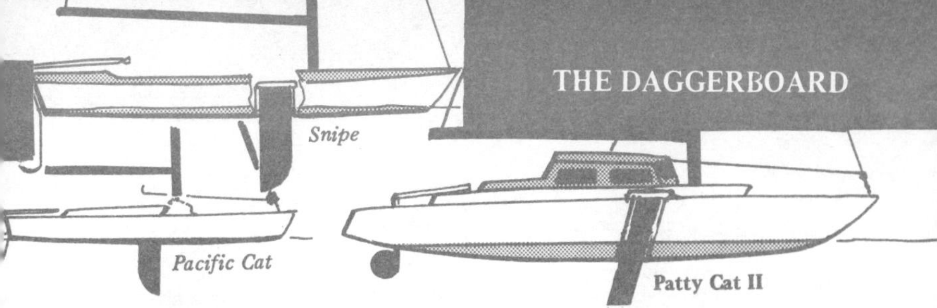

- **The advantage.** The Snipe Class provided a choice so owners could race a centerboard or daggerboard hull. Around 1960 the daggerboard with the better board aspect ratio could point higher and foot faster than a centerboard Snipe. Will your one-design class rules permit the longer edge of your daggerboard as shown above to become the leading edge? This can also improve the pointing and footing ability of racing dinghies.
- **Daggerboard well.** It requires less cockpit space than a centerboard well, also decreasing the turbulence of the longer underwater centerboard slot. The daggerboards on the 44' ***Pattycat II*** above and on page 83, are raised out of the way for protection in their own compartments.
- **Disadvantages.** If the daggerboard is removed from the well of a dinghy racing downwind, the board becomes a clumsy, wet object to trip over. If a dinghy with the board down hits a solid underwater object, damage can be caused to the daggerboard and well structure.

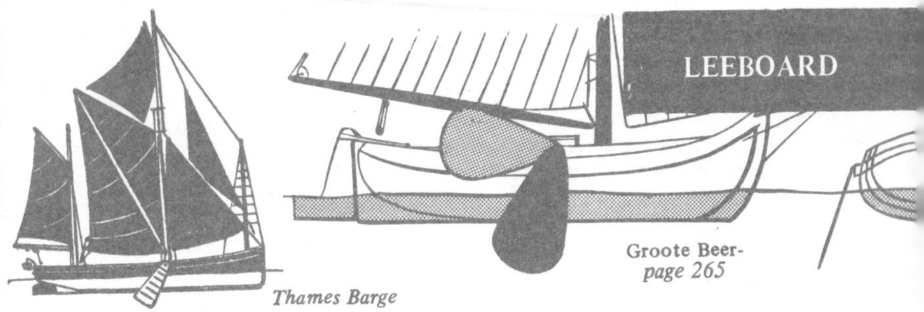

- **Leeboards** pivot down the leeward side to reduce leeway when sailing upwind with the Naples Sabot, page 29, popular in Southern California.
- **European cargo sailing vessels.** Leeboards are used in areas with large tidal ranges, an example being the ***Thames Barge,*** page 270.They have to settle down hard on their bottoms occasionally on mud flats or marshes at low tide with the leeboards raised.
- **Yangtze-estuary junks.** Some of these flat bottom cargo-carrying junks also prefer lee boards. They are raised as the vessels run up on a sandy beach to unload cargo. Where sailing efficiency is a more important factor for junks in shallow water, the centerboard is preferred.

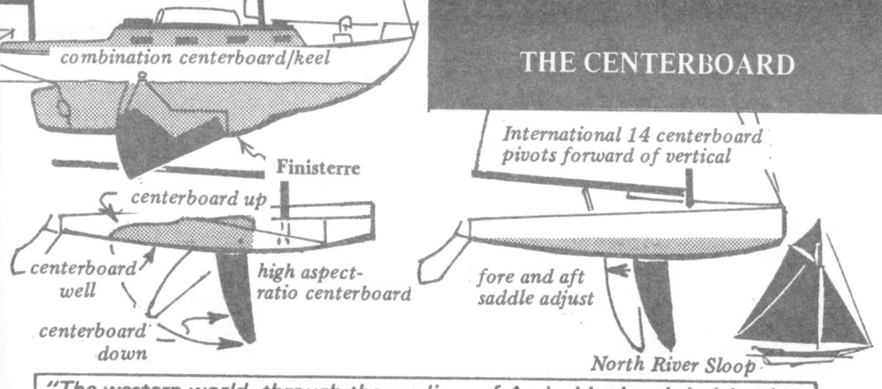

"The western world, through the medium of Arab shipping, is indebted to China for the lee-board, the centre-board, the balanced and slotted rudder, the windlass, and above all, the watertight compartment, unknown in the Mediterranean at that time"—**The Junks & Sampans of the Yangtze,** G.R.G. Worcester. Naval Institute Press, address page 278.

- **Pivoting centerboard.** It was introduced by early Dutch settlers along the Hudson River on their *inland sloep,*page 264. This was to help extend their trading in the shallow waters above Newberg which was the limit of their keel sloops. Such was the beginning of the large **North River Sloops.**
- **Centerboard advantages.** When in the down position for upwind sailing to reduce leeway,if the board hits a solid object, the centerboard may pivot up into its trunk with minimum damage. For downwind sailing, raise the centerboard into its trunk to minimize drag, which increases the speed.
- **Combination centerboard/keel.** It is used in the yawl *Finisterre,* pages 66-9, to reduce draft and hull weight. This permits it to sail or anchor in shallower water than an identical yawl with a deeper fixed keel.

  The centerboard is down all the way when beating to windward in a light breeze. As the wind increases, the centerboard is raised sufficiently to trim the rudder to reduce weather helm rudder drag, pages 132-135.
- **International 14.** This is a development class, the proving grounds to test new ideas since the turn of the century. The long slim centerboard in the down position pivots slightly forward of vertical. This provides a high aspect ratio leverage with minimum parasitic drag. As the wind keeps increasing a **saddle** rigging arrangement is used, page 250. This permits fore and aft centerboard trim to minimize weather helm...without raising the centerboard.
- **Centerboard/keel sloop AND yawl?** The 45′ *Salty Tiger* had such an unusual idea. The centerboard pivot point could move six feet to trim out weather helm, as well as the ability to change from a sloop to yawl rig, or visa versa.

Note— we provide numerous references to products and manufacturers to help readers. This does not indicate implied nor paid-for advertising but products we have used thru the years. *Warning*— some established products may have been taken over by later organizations with different standards. Study the manufacturers recommendations, obtain as much technical information as possible, and hang onto your warrantees for your protection.

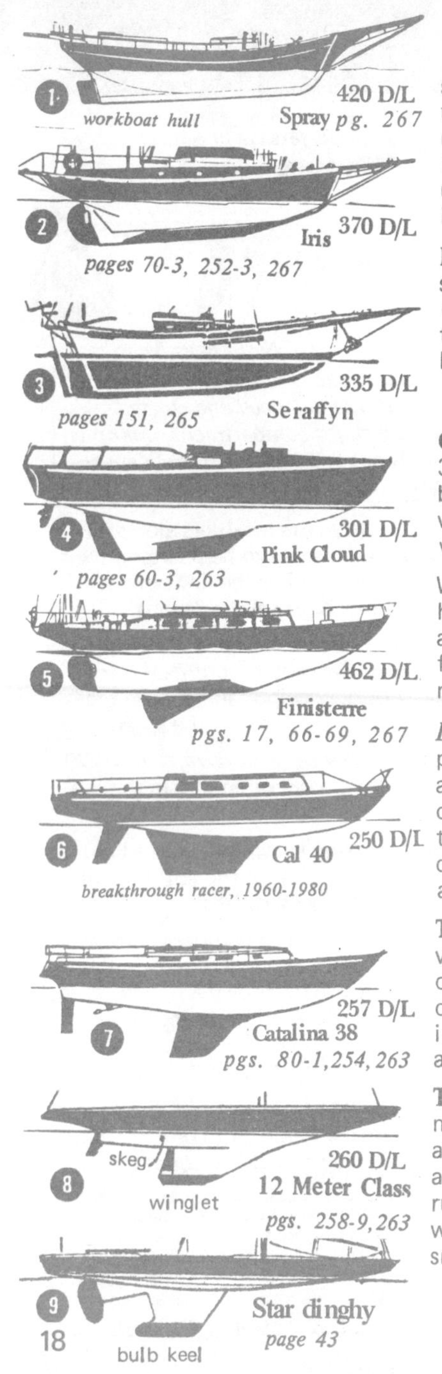

Keels and rudders have a variety of shapes. A major function is to provide **ultimate stability,** with resistance to upset, which increases with heel angle. If hull doesn't stop at 90 degrees during upset, it will roll 360 degrees to right itself without sinking.

Directional stability is ability for a sailboat with correct keel and rudder design, plus correct sail trim and weight trim, to sail itself for long periods with little rudder correction.

keel-mounted rudders

Cargo-carrying capacity. Hulls 1, 2, and 3, are old designs with *Spray* originally built 300 years ago. All are designed with long keels to sail long distances with self-steering ability.

While hull 3 is designed to sail for many hours without changing course, hull 4, a similar length has a **cutaway forefoot** for rapid course changes sailing thru tigh moorings, with easier docking potentials

***Finnisterre's* centerboard/keel,** pgs. 66-9 permitted it to sail in shallower water and anchor further inshore than deep-ke competitors. The Dutch developed it wi their North River Sloop, page 263, to carry cargo and passengers in the shallow areas of the Hudson River to Albany.

The winged keel introduced in the U.S. vs Australian 12 meter races, seems an outgrowth of the 1911 Star **bulb keel** dinghy design. The low-placed ballast increased leverage resistance to upset, pl ability to carry more sail than the fin k

Twin rudders? The single-purpose 12 meter racer steering ability begins with a long skeg to minimize size and drag of aft-steering rudder. The keel-mounted rudder trims out the weather helm which would be a problem otherwise with the small aft steering rudder.

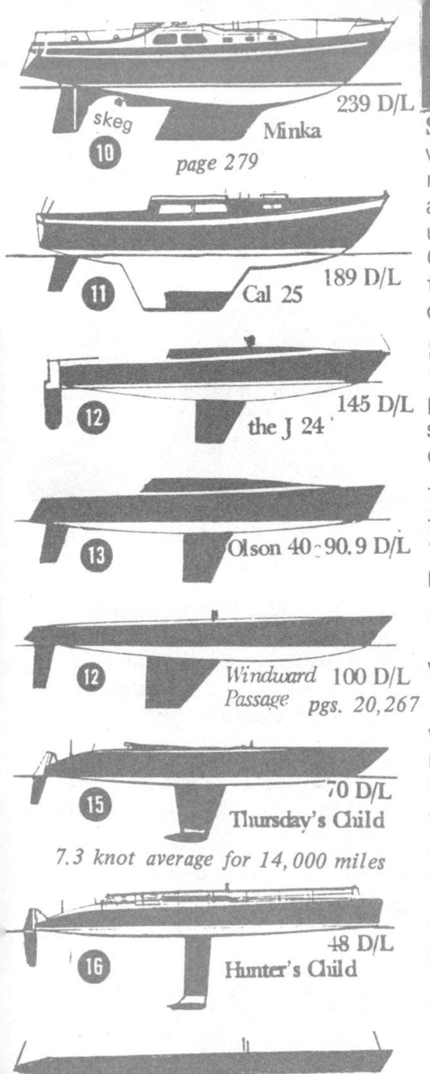

Sailing Illustrated

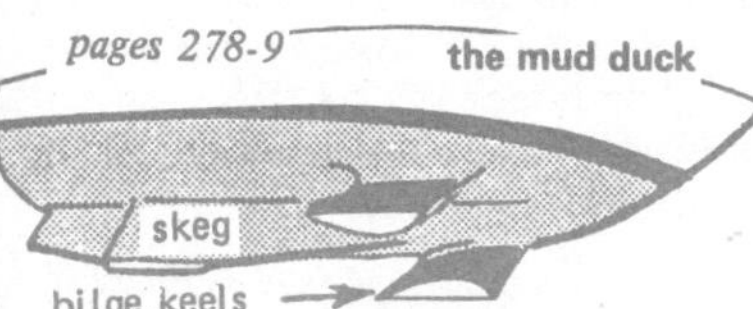

SEVENTEEN KEELS

Separate fin keel/spade rudder. Cal 40 was the leader for 20 years, breaking more racing records worldwide than any one-design racer. The Catalina 30 used for over ten years with the Congressional Cup Series, has a shorter fin keel, with thinner rudder blade carried further aft for leverage.

Skeg. It protects the rudder on hull 10 from deadheads, grounding, and porpoises. While the fully-exposed spade rudder has better leverage, it doesn't have such built-in protection.

The Cal 25 appearing in 1965, proved the all time popular racing/cruiser 'pocket' cruiser with excellent performance in strong winds.

Stern-mounted rudder. The J 24 was lighter and leaner for overnight racing with minimum creature comforts below.

The first ULDB maxi launched 1968, was the ***Windward Passage.*** It won more races worldwide than any large racer in history.

The 1980's saw a new breed of lean ocean racers with hull 15 breaking the square rig racing record from New York to San Francisco. Hull 16 is a leaner, lighter world racer using water ballast for upwind sailing, which was pumped to the other side coming about. Much water weight can be pumped overboard sailing downwind.

America's Cup Class. The lean new 75 footer is the latest all-out racer.

British **mud duck** settles upright on its 3-point suspension bottom at low tide.

Swing-keel lock is required in knock-down to prevent centerboard pivoting up into its well compounding problem.

A century of blue-water hulls.

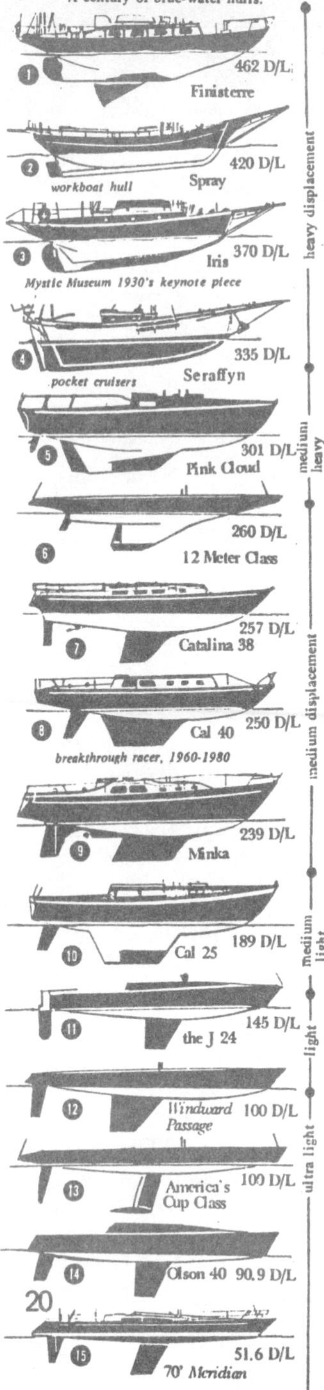

Many thanks to naval architect Robert Perry for his help to numerically analyze and evaluate cabin sailboats of varying lengths.

Since the racing personality will seldom be happy with *Spray*, and the cruising personality with an Olson 40, you begin to understand the importance of choosing the D/L ratio of a sailboat that best matches your personality, though shorter or longer with the same D/L rati

We have found in past experience that probably a third of owners make a good choice for their first sailboat without first analyzing the **D/L or displacement to length ratio.** Many rely on the local salesmans personality, limited to boats he has in stock, and/or advertising slogans, may have much to be desired.

The IOR D/L ratio accurately predicts racing potentials though still on the drawing board, a European idea introduced to the U.S. in 1970.

320 and above-- heavy displacement
280 to 320-- medium heavy displacement
220 to 280-- medium displacement
160 to 220-- medium-light displacement
110 to 160-- light displacement
110 and below-- ultra-light displacement

Age is an important factor. Younger sailors are more interested in competition performance, wi less creature comforts below.

By middle age many sailors become interested in slower craft with more cargo-carrying capacit Many owners face ample competition to make a living, with creature comforts now more import

It has been fascinating to sail on several of the sailboats at left, plus others in the same D/L rat some smaller, and others longer. All range from good to excellent if well built, and if used, are they well maintained? Sailing ain't like Detroit where nothing is older than last years auto model

ULDB big dinghy sleds proved a whole new outlook on sailing beginning around 1980. The ULDB home is Santa Cruz, south of San Franci an outgrowth of the 1970 505 dinghy world competition. The honor of the first maxi ULD goes to *Windward Passage* launched 1968, winni more races worldwide than any competitor.

Sailing Illustrated

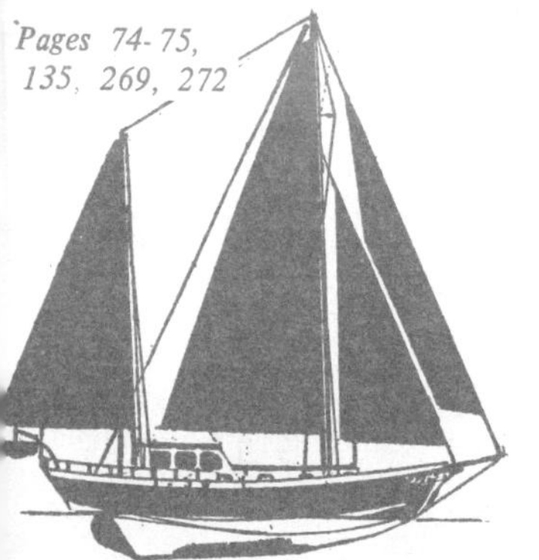

40' Newporter Ketch

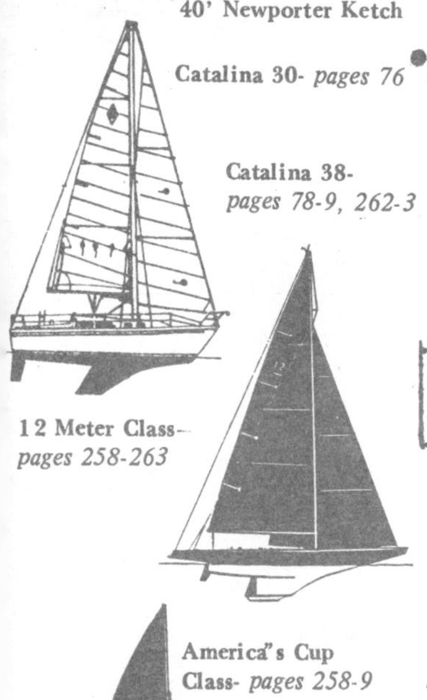

Catalina 30- pages 76

Catalina 38- pages 78-9, 262-3

12 Meter Class- pages 258-263

America's Cup Class- pages 258-9

Motorsailers are under rigged. The Newporter ketch carries an 85% sail rig to operate under engine power in light winds, reaching hull speed in stronger winds than sailboats with full sail rigs.

The most important performance ratios are the D/L on the left page, and SA/D, sail area/displacement ratios below. A sailboat with two ratios–

- ***15.2 SA/D ratio***– is the normal sail rig of a Catalina 30 with a 291 D/L ratio.
- ***17.2 SA/D ratio***– is the tall sail rig of a Catalina 30 with a 291 D/L ratio, a mast almost 2' taller for lighter winds.

Cruising sailboat ratios–

12.97– Nicolson 35	413 D/L
14.4– Crealock 37	334 D/L
15.04– 22' Falmouth Cutter	365 D/L
15.5– Crealock 34	320 D/L
15.73– Sou'wester 42	298 D/L

16.0 SA/D ratio–indicates a fast offshore cruiser, good for light winds, and normal heavy weather reefing, wind scale, pg. 137.

16.02– 28' Bristol Channel Cutter	345 D/L
16.2– Catalina 38	257 D/L
16.22– Nicholson 58	242 D/L
16.5– Alden 44	missing
17.0– Shannon 28	346 D/L
18.0– Shannon 43 ketch rig	250 D/L
18.9– Sweden Yachts 41	236 D/L
21.93– 40' Beneteau 404	183.23 D/L
24.1– Swan 43	230 D/L

The big dinghies–

The 12 meter one-purpose class afternoon racer– ***19.6 SA/D*** has a ***260 D/L.*** with an 8½ story tall mast.

The America's Cup Class, another afternoon racer– ***42 SA/D*** has a ***100 D/L***, with an 11 story tall mast. While the AC Class has 2000 more square feet of sail, the 12 meter is 20,000 lbs. heavier, pages 258-259.

Your complex sailing language.

The international sailing language exists in a unique world all by itself. It is a functional, colorful, spoken language developed from technical **slang terms** which have withstood the test of time, some possibly with a thousand year heritage. Rather than being developed by scholars, the language was passed on by word of mouth by sailors, few with any basic schooling. This becomes a challenge for writers trying to put the pieces together recording it in the printed word...beginning with halyard spelled three ways by various authors.

The sailing vocabulary. The best way we can help new sailors is with the idea a picture is worth a thousand words. Our emphasis is on visual terms to teach the functional parts of beach boats, dinghies, and cabin sailboats, then help you understand the reason for operational sailing terms with illustrations.

As you expand this knowledge you will enjoy talking to sailors, plus reading sailing magazines and excellent sailing books from Columbus to Slocum and Horatio Hornblower, plus many present day cruising books.

- **Beach boats and dinghies.** We begin with these two groups which vary considerably across the U.S. and worldwide. Two of the largest in numbers are the **Sunfish** which we see a few in our harbor, while at time of writing we have not seen an **Optimist.**
- **Naples Sabot.** Southern California has large fleets of them, page 29, with two of our own. A similar version in Northern California is the daggerboard **El Toro.** They are good basic dinghies for ages 9 to 12 as hardware can be installed with minimum tools...screwdrivers, wrenches, and a drill.
- **Penguin.** While junior dinghy classes vary considerably and justifiably so around the U.S., we go to the Chesapeake bay, home of the Penguin.They are built by owners, or as a yacht club group project with endless hardware variables. We show a rare fiberglass Penguin on page 28 to which we added the most advanced hardware. The class measurer said it was legal, then replied with a wry grin,"But don't expect to find one rigged that way".
- **Beach boats.** Take time to study their controls and cockpit layouts on pages 24, 25, and 26. With a little preparation you may climb into any of them, make last minute adjustments, then enjoy a spirited sail.
- **Olympic Finn** and the **International 14** are classics we have frozen in time which have been moved to pages 248-251. During one of our numerous revisions it became more practical to move these specialized dinghies to detail more beach boats.
- We never intended to detail a **Windsurfer,** but...

Our sailboat is docked across the bay from a beach where endless board boats without rudders are launched 365 days of the year, even in storms. Added to this are classes for beginners providing endless entertainment, punctuated by loud splashes. If you want to operate a rudderless sailing surfboard, study pages 80 and 81 of our ***Homestudy Guide.***

While this kind of sailing still doesn't make sense, we hope some of their owners may eventually want to operate a real sailboat. I've never been on one of those critters, and furthermore...

Optimist Dink

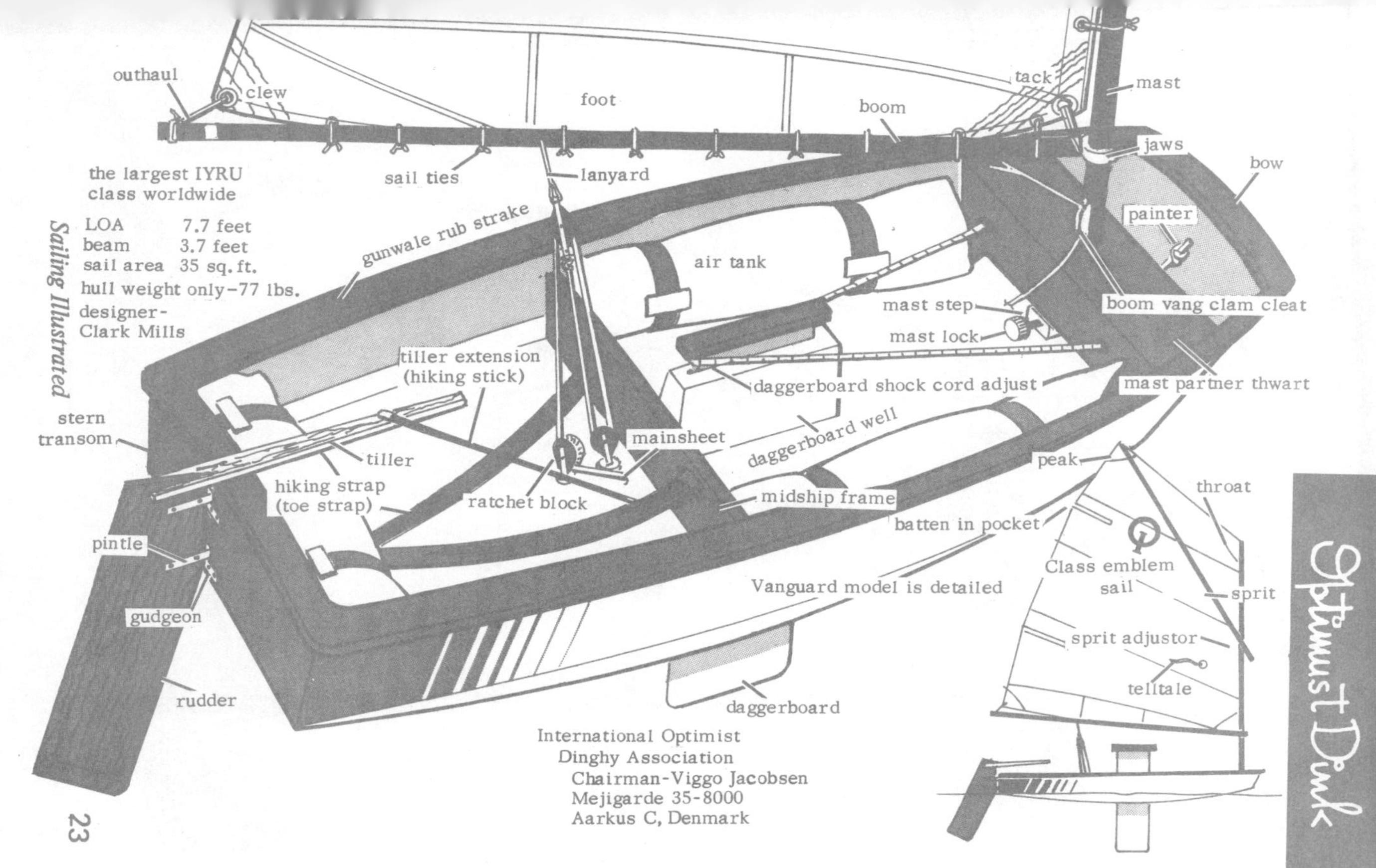

the largest IYRU
class worldwide

LOA	7.7 feet
beam	3.7 feet
sail area	35 sq. ft.

hull weight only–77 lbs.
designer-
Clark Mills

Sailing Illustrated

International Optimist
Dinghy Association
Chairman-Viggo Jacobsen
Mejigarde 35-8000
Aarkus C, Denmark

Force 5

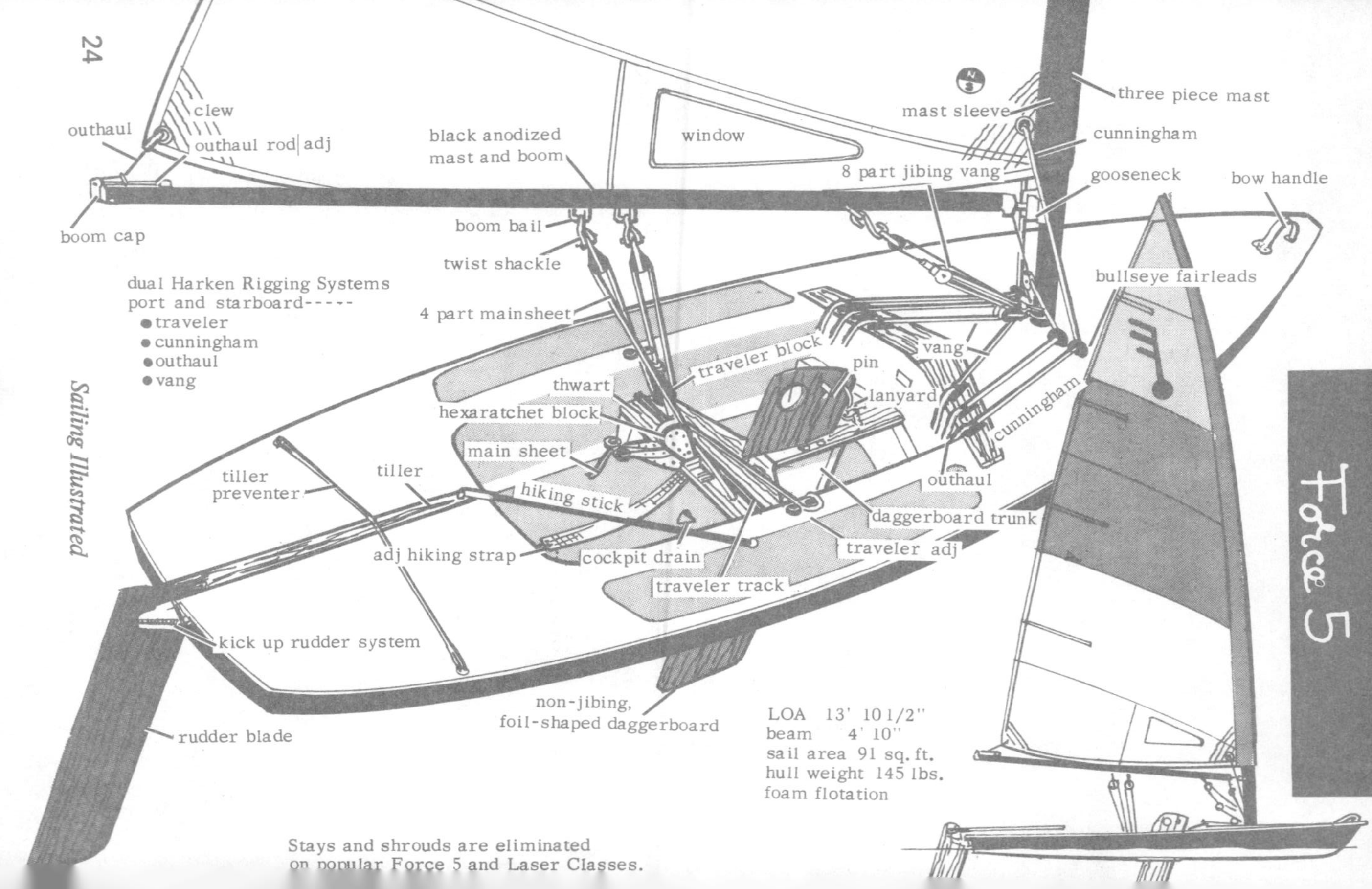

Stays and shrouds are eliminated on popular Force 5 and Laser Classes.

Laser

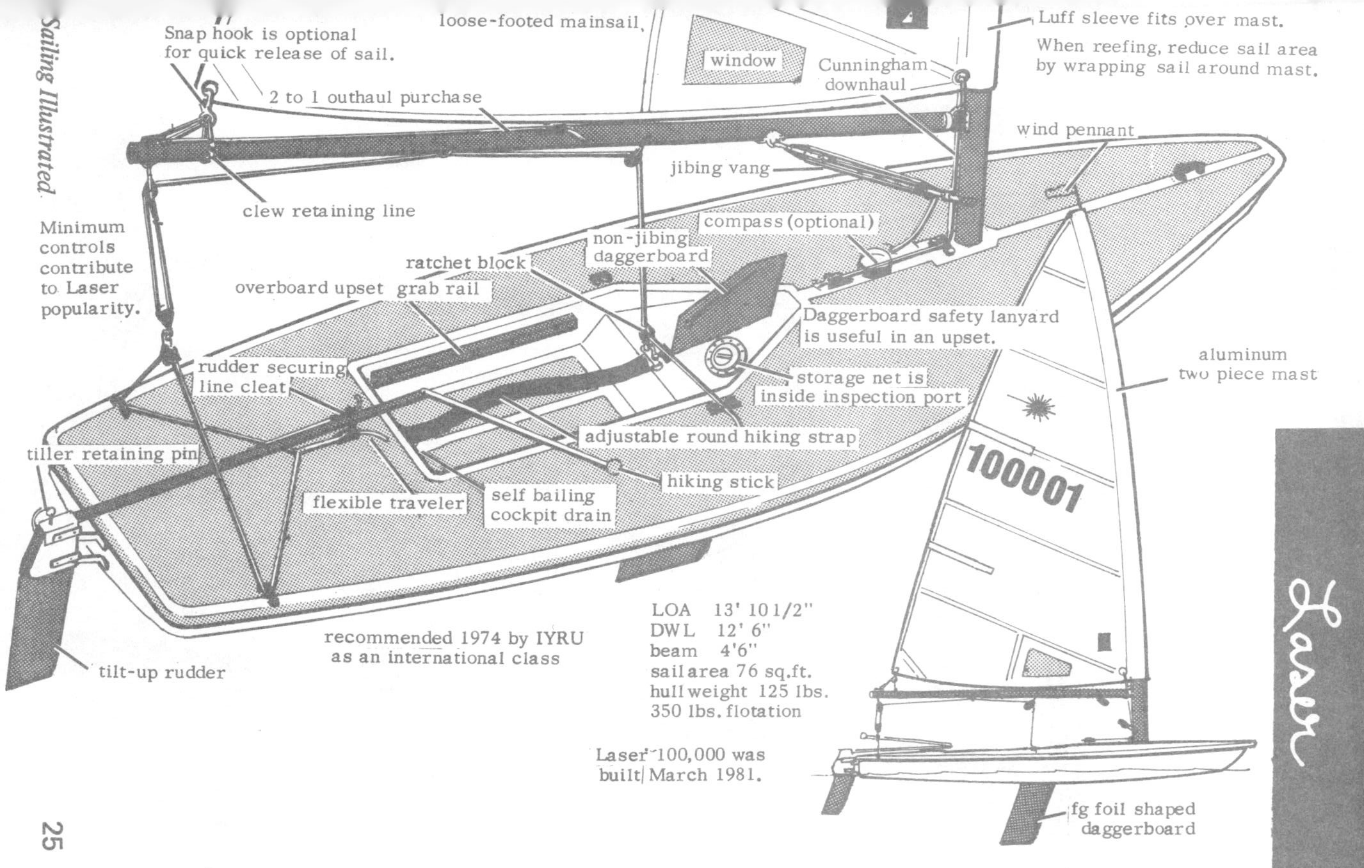

Minimum controls contribute to Laser popularity.

recommended 1974 by IYRU as an international class

LOA 13' 10 1/2"
DWL 12' 6"
beam 4'6"
sail area 76 sq.ft.
hull weight 125 lbs.
350 lbs. flotation

Laser 100,000 was built March 1981.

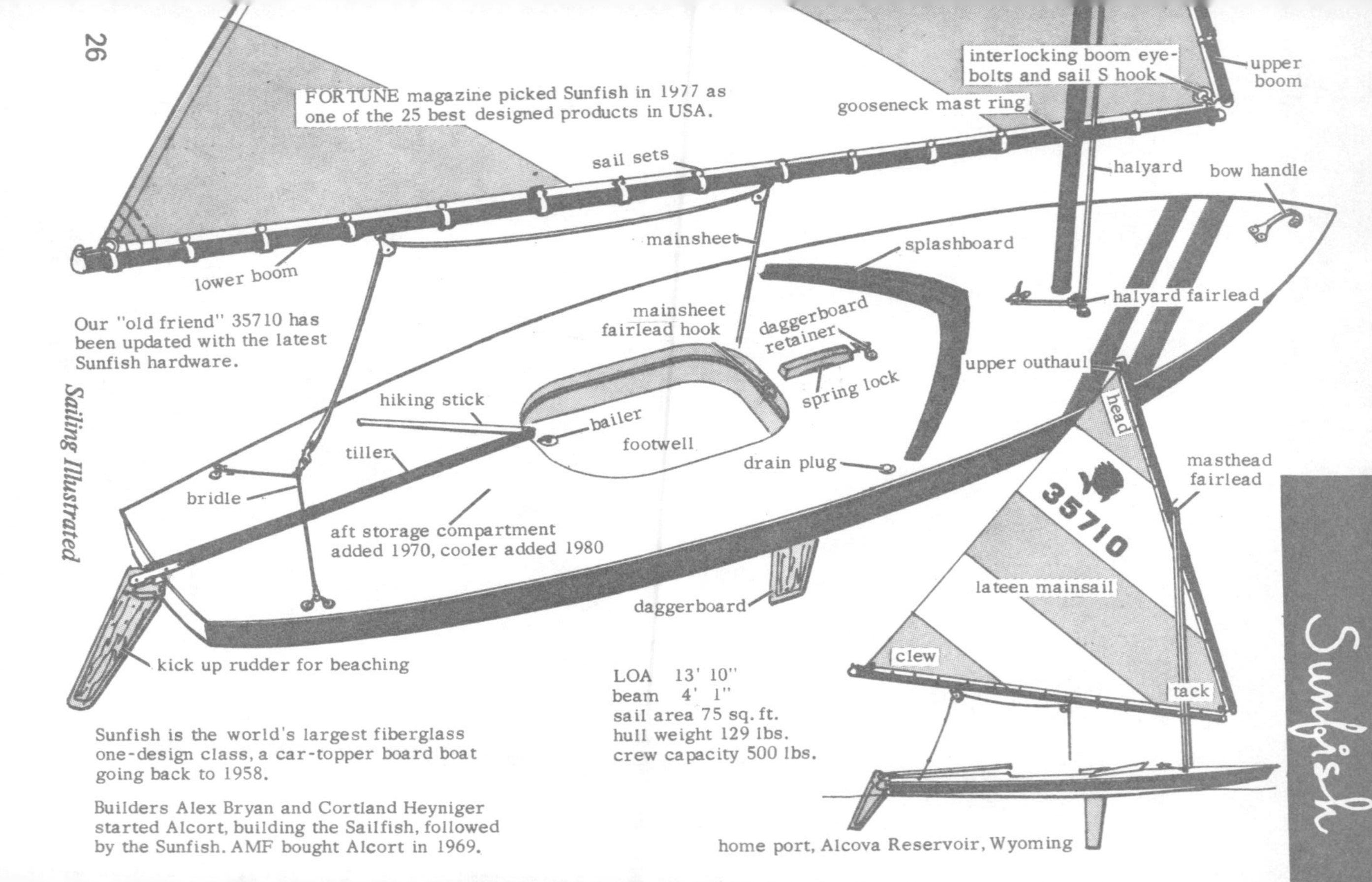
Sunfish
FORTUNE magazine picked Sunfish in 1977 as one of the 25 best designed products in USA.
interlocking boom eye-bolts and sail S hook
upper boom
gooseneck mast ring
sail sets
halyard
bow handle
mainsheet
splashboard
lower boom
halyard fairlead
mainsheet fairlead hook
daggerboard retainer
Our "old friend" 35710 has been updated with the latest Sunfish hardware.
upper outhaul
spring lock
hiking stick
bailer
head
footwell
tiller
drain plug
masthead fairlead
bridle
35710
aft storage compartment added 1970, cooler added 1980
lateen mainsail
daggerboard
clew
kick up rudder for beaching
LOA 13' 10"
beam 4' 1"
sail area 75 sq. ft.
hull weight 129 lbs.
crew capacity 500 lbs.
tack
Sunfish is the world's largest fiberglass one-design class, a car-topper board boat going back to 1958.
Builders Alex Bryan and Cortland Heyniger started Alcort, building the Sailfish, followed by the Sunfish. AMF bought Alcort in 1969.
home port, Alcova Reservoir, Wyoming

Windsurfer

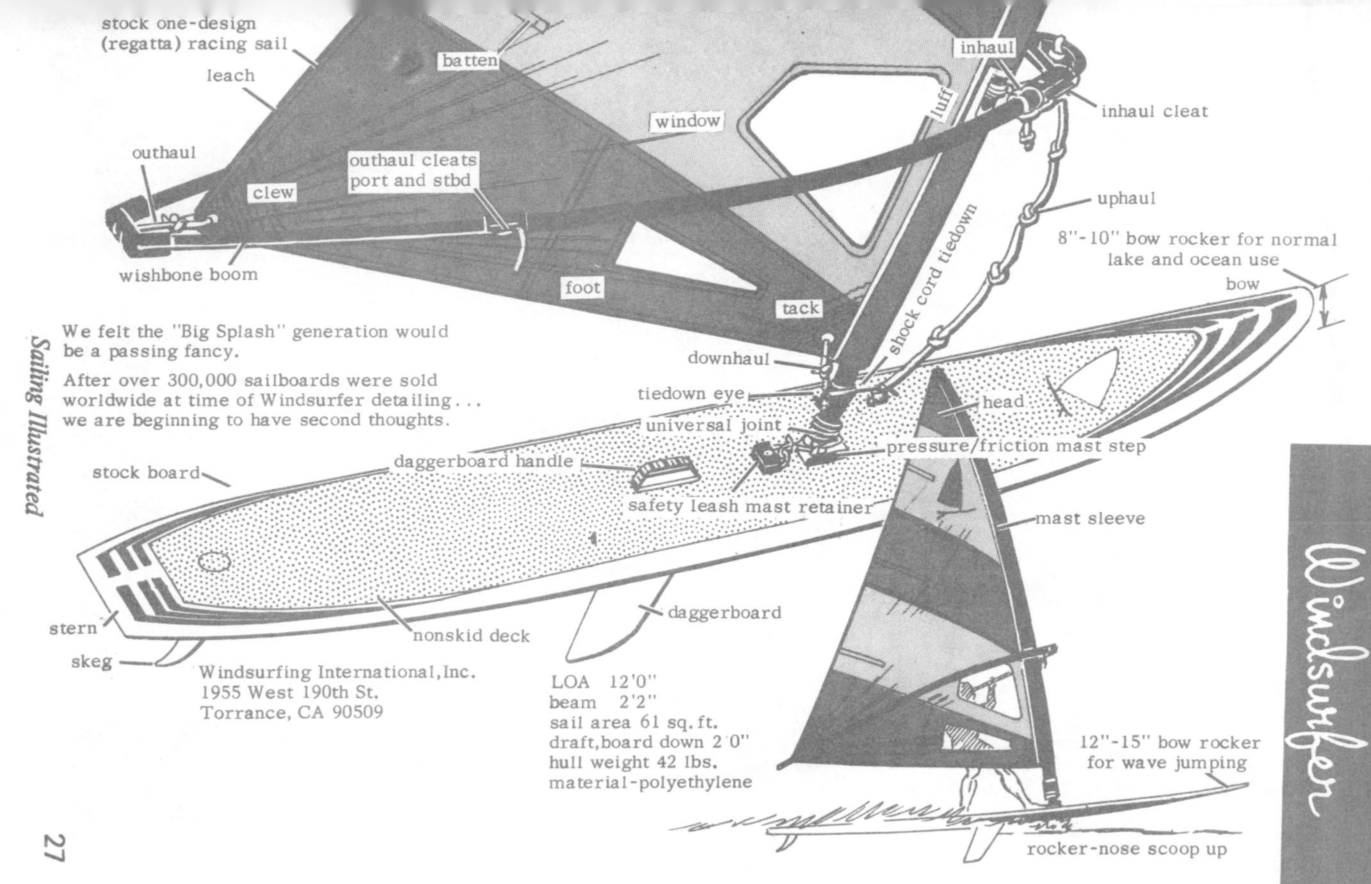

We felt the "Big Splash" generation would be a passing fancy.

After over 300,000 sailboards were sold worldwide at time of Windsurfer detailing . . . we are beginning to have second thoughts.

Windsurfing International, Inc.
1955 West 190th St.
Torrance, CA 90509

LOA 12'0"
beam 2'2"
sail area 61 sq. ft.
draft, board down 2'0"
hull weight 42 lbs.
material-polyethylene

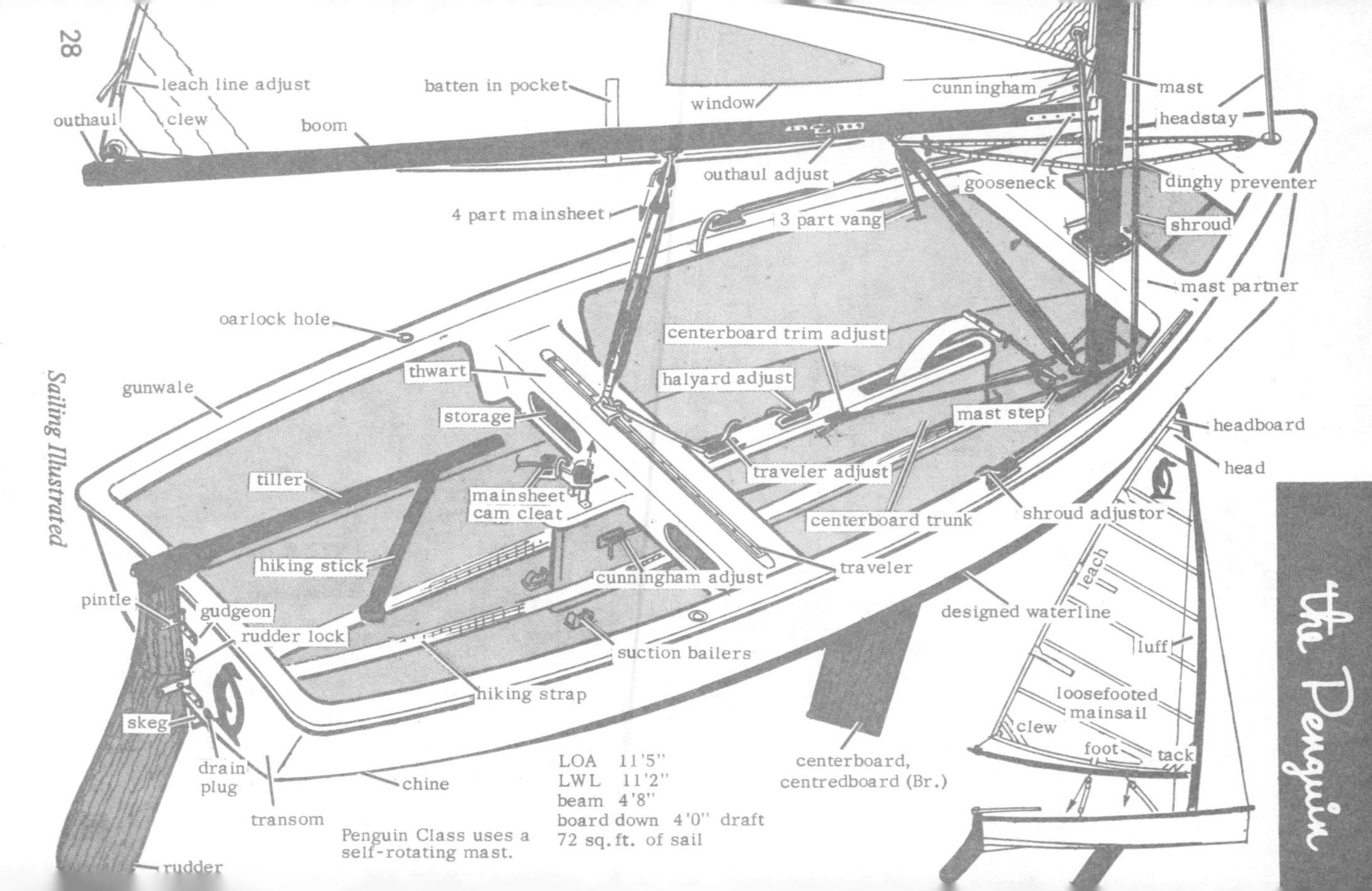
the Penguin
mast
headstay
dinghy preventer
shroud
mast partner
headboard
head
luff
leach
loosefooted mainsail
tack
foot
clew
designed waterline
shroud adjustor
mast step
centerboard trunk
traveler
centerboard, centredboard (Br.)
cunningham
gooseneck
window
outhaul adjust
3 part vang
centerboard trim adjust
halyard adjust
traveler adjust
cunningham adjust
suction bailers
batten in pocket
4 part mainsheet
mainsheet cam cleat
storage
thwart
hiking strap
chine
boom
oarlock hole
tiller
hiking stick
rudder lock
gudgeon
transom
drain plug
leach line adjust
clew
outhaul
gunwale
pintle
skeg
rudder
LOA 11'5"
LWL 11'2"
beam 4'8"
board down 4'0" draft
72 sq. ft. of sail
Penguin Class uses a self-rotating mast.

Naples Sabot

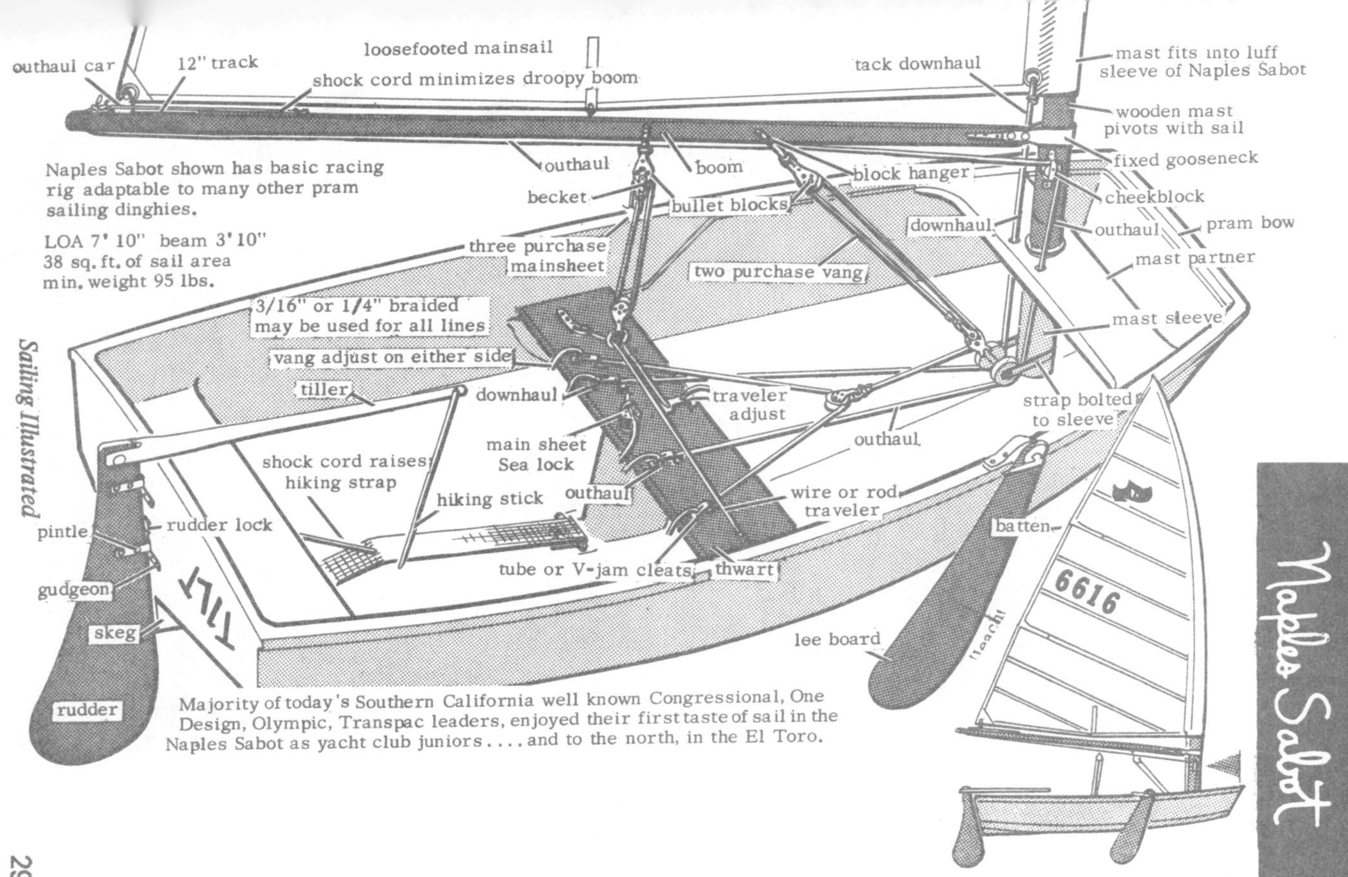

Naples Sabot shown has basic racing rig adaptable to many other pram sailing dinghies.

LOA 7' 10" beam 3' 10"
38 sq. ft. of sail area
min. weight 95 lbs.

Majority of today's Southern California well known Congressional, One Design, Olympic, Transpac leaders, enjoyed their first taste of sail in the Naples Sabot as yacht club juniors . . . . and to the north, in the El Toro.

Lido, Thistle, and Snipe.

We detail three 2 person sloop sailing dinghies for your analysis. Each have specific, and considerably different advantages depending on your background, experience, and whether your interest is sailing for fun and relaxation, part-time racing, or full-time racing.

- **Lido 14.** It appeared locally in 1958, one of the first quality fiberglass dinghy hulls.The Lido, a ***strict one-design class***, has adequate and efficient rigging controls. They help to make the Lido a happy boat to sail that is delicate to the helm, and very sensitive to weight distribution.

After teaching on more than 40 Lido's, we found it excellent for that first sailboat. After a year of sailing, the owner is able to move up to a high-performance dinghy, or a large cabin sailboat. One Lido I taught on had three owners at different periods who gained sufficient exposure on the Lido to buy and enjoy sailboats 30' to 45' long.

The Lido becomes a spirited dinghy that is a lively performer in a good wind. It is an excellent choice for the new sailor, plus high school, college, and public instruction for which we have a large local fleet.

- **Thistle.** It first appeared in 1945, a Sandy Douglass design. I saw the first Thistle a few years later while sailing out of Freeport, Long Island...with the beautiful varnished hull gleaming in the summer sun.

The Thistle, detailed page 32, is an open 17' dinghy with air tanks to keep it afloat in a capsize, a big brother to the **International 14,** page 250. It planes easily and seems ready to take on her share of newcomers.The Thistle has a distinctive personality frozen in time so the oldest and new members of the fleet stay competitive.

A discussion as to whether the Thistle could beat the Lightning, started the first ***YACHTING'S One-Of-a-Kind-Races*** in 1949,page 2. As the Lightning was 200 pounds heavier, the Thistle with a flatter planing bottom came in first. But it was the public that became the winner as this race started the ***OOAK Series*** races held every three years in five divisions.

- **The Snipe.** It was the largest one-design class until the late sixties, designed in 1931 by William F. Crosby. We have included a Snipe in every edition of our book due to continuous self improvement within the rules of the class. After our basic Snipe, the next two belonged to sailmaker Earl Elms who dominated the Snipe World's competition for over a decade.

Snipe 24001 detailed on page 33, was one of a dozen identically rigged Snipes prepared for the 1979 Pan-American Competition. They were built by ***Phoenix Boat Company, Long Beach, CA 90813.***

Snipe competition is tremendous. It helps to have previous exposure and success in a less competitive class. When you want to be a Snipe candidate, contact the class secretary for the latest information. Study page 33 of this book, and page 91 of our ***Homestudy Guide*** to analyze the basic rigging needs of this class, to understand the new ideas which have developed in the meantime. You will need the latest hardware and rigging to make your Snipe competitive in a highly competitive one-design class.

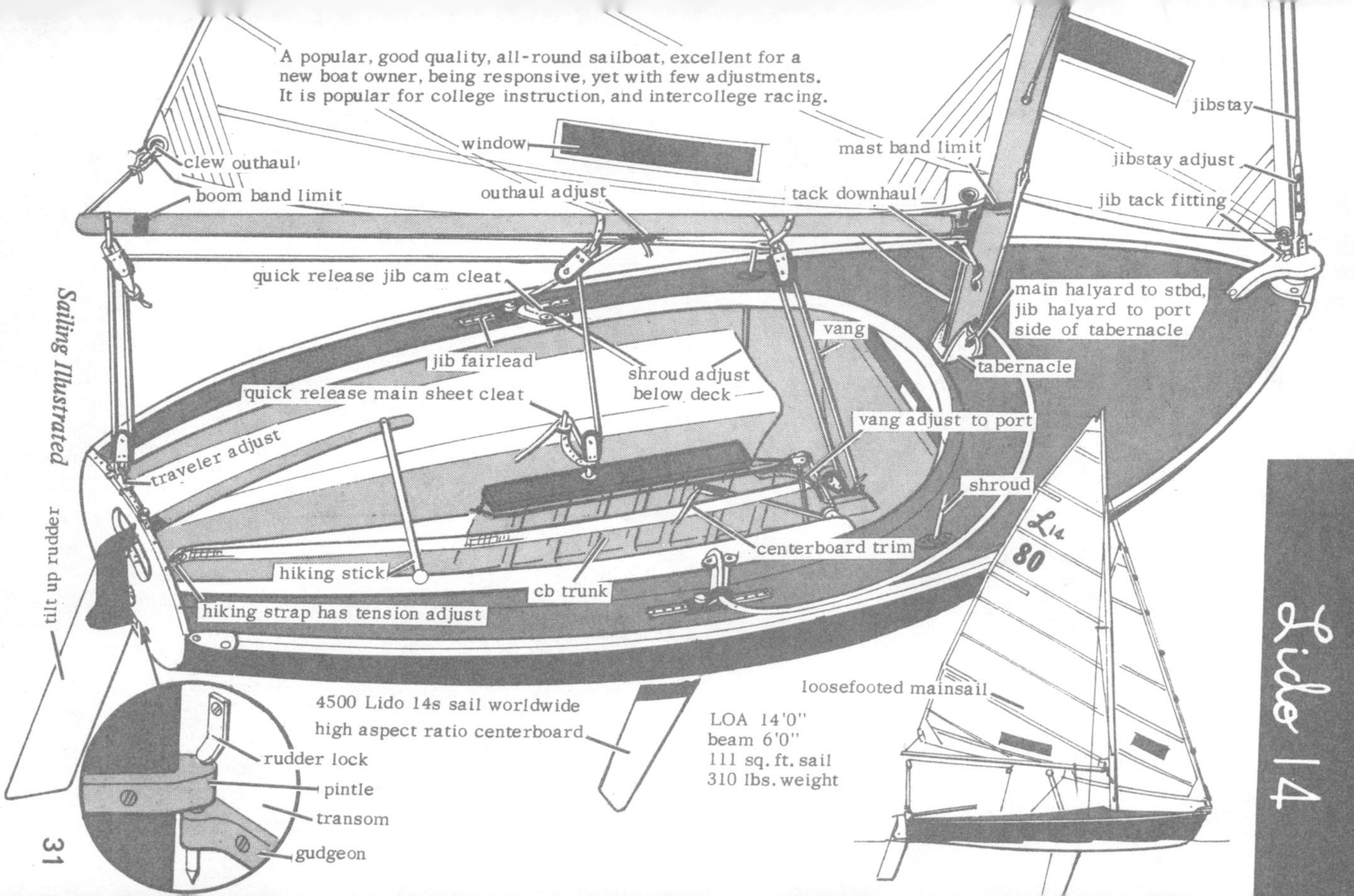

Lido 14
A popular, good quality, all-round sailboat, excellent for a new boat owner, being responsive, yet with few adjustments. It is popular for college instruction, and intercollege racing.
window
clew outhaul
boom band limit
outhaul adjust
mast band limit
tack downhaul
jibstay
jibstay adjust
jib tack fitting
quick release jib cam cleat
main halyard to stbd, jib halyard to port side of tabernacle
vang
tabernacle
jib fairlead
shroud adjust below deck
quick release main sheet cleat
vang adjust to port
traveler adjust
shroud
centerboard trim
hiking stick
cb trunk
hiking strap has tension adjust
tilt up rudder
4500 Lido 14s sail worldwide
high aspect ratio centerboard
rudder lock
pintle
transom
gudgeon
LOA 14'0"
beam 6'0"
111 sq. ft. sail
310 lbs. weight
loosefooted mainsail

Thistle

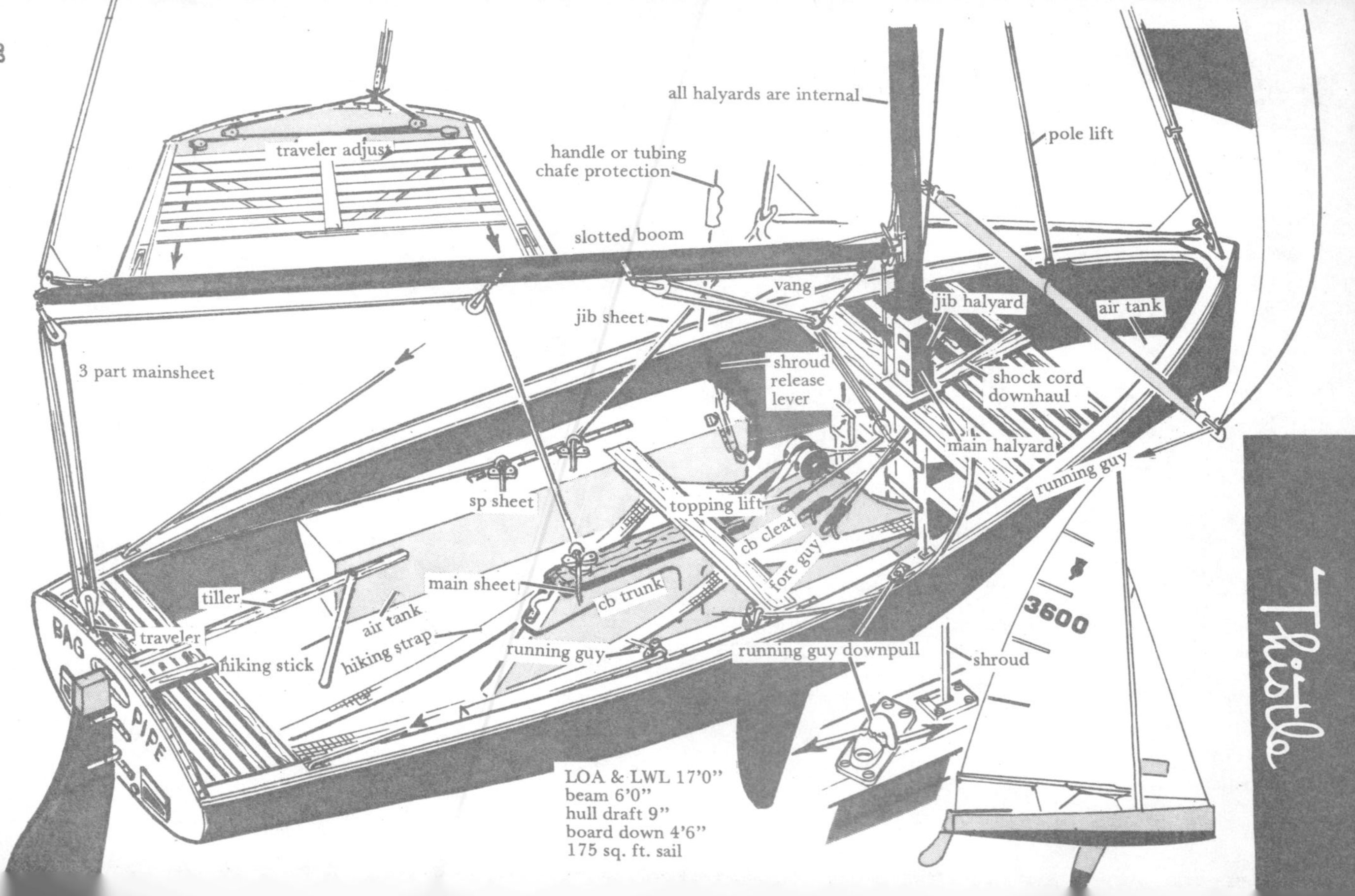

LOA & LWL 17'0"
beam 6'0"
hull draft 9"
board down 4'6"
175 sq. ft. sail

the Snipe

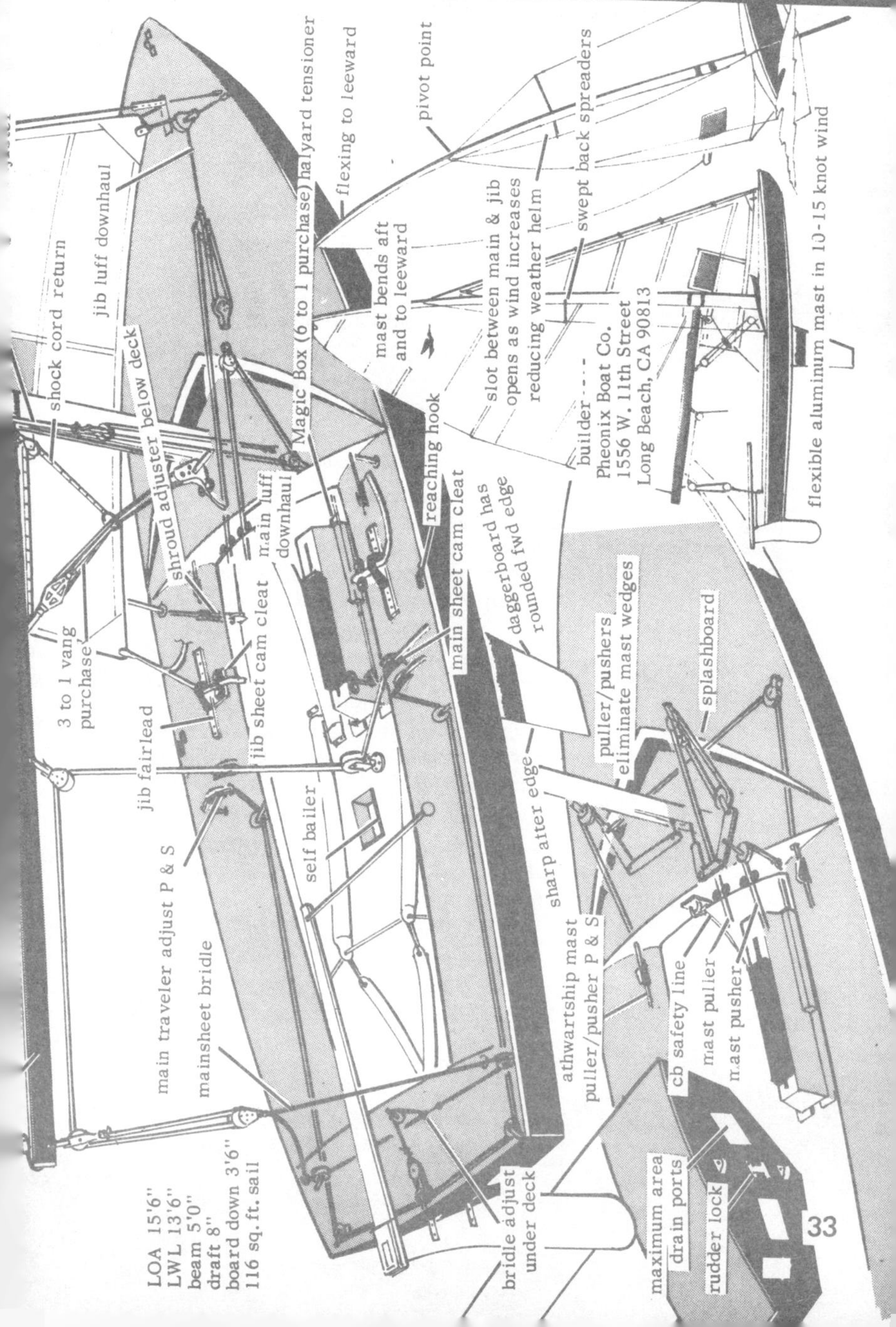

LOA 15'6"
LWL 13'6"
beam 5'0"
draft 8"
board down 3'6"
116 sq. ft. sail

main traveler adjust P & S
mainsheet bridle
jib fairlead
3 to 1 vang purchase
shock cord return
jib luff downhaul
shroud adjuster below deck
jib sheet cam cleat
main luff downhaul
Magic Box (6 to 1 purchase) halyard tensioner
self bailer
flexing to leeward
mast bends aft and to leeward
pivot point
reaching hook
main sheet cam cleat
slot between main & jib opens as wind increases reducing weather helm
daggerboard has rounded fwd edge
sharp after edge
bridle adjust under deck
athwartship mast puller/pusher P & S
swept back spreaders
puller/pushers eliminate mast wedges

builder - - -
Pheonix Boat Co.
1556 W. 11th Street
Long Beach, CA 90813

maximum area drain ports
cb safety line
mast puller
mast pusher
splashboard
rudder lock
flexible aluminum mast in 10-15 knot wind

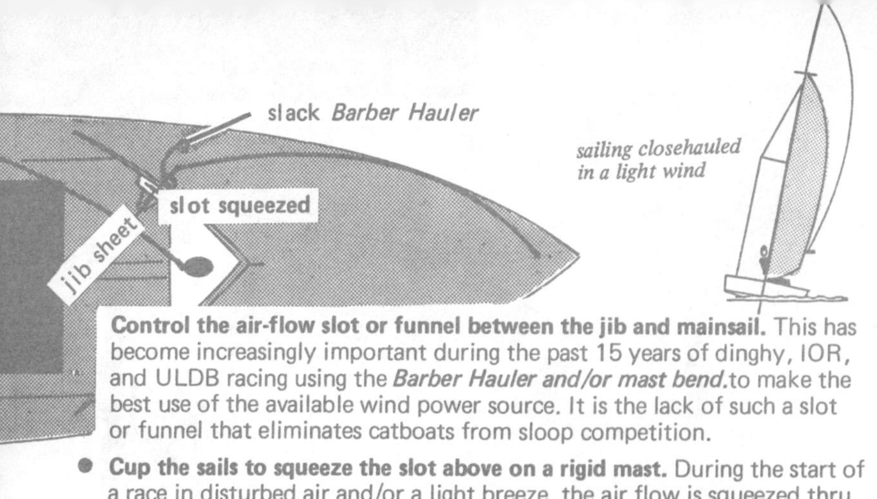

Control the air-flow slot or funnel between the jib and mainsail. This has become increasingly important during the past 15 years of dinghy, IOR, and ULDB racing using the *Barber Hauler and/or mast bend.*to make the best use of the available wind power source. It is the lack of such a slot or funnel that eliminates catboats from sloop competition.

- **Cup the sails to squeeze the slot above on a rigid mast.** During the start of a race in disturbed air and/or a light breeze, the air flow is squeezed thru the slot to increase its speed by easing the backstay to increase mainsail draft. The jib sheet is hardened, while the jib wire and jib cloth adjustments are eased. See control details on the facing page.
- **Flatten the sails to open the slot below left on a rigid mast.** As the wind increases while racing closehauled or reaching, both backstay and main sheet are hardened to open the slot.The *Barber Hauler,* named after the inventors, the identical Barber twins of San Diego, is hardened. The jib-wire luff, and jib cloth adjustments are hardened to flatten the jib to remove jib-luff wrinkles.
- **The flexible aluminum mast on a fractional sloop, below right, provides automatic slot control.** As the wind increases, the amount of mast rake or bend also increases to flatten the mainsail. ***Mast bending opens the slot to reduce crippling heel forces.*** Mast bending turns most of the wind power into forward drive for dinghies and ULDB's,which are designed to sail upwind with minimum heel and minimum weather helm.
- **Excessive mast bend** with a flexible mast in a strong wind **permits the upper part of the mainsail to feather aft.** This idea pioneered by the Star Class reduces the heel angle, permitting the sailboat to point and foot efficiently upwind, see details on page 35 of our *Homestudy Guide.*

The rigid mast on an identical sailboat without this pressure release, requires the mainsail to be reefed to reduce excess heel. Otherwise the excess weather helm may cause a capsize and equipment failure.

slot opened to maximum

sailing closehauled
in a strong wind

jib sheet

Barber Hauler **hardened**

Lightning

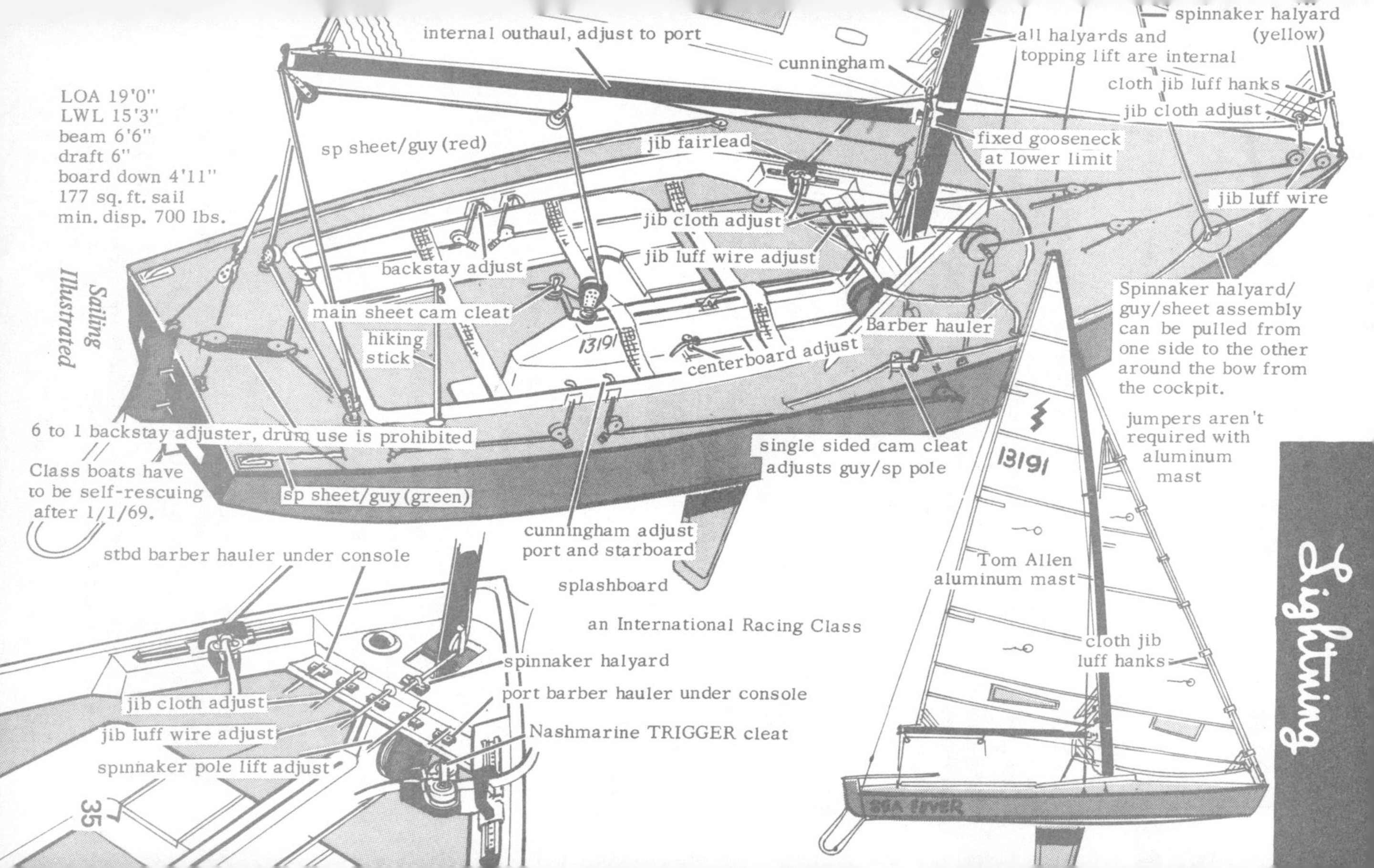

LOA 19'0"
LWL 15'3"
beam 6'6"
draft 6"
board down 4'11"
177 sq. ft. sail
min. disp. 700 lbs.

Class boats have to be self-rescuing after 1/1/69.

Sailing Illustrated

More than 10" separates Lightning and Flying Dutchman Classes.

The Lightning given International Racing Class status in 1962, is the best-loved centerboarder sailed worldwide.The association has existed since 1939, with over 460 chartered Lightning fleets worldwide at present. The Lightning began as stock design 265 by Sparkman and Stephens.

Lightning sailors are highly competitive. Their boat is also comfortable for family afternoon sailing...while some racing classes that are not as kindly and comfortable, seldom leave the dock if not racing.

The unique Lightning **spinnaker,halyard, sheet, and guy assembly** shown on page 35, has a bow tang support. The crew can pull this assembly from one side of the Lightning to the other without leaving the cockpit.

The spinnaker halyard,sheet,guy assembly is usually secured to the chute at the dock before the race, page 37, with most triangular course races leaving the marks to port. The pole is secured just before reaching the mark, the halyard is raised as the mark is turned, then the spinnaker sheet is set as the jib is dropped and secured under the bow shock cord.

Aluminum mast. When it was accepted by the Lightning Class,the jumper strut shown on the older wooden mast page 7, was eliminated. The controls producing mast-bend flexibility permitted the same crew to race more efficiently in a wider variety of wind and water conditions.

Sea Fever is the third Lightning we've detailed. Owner Mike Boswell told us, "Owners love their boats staying with this class a long time"...which is an important Lightning factor to also consider. Much of the credit for keeping such a large worldwide class growing and improving, goes to the secretary Donna Foote, and the excellent Lightning organization.

The **Flying Dutchman** though small in numbers, is an important development class. While the FD is only 10" longer than the Lightning, these two classes are as different as we could find for your examination and analysis.

The FD is easy to sail though difficult to sail well...and not all are equally competitive. The strict hull and mast rules, with elastic deck and equipment rules, produce considerably different cockpit layouts. Later FD's have double-bottoms forward with the weight being increased to 374 pounds.

The Flying Dutchman was designed by Uffa Van Essen of Holland. It was selected as the two-man centerboarder for Olympic competition, participating in all Olympic Games since 1960.

We have frozen in time, a rare, classic, fiberglass 1967 FD, detailed on pages 38 and 39. After considerable study of the rigging complexity, you soón find the ideas are simple, functional, and efficient. We use the same FD in our *Homestudy Guide* page 14,to provide a foundation for all complex racing dinghies, plus those wanting to crew on large IOR and ULDB racers.

Competitors from Thistle to Star classes when offered an FD in a race at the last moment, even the nationals with no previous experience in this class, often place high in FD competition.

Lightning

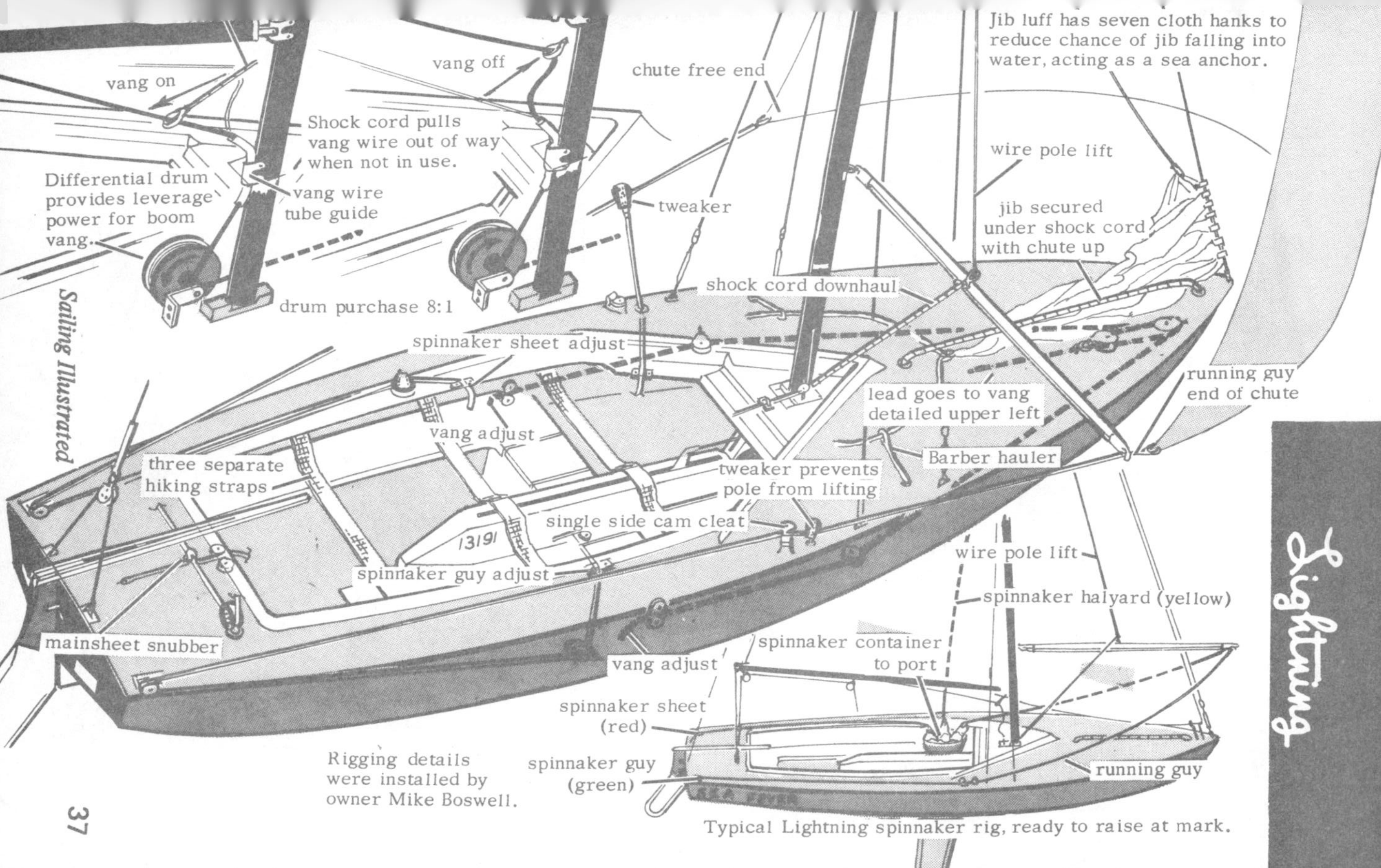

Rigging details were installed by owner Mike Boswell.

Typical Lightning spinnaker rig, ready to raise at mark.

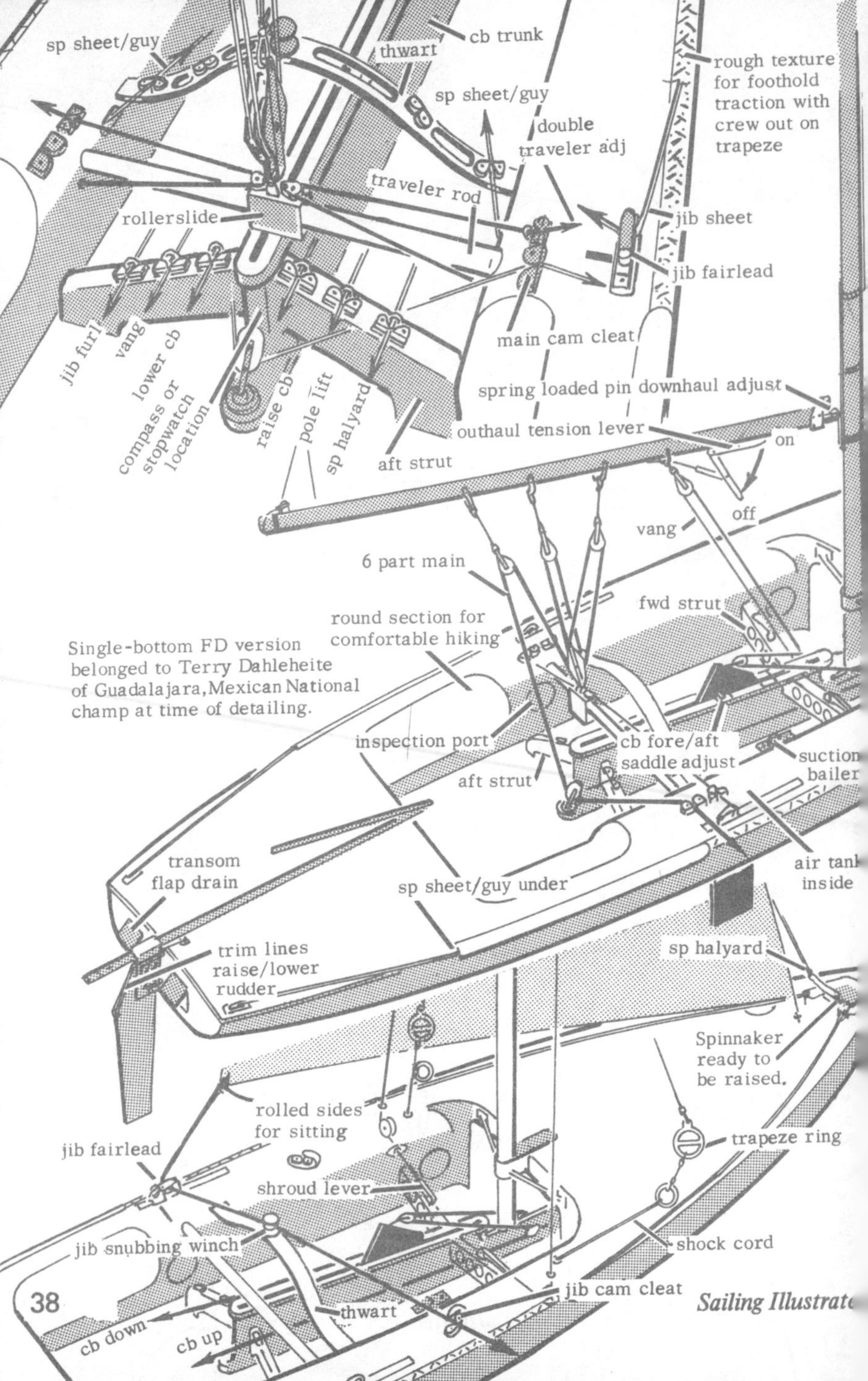

sp sheet/guy
cb trunk
thwart
rough texture for foothold traction with crew out on trapeze
sp sheet/guy
double traveler adj
traveler rod
rollerslide
jib sheet
jib fairlead
jib furl
vang
lower cb
compass or stopwatch location
raise cb
pole lift
sp halyard
main cam cleat
spring loaded pin downhaul adjust
outhaul tension lever
on
aft strut
off
vang
6 part main
fwd strut
round section for comfortable hiking
Single-bottom FD version belonged to Terry Dahleheite of Guadalajara, Mexican National champ at time of detailing.
inspection port
cb fore/aft saddle adjust
suction bailer
aft strut
transom flap drain
sp sheet/guy under
air tank inside
trim lines raise/lower rudder
sp halyard
Spinnaker ready to be raised.
rolled sides for sitting
trapeze ring
jib fairlead
shroud lever
jib snubbing winch
shock cord
jib cam cleat
thwart
cb down
cb up

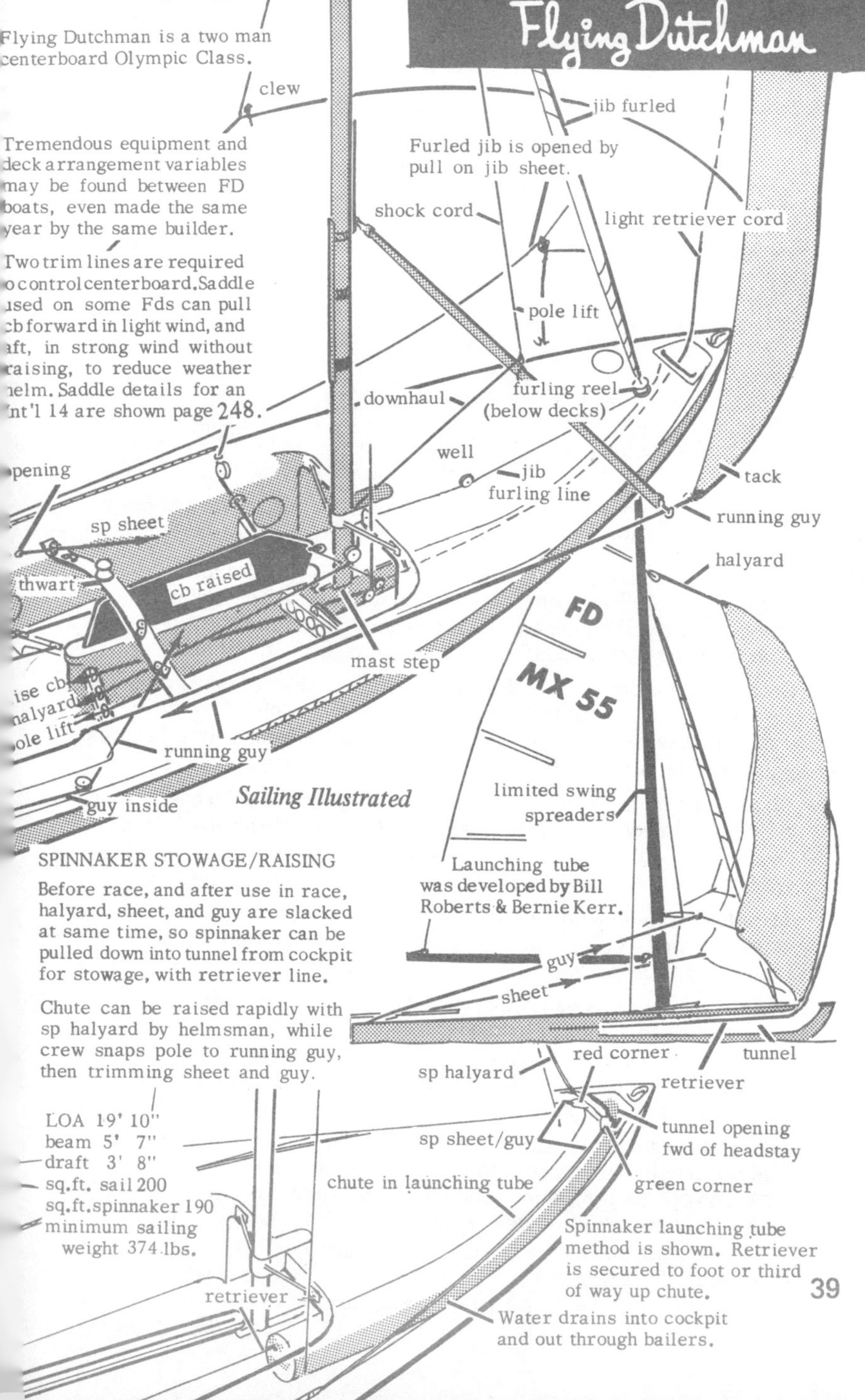
Flying Dutchman
Flying Dutchman is a two man centerboard Olympic Class.
clew
jib furled
Tremendous equipment and deck arrangement variables may be found between FD boats, even made the same year by the same builder.
Furled jib is opened by pull on jib sheet.
shock cord
light retriever cord
Two trim lines are required o control centerboard. Saddle ised on some Fds can pull cb forward in light wind, and ıft, in strong wind without raising, to reduce weather ıelm. Saddle details for an nt'l 14 are shown page 248.
pole lift
downhaul
furling reel
(below decks)
well
pening
jib furling line
tack
sp sheet
running guy
thwart
cb raised
halyard
FD
MX 55
mast step
ise cb
ıalyard
ole lift
running guy
limited swing spreaders
guy inside
Sailing Illustrated
SPINNAKER STOWAGE/RAISING
Before race, and after use in race, halyard, sheet, and guy are slacked at same time, so spinnaker can be pulled down into tunnel from cockpit for stowage, with retriever line.
Chute can be raised rapidly with sp halyard by helmsman, while crew snaps pole to running guy, then trimming sheet and guy.
Launching tube was developed by Bill Roberts & Bernie Kerr.
guy
sheet
red corner
tunnel
sp halyard
retriever
LOA 19' 10"
beam 5' 7"
draft 3' 8"
sq.ft. sail 200
sq.ft. spinnaker 190
minimum sailing weight 374 lbs.
sp sheet/guy
tunnel opening fwd of headstay
chute in launching tube
green corner
Spinnaker launching tube method is shown. Retriever is secured to foot or third of way up chute.
retriever
Water drains into cockpit and out through bailers.

The old man's pet...

When square riggers met on the ocean, a few carried a small, open dinghy aboard. It was the old man's pet upon which the ship's carpenter lavished considerable attention. The purpose was to make gambling bets similar to horse racing, though survival sometimes became the major factor. This was the spawning ground of a distinct line of racing dinghies we see today including the **International 14, 420, 470, 505, FD, and C 15.**

- **International 14.** Its ancestor dates back to 1887 as a gaff-rigged, clinker-built racer. It became the National 14 in England in 1922, and the new International 14 in 1927, the first IYRU dinghy. It is the oldest existing dinghy class, ***a one-design development class*** to allow experimentation and continuous development thru the years. Pages 250-251 show the unique ***Daring*** winning the 1965 YACHTING's OOAK, while in 1964, it was the first American boat to win England's Prince of Wales Cup.

  Traditional characteristics are an open, overcanvassed dinghy requiring skill and seamanship to stay upright while racing in a stiff breeze.

- **Coronado 15.** It began racing in 1967, also following the square-rigger heritage. It has high-aspect ratio underwater blades. The hull narrows forward for weatherliness, while broadening aft of the chain plates to have a wide, stable bottom platform to aid planing lift and stability.

Crew seating is on rolled cockpit side air tanks that are comfortable for hiking out. An unusual feature is the high boom to eliminate the need for ducking while changing tack, while several **decksweeping classes** starting with the Finn have low booms to dodge when changing tack.

Snipe and C 15 are almost identical in length, yet the C 15 has 8" more beam, and an additional 23 square feet of sail. This gives the C 15 an advantage in light winds to keep moving in the San Diego Mission Bay while a light crew on a trapeze in a strong wind helps sail the boat flat.

Mainsheet traveler adjust is important for the high boom. The traveler is usually carried to windward for upwind sailing. Maximum mainsail efficiency require adjustments with the continuous traveler adjust, see illustration.

The first pouches. They were developed by early C 15 class members to contain the bitter ends of halyards, sheets, etc.,otherwise with all lines coming to the cockpit, could resemble a ***snake pit*** even if color coded.The pouches are also used on the C-38 detailed on page 81.We added the shock-cord retractor so the **vang** is out of the way when not being used.

The **centerboard** can be trimmed to port or starboard. The centerboard is held down with a shock cord that lets the centerboard swing up when hitting an obstruction, then returning the board to down position. The C-15 rudder and centerboard are fully retracted for beaching.

The C-15 is a small, spirited, and highly competitive class. The nationals which are held yearly, draw many top inland and larger ocean one-design competitors to the California Huntington Lake Regatta.

Coronado 15

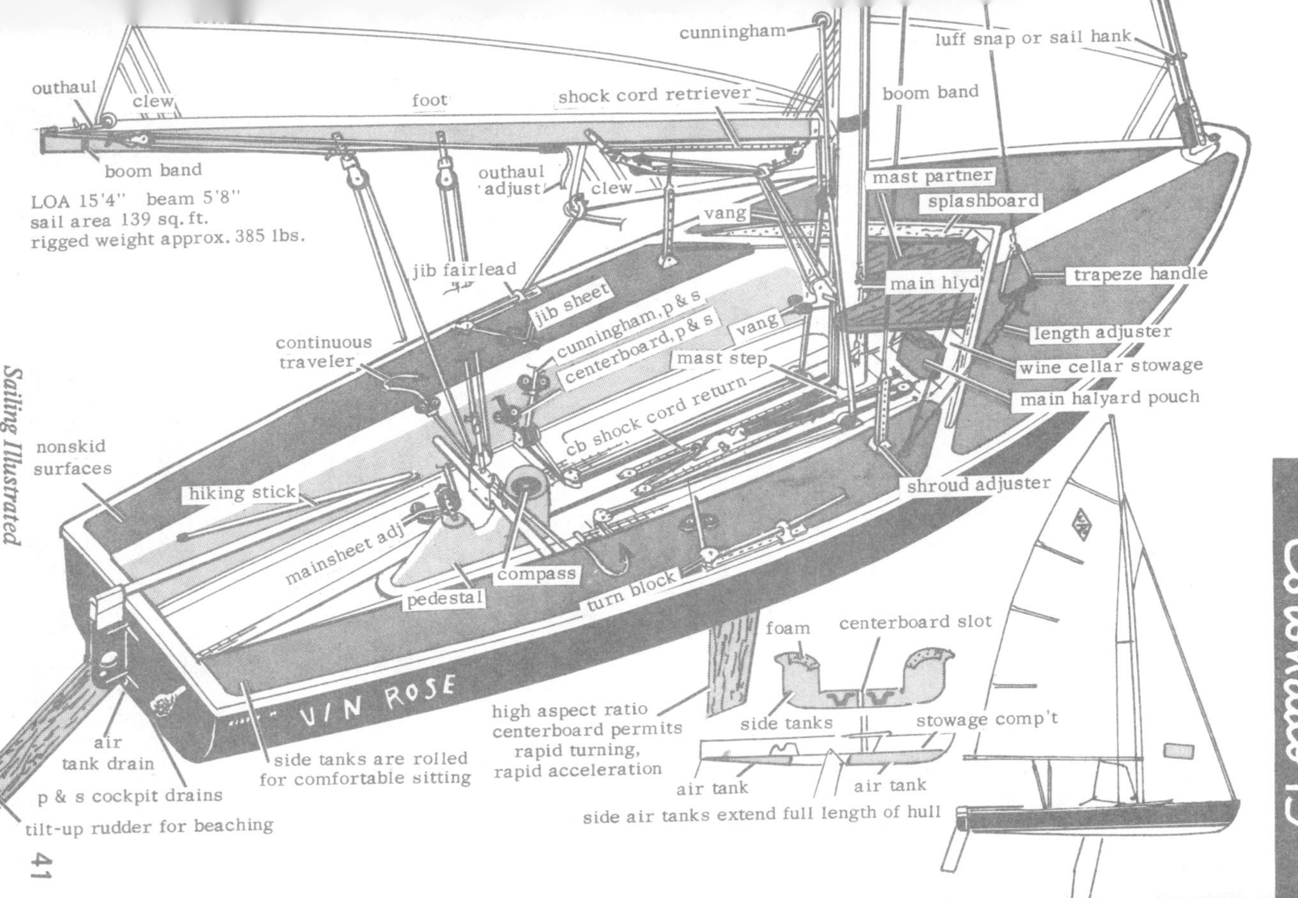

LOA 15'4" beam 5'8"
sail area 139 sq. ft.
rigged weight approx. 385 lbs.

The unique Star has a 75 year engineering heritage.

Do you have the time, interest, background, and dedication to own a dinghy that is seldom sailed for pleasure? The Star has a tremendous variety of controls and adjustments developed thru 75 years of engineering **to fine tune...then super fine tune every system.** The complexity is best summarized with equal trophies going to skipper and crew.

The Star is a *born-again* class. Many times when its popularity goes down the Star bounces back to life, the last time to gain 1984 Olympic status.

Since the number of active, competitive Stars is small, the best way to analyze the class is to meet its members. Most are dedicated *yachties* with many years of competitive class and ocean racing backgrounds.

- **A $260 poor man's boat** was the goal of the Star designer William Sweisguth in 1911. Have you checked sailaway prices recently? The high-peaked gaff main was changed in 1921 to a low-headed marconi main...which proved too tame. The first lofty, flexible rig was introduced in 1929 with a wooden mast. It was replaced by the ***wet noodle aluminum*** Star mast, the most efficient and best controlled of all flexible masts.

- My association with the Star class began when contacting Carl Eichenlaub who built Lowell North's ***North Star,*** launched March,1963. Carl began, "Fully detail another one in the recent Star World's competition...then you will begin to understand the questions to ask Lowell North".

  Carl's advice was an understatement. Soft talking Lowell North helped continuously during the four days required to finish my preliminary drawings of his Star. I was dressed as a worker going into his office without an appointment when stopped by a customer, "How can you continuously go in and out of his office? I flew from Long Island just to thank him for my new sails that cost over $16,000. And after six hours of waiting..."

  Lowell, working on several jobs at the time, asked how I handled the situation. My reply,"I am sorry for any inconvenience as I just work here". His grin was more satisfaction than hoped for.

- When looking for a Star to detail with 1984 Olympic potential, the local Stars rapidly moved out of town to hide their "secret details". A marine hardware manufacturer*,Harrison Hine, enjoyed the irony of the situation. He offered his ***Yawaes,*** and later his ***Rapidamente,*** both having 17 diverse rigging systems, with both in the Olympics. Harrison provided records of their 130 blocks with catalog numbers, the length, diameter, and color of all lines, plus detailed photos. Harrison said his rigging installations were not to either extreme, but in the middle of the Star class. A month after detailing ***Yawaes*** I attended a regatta in Wyoming with 7 Stars from four western states. ALL had rigging almost identical to ***Yawaes.***

- ***Do you want to race Stars?*** A major purpose of our **Homestudy Guide** is to teach the complex rigging systems and hardware with many sailboats detailed in our book, using larger illustrations without terminology. The final test is to analyze and familiarize yourself with the ***Rapidamente.*** We don't know any method as practical to gain a foundation for enthusiasts interested in a class with 75 years of engineering background.

 ****Seaway Marine Catalog- 4201 Redwood Ave,, Los Angeles, CA 90066***

the Star

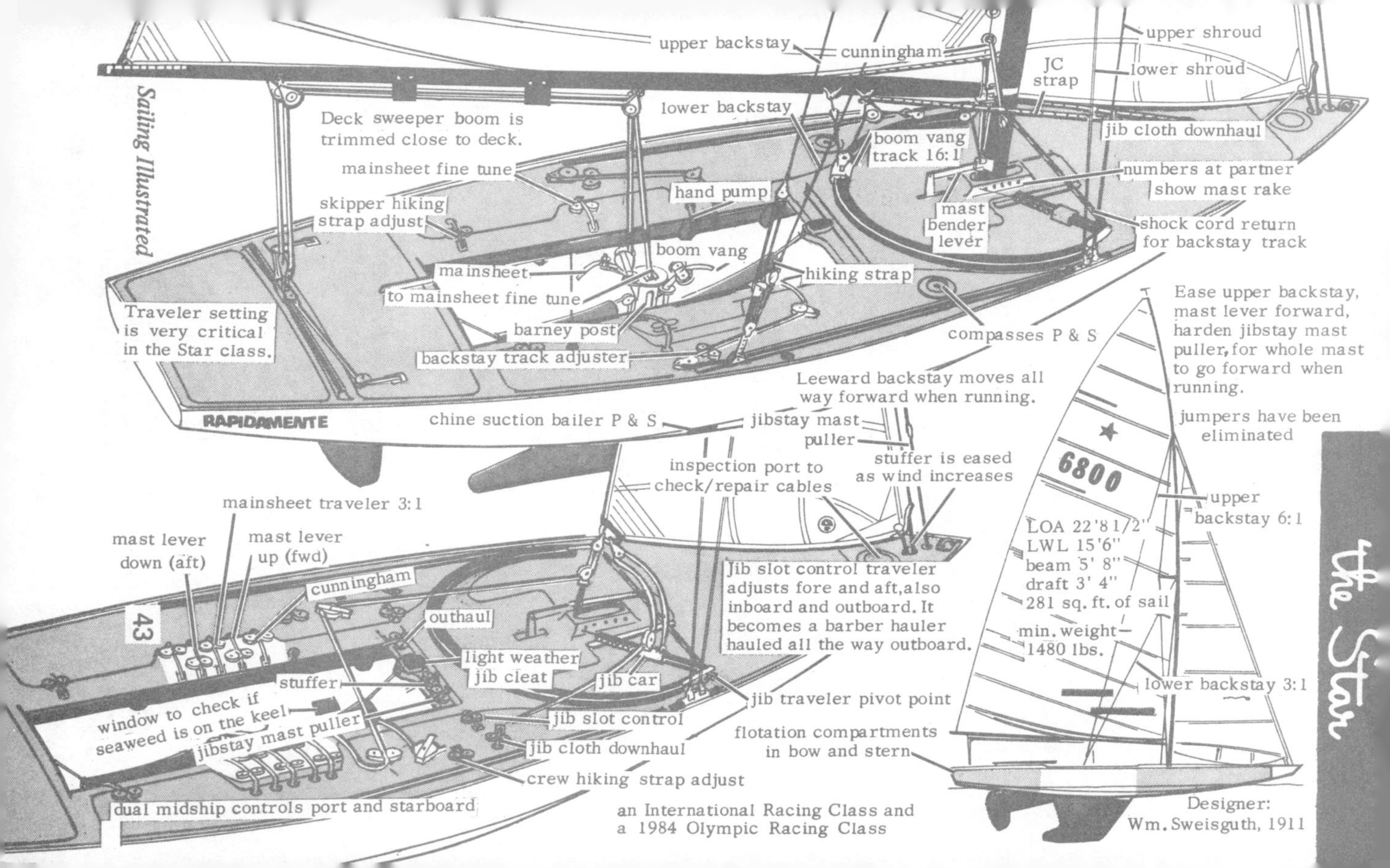

upper backstay
cunningham
upper shroud
JC strap
lower shroud
lower backstay
jib cloth downhaul
Deck sweeper boom is trimmed close to deck.
boom vang track 16:1
mainsheet fine tune
numbers at partner show mast rake
hand pump
mast bender lever
skipper hiking strap adjust
shock cord return for backstay track
boom vang
mainsheet
hiking strap
to mainsheet fine tune
Traveler setting is very critical in the Star class.
barney post
compasses P & S
backstay track adjuster
Ease upper backstay, mast lever forward, harden jibstay mast puller, for whole mast to go forward when running.
Leeward backstay moves all way forward when running.
RAPIDAMENTE
chine suction bailer P & S
jibstay mast puller
jumpers have been eliminated
stuffer is eased as wind increases
inspection port to check/repair cables
6800
upper backstay 6:1
mainsheet traveler 3:1
mast lever down (aft)
mast lever up (fwd)

LOA 22'8 1/2"
LWL 15'6"
beam 5' 8"
draft 3' 4"
281 sq. ft. of sail
min. weight 1480 lbs.

cunningham
Jib slot control traveler adjusts fore and aft, also inboard and outboard. It becomes a barber hauler hauled all the way outboard.
outhaul
light weather jib cleat
jib car
stuffer
lower backstay 3:1
window to check if seaweed is on the keel
jib traveler pivot point
jibstay mast puller
jib slot control
flotation compartments in bow and stern
jib cloth downhaul
crew hiking strap adjust
dual midship controls port and starboard
an International Racing Class and a 1984 Olympic Racing Class

Designer:
Wm. Sweisguth, 1911

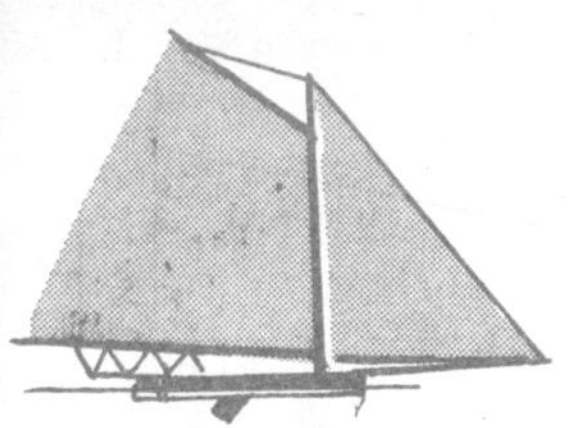

sandbagger *Bermuda 14* *Aussie 18*

Then we come to those not satisfied with ordinary sailing.

- **Sandbaggers** were popular from 1870 to 1900 in the New York and Boston harbors...with sloop or catboat rigs. While they had four classes from 20′ to 30′ long, they could measure 70′ from bowsprit to boom end, while carrying up to 1600 square feet of sail. Gambling predominated with betting and large prizes, while wealthy owners on nearby chartered steamers cheered on their captains and professional crew members.

  They carried 700 to 800 pounds of lead low as possible to keep their craft upright at anchor. Upwind racing stability depended entirely on heavy canvas bags with rope handles containing 50 to 60 pounds of gravel each. Competitors coming too close were often ***sand bagged*** with these bags.

- **14′ Bermuda Racing Dinghies** had the choice of three rigs according to the weather, the largest including a 700′ foot spinnaker. Races were beats and runs with spinnaker, pole, and lines sometimes thrown overboard at the mark to change to a beat. Live ballast was expendable...can you swim? The request when underway, "Will you bend on another jib", bears second thoughts with the naked bowsprit extending 9½ feet past the bow.

- The **Eighteen or Aussie 18** monohull may only weigh 200 pounds though it carries a working sail area of 440 sq. ft., plus an almost 1000 sq. ft. chute. The 18 is a sportsman's dream with a crew of three. Their 500 to 550 lbs. maximum weight on an aluminum rack or trapeze including the helmsman, can reach 15 knots upwind...and to 30 knots downwind.

- The **Malibu Outrigger** with Pacific ancestors thousands of years old, was the first recreational craft able to sail out, and to return to our Southern California beaches . It was replaced by the Hobies. We have many fond memories of the Malibu ***lot club*** sailors, gourmet gopher problems that dined on outriggers, plus the wildest sail of my life on an outrigger in a force 5 coming into the beach thru high breakers!

- **Scow** is a magic word causing the pulse of inland sailors to quicken. The shallow draft, square bow, wide-beam scows are found in various classes.

  Souped-up racing machines. They are light, lively, and extremely tender, designed to sail at extreme heel angles on protected inland lakes, not the ocean.The crew hangs out on a ***monkey bar*** with both feet resting on twin centerboards or bilgeboards.

the Scow

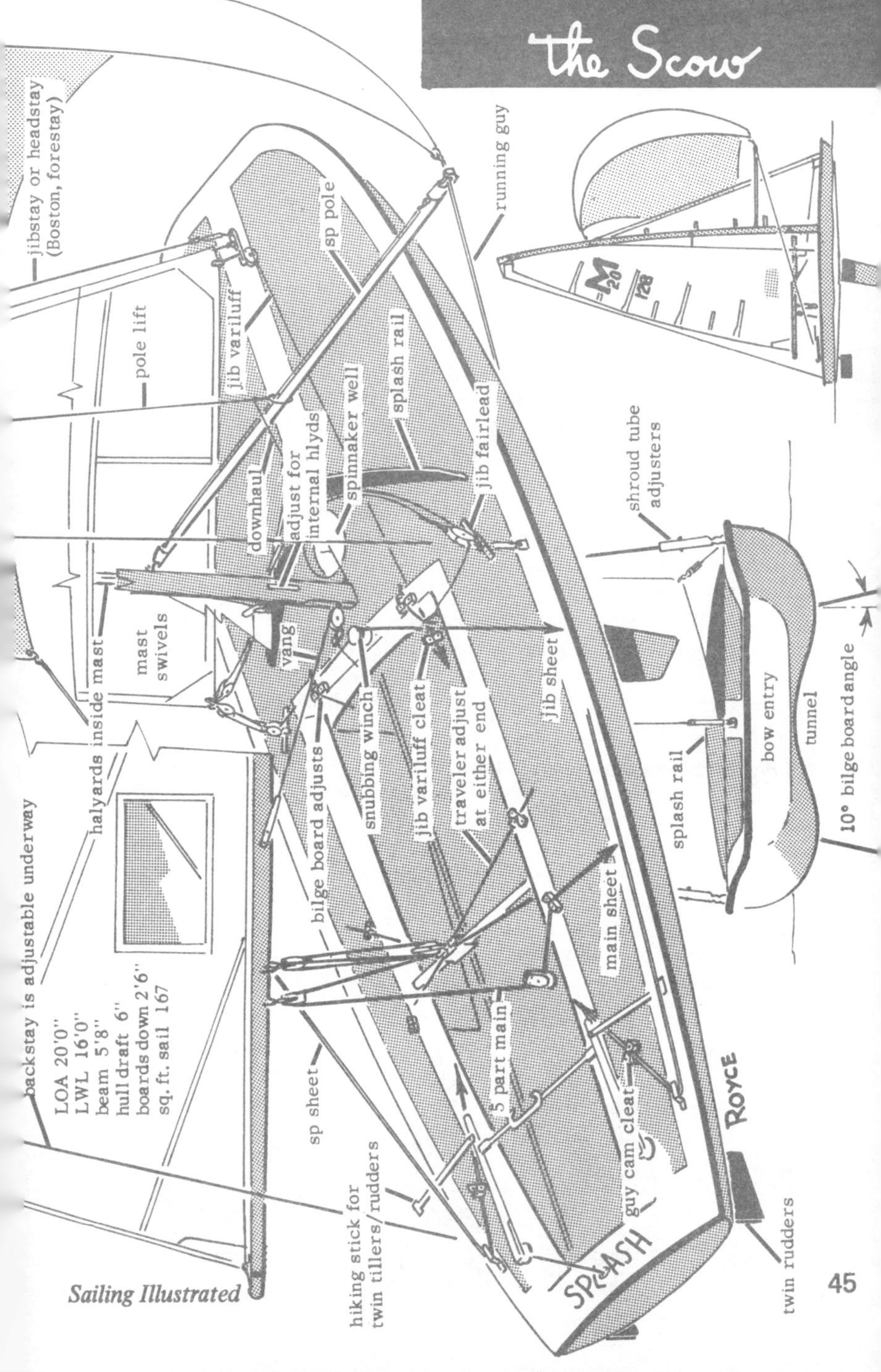
jibstay or headstay
(Boston, forestay)
running guy
sp pole
pole lift
jib variluff
splash rail
spinnaker well
adjust for
internal hlyds
downhaul
jib fairlead
shroud tube
adjusters
mast
swivels
vang
jib sheet
halyards inside mast
bilge board adjusts
snubbing winch
jib variluff cleat
traveler adjust
at either end
bow entry
tunnel
splash rail
10° bilge board angle
backstay is adjustable underway
LOA 20'0"
LWL 16'0"
beam 5'8"
hull draft 6"
boards down 2'6"
sq. ft. sail 167
main sheet
5 part main
sp sheet
guy cam cleat
ROYCE
SPLASH
hiking stick for
twin tillers/rudders
twin rudders
M 20
128

Brinkmanship is flying a single hull!

Multihull day sailing is a specialized sailing world. The dream is to fly a hull clear of the water for long periods with the wind and spray singing through the rigging while everything is on the ragged edge. Will a sudden puff flip your cat...or will the lee bow stub it's toe to cause a cartwheel, to be followed by boneyarding. It certainly beats the Monday morning office blaaahhhs!

- **Trampoline cats.** The Hobie 14 appeared in 1968. It was a natural step up for surfers who could now sail away from the beach, return thru the surf which was their expertise, then trailer their light craft home.

The **Hobie cat/cat** had sailing limitations. Owners may obtain factory kits for conversion, adding the jib with required hardware to the 14′ **Turbo cat/sloop** rig to improve both tacking and maneuverability.

The **Hobie 16 cat/sloop** arrived in 1970. It opened new storage potentials when not in use with many trampoline cats stored on our Southern California beaches. While most monohull centerboard and keel sailboats require storage on a dock or trailer, trampoline cats became popular for inland use where after a sail they could be run up on a sandy beach in front of the owners cottage, the sails removed, and be ready for the next vacation.

Running rigging. The Hobie 16 has a continuous jib sheet, with a jib-traveler adjust. Mainsheet rigging starts from the bitter end. It goes to an eye on the main sheet block, then returns to the traveler control cleat for traveler adjusting. It goes to the main sheet cam cleat, which controls the traveler and main sheet with one line.

- **Rigid-deck catamarans.** Many classes exist nationwide. Their numbers are small due to production/equipment costs, and the 26′ by 8′ trailering limitations without requiring special permits.

American and English wooden catamarans appeared with endless publicity. Due to unknown stress factors most exploded in 4 to 6 months. After minor changes, new classes were announced with more publicity to repeat the problem. The fiberglass Carter Pyle 18′ 9″ **Pacific Cat** appeared in 1960 with the first ***P-Cat*** still competitive twenty years later.

The second generation **Pacific 2/18** is shown on page 49. The chute has been eliminated as the 2/18 sails faster than the spinnaker in all but very light breezes.

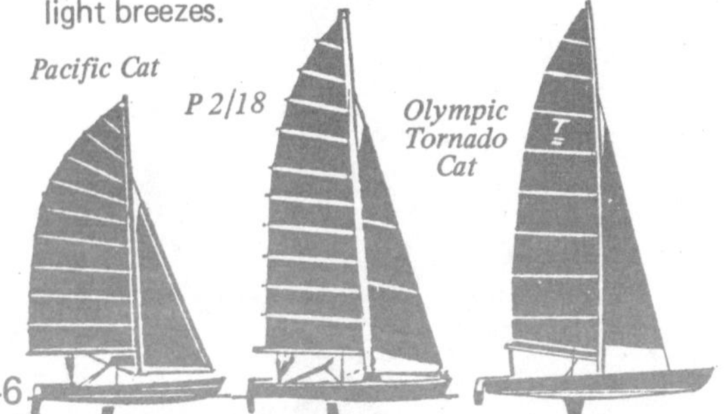

Aspect ratio, 1960 to 1990. The 1960 P-cat mainsail carried a full roach. The later P 2/18 with same length and sail area has a taller mast with high-aspect ratio main, also full battened with a minimum roach.

Hobie 14

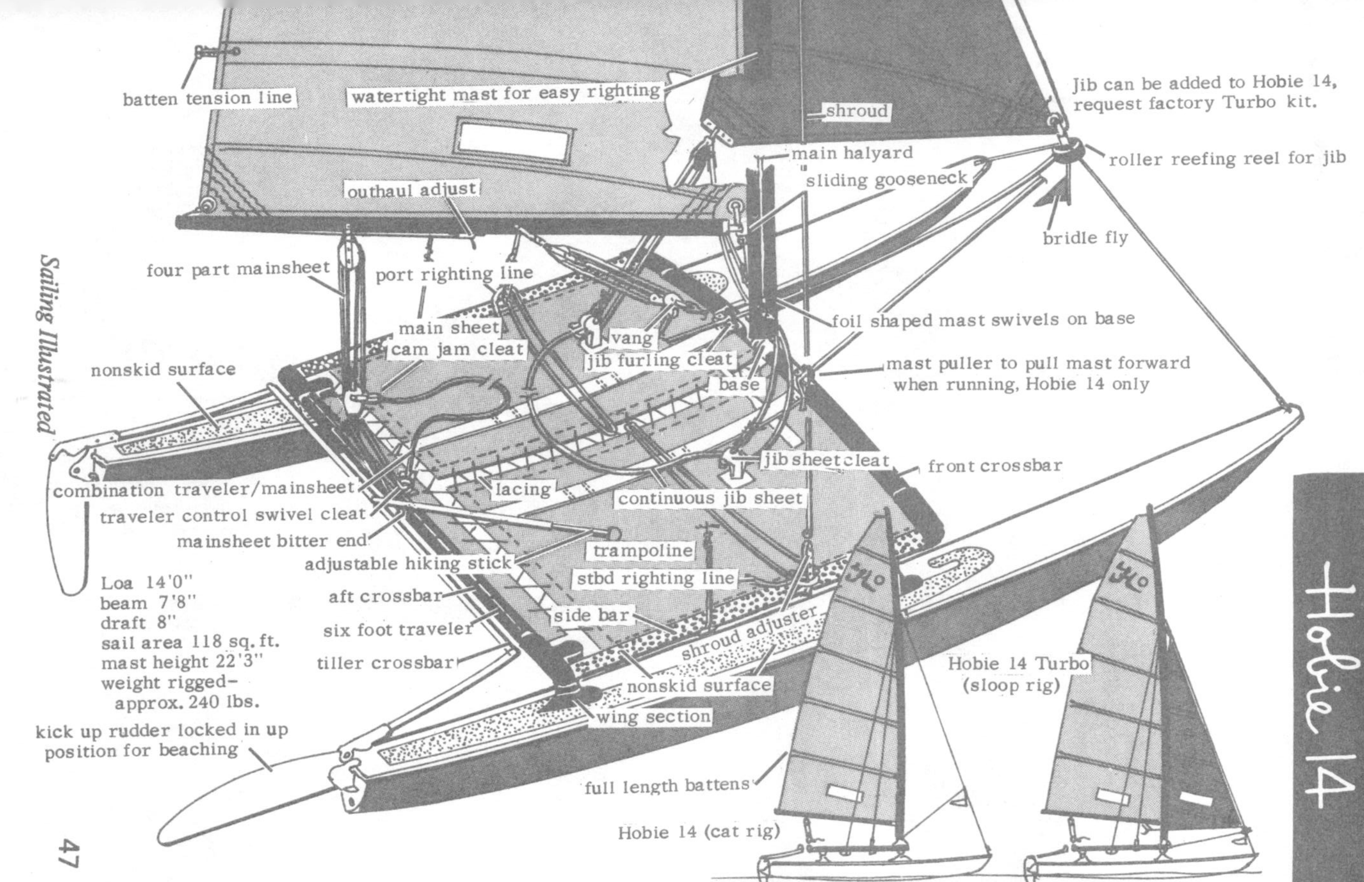

batten tension line
watertight mast for easy righting
shroud
Jib can be added to Hobie 14, request factory Turbo kit.
main halyard
roller reefing reel for jib
sliding gooseneck
outhaul adjust
bridle fly
four part mainsheet
port righting line
foil shaped mast swivels on base
main sheet
vang
cam jam cleat
jib furling cleat
nonskid surface
mast puller to pull mast forward when running, Hobie 14 only
base
jib sheet cleat
front crossbar
combination traveler/mainsheet
lacing
continuous jib sheet
traveler control swivel cleat
mainsheet bitter end
trampoline
adjustable hiking stick
stbd righting line
Loa 14'0"
beam 7'8"
draft 8"
sail area 118 sq. ft.
mast height 22'3"
weight rigged– approx. 240 lbs.
aft crossbar
side bar
six foot traveler
shroud adjuster
tiller crossbar
Hobie 14 Turbo (sloop rig)
nonskid surface
wing section
kick up rudder locked in up position for beaching
full length battens
Hobie 14 (cat rig)

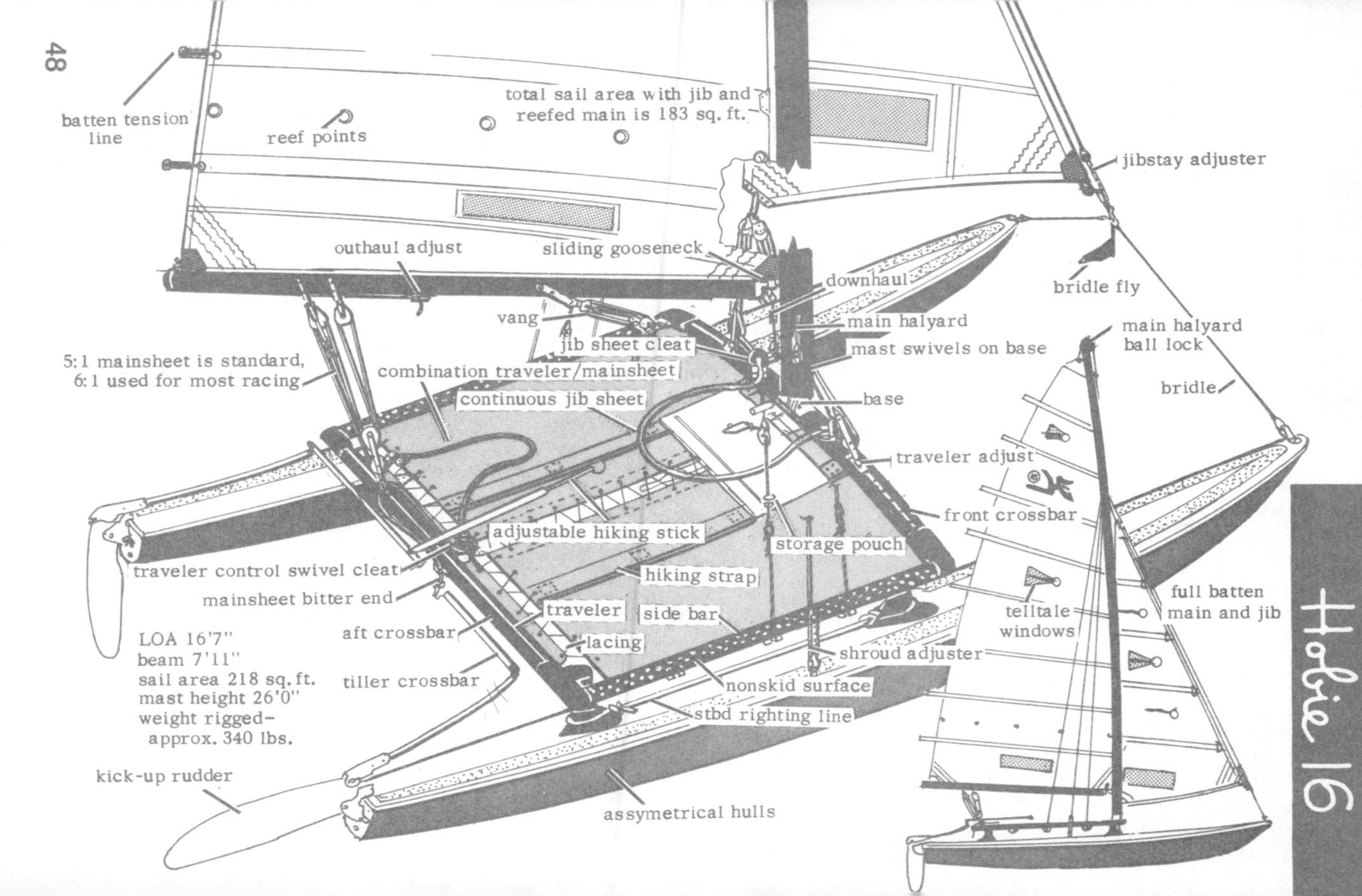

batten tension line
reef points
total sail area with jib and reefed main is 183 sq. ft.
jibstay adjuster
outhaul adjust
sliding gooseneck
downhaul
bridle fly
vang
main halyard
main halyard ball lock
jib sheet cleat
mast swivels on base
5:1 mainsheet is standard, 6:1 used for most racing
combination traveler/mainsheet
continuous jib sheet
base
bridle
traveler adjust
front crossbar
adjustable hiking stick
storage pouch
traveler control swivel cleat
hiking strap
mainsheet bitter end
full batten main and jib
traveler
side bar
telltale windows
aft crossbar
lacing
LOA 16'7"
beam 7'11"
sail area 218 sq.ft.
mast height 26'0"
weight rigged–approx. 340 lbs.
shroud adjuster
tiller crossbar
nonskid surface
stbd righting line
kick-up rudder
assymetrical hulls

Hobie 16

Pacific Cat P 2/18

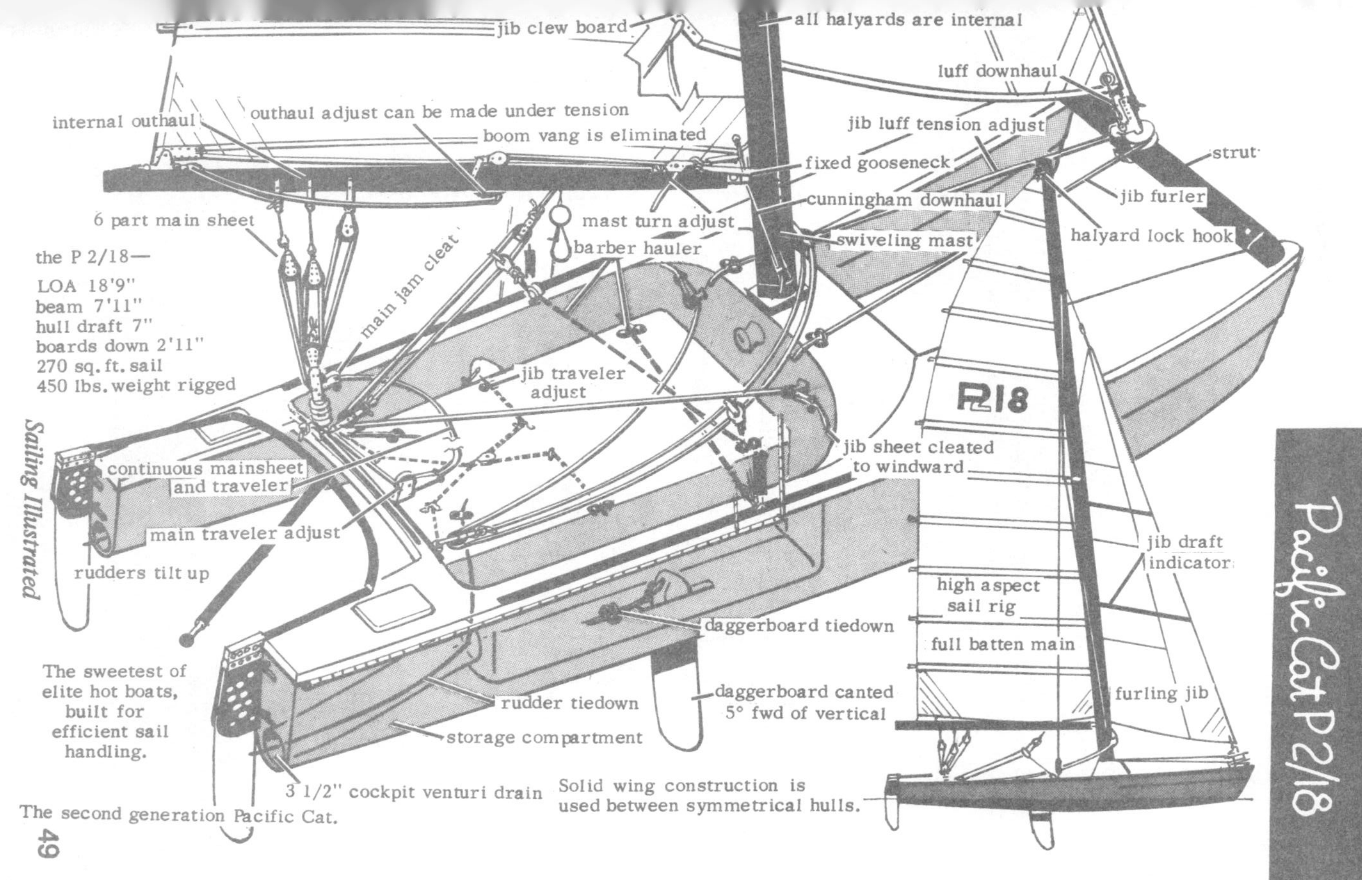

the P 2/18—

LOA 18'9"
beam 7'11"
hull draft 7"
boards down 2'11"
270 sq. ft. sail
450 lbs. weight rigged

The sweetest of elite hot boats, built for efficient sail handling.

Solid wing construction is used between symmetrical hulls.

The second generation Pacific Cat.

Eighty seven one-design class associations—Albatross to Yngling

A **Albacore**–Roger C. Thomas,7905 Anne Ct.,Clinton,MD 20735
Atlantic–Steve Kurlansky,29 Sequin Rd.,W.Hartford,CT 06117

B **Banshee**–Wm B.Haile,18579 Ravenwood Dr.,Saratoga,CA 95070
Beetle Cat–40 Juniper Rd.,Holbrook,MA 02343
Blue Jay–Julie Dunbar,937 Lagoon Ln.,Mantoloking,NJ 08738
Buccaneer–Vincent Wright,105 Dolington Rd.,Yardley,PA 19067
Bullseye–Emily Wick,37 Atlantic Ave.,Rockport,MA 01966
Butterfly–Dan Darrow,15342 W.Clover,Libertyville,IL 60048

C **Cal 20**–Norm Yett,1320 Hart St.*201,Honolulu,HI 96817
Catalina 22–Loal Scofield,Box 7885,Eugene,OR 97401
Celebrity–Edward Lippman,Box 1029,Morrisville,PA 19067
Comet–Josh Goldman,60 E. 96th St.,New York,NY 10028
Coronado 15–Jon Otto,2591 Troy Ct.,West Linn,OR 97068
Cyclone–S.Toller,28710 Canwood St.,Agoura Hills,CA 91301

D **Day Sailer**–Dolores Bayer,Box 1918,Gulf Shores,AL 36542
Dragon–Jean Fraley,202 Lake Wash.Blvd.,Seattle,WA 98122

E **E-22**–Gay Lynn,3815 Paces Ferry Rd.NW,Atlanta,GA 30327
El Toro–Edna Robinson,Box 487,Sn Leandro,CA 94577
Ensign–Warren Hamm,3400 E.Virginia Ave.,Denver,CO 80209

F **FJ**–Mike Wyatt,475 Manhattan Pkwy.,Painesville,OH 44077
Finn–John McIntosh,Jr.,Box 22669,Savannah,GA 31403
Fireball–Charles Hooker,775 Sterling Dr.,Charleston,SC 29412
505–Ruth Tara,4155 Emerald St.,Oakland,CA 94609
FD–Peter Wells,Box 152,Rindge,NH 03461
Flying Scott–Ed Eubanks,Box 11187,Columbia,SC 29211
Force 5–Lee Parks,1 Oakwood Terr.*7,Newport,RI 02840
470–Dave Kellog,Box 355,Oyster Bay,NY 11771
420–Debbie Callahan,38 Lincoln St.,Hingham,MA 02403
Int'l 14–Neil Gallagher,70 Evarts,Newport,RI 02480

G **GP-14**–Harry Loeb,600 E.Manoa Rd.,Havertown,PA 19083
Geary 18–Joan Busch,Box 99783,San Diego,CA 92109

H **Hampton**–C.Zimmerman,Jr.,2204 Chesapeake,Hampton,VA 23661
Highlander–Alan Singer,4600 Logan NW,Canton,OH 44709
Hobie–Michele Krcelic,Box 1008,Oceanside,CA 92054
Humbug–543 El Modena, Newport Beach, CA 92663

I **Interlake**–Diane Locker,Box 2965,Ann Arbor,MI 48106
Int'l Catalina 27–1007 Woodview Ln.,West Chester,PA 19380

J **J-22**–Box 843,Franklin,TN 37064
J/24–Dick Tillman,Box 2578,Satellite Beach,FL 32937
J/30–Thomas Babbitt,Box 593,York Harbor,ME 03911
Javelin–Mrs.D.Reiber,874 Beechers Brook,Mayfield,OH 44143
Jet 14–Mary Ungemach,26 Pontiac Dr.,Wayne,NJ 07470

L **Laser**–Fiona Kidd,Box 569,Hawkesbury,On.,Canada K6A 3C8
Lido 14–Box 1252,Newport Beach,CA 92663
Lightning–Donna Foote,808 High St.,Worthington,OH 43085

M **M-20**—John Sharpless,2114 Regent St.,Madison,WI 53705
Mercury—Joanne Lusignan,12 Warren Rd.,San Mateo,CA 94401
Mini-12—2265 Westwood Blvd.,*453,Los Angeles,CA 90064
Mirror—John Borthwick,5305 Marian Dr.,Lyndhurst,OH 44124
Mobjack—F.Whittemore,1 Huntly Rd.,Richmond,VA 23226
Moore 24—159 Franklin St.,Napa,CA 94559
Moth—Ben Krothe,705 S.Shore Rd., Rt.9,Marmora,NJ 08223
Mutineer—Ernie French,Box 189,Lexington,NE 68850

N **Nacra**—Box 1153,Simi Valley,CA 93062
Naples Sabot—Peggy Lenhart,690 Senate St.,Costa Mesa,CA 92627
Nat'l One Design—Jolly Booth,1225 E.Bronson,South Bend,IN 46615

O **Olson 30**—Vicki Shelton,1955 Weston Rd.,Scotts Valley,CA 95066
Int'l 110—Jeffrey Adam,Box 1314,Newport,RI 02840
Int'l One Design—Robert McCann,391 Ocean Ave.,Marblehead,MA 01945
U.S.Optimist—S.Lippincott,1374 SE 14th,Ft.Lauderdale,FL 33316

P **Pacific Cat**—Rocky Hodges,7405 Middlebrook,Bakersfield,CA 93309
Penguin—Steve Shepstone,26 Sheppard St.,Glen Head,NY 11545
Pintail—Dave Long,2420 Provicial House Dr.,Lansing,MI 48910
Prindle—Leslie Lindeman,848 Airport Rd.,Fall River,MA 02720

R **Raven**—Edward Horrocks,3500 Bluff Ct.,Godfrey,IL 62035
Rebel—Debra Blough,RD 1 Shenks Ferry Rd.,Conestoga,PA 17516
Rhodes Babtam—Kay Wallace,136 Strongwood,Battle Creek,MI 49017
Rhodes 19—Fred Brehob,17 Corinthian Ln.,Marblehead,MA 01945

S **San Juan 21**—Fred Rehm,1900 North Lane,Camden,SC 29020
San Juan 24—Chris Wilde,Box 66421,Seattle,WA 98166
Shields—Hoke Simpson,813 Urie Hall,Columbia U.,NY 11050
Int'l Snipe—Thomas Payne, Rt. 16, Box 694, Gainesville, GA 30506
Sol Cat—2750 S.Wadsworth,*A,Box 331, Denver,CO 80227
Soling—C.T.Floyd,2841 Aspen Rd.,Northbrook,IL 60062
Int'l Star—Doris Jirka,1545 Waukegan Rd.,Glenview,IL 60025
Sunfish—Lee Parks,1 Oakwood Terr.*7,Newport,RI 02840

T **Tempest**—Dave McComb,151 Butterfield Hollow,Acton,MA 01718
Thistle—Honey Abramson,1811 Cavell Ave.,Highland Pk.,IL 60035
Thunderbird—Mark Clemmens,709 35th Ave.S,Seattle,WA 98144
Tornado—Gary Ebdon,202 Blue Point,Kemah,TX 77565
Triton—Thomas Stevens,300 Spencer Ave.,E.Greenwich,RI 02818
Int'l 210—Suzanne Anderson,88 Fearing Rd.,Hingham,MA 02043

W **Wayfarer**—Leigh Smith,Jr., 5900 Bloomfield Glens, W. Bloomfield, MI 48033
Windmill—Walter Bailey,Box 43564,Birmingham,AL 35243
Windsurfer—Diane Schweitzer,1955 W.190th St.,Torrance,CA 90509

Y **Y Flyer**—G.W.Kieffner,489 Redwood F.Dr,,Manchester,MO 63011
Yngling—N.Field,Jr.,2200 Fleet Bank Bldg.,Providence,RI 02903

If you desire the address of other class secretaries, write to USYRU, Box 209,Newport,RI 02840...or phone (401) 849-5200.

The unique, specialized world of the portable cabin sailboat.

A variety of trailerable cabin sailboats have been produced from 20′ long to the 26′ x 8′ maximum limit without requiring special permits. The best choice may be an overnighter with minimum but sufficient necessities, a sailboat that can be towed behind the family auto or camper.

Trailerable cabin sailboats began to appear in 1970. Many went to inland lakes and rivers where the sailing bug was beginning to bite such as Oklahoma and Arkansas. Others went to shallow water areas such as the Puget Sound and New England for ***gunkholing*** use.

Many went to areas similar to Arizona, New Mexico, and the Great Lakes where portability and vacation factors were primary reasons...plus the advantage of a backyard home-port storage area.

- **Fair-weather sailors.** The trailer sailor lives in his own unique environment restricting his sailing to fair weather. On the plus side, it opens new, shallow water sailing areas, rivers, etc., full-keel relatives must avoid. Consider it similar to camping out with more comforts. Also at the end of the day you don't have to worry about snakes or ants in your sleeping bag.

- **Sailboat size is confusing.** If other factors are proportional, the 24′ cabin sailboat is not just 4′ longer...the 24′ sailboat will have **twice the cubic capacity** of a 20′ sailboat, twice the weight, twice the towing windage,etc.

Size becomes the critical factor when choosing the portable cabin sailboat. The 24′ cabin sailboat will be more comfortable and have a lot more storage area. The larger cubic capacity and weight must be considered for storage, while trailering, and for launching, and loading.

- **Rerig this kind of sailboat. This is a critical factor** as all sheets, halyards, reefing lines, the anchor and anchor lines can be singlehanded from the cockpit for normal AND sudden storm conditions, see pages 58 and 59.

Lighter trailerables. Not only does it make trailering easier, but since less fiberglass, resin, lead in the keel, etc., will be required than standard-keel sailing craft the similar length, the price will be less.

Launching? What kinds of launching ramps and/or hoists can your portable sailboat use...as they may vary considerably across the U.S. and Mexico.

- **Fully-retractable swing keel?** Can your portable sailboat be run up on a sandy beach, or be caught high and dry at low tide without damage? A swing keel locking method is required for a knockdown, see page 19.

Ocean hull vs inland hull. The Balboa 21 hull had a strange movement on long ocean waves with much spray. On the Puget Sound Hood Canal with a short steep chop, also in a force 4 to 5, the Balboa 21 *Felix* proved to be an excellent performer with a dry, comfortable ride. A similar trailerboat hull would be high on our list if we moved to a similar inland bay or lake.

Catalina 22

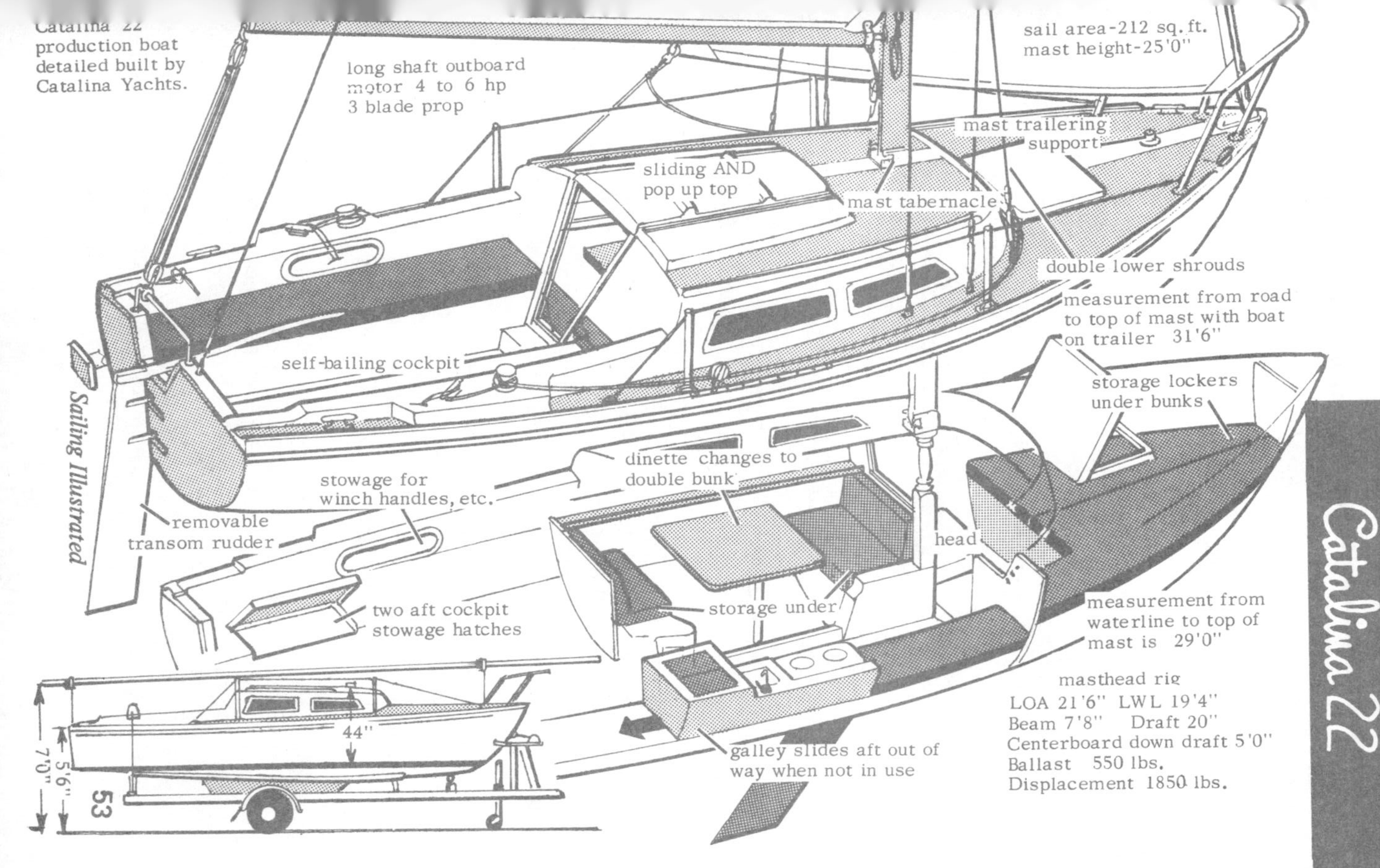

Catalina 22
production boat
detailed built by
Catalina Yachts.
long shaft outboard
motor 4 to 6 hp
3 blade prop
sail area-212 sq. ft.
mast height-25'0"
mast trailering
support
sliding AND
pop up top
mast tabernacle
double lower shrouds
measurement from road
to top of mast with boat
on trailer 31'6"
self-bailing cockpit
storage lockers
under bunks
dinette changes to
double bunk
stowage for
winch handles, etc.
removable
transom rudder
head
two aft cockpit
stowage hatches
storage under
measurement from
waterline to top of
mast is 29'0"
masthead rig
LOA 21'6" LWL 19'4"
Beam 7'8" Draft 20"
Centerboard down draft 5'0"
Ballast 550 lbs.
Displacement 1850 lbs.
galley slides aft out of
way when not in use
44"
5'6"
7'0"
Sailing Illustrated

How important is trailer capacity?

How much portability do you want? Our boat trailer experience started in late 1957 while testing a variety of trailers and outboard rigs. Considerable research was necessary to be able to publish our 1960 **Trailerboating Illustrated,** the first book on the portable, planing outboard hull.

▲**How many miles will you trailer your boat yearly?** While many owners in the northeast may trailer their boats 50 or so miles yearly, we have worked with owners in the southwest that are active all year. They want efficient, ample-capacity trailers for their fully loaded boats that can move on short notice. If New Englanders also considered long-haul trailers, instead of minimum ones for short hauls, they could look forward to one or two sun-belt sailing vacations during the winter months.

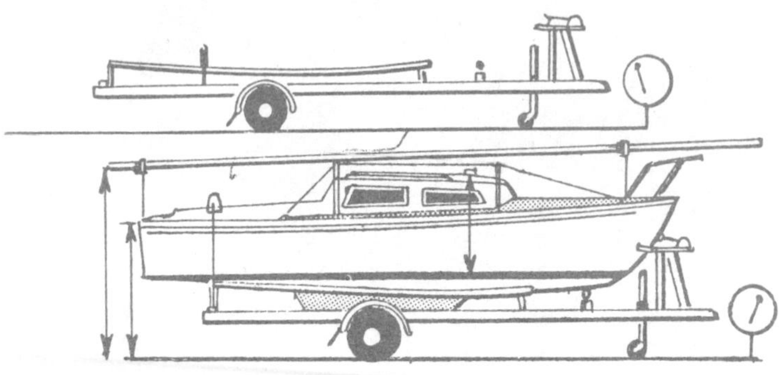

▲**Will the weight of the fully-loaded boat exceed the maximum capacity of the trailer which was ample for your new boat when it was empty?**

❶ **Weigh the empty trailer** on local public scales without the boat.

❷ **Weigh the trailer with the empty boat as it came from the factory.** You can subtract the trailer weight...to find the weight of your boat.

❸ **Weigh the fully-loaded sailboat on its trailer.** This includes the outboard motor, anchors and anchor line, tool kit, radio, cooking gear, food, etc. Weight of such carry-aboard items normally increase the longer you own your boat. Fill your water tanks at your destination with water at 8.3 lbs. per gallon, and gasoline at 6.8 lbs. per gallon, if possible.

▲**The 15% safe load factor** is ample for an empty boat. This capacity is often exceeded when fully loaded reducing the useful lifespan of the trailer and tires considerably. The overloaded trailer is a hazard due to unexpected metal fatigue such as springs breaking that cause steering problems. We hope you buy your first trailer with a larger safe load factor... the reason most owners choose better trailers the second time around.

▲**Keep trailerable sailboats on a continual diet.** Your sailboat or powerboat will then be able to perform to the best of its ability on the water...and what is equally important, is on the highway.

TROLLEY TRAILER

A fresh approach to an old problem.

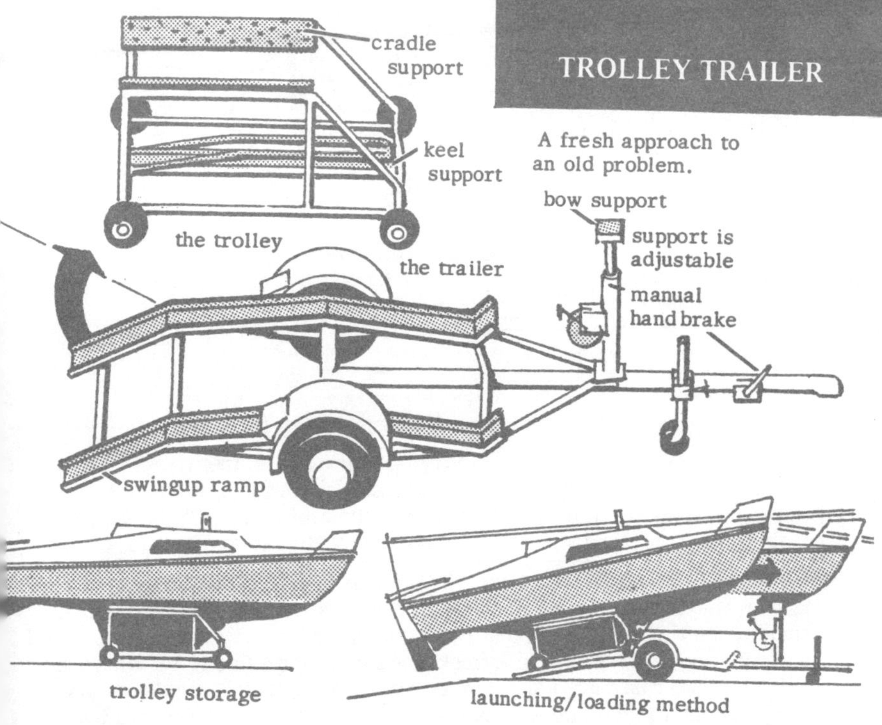

Combination trolley/trailer. It provides excellent flexibility for sailboat storage. Several Varianta's in the Bonn, Germany area, have their own trolleys using one trailer. Auto hubs are used and corrosion problems are reduced as the trailer and trailer lights aren't submerged.

The 21'4" Varianta. It is a cb/keel sloop, a E.B. van de Stadt design with over 3000 class sailboats throughout Europe. What makes it unique is its trolley/trailer with the boat and trolley/trailer made at the Dehler Factory in Hamburg, Germany. The *Menina*, shown above, is owned by our sailing language expert, Karl Freudenstein of Bonn, Germany.

Loading the trailer. The winch cable snap hook is secured to the underwater eye on the forward edge of the keel to pull the boat onto the fully submerged trolley. A fender tied to the front end of the trolley, its rope length a couple more inches than the boat draft, helps to position the boat keel on its submerged trolley.

Boat and trolley are winched aboard the trailer until the bow of the boat rests on its Y-shaped bow support. Then the "slipping rails" or ramps are raised and locked vertically. Tiedowns are added to secure the sailboat to the trailer, and the rig is ready to move out. While we feel the trolley/trailer has excellent potentials for portable sailboats and powerboats, none are presently made in the U.S.

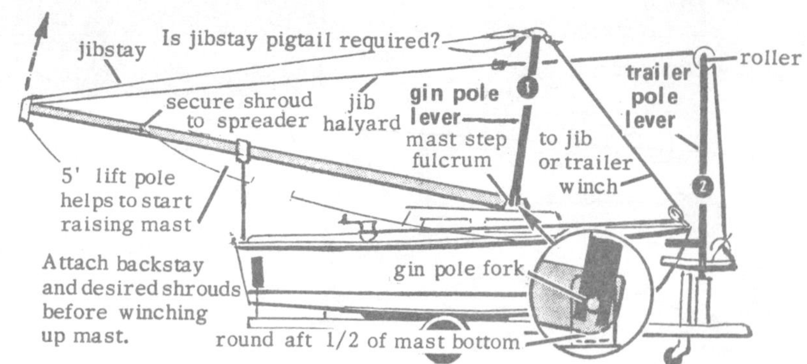

Poorly planned mast raising methods can be hazardous.

One or two people at the launching ramp, at the last moment, often climb on top of the cabin to push the mast up using brute force. If anyone trips during this operation, it isn't the fall from the cabin top...but the sudden stop on the concrete ramp 5' to 7' below...that should be the major concern.

❶ **Gin or jockey-pole lever.**–Islander 24 number 1, May 1964. We secured the base of the mast to the tabernacle. We found a strange pole aboard with a ring on one end, while the other fitted into a saddle on the mast. We secured the pole ring to the jibstay turnbuckle. We next tied a line to the ring, then led it forward to a turn block that led aft to the jib winch. While one used the jib winch to crank up the mast, another crew member held onto the backstay, which helped to prevent the mast from swinging sideways.

Lowering the mast. Release the jibstay turnbuckle from the stemhead fitting. Secure a line to the turnbuckle end leading it forward to a turn block so the line going to the jib sheet winch provides full control when lowering the mast.

❷ **Trailer-pole lever.** Secure bottom of mast to turnbuckle, then connect both backstay and lower shrouds to their chainplates. Secure bitter end of the jib halyard to the port mast cleat, then secure a line to the jibstay snap.

Put this line over the top of the roller. Install the pole in the trailer bow fitting with a V-shaped collar resting against the bow. Start to raise the mast with the trailer winch.

After the mast is vertical, reach the jibstay turnbuckle with a boat hook, then lock the turnbuckle to the bow tang. Flip the released raising line off the roller. Remove and secure the pole to the trailer frame out of the way.

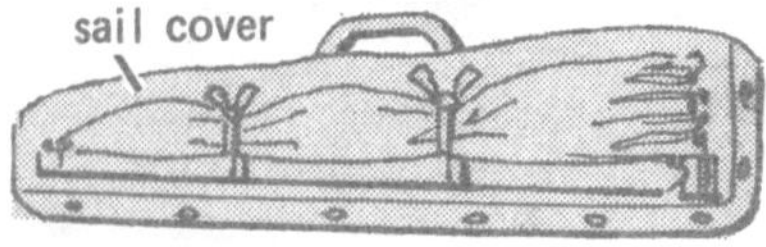

Add slugs to the mainsail luff and foot as shown on page 87. Finally have a sail cover designed so it can protect the sail on its boom when stored ashore or in the boat while trailering.

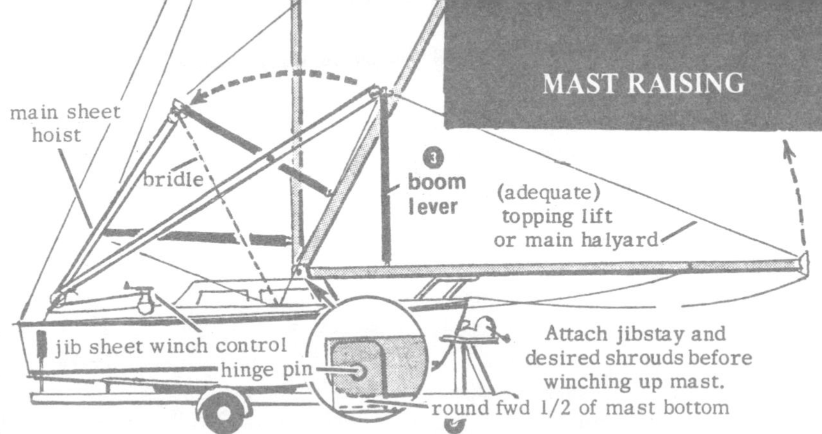

3 The boom lever is excellent for on-board mast raising.

The Dutch mast-raising method used on our *Pink Cloud* is needed for most cabin sailboats entering nearby Huntington Harbor in Southern California, due to a low highway bridge inside the jetty entrance.

- "Why do you prefer **most masts to tilt forward?"** , we asked Fred Lanting, who made most of these installations as he was working on our boat.

"When I was a boy in Holland I often worked on my father's floating general merchandise store. He didn't want to waste time nor pay endless bridge keepers to raise their bridges when he made the monthly rounds. He used this method on his 60' sailboat to lower and raise the mast single-handed from the cockpit with the main sheet. It was easy to go under the numerous bridges...which didn't please most local bridge keepers".

- **A bridle is used** while raising and lowering a mast to prevent it from swinging sideways. Our upper shroud required a 3" spacer added to provide a pivot point in line with the pivot of the mast...while other sailboat rigging designs may find the lower shroud pivot more practical.

- **Quick-disconnect turnbuckles** are required for the backstay and lower shrouds on our boat...and **a longer mainsheet is required.** After a redwood stiffener was added for support in the mast pivot area, the forward bottom part of the mast had to be rounded as shown, to permit the lower end to be raised or lowered without catching on anything.

To summarize–

- **Dockside raising–**the gin pole method is good for sailboats to 26' long. The boom lever method is used for sailboats to 60' long to go under low bridges, to replace burned out light bulbs, to paint the mast, and to check and replace mast fittings if necessary.

- **Launching ramp mast raising–** consider the trailer pole lever method for trailerable sailboats. Most adults can step on the trailer frame to secure the base of the mast to the tabernacle.

This eliminates the need to climb on top of the cabin...and the chance of a fall with a sudden stop on the concrete five to seven feet below on the concrete launching ramp.

Rig for single-handed operation.

How often will you want to use your sailboat ...is the primary consideration. The sailboat with clumsy, partially thought-out running rigging controls takes the fun out of sailing. Consider rerigging your portable cabin sailboat and larger sailboats so all controls come to the cockpit and operate easily. *The boat that is easy and fun to sail will be used more often.*

- **Rigging efficiency.** Many fleets of portable cabin sailboats have been launched since 1970.Many had minimum, poorly planned rigging and hardware to cut cost in a competitive field, Many have become unloved derelicts...which may become a blessing in disguise for those with a sailing background.
- **Fair-weather sailing and gunkholing.** They are light compared to a similar length ocean keel sailboat. **Owners have to be on the defensive** since, if a fast moving storm hits without reefing, they will heel considerably which can wipe out most steering control.
- **A knockdown** can rapidly follow. If the *weighted centerboard* doesn't have a stout *shock cord tiedown,* the board will swing up into its well to cause a rapid 180 degree upset with a possible sinking. A major concern I have is the total absence of basic reefing methods on portable sailboats, that can be single handed from the cockpit.
- **Rigging variables.** The rigging details on the facing page and our *Homestudy Guide* page 107 resulted after two sailing students from Lake Tahoe faced a similar situation in their new portable sailboat in a fast moving storm. Analyze the functions of the necessary control lines using quick-release cam cleats with all lines trimmed and released from the cockpit.

  When a storm moves in—**release main halyard** to starboard, storing it in its pouch so it can't go overboard and wrap around propeller. **Snap the boom-mounted shock cord** over the mainsail so it can't fill and lift.

  If you still carry too much sail—**release jib halyard** to port, with the halyard stored in its pouch. The **jib downhaul** is required to prevent the jib from lifting and filling, producing erratic steering action.
- **The anchor and anchor line** must be handled from the cockpit in a storm without going forward. The alternative, is to run downwind with bare poles.
- **Jam cleats jam at the wrong time!** Replace with **cam cleats,** page 144, which are easy to adjust or release under pressure. The best one we can recommend is the versatile *Nashmarine Trigger Cleat* *, see page 35.
- **Bitts should replace bow cleats,** page 190. They are lighter, require less area, and handle larger size anchor and dock lines. **Locking skene chocks** in a larger size without sharp edges, page 190, should replace straight bow chocks with sharp edges, which are easy for dock lines and anchor lines to jump out of in wave action. **Backing plates are required** for bitts and cleats to spread the stress over larger fiberglass areas so bolts can't be pulled out.

You will enjoy many more pleasureable hours sailing trailerable to large ocean sailboats rigged for single-handed operation from the cockpit, if all hardware and rigging leads are simple, functional, and practical.

***Nashmarine, 32906 Avenida Descanso, San Juan Capistrano, CA 92675**

RIG COCKPIT CONTROLS

The better prepared a sailboat is for single-handed operation, the more it will normally be used. We show basic rigging patterns for your analysis.

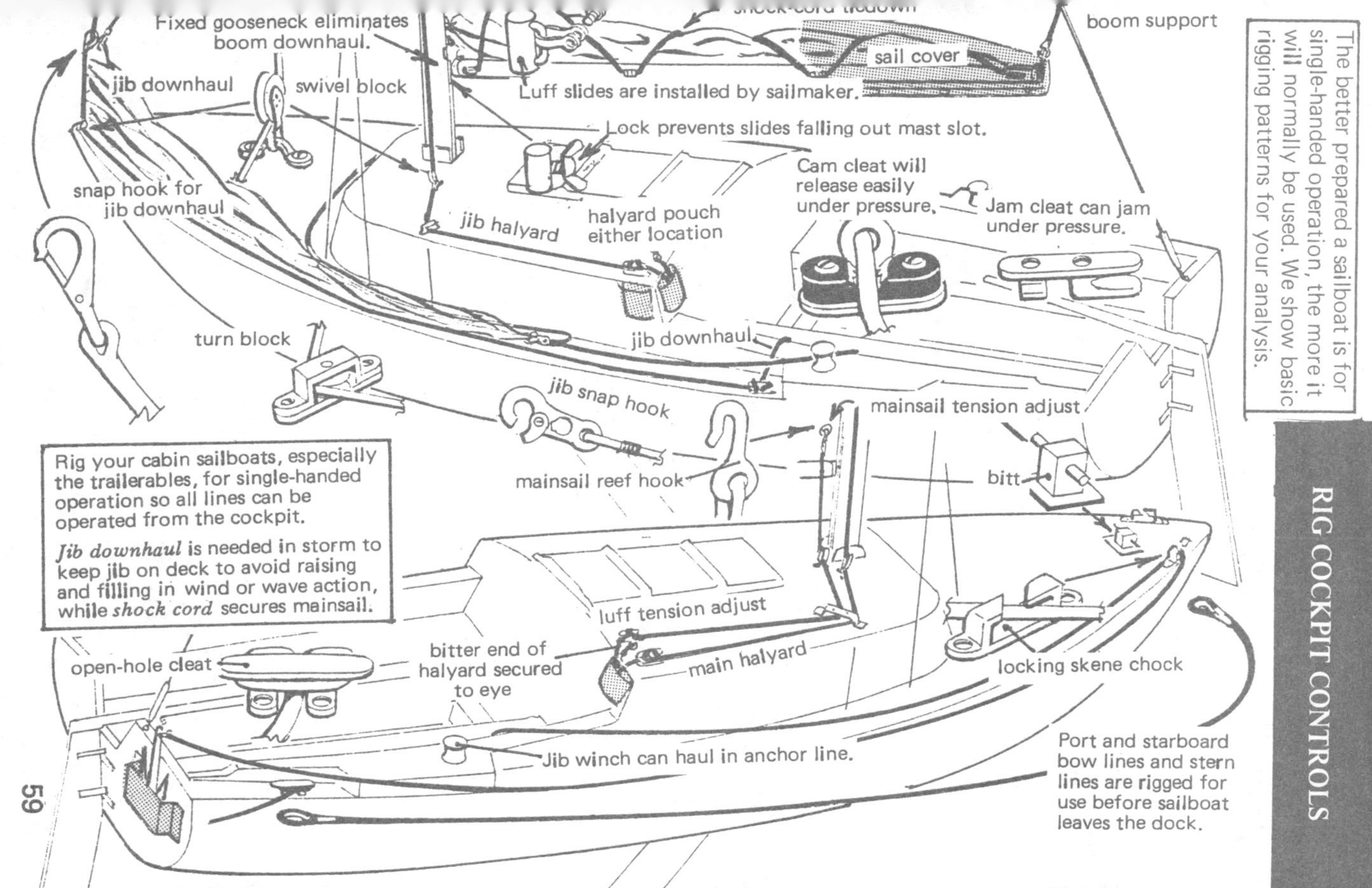

Rig your cabin sailboats, especially the trailerables, for single-handed operation so all lines can be operated from the cockpit.

Jib downhaul is needed in storm to keep jib on deck to avoid raising and filling in wind or wave action, while *shock cord* secures mainsail.

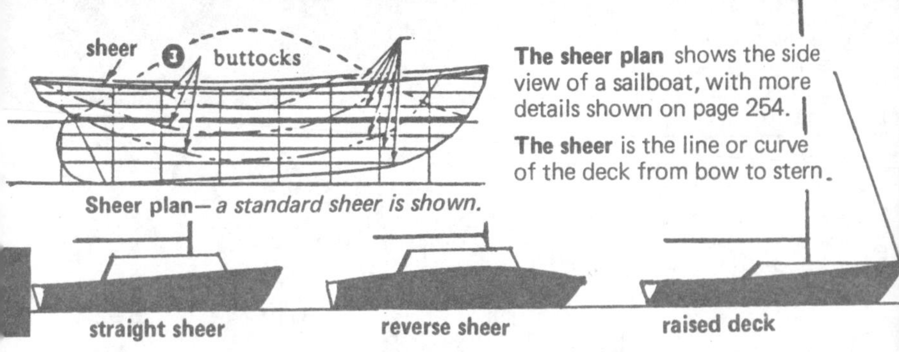

Sheer plan—*a standard sheer is shown.*

The sheer plan shows the side view of a sailboat, with more details shown on page 254.

The sheer is the line or curve of the deck from bow to stern.

▲**Walk around vs walk-over deck.** Standard, straight, and reverse sheer hulls have a trunk cabin with a walk-around deck...while a ***raised-deck hull*** has a walk-over deck extending the full width of the cabin.

● **Standard sheer.** Sailboats 40′ and longer made of wood were common in 1950.The bow and stern were higher so waves and spray coming aboard would drain to the low point in the center of the sheer to drain overboard.

● **Cubic capacity** becam a major factor when the smaller fiberglass sailboats emerged in the 1960′s for a market of first owners looking for low maintenance craft, with minimum need for the standard sheer drainage.

● **The straight sheer** became popular for the new fiberglass sailboats as it increased the cubic capacity below. ..while other builders introduced the **reverse sheer,** increasing the cubic capacity below even more than a standard sheer hull the same length. Some sailboats have a small reverse sheer while the extreme reverse sheer above had little public acceptance.

▲**The raised-deck** 24′ Columbia Challenger is shown at right...while the same hull was used in the Columbia 24 with a trunk cabin.The comparison of these two sailboats is important for pocket-cruiser owners where cubic capacity, and comfort are more critical than on sailboats over 30′ long.

● **24′ trunk-cabin version.** It has a small cockpit, a narrow walk-around deck, while the high cabin blocked much view, especially with a large genoa. It has 6′2″ standing room in the main cabin. Sitting in the main cabin was uncomfortable as the junction of the deck and cabin hits me in the back of the neck. This situation commonly happens to me on trunk cabin sailboats to 32′ long as I am 6′7″ tall.

● **The 24′ raised-deck version** is a better performer with less weight and less windage. The cost is less as not as much material and hand work are needed. The cockpit is large and comfortable for 6 to 8 adults where we spend most of the daylight hours underway or at anchor. Visibility was excellent for teaching over 1600 students with full day sailing lessons. Because of the full width cabin, I am comfortable when sitting, or sleeping below.

If you are faced with a choice of the two identical length sailboats above,the trunk cabin provides a better weekend bungalow while staying below for long periods.The active sports-minded sailor may prefer the raised-deck hull with the large comfortable cockpit when underway or at anchor if he enjoys sunshine, scenery, and varied water sports.

Pink Cloud

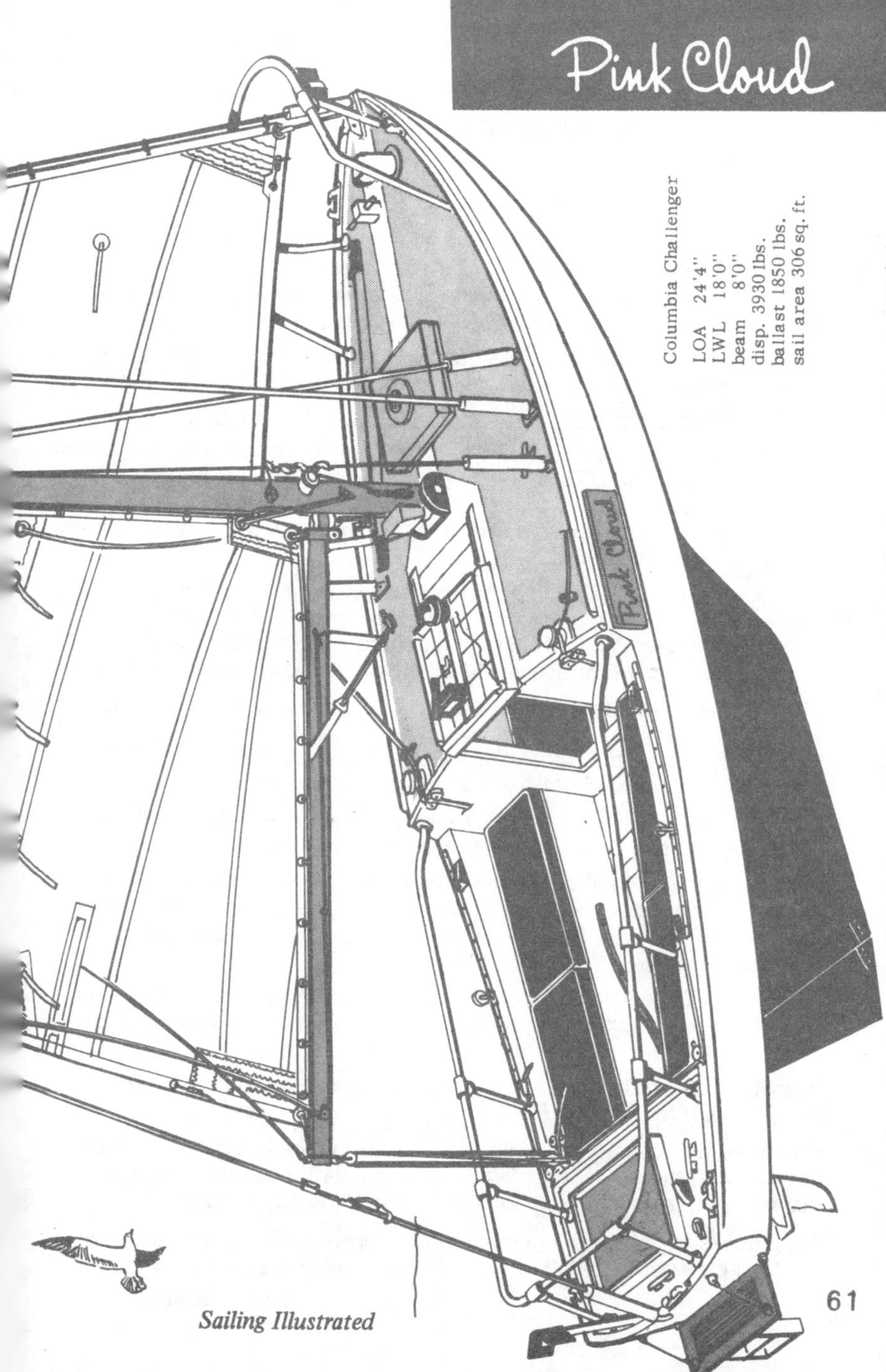
Columbia Challenger
LOA 24'4"
LWL 18'0"
beam 8'0"
disp. 3930 lbs.
ballast 1850 lbs.
sail area 306 sq. ft.
Pink Cloud

The racing fraternity has clouded the term cruising sailboat.

It is sailing for pleasure. When sailing ceases to be fun and no longer makes sense on a racer with spartan accommodations slugging to windward on a leftover ocean in a dying wind...the pocket cruiser or the long distance cruiser is snug in the world of its choice.

It may be at a dock, riding to a mooring, or anchored near isolated Santa Barbara Island with a chorus of sea lions arguing in the distance. Or it can be a pocket cruiser anchored to a sand bank on a large western reservoir... or surrounded by cattails with the bow snuggled into an eastern river bank.

The crew is below exchanging ideas of the day while enjoying a hearty meal with background music furnished by seagulls and terns...or meadowlark, whipporwill, and bull frogs.

- **The pocket cruiser** from 22′ to 27′ long has many potentials, with a challenge due to miniaturization. Take time to rig it efficiently topside for your kind of sailing. Take ample time to choose the built-in comforts below as shown on the facing page to make it a comfortable bungalow with changing scenery for weekends and vacations.

Storage space is critical. Each person can be assigned one bulkhead storage bag for clothing...add grommet drains beneath them to eliminate mildew. Store sleeping bags in pillow bolsters for daytime use. Seat belts make excellent **bunk straps** for sleeping in sloppy weather underway or at anchor.

Electrical requirements are important to provide for your needs on a mooring or at anchor using 12V battery power, plus a 110V dockside hookup for lights and to charge the battery. Study page 140 of our *Homestudy Guide* for a detailed electrical installation of the pocket cruiser shown at right.

Cockpit sun shades are important...avoid white ones due to tremendous glare. Colorful red, green, or blue *Acrilan* will eliminate the glare.

- **Running rigging and sail adjustments should be easy to reach and operate.** Replace standard cleats and jamcleats with quick, easy to release cam cleats for main and jib sheets, page 59, so they can be easily released when under considerable pressure in storm conditions.

A topping lift and a boom lift should be added to the boom, page 96. They serve different purposes and should be easy to reach. The mainsail needs a jiffy reef which should be easy to reef from the cockpit, page 148.

Autopilots are important for ocean operation under sail and/or power. The Hill pilot used for 15 years was replaced with a *Tiller Master.*

Pocket cruiser operation flexibility requires various basic instruments. This includes a depth sounder, page 245, an rdf, page 245, a barometer, page 213, a combination speedometer/odometer, and a *Sea Temp*, page 228.

Fog requires a temperature/humidity indicator to predict an incoming fog, and to know whether it will be light or heavy, see page 219.

pulpit
working jib
jib foot adjust
17" jib pennant
bitt
whisker/spinnaker pole
shroud roller
jib hlyd to stbd
main hlyd to port
jib hlyd to port
telltale
tabernacle
humidity indicator
double lower shrouds
bulkhead storage bags
stowage for flopper stoppers, Para-Anchor, etc.
15 gal. water tank
bunk straps
head
clinometer
alcohol stove
Sea Temp
preserver locker
cunningham
downhaul
compass
midship cleat
chart
rdf
"Tiller Master" auto pilot
mast step
barometer
depth sounder transducer
extinguisher
odometer and speedometer
outboard controls
boom vang/preventer
jib sheet cam cleat
cockpit railing
genoa fairlead
main sheet cam cleat
mainsheet traveler adjust
dockside power inlet
electrical switch panel
12v 110 amp battery
shock cord tiedown
jiffy reef
outhaul
skene chocks
swim, dive platform
rope locker below
Lewco battery charger
7 1/2 hp outboard, pg. 180
topping lift
topping lift cleat
boom lift
telltale
stern light
vents

Naval Architect Bill Crealock is defined as the "Man of 8000 Boats", in the first 2/1993 edition of SEA *Waterfront News.* Bill has been my cruising sailboat advisor since the early 1960s when he opened a local design office, and the first, much needed nautical bookstore.

Bill had an English heritage with an engineering training background in a Glassgow, Scotland shipbuilding firm, with up to three weeks to design a ship bulkhead. When boredom set in he began to dream of small cruising sailboats. Bill had the traditional North Atlantic heavy-weather background, plus the Pacific with probably 100,000 miles under his keel before arriving in Newport Beach.

He arrived at an opportune time when the first production fiberglass sailboats were produced in Orange County, rapidly spreading thruout neighboring counties. Everyone was in a learning process with this new medium. The young designers rapidly found they had a good market with sailing interest and spendable income. Racing sailboats soon took the advertising lead for our light westerly winds. Builders soon realized their sales didn't increase as advertisers promised. A survey soon found one owner was a hardened racer, three to four were interested in some racing, the rest of ten were interested in leisurely cruising.

Crealock agreed to a 2½ hour lecture for our evening sailing classes open to the public, with some local designers unobtrusively slumped in back row seats. Everything Bill said with his traditional cruising and wooden boatbuilding expertise was new. In the two 5 minute breaks students stayed in their chairs saying little. After the lecture was over, they still waited hoping for more of his specialized information.

While Bill designed 70 to 80 sailboats and powerboats for various companies, He designed the Dana 24, Pacific Seacraft 31, plus the 34, 37, and the new 44 with his name for Pacific Seacraft.

Bill is quiet, modest, slim, and soft spoken, with his blue eyes always on the move taking in endless details. We were in his Carlsbad office when he surprised us with a broad grin, "I was just informed that I now have an exclusive agreement to design Pacific Seacraft sailboats!"

Bill had ample time thru the years to answer my questions, often from cruising sailors worldwide when having problems. He supplied me with full engineering drawings of his Dana 24 I started to detail. We were looking at a 24 at the factory as more information was needed. "Wait two weeks and we'll have this 24 in a slip near your sailboat".

We arrived midafternoon as the magazine photographers left. My wife tugged and eased various docklines, while Bill walked fore and aft, and side to side to provide the missing details for our camera.

Each Pacific Seacraft sailboat is made one at a time with loving technical care. They are expensive bought by experienced sailors, NOT first time owners. Crealock and Pacific Seacraft are a happy combination.

Dana 24

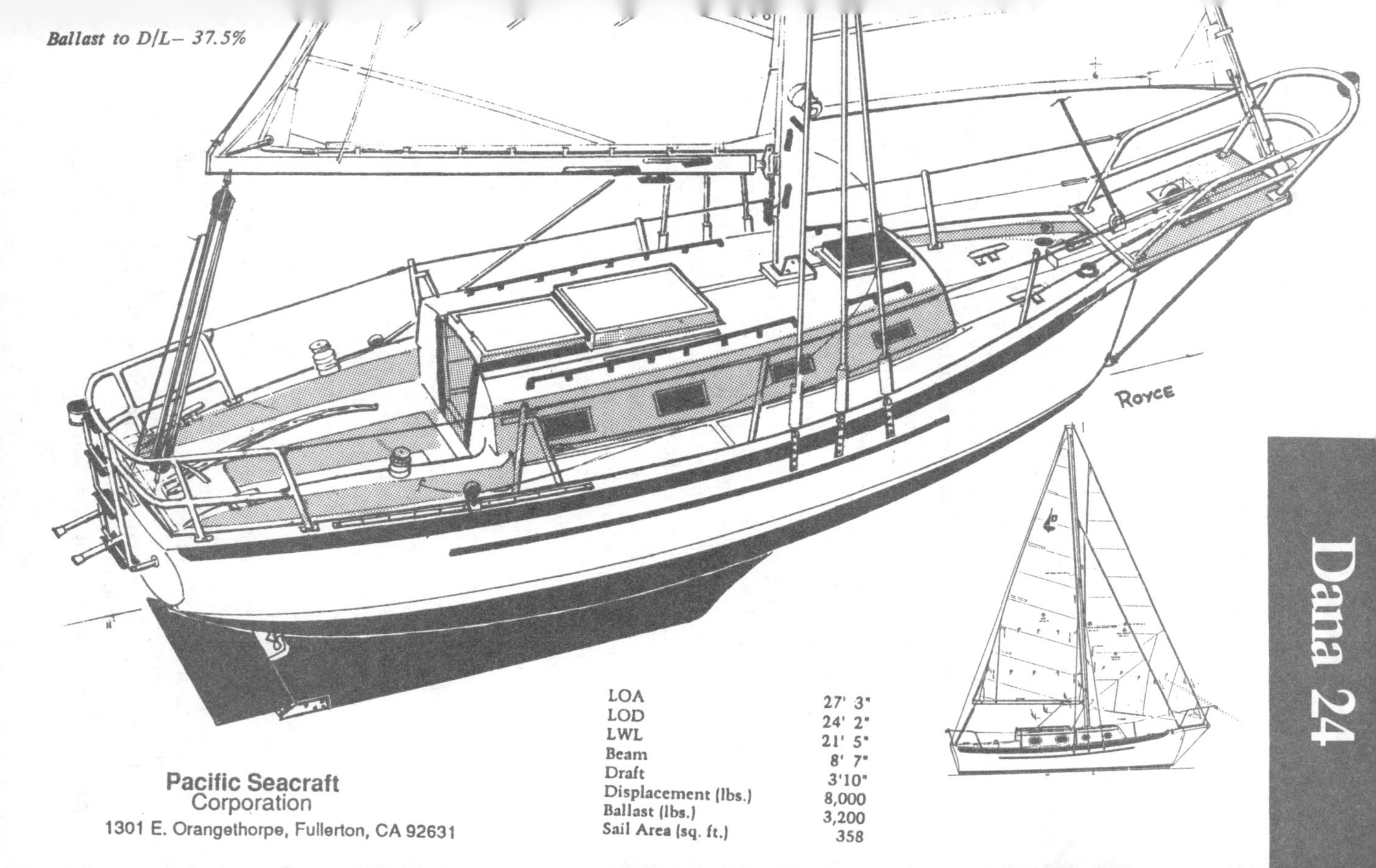

Ballast to D/L– 37.5%

LOA	27' 3"
LOD	24' 2"
LWL	21' 5"
Beam	8' 7"
Draft	3'10"
Displacement (lbs.)	8,000
Ballast (lbs.)	3,200
Sail Area (sq. ft.)	358

Pacific Seacraft
Corporation
1301 E. Orangethorpe, Fullerton, CA 92631

The little publicized world of wooden cruising sailboats.

Tahiti is the crossroads of the mid Pacific. When we visited Papeete in 1973 we found 53 tired sailboats stern to the quay with only a couple from the U.S. The majority were wooden hulls, a few metal hulls, and the only excellent cement hull I've known...and no fiberglass hulls. We can provide no better example of the popularity of wooden sailboats for long-distance cruising though receiving little publicity in sailing magazines.

Tahiti provides a continually changing world for cruising sailboats. A friend owning the Tahiti ketch *Fat Squaw* visited Papeete 20 years ago to find no Tahiti ketches as the majority of the craft were trimarans.

Many good wooden cruising sailboats can be found in saltwater ports worldwide. This is the environment that is kind to wood **if the boat is well designed, well ventilated, and adequately maintained.**

The marine surveyor is a necessity when buying a wooden or fiberglass cruising sailboat to avoid unnecessary and expensive problems beginning with rot. Add to the initial agreement that the owner will pay the surveyor if the vessel won't pass the survey to save you time and money. Listen closely and make many notes for ideas the surveyor may recommend.

- **Finisterre** was launched in 1954, which is the classic of that period. She spawned an endless number of look-alikes to 55' long which seem ageless and are in mint condition, still sailing worldwide. The latest we saw was the 40' *Dreamer* which was on a nearby mooring after returning from a 3 year cruise of the South Pacific which looked like a brand new sailboat.

Traditionalists at the time of launching called **Finisterre** an ugly duckling when the sleek, wet, narrow beam, heavy displacement hulls were popular. After the combination racing/cruising sailboat won the Bermuda Race first overall in three consecutive races...the beamy yawl rig became popular.

Finisterre was beamy with a heavy 10 ton displacement. Her centerboard provided a 7'7" draft when down, and a 3'11" draft for sailing in shallow water or anchoring.

- **Iris** is shown on pages 70 to 73, a yawl carrying the early gaff cruising rig the owner recommended showing. It was owned by John Martucci who passed away in 1956 a week after seeing his sailboat in our new book. It was featured in many magazine articles, also winning the 1939 Blue Water Cruising Award for sailing to Italy, and returning to Brooklyn.

- **Medley,** *ex Kenetta,* is a 38' Alden designed schooner built nearby, that was launched in 1940. She has a long career in short and long races, and has cruised the Pacific as far as Australia...a former crew member told us.

Though the schooner *Medley* is two feet longer than the yawl *Iris,* their lines seem almost identical. *Medley* is beamier and lighter than some of the narrower, heavier, meter-type hulls built in the same time frame that I've sailed on. The difference becomes apparent in light winds when *Medley* is still responsive with a light touch...while narrower, heavier, slack-bilge hulls bog down,losing steering control.

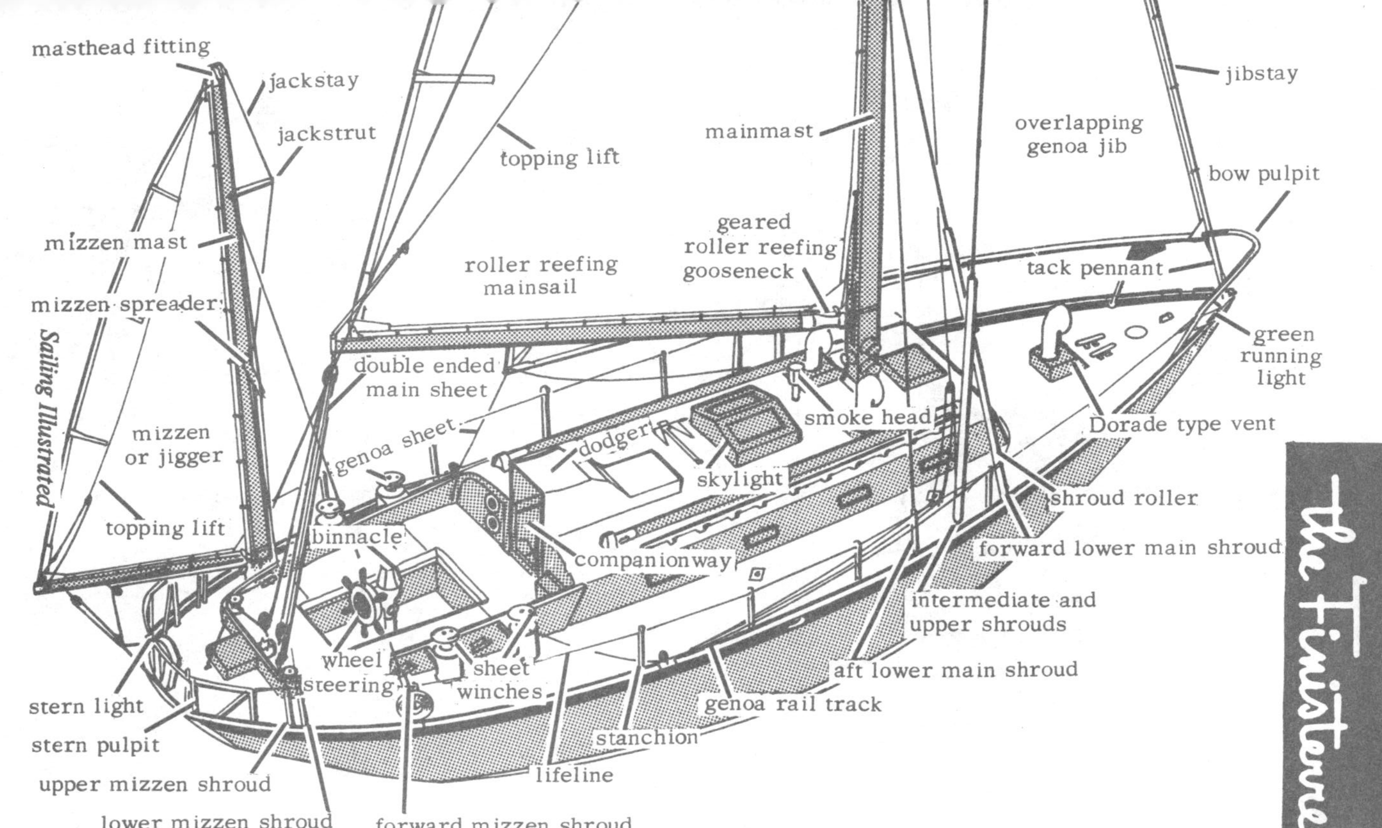
the Finisterre
masthead fitting
jackstay
jackstrut
topping lift
mainmast
overlapping genoa jib
jibstay
bow pulpit
mizzen mast
roller reefing mainsail
geared roller reefing gooseneck
tack pennant
mizzen spreader
green running light
double ended main sheet
Dorade type vent
smoke head
mizzen or jigger
genoa sheet
dodger
skylight
shroud roller
topping lift
binnacle
companionway
forward lower main shroud
intermediate and upper shrouds
wheel steering
sheet winches
aft lower main shroud
genoa rail track
stern light
stern pulpit
stanchion
upper mizzen shroud
lifeline
lower mizzen shroud
forward mizzen shroud
Sailing Illustrated

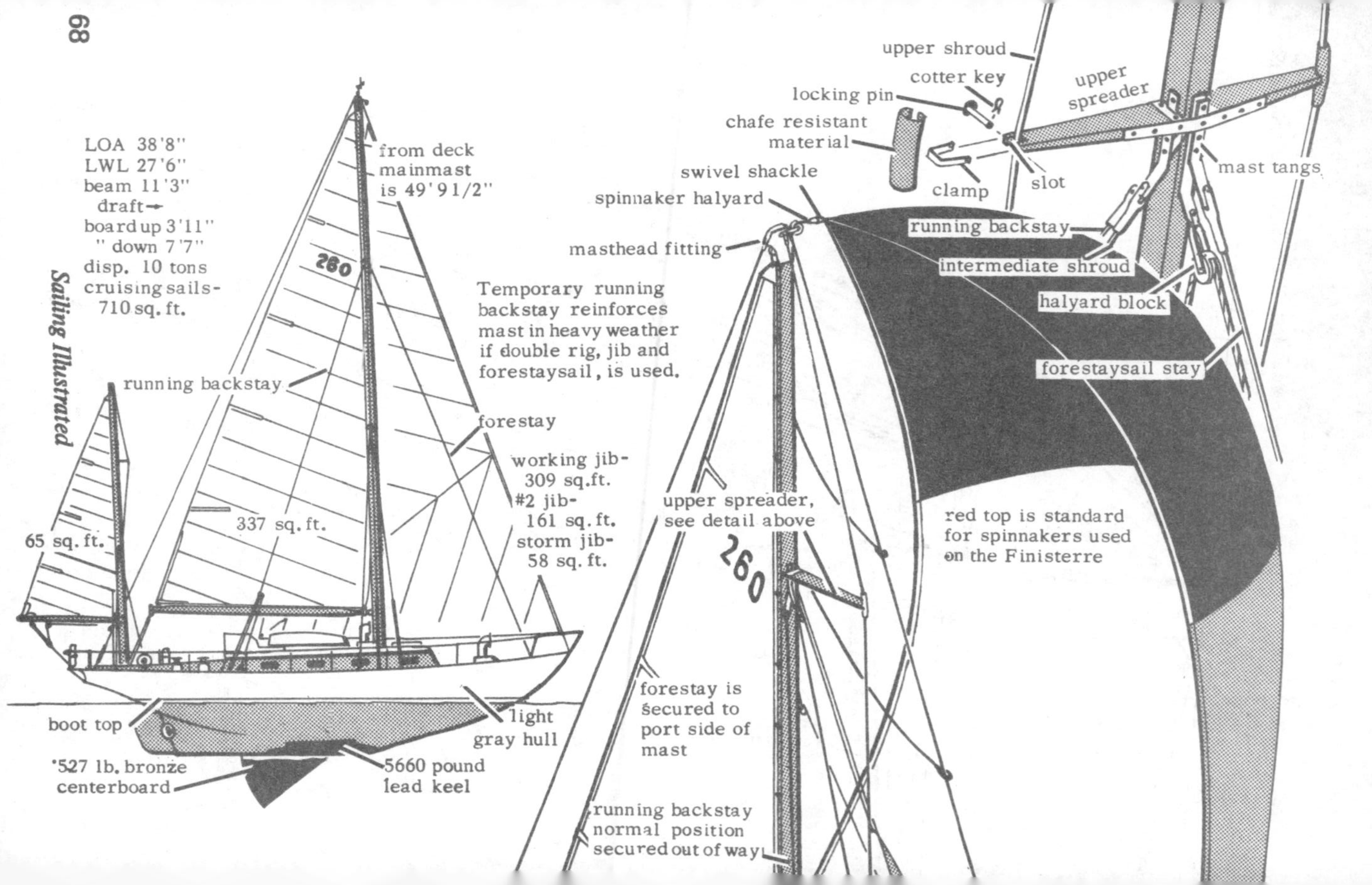
LOA 38'8"
LWL 27'6"
beam 11'3"
draft→
board up 3'11"
" down 7'7"
disp. 10 tons
cruising sails-
710 sq. ft.
from deck
mainmast
is 49'9 1/2"
260
running backstay
Temporary running
backstay reinforces
mast in heavy weather
if double rig, jib and
forestaysail, is used.
forestay
working jib-
309 sq.ft.
#2 jib-
161 sq. ft.
storm jib-
58 sq. ft.
337 sq. ft.
65 sq. ft.
boot top
light
gray hull
'527 lb. bronze
centerboard
5660 pound
lead keel
upper shroud
cotter key
locking pin
chafe resistant
material
upper
spreader
mast tangs
slot
clamp
swivel shackle
spinnaker halyard
masthead fitting
running backstay
intermediate shroud
halyard block
forestaysail stay
upper spreader,
see detail above
red top is standard
for spinnakers used
on the Finisterre
260
forestay is
secured to
port side of
mast
running backstay
normal position
secured out of way

the Finisterre

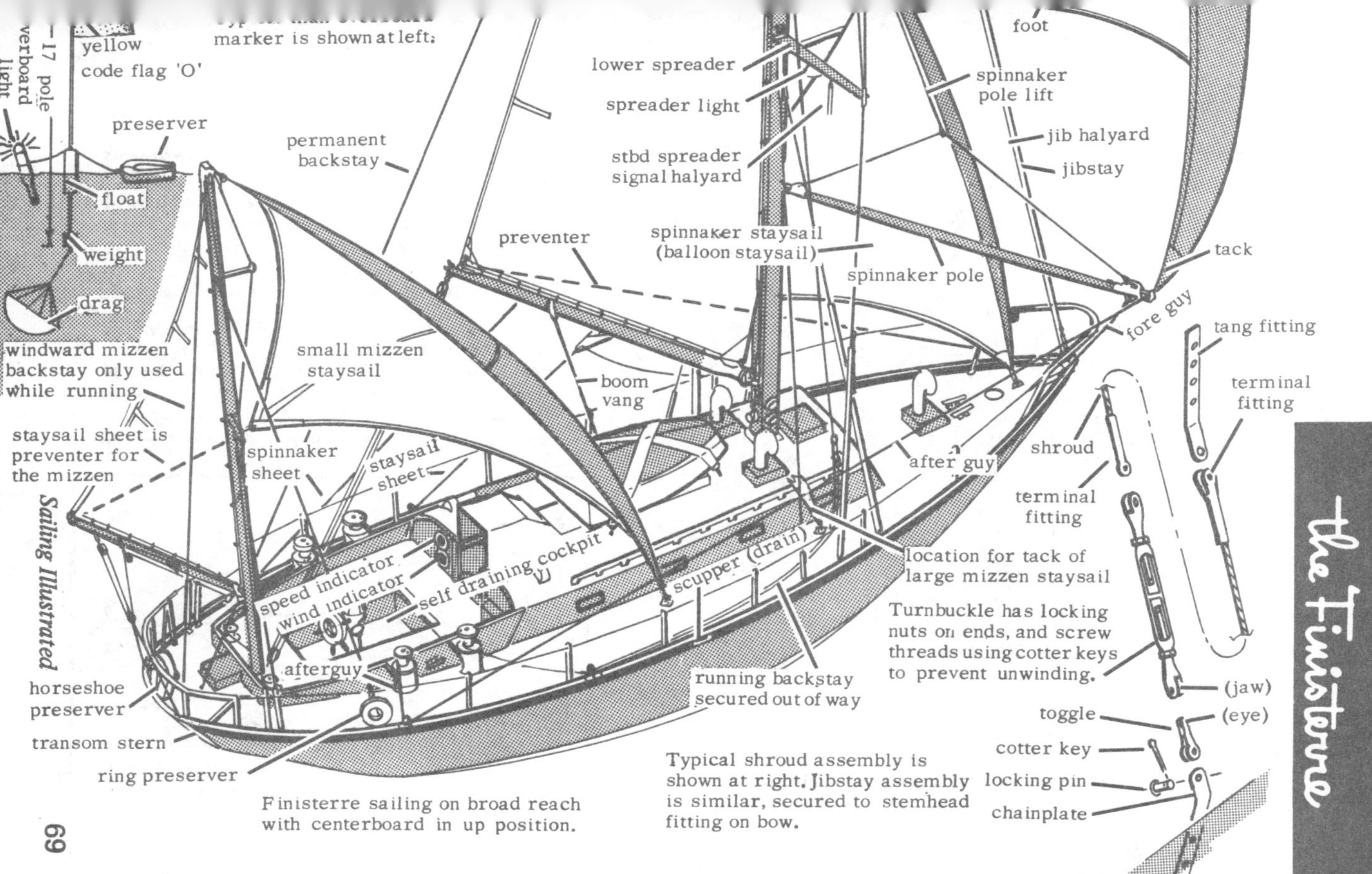

Turnbuckle has locking nuts on ends, and screw threads using cotter keys to prevent unwinding.

Typical shroud assembly is shown at right. Jibstay assembly is similar, secured to stemhead fitting on bow.

Finisterre sailing on broad reach with centerboard in up position.

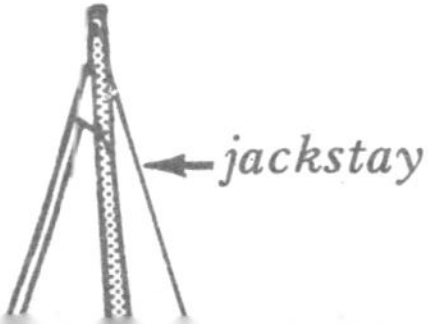

Homestudy Guide—pages 103 and 121

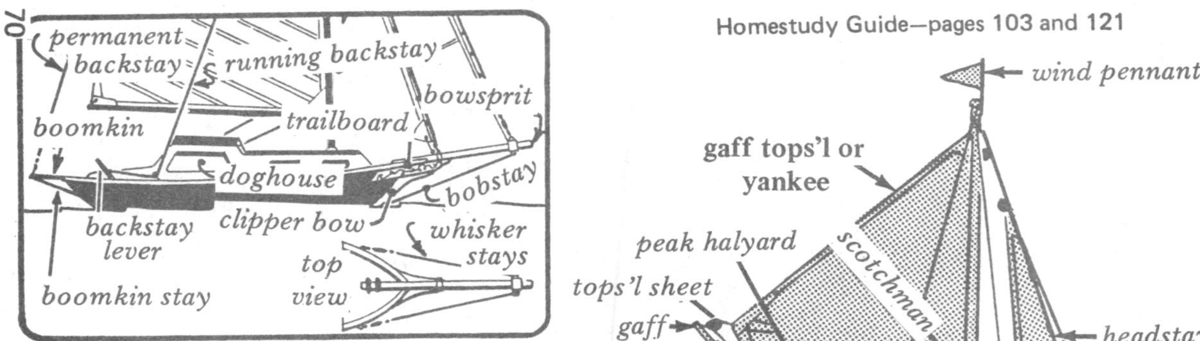

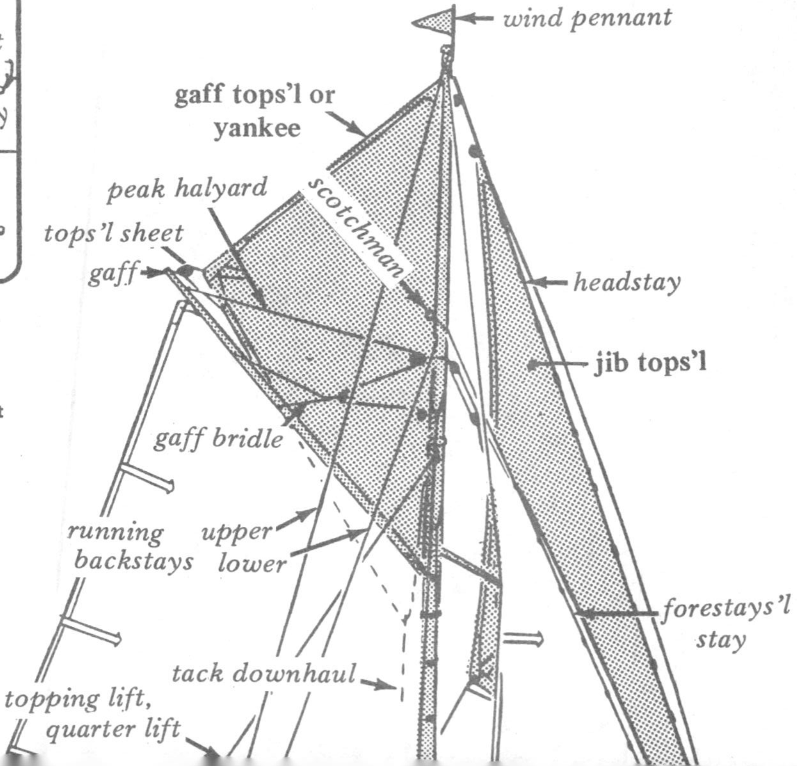

We provide considerable coverage of IRIS, designed in 1937 for John Martucci, see the lines drawings on pages 254-5. John spent a year making a model of IRIS plank by plank which is the keynote piece for the 1930 yachting exhibit at the Mystic Seaport Museum in Mystic, Connecticut.

IRIS had a special mooring area near Sheepshead Bay, Brooklyn, New York. We liked to paddle out of Jamaica Bay in our kayak to look at her tall rig, and wave at her owners. Little did we realize how important IRIS would be to sailing history.

staysail—159 sq. ft.
mainsail—378 sq. ft.
mizzen—129 sq. ft.

total— 666 sq. ft

IRIS – our 1938 yawl

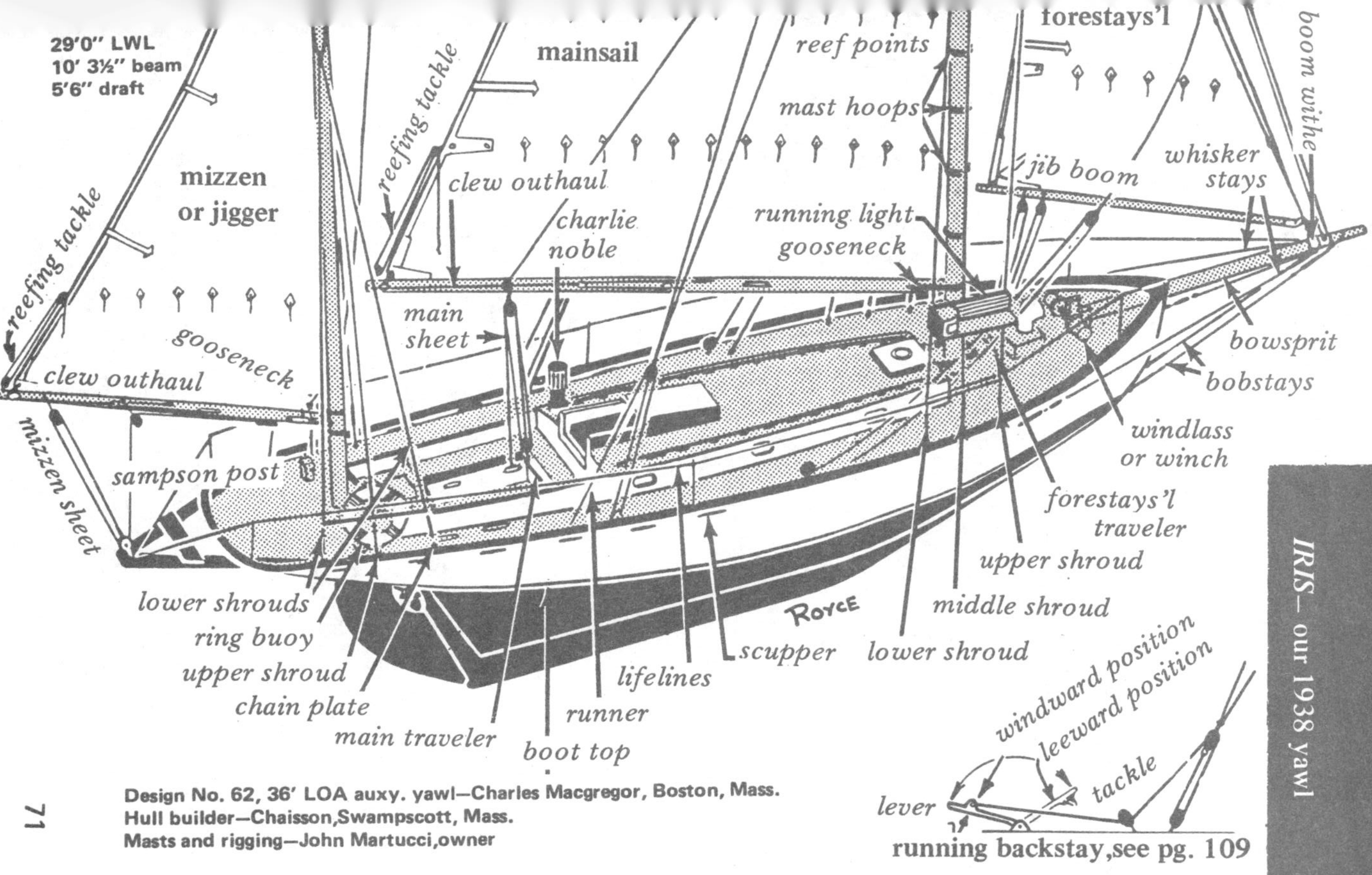

running backstay, see pg. 109

Design No. 62, 36' LOA auxy. yawl—Charles Macgregor, Boston, Mass.
Hull builder—Chaisson, Swampscott, Mass.
Masts and rigging—John Martucci, owner

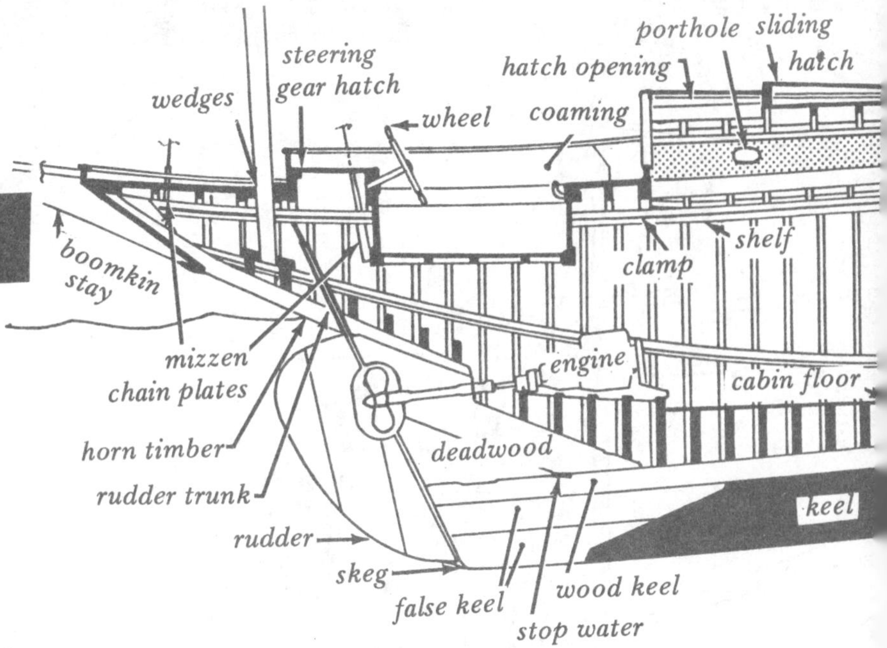

After owner and naval architect agreed to preliminary plans of IRIS, the next step was for the architect to prepare the lines drawings, pages 254-5, to show the hull shape from three views—profile, plan, and sections.

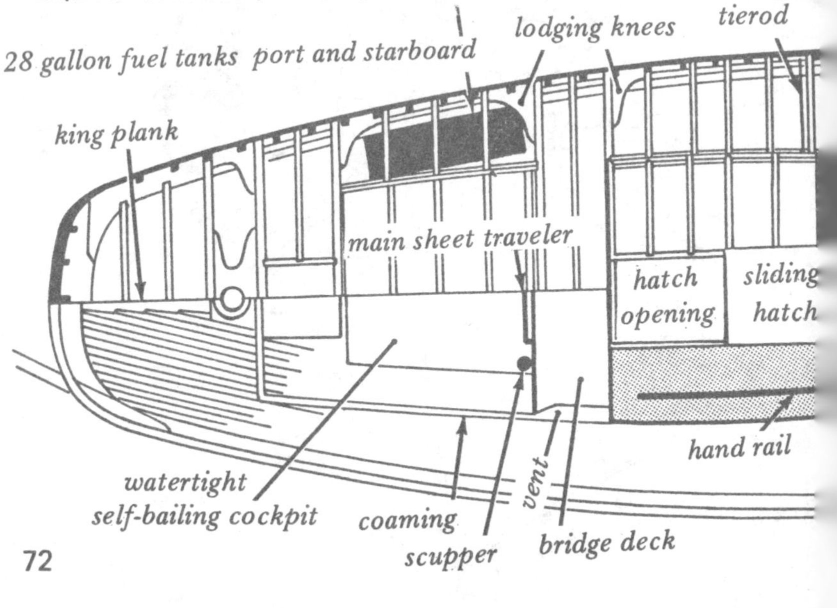

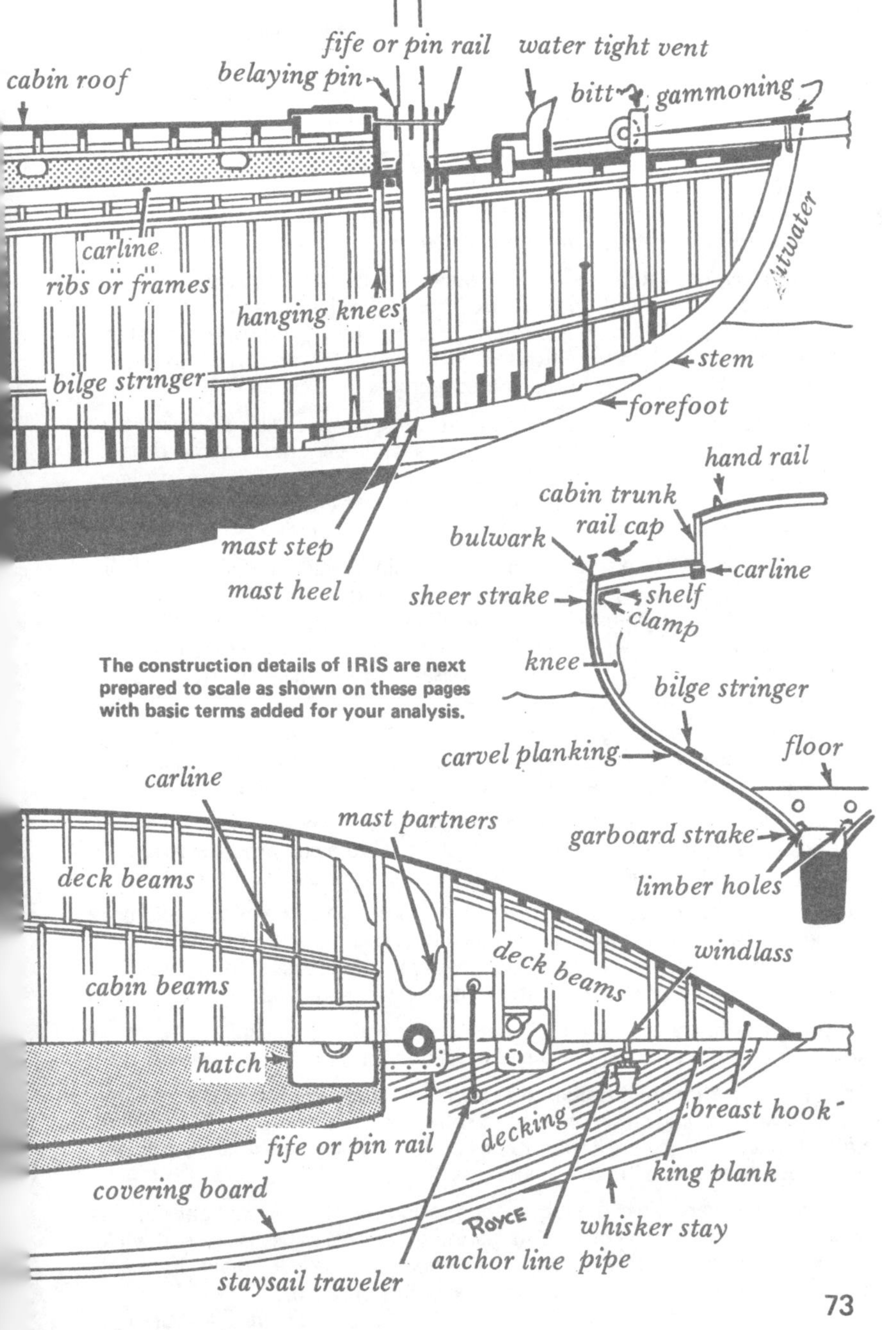

The construction details of IRIS are next prepared to scale as shown on these pages with basic terms added for your analysis.

Long-distance cruising sailboats are deceptive.

The practical long-distance cruiser often averages 35′ to 40′ long. It will be of medium to heavy displacement for considerable cargo-carrying capacity with 2 to 3 people aboard for long periods at a time . **Cubic capacity is the major factor** as a 31′ sailboat may have half the capacity of a 35′ sailboat...while a 44′ sailboat may have twice the capacity of a 40′ sailboat.

Human engineering is important to live comfortably and harmoniously in tight quarters underway, and with half the time dockside or at anchor.

- **The 40′ Newporter ketch.** We feel it was the first sailboat specifically designed for cruising by designer/builder "Ack" Ackerman. He began building his 45′ schooner *Island Girl* which was interrupted by WW II, and was completed afterwards. Ack and his wife lived aboard for over 22 months while they cruised over 15,000 miles in the Pacific going as far west as Tahiti.

His goal was to build the perfect sailboat for offshore cruising. He spent 4 years as a marine surveyor after returning while designing an improved, smaller version of his *Island Girl.* The first few Newporters were gaff-rigged ketches, later changed to marconi rigs. A few were cutter rigged which could point with the rest of the racing fleet in the 1960's.

We've spent many weeks on Newporters cruising, racing, vacationing, diving, and partying, plus an ample share of stormy weather. The Newporters had endless storage areas, plus ample room below and topside to get lost in to reduce temper clashes when required. Many other cruisers before 1970 were good for weekends, with compromises for long-distance cruising.

- The charter-business then caused a change to improve the human engineering needs for their expanding field. This improved the efficiency and comfort topside and below for a minimum-size crew using self-tailing winches and excellent running rigging layouts for easy, even single-handed operation.

- **Avoid** older, lean, narrow beam, wet, heavy sailboats with spartan accommodations. The tight living with minimum storage areas can produce serious temper clashes after the first week underway even under ideal conditions.

Heavy, sluggish, undercanvassed gaff rigged sailing vessels may look picturesque to the novice. Though capable of sailing downwind in a blow, will they be cranky and dull above a beam reach? Many remain dockside to impress relatives, or are dying a slow death on moorings due to neglect.

- **Consider chartering** a cruising sailboat of your choice or a similar one, to find any compromises or changes needed in its operational potentials.

- **Spend at least three nights aboard** at anchor or dockside examining the interior layout from sleeping arrangements, to galley, to lighting, to the storage areas. Will it have enough ventilation to be comfortable in the tropics, or become an unadvertised sauna? Is the engine easy to work on?

After you have analyzed the market and found the cruising sailboat that fits your needs whether new or used, a marine surveyor's expertise gained while checking hundreds of sailboats and powerboats, becomes of major importance, and he is also required for your sailboat insurance.

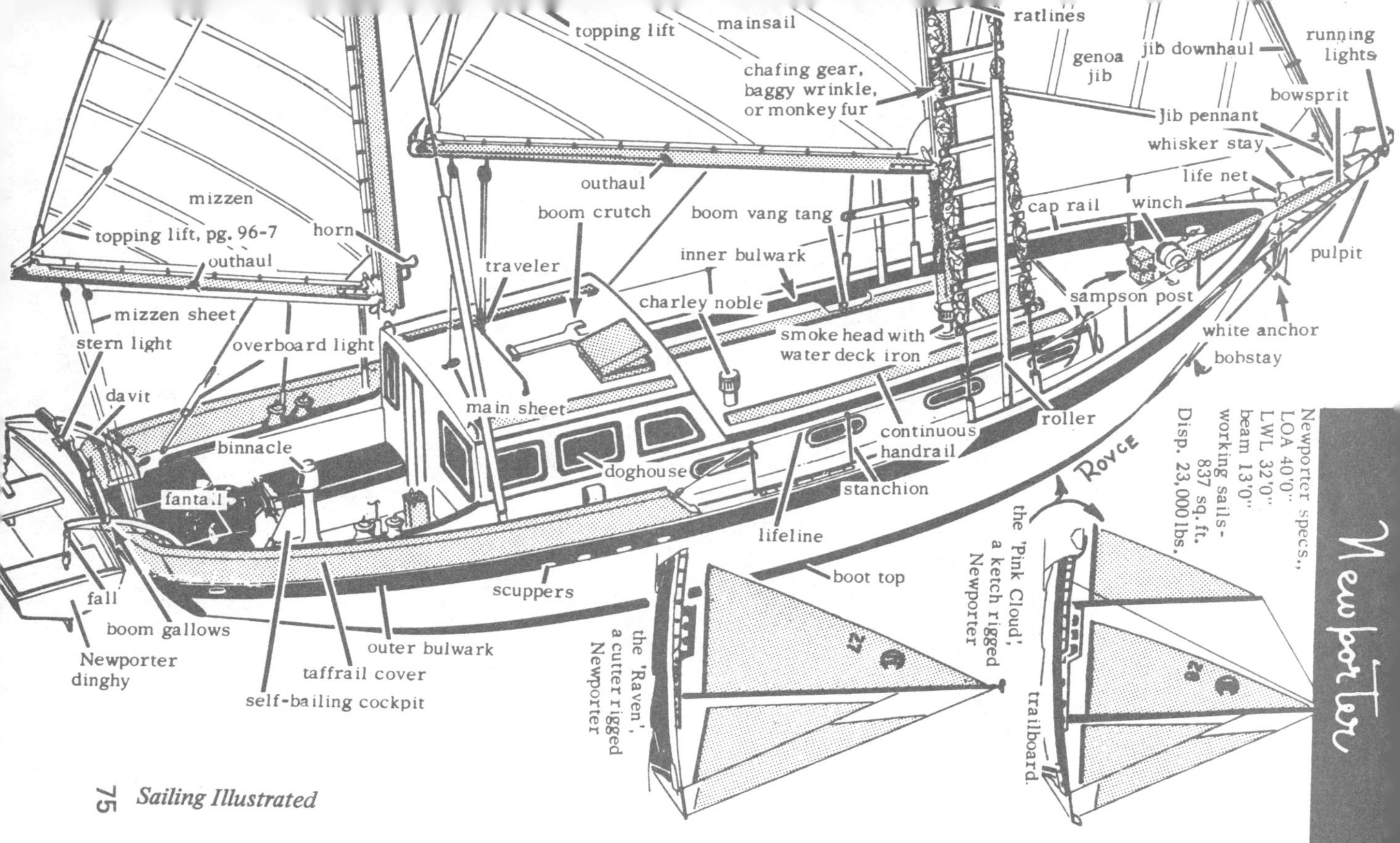
topping lift
mainsail
ratlines
running lights
genoa jib
jib downhaul
chafing gear, baggy wrinkle, or monkey fur
bowsprit
Jib pennant
whisker stay
life net
outhaul
mizzen
boom crutch
boom vang tang
cap rail
winch
topping lift, pg. 96-7
horn
pulpit
outhaul
traveler
inner bulwark
charley noble
sampson post
mizzen sheet
smoke head with water deck iron
white anchor
stern light
overboard light
bobstay
davit
main sheet
roller
binnacle
continuous handrail
doghouse
ROYCE
fantail
stanchion
lifeline
boot top
fall
scuppers
boom gallows
outer bulwark
Newporter dinghy
taffrail cover
self-bailing cockpit
Newporter
Newporter specs.,
LOA 40'0"
LWL 32'0"
beam 13'0"
working sails-
837 sq. ft.
Disp. 23,000 lbs.
the 'Pink Cloud',
a ketch rigged
Newporter
trailboard.
the 'Raven',
a cutter rigged
Newporter

The most popular 30 footer worldwide is the Catalina 30, relying on owner enthusiasm with little advertising or publicity.

Catalina 30 has many surprises for those shopping for a new sailboat. Most buy a number on the assembly line with a choice of installations, to be ready in about four months. You can choose any color desired... as long as it is white. The manufactures is one of the first in industry to offer a five year warranty protection against fiberglass blisters or pox facing fiberglass hulls during the 1980s.

The Catalina 30 is excellent for normal weather use, becoming fun and spirited in force 5 and 6 winds. After sailing on several of the 30s thru the years, I found it excellent for weekend sailing and week or longer vacations for owners, and those who prefer to charter. It is fun to race in the Thirsty Thursday beercan races, our five day Midwinter races, and the downwind overnight race to Ensenada.

While the 30 footer is a popular size produced by many builders during the years, most are replaced by later models. Catalina 30 is an exception looking very similar during the past 20 years. It undergoes periodic majc engineering improvements topside to improve rigging controls for short-handed crews, and improved below-deck arrangements. Tiller steering wa common in the early years, with wheel steering taking over in later yea requiring a different cockpit arrangement shown at right.

Four Catalina 30 versions have evolved thru the years with a standard keel 291 D/L, and a wing keel 294 D/L. The standard keel standard sail rig has a 15.20 SA/D, and the tall rig with a mast two feet longer, has a 17.20 SA/D. Both sail rigs can also be ordered with the wing keel with a 15.10 SA/D, and the tall rig, 17.10 SA/D.

The Catalina 30 is excellent for year-round California use with tall rigs often chosen to the south for lighter winds. While racers may still prefer the tall rig, many choose the standard sail rig for the stronger westerlies from Monterey north.

Versatility is important. The Catalina 30 serves many purposes, best shown with comparison of similar length sailboats in the same area. An excellent Canadian-built 30 footer aboard several times seemed unhappy in our light breezes. It came to life with strong santanas on the ocean rapidly changed from force 3 to upper force 6 with its excellent sail trim controls designed for heavy weather.

A 30 footer with freestanding mast, full-batten main, and small self-tending jib I sailed on several times with limited sail trim changes, appealed to women. Men became unhappy as passive passengers with their limitations without tending jib sheets when coming about.

The major secret... it is a wide beam **30 foot big dinghy** very sensitive to crew weight with a light steering touch. It has tremendous maneuve ability for sailing thru tight moorings. Backing the jib, page 170, perm it when required to change tack rapidly upwind in little more than its length, becoming a high-spirited experience in good winds.

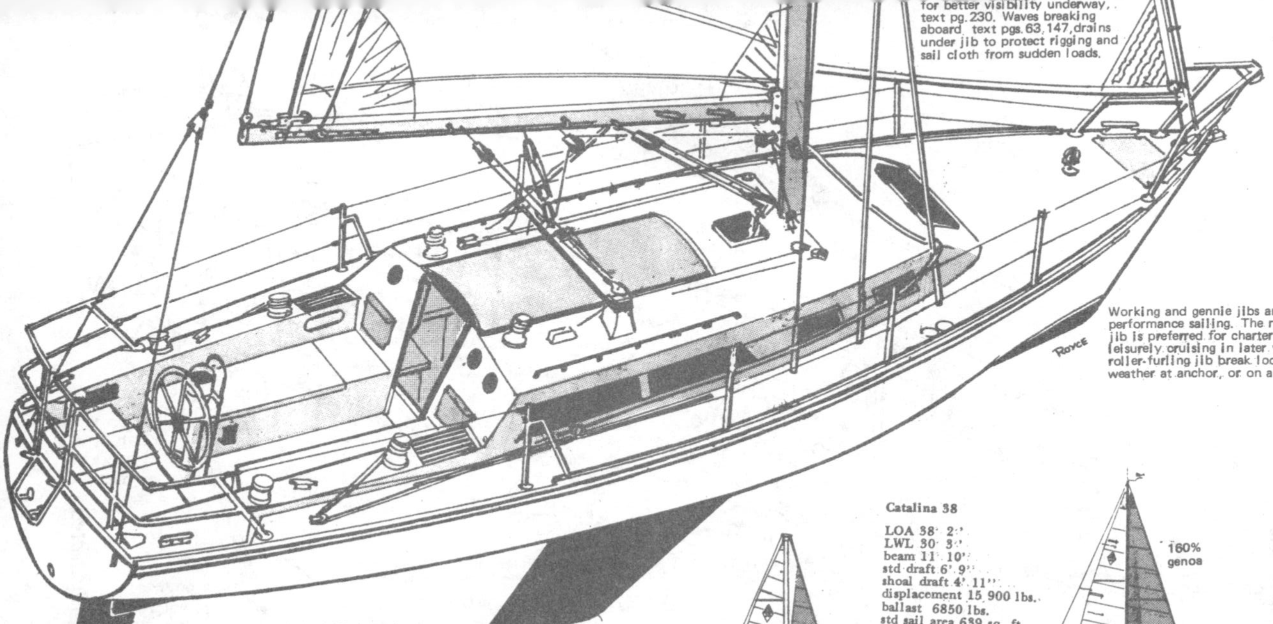

CATALINA 30

for better visibility underway, text pg. 230. Waves breaking aboard, text pgs. 63, 147, drains under jib to protect rigging and sail cloth from sudden loads.

Working and gennie jibs are preferred for performance sailing. The roller-furling jib is preferred for charter sailing, and leisurely cruising in later years. Will the roller-furling jib break loose in heavy weather at anchor, or on a mooring?

Earlier Catalina 30s had tiller steering. Later models used wheel steering that required a different cockpit seating arrangement.

Catalina 30

LOA 29' 11''
LWL 25' 0''
beam 10' 10''
std draft 5' 3''
shoal draft 3' 10''
displacement 10,200 lbs.
ballast 4200 lbs.
std sail area 446 sq. ft.

standard keel, D/L– 291
standard rig SA/D– 15.2
tall rig Sail/Disp.– 17.2

standard sloop rig

100% working jib

Catalina 38

LOA 38' 2''
LWL 30' 3''
beam 11' 10''
std draft 6' 9''
shoal draft 4' 11''
displacement 15,900 lbs.
ballast 6850 lbs.
std sail area 639 sq. ft.

conservative Catalina 38
D/L ratio– 257
Sail/Disp. ratio– 16.2

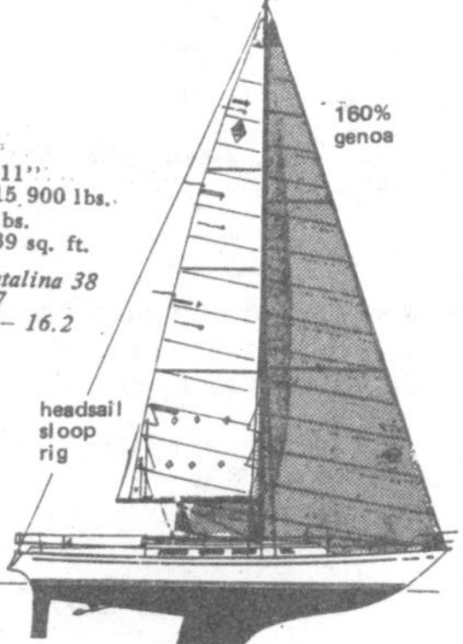

headsail sloop rig

160% genoa

The Catalina 30 sailing since 1970, is the most popular 30 footer worldwide. It undergoes periodic engineering improvements topside and below to improve operational efficiency.

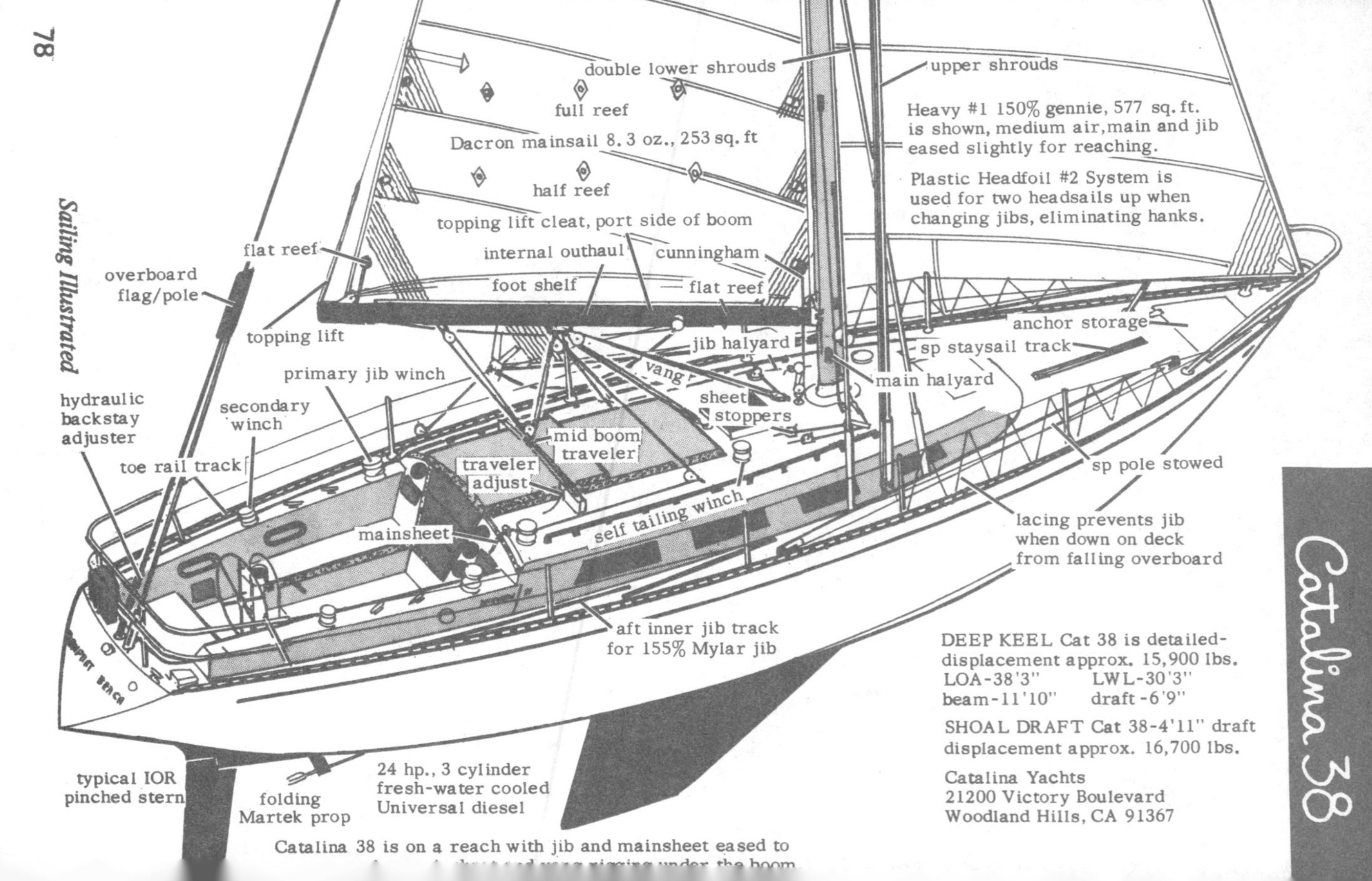

Catalina 38 is on a reach with jib and mainsheet eased to

Catalina 38

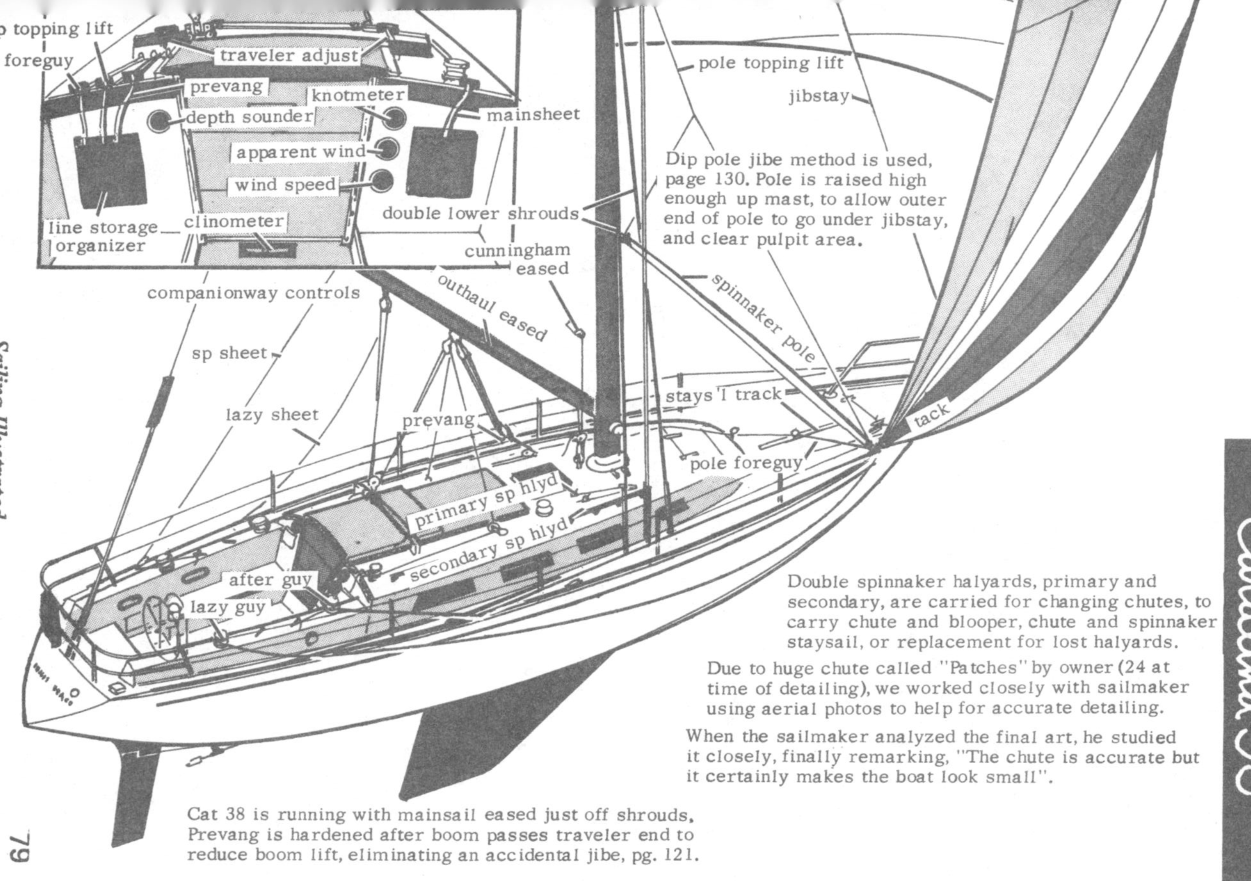

Dip pole jibe method is used, page 130. Pole is raised high enough up mast, to allow outer end of pole to go under jibstay, and clear pulpit area.

Double spinnaker halyards, primary and secondary, are carried for changing chutes, to carry chute and blooper, chute and spinnaker staysail, or replacement for lost halyards.

Due to huge chute called "Patches" by owner (24 at time of detailing), we worked closely with sailmaker using aerial photos to help for accurate detailing.

When the sailmaker analyzed the final art, he studied it closely, finally remarking, "The chute is accurate but it certainly makes the boat look small".

Cat 38 is running with mainsail eased just off shrouds. Prevang is hardened after boom passes traveler end to reduce boom lift, eliminating an accidental jibe, pg. 121.

Engine operation is equally important to cabin sailboat owners with 2 cycle and 4 cycle engines. Batteries, marine wiring, and hull blisters are also analyzed in the authors 416 page **Powerboating Illustrated.**

Outboard motors. Not many sailors realize more sailboats use this portable powerplant for sailboats, than inboard engines. Study your new friend in the language of marine mechanics

Marine metals– start with our corrosion chapter page 355. Analyze the self protection and self destruction details of the five basic metal families. It requires considerable study to know the reasons and choices for the difference between topside metals and those below the water we briefly cover on pages 180-1 of *Sailing Illustrated.*

Blisters, pox ????? This new hazard became obvious in the late 1970s. Many years were required to understand the problems, then predict answers none of us could have predicted. Twenty complex steps are required to produce quality fiberglass/composite hulls... taking place in critical time frames. If 15 hulls are on the production line, one for example, may develop blisters in a few years ranging from minor to major damage. Study pages 399 to 409 of our powerboating book to develop an understanding of the blister underworld. For composite hull details by quality major builders, read *The World's Best Sailboats* by Ferenc Mate. This is an expensive, quality book... does your library have one available?

Wood. Some quality wooden sailboats are still operating almost 100 years later. Requirements are good designs, quality woods and competent owners who know and care for their sailboats. For an opposite view is a five year old 57' sailboat reported by Calahan with so much wood rot, it had to be cut into sections for burning in an isolated part of the yard. Pages 389 to 392 are important reading for ALL owners.

Sails. Learn as much as possible, and think twice before investing in high-tech sails for regular use. Variables are endless in design during the past ten years. For cruising sailboats, consider buying new sails without battens... the first sail areas to fail in strong winds. On the other extreme, full-batten sails have come into their own for protected weekend racing and cruising. A popular example is the stayless, and shroudless Freedom 30 with large main and small self-tending jib.

Marine electricity. It has tremendous complexity. Study the negative and positive ground pages 326-7. Dockside plugs provide a liberal education, pages 330-5. Know your electrical systems thoroughly to replace weak points before failure with periodic maintenance.

Marine batteries– pages 338-353. Study one or two pages a day to develop a working foundation in this field, probab[y the least understood marine field... until that first major battery failure.

One-design dinghies– Write your class secretary, pages 50-1, to find as much background as possible for an active class in your area. Find a racer with experience in that class to check dinghies for sale as age and condition are important, also to know potential defects. When a friend wanted to buy a new 14' dinghy for $3600, I recommended a used Lido 14. They found one 3 years old in excellent condition for $1500. New tires and bearings were added plus minor sail repairs before sale. A major advantage, the Lido had the last Mission Bay Yacht Club dinghy parking space available.

Cabin sailboats. A tremendous variety are for sale to choose from with a couple of years water under their keels. You have a wide variety to choose from with plusses and minuses that must first fit your personality. We recommend taking ample time to study our Sail Course to develop a good 'dry-land' foundation first in the sailing language, then the variety of hulls to find your dream boat.

Sailboat listings. Some cover local areas, while others have nationwide listings with location, age, price, etc. When you find a good candidate, have the owner take you for an afternoon sail. Then request staying on board overnight as you will find many new ideas not obvious in daytime.

Potential dreamboat. After this exposure, it is time to find a systematic boat detective *marine surveyor* searching for obvious problems, and those obvious only to the trained eye. If a current marine survey has been made for insurance purposes... request a full copy to study.

Sales contract. A perfect sailboat is rare, with the owner listing items that may need repair. Stipulate in the contract that if the sailboat passes survey except for items listed, you pay the surveyor, if not, the owner pays the surveyor. If the owner objects, take another look at the boat. Did the owner omit a major item that should be listed on the survey?

We recommend a survey even if I were buying a new sailboat. A friend wanted me to check a 26' sailboat he wanted to buy. I recommended a 30 footer with double the cubic capacity. He found his 30 footer in much better condition than in the survey report... a very happy owner.

Maintenance is critical. The best all-purpose foundation we can recommend is our new *Powerboating Illustrated.* It has 200 pages of maintenance that is applicable to ALL sailboats and powerboats. **Your engine.** Analyze the inboard, pages 227-237, 268-9, 363, and 370. More outboard motors power sailboats than inboard engines for which we have endless coverage, a very dependable critter. You soon find temperamental outboard motors usually have 'temperamental' owners.

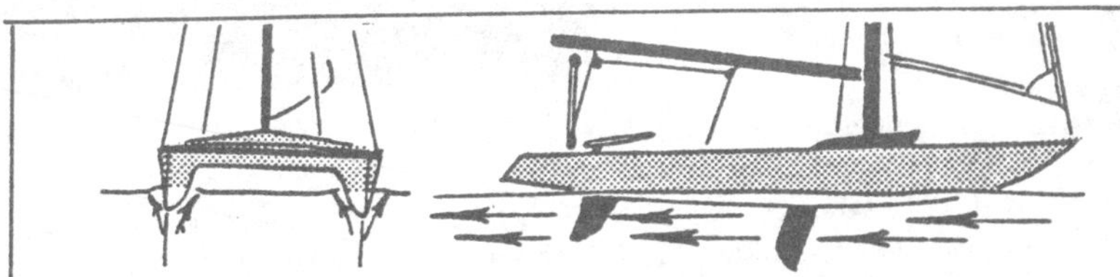

The first *Patty Cat* shown above, was 26' long. It illustrates the long, slim displacement hull lines favored by catamaran designer Rudy Choy. The hulls are designed to minimize lift by releasing water pressure buildup, to eliminate the monohull bow/stern wave trap discussed on page 140.

His large catamarans use twin-hull leverage for resistance to heel permitting more efficient use of wind pressure. This leverage eliminates monohull keel dead weight permitting much lighter construction.

- **Assymetrical hulls** provide excellent directional stability on all courses with minimum leeway. Symmetrical hulls sailing upwind have to rely more on daggerboard resistance increasing the underwater parasitic drag.

Soft water support permits a comfortable ride in wave and wind action with minimum water lift. The 44' *Patty Cat II* held an easy 20 knots with two finger steering and minimum wake in a force 5 reach. When I crewed on the 56' *Seasmoke* in its first race, the speedometer reached 24 knots several times on a reach for over an hour. *Seasmoke* developed a considerable roostertail above 20 knots though hull wake was minimal.

- My first multihull exposure was on the 26' *Patty Cat* in a Thirsty Thursday Race. The race committee permitted us to start unofficially AFTER the last of over 400 monohulls had started in light winds. We continually outpointed and outfooted larger sailboats, receiving glares from many skippers and sharp remarks from the owner of the 10 meter *Coquille.*

We overtook and passed all participants but the 14 meter *Barlovento* with its tall mast making the most of the upper wind light breezes. Six to eight weeks later some of my monohull racing friends began to speak to me again.

Rudy Choy is the pioneer in light hull construction for ocean racing. Over a decade later his engineering concepts started to be applied to the long, lean ultralight monohulls called ULDB's, page 79. The lean, all-muscle ULDB's often registered continuous speeds beyond previous monohulls.

- **Catamaran upset?** As a reporter enjoying all kinds of sailing, monohull critics often question the safety potentials of large catamarans. The answer—while catamarans may flip and float, monohulls can be holed or have a knockdown that can cause flooding and sinking. The choice is that of the sailboat owner.

Big catamarans have minimum heel angle, with both hulls having to be in the water at all times. A **mainsail sheet safety valve is used** to remove excess wind pressure when a big cat is overpowered. The mainsheet is rapidly slacked 3 to 5 feet...then resheeted immediately. The same method is very efficiently used to keep monohulls racing on their fore and aft lines without excess heel going to windward in strong and puffy winds.

the Big Cat

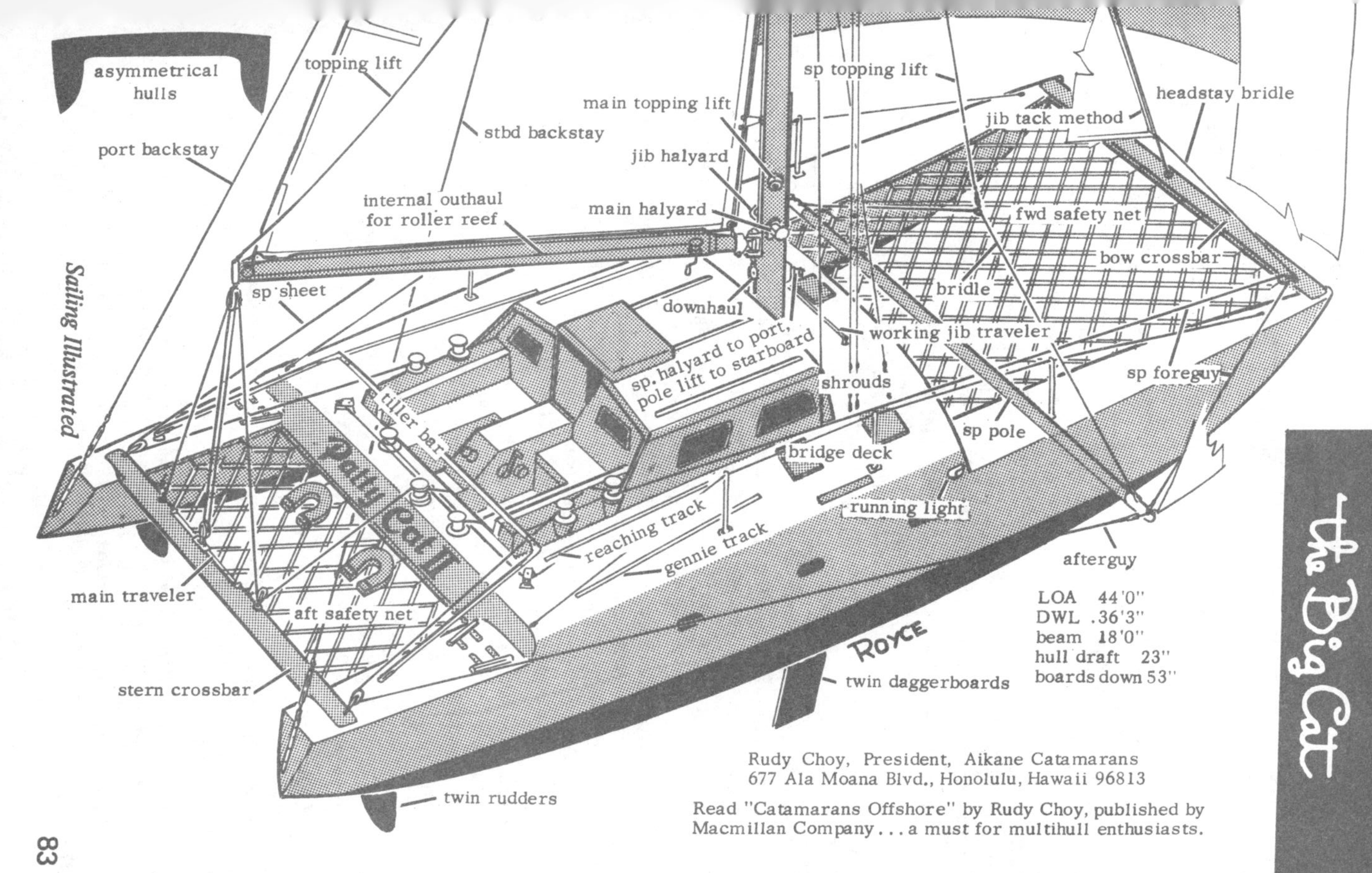

LOA 44'0"
DWL .36'3"
beam 18'0"
hull draft 23"
boards down 53"

Rudy Choy, President, Aikane Catamarans
677 Ala Moana Blvd., Honolulu, Hawaii 96813

Read "Catamarans Offshore" by Rudy Choy, published by Macmillan Company . . . a must for multihull enthusiasts.

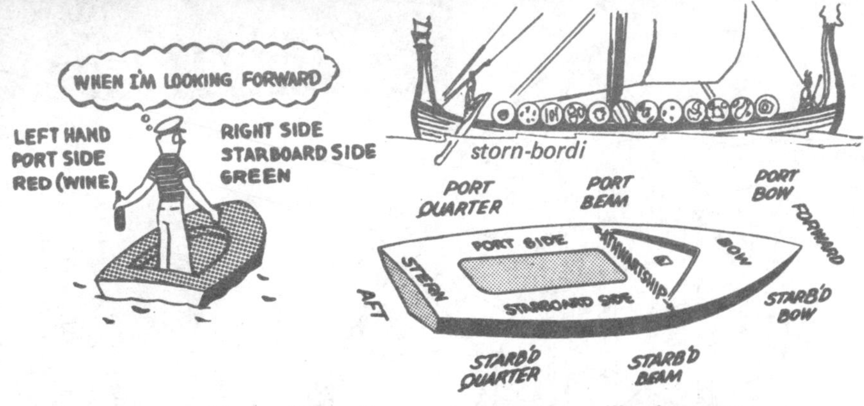

The traditional international spoken sailing language.

The captain of a square rigger had to be a man of few words. His commands were specific, clear, and concise, as they had to be understood and put to use in seconds by crews from various nations barely able to talk with each other in their homeland languages. The universal language of the sea was developed to fit this specific need.

- **Technical slang terms?** Today's sailing vocabulary is a functional and colorful spoken language developed from sounds of various languages, some more than a thousand years old which have withstood the test of time.

- **Starboard vs larboard.** Starboard comes from the Scandinavian ***stjorn-bordi,*** a vessel's side or board where the steering was done. To protect the rudder slung from that side, vessels tied up to the docks on the opposite side to be loaded was called the ***lade-board*** or ***laddeboarde*** in middle English. Since the term was later pronounced and spelled **larboard** which could be easily confused with a **starboard** command in a storm, the term **port*** for the port side was adopted by the British in the mid 1700's.

- **A spoken language.** Our sailing language developed as a spoken language, and only in the last 50 or so years have we tried to record it also as a written language with many loose ends, such as halyard spelled three ways, and different terms for the same function such as sail course terms, pg. 99.

Considerable effort will be required to learn, then become conversant in the unusual sailing language. It is the only effective method to explain your intentions to your crew or other sailors, and obtain technical answers.

- **Avoid shortcuts.** Without a good foundation in our sailing language you will feel lost when trying to expand your knowledge while reading sailing books and magazines. You will lose much not being able to enjoy the maritime jems from Columbus,to Josh Slocum ,and the Hornblower series as well as the adventures of Lin and Larry Pardey sailing around the world.

*Thanks go to Karl Freudenstein's unusual hobby, the sailing language.He is an international professional linguist who has provided many of those difficult answers to the history of sailing terms. My first contact with him was a letter questioning my use of larboard with his research going back several hundred years which he also checked thru five or more languages. Also see pg. 55.

- **Compass bearings.** In the traditional days of sail, seamen used a compass circle for navigation divided into 32 points...each of 11¼ degrees.

- **Relative bearings.** Seamen also used the same point system based on the ship's fore-and-aft centerline. It was used daily by lookouts to indicate the direction of other vessels to avoid collision potentials, deadheads, whales, plus land and other stationary objects.

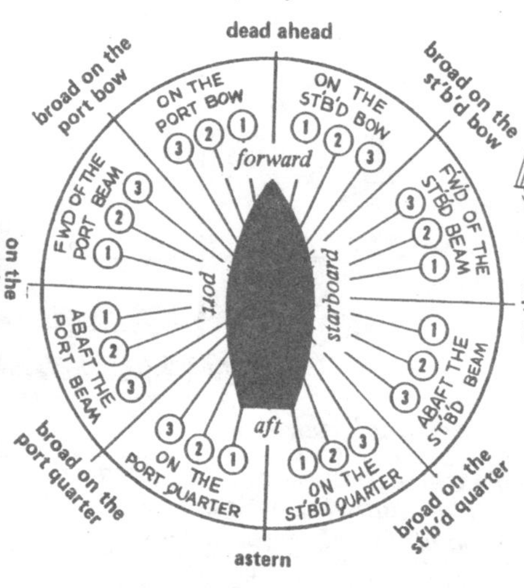

The traditional relative bearing reporting system is still used as standard procedure on larger sail training vessels.

This includes the ***Eagle***, page 286, the 68' Sea Scout topsail ketch ***Argus*** on page 269, and others.

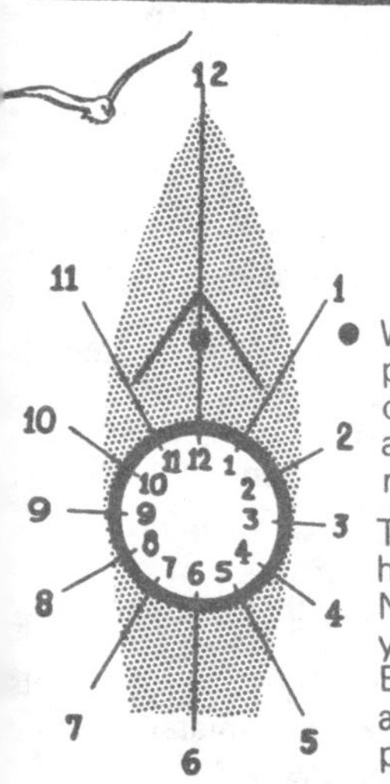

- We found the **Air Force clock reporting system** very practical for heavy New York Harbor traffic. A novice could easily report, "Tanker at 7 o'clock and a tug at 4. Change course immediately to miss a deadhead near the bow at 11 o'clock".

The clock reporting system is just as efficient to dodge heavy sail and powerboat traffic on weekends in our Newport Harbor. We found it mandatory for the yearly race beginning off our harbor entrance to Ensenada, Mexico. Over 1000 sailboats are milling above the starting line trying to miss each other... plus a large spectator fleet under sail and power.

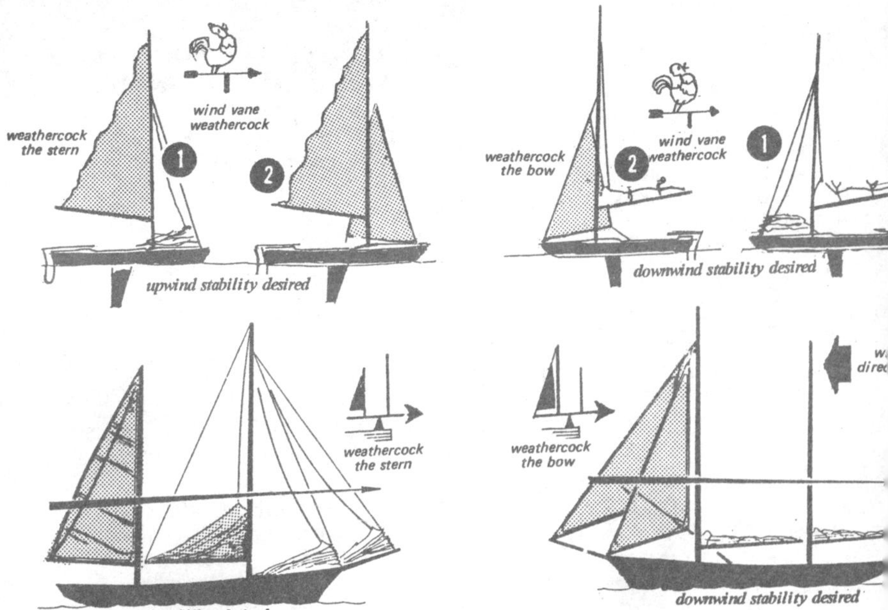

Sail raising directional stability

> *Experienced sailors can relate endless embarrassing comedies, and expensive damages resulting in a spirited wind when sails are raised in the wrong sequence... and sometimes soon afterwards when underway**

- **Raising sails upwind**--directional stability sequence for sloop, yawl, ketch, and schooner, are best explained with the ketch. The sailboat is *weathercocked* with the mizzen raised first to ride quietly into the wind. The mainsail, inner jib, then outer jib are raised in this sequence for upwind directional stability.

- **Raising sails downwind.** The ketch is drifting downwind under bare poles. The sailboat is *weathercocked* with the outer jib raised first, followed by the inner jib. While main and mizzen can be raised without changing course in a very light wind, it should be avoided in a spirited wind as wind will be in main and mizzen as they are raised with battens catching in spreaders and shrouds with jibing potentials. After jibs are raised, turn upwind to minimize problems with mizzen first, then main with wind in the sails. Continue sailing upwind, or turn to downwind tack.

*Six ten meter cutters 55′ to 60′ long, had a perfect start in tight quarters, wind force 5 racing neck and neck on starboard tack at hull speed. At the first mark changing to port tack, I found the jib sheet to starboard, between the mainsail halyard and mast...with a red faced author raising the mainsail. The 10 meter owner 20 years later still greets me with a dirty grin...yet the sailor who has never made a mistake has never left the dock. Can I provide a better reason for one last check?

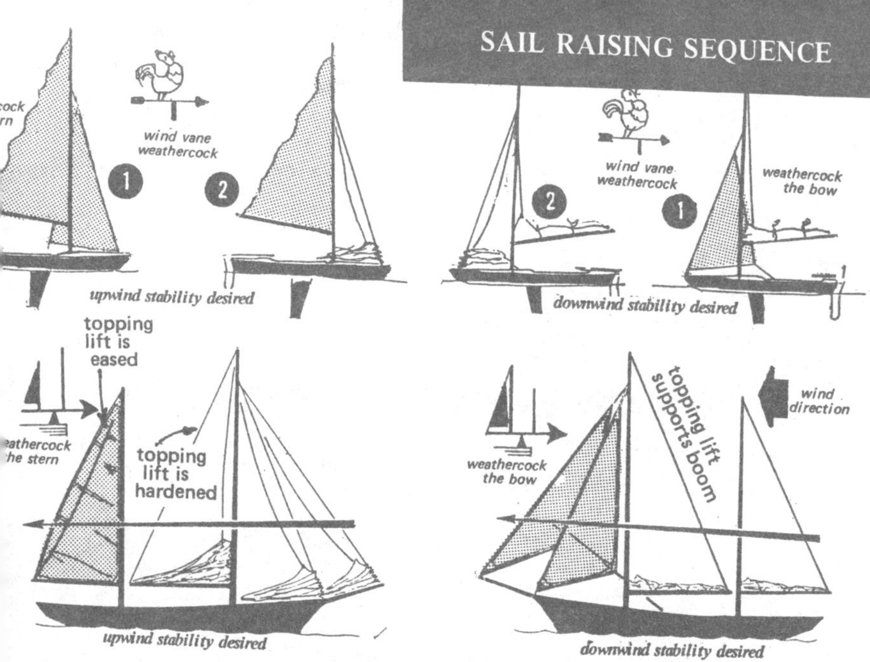

Sail lowering directional stability

Lowering sails upwind. Directional stability sequence for sloop, yawl, ketch, and schooner, are again explained with the ketch. The sailboat is *weathercocked* bow to wind with outer jib dropped first, then the inner jib. The mainsail is dropped followed by the mizzen coming down last for upwind directional stability as it rides quietly.

Lowering sails downwind should only be attemped in a very light wind. If you have a downwind dock or slip, plan your approach so you are upwind dropping main, then mizzen, before turning downwind. Drop inner jib, then outer jib to reduce speed, now with bare poles. If you still have too much way on, head up to a broad reach with the hull stalling out to reduce downwind thrust. If you want to reduce speed more when entering a slip, drop a bucket, or group of buckets secured to stern cleats at the last moment.

Downwind, dead-stick landings become very practical and interesting as a sailor gains experience with the capabilities and limitations of his sailboat, with variables when comparing different hulls and rigging.

Our *Homestudy Guide*, pages 43 to 49, cover various methods to raise sail and leave docks, then make landings that become increasingly interesting as you progress step by step thru this sequence. This exposure provides critical planning required for a variety of docking situations on various sailboats you may enjoy in your sailing future.

Bending a Main

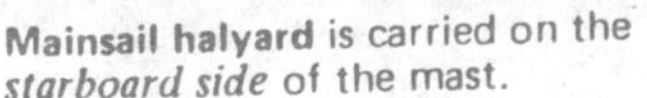

Mainsail halyard is carried on the *starboard side* of the mast.

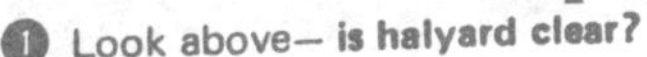

1. Look above– **is halyard clear?**

2. Secure halyard shackle to eye in mainsail luff headboard.

3. Put **mainsail luff slides** into track on aft side of mast.

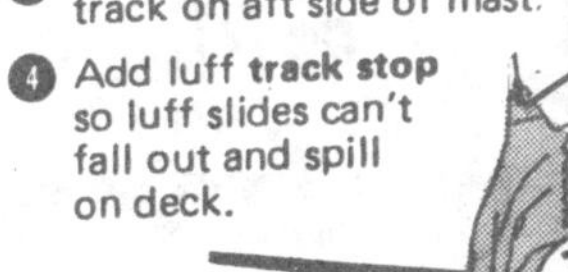

4. Add luff **track stop** so luff slides can't fall out and spill on deck.

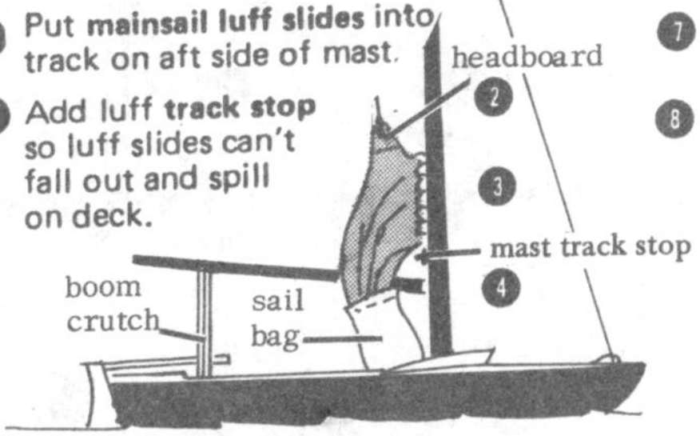

5. Run slides out boom.

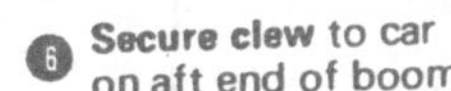

6. **Secure clew** to car on aft end of boom.

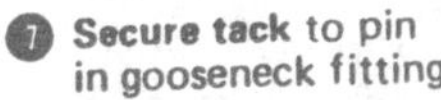

7. **Secure tack** to pin in gooseneck fitting.

8. Add battens to leach.

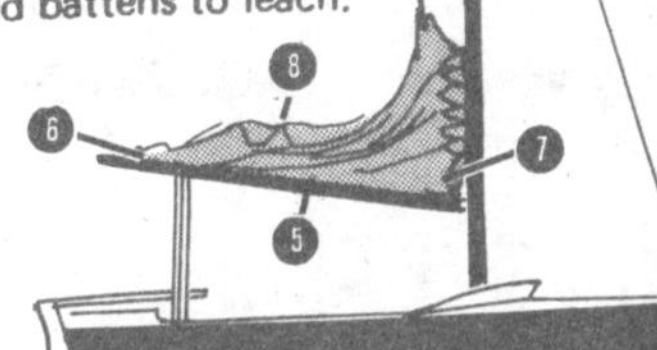

Cabin sailboat– the foot is usually added to the boom first if the mainsail isn't stored on the boom. On a small dinghy this increases the risk for the sail to fall into the bilge producing dust or water stains, or be walked on.

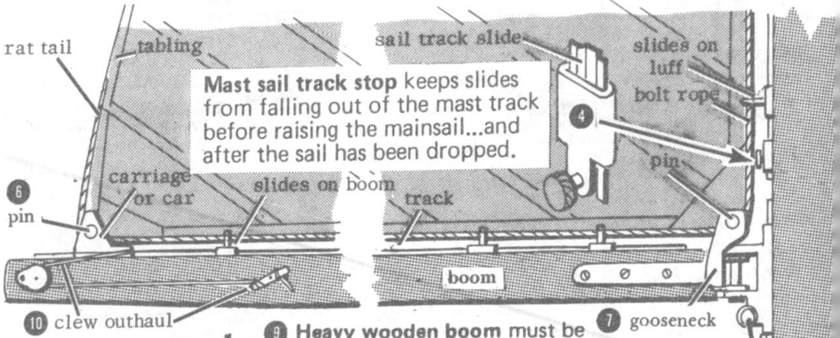

Mast sail track stop keeps slides from falling out of the mast track before raising the mainsail...and after the sail has been dropped.

9. **Heavy wooden boom** must be supported while raising or lowering mainsail to avoid stress points on luff cloth...see note.
10. **Adjust outhaul.**
11. **Adjust downhaul.**
12. **Sheet should be slack** to avoid filling prematurely until underway.

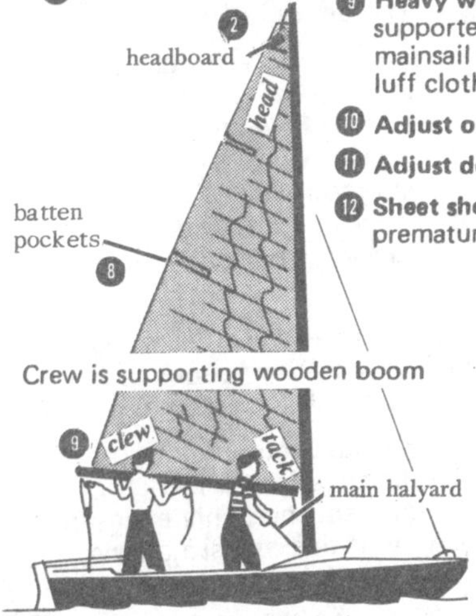

Crew is supporting wooden boom

9 **New, blown-out Dacron mainsail?**

An owner complained his boat couldn't sail above a beam reach though his sails were five months old.

Boom crutch, boom lift, and topping lift were missing. Mainsail halyard pulled up sail AND heavy boom producing luff stress areas. If you want a new blown-out main...

Bending a Jib

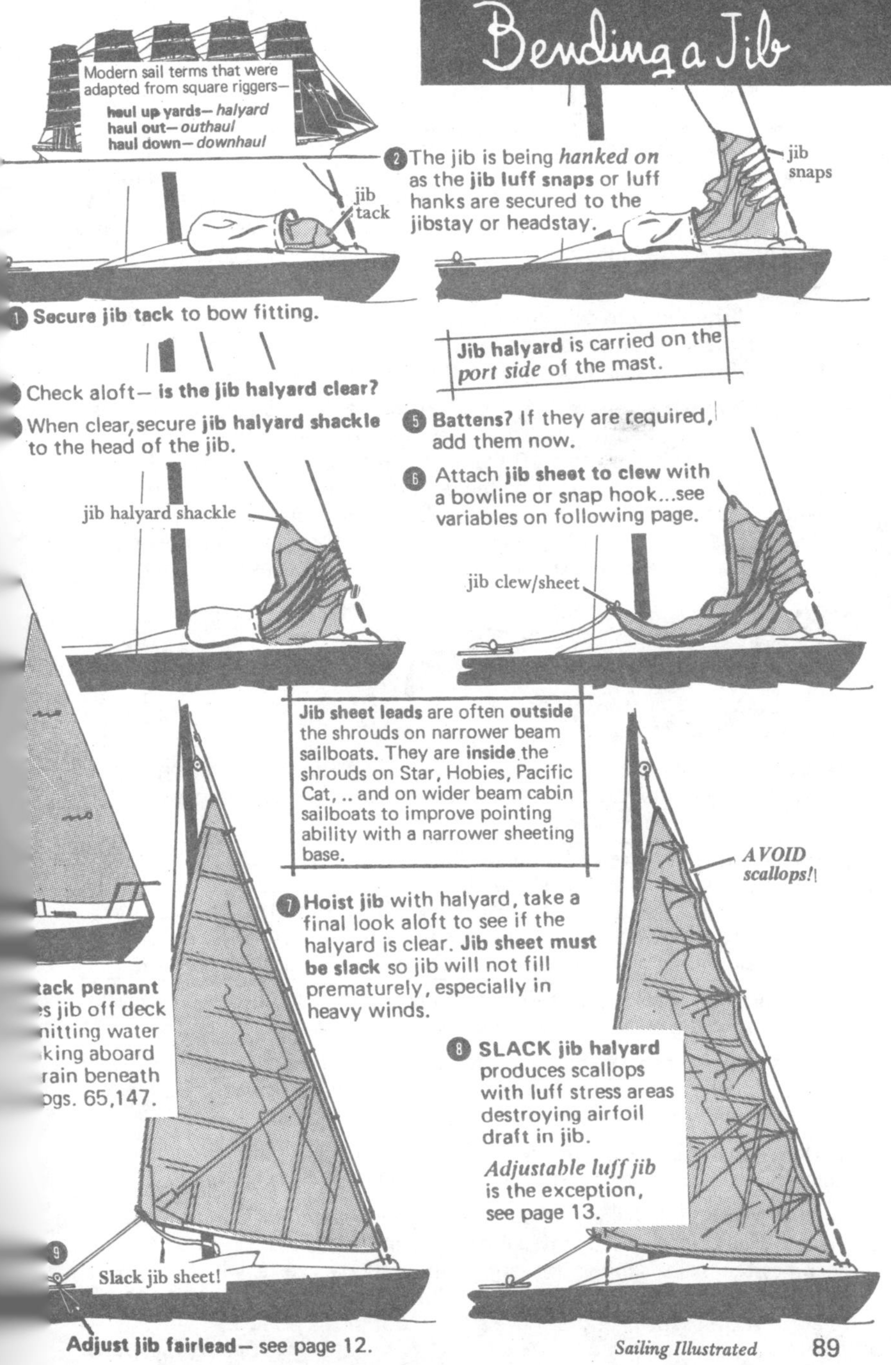

1 **Secure jib tack** to bow fitting.

2 The jib is being *hanked on* as the **jib luff snaps** or luff hanks are secured to the jibstay or headstay.

3 Check aloft— **is the jib halyard clear?**

4 When clear, secure **jib halyard shackle** to the head of the jib.

Jib halyard is carried on the *port side* of the mast.

5 **Battens?** If they are required, add them now.

6 Attach **jib sheet to clew** with a bowline or snap hook...see variables on following page.

Jib sheet leads are often **outside** the shrouds on narrower beam sailboats. They are **inside** the shrouds on Star, Hobies, Pacific Cat, .. and on wider beam cabin sailboats to improve pointing ability with a narrower sheeting base.

7 **Hoist jib** with halyard, take a final look aloft to see if the halyard is clear. **Jib sheet must be slack** so jib will not fill prematurely, especially in heavy winds.

8 **SLACK jib halyard** produces scallops with luff stress areas destroying airfoil draft in jib.

Adjustable luff jib is the exception, see page 13.

…ack pennant …s jib off deck …itting water …king aboard …rain beneath …pgs. 65,147.

9 **Adjust jib fairlead**— see page 12.

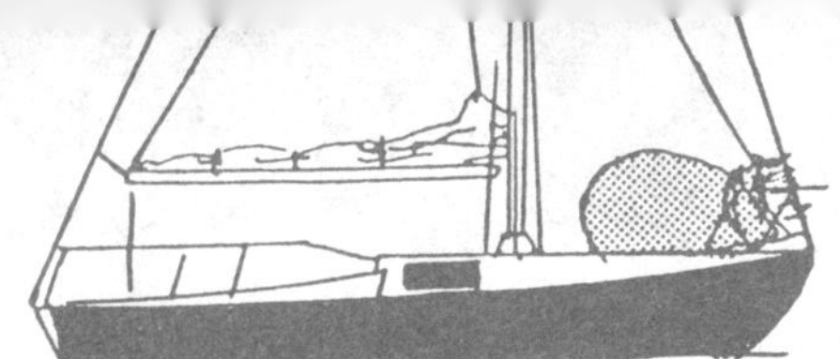

• **Leaving downwind?** The present slip for our 24' sailboat pointing into the westerlies is easy to make a landing, but leaving is another situation. We bend on and raise our genoa or working jib **without attaching the jib sheet.** The jib is dropped into and stored in its sailbag shown above. The mainsail cover is removed, and the main halyard is secured to its headboard.

After a little shove to gain sternway, the tiller is turned away from the dock so the hull comes to a stop with the stern into the wind. Then the boat begins moving in a downwind channel under bare poles.

• **The jib is raised at leisure.** After it is up and halyard cleated, the clew is taken in and secured to a Swedish snap hook on the jib sheet, then the jib is sheeted in. After another 200' or so the mainsail topping lift is hardened and the boom lift is released.**As the boat heads up to a reach** the mainsail gaskets are removed. The mainsail is raised rapidly and its halyard tail is cleated.The downhaul is hardened and the sails sheeted in for the next course. This downwind sequence can be used on all sizes of sailboats.

• **A bowline** jib sheet attach to the clew is practical for ocean racing. It has questionable limitations for wide beam craft in crowded harbors with tall buildings on the shoreline.

Downdraft wind currents. Docks on the lee side of tall buildings can back-wind docking sailboats jibs. If the jib sheet can't be released instantly, all steering control is lost hitting the dock or other boats. The jib sheet snap hook can easily release the jib in that situation. The luffing jib becomes an air brake reducing boat speed with the sailboat under full control.

• **Large jib sheet snap shackles**—*avoid!* They are large and heavy (blackjack?) which can hurt a crew member especially if it hits a head.

• **Swedish snap hooks.** We have used them on our jib sheet since 1964. They are small, light, and easy to snap onto the jib clew. It keeps the foredeck clear with one less item to trip over when the jib is down.

• **Barient J locks** are excellent for jib sheet use on larger sailboats. They are light and small with load capacities from 3,000 to 14,000 pounds.

• **Jib luff tension** is provided on a FD dinghy with the jib-luff wire as the jibstay is just strong enough to support the mast at the dock. The jibstay becomes the major support for larger cabin-sailboat masts, while the jib-luff wire becomes a minor support. Jib luff tension should be tight enough to avoid scallops, page 89,nor have a hard spot in the jib luff.

Leave Mooring

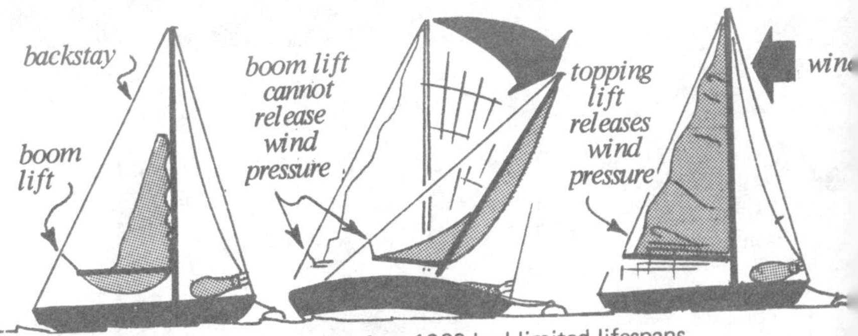

- **Canvas sails** commonly used before 1960 had limited lifespans

Raising a mainsail. Heavy wooden booms required topping lifts to ***top up the end of the booms*** on mainsails and mizzens while raising the sails until they were up and the halyards cleated. This avoided stretching the luffs which destroy airfoils. After the sails were dropped, the topping lifts were eased with booms supported by **permanent gallows or boom crutches**, 74.

- **Stronger Dacron sail cloth** on lighter, stronger aluminum booms now need a **boom lift** secured to the backstay. This eliminates the need for boom gallows except on large sailboats.
- **Traditional topping lift** is still required for large sailboats for raising and lowering mainsails in all but very light winds.

Sailing lessons soon proved the boom lift AND the topping lift were needed for our 24' sailboat. The topping lift became very important for raising and lowering sail in strong winds, and for unusual docking situations.

- **Trailerables?** An owner of a new Catalina 21, page 51, stopped by to ask some interesting questions providing a new exposure to the topping lift.

The topping lift which can be operated from the cockpit, can be of vital importance to the light trailerables which are very sensitive in rapidly changing weather conditions.

> The topping lift is going to be around in increasing numbers for future generations of sailors who want to handle their sailboats in a wider variety of sailing conditions. Will a topping lift help your sailing operation?

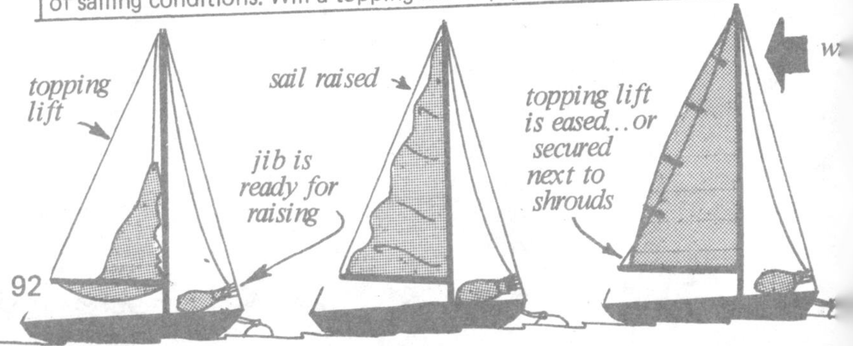

Flexible Mast

The best way to check the setting and trim of your sails underway is to take photos of them from another boat.

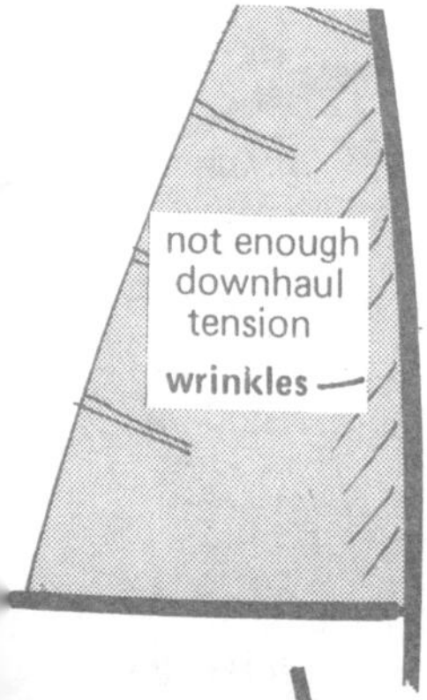

not enough downhaul tension
wrinkles

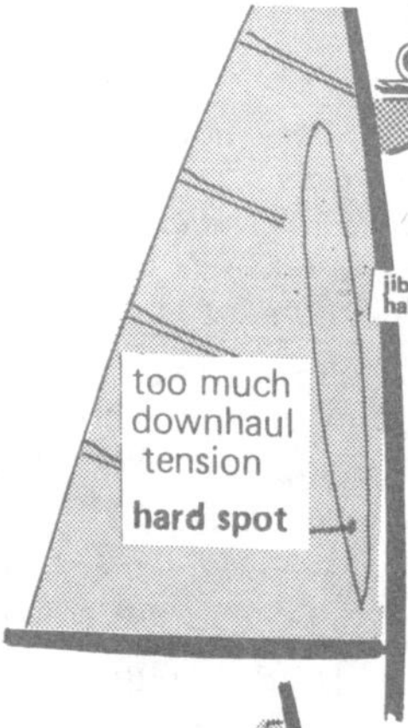

too much downhaul tension
hard spot

Add snaps to ends of halyards and downhaul, Secure the three snaps together so halyards cannot be lost in sloppy weather.

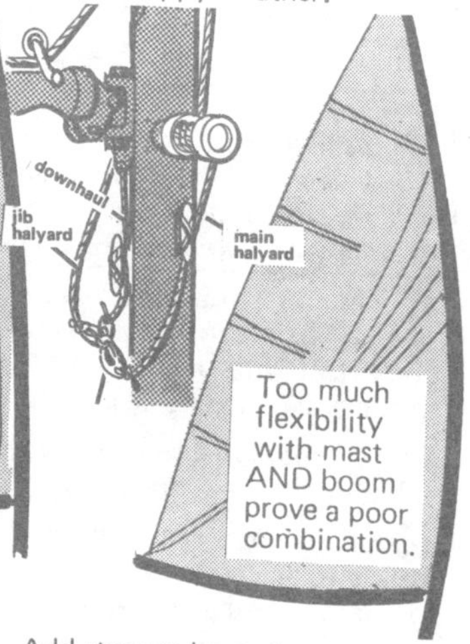

downhaul
jib halyard
main halyard

Too much flexibility with mast AND boom prove a poor combination.

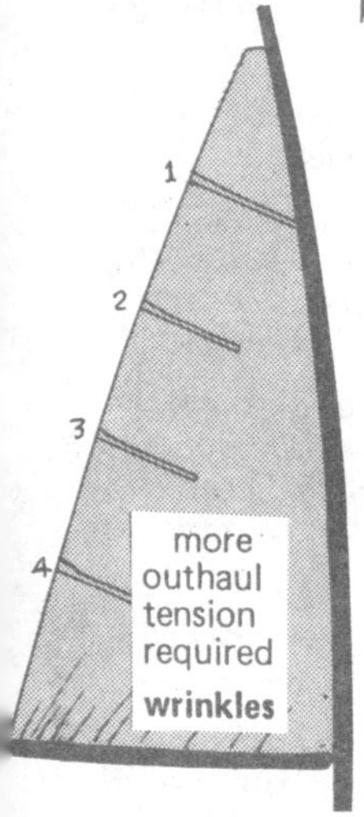

1
2
3
4

more outhaul tension required
wrinkles

number your battens

too much outhaul tension
hard spot

Add stopper knots to prevent rope halyards from accidentally being pulled out of their sheaves.

Battens should be light, rigid, and without sharp edges. Wooden battens break easily, while some fiberglass battens are too flexible.

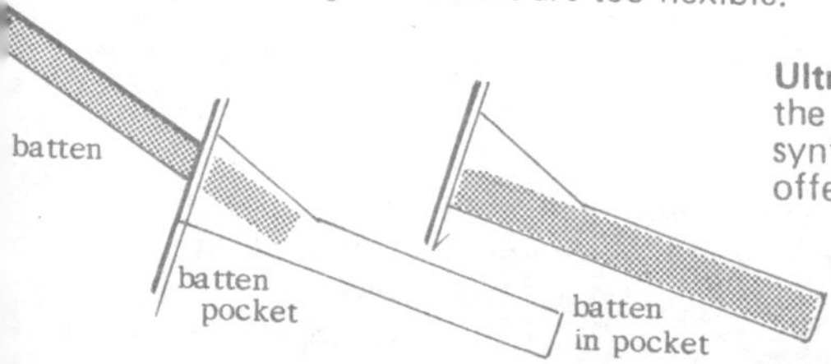

batten
batten pocket
batten in pocket

Ultraviolet rays and sails flapping in the breeze are major enemies of your synthetic sails. *Acrylic* sail covers offer the best insulation, especially for roller-reefing jibs.

The ideal dock for dinghies and keelboats. It requires enough draft so your boat can tie up at any of the three sides. At the correctly timed moment the sailboat heads into the wind with uncleated sheets.following the black arrow with the sail air brakes stopping your boat alongside the dock.

When one or two sides of the dock are blocked with boats plus inflatable dinghies on the third side, you have a situation commonly found today. While we only have room to show the basics in this book, we cover 30 specific situations in our Homestudy Guide ***pages 44 to 47 from dinghies to large yawls, ketches, and schooners for your evaluation.***

❶ The outer side is preferable with your sailboat heading up to stop on side B. The second choice is side A. After the bow line is secured to the dock cleat with sheets fully released, a stern line can pull your sailboat to the dock with its beam into the wind.

Side A problem– can your crew reach the dock cleat, will he have to climb up over a tippy bow, or will help be needed by someone on the dock?

❷ Side A has an easy approach .Head up with sheets released and sails luffing to stop at dock, then tie bow and stern lines. Side B is more spirited for landing without sheets tangling on dock pilings and/or cleats.

Downwind approach– side C. Head up momentarily to drop mainsail, return to downwind course, drop jib far enough out to make a soft dead-stick landing. In a stiff breeze a 180 degree turn can stop your boat on side C...or drop a bucket overboard tied to the center of the boat stern.

❸ Side A timing is a little tighter. You release sheets earlier to round up with an easy beam to dock stop.If sides B or C are chosen– head up, drop mainsail, head down and drop jib to make a deadstick landing. Speed can be reduced by heading up to a broad reach to stall the hull, then return to downwind course to make a soft landing.

Low tide problems–if tarred wooden pilings are used with a considerable drop of the dock at low tide, how can you protect your sails,sheets, and hands from the preservatives on the pilings?

❹ Sides A and C make easy landings by heading up into the wind a short way out. Release the sheets so your boat can glide to a stop with your luffing sails as airbrakes.Side B will be easy to land on...IF your sheets are first released all the way, otherwise...

Fond memories? Every club has its share of classic landing experiences that suddenly went sour. Many began with stuck main or jib sheets, the reason to use easy to release sheet cam cleats. I fondly remember a movie actor landing his new 36′ sailboat in a strong wind. His two crew members made pierhead leaps to cleat the docklines not cleated to his sailboat. I've also made more of my own contributions than I want to remember.

On those precious days when nothing goes right, take solace in the idea that the only sailors who haven't contributed to memorable docking catastrophies...are the rocking chair experts who never leave the dock.

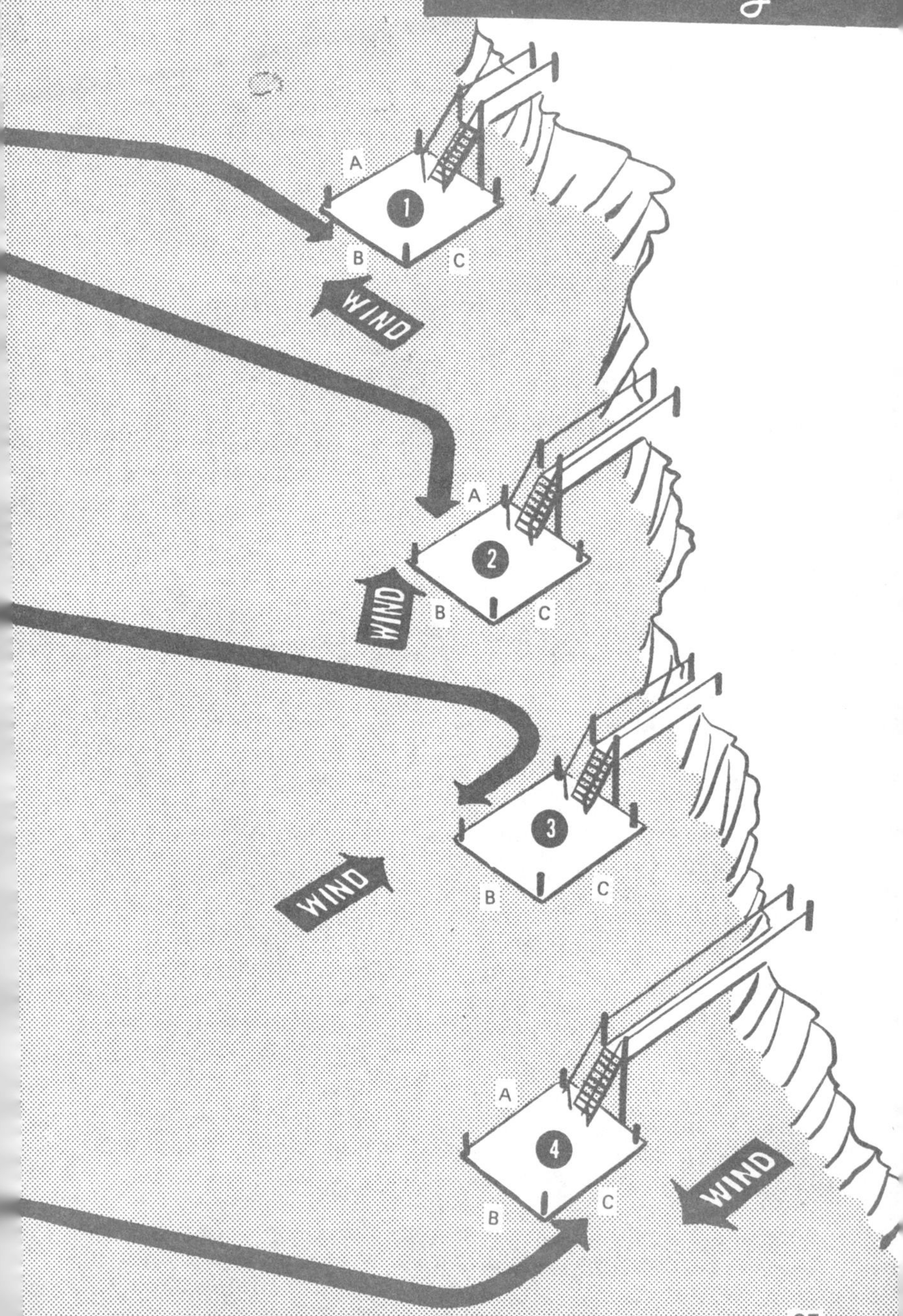
A
1
B
C
WIND
A
2
B
C
WIND
3
B
C
WIND
A
4
B
C
WIND

● **Folding sails.** We returned from a spirited dinghy sail to the Mission Bay YC while revising this page to watch racing sailors fold their sails. A nice stretch of lawn near the dinghy hoist had a steady procession of sailors using ***the loft*** or ***accordian fold*** to minimize wrinkle formation with minute drag areas. After racing sails are repeatedly folded this way, sharp creases develop which mean little as they are horizontal, parallel to the air flow.

This folding method is common for racing mainsails and jibs for dinghies to large ocean racers. A sufficiently dry lawn is an excellent place to learn to fold sails; just watch out for those friendly four legged critters walking across the lawn following the call of nature. The competitive racer crewing on a variety of craft is soon folding sails on tight docks, and on pitching IOR and ULDB racers while avoiding to step on the sails.

● **Mylar, Kevlar, and ?** Brittle sail material should be rolled around the boom of a dinghy to avoid creases. After a cover is added to keep the sail clean, the mainsail and its boom are stored ashore.

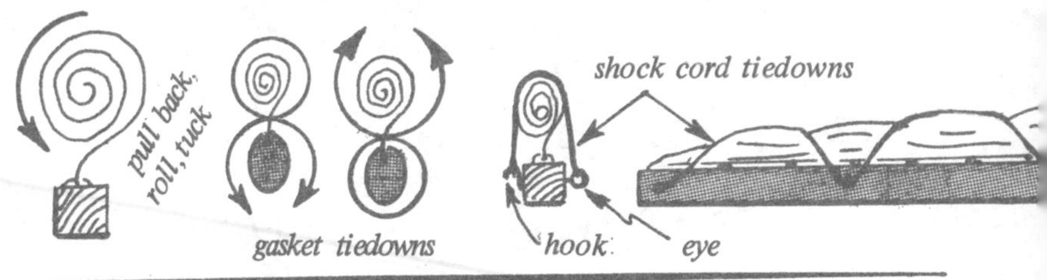

● **Furling the mainsail.** Start near the upper part of the leach ***with a pull AFT, followed by a roll and a tuck,*** repeating the process a few times as you work your way down to the bottom of the leach. The pull and roll sequence protects the battens as they lay parallel to the boom.

● **Gasket tiedowns** go around the boom and around the sail in a figure eight as shown above, so the mainsail will stay on top of the boom for storage in a neat roll. ***Avoid tight gaskets*** even on Dacron mains, as a slight air flow will reduce the potentials of mildew stains.

● **Sail covers** help to keep the mainsail clean and provide protection from a major enemy of synthetic sails, the ultra-violet rays of the sun. with *Acrylic* covers providing the best sun screen.

● **Boom shock cord tiedowns.** Ocean winter sailing is excellent in our area on larger cruising sailboats. Gasket tiedowns for main and mizzen require too much time to use in a fast moving storm. We tested the shock cord tiedown on the Newporter ketch, page 75, requiring less than half the time to secure the sails to their booms. The shock cords shrink to normal length out of the way on the boom when not in use.

We still see a few canvas sails which were commonly used before 1960. They need to be dry and have lots of air pockets to reduce mildew potentials when stored in sail bags or on the boom.

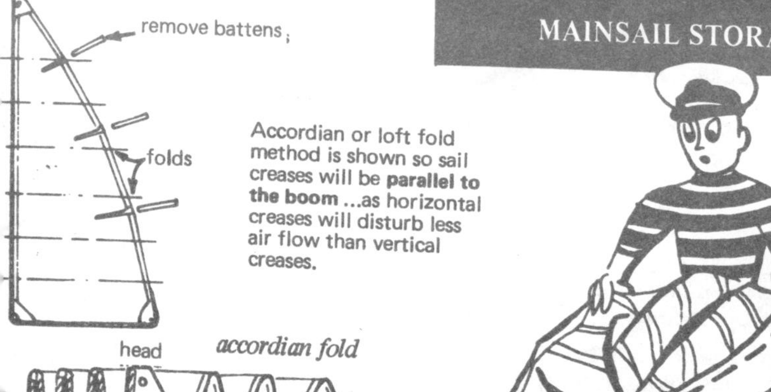

Roll mainsail parallel to the boom as folds will develop vertical creases causing wind flow disturbance.

When stuffing a jib into a sail bag, the corner you want to come out first...is stored last.

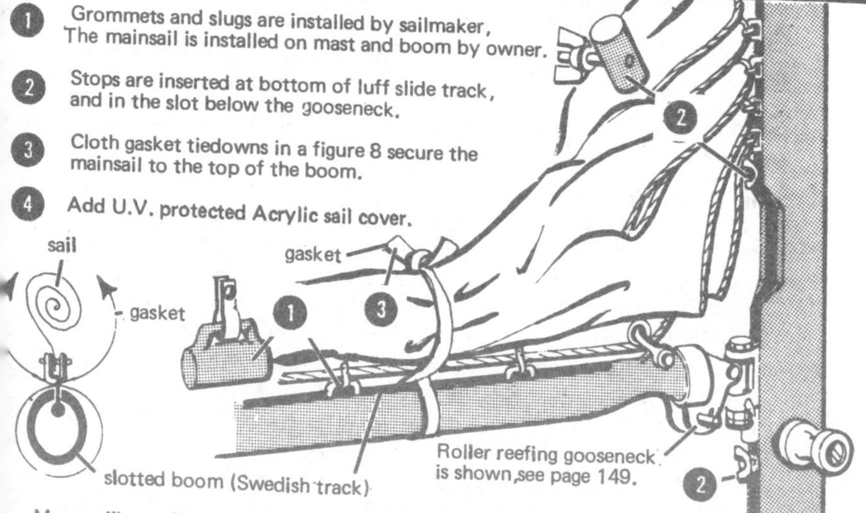

Many sailboats 20' and longer have slotted aluminum masts and booms. Changes are required if you want to store the mainsail on the boom when not in use, and to prevent the luff from spilling onto the deck when applying a reef in heavy weather, page 149. The answer is to have your sailmaker install slugs on the luff and foot of the mainsail, and carry along spare slugs, as they occasionally need replacement.

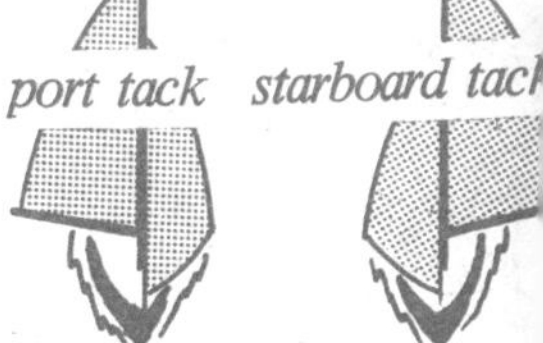

Homestudy Guide–28,29

● **Port tack**– *a sailboat is on a port tack when the wind comes over the port bow, beam, or quarter.*

● **Starboard tack**– *a sailboat is on a starboard tack when the wind comes over the starboard bow, beam, or quarter.*

● **Main boom location**– *a sailboat is on a tack opposite to the side on which the main boom is carried. When a sailboat is running and the boom is carried on the port side...the sailboat is on a* **starboard tack.**

● **Sailboat course**– *it is determined by the angle at which the vessel is sailing into...or away from the wind.* We include a variety of course terms at right. Some are square rigger terms only found in books or movies about square riggers. The rest are fore-and-aft course terms used today,with the most commonly used terms following.

Closehauled– the sailboat is sailing as close to the wind as efficiency permits, with the sheets hauled as tight as efficiency permits whether on an elderly cruising sailboat, or the most efficient 12 meter craft. The term **beating** is more commonly used when racing than the term closehauled.

Running– the sailboat is sailing before the wind coming over the stern with the sails on opposite sides of the sailboat,called **wing and wing.**

Reaching– this includes all courses between sailing closehauled and running, from a close reach, to a beam reach, to a broad reach.

●

● **Beam reach limit.** It existed up to the 1700's on bluff-bow square riggers with heavy canvas sails using flexible hemp for standing and running rigging. As the hull lines slimmed down, square-rigged clippers with clean bottoms could point 20 degrees higher, or 70 degrees from the eye of the wind. With considerable bottom growth they couldn't sail above a broad reach, then soon drift out of control to the whims of wind or current.

● **Fore and aft rigged sailboats.** Two masted cruisers may point to within 50 degrees of the eye of the wind, the racer/cruiser, to 45 degrees.12 meter and IOR racing machines may point up to 30 or 35 degrees of the eye of the wind...which the International 110 class attained many years ago.

● **The barrier is reached** *when this limit is passed and the sails become* **air brakes. The sails lift...and their flexible airfoils break, called luffing,** with the wind hitting both sides of the sails. The sailboat drifts to a halt with all control disappearing as it goes into irons, then begins drifting backwards. This is a major reason for dinghy upsets with the details covered on page 70 of our *Homestudy Guide.*

Sail course terms originated on square riggers. Some are popular today, others are still used on traditional craft.

A sail course is the angle a sailboat points into, or away from the wind...or the direction a vessel steers to a magnetic compass course.

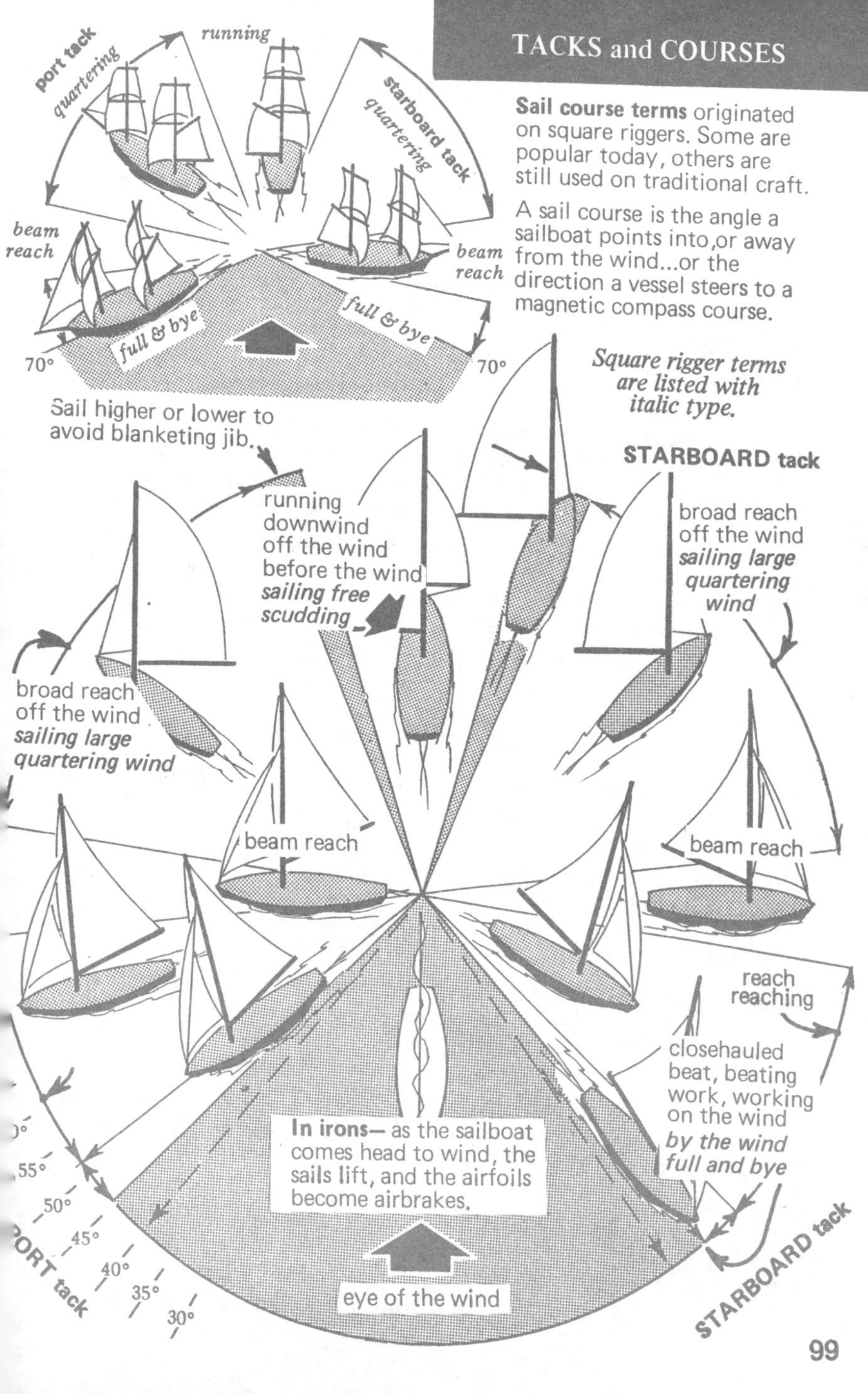

The sailboat is heeling, not keeling.

- **Wind pressure relief valve**—a sailboat begins ***to heel as the wind increases*** on an upwind course. Hike to the high side as the heel angle increases to reduce wind pressure spilled from the sails, with an increase in hull speed.
- **Wind direction – stationary true wind indicators** are important to sailors. These are wind indicators on shore which are obvious such as flags, smoke from chimneys, plus the movement of trees and bushes.

  Apparent wind direction on a sailboat underway will be somewhat different in direction from stationary wind indicators on shore.

  Daytime apparent wind indicators. Light feathers secured to shrouds and stays, plus orange threads or ribbons sewn to the luff of mainsail and jib indicate the direction and strength of the wind entering your sails. Daytime indicators become even more important in confused wave action.

  Masthead telltale. It is excellent on larger sailboats recorded on a cockpit dial which is easy for the helmsman to read. For visual use only on smaller sailboats,it is often blocked by the head of the mainsail...which produces a stiff neck if constantly watched. Rely on shroud and backstay indicators.

  Nighttime apparent wind indicators. White telltales on shrouds and backstay are easier to see than orange telltales. A masthead telltale may be illuminated with a masthead light directly beneath. Use this light with care if commercial vessels are in the area as it might give them a false signal.

- **Advancing or working to windward.** The fore and aft rigged sailboat will advance to windward on a course that is closehauled with the sails full and pulling, averaging about 45 degrees from the eye of the wind.
- **Changing the wind over the bow.** The same sailboat will change tack by ***coming about*** when advancing to windward by changing the wind over the bow. If it points higher the sails will lift, the airfoils break...and the luffing sails bring the sailboat to a halt with loss of steering control.
- **Wearing** ***(to ware*)***– changing wind over the stern. Square riggers followed complex worldwide tradewind current routes with the wind aft to abeam, see pages 210 to 213. If they changed tack changing the wind over the stern called wearing,see right, the disadvantage was losing considerable ground.

caught aback!

- **Tacking ship** ***(tacking expeditiously*)***– was used to change tack by changing the wind over the bow with all sails momentarily caught aback.

  Square rigger balance was more critical than most of us realize. Dismastings, knockdowns, and sinkings could result if square riggers were **caught aback** in heavy weather, and/or if the cargo shifted.

**Lever's*–pages 184, 286.

WINDWARD TERMS

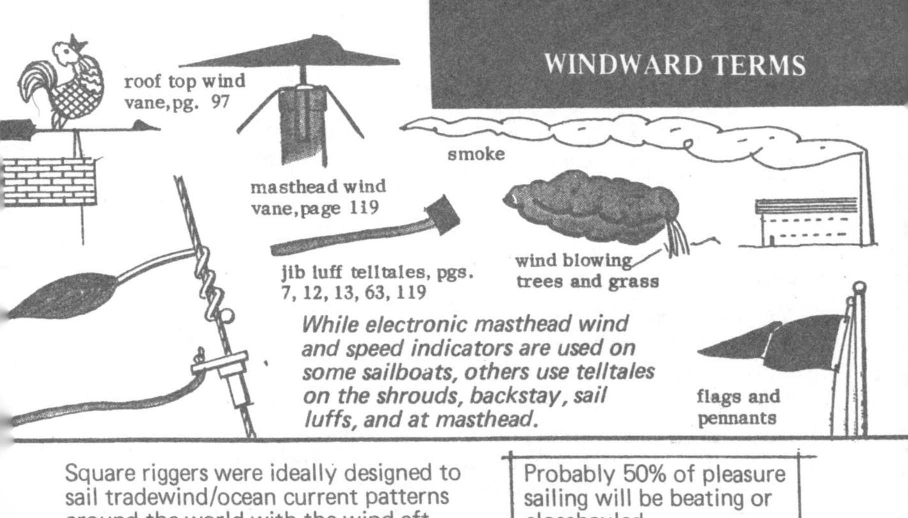

While electronic masthead wind and speed indicators are used on some sailboats, others use telltales on the shrouds, backstay, sail luffs, and at masthead.

Square riggers were ideally designed to sail tradewind/ocean current patterns around the world with the wind aft to abeam.

Within 50 to 100 miles of shore they faced land and sea breezes, pages 214 and 270, only able to point to 7 points of the apparent wind (70 degrees).

The complexity of square rigger ***tacking expeditiously*** and ***waring*** are thoroughly detailed in ***Lever's*** 1819 text for sea officers.

Probably 50% of pleasure sailing will be beating or closehauled. 25% is reaching, and the rest, from a broad reach to a run.

wind direction

sailing upwind, closehauled, or beating

Fore and afters can point upwind to within 4 to 5 points of the compass.

Wearing requires 20 points of the compass. *

sailing full and by (bye)

port tack

coming about

starboard tack

short leg or short board

coming about

port tack

coming about (tacking is the commonly used racing term)

starboard tack

long tack or long board

Tacking is the term used on the ***USCG Eagle*** today for changing the wind over the bow with all yards temporarily **caught aback.**

A minimum of 6, to a maximum of 12 knots hull speed is required for ***Eagle*** pg.286, tacking head to wind thru 12 points of the compass.

****A compass has 32 points, one point is 11¼ degrees.***

How does a sailboat sail upwind?

The flexible low-speed sailboat airfoil. *It provides* **upwind lift** *for sailing above a beam reach...and an* **air bag** *for sailing downwind. The sails are then used as* **air brakes** *so a sailboat is able to stop at a mooring or dock, or anchor.*

The combination of these three functions are systematically covered on pages 44 to 48 of our *Homestudy Guide.* We provide 30 varied patterns for catboats, to dinghies, to sloops, and large yawls, ketches, and schooners leaving, then returning to docks or moorings in a variety of conditions.

A rigid, horizontal airfoil is used by an airplane to support it in the air, while **flexible, vertical airfoils** are used to provide upwind air lift on a sailboat advancing to windward. Both airplanes and sailboats rely on a slight but adequate difference in wind pressures on both sides of the airfoils.

- **Flexible low-speed airfoils.** Upwind sail lift is developed with a slight but adequate difference with an increased pressure on the windward side, and a slight pressure decrease on the leeward side of the sail. This theory is sometimes defined as suction, which instead refers to a complete vacuum.

  Note the considerable curvature in the low speed airfoil of the monohull catboat sailing upwind. While the entire sail area is required, the most important drive area,of maximum curvature is indicated by the vertical shaded area. for upwind sailing efficiency. Jib telltales should be in the center of shaded area. Many are too far forward sending false signals.

- **Semi-rigid, full-batten, high-speed airfoils.** High performance catamarans and iceboats require flatter, shallower airfoils for upwind sailing,such as the iceboat starting on a closehauled course. After picking up speed it will have to drop to a reach, to a beam reach, then to a broad reach at maximum speed to keep the sails full and not run out of the apparent wind...while the sails are still trimmed to the apparent wind for a closehauled course.

- **Shallow, semi-rigid, full-batten lug sails.** Our western culture has just begun to explore the potential of the balanced lug rig, pages 279-281, which has powered Chinese junks for possibly 2000 years.

  These semi-rigid rigs sail easily upwind and downwind, changing tack easily upwind, and jibing easily downwind. It eliminates the tremendous pivoting torque forces involved with the boom when jibing our fore and aft rigged boats.

- **A flat rigid sail.** It can sail dead downwind. Yet when rolling action develops, the continuous changing direction surge of unstable air flow across the flat plate provides a braking action reducing downwind speed.

  If the sailboat with the flat rigid sail turns from a run to a broad reach, a disturbance develops on the leeward side of the sail. The resulting stall will produce leeway, drift, and lack of steering control.

- **Flexible sail cloth downwind.** The airfoil must be eliminated, with large cups developed in mainsail and jib. This stabilizes both sails,which helps to develop maximum downwind drive. While we report the basics of sail trim which have been underway for thousands of years...we wonder how sail design and sail trim will change in another 100 years.

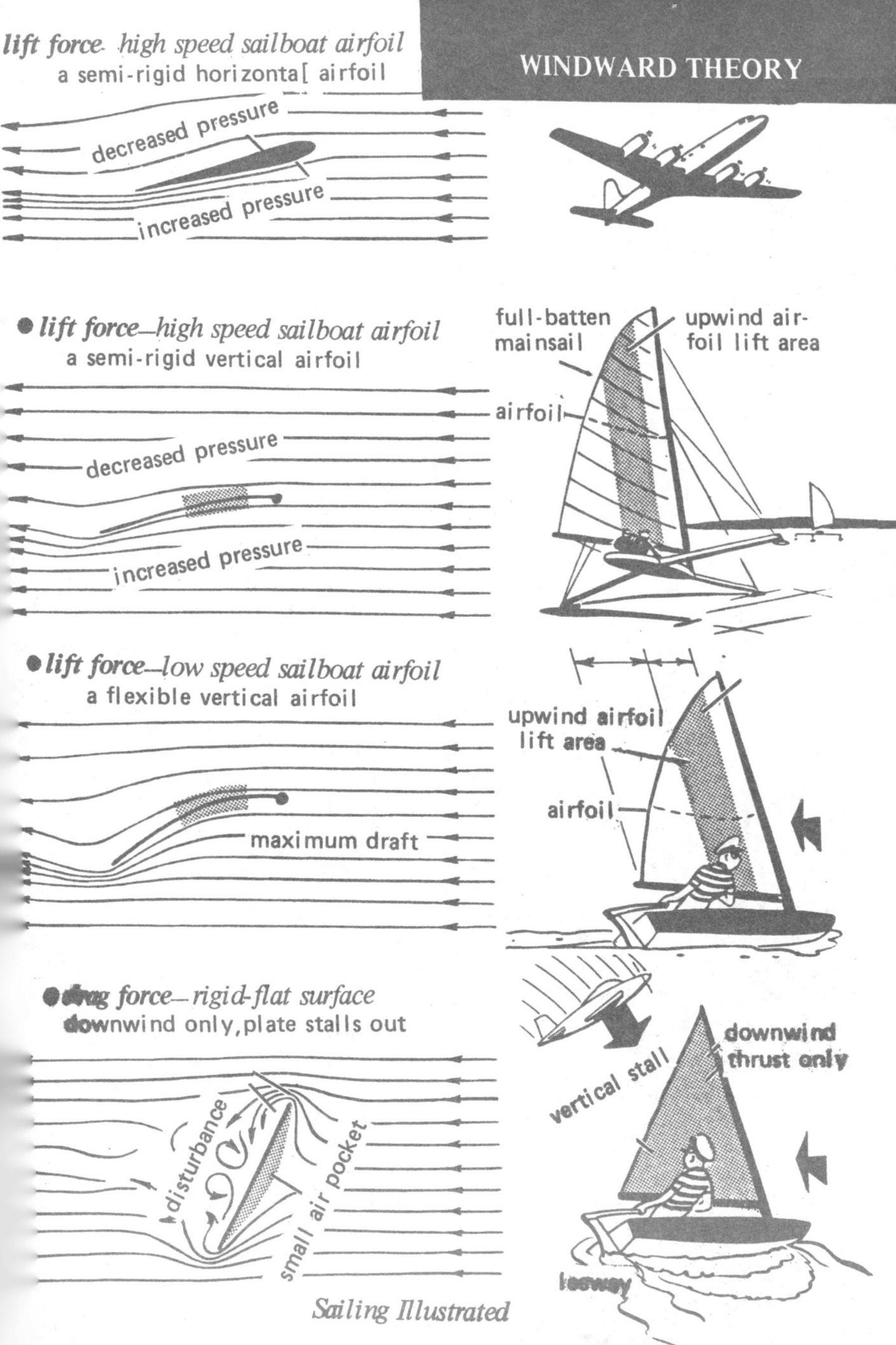
lift force- high speed sailboat airfoil
a semi-rigid horizontal airfoil
decreased pressure
increased pressure
● lift force—high speed sailboat airfoil
a semi-rigid vertical airfoil
decreased pressure
increased pressure
full-batten mainsail
upwind airfoil lift area
airfoil
● lift force—low speed sailboat airfoil
a flexible vertical airfoil
maximum draft
upwind airfoil lift area
airfoil
● drag force— rigid-flat surface
downwind only, plate stalls out
disturbance
small air pocket
vertical stall
downwind thrust only
leeway

Nature provides flexible, sensitive airfoils with a variety of complex factors for upwind sailing shown at left. Since not all sailors excel in the same areas, large racing craft often change helmsmen from downwind to upwind courses.

Closehauled sailing is the most difficult skill facing new sailors. The hull ❶ is pointing as high *as efficiency permits...*and the sails are trimmed as tightly *as efficiency permits.*

Closehauled boom positions vary considerably ❷ as you *trim your mainsail to the horizontal center of the mainsail,* not to the boom. Due to the flexible sail cloth, the boom may be over the quarter of a 7'10" Sabot...while the boom may appear almost amidship on the 12 meters beating or sailing closehauled.

Three incorrect variations are—

❸ **Pinching— the hull is pointing too high into the wind.** The sail drive area stalls, boat speed is reduced, the boom lifts, and the airfoil breaks, which is a good way to stop a sailboat.

❹ **Stalled condition with the sails trimmed too tight.** The hull is on a closehauled course yet the sails are trimmed too tight to develop an airfoil due to turbulence on the aft side. Speed slows down, the sailboat heels excessively, and sideway drift or leeway increases.

❺ **Luffing— with sheets slacked excessively.** The hull is on a closehauled course with the sheets slacked too far, with the airfoils disappearing. Luffing is an excellent way to reduce speed to stop at a dock or mooring using the sails as brakes.

Maximum efficiency— requires both jib and mainsail to be trimmed just above a luff condition...with the hull on a closehauled course. This combination under normal conditions develops maximum drive with minimum heel and minimum leeway.

Practice sailing closehauled until you are able to put this basic information to use. Then it is time to fine tune these ideas with pages 23, and 32 to 35 of our *Homestudy Guide.* so you are able to blend together the science and art of sailing.

 Sailing Illustrated

● **Wind funnel.** If all factors could be equal on a catboat and a sloop sailing closehauled, the sloop will point higher and sail faster due to the wind funnel increasing wind speed flowing past the leeward side of the mainsail.

● **Backwinding.** Genoa trim is critical to avoid backwinding the mainsail except when the ***fishermans reef*** is required, page 174. Jib trim is critical also on a ketch. If the jib backwinds the main, the mainsail can also backwind the mizzen...ease the sheets or fall off a few degrees.

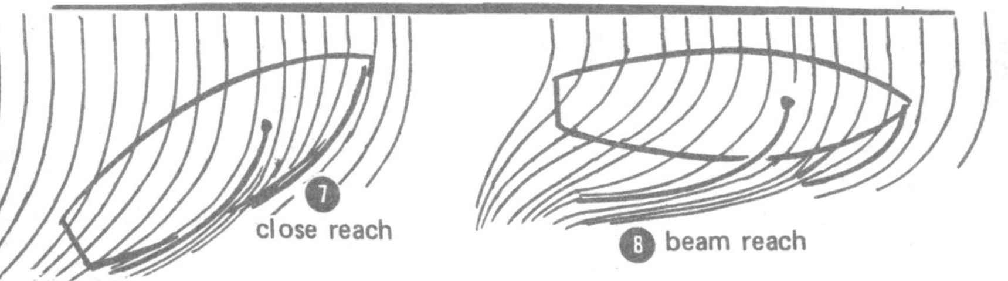

● **Reaching.** Fall off a few degrees and ease sheets so the sailboat can hold a straighter course for longer periods on a **close reach.** Slack the sheets more to maintain maximum airfoil efficiency when dropping to a **beam reach.** If the sheets aren't eased sufficiently, the stalled mainsail will increase heeling action with a speed loss, see stalled condition on the facing page.

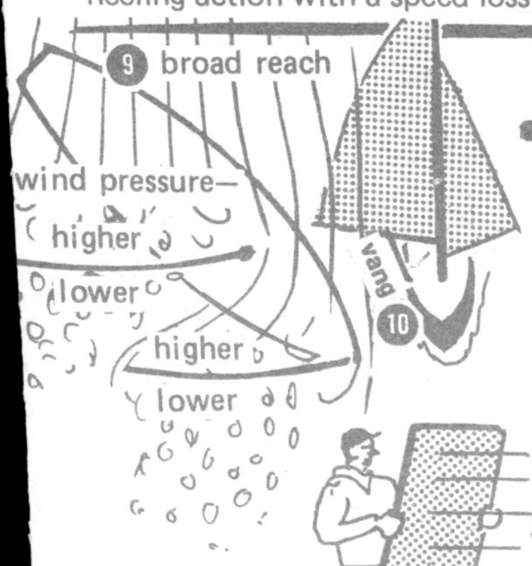

● ***Sails must change from airfoils to air bags when dropping below a beam reach.***

Sheets and sail adjustments are eased to increase depth in center of main and jib. Add and harden **boom vang** to stabilize and prevent the boom from lifting and moving excessively when sailing downwind.

A boom without a vang will have excessive movement that disturbs the mainsail. If the boom isn't stabilized, it will reduce the sailboat speed considerably.

● **Vang variables.** While wide-beam sailboats can use the boom vang up to a reach, the overcanvassed International 14 may need to use it sailing closehauled.

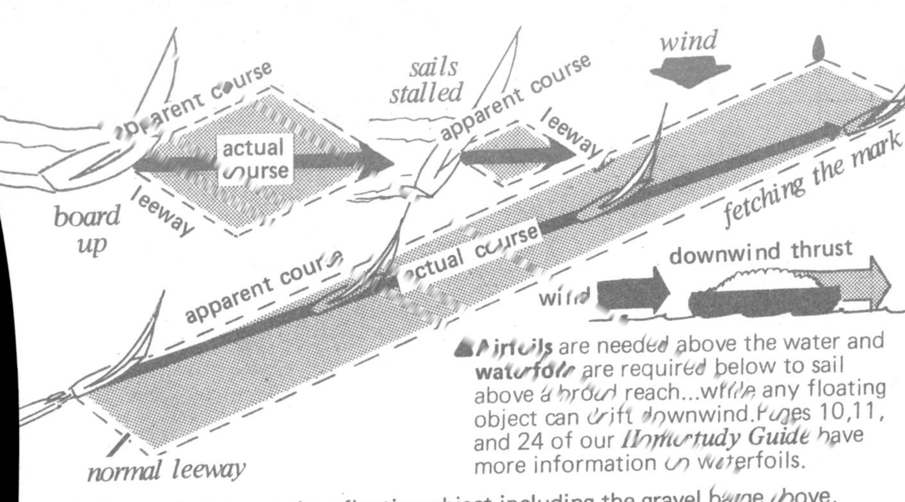

▲**Airfoils** are needed above the water and **waterfoils** are required below to sail above a broad reach...while any floating object can drift downwind. Pages 10,11, and 24 of our *Homestudy Guide* have more information on waterfoils.

- **Downwind thrust.** Any floating object including the gravel barge above, can be pushed downwind drifting without control...which sounds like a strange way to begin most of our full day sailing lessons.

We left our dock downwind under bare poles to provide exposure to tiller movement for students. Wind pressure aft was able to provide ample steerageway with our drifting sailboat answering to the rudder.

- **Bare pole downwind limitations.** After sufficient familiarity with tiller movement, we would have students head upwind until the hull stalls out just below a beam reach.After the boat falls back to a run to regain speed, students tested it on the other tack until the waterfoils stalled out again.

After this exposure it was time to raise the sails for familiarity with a faster, more responsive tiller action from a run up to a beam reach.

- **Upwind airfoil lift.** From noon on students practiced closehauled sailing on the ocean, then we returned to the harbor. They were now usually able to sail a closehauled course heading up in a puff, and falling off in a lull.

- **Airfoil brakes.** When the cabin racer/cruiser tries to point higher above closehauled, pinching begins, speed is reduced, the sails lift, and the flexible airfoils break. It is an excellent way to stop at a dock or mooring.

The higher a sailboat points to windward, the greater becomes the sideway force or leeway, with a decrease in forward drive with a waterfoil stall.

- **Waterfoil stall.** Single-purpose 12 meters, page 258, can point higher than racer/cruisers with the sails looking good and pulling though it is coming to a stop. Their limit is passed when the ***sideway force has overpowered the drive force,*** stalling out the underwater keel and rudder waterfoils.

The challenge to gain advantage in upwind sailing is centuries old, to carry cargo, or to outsail the enemy or pirates. Technological advantages are even more rapid today in recreational sailing with competition of your choosing from dinghies, to racer/cruisers, 12 meters, IOR, and ULDB racers.

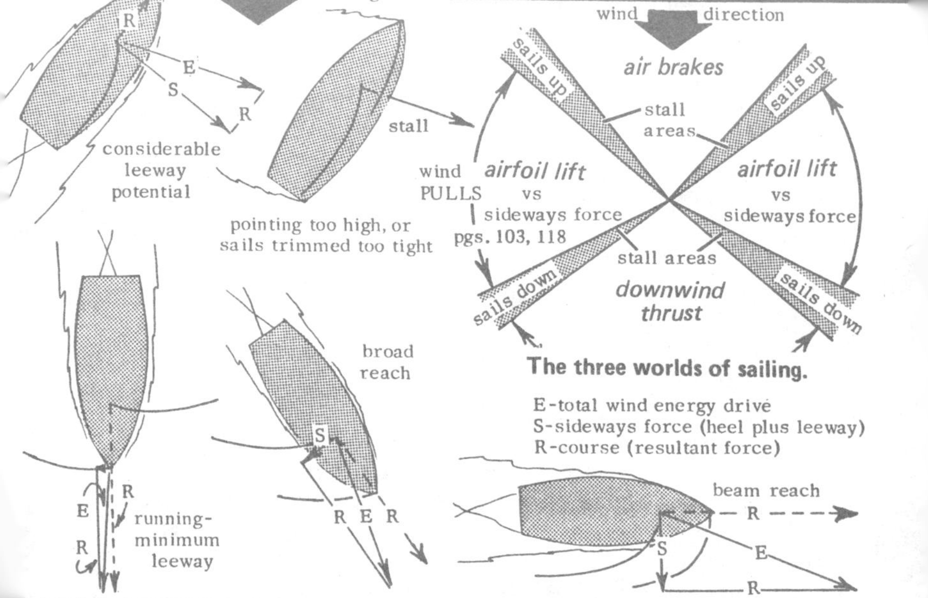

closehauled
wind direction
sailing bare
R
E
S
R
considerable leeway potential
stall
pointing too high, or sails trimmed too tight

wind direction
air brakes
sails up
sails up
stall areas
airfoil lift vs sideways force
airfoil lift vs sideways force
wind PULLS
pgs. 103, 118
stall areas
sails down
sails down
downwind thrust

The three worlds of sailing.

E-total wind energy drive
S-sideways force (heel plus leeway)
R-course (resultant force)

running-minimum leeway
E R R
broad reach
S
R E R
beam reach
R
S
E
R

Sailboat below is 30′ long with 400 sq.ft. of sail. Wind force 5-.96 to 1.4 lbs. sq. ft. pressure may have a total pressure ranging from 384 to 560 lbs.

Upwind. Wind pressure is increased by airfoil lift as sails push mast pulling stays, shrouds, and sheets forward to propel sailboat.

Minus factors— sideway forces of heel and leeway, bow and stern wave trap, parasitic drag of wetted surfaces. Others are mast, stays, shrouds, plus hull and cabin surfaces that don't provide airfoil lift.

Heeling safety valve spills excess pressure in a strong sudden puff.

Downwind. Wind pressure and speed are reduced considerably.

Total hull area, sails, mast, shrouds, stays, cabin, and crew in cockpit are thrust areas pushing downwind.

Dismastings may occur downwind in heavier, slower monohulls without a normal method to release excess wind pressure.

Minus factors— parasitic drag from wetted hull underwater surfaces, bow and stern wave trap.

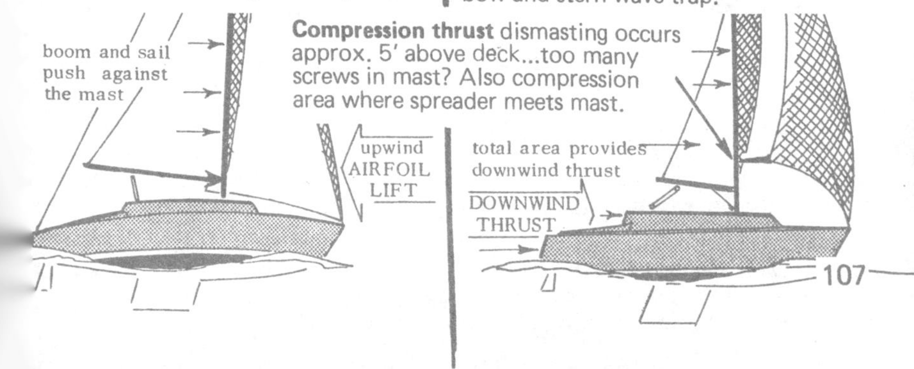

Compression thrust dismasting occurs approx. 5′ above deck...too many screws in mast? Also compression area where spreader meets mast.

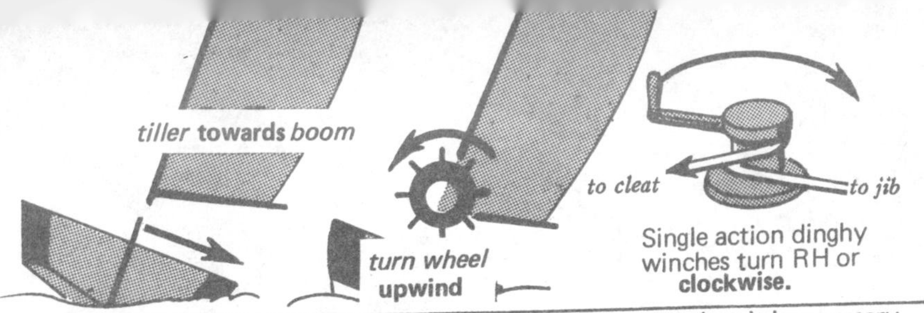

Coming about (*racing term is* **tacking**). The time comes when it is necessary to change tack by changing the wind from one tack thru the wind wall over the bow to the new tack with the sails full and pulling, and the boat underway.

Backing the jib on the facing page, involves weight, beam, keel or board shape, plus wind and wave action. We discuss its use on specific sailboats on page 170 of this book, and page 36 of our *Homestudy Guide.*

- **Sufficient inertia.** It is required for a sailboat underway to push the bow of a sailboat from one tack thru the wind wall...to the new tack with the sails full and pulling with the hull moving easily thru the water.

  When a keel sailboat runs out of inertia while changing tack and goes into irons, it can be an inconvenience, or a hazard due to lack of rudder control. When a centerboard or a daggerboard dinghy runs out of inertia in a stiff wind, a capsize we call **the big splash** can rapidly result, see page144.

Shorter, lighter, wide-beam sailboats.

- **Minimum inertia.** The wide beam fiberglass racer/cruiser became popular in the 1960's with excellent examples our 24' Challenger and the Catalina 30. They were lighter, much beamier, and with shorter keels than previous narrower beam, heavier hulls. The new light, wide-beam sailboats had to change tack rapidly to avoid running out of inertia...and steering control.

  Backing the jib is required. The sequence is amply shown on the facing page with the bow going into the eye of the wind. The wind catches the wrong side of the jib as the tiller comes amidship.The bow is pulled down to the new tack when the order *"CUT"*, is given AFTER the mainsail fills. The jib is resheeted as most of the boats are able to come about in little more than their own length. ***This tacking method provides excellent maneuverability in tight mooring areas*** which few sailors still realize.

- **Ample inertia.** Above 35' long, with the Catalina 38 an excellent example, many sailboats have enough weight and inertia so backwinding is an over-correction except in very light winds, see the variables on page 170.

- **Maximum inertia.** Most IOR and meter boats can come about changing tack so easily it presents a new problem... best defined on the 10 meter *Branta* page 265. As it goes up into the wind the helmsman goes a few more degrees. The jib sheet is released, the genoa clew is taken by hand around the mast, and aft to the winch ,with other crew members cranking rapidly.

  The helmsman then turns the bow the rest of the way to the new tack with the genoa sheet cleated, and the sail set so it is full and pulling for the new tack. If you try to sheet in such a big genoa in a stiff wind AFTER the sailboat is on course with wind in the jib...rotsa luck!

Coming about is the method used to change the wind's direction over the bow of a sailboat going to windward.

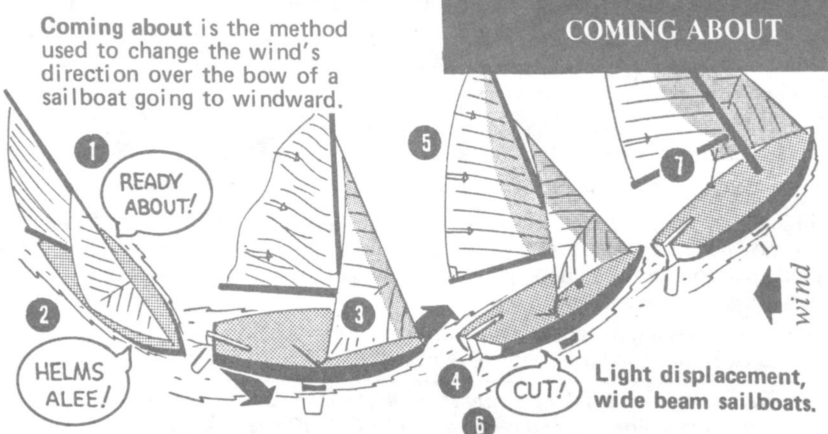

Light displacement, wide beam sailboats.

The command ❶ *Ready About* is given to alert crew. Helmsman gives ❷ command *Helms Alee* the moment he pushes tiller towards the boom. As the bow approaches head to wind ❸ the jib begins to fill on the wrong side backing the bow to the new tack as the helmsman ❹ pulls the tiller amidship. When the ❺ mainsail fills he gives the order at ❻ *CUT* to release the jib sheet and ❼ recleat jib sheet for the new tack.

Monohull mainsheet should automatically adjust itself when coming about...while **multihull mainsheets need to be released every time** when changing tack by coming about upwind.

Heavier displacement, longer, narrower hulls and larger racers with running backstays.

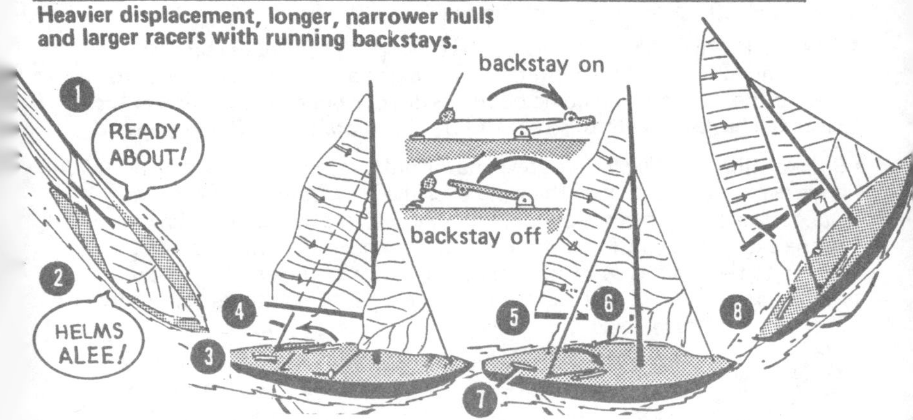

❶ and ❷ are same as above, while at ❸ the tiller is pulled midship. The windward backstay ❹ is cast off, and the other ❺ running backstay is taken in and locked. The clew of the genoa meanwhile has been taken around the mast at ❻ and the jib sheet trimmed in. The tiller is pushed over at ❼ for the boat to fall off on the new tack at ❽ .

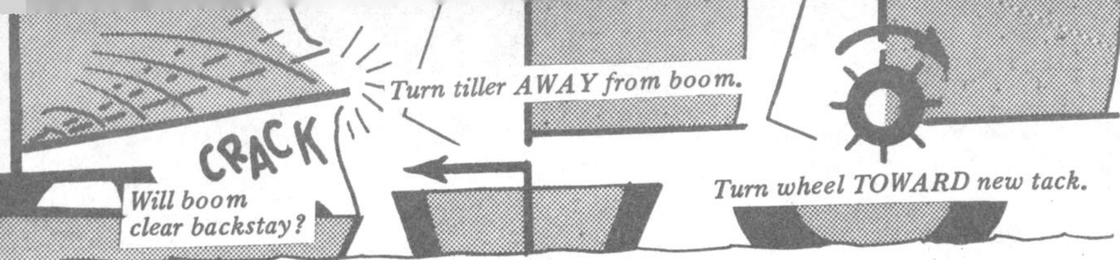

Changing tack with the wind over the stern.

Jibing is the method used to change the wind direction over the stern from one downwind tack to the other on a fore and aft rigged sailboat. Various jibing methods are used depending on crew experience, size of the vessel, plus wind and wave action.

Jibing becomes a normal procedure after practice to gain familiarity, and to improve timing, which becomes a lot more spirited in a strong wind.

Personal experience teaching jibing to endless students caused us to revise traditional term **Jibe—O.** *The command* **Jibe-O-DUCK** *is more practical in a strong wind for your crew to avoid the boom whizzing overhead.*

- **The controlled jibe.** It is standard procedure for jibing in light to medium winds. In light airs the boom may be pulled amidship while running dead downwind, then released after the wind catches the other side of the mainsail. In a medium wind the main sheet may be snubbed temporarily to a cleat to take the punch from the swinging boom, then released or eased out.
- **The flying jibe.** It is normal procedure while turning a downwind mark when racing on dinghies, IOR, and ULDB craft in medium to strong winds ...also on cruising sailboats. *The problem*—the swinging boom can develop tremendous torque forces similar to a running bulldog hitting the end of his chain...which must be compensated for.
- **The North River Jibe** was used by large sloops in the upper reaches of the Hudson River, page 263, with the hull making a rapid course change to absorb the forces of the jibing boom...**will your boom and mainsheet tackle clear the backstay** with this type of jibe? See *Homestudy Guide, page 38.*
- **Chicken jibe** *(wearing?).* In strong and/or puffy winds we occasionally find it more practical to change the wind over the bow from one downwind tack to the other downwind tack. We have used it successfully a few times on the Lido 14 (don't forget to momentarily lower the centerboard) to change to the other downwind tack...to avoid swimming home. If you are sailing downwind in a narrow channel reaching a turn without room for a chicken jibe, find ways to drop the main, then jibe the jib.

- **The goosewing jibe.** It occurs when only the lower half of the mainsail jibes...with the boom going vertical. Sheet down the main, jibe back, and make a second try.After your first goosewing jibe the symptoms are easy to recognize. It will then be easy to eliminate one in the developing stage. The boom torquing leverage was so great in our first exposure in a high wind, that two of our mast wedges flew skyward over the top of our mast and disappeared.

The fore and aft rigged sailboat jibes from one tack to the other by changing the wind over the stern.

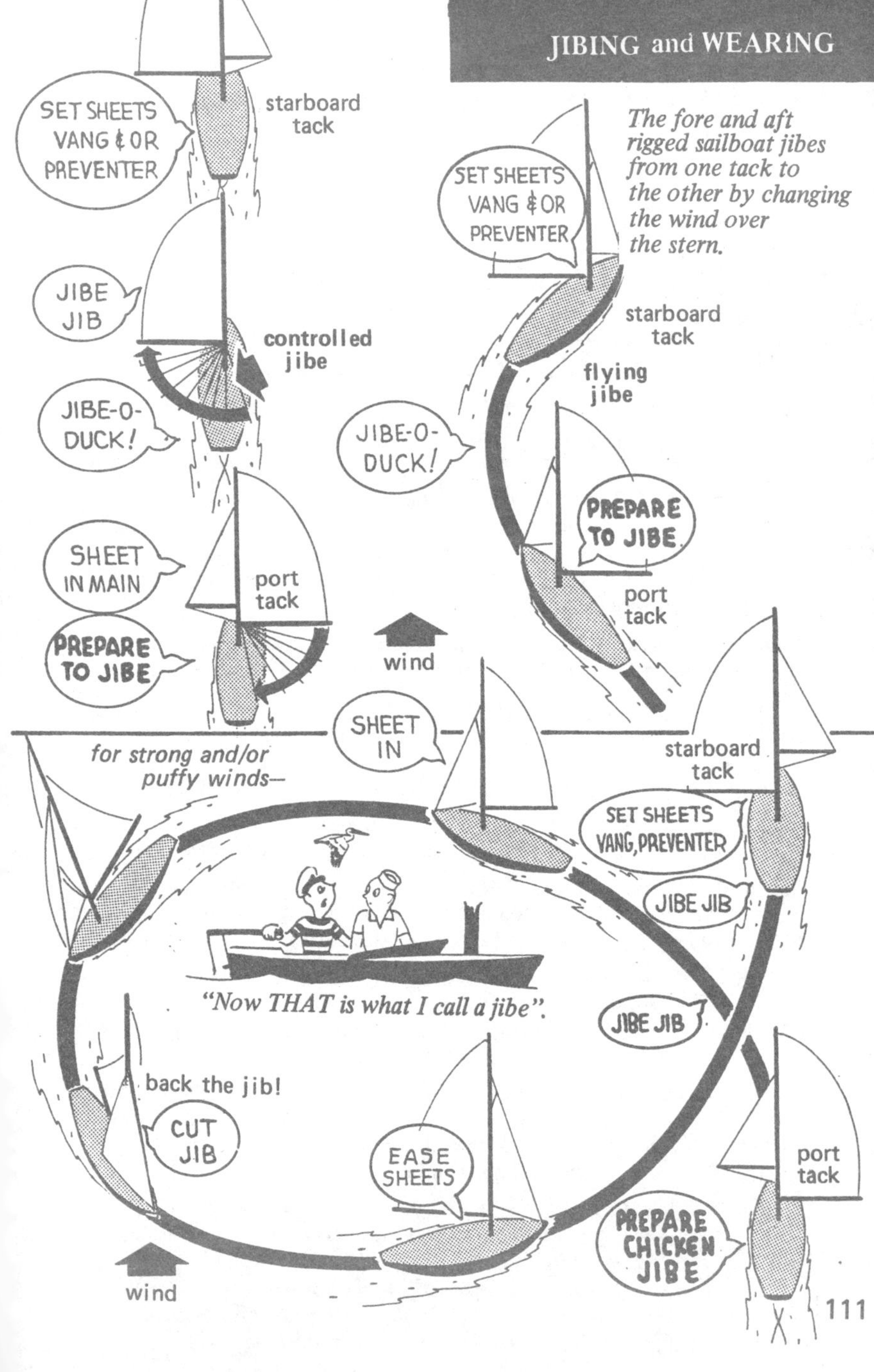

"Now THAT is what I call a jibe".

Wind power action...is transferred to the hull, the reaction.

To bend like a tree in the wind— is the theory of the unstayed Chinese pole mast used for over 2000 years with wind force transmitted to the hole thru the deck, and to the mast base. American builders launched many catboats, cat ketches, etc., since 1975 also using the unstayed pole mast theory.

Rapid acceleration. Wind pressure on a 30' sloop is transferred from the sails to the mast, to the cabin support, and, if keel mounted, to the bottom of the hull...*PLUS* sheets, shrouds, jibstay, and backstay. Over 100 parts are used in the **standing rigging** to support the mast, and transfer wind pressure to the hull, requiring turnbuckles, shackles, locking pins, etc.

When sails and mast go faster than the hull...a dismasting results due to failure of a few standing rigging parts. Most dismastings can be eliminated with periodic checks of all standing rigging parts.

- **Flexible or bendy dinghy mast.** Obtain rigging tension standards from your one-design class secretary, then compare these with the shroud and stay tensions of the present class fleet champion.
- **Tall IOR and ULDB masts.** Most are under tension even when dockside. Professional riggers should set them up with tension meters following the factory specifications. **Large catamaran and trimaran** rigging tension spec's are very critical. They should be provided by their designers and be set up using (aircraft?) tension meters.
- **Cabin racer/cruisers to 40' long with masthead and fractional rigs** follow similar rigging patterns with owners often setting their own tension standards.

  Rigging too tight is the most common mistake. Tight rigging sets up abnormal action/reaction tension forces. While shrouds and stays try to pull up the bow, stern, and sides, they try to push the mast heel thru the top of the cabin, or if mounted below, thru the keel. ***The sailboat has NO sensitivity.***

  Rigging too slack. This is fortunately rare. In a sloppy sea the mast can bounce up and down like a pile driver, also causing damaging action/reaction forces.

  Rigging tension compromise. Are they provided by your builder? Sufficient tension is required to keep the mast *in column* with probably a little more backstay and jibstay tension to reduce unnecessary jibstay sag to windward.

▲ **Pumping?** Many sailboats to 30' have an upper shroud, and a single lower shroud. In wave action the mast response to the hull is momentarily delayed with the mast going one way, and the hull the other, called **pumping.** Add a second lower stay as shown to minimize chances of a dismasting.

▲ **Change to double lower shrouds,** see facing page. When making this change our hull and mast worked together as a team with instant response reducing the chance of dismasting. This idea will only make sense AFTER the owner has had an exposure to pumping action in heavy weather.

- **Avoid tight, snug shroud covers** in which hygroscopic ocean water can collect, and due to blocked air flow can cause oxygen starvation. This contributes to ***stainless intergranular corrosion*** indicated by broken strands. **Shroud covers should roll easily against jib and jibsheet** when changing tack. Pages 126 to 135 of our *Homestudy Guide* cover the complex subject of seagoing metals, corrosion potential, and protection methods.

RIGGING TENSION

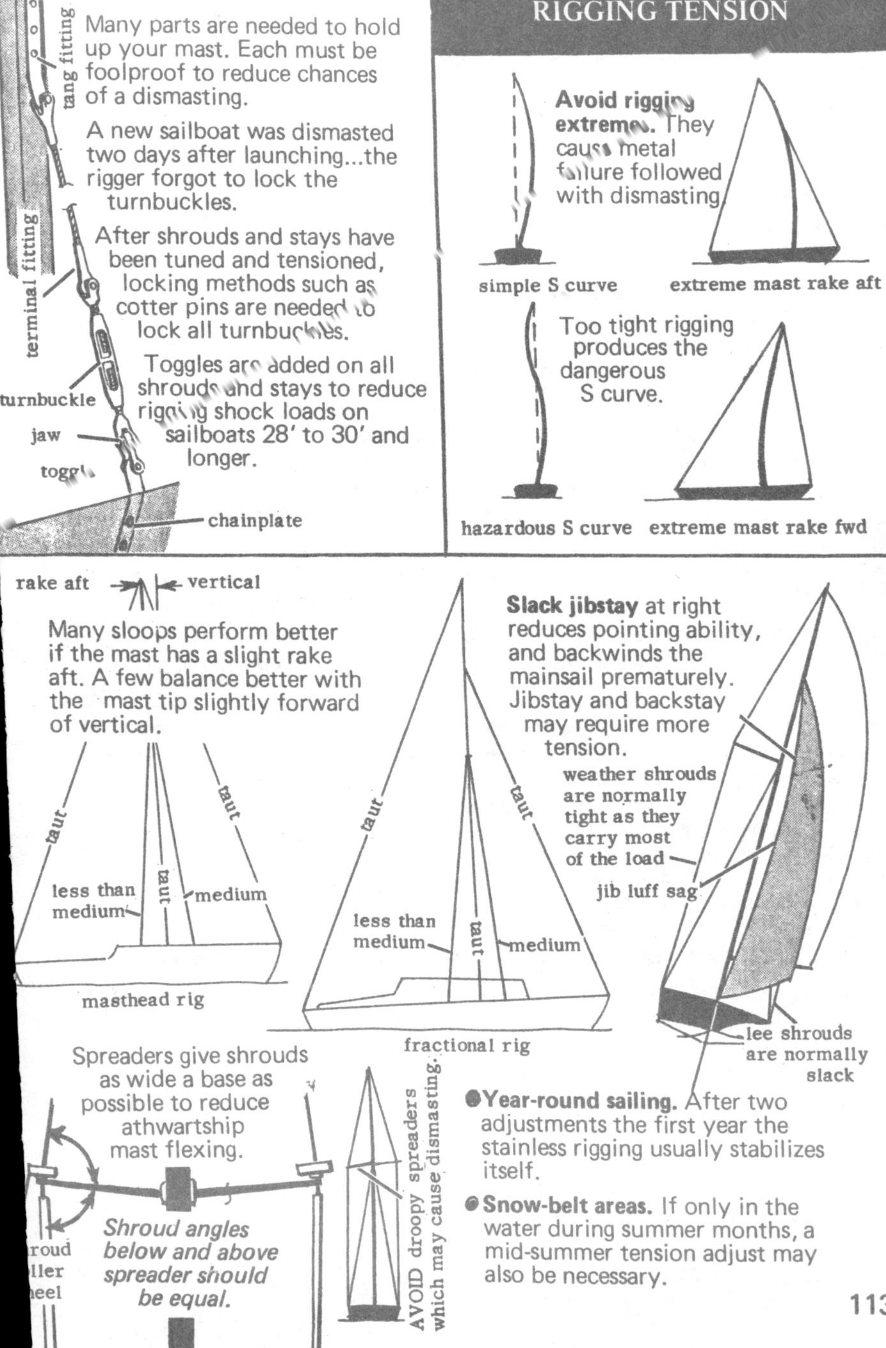

The technology and art of boatbuilding and sailing predates recorded history with many interesting ideas. No two wooden masts in history for example were identical... as each tree has its own individual characteristics.

- **Viking quality control** They had a fascinating method used for centuries to provide excellent masts. They planted a fir tree...then shortly afterwards planted a circle of trees around it. While this provided a wind break for the center tree to grow taller, it also reduced the number of limbs as the center tree potential mast tried to outgrow surrounding trees.

- **Early Arab traders were excellent sailors** with their vessels reported to arrive in Chinese ports by 787 A.D. Though we have no authentic record of their early masts, in the last century, due to a poor wood source masts and tree yards were made of many tree trunks lashed together, see page 276.

- **Chinese pole masts.** Chinese traders carried on extensive commerce under sail with Indo-China and Korea for 2000 years. While using locally grown pine for their 30' to 90' masts, in the last century they preferred Oregon pine. They bury their masts in damp ground, while we cure wood above the ground to reduce moisture content, see ***Homestudy Guide,*** page 137.

  Most Chinese lug-rig masts without stays or shrouds have several iron bands for support as did our square riggers. Some of these masts served on many junks in their lifetime costing more than they junks using them.

- **European pole masts** began with single trees. As taller masts were required, several pole masts were stepped together. The ***Cutty Sark*** mainmast was made of four pole masts or trees, reached 150' above the deck, page 284.

- **Ban Christmas trees!!!!!** As the market for wooden masts increased, availabilty of quality wooden masts decreased. Sailboat designer Herreshoff was outspoken trying to discourage the practice of cutting down fir and spruce evergreens before the turn of the century. He predicted yearly Christmas tree demand would result in our running out of trees for sailboat masts. On December 1987, an estimated 33,000,000 Christmas trees were sold.

- The **aluminum mast** entered the market with standardization for the first time. It produced predictability in performance with the rigid mast...and later controlled flexibility with dinghy, IOR and ULDB aluminum masts.

- **Snipe aluminum mast.** An invitation was held by the Mission Bay Yacht Club to test the first Proctor aluminum masts. As a puff moved in, the Snipe with a wooden mast would heel first, then start moving. A Snipe with the semi-flexible aluminum mast would accelerate with minimum heel.

  As wind speed increased, wooden masts backwinded mainsails while the slot opened on more flexible aluminum masts to improve the pointing and footing ability of the Snipe. Several of us held a wake at the clubhouse bar that night with accordian music furnished by a wooden mast builder.

  We wished Nat Herreshoff could have joined us at the wake before running out of evergreens. How many times has a new technology obsoleted older ideas such as a Michigan manufacturer redesigning his buggy whip as the best answer to compete with the new horseless carriage.

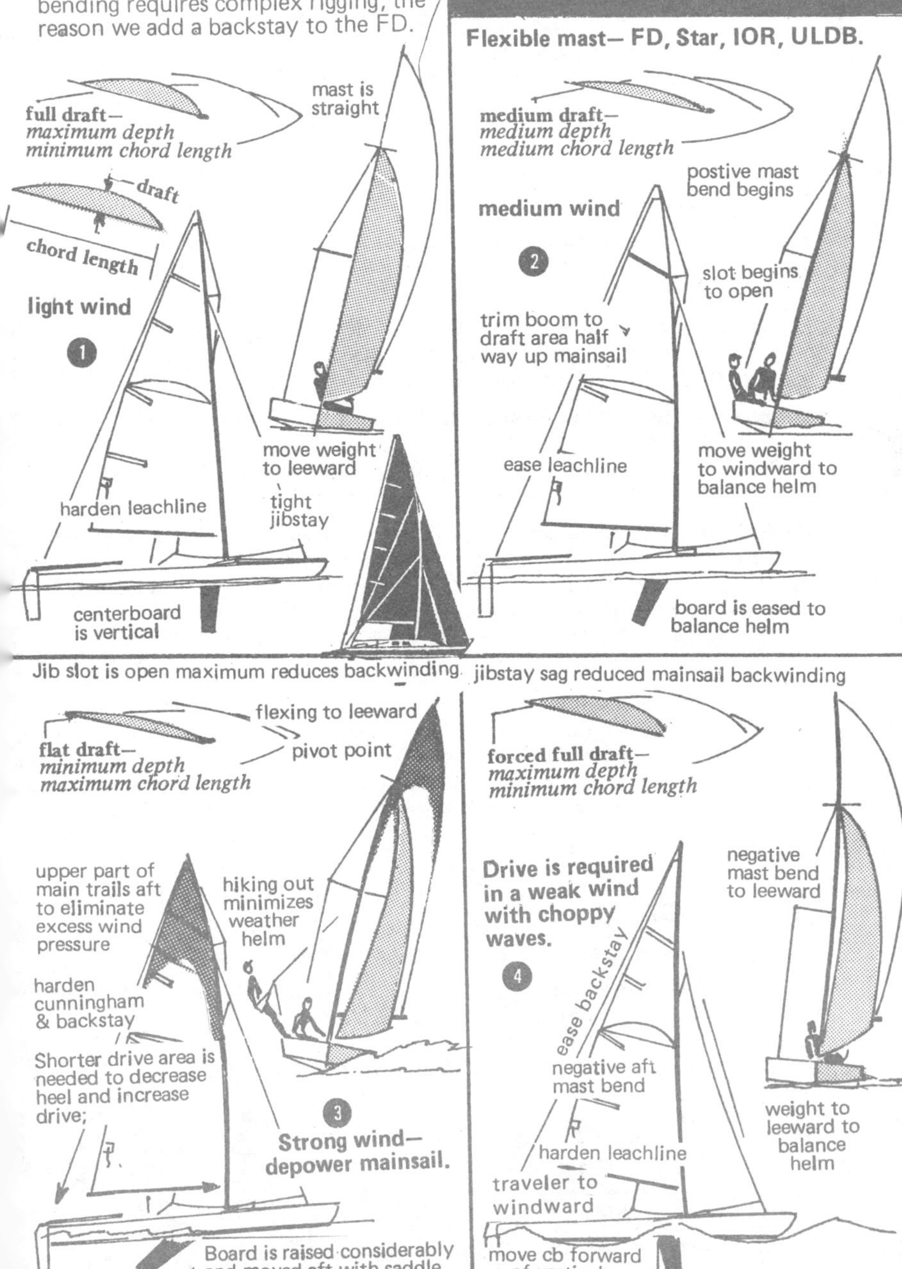
Theory is similar though IOR mast bending requires complex rigging, the reason we add a backstay to the FD.
Flexible mast– FD, Star, IOR, ULDB.
full draft–
maximum depth
minimum chord length
draft
chord length
mast is straight
light wind
1
harden leachline
move weight to leeward
tight jibstay
centerboard is vertical
medium draft–
medium depth
medium chord length
postive mast bend begins
medium wind
2
slot begins to open
trim boom to draft area half way up mainsail
ease leachline
move weight to windward to balance helm
board is eased to balance helm
Jib slot is open maximum reduces backwinding
jibstay sag reduced mainsail backwinding
flat draft–
minimum depth
maximum chord length
flexing to leeward
pivot point
upper part of main trails aft to eliminate excess wind pressure
hiking out minimizes weather helm
harden cunningham & backstay
Shorter drive area is needed to decrease heel and increase drive;
3
Strong wind–
depower mainsail.
Board is raised considerably and moved aft with saddle to reduce weather helm.
forced full draft–
maximum depth
minimum chord length
Drive is required in a weak wind with choppy waves.
4
ease backstay
negative mast bend to leeward
negative aft mast bend
harden leachline
traveler to windward
weight to leeward to balance helm
move cb forward of vertical

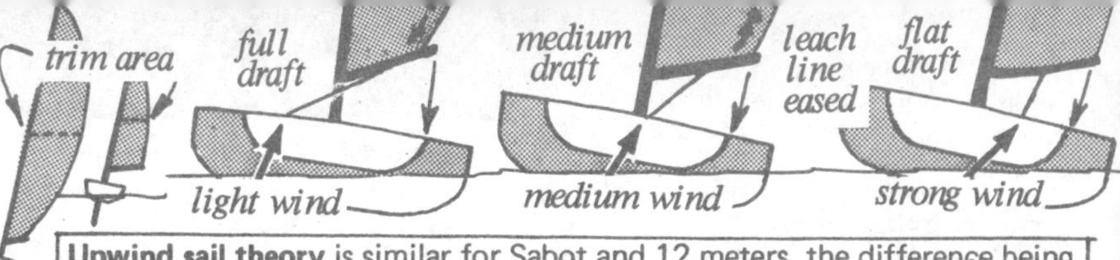

Upwind sail theory is similar for Sabot and 12 meters, the difference being flexible twist of the sail cloth.Both are trimmed to the horizontal center of the mainsail, see upper left, with the 12 meter closehauled boom position almost midship...while end of main boom on Sabot is beyond the quarter.

- **Boom trim reference point** is shown above for a Flying Dutchman sailing closehauled. The end of the boom is carried on the same point above the corner of the stern...which is similar for many smaller sailboats.
- **Light wind—maximum airfoil depth.** The leach line is hardened, and the mainsheet traveler car is sheeted to the high side or windward to develop a maximum cup across the horizontal center of the mainsail.
- **Strong wind—minimum airfoil depth.** The leach line has been eased all the way, and the mainsheet traveler car is eased all the way to the leeward end of the track. The end of the main boom is still at the same trim point on the corner of the stern...though much lower due to the shallower airfoil.
- **Medium wind—medium airfoil depth.** It covers a variety of settings between the extremes of light wind to heavy wind. For many sailboats the mainsheet traveler car will be sheeted somewhat leeward of the center of the track, with the leach line eased. ***The action*** becomes the horizontal center of the mainsail to trim to. ***The compensating reaction*** is the end of the boom reference point on the stern of your sailboat, see trim ideas above.
- **A loosefooted mainsail** may be excellent for local racing with adjustments shown for the 40′ ***Dolphin.*** It provides a flexible variety of sail draft conditions using the outhaul and topping lift for light San Diego breezes. Since most rules permit only one mainsail for long distance racing, the loosefooted mainsail is restricted for afternoon racing.The loosefooted mainsail has a long history shown on page 265 with an end boom attach on the **Groote Beer,** and no boom on the English **Pilot Cutter.**
- **End-boom sheeting—masthead rig.** While leachline and downhaul may be hardened to flatten the airfoil, various foot reef methods may be used. The end boom attach advantage—the mainsheet is aft of the cockpit.
- **Mid-boom attach—fractional rig.** It provides more setting for the controlled flexibility of the FD, Star, IOR, and ULDB **bendy mast** shown on previous page. If the mast is flexible the boom must be rigid, and if the boom is flexible such as on the 12 meter **Vim,** the boom must be rigid. If both are flexible an overbend results as they fight each other.

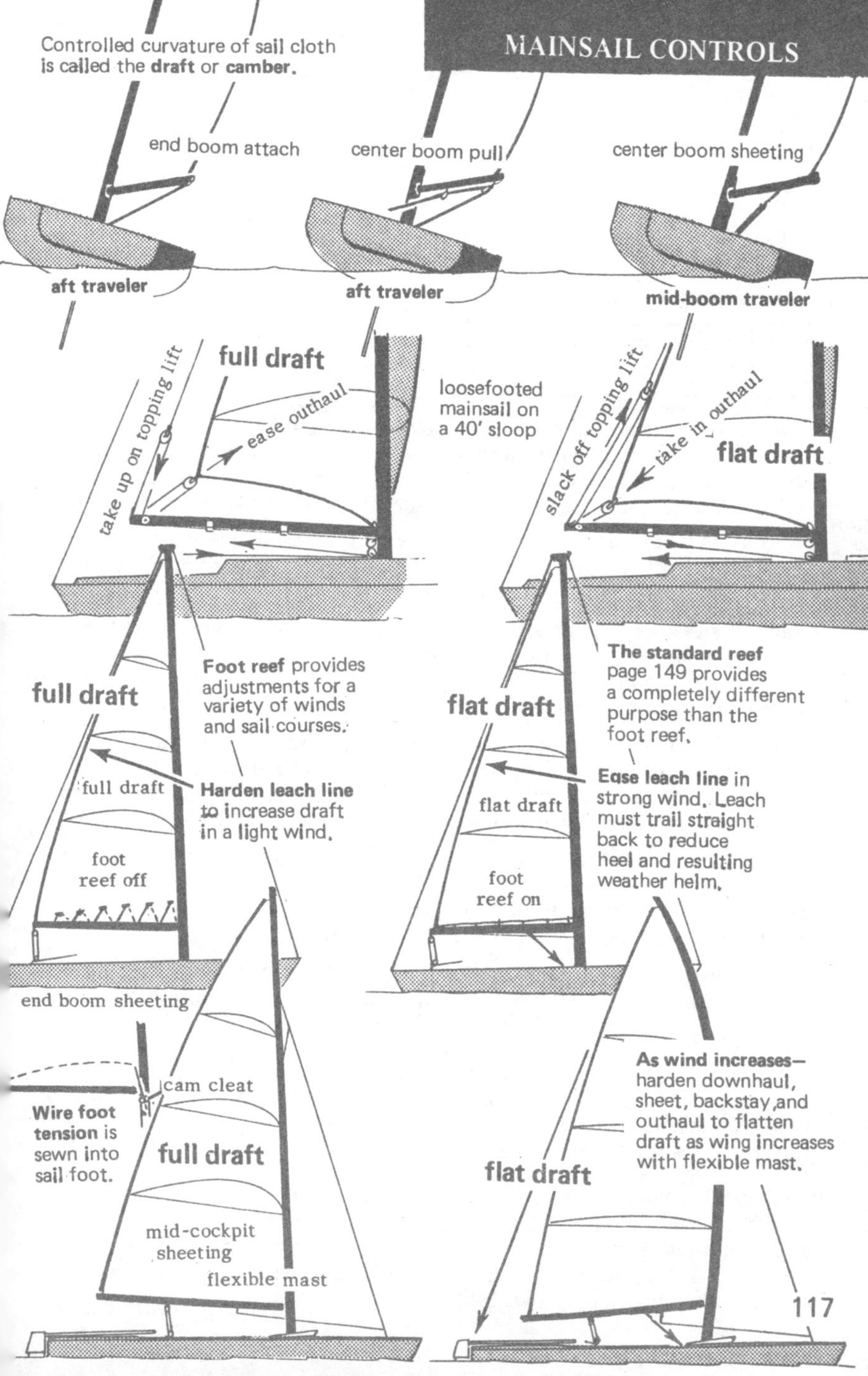
Controlled curvature of sail cloth is called the **draft** or **camber.**
end boom attach
center boom pull
center boom sheeting
aft traveler
aft traveler
mid-boom traveler
full draft
take up on topping lift
ease outhaul
loosefooted mainsail on a 40' sloop
slack off topping lift
take in outhaul
flat draft
full draft
Foot reef provides adjustments for a variety of winds and sail courses.
full draft
Harden leach line to increase draft in a light wind.
foot reef off
flat draft
The standard reef page 149 provides a completely different purpose than the foot reef.
flat draft
Ease leach line in strong wind. Leach must trail straight back to reduce heel and resulting weather helm.
foot reef on
end boom sheeting
cam cleat
Wire foot tension is sewn into sail foot.
full draft
mid-cockpit sheeting
flexible mast
As wind increases—harden downhaul, sheet, backstay,and outhaul to flatten draft as wing increases with flexible mast.
flat draft

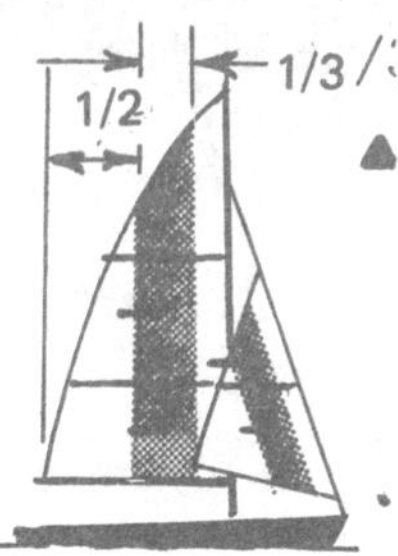

▲ **Self steering with sail trim and hull trim.** Trim mainsail and jib, then crew weight so your boat can sail on its lines fore and aft. The goal for small to large sailboats in steady wind and wave action...is self steering for long periods with the rudder used only for a minimum of steering corrections.

For lighter winds– cup the sails, move weight to leeward and further forward. For heavy winds– move crew weight to the high side and further aft to trim for self steering.

After you understand these basic requirements for upwind sailing, we add more mechanical methods you can use to increase sail draft in light winds, and decrease the draft in heavier winds.

- **Clinometer and speedometer.** The majority of boats I've sailed on usually go faster closehauled with a minimum of 3 to 4 degrees heel to balance the hull, page 134, while an identical boat sailed flat may be dead in the water. A clinometer and sensitive speedometer will provide your answers.
- **Shroud telltales.** Orange yarn telltales provide an excellent answer for closehauled sailing down to a broad reach whie a **backstay telltale** is used for running when the wind currents are disturbing the shroud telltales.
- **Sail telltales** are sewn in the gray areas upper left, to help you fine tune your closehauled sail trim to stay between pinching and luffing. This location is critical, as I found sailing an IOR boat. The jib telltales sewn on the forward edge of the gray area provided false signals.
- **Leach lines** are commonly used on mainsails and some jibs to cup the airfoil for light air upwind use, and for all wind strengths to cup the mainsail while running. As wind speed increases sailing upwind, leach lines are eased to reduce mainsail airfoil depth...and unnecessary heeling.
- **Centerboard vs weather helm.** At a certain point in a strong breeze sailing upwind with excess heel, the weather helm becomes overpowering which also reduces pointing ability. Centerboards and daggerboards may be raised somewhat to reduce the crippling weather helm.
- **The saddle.** Both International 14 and Flying Dutchman classes use this arrangement so their centerboards may be moved aft without raising to balance the helm while maintaining efficient pointing ability.
- **The barber hauler** was introduced by the San Diego Barber twins during a Lightning Regatta. A month later in South America where the Lightning World's was held, almost all competitors had barber haulers to open the slot to reduce heel and increase drive due to excellent class communication.
- **Backwinding the mainsail** can prove advantageous for keel sailboats with rigid masts and rigid booms. When sufficient heel develops to start producing crippling weather helm such as on our sailboat...the mainsail is automatically backwinded. This eases the excess weather helm caused by heeling, without affecting the normal pointing ability.

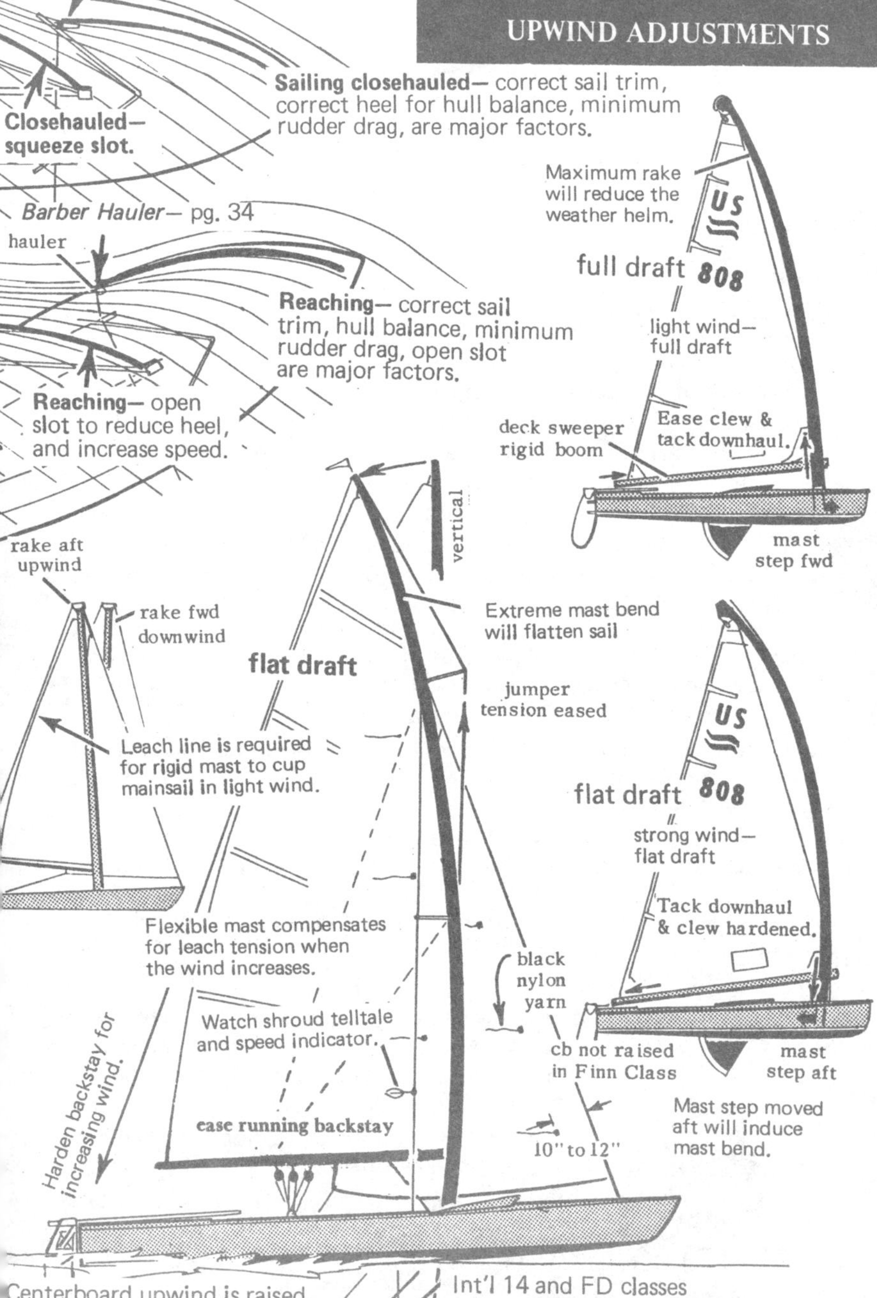
Sailing closehauled— correct sail trim, correct heel for hull balance, minimum rudder drag, are major factors.
Closehauled— squeeze slot.
Barber Hauler— pg. 34
hauler
Reaching— correct sail trim, hull balance, minimum rudder drag, open slot are major factors.
Reaching— open slot to reduce heel, and increase speed.
Maximum rake will reduce the weather helm.
US
full draft
808
light wind— full draft
deck sweeper rigid boom
Ease clew & tack downhaul.
mast step fwd
rake aft upwind
rake fwd downwind
vertical
flat draft
Extreme mast bend will flatten sail
jumper tension eased
Leach line is required for rigid mast to cup mainsail in light wind.
US
flat draft
808
strong wind— flat draft
Tack downhaul & clew hardened.
Flexible mast compensates for leach tension when the wind increases.
black nylon yarn
Watch shroud telltale and speed indicator.
cb not raised in Finn Class
mast step aft
Harden backstay for increasing wind.
ease running backstay
10" to 12"
Mast step moved aft will induce mast bend.
Centerboard upwind is raised progressively as wind increases
Int'l 14 and FD classes use a saddle adjust, pg. 248

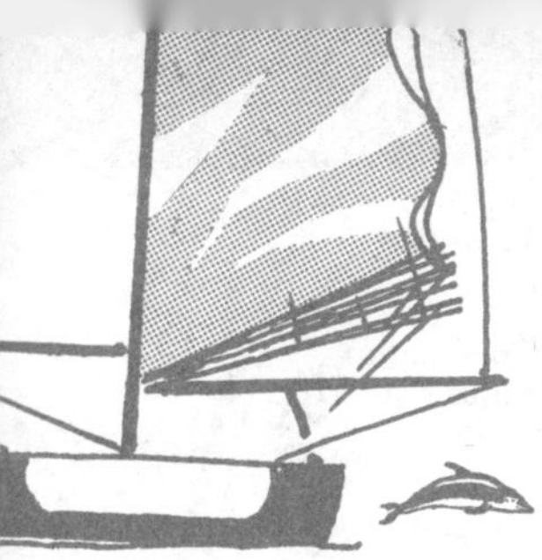

When most monohulls drop below a reach including our FD, the mainsail boom is outside of the hull and to leeward of the traveler track. The mainsheet is no longer able to provide a vertical downpull.

The end of the boom under minimal control starts to lift, and the confused boom movement produces disturbe wind patterns on both sides of the mainsail. While it reduces hull speed, unnecessary chafing also results.

● **Monohull boom lift.** The boom is beyond the control of the traveler track on monohulls between a reach and a beam reach. Narrower hulls lose control earlier, while wider beam monohulls with longer traveler tracks may usually have mainsheet control over a larger radius.

Mainsail trim is now transferred from the sheet to the forward end of the boom with the use of a **boom vang.** The vang stabilizes the boom and the mainsail with wind pressure again producing forward drive.

● **Multihulls**— large catamarans and trimarans provide a much wider traveler track with a vertical mainsheet pull often down to a broad reach.

▲The **vang** stabilizes the mainsail sailing downwind, yet it cannot prevent an accidental jibe. The traditional **preventer** leads forward to prevent an accidental jibe, it must be reset after every jibe. It also requires a vang as it doesn't hold the boom down. The **prevang** is a combination preventer and vang. It can be set and released on our sailboat, page 65, most of the time without leaving our cockpit, or going forward of the mast on larger sailboats.

● **The mainsail rides on the lee shrouds** running downwind. This breaks the mainsail surface into two areas with chafe problems when done for long periods on ocean cruisers.

● **FD and Thistle shroud levers.** They are cast off on the leeward side of the mainsail while running, see illustration at right, with a plastic tube or bicycle handle to reduce shroud chafe against the boom. It may be a good idea to lock the leeward lever again...before jibing. It has my curiosity when the shroud lever release will become the latest 12 meter, IOR, and ULDB secret weapon. Such heady dreams keep me awake at my typewriter.

▲ **Downwind air cup or air bag.** All traces of the airfoil are removed below a beam reach. Leachline, outhaul, and downhaul may be eased to increase and stabilize the mainsail air cup.

Total sail area is the major factor running downwind with minimum disturbed air flow off the sails, pg. 105

● **Backstay tension may be eased, and jumper tension increased** on some 5.5 meter and Int'l 14 racers. With the tip of the mast forward, downwind drive increases to provide a lighter tiller touch.

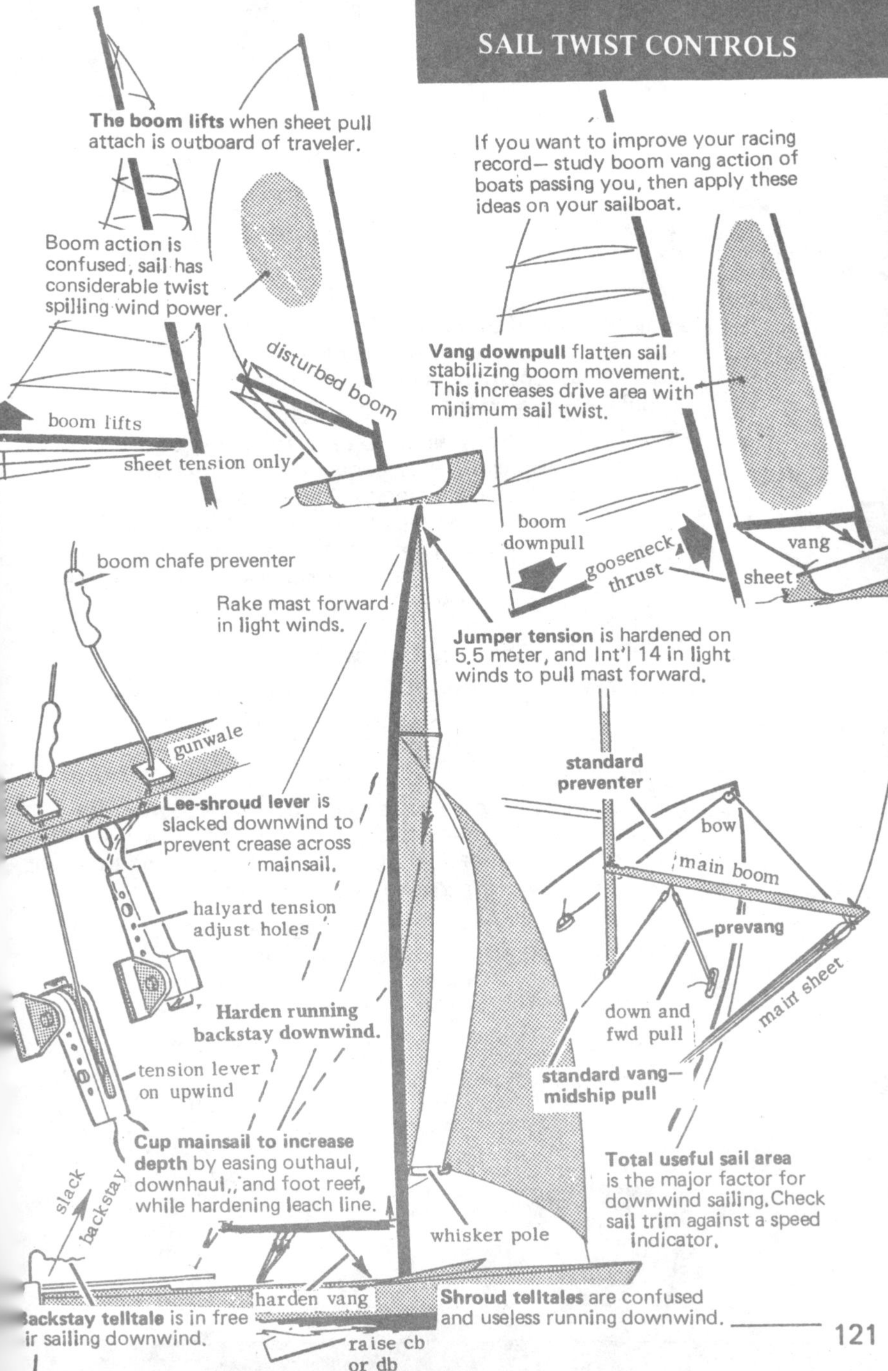
The boom lifts when sheet pull attach is outboard of traveler.
Boom action is confused, sail has considerable twist spilling wind power.
boom lifts
sheet tension only
disturbed boom
If you want to improve your racing record— study boom vang action of boats passing you, then apply these ideas on your sailboat.
Vang downpull flatten sail stabilizing boom movement. This increases drive area with minimum sail twist.
boom downpull
gooseneck thrust
vang
sheet
boom chafe preventer
Rake mast forward in light winds.
Jumper tension is hardened on 5.5 meter, and Int'l 14 in light winds to pull mast forward.
gunwale
Lee-shroud lever is slacked downwind to prevent crease across mainsail.
halyard tension adjust holes
standard preventer
bow
main boom
prevang
main sheet
down and fwd pull
standard vang— midship pull
Harden running backstay downwind.
tension lever on upwind
Cup mainsail to increase depth by easing outhaul, downhaul, and foot reef, while hardening leach line.
slack backstay
whisker pole
Total useful sail area is the major factor for downwind sailing. Check sail trim against a speed indicator.
harden vang
Backstay telltale is in free air sailing downwind.
Shroud telltales are confused and useless running downwind.
raise cb or db

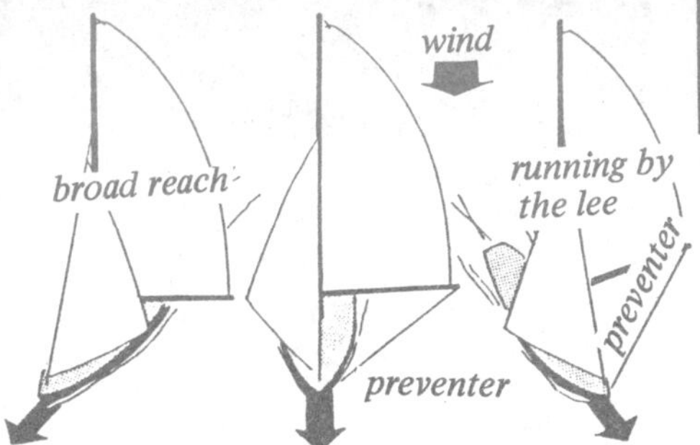

SAILING DOWNWIND

Sailing downwind in strong or puffy wind conditions has spirited moments. While you may have the least problems on a broad reach, the worst condition is to sail **by the lee** ...providing endless tempations for the main to jibe.

- **Reach or run.** If the wind at left is steady but light,you may cross the finish line earlier on a monohull by tacking downwind. If all conditions are equal in stronger winds,the boat running downwind should finish earlier.
- **The fine line between sailing art and technology.** Several of us were discussing this idea wondering what wind strength would be the factor for running downwind. We had an excellent chance to test the idea a week later on an ocean race. I was on the boat choosing the run for Ensenada while the other similar boat chose the broad reach. After changing tack and jibing the spinnaker a few times, an hour later it was back on the same spot 50' under our stern, which is the kind of challenge that makes sailing fun.
- **Wind funnels.** They can be spirited as we found on Lake Mead,page 210, where conditions were ideal to triple the speed of the basic wind flow.

San Francisco Bay thru the Sacramento Slough has a wide wind funnel with steady force 4 to 6 westerlies coming off the ocean for many summer days at a time. You may leave your marina in a force 2 wind,then turning a headland to meet a force 6 wind increased by a wind funnel.

The spirited bay area with steady year-round conditions was the proving ground for the **jiffy reef,** Timing can be critical to which is added a variety of local conditions such as wind coming off the high, steep hill lower left.

We misplaced a photo of the two racers at left in the bay area. The racers were heading for the finish on opposite tacks less than 50' apart sailing on parallel courses.

Sailing Illustrated

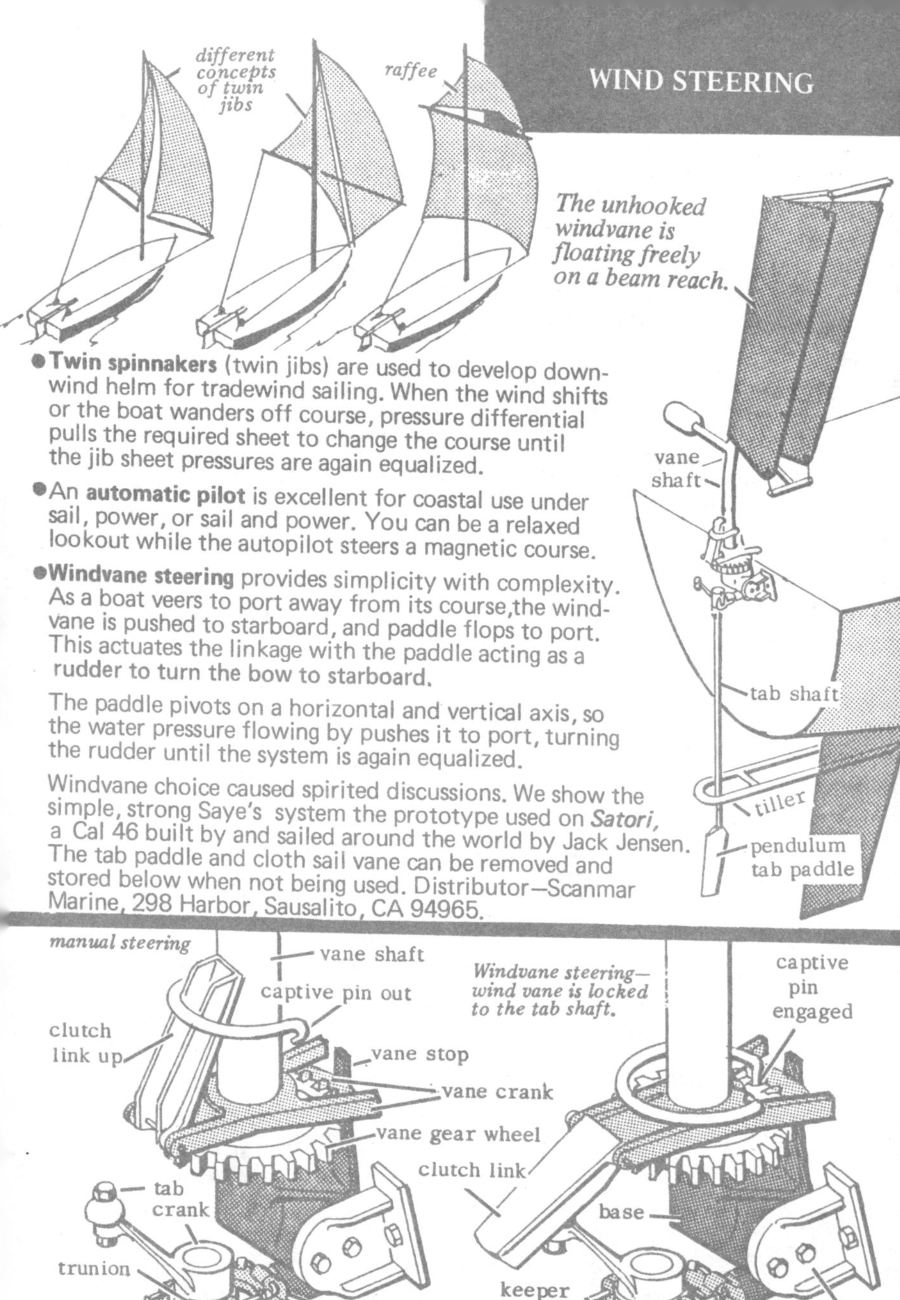

- **Twin spinnakers** (twin jibs) are used to develop downwind helm for tradewind sailing. When the wind shifts or the boat wanders off course, pressure differential pulls the required sheet to change the course until the jib sheet pressures are again equalized.
- An **automatic pilot** is excellent for coastal use under sail, power, or sail and power. You can be a relaxed lookout while the autopilot steers a magnetic course.
- **Windvane steering** provides simplicity with complexity. As a boat veers to port away from its course,the windvane is pushed to starboard, and paddle flops to port. This actuates the linkage with the paddle acting as a rudder to turn the bow to starboard.

The paddle pivots on a horizontal and vertical axis, so the water pressure flowing by pushes it to port, turning the rudder until the system is again equalized.

Windvane choice caused spirited discussions. We show the simple, strong Saye's system the prototype used on *Satori,* a Cal 46 built by and sailed around the world by Jack Jensen. The tab paddle and cloth sail vane can be removed and stored below when not being used. Distributor—Scanmar Marine, 298 Harbor, Sausalito, CA 94965.

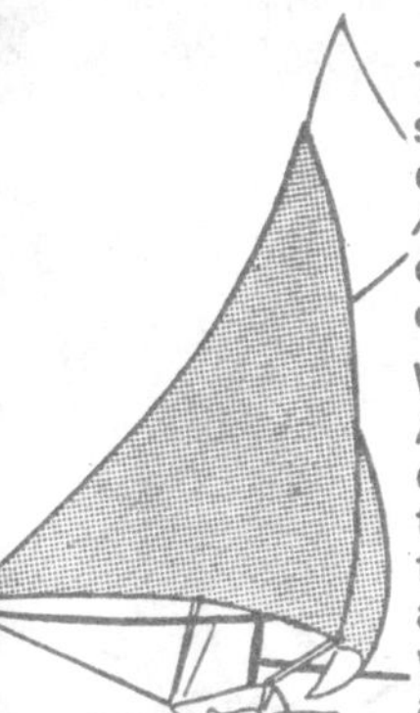

The 47 ton cutter *Spinx* broke out a strange,huge, triangular staysail in 1866 during a Cowes regatta instead of a square sail competitors used for downwind sailing. It was called *Sphinx's Acre or Sphinxer,* evolving into the term *spinnaker.* Was it an outgrowth of the Thames barge, pages 18 and 271, booming out large fore staysails for running downwind?

We show this new staysail on *Mischief,* winner of the 1881 America's Cup Series. The huge sail kept growing until a cruising sailboat with 750 sq.ft. of working sail carried "circus tents" with up to 3000 sq.ft. of staysail area. During jibing the sail had to be dropped,the boom changed to the other side and the sail raised again. Due to the heavy cloth it didn't want to lift, often dragging across the deck with the long foot, and sometimes the foot fell into the water.

Sven Salen in 1927 for his 6 meter *Maybe* made both sides of the spinnaker identical so it could be jibed without dropping. He increased the width at the head or upper area to help it lift clear of the deck. It underwent another name change becoming the parachute spinnaker we irreverently call the *chute.*

The British used the new sail for running while Americans also started to use it for reaching. We show ③ an early full cut running chute with broad shoulders, and a ① flat cut reaching spinnaker with narrow shoulders. A smaller storm spinnaker with heavier cloth was used for stronger winds.

- **Confusion occurred in the 1960's development period.** It is summarized by a student buying a 50' cutter, finding he also bought a garage full of 13 spinnakers...which were so expensive the previous owner had to sell his boat.
- The **star-cut spinnaker** arrived to fill the awkward gap between his almost new 13 reaching and running spinnakers. It proved better for stronger winds due to better construction, and the flatter cut reduced oscillation.
- **12 meter Cup competition has produced many spinnaker improvements** beginning with the dip-pole jibe which was introduced by *Vim. Intrepid* in the 1974 Cup trials introduced the all-purpose tri-radial chute to out-maneuver *Courageous* having to change from reaching to running spinnakers. *Courageous* was however chosen,using the new chute to win the series.The tri-radial chute was complex to design and build. The stresses theoretically fall on thread lines,loading,then unloading the entire chute at the same time.

During preparation for the 1987 America's Cup Series off the Australian coast,stronger winds caused spinnaker problems. The answer was to reverse our thinking,finding a fuller cup chute more stable than a flatter one.

- We were discussing new 12 meter technologies involved to return the *Grand Ould Mug* to the U.S. with boat designer Dick Reineman, owner of 10 meter *Branta,page 263. He summarized,* "We must have done a few things right in Australia which shows the fine line between sailing art and technology".

Research and improved engineering is continuous with the spinnaker we call *the emotional sail.* We show 120 years of history beginning with the *Sphinxer* to help you anticipate and develop future trends. After such colorful and unpredictable spinnaker development patterns in the past, we have no predictions for future spinnaker trends...but neither did Sven Salen's competitors. I wish he were around today to enjoy the highly complex and expensive technical mischief he started in 1927 with his *Maybe.*

Spinnakers

Sven Salen used the first parachute spinnaker in 1927 on his 'Maybe', helping him win the Seawanhaka Gold Cup. A few months later he introduced the 'Swedish Jib' at a race in Genoa, Italy, nicknamed the genoa jib'.

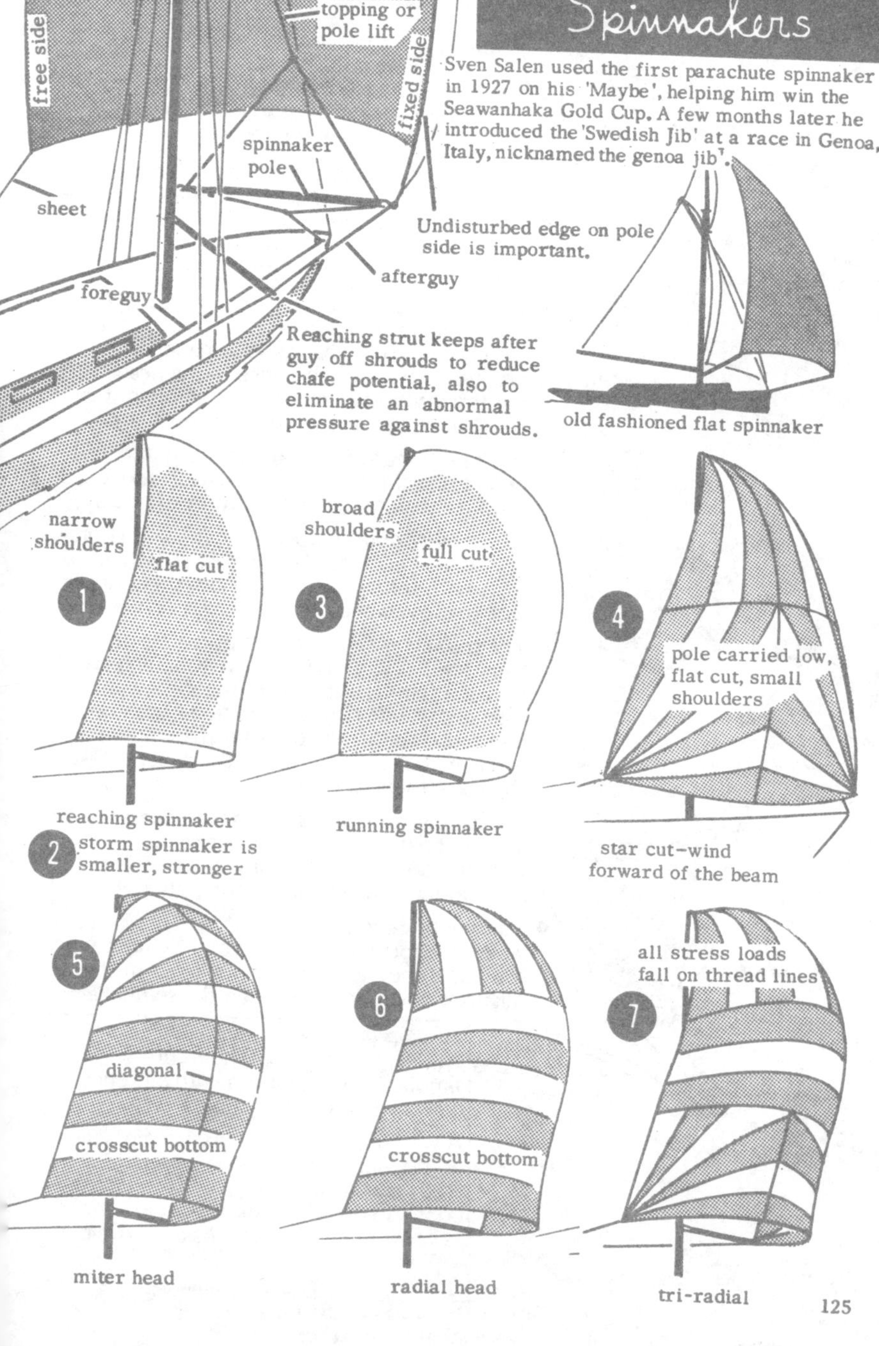

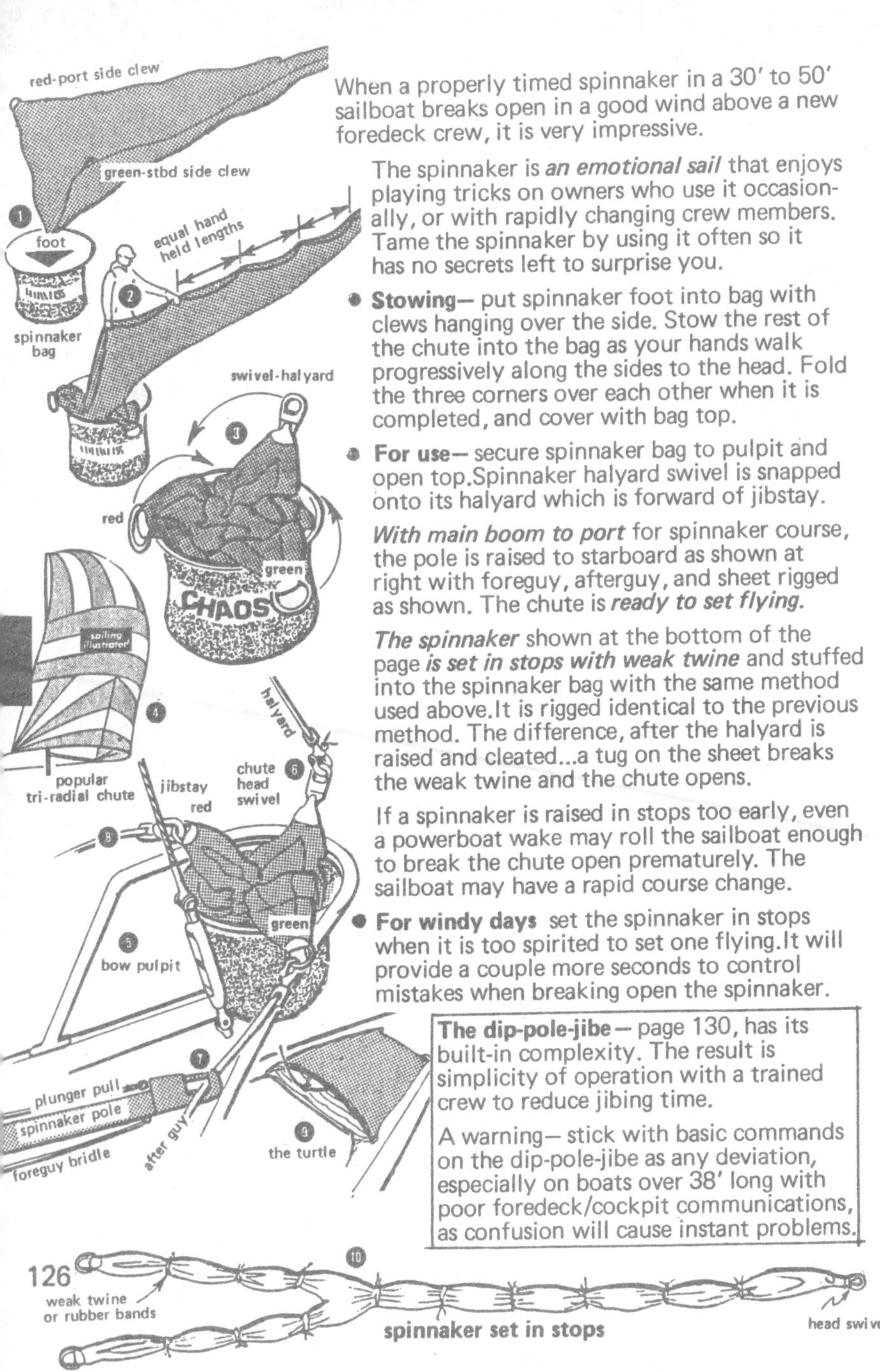

spinnaker set in stops

When a properly timed spinnaker in a 30′ to 50′ sailboat breaks open in a good wind above a new foredeck crew, it is very impressive.

The spinnaker is ***an emotional sail*** that enjoys playing tricks on owners who use it occasionally, or with rapidly changing crew members. Tame the spinnaker by using it often so it has no secrets left to surprise you.

- **Stowing**— put spinnaker foot into bag with clews hanging over the side. Stow the rest of the chute into the bag as your hands walk progressively along the sides to the head. Fold the three corners over each other when it is completed, and cover with bag top.
- **For use**— secure spinnaker bag to pulpit and open top. Spinnaker halyard swivel is snapped onto its halyard which is forward of jibstay.

With main boom to port for spinnaker course, the pole is raised to starboard as shown at right with foreguy, afterguy, and sheet rigged as shown. The chute is ***ready to set flying.***

The spinnaker shown at the bottom of the page ***is set in stops with weak twine*** and stuffed into the spinnaker bag with the same method used above. It is rigged identical to the previous method. The difference, after the halyard is raised and cleated...a tug on the sheet breaks the weak twine and the chute opens.

If a spinnaker is raised in stops too early, even a powerboat wake may roll the sailboat enough to break the chute open prematurely. The sailboat may have a rapid course change.

- **For windy days** set the spinnaker in stops when it is too spirited to set one flying. It will provide a couple more seconds to control mistakes when breaking open the spinnaker.

The dip-pole-jibe— page 130, has its built-in complexity. The result is simplicity of operation with a trained crew to reduce jibing time.

A warning— stick with basic commands on the dip-pole-jibe as any deviation, especially on boats over 38′ long with poor foredeck/cockpit communications, as confusion will cause instant problems.

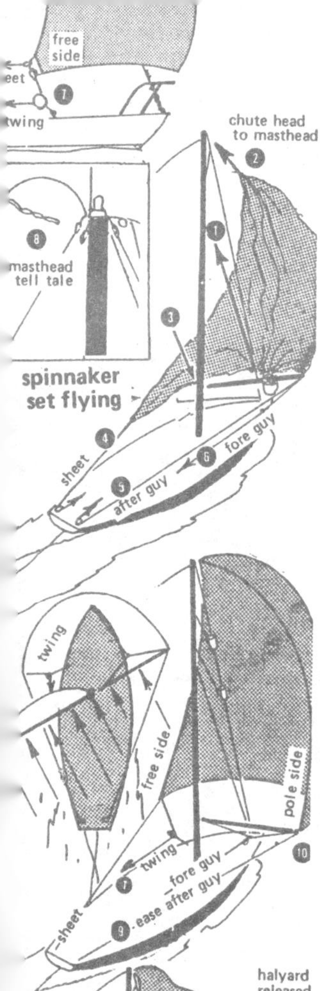

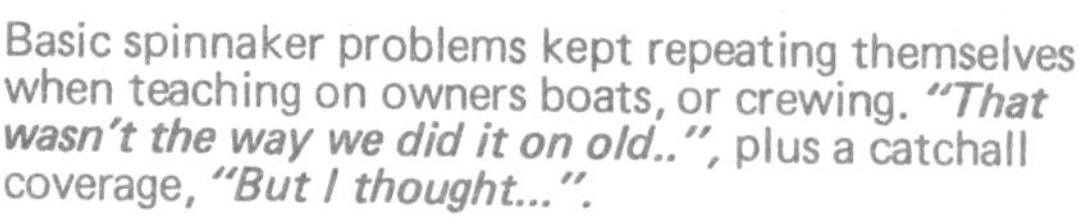

Basic spinnaker problems kept repeating themselves when teaching on owners boats, or crewing. *"That wasn't the way we did it on old..",* plus a catchall coverage, *"But I thought...".*

When the turn mark approaches— systematically rig the pole for the new course, plus afterguy, foreguy, and chute. During the turn *only one person gives the orders* in the following sequence.

- *Raise halyard*—it is raised AND cleated.
- *Haul in sheet*— comes 2 to 4 seconds later.
- *Set afterguy and foreguy*— an additional 2 to 4 seconds later. Then it is time to make final adjustments to sheet, guys, and topping lift.

The halyard must be cleated first. If sheet, or afterguy, or both are hardened before the spinnaker halyard is cleated in a good wind, the tailer may let loose of the halyard...or it may pull him 20' to 30' off the deck to enjoy some unexpected scenery.

If the spinnaker halyard is cleated first, and the ***sheet or afterguy is hardened too late*** in a good wind, the spinnaker may wrap around the headstay.

The wrap— begins in the upper half of the spinnaker which wants to go in an opposite direction to the lower half of the chute which lifts. The resulting hourglass wrap may only be a momentary problem, or the reason to buy a new spinnaker.

Preventing a wrap. ***Our* first** exposure was on the 36' *Sunda* in a 1959 Ensenada Race. In the slackening wind, sheet trim to counter a wrap disturbed the spinnaker, becoming counterproductive.

We installed a spinnaker twing or vang as shown which was momentarily hardened to stop a wrap. The masthead coathanger telltale proved the best protection. In a momentary lull when the telltale swings aft, you have 3 to 5 seconds to pull down the free side to stop a wrap and hold, until the telltale flows forward.

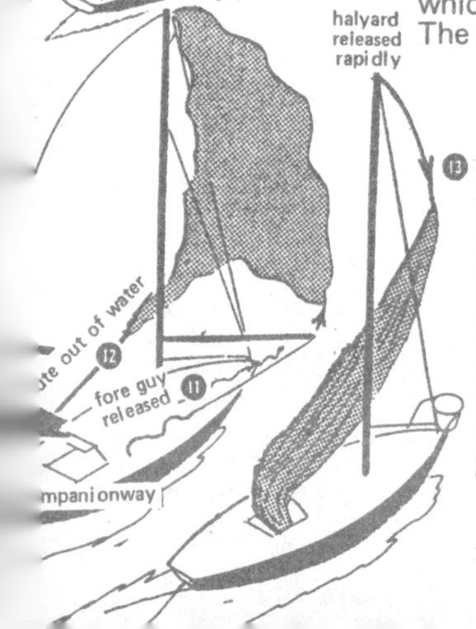

The broach— ***"The tiller overpowered me and I couldn't stop the knockdown".***

The wind was spirited raising the stern and depressing the bow, page 122. The helmsman MUST hold the downwind course when it wants to head up. If the bow turning tendency isn't counteracted immediately. the developing forces can soon overpower the rudder causing a broach with a knockdown.

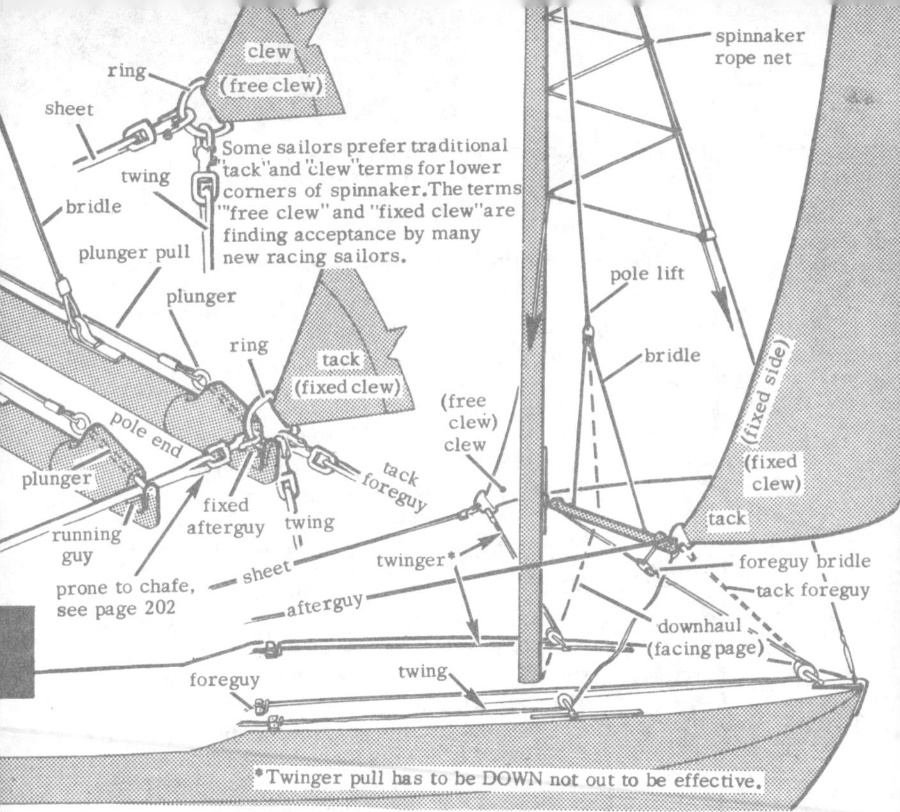

Double-ended pole, or end-for-end jibing method is used for most boats to 40'. Larger boats may use the dip pole method shown pg. 130. Method shown right, is used for open one-design boats, with pole downhaul coming back to lower part of mast.

Similar jibing method is used on boats to 40', except foreguy must also be changed if secured to ring on corner of chute. Foreguy coming to bridle under the pole, eliminates this extra operation. Running guy seems used on majority of boats for short races. On long ocean races, afterguy is secured to ring on chute, reducing chafe on afterguy.

Discussion of "twing" or "tweaker" will produce varied reactions. We've had considerable luck with it on wide beam monohulls over 30' to make chute trim changes in preference to sheet, yet with little luck, on narrow beam hulls. We used a stout shock cord 'twing' on wide deck "Tri Star" pg. 81, providing better trim, also eliminating spinnaker net. Wrap potentials are maximum on rolling monohull, running in sloppy seas with puffy winds, while multihull beam reduces rolling, minimizing wrap in same conditions. Spinnaker net made of rope above has stowage problem, minimized if it is wrapped in a cloth roll.

Balance of sailboat carrying spinnaker is critical in all winds, yet most obvious on monohull rolling considerably in strong winds with tendency to bury bow, pg. 123, causing erratic steering action. Steering action may be reduced by moving crew aft to level hull under these conditions, see page 115.

When people wander around the deck with spinnaker up, extra rudder compensations are required, reducing boat speed. If twinger & foreguy adjustments may be made from cockpit in a short race instead of on the foredeck, it may improve your racing record.

Spinnaker Jibing

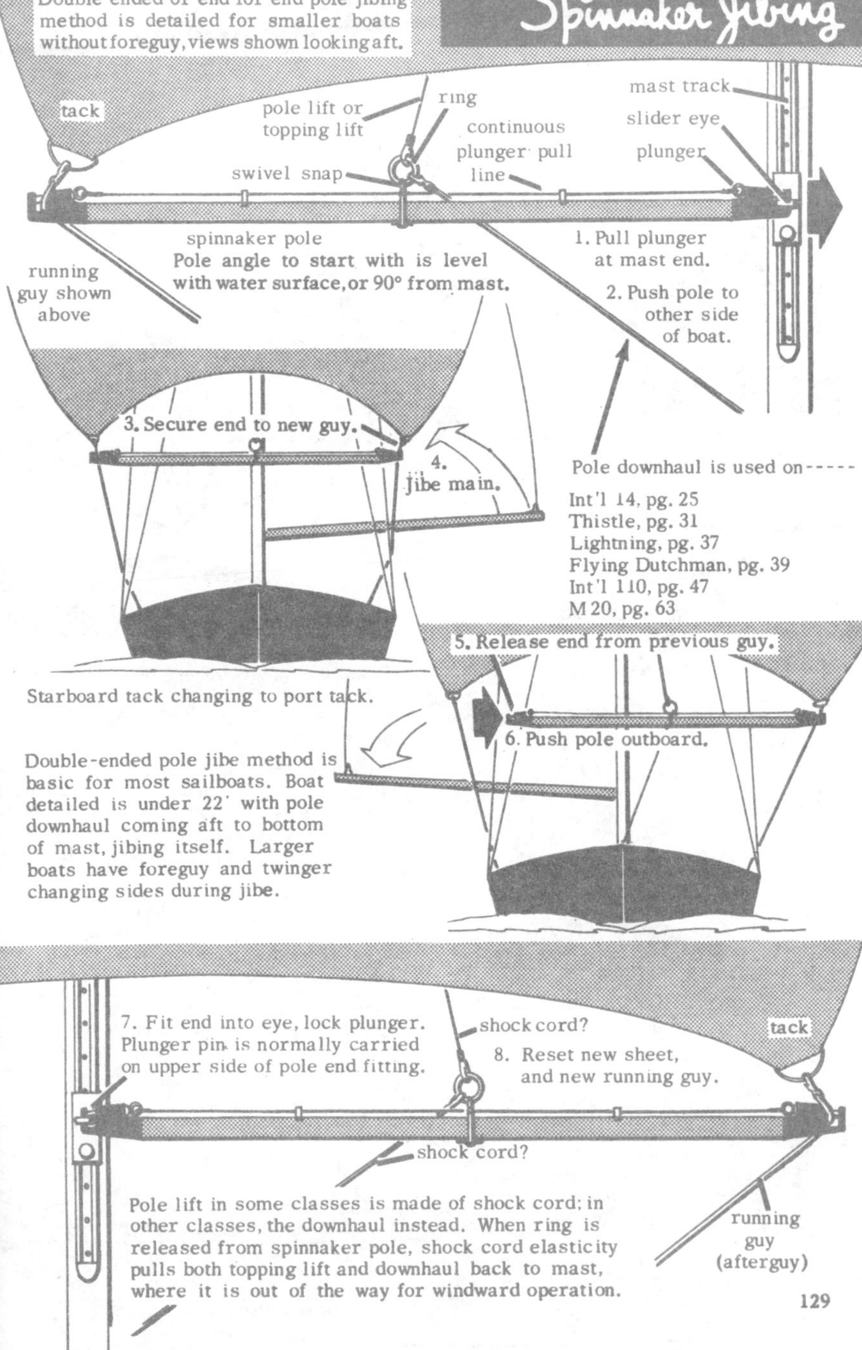

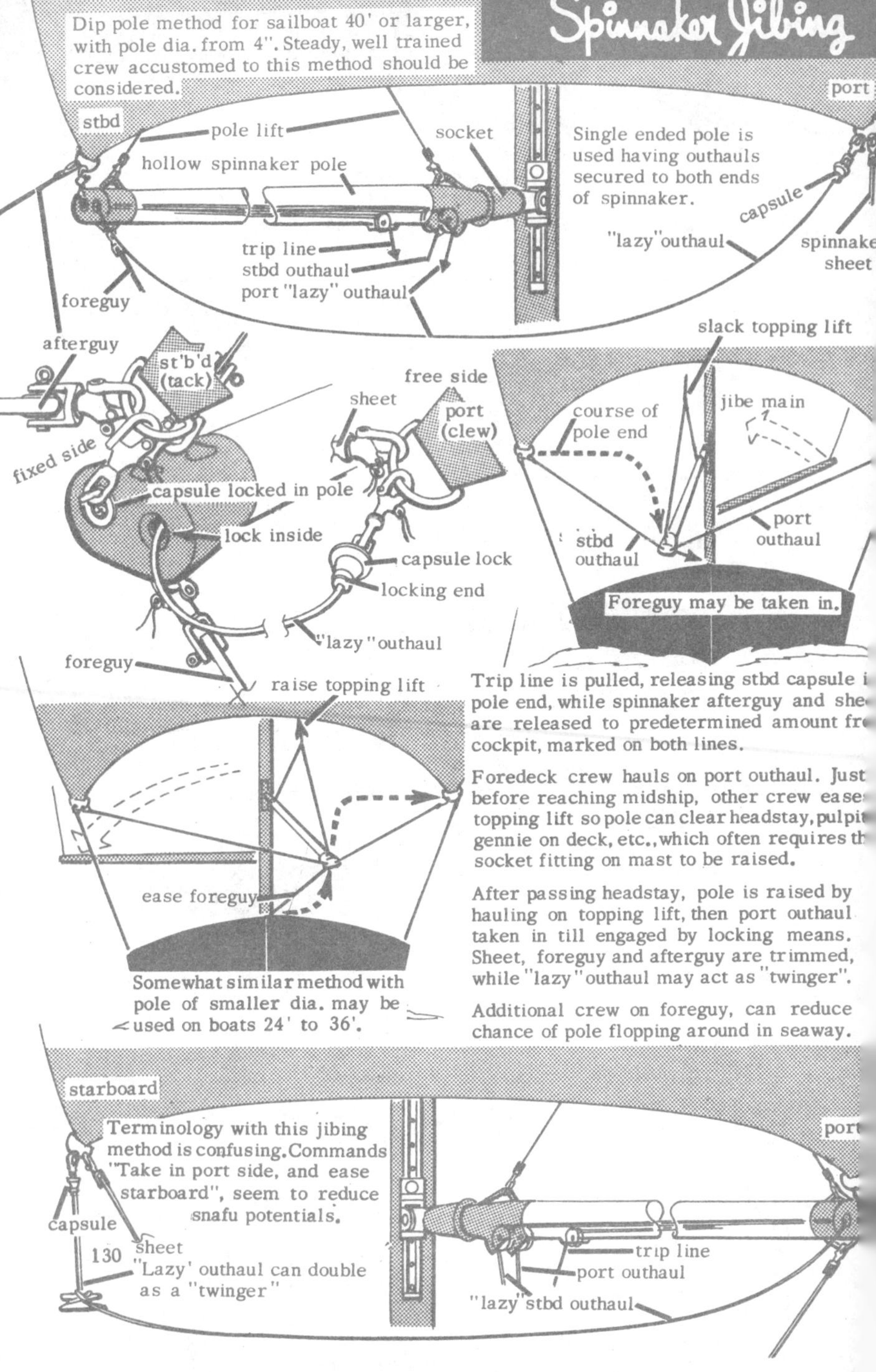
Spinnaker Jibing
Dip pole method for sailboat 40' or larger, with pole dia. from 4". Steady, well trained crew accustomed to this method should be considered.
stbd
port
pole lift
socket
hollow spinnaker pole
Single ended pole is used having outhauls secured to both ends of spinnaker.
capsule
"lazy"outhaul
spinnake
sheet
trip line
stbd outhaul
port "lazy" outhaul
foreguy
afterguy
st'b'd (tack)
free side
sheet
port (clew)
fixed side
capsule locked in pole
lock inside
capsule lock
locking end
"lazy" outhaul
foreguy
slack topping lift
course of pole end
jibe main
stbd outhaul
port outhaul
Foreguy may be taken in.
raise topping lift
ease foreguy
Somewhat similar method with pole of smaller dia. may be used on boats 24' to 36'.
Trip line is pulled, releasing stbd capsule i pole end, while spinnaker afterguy and she are released to predetermined amount fr cockpit, marked on both lines.
Foredeck crew hauls on port outhaul. Just before reaching midship, other crew ease topping lift so pole can clear headstay, pulpit gennie on deck, etc., which often requires th socket fitting on mast to be raised.
After passing headstay, pole is raised by hauling on topping lift, then port outhaul taken in till engaged by locking means. Sheet, foreguy and afterguy are trimmed, while "lazy" outhaul may act as "twinger".
Additional crew on foreguy, can reduce chance of pole flopping around in seaway.
starboard
port
Terminology with this jibing method is confusing. Commands "Take in port side, and ease starboard", seem to reduce snafu potentials.
capsule
sheet
"Lazy' outhaul can double as a "twinger"
trip line
port outhaul
"lazy" stbd outhaul

The floating teeter totter. Always sail your boat upwind and downwind **on its fore and aft lines** for which the hull was designed.

Install a simple carpenter's level. It should be easy for the helmsman to observe when steering the boat so he can request the crew to move fore or aft to pull the sailboat back onto its lines with the level parallel to the water line of your sailboat.

▲ **Lido 14 balance is critical.** An inch movement of crew weight fore or aft may be enough for the Lido to start gaining on the racing fleet...or watch other competitors pass your Lido one by one.

The level proved important on our *Pink Cloud.* New sailors soon realized the sensitivity our boat had to movable weight placement, plus the variable wind power source to test pointing ability and speed potential. After such an exposure, the level proved itself with few questions.

▲ **A double-ended** 50′ Caulkins cutter was averaging 7 knots in an Ensenada Race with a cranky helm. Three of us at the shrouds moved a foot forward to raise the dragging stern with a speed increase to over 8¼ knots. A level I taped to the side of the cabin indicated too much cockpit weight.

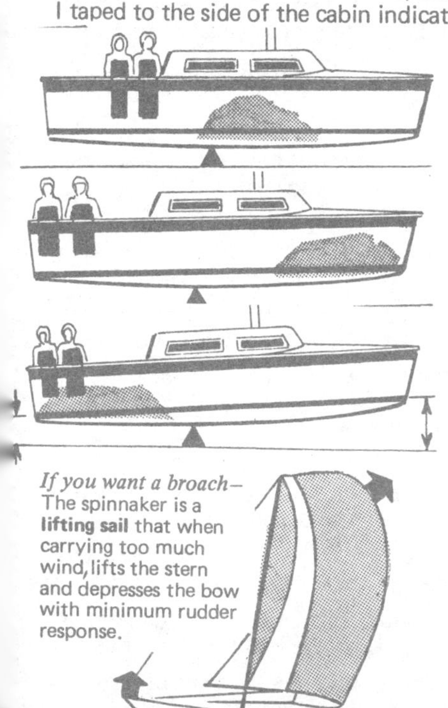

If you want a broach— The spinnaker is a **lifting sail** that when carrying too much wind, lifts the stern and depresses the bow with minimum rudder response.

● **A rapid teeter totter is desired**— showing the hull is balanced...as it recovers rapidly to meet a new wave angle with minimum hesitation and little water disturbance.

● **A slow teeter totter**— indicates a confused hull that is out of balance. Hull speed is reduced upwind and downwind as it hesitates to adapt to the next wave.

● **Stern down, bow high.** The hull is out of balance and off its lines. It reduces speed AND pointing ability.

● **Pull at masthead depresses the bow** in a storm with a genoa jib or working jiblland flying a chute in a strong wind. The depressed bow has broach potentials.

Move crew weight aft, drop chute, or ??? until the level indicates your sailboat has returned to its fore and aft hull lines.

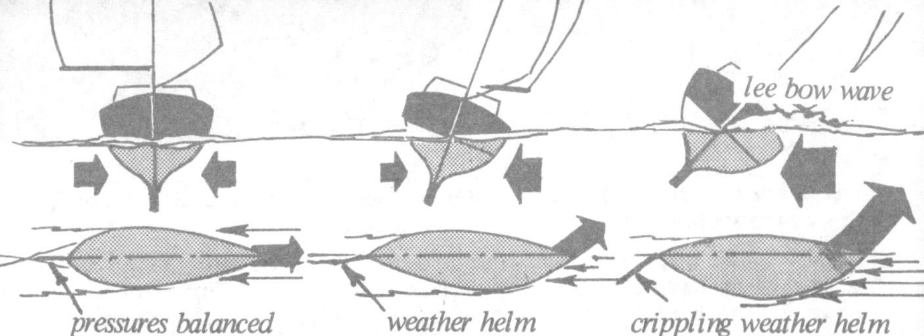

▲Sail wind pressure ***action..*** transferred to a monohull produces forward drive and heel forces ***reaction.*** Good hull designs face a delicate balance producing upwind drive and pointing ability, while compensating for heeling forces.

The **lee bow wave** is a major balance factor. As monohull heeling action is increased, it causes the immersed part of the hull to undergo a rapid shape change. As the ***action*** tries to push the bow higher into the wind, it produces a weather helm ***reaction*** so the sailboat doesn't go into irons, head to wind.

●This compensation with the rudder being carried at an angle to the hull produces **weather helm drag,** similar to driving an auto with the hand brake on.This excess weather helm heeling action develops unnecessary strains on the rudder, rudder shaft, and rudder fittings.The excess heel angle must be reduced by reducing OR changing the sail pattern to balance the hull and rudde

A square foot of **rudder drag** weather helm is comparable to 800 sq. ft. of hull and sail air drag as water and air are similar mediums. The basic difference is that water has the density 800 times that of air.

● **Minimum upwind heel angle** is common practice for most dinghy classes and ULDB's, page 79, also our ***Homestudy Guide*** on pages 35 and 113.

● **Considerable upwind heel angle** with minimum heel angle to 30 degrees we were told was designed into older, longer, heavy-displacement meter hulls. Was the extreme heel angle a sneaky way to keep the wives at home?

Balance compensations for the average racer/ cruiser shown at right in an increasing wind involve the interaction of a variety of complex factors.

❶ Use largest genoa, crew weight is on lee side of hull for a light tiller touch. As the wind increases, crew weight will move to high side of the boat to balance it to again produce a light tiller touch.

❷ After the heel angle reaches 16 to 18 degrees sailing upwind in an upper force 4 or lower 5, change to a working jib. This will counteract the lee-bow pressure weather helm to again produce a light tiller touch.

At upper force 5 the mainsail is reefed to counteract increasing weather helm heeling action, to again produce a lighter tiller touch with minimum drag.

❹ At upper force 6 you may have to drop the mainsail and used only the working jib to ease the weather helm and keep your sailboat under control.

If the wind still increases change to a **storm jib.** ..and only as a last resort use a ***fisherman reef,*** ,as a partial luffing jib may rip the sail cloth.

Homestudy Guide, pages 74-77

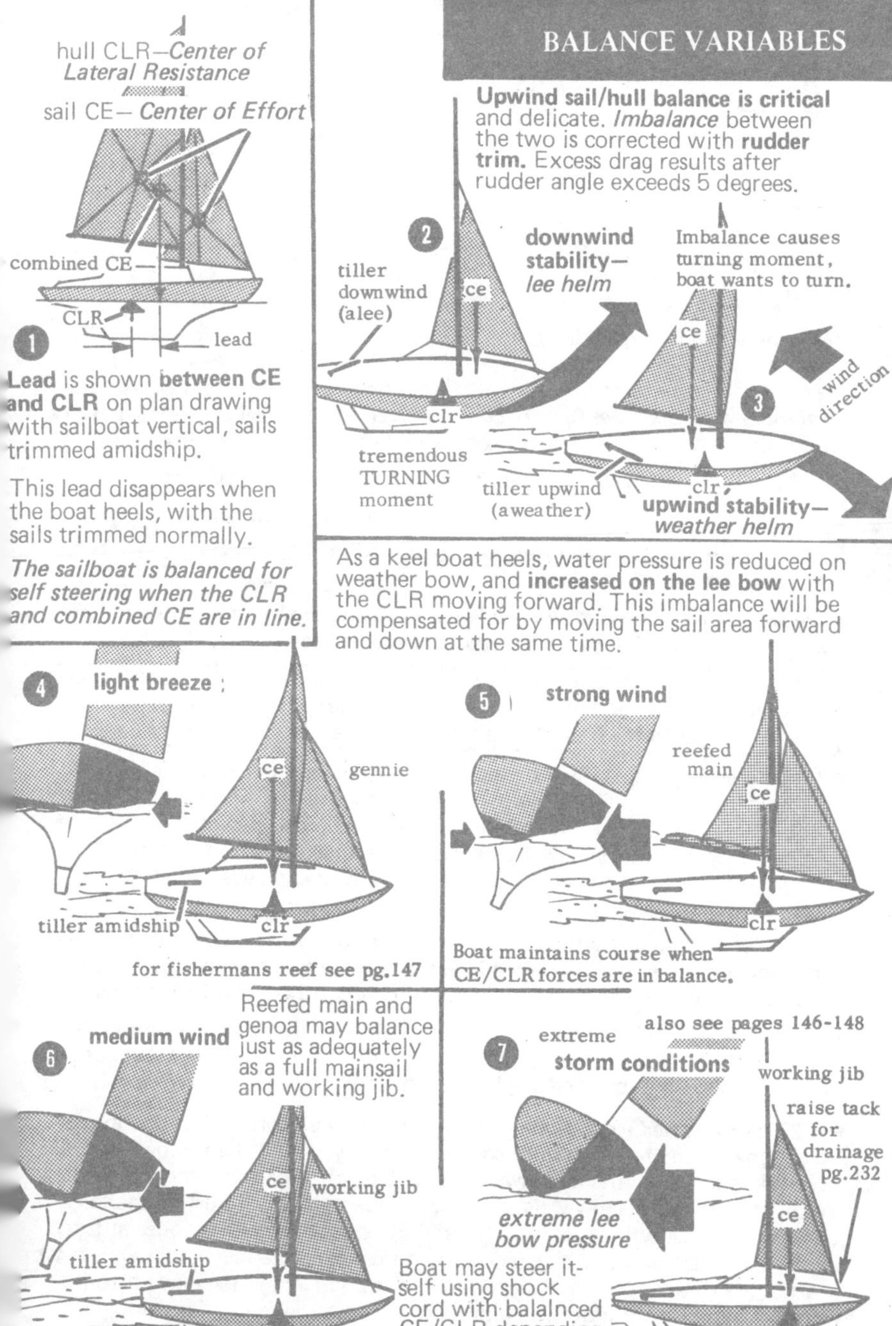
hull CLR—*Center of Lateral Resistance*
sail CE— *Center of Effort*
combined CE
CLR
lead
1
Lead is shown **between CE and CLR** on plan drawing with sailboat vertical, sails trimmed amidship.
This lead disappears when the boat heels, with the sails trimmed normally.
The sailboat is balanced for self steering when the CLR and combined CE are in line.
Upwind sail/hull balance is critical and delicate. *Imbalance* between the two is corrected with **rudder trim.** Excess drag results after rudder angle exceeds 5 degrees.
2
tiller downwind (alee)
ce
downwind stability— *lee helm*
clr
tremendous TURNING moment
Imbalance causes turning moment, boat wants to turn.
ce
wind direction
3
tiller upwind (aweather)
clr
upwind stability— *weather helm*
As a keel boat heels, water pressure is reduced on weather bow, and **increased on the lee bow** with the CLR moving forward. This imbalance will be compensated for by moving the sail area forward and down at the same time.
4
light breeze
ce
gennie
tiller amidship
clr
for fishermans reef see pg.147
5
strong wind
reefed main
ce
clr
Boat maintains course when CE/CLR forces are in balance.
6
medium wind
Reefed main and genoa may balance just as adequately as a full mainsail and working jib.
ce
working jib
tiller amidship
clr
7
extreme
storm conditions
also see pages 146-148
working jib
raise tack for drainage pg.232
extreme lee bow pressure
ce
Boat may steer it-self using shock cord with balalnced CE/CLR depending on wave action.
clr

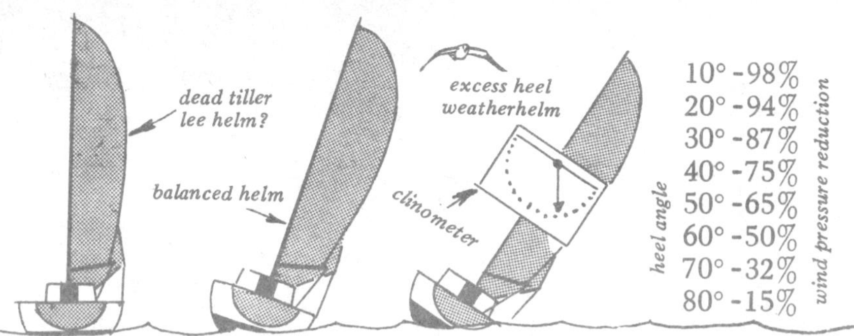

- **Minimum rudder drag.** Many monohull racer/cruisers are designed for self-steering hull balance thru a heel range of 5 to 15 degrees. When the rudder is beyond 5 degrees of the sailboat centerline to steer a straight course, the ***only way a sailboat can fight back*** to show it is out of balance is with excess weather helm usually caused by too much heel, which can be corrected.

If that compensation doesn't work, is the sailboat out of balance?

- ***The well- balanced self-steering sailboat begins with the integrity of the designer, followed by the competency of the builder.***

> Then it becomes the responsibility of the owner to have a thorough understanding of the sail and hull balance factors. The goal is to sail a boat efficiently and to the best of its ability with one, two, or three masts.

- It is interesting to test the self-steering ability of wooden sailboats 30 or more years old averaging 40' long. Some balance easily, while others have problems. A search starts for changes added without the knowledge of the designer..Most problems are basic such as large water or fuel tanks added to the ends of the boat...or a larger, heavier engine is added without forward weight compensation to level the waterline to balance the hull.
- A 40' ketch wouldn't quite balance out, with identical ones seeming to have the same problem, until a sistership easily outpointed us. The secret, he had 300' of heavy chain in the chain locker forward, others had 120' of chain.
- When fiberglass cabin sailboats had minimum sensitivity, it often improved rapidly if the mast tip was raked 2" to 3" aft. A rare case was a stubborn boat that wouldn't balance until the mast tip was raked 7" forward.
- **A 25' sailboat had a dead tiller.** The mast step had depressed the cabin top more than an inch due to tight shrouds and stays which had to be eased considerably...then the mast was raked a little aft. The short cockpit made it difficult to move crew weight, so we compensated by adjusting the moveable weight below for balance. The trailing edge of the wide rudder at force 3 vibrated considerably, which eased when it was rounded.We had a similar vibration which disappeared after the edges were sanded. When new bottom paint is added, our rudder will vibrate for approx. a month,and stop.

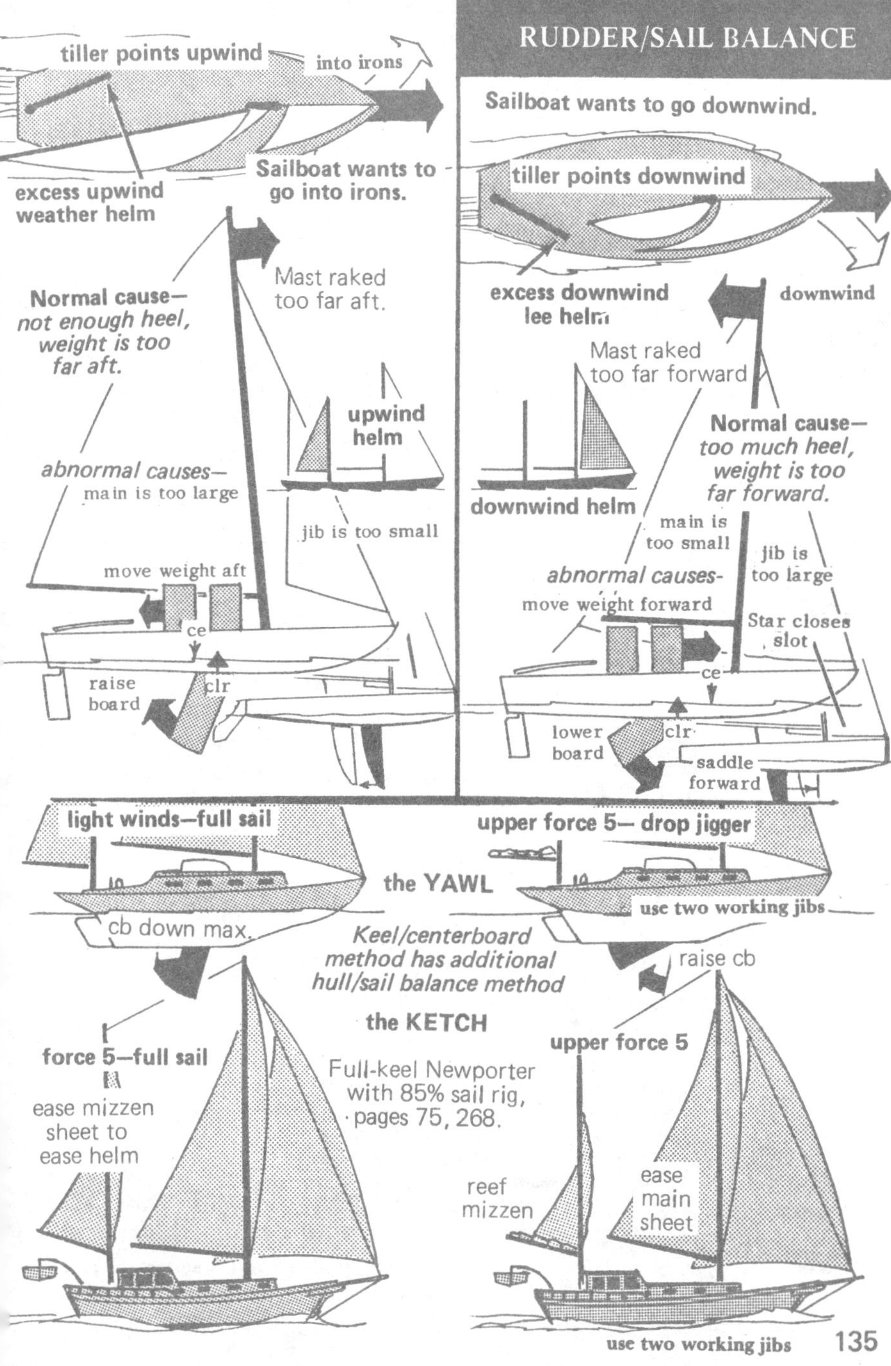
tiller points upwind
into irons
excess upwind weather helm
Sailboat wants to go into irons.
Sailboat wants to go downwind.
tiller points downwind
excess downwind lee helm
downwind
Normal cause—not enough heel, weight is too far aft.
Mast raked too far aft.
upwind helm
abnormal causes—main is too large
jib is too small
move weight aft
ce
clr
raise board
Mast raked too far forward
downwind helm
Normal cause—too much heel, weight is too far forward.
main is too small
jib is too large
abnormal causes-
move weight forward
Star closes slot
ce
clr
lower board
saddle forward
light winds—full sail
upper force 5— drop jigger
the YAWL
use two working jibs
cb down max.
Keel/centerboard method has additional hull/sail balance method
raise cb
the KETCH
upper force 5
force 5—full sail
ease mizzen sheet to ease helm
Full-keel Newporter with 85% sail rig, pages 75, 268.
reef mizzen
ease main sheet
use two working jibs

Your wind pressure scale evolved from square rigger use on the ocean.

Our weather bureau reports wind speed in miles per hour which is of little use as wind speed is invisible. Sailors need some kind of a visual measurement.

Wind speed produces visual ocean wave patterns that can be calibrated into wind pressure driving your sailboat. These wave patterns can be translated into existing wind pressure for use on all kinds of sailboats.

The wind force scale is easy to memorize— forces 1-2, ripples...forces 3-4, small waves...force 5, a few whitecaps...force 6, many whitecaps...force 7, ***small craft warning,*** tremendous wind pressure with whitecaps AND swells.

- Your wind force or pressure scale was developed by Admiral Beaufort in 1806 for the British navy. It recorded square rigger rudder action in light winds trying to develop steerageway, to force 5, reaching hull speed. Above that it indicated sail reductions patterns to force 12, after which vessels were under bare poles out of control, no longer able to carry sails.

We have slightly altered the traditional wind force scale to make it easier to remember and apply for recreational sailors.

110

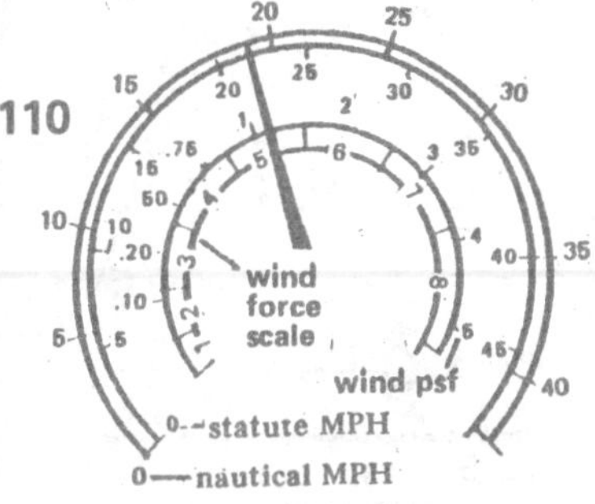

We show wind speed in statute miles and nautical miles per hour using a masthead wind gage cockpit dial...adding a dial for comparison with wind force or pressure.

We wish new wind speed dials showing speed in miles per hour could add a wind force scale so owners could know how much sail area to add or reef as the wind changes.

Meanwhile you can pick up wave patterns to estimate wind pressure, to know whether to reef for best efficiency, or increase sail area.

- **Variables are involved.** When a force 7 suddenly starts to blow over a flat ocean, time is required to catch up with the force 7 wave pattern. When the force 7 suddenly quits blowing, time is required for the wave patterns to fall out of sequence...then the waves flatten out. If you know this scale you will have your sails reefed the correct amount before the storm hits, while other sailboats are floundering around trying to reef their sails **after the storm hit...**for which they weren't prepared.

- **Currents.** When wind blows against the current, waves will be higher with the crests closer together. When wind blows with the current, waves will be shorter and crests farther apart...though having the same wind pressure.

▲ **Inland lakes.** The wind force or pressure scale was developed for ocean use over unobstructed stretches of water. While inland lakes don't have the area to develop ocean wave patterns, add 1, 2, or 3 forces to the wave action that is visible to compute the existing wind pressure on your sails and hull.

▲ **Wind funnels** can double,and even triple the overall wind pressure, pages 158 and 159, on inland lakes and hills next to the ocean...with predictable results using the water color and wave action. *Powerboating Illustrated*

WIND PRESSURE

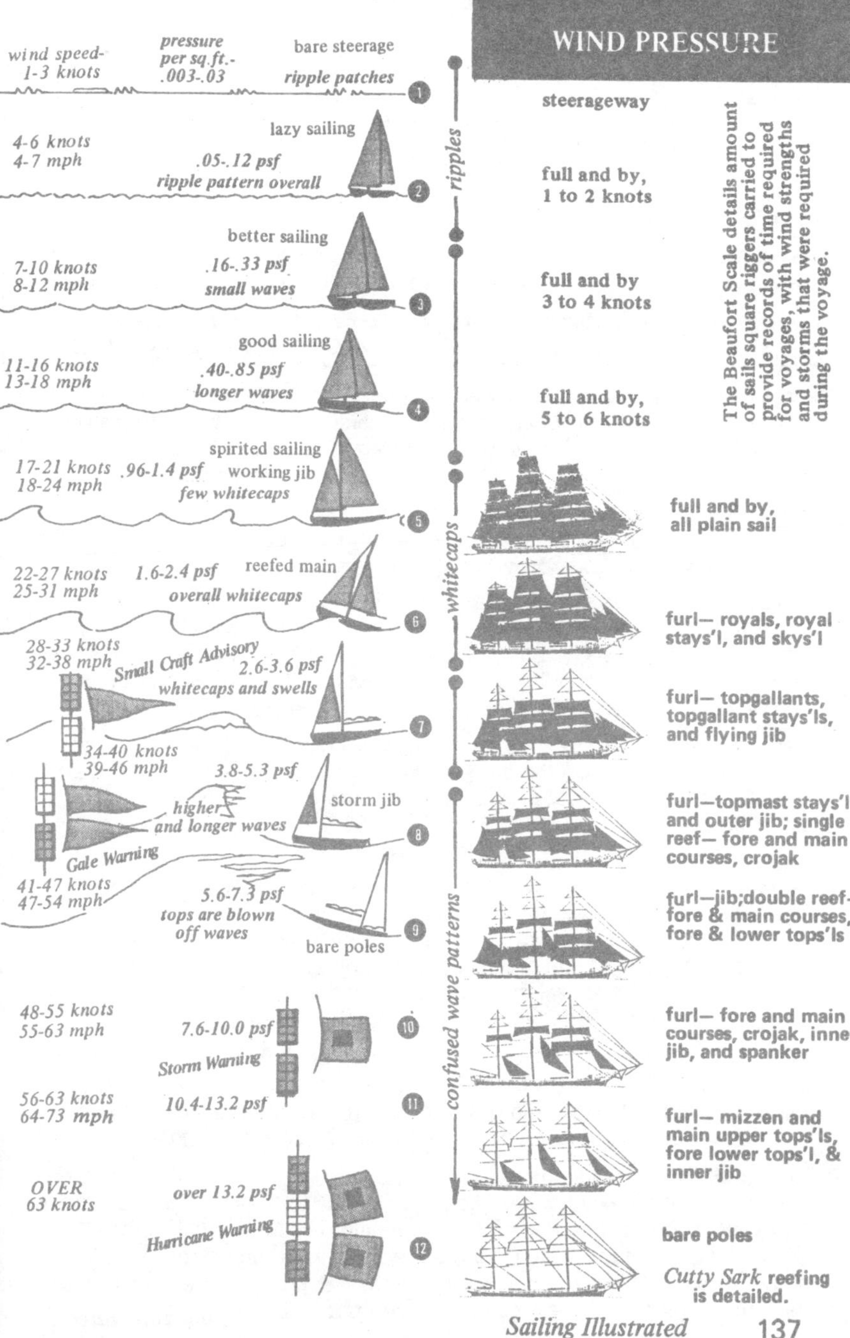

Our storm warning method based on the wind force or pressure scale was introduced in 1958. It was for wind forces 7 and above to provide an estimate of the strength of a storm moving in.

Most sailboats reach normal maximum hull speed at force 5. Since the wind force doubles from force 5 to 7, the sail area should be reduced by half to maintain the same force 5 maximum efficient wind pressure in the sails... to prevent dismasting, torn sails, etc.

Wind pressure doubles again from force 7 to force 9, requiring another half sail reduction...with the dynamic surface wave action increases considerably.

wind pressure—lbs.	**force 5**	**force 7**	**force 9**	**force 11**	**force 12**
per square foot—	*.96-1.4*	*2.6-3.6*	*5.6-7.3*	*10.4-13.2*	*over 13.2*

▲ **Many variables exist in heavy weather operation.** Is the water deep or shallow, is a current included. Is it a thunderstorm or long duration storm over a large area, to which we add 13 different responses for sailboats on our cover, width between crests, trough depth, and angle of wave fronts.

● **Force 7** is the practical limit for most sailboats on the ocean to 40' long for upwind sailing due to wave action. Most may operate easier on a reach to a beam reach, or sail downwind under working jib.

● **Bare poles.** If the pressure increases, all sails are dropped, and a sailboat can go downwind responding to the rudder with a broad reach to broad reach limit. A small drag such as the ***Mexican Hat*** page 152, or a variety of drags from chains to tires, can improve steering control by keeping the stern to the wind, and reduce bare-pole speed, see ***Homestudy Guide,*** page 77.

● **Large parachute.** Several months testing were required to tame it before the *para-anchor* was put on the market. While we designed it for powerboats with minimum heavy weather protection, sailors began using it to avoid being blown ashore, pages 155-157, 160, 161, while others used it as a deep water anchor at night with icebergs nearby, for fishing, etc.

● **Wind force 9.** It was blowing force 7 as we left San Francisco on a new 32' heavy-displacement headsail sloop rig with a definite $1.34\sqrt{WL}$ speed limit. It was force 9 the next afternoon soon dropping the small jib to bare poles. We had 5 unexpected equipment failures, a broach, and we were pooped three times.We had several miles visibility with wave action so high we saw a large lumber sbip half a mile away for less than 10 seconds. ***MOMMY—***

● **Wind force 10 or 11.** Wind rapidly increased from a force 5 on a 40' Newporter ketch with a knockdown before all sail was dropped. The boat bucked like a bronco until down to a beam reach when wind pressure on the high doghouse brought it under control at hull speed. Was it a ***doghouse reach?***

▲ **The windless storm** is a rare unpredictable monster without wind while the high waves are falling out of sequence, once due to the tail end of a Mexican hurricane, another time the tail end of a major Northern Pacific storm. Lash all objects and reduce chafe potentials, wear jackets, preservers, etc., for body protection.Have as many crew members as possible stretched out on the main cabin floor to reduce knockdown potentials.

SMALL CRAFT ADVISORY–
can indicate a thunderstorm squall*.

force 7– winds to 33 knots or 38 mph, pressure per sq. foot to 3.6 lbs.*(For low-powered,or boats to tugs with little freeboard.)*

GALE WARNING–

to force 9– winds to 47 knots or 54 mph, pressure per sq. foot to 7.3 lbs.

STORM WARNING–

to force 11– winds to 63 knots or 73 mph, pressure per sq. foot to 13.2 lbs

HURRICANE WARNINGS–

force 12 and above– winds over 63 knots or 74 mph,pressure over 13 lbs.

A tropical cyclone covering a large area of long duration is anticipated (*not a thunderstorm with just as strong winds seldom lasting more than 20 minutes.)

Note–shaded areas are red. *day signals* *night signals*

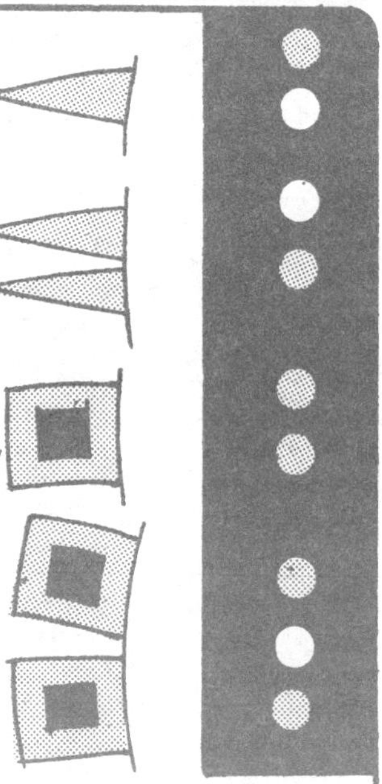

- **Boating safety vs education.** The definition of a sport is that some risk is involved. Sailing is a very healthy sport with minimum risks for sailors from 9 to 80 with training and awareness. It is a continuous lifetime education for active sailors from dinghies to cruising sailboats for which we enjoy the best of nature being paid back many fold with the joys of sailing.
- **Boating safety** is a strange religion we are supposed to accept and ask no questions. It perpetuates interesting kinds of mischief such as–
- **Operator licensing.** The 1972 USCG licensing push in the name of boating safety had much publicity.The real reason, DOT wanted more power to raise more taxes. After paying a fee and answering enough questions with probably true or false answers, we were to become safe boating operators.
- **USCG mandated boating course** surfaced quietly in 1977. It seemed to be a spur of the moment decision with many antiquated boating regulations which had been my hobby collecting thru the years.DOT tried another approach for power to raise taxes with little in return for boat operators.

Both pushes were quietly dropped when proving the real need was quality educational courses in sail and power to improve operator competency instead of penalizing us in the name of safety.As the proposed taxation source disappeared...so did the bureaucratic interest in "our" boating safety.

The unique heavy-displacement hull speed limiting factor depends on a sailboats waterline length.

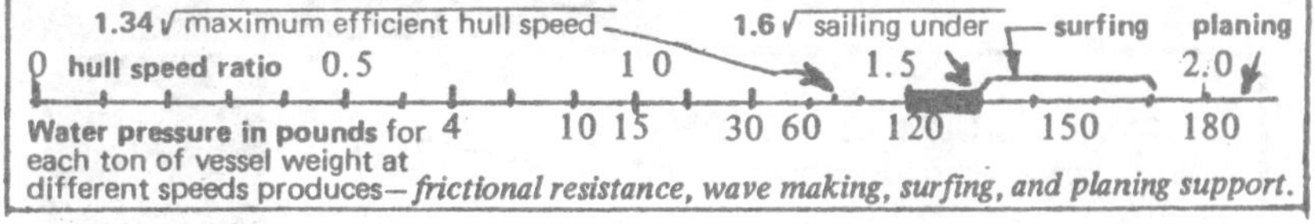

1.34 √ maximum efficient hull speed			1.6 √ sailing under	surfing	planing
0 hull speed ratio	0.5	1.0	1.5		2.0
Water pressure in pounds for 4	10 15	30 60	120	150	180

Water pressure in pounds for each ton of vessel weight at different speeds produces—*frictional resistance, wave making, surfing, and planing support.*

wind pressure—lbs. per square foot--	force 5	force 6	force 7	force 8	force 9
	.96-1.4	*1.6-2.4*	*2.6-3.6*	*3.8-5.3*	*5.6-7.3*

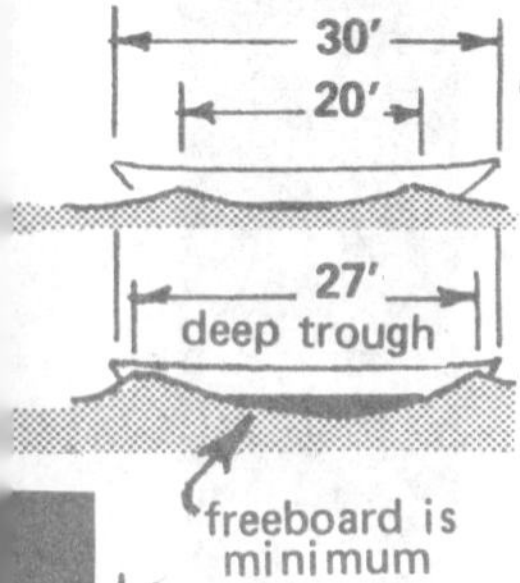

30′
20′
27′
deep trough
freeboard is minimum

Maximum efficient hull speed= 1.34√WL

wave speed in knots	wave length in feet
6	20.0
7	27.2
8	35.6
9	45.0
10	55.6
11	67.3
12	80.1
14	109.0
16	142.4
20	222.5
25	347.7
30	500.6

Nature makes strict limitations for ocean operation.

- **Displacement hull speed** is a primary one determined by the ***wave length/hull speed ratio*** of a vessel. The hull speed of a 30′ sailboat with a 20′ waterline length is theoretically 6 knots...coinciding with a trochoidal wave with peaks 20′ across also going at 6 knots.
- **Heavy-displacement hulls.** When the wave-length speed increases to 7 knots, the crest to crest wave distance increases to 27′. If the 30′ sailboat isn't dismasted or has tremendous overhangs, it settles into the deep trough... and may be sailed under. If the hull is sealed, it comes to a halt due to water density, and surfaces. The crew may have enough reefing time to reduce sail area before it passes the 6 knot wave length/hull speed ratio.
- **Square riggers** had strict wave length/hull speed limitations Some may have disappeared in violent, fast-moving storms sailing under as sails couldn't be removed fast enough, and/or hulls fractured with the extreme water pressure.
- **20 knot** heavy displacement hull speed? If you want to buy or build such a monohull, look for a 222′ waterline due to the strict wave length/ hull speed ratio at left.
- Monohull sailboats with maximum cargo-carrying capacity have been plagued for centuries with the wave length/hull speed ratio. **Multihulls** don't have this speed limitation... ***though they have even stricter cargo-carrying capacity limitations.***
- **Water frictional resistance** is the primary speed limitation factor of large oceangoing tankers, freighters, liners, and other large ocean vessels; While the majority of world shipping moves at speeds below an 0.8 $\sqrt{WL}$ (waterline length), large supertankers to conserve fuel operated at 0.6 $\sqrt{WL}$ at 14 to 15 knots, their most efficient displacement speed. When fully loaded, proportions of the hull underwater causing frictional resistance is vaguely similar to that of an iceberg.

Small coastal vessels, large liners, and some warship classes may operate at 1.0 $\sqrt{WL}$ speed which almost quadruples the water resistance per ton of vessel weight, while the practical operational speed of heavy displacement monohull sailboats is 1.34 $\sqrt{WL}$ which is the sailboat above with a 6 knot hull speed having a 20′ waterline length.

stern light

aft range light

green starboard light

VLCC—Very Large Crude Carrier over 200,000 tons
ULCC—Ultra Large Crude Carrier over 400,000 tons

forward range light

Nature provides strict displacement hull speed limitations for large power-driven vessels.Supertankers, crude carriers of 200,000 to 400,000 tons with one propeller, operate at economical speeds of 12 to 15 knots.

- **Tonnage vs speed.** Most large vessels operate below 1.0 $\sqrt{WL}$ (unity), while smaller vessels are often designed to operate from unity and above.

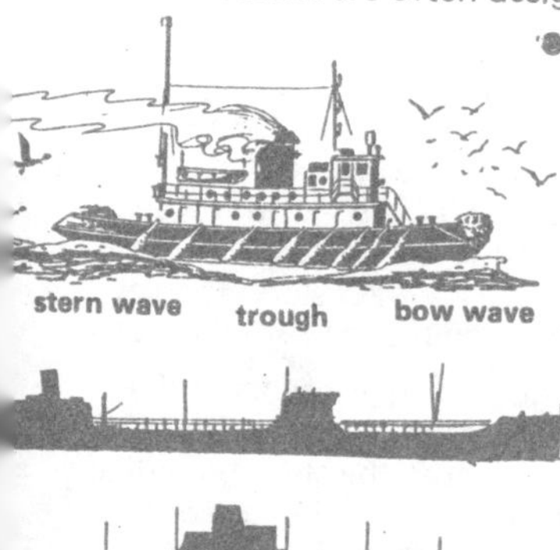

- **Maximum efficient displacement hull speed** is shown with tugboat bow and sterm waves as it loafs along at hull speed going to, or returning from a tow.

The peaks of these waves coincide with those of trochoidal waves the same distance.which is 1.34 $\sqrt{WL}$ in naval architecture terms.

Speed of a 70′ tug would be 11 knots with approx 9″ sinkage, more aft than forward. If pushed to 1.5 $\sqrt{WL}$ or 12½ knots the freeboard wuuld be reduced by two feet plus heavy wave-making resistance. If a great increase in power is added, then energy would go to wave making in this heavy displacement hull,with a negligible speed increase.

- **Frictional resistance.** Tankers and freighters prefer to operate at the slower economical speed around 0.6 $\sqrt{WL}$ as wave-making resistance is minimal at 3 to 4 lbs. pressure per ton. 60% to 80% of the energy is used to overcome the frictional resistance of the hull. The rest of the energy is use up in prop wash and wake.

Iowa Class **USS Missouri**— 880′ long
108′ beam 36′ draft 57,950 tons

33 knot top speed

- **Wave making & frictional resistance.** Liners and some warships operate between 0.7 $\sqrt{WL}$ to unity or 1.0 $\sqrt{WL}$. Wave making accounts for 50% to 70% of the total resistance, increasing to 10 to 15 lbs. per ton.Vessels in this range are usually too expensive to operate to carry freight.

- **Unity to 1.25 $\sqrt{WL}$.** This includes specialized, overpowered vessels such as the fastest warships not operated for profit, resistance is 30 lbs per ton.

▲**Sailboat D/L ratio** The *displacement to waterline ratio* is comparable to the **weight in proportion to length** . The D/L ratio accurately predicts sailboat speed potentials after maximum hull speed is exceeded.

▲**Heavy displacement hulls.** Square riggers caught in a heavy blow suddenly could be sailed under, or if lucky, be dismasted. Heavy displacement sloops under full sail at maximum hull speed in a sudden wind increase may find the mast and sails going faster downwind than the hulll...called dismasting.

▲**Medium heavy, medium light, down to the 100 /DL ULDB** ***Windward Passage*** ratios prove an excellent indication to sailboats that may pass the speed barrier in some situations...while those with smaller D/L ratios may do it quite often.

▲**The monohull reach pressure pocket—** begins with the idea water can't be compressed. Fiberglass sailboats of the 1960's started a new generation of lighter, wider beam, round-bilge hulls with finer lines, an evolution still underway. When they dropped to a reach with the hull speed of $1.6\sqrt{WL}$, water pressure lift helped the hull exceed the wave length/hull speed ratio, while narrower, slack-bilge heavy displacement hulls of the 1950's without lift at $1.6\sqrt{WL}$,dropped into their wave troughs and sailed under, page 140.

▲**Displacement/Hull ratio—**pg.112, ***Homestudy Guide.*** Our D/L 301 ratio *Pink Cloud,* was caught on a flat ocean on a beam reach with a sudden force 6 wind, the speedometer holding the 10 knot peg for an hour until reaching port. We found the lighter 189 D/L ratio Cal 25, able to reach surfing speeds easier and with less effort in our sailing lessons. In the Santa Barbara Channel under jib alone a Cal 25 held 10 to 15 knots for over an hour. The same students were on a heavy displacement 28' sloop the day before in a similar force 6 with a wet, miserable ride though reefed down.

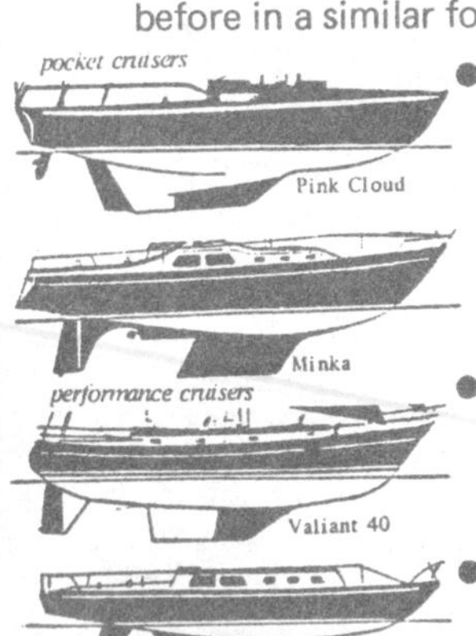

- **The Cal 40—** 250 D/L ratio. Transpac sailors in the race to Hawaii learned a new trick called ***surfing.*** They would catch a wave coming under the stern providing lift to increase hull speed going down the face of a long wave at $1.6\sqrt{WL}$ speeds and above, page 140. They were soon able to hold these surfing speeds with practice for much longer time periods.
- **The ULDB** developed due to our prevailing westerly wind pattern with many days of steady, predictable force 5 to 6 winds from San Francisco, south to Santa Cruz, and Monterey, California.
- **The 505 dinghy** World Championship in 1970 was held in Santa Cruz where the light 16'6" dinghy performed admirably. A few fascinated spectators began building **large, ultra-light** dinghies with long, lean hulls...using 20 knot speedometers.
- **ULDB'S—**110 D/L ratio or less, sail at a shallow heel angle, while carrying tall rigs to gain rapid acceleration as a puff moves in. A comparable length IOR racer may be a better closehauled performer. When both drop to a reach or beam reach with a $1.6\sqrt{WL}$ hull speed pressures, the lighter, long, lean ULDB's become faster performers.
- **Windward Passage—** 100 D/L ratio built in 1968, was the first ULDB, winning more races in the next 15 years worldwide than any large racer in history. When I studied the bow and stern lines, they looked very familiar. They seem almost identical to the Int'l 14, ***Homestudy Guide page 113.*** As for the reasons the ULDB's are called big dinghies...we rest our case.

- **Heavy displacement**—*Sovereign of the Seas,* page 210, was the first square rigger to sail 400 miles in 24 hours. A crew of 105 men and boys handled the 12,000 yards of sail.

- **Force 5**— bow and stern wave displacement hull speed is shown for our 301 D/L heavy ***Pink Cloud.*** Leeway forces are eased when dropping to a reach. A pressure pocket builds up under the hull providing hydraulic lift for our hull with a clean bottom to exceed the wave trap. The reach lift pocket is more efficiently used on long, light ULDB's for force 5 to 7 winds with 20 knot speedometers.

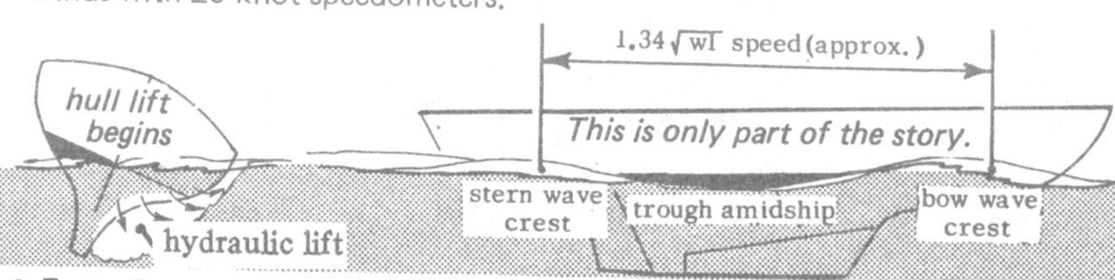

- **Force 6**— our boat held 10 knots for an hour on a reach, while the 189 D/L Cal 25 surfed easily at 10 to 15 knots for an hour. The 31′ 239 D/L ***Minka*** ranged from 8.3 to 8.9 knots downwind with a high haystack wave way aft of the stern. Page 77 of our ***Homestudy Guide*** will provide more details.

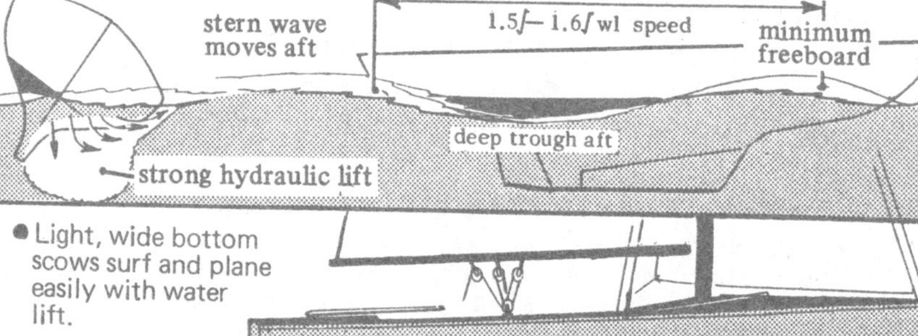

- Light, wide bottom scows surf and plane easily with water lift.

Incompressible. *Action*— as dinghy hull speed increases... ***reaction***— water density 835 times that of air, hardens for hydraulic planing lift.

Movable ballast hastens upset on the water and at the boat hoist.

Fresh water weighs approximately 8.3 pounds per gallon.
Gasoline weighs approximately 6.6 pounds per gallon.
Diesel fuel weighs approximately 7.3 pounds per gallon.

- **Keel sailboat in irons.** It starts to drift backwards out of control producing excess strains on exposed rudder, plus a possible knockdown in heavy weather. ***Back the jib opposite to tack desired,pg.109.*** This pivots bow to a reach. Release jib sheet. Sheet in on correct side so sailboat moves forward.

- **The keel boat has ultimate stability.**The more it heels the stiffer it becomes as the C of G increases heel resistance. The keel boat with a 90 degree knockdown will normally right itself. If one has a 180 degree upset the C of G helps continue the roll till upright again...IF the hull is sealed off.

- **Centerboard/daggerboard dinghies.** The board boats provide leverage stability for those with soft chines, while V-bottom hulls with hard chines provide initial stability increasing leverage stability or resistance to heel.

- **The board boat goes into irons.** The jib should be backed continually,pg.109, when changing tack so the dinghy is on the new tack and underway before running out of inertia.If a scared, cautious, or confused owner in a strong wind doesn't back the jib, the boat goes into irons losing rudder control.

The big splash– ***the dinghy drifts backward, the bow turns and the sails fill. Instead of forward drive...the boat trips on its board.*** **The capsize is rapid.**

- **Upset on a tack.** After 45 to 50 degree heel angle,the C of G passes the C of B with the board boat ***becoming more stable in an upset position.*** This C of G action may be stopped and reversed if a person momentarily stands on the board, then comes back aboard. **Metal daggerboard** should be secured to the dinghy so it can't fall out and sink in a capsize.

90 degree upset. Check crew, lash floating objects to boat, release halyards, and swim to top of mast. Secure float as shown to mainsail halyard shackle to prevent a 180 degree roll. Drop sails, right boat, and begin bailing. Remove float, shackle halyard to mainsail, raise sails and resume sailing.

- **Plug cb or db well before bailing.** A Lido 14 upset on a cold, blustery March morning. Cold, weary crew members were still trying to bail the righted boat 20 minutes later. ***Water was still flowing in the cb well which was underwater.***

- **180 degree–turning turtle.** Check crew, then release sheets all the way from cam cleats to avoid dismasting. Rig a line across bottom, use your body as a lever to right the dinghy,drop sails, start bailing. **Self-rescuing classes**– rethread sheets, climb aboard, start sailing with stern scuppers open.

- **Salt water upset**–***remove water-seeking hygroscopic salts.*** Wash sails with fresh water, then allow them ample drying time. Hose down all metal parts and mast with fresh water. After drying, wax mast to minimize corrosion.

Enjoy a spirited sail ***as capsize potentials multiply when sailing cautiously!*** **Keep your speed up, and back the jib continuously when rapidly changing tack to stay upright having ample speed, maneuverability, and stability.**

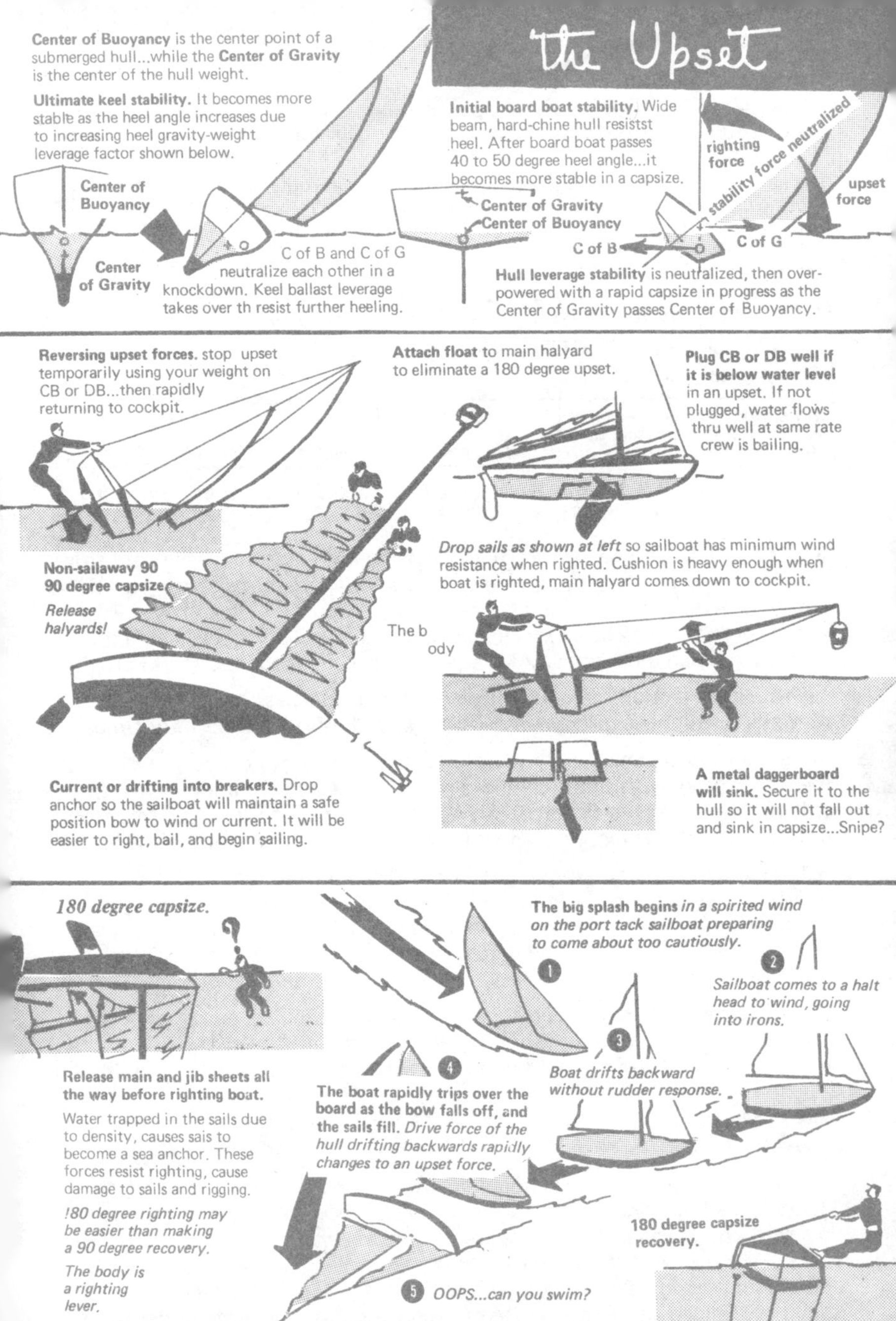

180 degree recovery. After releasing sheets all the way, use your body as a righting lever. As the capsized boat slowly then rapidly begins righting momentum...can you fall clear of righting hull?

Active ocean sailors should study, and periodically review complex U.S. and worldwide weather patterns covered in depth on pages 56-68 of our *Homestudy Guide*, Pages 69 to 77, cover much more information of the complex variables of heavy weather operation.

The fascinating, difficult to find worldwide square-rigger routes are covered on page 78 of our *Guide*. We found endless surprises when preparing the illustration such as 55 days taking the shortest route from New York to Rio. Time was reduced to 38 days if square riggers went east to mid Atlantic...then turned south.

The unique heavy-displacement hull speed limiting factor depends on a sailboats waterline length.

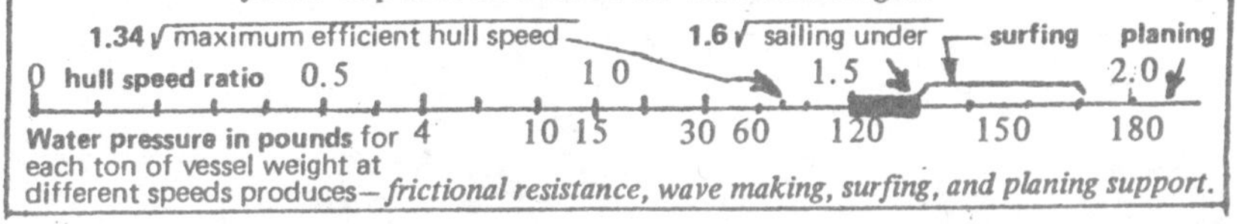

1.34 √ maximum efficient hull speed — **1.6 √ sailing under** — **surfing** — **planing**

hull speed ratio	0	0.5	1.0	1.5	2.0

Water pressure in pounds for each ton of vessel weight at different speeds produces—*frictional resistance, wave making, surfing, and planing support.* 4 10 15 30 60 120 150 180

wind pressure—lbs. per square foot—	**force 5**	**force 6**	**force 7**	**force 8**	**force 9**
	.96-1.4	*1.6-2.4*	*2.6-3.6*	*3.8-5.3*	*5.6-7.3*

Short duration thunderstorms. A fast moving low pressure with a cold front enters your area with a squall line of ***frontal thunderstorms*** coming from the SW,W, or NW. Though most last under half an hour, they may have violent winds up to force 12 strength changing direction rapidly, page 206.Static increasing on an inexpensive AM radio is an excellent thunderstorm predictor.

Lightning protection methods for wooden and fiberglass hulls we feel need rethinking which we discuss on pages 64 and 65 of our *Homestudy Guide.*

Long duration storms. We show wind pressure/reefing patterns of a yawl on the facing page, with sloop reefing, similar. We begin with a force 5 as the sailboat moves at an efficient 1.34 √WL hull speed...with the wind increasing to force 7, as the sailboat is reefed down to storm jib and storm trysail.

- **Sailing upwind— weatherhelm warning.** A sudden wind increase as a storm moves in causes the sailboat to heel excessively. The reaction, is to fight the tiller or wheel due to excess rudder angle...which provides an automatic warning to reef your sails.The unpleasant alternative with the stress loads, is for the mast and sails to go faster than the hull...called dismasting.

- **Sailing downwind provides no similar warning.** Page 77 of our ***Homestudy Guide*** details this situation faced on the medium displacement 31'4" ***Minka*** with a 25' waterline for a 6.2 knot hull speed. Wind increased so rapidly the speedometer peaked at 10.7 knots before we could drop all sails to go under bare poles. Before the sails dropped,we had a 55' wave trough with inches of freeboard at the bow, and a huge haystack stern wave behind us.

An elderly 30' wooden cutter going downwind under gaff rig was hit by a white squall blowing the Chesapeake Bay flat momentarily as it climbed on a screeching plane. Drags were used to reduce planing speed to drop sails. Timing was tight as extreme water pressure on the hull was within seconds before compression stresses could have crushed the hull...even a dismasting may have helped this extreme situation. ***Always have a crew member facing aft*** when sailing downwind if storm conditions exist.

Reefing

A fisherman's reef is temporarily used in strong puffy winds. Release or ease the mainsheet to reduce excess heel causing crippling weather helm.

Harden the jib sheet while easing mainsheet.

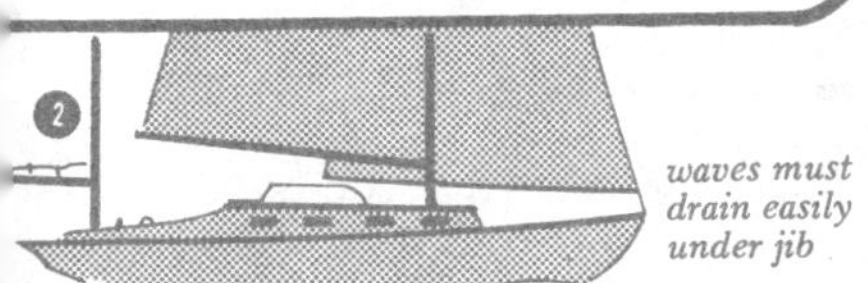

Force 5— the jigger is dropped to reduce heel for maximum efficient hull speed.

If the wind still increases...add first reef to mainsail. Change to double headsails which increase drive potentials while reducing excess heel causing crippling weather helm.

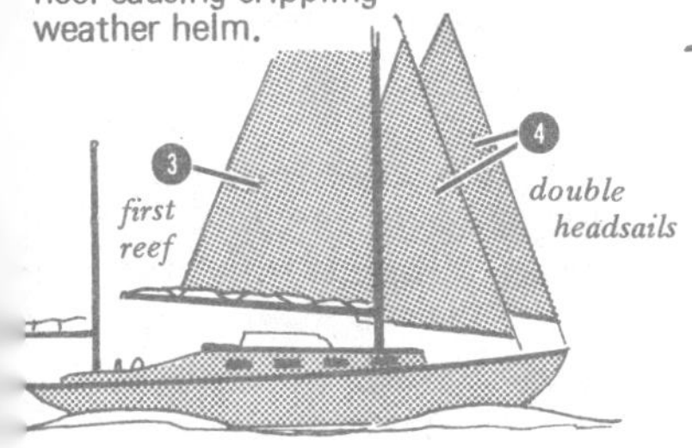

Force 6 to lower force 7— requires second reef tied onto mainsail. A strong working jib is used so sail wind pressure will still hold boat shown below to maintain an efficient 7 knot hull speed.

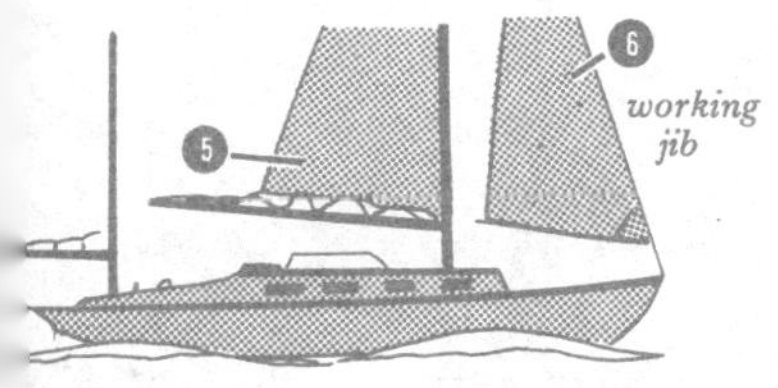

Reefing sequence shown is for a 40' yawl with a 27' waterline.At a force 5 it will be operating at its maximum efficient 7 to 8 knot hull speed.

As wind speed pressure increases— ***sail area has to be proportionally decreased so as not to exceed the force 5 wind pressure producing the 7 knot hull speed.***

- **Upper force 7**— a small storm jib and small trysail are used. Trysail is laced to the mast so it cannot pull out of the sail track.It can only be raised to the first mast projection...then engine light, or lower spreader.

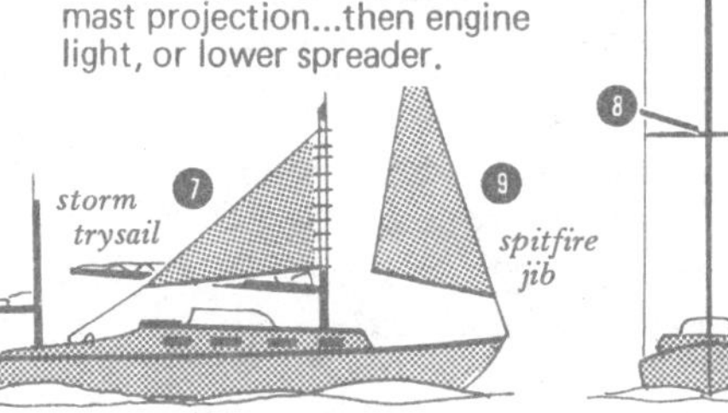

- **A switch track** below permits the mainsail to be dropped, and the storm trysail raised immediately.

The trysail with sail slides can be raised much higher if needed to prevent sailboat being temporarily becalmed in deep wave trough.

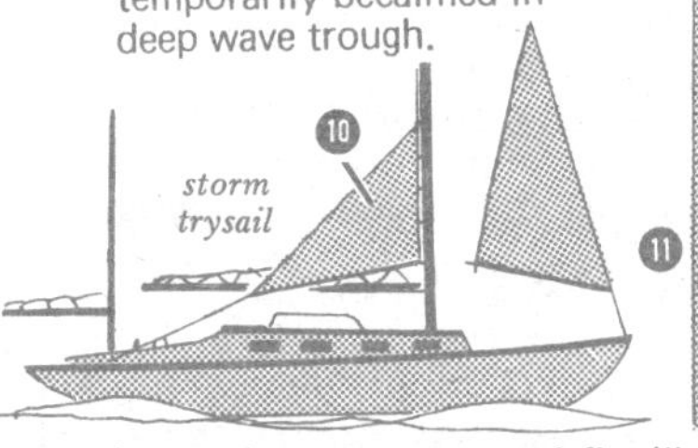

- A working, storm, or spitfire jib may be preferred for a yawl or ketch sailing downwind, and for a sloop up to a reach in force 7.

The **trysail** is added to a ketch or yawl for sailing a beam reach or higher to balance the helm.

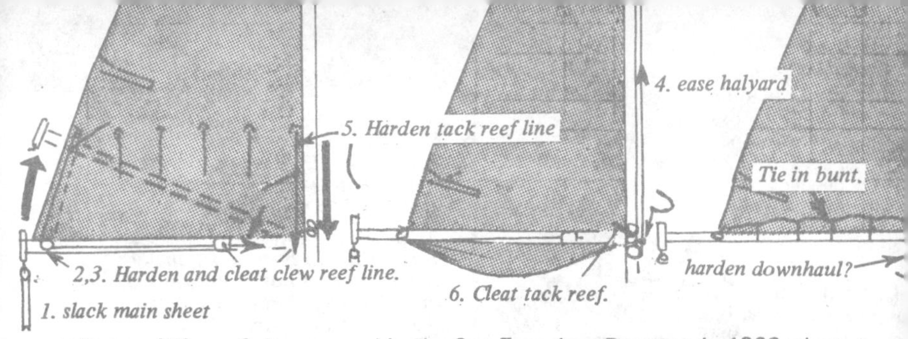

- **Slab or jiffy reef.** It appeared in the San Francisco Bay area in 1968 where it is common to sail in a force 2 in one area, then when turning a headland, to face a stimulating force 6 with the lee rail under. Our Challenger fleet champ gave me a demonstration of it shortly afterwards, reefing his mainsail smoothly and efficiently, having it pulling again in ten seconds.

  All of the reef lines should lead to the cockpit of racing craft for maximum efficiency. ***The basic jiffy reef***– 1. Slack mainsail sheet. 2. Pull clew reef line to raise the end of the boom. 3. Cleat the reef line. 4. Ease halyard to halyard marker on mast. 5. Harden tack reef line pulling the mainsail tack down at an angle to the mast. 6. Cleat reef line to mast. 7, Your sailboat is underway as you haul in the mainsheet. ***Take a last look***– will it be necessary to harden the downhaul?

- **Major mainsail strees points** are the foot and clew. If you tie in the reef points, the mainsail bunt cloth will look neater, while also improving the helmsman's visibility under the boom.

- **Specialized reefing methods.** There are various methods used to reduce sail area depending on the type of craft. The ***ketch*** below is operating in an upper force 6 being balanced to hold a long course under jib and mizzen. When tacking up a narrow harbor the ketch is better balanced for short tacks and coming about with the mainsail only...and the engine on.

  A ***sloop*** may have the advantage to a force 6, while the same length ***cutter*** gains the advantage iñ a force 7. It can be balanced and make headway with the inner jib (forestays'l), while the sloop becomes awkward under storm jib, or bare pole.If the wind still increases, the cutter preferred by English harbor pilots, page 264, can heave to using inner jib only.

- **Scandalizing** is a temporary reefing method used on gaff rigs to rapidly reduce sail area by half. Harden boom topping lift, and release peak halyard located on port side of mast. This temporary measure may be more than 300 years old, when necessary to sail out of a difficult situation or anchorage.

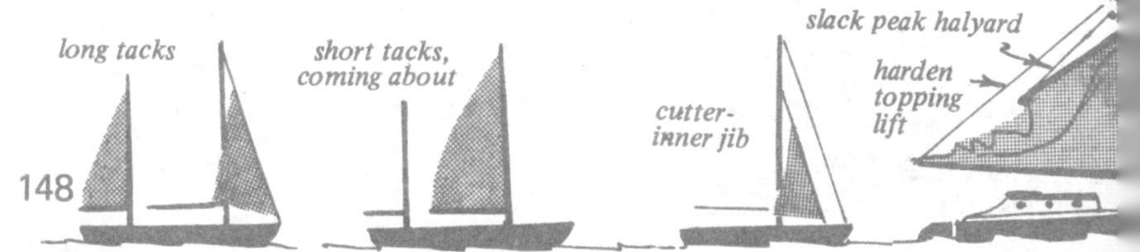

Reefing Methods

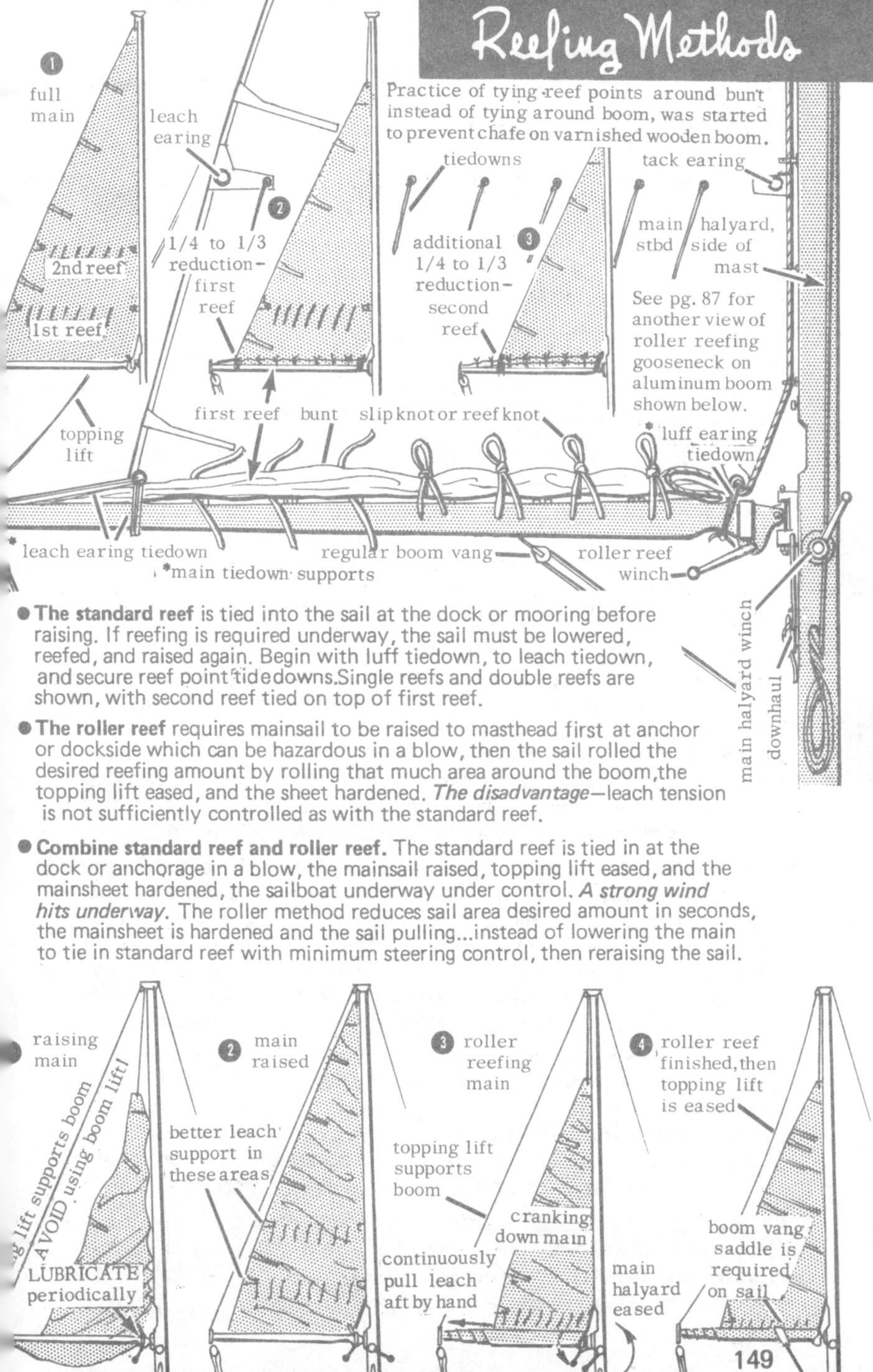

- **The standard reef** is tied into the sail at the dock or mooring before raising. If reefing is required underway, the sail must be lowered, reefed, and raised again. Begin with luff tiedown, to leach tiedown, and secure reef point tiedowns. Single reefs and double reefs are shown, with second reef tied on top of first reef.
- **The roller reef** requires mainsail to be raised to masthead first at anchor or dockside which can be hazardous in a blow, then the sail rolled the desired reefing amount by rolling that much area around the boom, the topping lift eased, and the sheet hardened. ***The disadvantage***—leach tension is not sufficiently controlled as with the standard reef.
- **Combine standard reef and roller reef.** The standard reef is tied in at the dock or anchorage in a blow, the mainsail raised, topping lift eased, and the mainsheet hardened, the sailboat underway under control. ***A strong wind hits underway.*** The roller method reduces sail area desired amount in seconds, the mainsheet is hardened and the sail pulling...instead of lowering the main to tie in standard reef with minimum steering control, then reraising the sail.

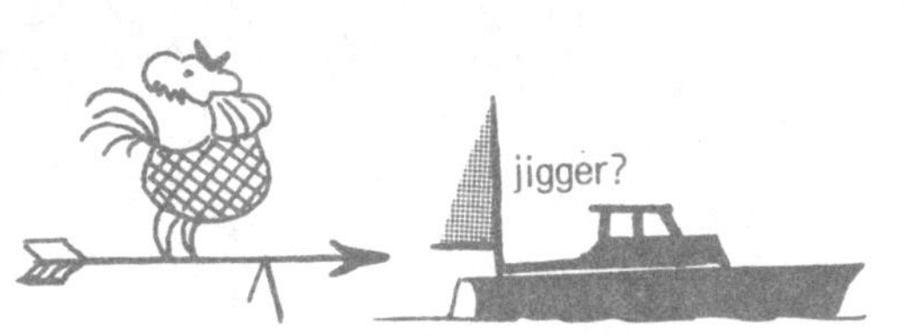

● **Weathercock** the bow so the boat will head into the wind without requiring a bottom anchor to hold position.The lobster boat uses the small aft jigger to pick up several lobster pots or trot lines in a day without using an anchor.

● **Temporary jigger.** ***Tinkerbelle*** used one plus a bucket to keep the boat headed into the waves, to avoid the major hazard of waves hitting the beam and rolling the boat at night when Manry was asleep. Sloops and cutters can use the same idea in a similar situation, or at anchor in bad weather.

We've used the same idea on ketches and yawls as shown above with the aft sail up and sheeted amidship.

● **Heaving to** is a method use to maintain drifting position with your sails and rudder counterbalancing each other.Try heaving to on your sailboat in good weather as hull action varies due to weight and keel shape.We enjoy trolling under sail with pole holders on the transom. In a hookup it is necessary to heave to going upwind, or beam to when going downwind.

The best example I remember was on the 31' ***Minka*** with most sailing in the winter months. After slogging upwind in a noisy upper force 5 with cold spray continually coming aboard,the boat would heave to easily to go below for an hour to have supper. The noise was minimal below, the ride was comfortable, and the owner a good cook.Sailboats with spade rudders seem to heave to with less effort than those with keel mounted rudders. The space between the spade rudder and keel seems to provide a stabilizing factor to ease water resistance below the waterline.

● **Heave to under bare poles** was a common practice with fisherman over a century ago. ***Spray*** was a heavy-displacement lobster boat that had to ride out many major storms during its long career. It was built before 1800, then rebuilt by Slocum, and launched again in 1895, page 267. ***Igdrasil*** was an exact copy sailing twice around the world. The new owner Ed King, a retired admiral and his wife were having supper near Santa Cruz Island. The boat was drifting under bare poles when a major storm hit.

Ed lashed down the rudder hard aport, and tied down anything loose topside. Since the storm was too vicious to maintain a lookout, the only answer was to seal all hatches, then go below to ride out the storm. The heavy-displacement hull fighting the rudder, balanced nicely keeping the bow to windward, reducing the sternway considerably.The ride below was quiet and comfortable for eating, reading, sleeping, and talking.

On the second morning the storm eased enough so he could take a sun shot, finding ***Igdrasil*** was 110 miles west of San Diego with two well rested crew members aboard a hull design over 200 years old.***The first job when reaching port was to check all rudder fittings.***

Sails are counterbalanced with wind backing sails on forward mast to maintain position.

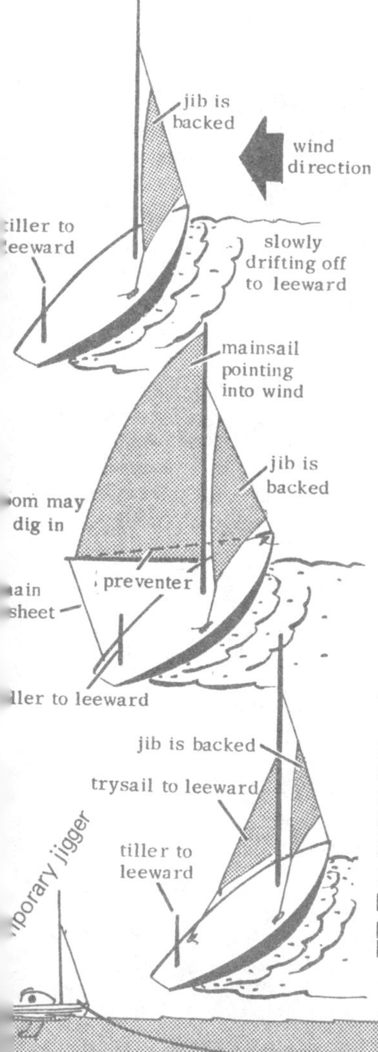

Square riggers hove to to maintain their position by counterbracing fore yards and main yards in opposite directions.

After picking up a pilot, or exchanging passengers and mail in midocean, they could soon be underway.

A similar practice is used on our sailboats today to maintain position with sails and rudders counterbalancing each other. Hull variables are considerable, so try the methods at left on your own sailboat.

Pink Cloud

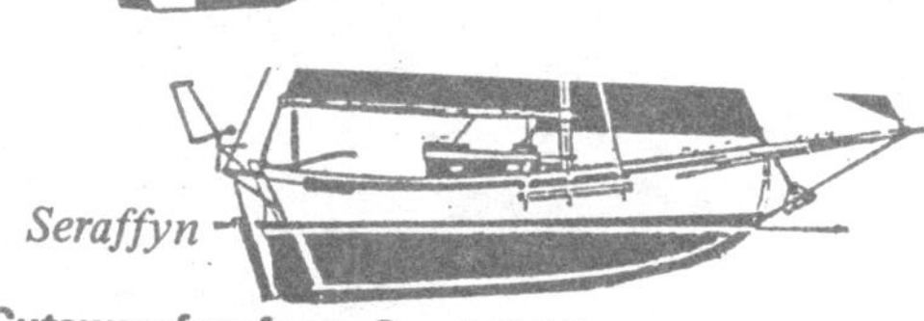

Seraffyn

Cutaway forefoot. Our 24'4"long *Pink Cloud* can change tack easily in its own length in tight moorings. The bow entry is a disadvantage when heaving to in a confused seaway.

Long keel. The 24'6" *Seraffyn* sailed around the world holding course on its own for long periods. It heaves to easily in the same situation, though crankily maneuvering thru same tight moorings.

Tinkerbelle— written by Robert Manry, Dell Pub.Co.Inc. He delighted readers by buying a 30 year old beat up 13½'x5¼' Old Town dinghy and rebuilding it in Cleveland,Ohio. He left Falmouth,Mass., 8/17/1965, requiring 78 days to sail his little boat to Falmouth, England.

He 'parked' his boat at night to a canvas bucket with a 150' length of ½" nylon, plus a makeshift jigger on the stern.Robert Manry is one of our sailing heroes.

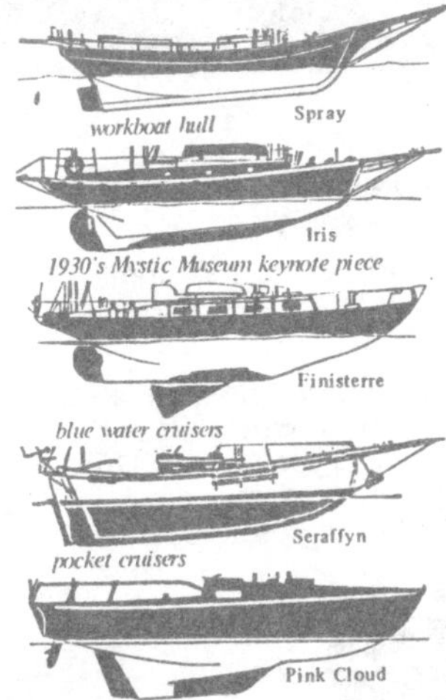

Storm action hull movement. Our 13 hull forms with varying degrees of draft and underwater area dampen the confused surface wave action.

The longer, heavier, deep-keel cruising hull with a deeper bite and more surface area, will be more stable and comfortable in storm action. In a maximum, long-duration storm when unable to carry any sail, the ***Spray,*** if heavily loaded, a design 100 years old before being rebuilt and launched in 1895, may be the most comfortable to lock the hatches, and let the boat ride it out on its own.

The most active and least comfortable hull shape influenced by surface wave action may be light displacement, wide beam, shallow draft, with cut-off forefoot. As it is more fatiguing to a helmsman, shorter watches will reduce potential mistakes.

- **Forward movement protects the rudder,** rudder fittings, and rudder shaft. As a sailboat is designed to only go forward, backward drift must be kept to a minimum to reduce abnormal stresses on large sailboat rudders.
- **Shallow draft, wide-beam planing powerboat.** It is subject to unpleasant fore and aft pitching, while high freeboard windage escalates rolling action in a storm. If it loses power, the hull wants to drift beam to the wind and waves. The rolling and pitching action combine to amplify each other as it is totally influenced by surface wind and wave action. Without the dampening action of a sailboat keel, a high sided powerboat may roll in even a minor storm. It was the reason we tested and introduced the **para-anchor,** page 157.
- **Crest to crest wave variables.** We returned from Ensenada to San Diego after a race in a 24' trunk-cabin sailboat under power with an upper force 6 wind. Twelve hours were required with the hull riding the close, steep crests like a duck with only one wave breaking aboard.

  A 59' 10 meter sailboat under power with long overhangs, required 16 hours to go 2/3 the distance. When coming off the top of a steep wave, the bow would drop, dig deep into the face of the next wave, and come to a stop. After gaining buoyancy, the bow would lift causing tons of water to sweep aft over the deck before the meter hull was underway again.
- **Ocean waves show no favoritism** with the wave crests spreading out the following day in a similar wind force. The large reefed sailboats now in their element were at hull speed...while we had a wet, miserable ride.
- **Drogue steering aid.** If a breaking wave poops the stern of the sailboat below entering a jetty, a broach and knockdown can result. The drogue needs **enough heavy chain** to stay fully submerged, **enough bite** to keep stern to the waves, and a **trip line** if it suddenly becomes counterproductive.

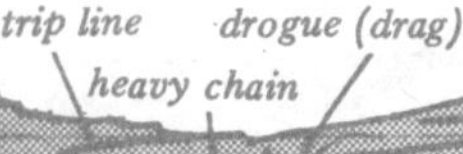

Broach, Pitchpole

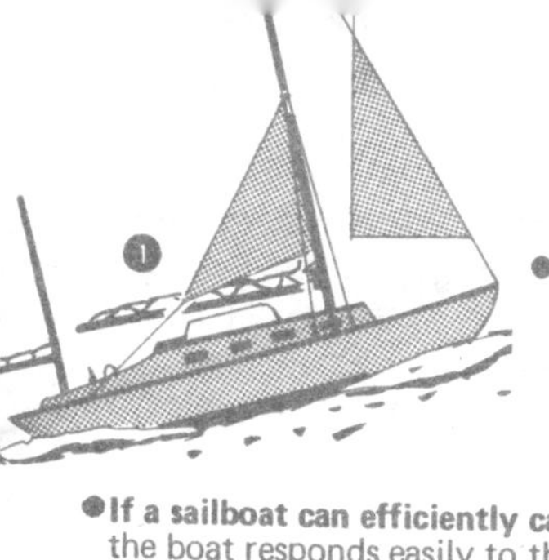

- **An easy helm** is needed to protect rudder and rudder fittings, and not to fatigue the helmsman.

- **If a sailboat can efficiently carry storm sails**— keep jogging along easily so the boat responds easily to the helm. Avoid pointing too high even temporarily to avoid losing rudder control at the worst possible moment.
- **Have short watches** as long watches produce fatigue with bad judgment at critical moments. **Avoid overmedication** for seasickness as it can cause seasickness plus many side effects at the wrong time.

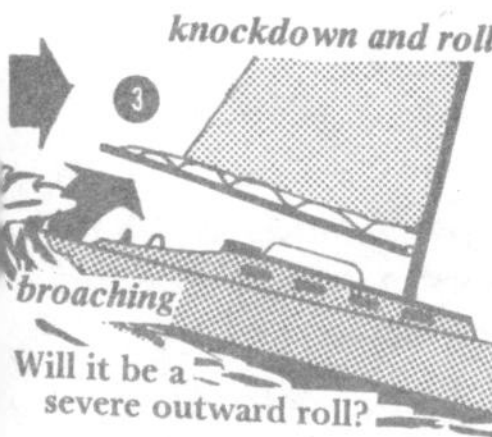

Will it be a severe outward roll?

- **Avoid the curl**— the boat at right on a beam reach is caught in a breaking wave which may cause a knockdown or 360 degree roll.

the curl

A knockdown and roll.

- **The broach.** A sailboat going downwind with *large mainsail only* has upwind helm. The bow wants to slew around out of control to windward **rolling outward to catapult crew overboard.** If the hull is caught in a **wave curl,** it can cause a knockdown or roll with dismasting. A spade rudder headsail sloop with small mainsail will have less broaching tendencies.

Broach, knockdown, roll?

pitchpole

The bow suddenly stops to become a pivot for the stern to go end over end.

- **Pooped**—*if overtaking waves go faster than the boat,* an overtaking wave may overtake and break aboard the stern. When this occurs, try to prevent the bow slewing around beam to wind to avoid a broach and roll.
- **Broach and roll**— *if the boat is going faster than wave speed,* the sailboat may come off the top of a steep wave...and the bow dig deep into the next facing wave before flotation lifts the bow. If the bow stops it becomes a pivot for the stern slewing to a beam reach with a broach, knockdown or pitchpole.
- **Wave action**—*shallow vs deep water action.* Stay in deep water with a keel boat where waves look mountainous but your boat rides them like a duck. Waves are retarded at their base to become steeper as they move into shallow water. When crest to trough ratio is 7 to 1, breaking waves release tremendous energy. Waves are most dangerous at an 8 to 9 ratio, with steep, almost vertical wave fronts...just before the wave crests break.

normal waves

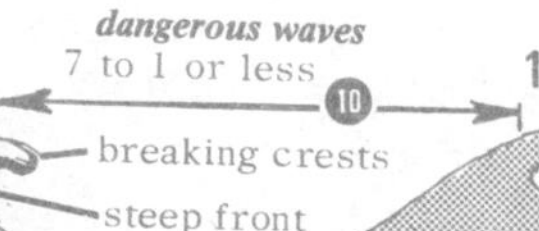

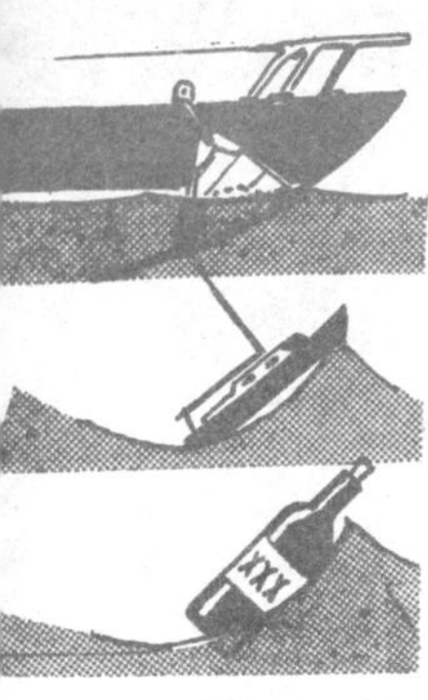

The seaworthy sailboat is one that will take care of you when you are no longer able to take care or control your sailboat.

A bottle can ride out the wildest hurricane on the ocean IF the top is sealed, and the bottle doesn't hit a solid object such as a rock, a reef, or floating debris. Heavy weather sailboat operation is almost identical...seal the hull, close all overboard valves, and stay in deep water so your hull can't thrust against similar solid objects.

The seaworthy sailboat is one that is prepared for stormy weather so your sailboat is ready to take care of itself.

- **When a boat is holed in a collision**– use a sail as shown upper left to cover the hole so outside water pressure against the sail will plug the opening. Before shoring up and plugging the hole from inside the boat, have everything prepared and ready to go...**then rapidly shove the plug into position.** If the plug is moved slowly into position, the inward water pressure on the sail cloth ceases, with water flowing between the hull and sail.
- **Use double stainless steel clamps** on all hoses. For ocean use all parts, band, clamp, and housing should be ***300 stainless.*** Avoid clamps mixing ***300 and 400 stainless*** which may corrode and fail, ***Homestudy Guide*** page 133.
- **Bunk straps** should be standard equipment on all ocean-going sailboats. We've tested many designs, yet the best and least expensive kind is seat-belt webbing, page 65. They provide a peaceful rest or nap at anchor in wave action, or underway in a rough sea. The next crew going topside will be well rested, while a crew without bunk straps, are fatigued with little sleep.
- **Bolt all structural parts** such as cleats, bitts, lifeline supports, etc., using corrosion resistant metals. Avoid wood screws in fiberglass sailboats for similar use as they may pull out easily under extreme impact.
- **Batteries become dangerous** in a knockdown or roll if not firmly secured and bolted down.If they don't have strong retainers, batteries have flown out of their containers with their 40 to 100 pound catapulted weight breaking hoses and equipment in the way. When hitting a solid object, battery parts and sulfuric acid cause unnecessary damage to equipment and people aboard, starting chain reactions that may produce fatalities.
- **Lack of marine head maintenance** has sunk many boats as several parts are involved having a good but limited lifespan. Overboard gate valves are questionable as they don't have positive sealing at all times in a closed position. **Seacock-overboard valves** are preferred but...they stick easily without continual use. Turn them on and off a couple of times everytime going aboard to reduce their chance of sticking.
- **Pocket cruiser electrical systems** have their own complexity. They can be owner installed with our installation on page 140 of our ***Homestudy Guide*** thoroughly detailed for your use. We searched endless places for such a captive electrical system using dockside charging only. .. until the first mate with a smirk asked, "Why don't you detail ours?"

Will you BEAT or RUN?

Heavy weather mistakes result from fatigue, lack of preparation, training, or awareness of changing conditions.

The reach. Can your reefed sailboat jog along easily in high wave action with water easily draining under a high-tacked jib? Bow entry is better prepared for wind and wave action with minimum flat surfaces for waves to thrust against.

Broad reach to run. Stern may have a flat surface to thrust against with waves overtaking and breaking over the stern. This may depress the stern which pivots around to cause a broach.

If a boat comes over the top of a steep wave going faster than the wave crests, the bow may dig deep into the next wave face coming to a stop, ***a pivot for the moving stern.*** The stern can slew around with a broach catapulting the crew overboard in an outward roll, have a knockdown, roll, or end for end pitchpole. A **small drogue** pgs. 152,157,may be sufficient to keep the stern to wind.

- **Doubloon,** a keel/cb yawl. It ran under bare poles in May with 40-65 knot winds off the Carolina coast with seas to 25′ fighting the Gulf Stream. When changing to a broad reach *Doubloon* had a beam knockdown.

  After *Doubloon* righted, the centerboard was lowered for stability with course changed to 60 to 70 degrees from the wind. A beams-end knockdown resulted with two 360 degree rolls losing masts and booms.

  A makeshift sea anchor was made with sailbag, sails, and anchor to keep the bow 50 to 60 degrees from the wind with 45 degrees desired.Mattresses were lashed to the stern pulpit to weathercock the bow to windward.

- **Mambo.** A couple of months later the owner of *Mambo* purchased a 24′ diameter **para-anchor** for protection if it had to face a parallel situation. *Mambo* and *Doubloon* were almost identical to ***Finisterre,*** pages 66-69.

  An unsolicited letter from the owner of ***Mambo*** tells his first use of the **para-anchor** in the Gulf Stream with 40-60 knot winds and seas averaging 25′ high. The major problem encountered was chafe of the nylon line going thru the bow chock. The owner reported only one man was required to take in the **para-anchor** afterwards with the trip line in heavy seas.

- Test ALL parachute anchors in good weather to understand their problems and avoid them in heavy weather as some have filled with air going skyward before being submerged...**pull trip line** to dump the wind, and learn the shroud rigging requirements so the chute fills easily without snafu's. We recommend 300′ of one inch diameter nylon to hold the bow to wind in a major storm. How well braced is your bow bitt,and foredeck able to take these stresses?

Owners trying to impress us with surplus sea anchors found the drogue drifting as fast as the boat, and the parachute disintegrated under tension. When we were caught in a sudden upper force 6 storm in our 17′ outboard returning from Catalina, a makeshift sea anchor drifted faster than the boat. It was a survival trip to reach port with seven hands bailing,one hand steering.

Commercial fishing boats attempted for over 15 years to use large parachutes as surface anchors...with major problems. A wooden boat off San Miguel Island started to be pulled apart at 50 knot winds. The anchor line chafed thru saving the boat as the float and trip line hadn't been introduced.

A tuna boat used a large parachute to stay in a large school of fish. The chute without a float soon developed a vertical pull with the bow deck down to the water level. A sharp knife cut the lines preventing the bow from being pulled under. The skipper was happy to lose his parachute.

We spent five months of intensive testing to tame the powerful **para-anchor** before releasing it with our approval for surface anchoring in good weather, and for survival conditions in bad weather. Testing to make it foolproof was on 18′ to 38′ powerboats, and a variety of 21′ to 40′ sailboats.

- **Switzerland** had many early orders as it was their first practical answer in history...as their lakes were too deep to use bottom anchors.
- **Fishing boats worldwide** were major early customers for the new surface anchor to stay in a school of fish, to hold position overnight close to shore in water too deep for a mud hook, and to ride out storms. It became standard equipment for Japanese fishing vessels after much of their fleet was lost in a 1964 typhoon, in order to prevent a similar disaster.
- **Mambo** proved the large parachute excellent for ocean sailboats in a survival situation. ***Shallower-draft hulls*** are less comfortable in a major storm responding more rapidly to surface wave action, which is an advantage to ease hull pressures. ***Older, deeper, narrower heavy-displacement hulls*** had a deeper, stronger bite in the water. As they had difficulty in releasing these pressures, it increased their chances of a broach, knockdown, and roll. The *Doubloon* probably tripped over its deep centerboard in the down position.
- The **two-pennant storm anchor** was tested in 1969. Though only 6′ in diameter, and size of a pillow when stored, the heavy open-weave nylon chute has minute bleed holes releasing small streams of water for stability. While the large parachute opened earlier, had more bite, and collapsed earlier...the smaller one required more pressure to open, and to trip, and collapse.
- The large parachute with a stronger bite proves better to protect large sailboat rudders. The smaller one is better for powerboats with small rudders due to less bite and some drift in a storm,easing the pressures on powerboat hulls.
- **Considerable misinformation** exists in this field,for which I tested and introduced the 6′ and 24′ surface anchors. A **float** is required to keep the chutes near the surface, and a **trip line** to collapse them with little effort,especially in storm conditions. A strong **swivel** is mandatory as the violent turning action has to be seen to be believed. Use these anchors only off the bow in bad weather survival conditions to protect the hull with minimum flat surfaces. Scarcity is the problem as U.S. surplus sources have disappeared. Contact—

Two-pennant storm anchor— Lissaur Company, 2529 Chambers St., Vernon, CA 90058

12′, 18′, 24′, 32′ chutes— Para-Anchors International, Box 19, Summerland,CA 93067

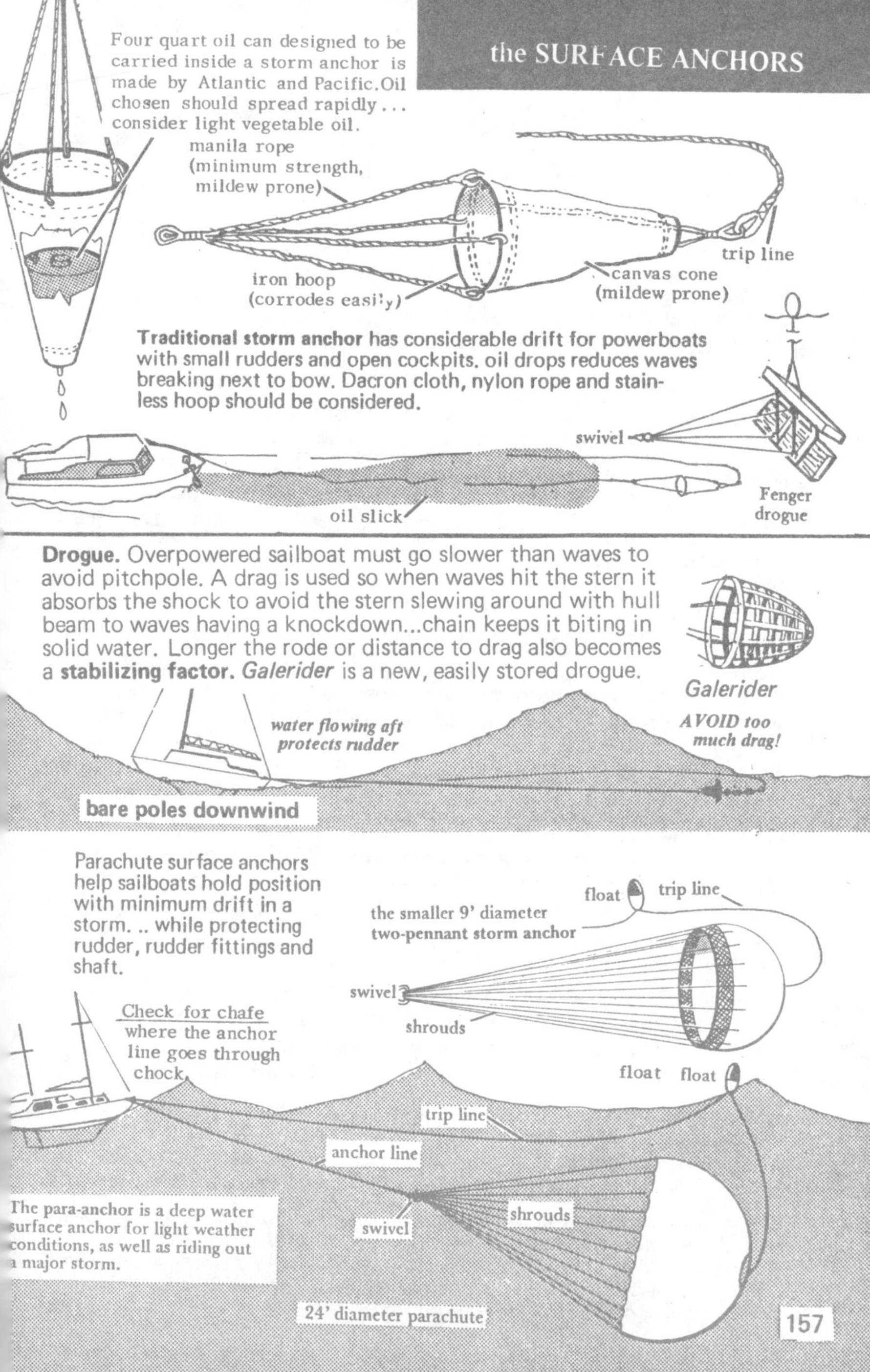
the SURFACE ANCHORS
Four quart oil can designed to be carried inside a storm anchor is made by Atlantic and Pacific. Oil chosen should spread rapidly . . . consider light vegetable oil.
manila rope (minimum strength, mildew prone)
iron hoop (corrodes easily)
canvas cone (mildew prone)
trip line
Traditional storm anchor has considerable drift for powerboats with small rudders and open cockpits. oil drops reduces waves breaking next to bow. Dacron cloth, nylon rope and stainless hoop should be considered.
swivel
oil slick
Fenger drogue
Drogue. Overpowered sailboat must go slower than waves to avoid pitchpole. A drag is used so when waves hit the stern it absorbs the shock to avoid the stern slewing around with hull beam to waves having a knockdown...chain keeps it biting in solid water. Longer the rode or distance to drag also becomes a stabilizing factor. Galerider is a new, easily stored drogue.
Galerider
water flowing aft protects rudder
AVOID too much drag!
bare poles downwind
Parachute surface anchors help sailboats hold position with minimum drift in a storm. .. while protecting rudder, rudder fittings and shaft.
float
trip line
the smaller 9' diameter two-pennant storm anchor
swivel
shrouds
Check for chafe where the anchor line goes through chock
float
float
trip line
anchor line
The para-anchor is a deep water surface anchor for light weather conditions, as well as riding out a major storm.
swivel
shrouds
24' diameter parachute
157

Your author has gone aground, and assisted more sailboats and powerboats that have gone aground than he cares to remember. Almost all were caused by carelessness or shoaling, one was a steering failure.

Think twice before requesting or taking assistance when putting a boat aground. We've seen tremendous, unnecessary, and expensive damage from eager, unthinking, and untrained or partially trained rescuers.

- **A shoaling grounding.** I put a 40' Newporter ketch aground in San Diego harbor under power. An overly eager Navy tug came to help, the crew trained to handle large indestructible USN vessels. Our major problem was to keep the tug at a distance to avoid pulling our sailboat apart.

  Both genoa and mainsail were raised and left luffing on a beam reach. As a puff moved in, both sails were sheeted hard, while a crew member swung out on the mizzen halyard. The sailboat heeled sufficiently in a force 4 wind to break loose from the sticky mud. The lee helm helped the bow swing into deeper water. The only damage was to the author's pride which was eased by the confused, cheering tugboat crew.

- **Panic is the first emotion** in a grounding or capsize. Rational thinking then starts to return with a common problem a **180 degree capsize with the mast stuck in the mud.** An overeager rescuer or harbor patrolman in a hurry to tow your dinghy into deeper water, can cause an expensive and unnecessary dismasting, page 145. If it were your dinghy, how could you right your boat while protecting the mast?

- **Depth sounders.** Earlier ones without alarms had a pulsating light that could soon hypnotize a person watching it. Our 1967 vintage Vexilar was the first we believe marketed with an alarm in the U.S. You could preset the alarm from 10' to 140' to warn of shallowing water.

  Over 15 years later a lifeguard supervisor dropped by to report during our afternoon pea soup fog, five keel sailboats to 43' long were hard aground in the breakers on our local beach. The rescue and repair costs far exceeded the savings by not buying a depth sounder, see page 231.

- *The full moon/ maximum tide ranges increase the risk of grounding. It also increases the positive ion affecting the thinking and judgment process affecting ALL boat operators. More analysis time is required when it is necessary to make critical decisions. Page 68 of our* Home-study Guide *covers it in greater depth.*

Can you turn sailboat around with sails up? Is it necessary to drop sails and back out under power?

- **What help do you have**— wind and/or current direction. Is the tide ebbing or flooding...is time working for or against you?

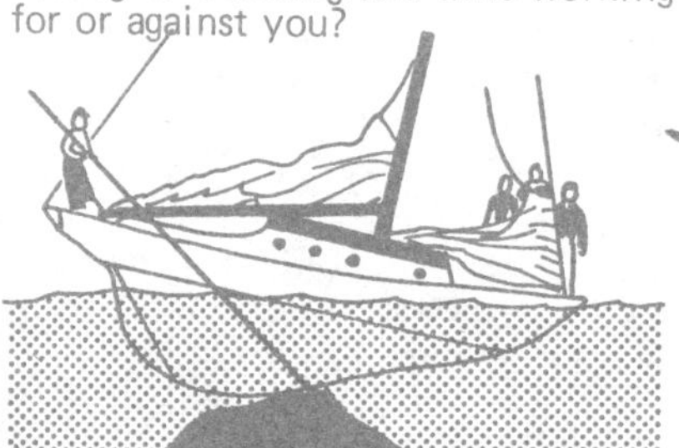

- **Movable ballast** may break boat loose.
- **Powerboat wake**— will it help to break your sailboat loose?

Main, mizzen, jib halyard. Crew member swinging out on halyard may help break suction of sticky mud. Powerboat pulling on halyard may break boat loose from mud or sandy bottom.

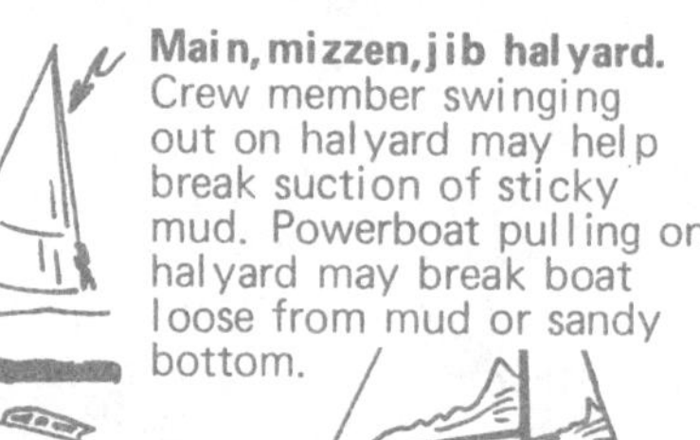

- **Avoid using the engine** if your boat is hard aground on a sandy bottom. Suction may pull in sand plugging and scouring the cooling system.

Do you have a dinghy to carry out your anchor? The sailboat is kedging out and winching off. Would it help for all movable weight to be on one side of boat?

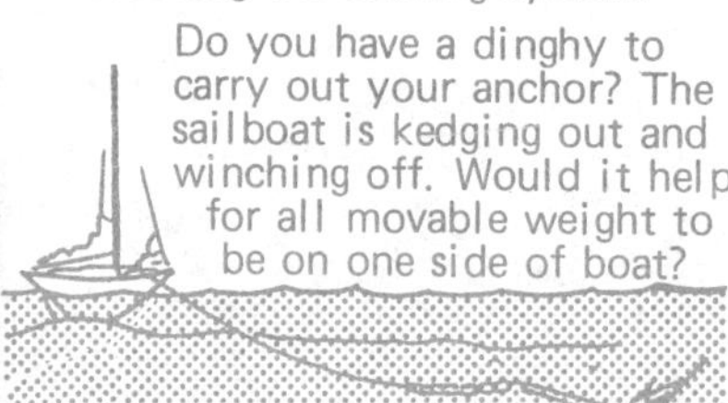

HARD AGROUND

- **Ebb tide warning**— put anchors out.

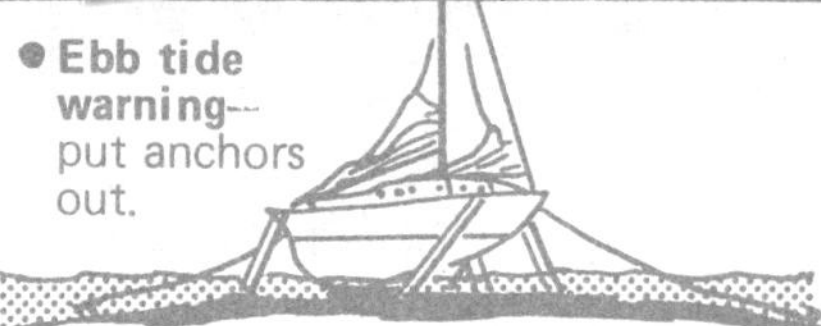

- **If boat is hard aground**— prop up the boat. *If that isn't practical*—

Let the boat fall so the cockpit and cabin won't be swamped before refloating. Seal all hatches and portholes to prevent cabin from being flooded.

- Cockpit and cabin of sailboat below may be flooded.

- Can you turn around and sail the centerboard out? Is it necessary to drop sails, raise centerboard and remove rudder to paddle over, or back off the obstruction?

- A sailboat was hard aground on the Jamaica Bay, the owner surrounded by swarms of gnats and mosquitos. How would you handle the situation?

Trapped air causes mildew.

hot air rises

suction air flow

Mildew potentials vary from annoyance to problems on many sailboats and powerboats. The answer is to provide a history of it on our 24' sailboat launched June, 1964.

Condensation developed below on all fiberglass surfaces as water droplets from condensation collecting and growing into puddles. Black mildew spots began growing on the overhead, cabin sides, on top and below the cushions, with major growth in all lockers.

A built-in air flow system is also required for fiberglass sailboats. We drilled twenty two 2" vents in our bulkheads and lockers, plus a 4" air scoop on the bow. We turned our bunk cushions on their sides when leaving the boat for better air flow.

- **Built-in headers.** They appeared in 1965 on the overhead in the cabin to absorb moisture during periods of high humidity. It released some of the moisture when the humidity dropped during the daytime. Headers proved a stabilizing influence to minimize condensation, which in turn limited mildew potentials inside a sailboat.
- **Pressure air flow.** We pointed our forward air vent into the westerlies as a storm moved into our area. After three days of rain, and a hot sunny day... we found a healthy fungi farm growing below. Many hours of scrubbing and ventilation were required to removed the black mildew and its smell.
- **Suction air flow.** A few months later when leaving Catalina we turned our forward air vent aft to avoid heavy spray from going below. We were soaked and tired after a spirited sail home...forgetting to turn the vent into the westerlies. After two days of heavy rain, and two hot sunny days we returned to our boat to find minimal mildew growth.
- **Convection air currents** ***begin a suction flow coming from the aft part of the cabin, which flows forward to exhaust the moist humid part of the air out the forward vent*** shown above. Mildew problems became a minor nuisance until the 1982-3 *El Nino* caused havoc worldwide. All boats, ours included, that we examined had abnormal mildew problems.
- **Circular suction vent.** We installed one on our forward cabin hatch...yet the following winter it didn't rain. When our 1984-5 winter season moved in, we had our normal amount of rain. We were very happy to find after 20 years thanks to our stainless circular vent above, we faced a fresh, clean smell when opening the companionway hatch. Why wasn't this efficient low-profile vent invented 24 years earlier?
- **A new fiberglass hull** may look smooth though it has small microscopic pores that enlarge with aging. Mildew will collect and grow in these pockets when conditions are ripe, which is a cosmetic problem.
- **Wax** the exterior of fiberglass hulls every two years to plug these holes, providing a smooth surface. It will be easy to remove any black mildew growth trying to attach to the slippery wax surface.

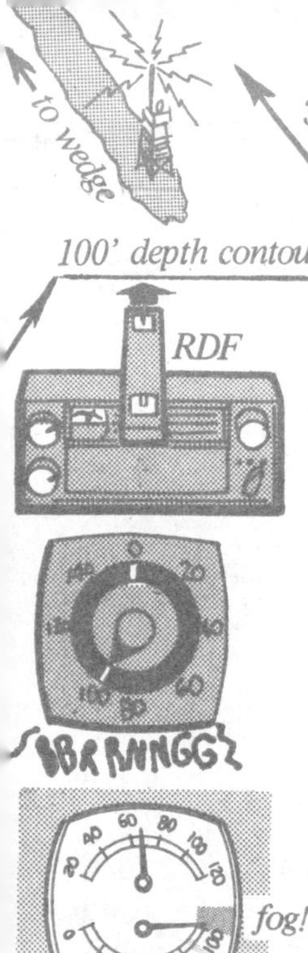

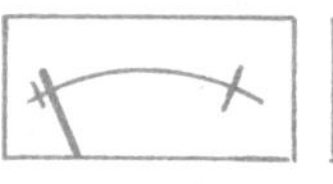
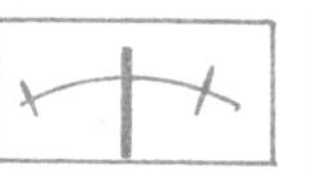
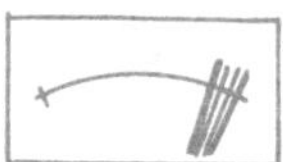

Fog operation becomes a spirited challenge for a sailboat with an accurate compass after adding 3 basic instruments.Practice with these instruments entering harbors in your area to eliminate surprises and easy to make mistakes without such familiarity.

The panic a new sailor faces suddenly caught in a peasoup fog on his new boat can be considerable. In time he realizes he can operate normally in an open cockpit,steering accurate compass courses on a sensitive displacement hull under sail or power.

The situation is much worse on a planing powerboat that has to throttle down becoming clumsy to steer accurate compass courses at displacement speed, and with inside controls, the windshield continually fogs over.

A displacement hull powerboat may operate almost as efficiently as a sailboat in fog conditions. The planing powerboat owner should avoid going to sea and stay dockside even if it is a light fog.

- **A humidity indicator** pages 94-5, is required to provide ample warning of a fog moving in to prepare for it...and also when moving out.
- **Depth sounders** should be standard equipment on ocean-going sailboats to learn underwater contours to avoid shoals and entering harbors, see page 158.
- **Radio Direction Finder (RDF)** is an excellent homing instrument to help you outwit a peasoup fog, though the less expensive ones may have an 180 degree error which is easy to compensate for. The problem, few owners ever seem to use them for familiarity even in good weather.

The basic RDF above could pick up our low-powered radiobeacon six miles from our local jetty which was excellent for student practice. They would ***steer on the NULL*** as the signal grew louder, and was finally overpowered. We were leaving deep water with the bottom shallowing rapidly.The preset depth sounder alarm went off indicating a 100' depth.

A sharp right turn on the 100' depth contour takes the boat to the entrance buoy, followed by a hard left turn to enter the jetty into the harbor.For entering harbors in heavy fogs, ***use magnetic courses only*** on your charts to eliminate juggling the differences between true and magnetic courses when maneuvering is tight, and critical.

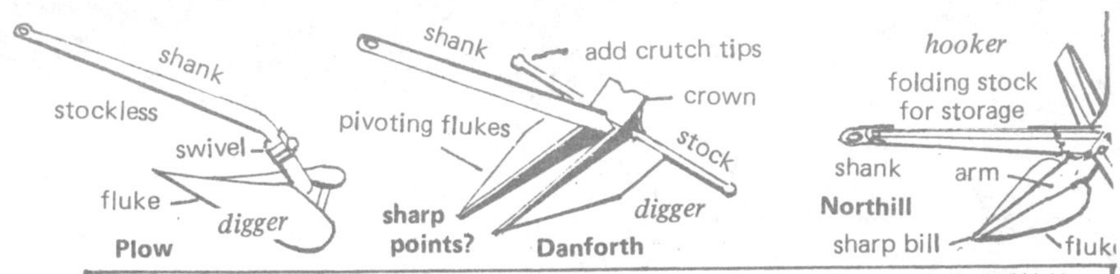

Our navy needed a new, light, efficient anchor for landing craft in WW II. The job was assigned to Fred Kissner choosing a tractor and a sandy beach. Tractor power broke out all the anchors except Danforth...it dug deeper.*

Kissner bought our first anchor, a 16 lb. Danforth.We pulled into a small cove near Jones Beach Inlet on Long Island on 6/4/48 in the afternoon with wall to wall large powerboats and our sailboat bow into the beach, plus a tahiti ketch in the middle with 6 anchors out. The stuffy gent next door peered down at me over the railing of his 54' powerboat with grinning servants on either side holding his dainty liqueur glass,"I say chap, why are you using an anchor twice the size of mine?"

A squall hit at 0200 recorded at 98 knots at the nearby USCG base. Only 4 out of 54 powerboats held...while our anchor dug in a couple more inches. The last I saw of my glassy-eyed neighbor, his nightshirt was wrapped around his neck. He was trying to hang onto his red night cap while hollering at his terrified servants clinging to him. His 54' boat was drifting backwards into the tahiti ketch, its owner trying to hang onto his night cap with his red nightshirt wrapped around his neck. My anchor interest was no longer passive.

- **Paint mud-hook anchors white.** When returning to a Newporter ketch after a September dive at Catalina I could see the anchor had broken loose, the water was clear, at a depth of 84'. We no longer kidded the owner who had painted the anchor white, it saved his boat. I've dived many times to check anchors which disappear rapidly and are hard to find if not painted white.
- **Imported anchor imitations**— who makes them? After an Ensenada Race a new 46' ketch was anchoring at nearby Todo Santos Island near us in an upper force 6 wind. One of the flukes bent double on the new anchor with the boat drifting thru shoal water with a rocky bottom; was it a bargain?
- **Plow anchors** were introduced in England. Their popularity came much later in the U.S. Cruising sailors from Mexico reported the heavier plow had a better bite, it broke out later, and set more rapidly without fouling.

Our testing with the lighter Danforth found it gaining lift at 3 to 4 knots planing above the bottom, becoming helpless when catching seaweed. We tested the plow at similar speeds finding it digging in due to the negative angle. Kelp didn't seem a problem when drifting thru kelp beds.

- **Bruce anchor**— a good basic design with no moving parts.Though not using one at time of writing, reports indicate it is an efficient design.
- **Anchor shackle bolt.** We prefer monofilament fishing line as a locking method, others choose noncorroding wire. Use a hammer and punch if you want to lock the shackle threads permanently.

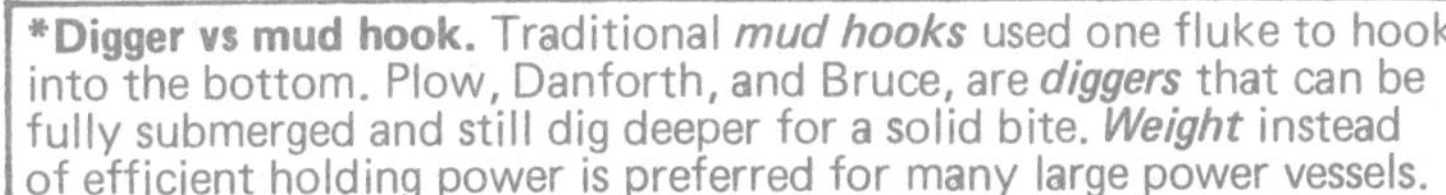

***Digger vs mud hook.** Traditional *mud hooks* used one fluke to hook into the bottom. Plow, Danforth, and Bruce, are *diggers* that can be fully submerged and still dig deeper for a solid bite. *Weight* instead of efficient holding power is preferred for many large power vessels.

Light efficient **diggers, mud hooks** relying on one fluke, stockless relying on **weight.**

the BOTTOM ANCHORS

- **Stones** were our first primitive anchors. They are still preferred for a large Utah lake with a rocky bottom. Self-tailing sailboat winches evolved from the first self-tailing winch designed to raise heavy rock anchors in Utah.
- **Traditional mud hook** with a 3000 year history was used on square riggers, schooners, and naval vessels. Up to 180 men were assigned to anchor detail on the *USS Constitution* with six anchors—a 5,443 lb. **sheet anchor,two bowers** of 5,304 lbs. each, a 1100 lb. **stream anchor,** and two 403 and 700 lb. **kedge anchors.** Anchor cable had up to a 22" circumference in wartime..
- **Heavy stockless anchors** appeared around 1890 relying on weight rather than design for vessels with ample steam power to raise them with shanks stowed inside a hawsepipe; the aircraft carrier ***Midway*** used a 40,000 lb. stockless anchor.The basic design idea, if naval vessels were at anchor being shelled, they could steam out dragging the anchor though at reduced speed.
- The **heavy mushroom** used for permanent moorings is not an anchor but a *pivot* with the pull of a boat taken and absorbed by the heavy chain it is attached to.The small mushroom can be used as an anchor line *killick* and a nautical paper weight.Stockless anchors and small mushroom anchors with minimum holding efficiency are of little use to recreational sailing.
- **Danforth anchors** have ancestors with a 4000 year history in China, plus a 2000-year-old wishbone anchor found in Italy...but where is the plow anchor ancestor, a design used by farmers for how many generations? Mud-hook engineering has contributed more to civilization than we realize.
- **Hawaiian hook.** South Pacific sailors said it was excellent for coral though I've never used one.The **grapnel** is used to *grapple* for and pick up objects on the bottom such as anchor chain, etc. It isn't a basic anchor.

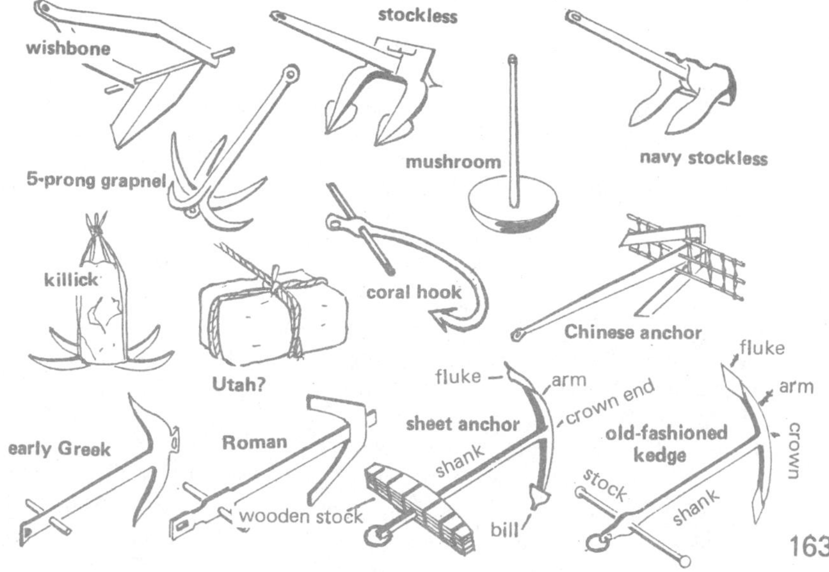

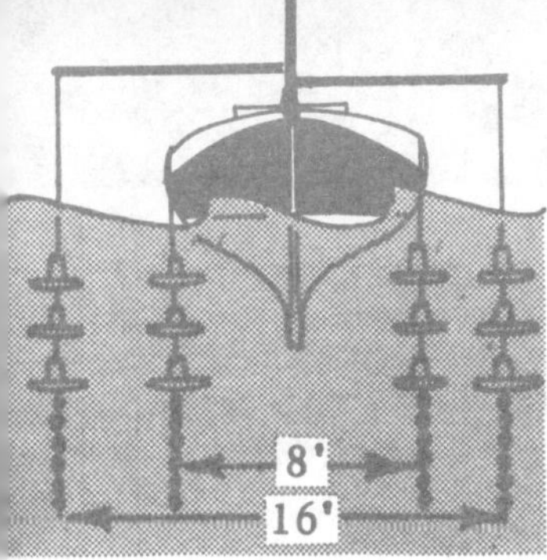

As all moorings were full in Avalon Harbor we had to anchor in an open roadstead. It was so miserable we returned to Newport. I asked the inventor of the new *Turbo-Flo* storm anchor to assemble some of his hats to test their action as flopper stoppers. They did a good job.

Our old hats are in good condition 20 years later. We still recommend the hats ***IF they are firmly locked to their stainless holding wire.*** Some produced in recent years without such a locking method can chafe on the stainless wire. It may reduce their useful lifespan.

Two anchors are needed for ocean cabin sailboats. Their sizes will depend on your sailing area, and the size of your boat.The larger one should protect your sailboat in a major storm, plus a lighter lunch hook easy to handle.

- **Nylon anchor line**— not everyone will agree with our emphasis against the extra elongation feature of 3-strand nylon. We feel it can be hazardous in some situations discussed on page 186.
- The **8 to 1 scope** for east coast hurricanes in shallow water provides wry remarks from local sailors with 1000′ to 2000′ depths a short distance offshore as the weight of that much anchor line would sink most boats. The parachute surface anchor is the best way to maintain position in deep water.
- **Summer sailing vacations**— 31′ sailboat...15′ of heavy chain and 300′ of ½″ double braid line should be ample. Chafe is present with rocks and sandy bottoms. At least the first three feet of line and thimble on the anchor end should be taped, page 199 to reduce chafe needing occasional replacement.
- **Long-distance cruising.** Use chain to eliminate the chafe of nylon anchor line; chain is also a shock absorber. Chain is nasty to handle requiring at least two pairs of quality leather gloves aboard to protect your hands.

I enjoyed considerable winter operation on the 31′ ***Minka*** in the nearby Channel Islands before it moved to Hawaii. We were anchored next to the San Pedro breakwater with a 30 lb. plow, 70′ of chain, and a few feet of ½″ nylon. As breakfast was ending we notice the boat drifting into the busy ship channel. An unseen diver with a chain cutter had cut it at the thimble stealing the anchor and chain. What an experience...if we were asleep????? The next anchor was a 25 lb. plow with 100′ of lighter chain, plus ½″ nylon. It was easier to handle and the longer chain helped the anchor dig in earlier.

- **Parachute anchors**— surplus sources have disappeared, though they can be obtained from the sources on page 156. **Warning**— practice with your new parachute anchor in good weather for familiarity. When first used in a storm, some chutes have filled and gone skyward providing an unexpected *Nantucket sail (sleigh) ride* without a whale.

When this occurs, collapse the chute with its trip line. Take below, repack the shrouds, and try again submerging it this time below the water.

Now just suppose you forgot to add the trip line....

Action— boat, wind, wave action pull against. **Reaction**—digging angle, anchor holding power.

A mud hook can be overpowered, while a digger anchor digs deeper.

Anchor line can foul on exposed mud-hook fluke as wind, current, or both change direction.

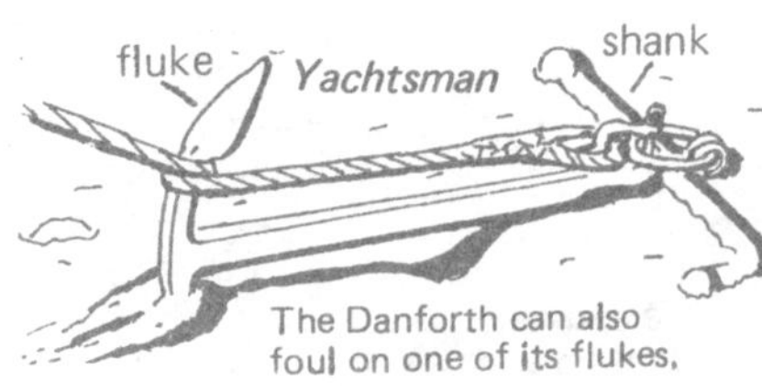

The Danforth can also foul on one of its flukes.

- **Normal practice**— drop anchor slowly to avoid hitches in the line, as well as anchor fouling on its own line.
- **Scope**— is ratio of anchor rode paid out to water depth with tidal changes. Tidal changes are extreme in periods of Hurricane high and low water.

2:1 scope— ¼ holding power

4:1 scope— ½ holding power

8:1 scope— maximum holding power in shallow water.

chafe

good weather · strong wind · major storm

nylon · chain · nylon · chain · nylon · chain

Use sufficient chain to improve anchor rode digging angle. Tape 3′ or so of nylon anchor line and thimble exposed on bottom to chafe from rocks, etc.

- *Traditional terms*— anchor line is called a **cable** usually 100 fathoms, 720′, or 1/10th of a mile. **Sheet anchor** is heaviest bower in reserve for emergency. Two **bower anchors** were carried on port and starboard bows. **Stream anchor** at stern is about 1/3 weight of bower, may also be used for ***kedging off.***
- **Rocky bottoms**— use a buoyed trip line secured to your anchor. Your anchor will be easier to locate if caught under a rock, see page 140.
- **Shorter scope, better catenary?** Use as much chain as possible. Send a ***weight**** down the line to improve the anchor digging angle. This will also improve shock loads on the hull fittings and nylon anchor line in wave action,pg. 188.
- **Alarm** indicates the sailboat is drifting and the anchor is dragging.
- **Chafe** is major problem for nylon anchor line in wave action. Wrap towels around line where it goes thru bow chock.

Periodically change the nip of the line where it goes thru the chock to also reduce chafe potentials.

float or plastic bottle

BRRRRING

better catenary

light line

cks

*Traditional weight term was ***killick*** or ***sentinel.*** The best weight pulling angle is a little more than halfway down the rode.

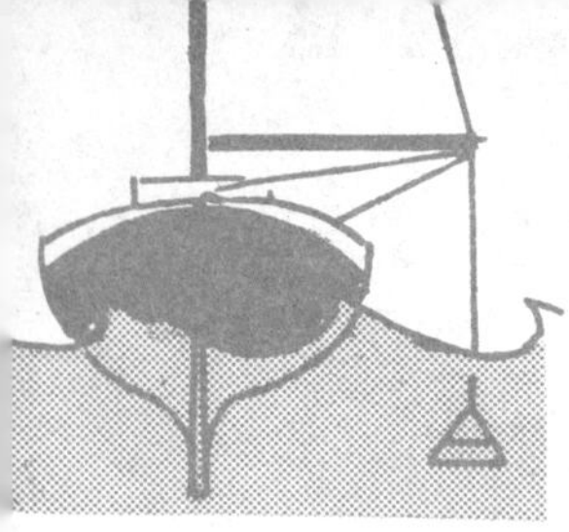

Nothing is as pleasant after a good sail, as falling asleep with the normal movement of a sailboat at anchor.

When movement is too active and uncomfortable, it is time to break out products such as the *Roll Control** stabilizer. A sailor never realizes how well this flopper stopper operates until taking it in preparatory to sailing as the boat begins to buck and roll again.

**Comfort Afloat–15146 La Calma Dr., Whittier,CA 90605*

Majority of sailboats lost in the Pacific occur after reaching protected water due to minor unexpected engine failures...which can also happen to you.

- The tahiti ketch *Fat Squaw,* named after the owner's ex-wife, was operating under power heading for a Mexican port with ugly swells on the stern when the engine suddenly quit. The owner heaved his white high-tensile 2½ lb. Danforth which dug in with the breakwater rocks only a few feet ahead. It held the stern into 35 to 50 knot winds for over 18 hours with ground swells breaking under the stern and into the cockpit. The spit-and-polish ketch was a mess while the little gray Danforth had a slightly bent fluke.

  We chose a rough anchorage for four days in 1966 to test braided anchor line with 3-strand anchor line , page 186. It became so rough we had to leave with the engine quitting after both anchors were in. I heaved our 2½ lb. high-tensile Danforth with braided anchor line similar to our heaving line. The anchor dug in saving our boat in the breaker line with big waves.

- **Heaving a small anchor**— we began teaching this new art to interested cruising students, see facing page.My best student was a movie stunt man who easily heaved our light Danforth over 100' on his second try. A man came down the dock asking,"Why hasn't this been taught before?" I recognized him as the owner of a 50' sailboat racing in Mexican waters less than 2 weeks earlier that had gone into the huge breaker line and was totaled, with the engine too weak to help. Could this idea have saved his sailboat?

- **Anchoring and the genoa winch.** We enjoyed taking the neighborhood kids fishing. It was easy to anchor several times in an afternoon by leading the anchor line up thru the bow chock and back to the cockpit winch. It wasn't necessary to leave the cockpit to anchor, or take up the anchor.

- **Twin bow anchors** can hold a boat in changing wind and/or tidal current conditions. Anchor the boat bow and stern first...then walk the stern line forward to secure it to the bow bitt or cleat.

  The bitter end. Owners of sailboats new to 30 years old aren't happy when I request they take out their 300' of heavy chain...until coming to the bitter end, finding it secured to the boat with weak,mildewed twine.

▲ A special truck was chartered to deliver 600' of heavy chain to a large, newly launched, privately-owned fishing boat. The proud owner is on the bridge rigging his poles for bottom fishing in deep water as his professional skipper in a flashy new uniform is at the bow doing the anchoring. You can write your own ending to this true *bitter end* story.

- **The bitter end**—It is easy to forget to secure that end of your anchor line.

Stories of the bitter end are hilarious ...if they happen to another person.

In an emergency— how far can you heave a small, highly efficient anchor?

AVOID using a 3 strand heaving line. Use braided line only which has been correctly stowed, page 194.

secure bitter end first

bucket with anchor line

- **Heaving an anchor** is dangerous if not done correctly. Begin on a quiet dock making at least 20 successful throws of the boat fender...before you consider heaving an anchor..

Ground tackle term includes anchor, anchor chain, line, and shackle assembly.

- **Anchor difficult to take in** due to wind or tidal current—use halyard winch or genoa winch for added leverage.

halyard winch

jib winch

float supporting coiled anchor line

Stuck anchor? Shorten anchor line, coil, and secure to float. Use a 2nd line, tie bowline around anchor line letting knot slip down until circling anchor shank. Pull opposite direction to break anchor out. ***Use Dacron or other line which won't stretch.*** If a nylon puller is used, unpredictable action of anchor under rubber band stress page 186, is dangerous.

puller

Our U.S. Buoyage System is numbered proceeding from the sea. The best way to remember the correct side to pass buoys is ***RRR or Red Right Returning*** to stay in the channel. When buoys can be passed on either side, the one preferred is indicated by the color of the topmost band.

- **Thirty major buoy systems** were used worldwide in 1976. Major collisions resulted especially in European waters with heavy ship traffic due to the variety of buoyage systems often in complete contradiction with each other. Buoyage systems are undergoing worldwide standardization.
- **Two basic patterns** evolved from the 30 systems. ***Region A—red buoys to port,*** and **Region B— red buoys to starboard** which was adopted by the Western Hemisphere nations, Japan, Korea, and the Phillipines*.
- **Revised U.S. Buoyage system.** It is to reach full compliance to meet the Region B buoyage system by 1989. Basic changes are the black buoys on the facing page being painted green. This is a change I question finding it difficult to spot green spar buoys in the Sacramento Slough area with green foliage in the background.
- **Mid-channel marker.** It is a round, white buoy with vertical red stripes which is also a landfall indicator. It is added to our system replacing the previous mid-channel buoy with black and white vertical stripes. Some lights have been made stronger for better identification in low visibility.
- **Isolated danger mark** is a continuing problem for an example, to indicate submerged pilings existing on Chart 1210 TR. Another, two systems meet and terminate with a rock between. A third, an unmarked hazard between two buoyage systems which can be an underwater obstruction or sunken vessel (recent?) not visible on the surface.
- **Hazard buoy—** a barber-pole buoy with red stripes curling up a black buoy could easily perform this function. USCG seems to have little interest to consider a hazard buoy until after 1989 though few are required.
- **After a storm—** question the location of floating buoys for your own protection...are lights out, and have they drifted off course? If such is the case, notify the closest USCG unit soon as possible to eliminate the hazard to help other sailors. If the buoys are state installed, contact your appropiate state officials.

Water depths on the east coast are charted ***from Mean Low Water...***while **west coast depths** are charted from ***Mean Lower, Low Water.***

The latest chart corrections in past years were added to the charts with the latest changes dated on the bottom of U.S charts. Most of the updating on our charts are now left to boat owners. The charts are produced by—

- **National Ocean Survey, NOOA—** Rockville, MD 20852
- **Defense Mapping Agency Hydrographic Center—** Washington, DC 20390

**IALA Maritime Buoyage Systems were developed by the International Association of Lighthouse Authorities. Their headquarters are— 13 Rue Yvon Villarceau 75116 Paris, France.*

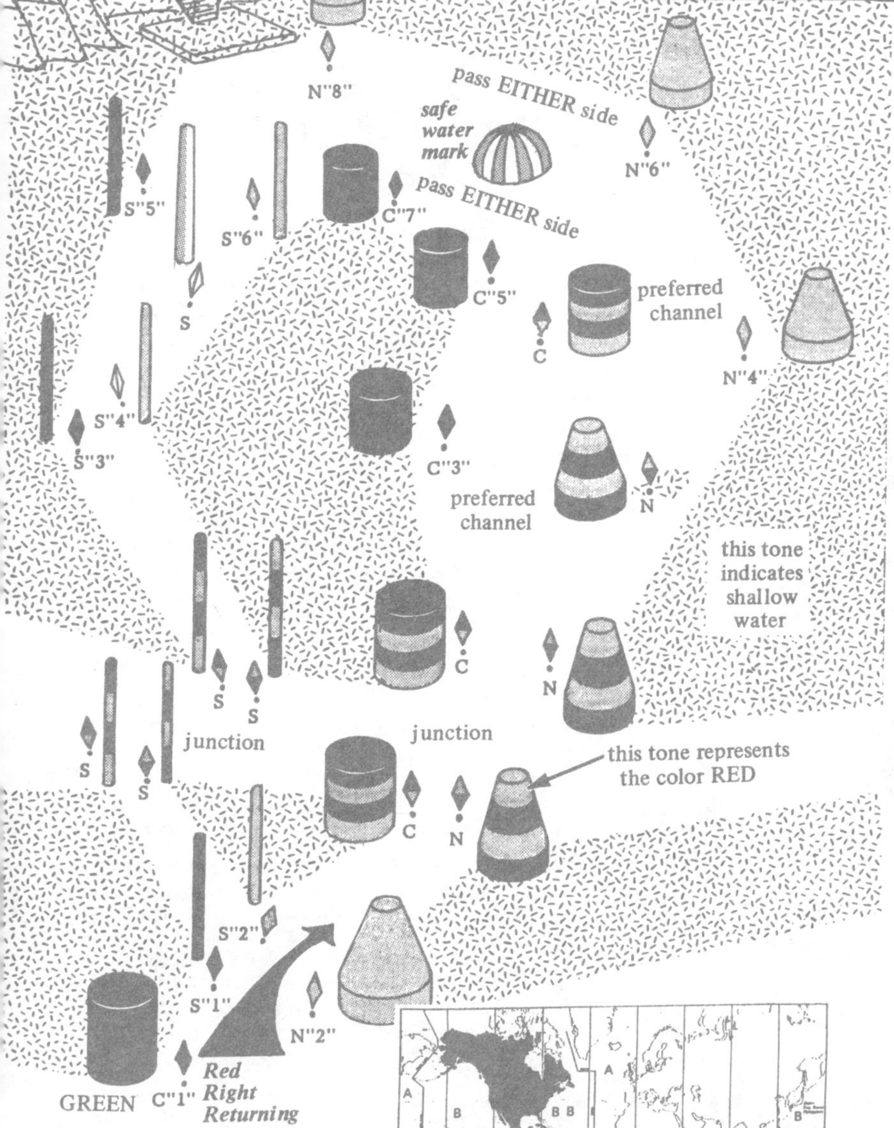

N"8"

pass EITHER side

safe water mark

N"6"

pass EITHER side

S"5"

S"6"

C"7"

S

C"5"

C

preferred channel

N"4"

S"4"

S"3"

C"3"

preferred channel

N

this tone indicates shallow water

S

S

C

N

junction

junction

S

S

this tone represents the color RED

C

N

S"2"

S"1"

N"2"

GREEN C"1"

Red Right Returning

Powerboating Illustrated

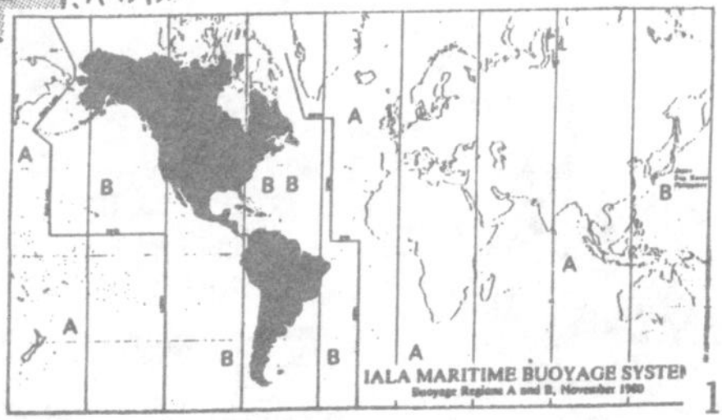

All black buoys will be changed to green by 1989.

A B B B A B A A B B A B

IALA MARITIME BUOYAGE SYSTEM

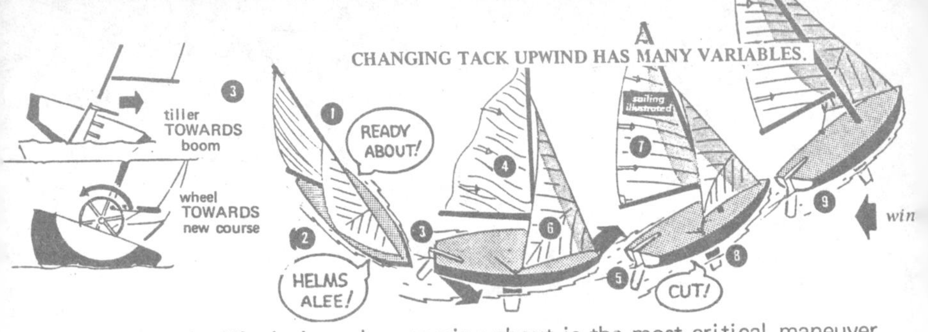

● **Backing the jib** timing when coming about is the most critical maneuver to be mastered for sailing upwind thru tight moorings. It is very simple but the most difficult idea to teach having no precedent in other fields.

After backing is mastered, sailing your boat thru tight moorings with every sense working to its optimum, provides much satisfaction. The slightest wind and/or weight change means being able to sail above, or go under the stern of sailboats and powerboats moored or at anchor.

The art of backing is complex when comparing various hulls as bow entry, beam, weight, inertia, and bottom growth become involved.

● **Cutaway forefoot** on our 24′ sailboat & Catalina 30, permits both to come about in little more than their own lengths. And if everything goes wrong, make a 180 degree turn to come out of a bad situation on a reverse course.

The Lido 14 with high aspect underwater blades, needs the jib backed in light and strong winds to be underway before losing steerageway.

● **Inertia.** Backing due to weight becomes an over-correction on *Iris,* Catalina 38, and similar hulls in normal operation,and to our surprise,the C 15. The underrigged 40′ Newporter ketch needs backing continually to maneuver in tight moorings.

● **Long keels.** We found the Thistle required the jib to be backed in all winds to come about efficiently, to be underway on the new tack with sails pulling.

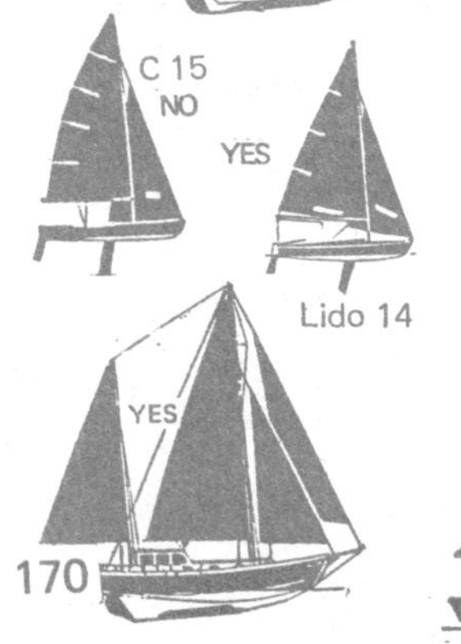

The owner of 48′ *Taku* said his long keel ketch could only comes about with engine on. The next day with five Navy Sailing Association friends aboard, we sailed for 8 hours continually backing the jib to come about successfully every time.

The helmsman had a difficult time adapting to the idea that after coming about, *Taku* was on the new tack under control with sails pulling a a full minute before it started moving.

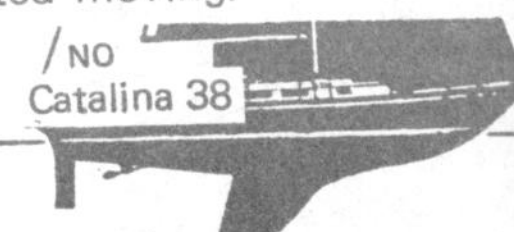

CROWDED MOORINGS

Many harbors have crowded mooring areas providing spirited moments for the unprepared sailor.

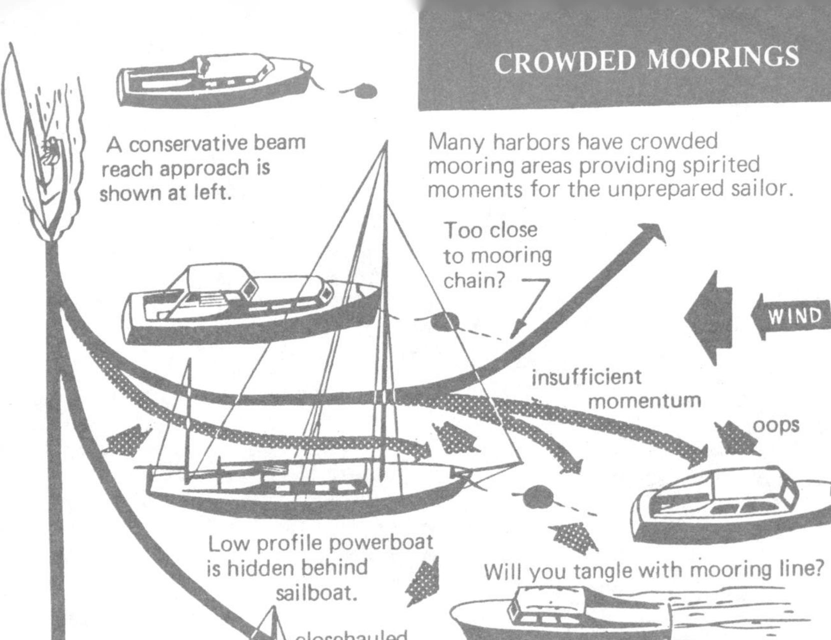

closehauled course

Shooting head to wind for short period with sails luffing for heavier keel boats.

The final part of our sailing lessons was thru tight mooring areas, the exposure providing anxious moments for students.

approaching your mooring now on a closehauled course.

Keel mounted sailboat rudder can slide over a rope mooring line if necessary, but–

Spade rudder? The same mooring line can pop up between the keel and rudder to stop your sailboat.

Watch for stern lines

Large moored powerboats cause much wind disturbance, low profile sailboats, will have minimum disturbance.

Cut jib sheet, then main to reduce speed.

Use air brakes to stop your boat next to pickup float.

pickup ring to mooring

mooring line

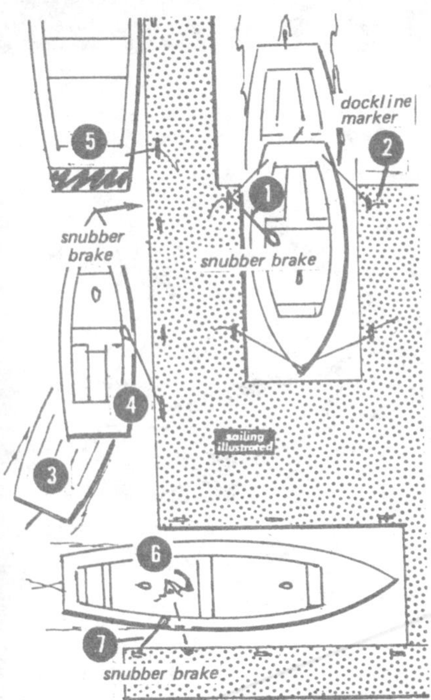

Eliminate many docking problems by—

Dockline markers. Position your boat in its slip with all of the lines adjusted correctly. Use nail polish to mark the location of the dock lines ***coming from the boat*** where the lines first touch their dock cleats.

Sew whipping markers with thread and needle on the nail polish markings. The lines should stay on the same boat and dock cleats so crew members can easily tie your sailboat in its slip even on a stormy dark night.

Dock snubber brake. When your boat is positioned in its slip, splice an eye long enough to loop over and around the dock entrance cleat.

Then splice an eye on the boat end so it will have a snug fit over a cockpit winch or cleat on your sailboat.

The next time your boat makes a landing in its slip, you or a crew member can pick up the open snubber eye, looping it over the cockpit winch or cleat to stop your boat from hitting the end of the slip in a hot landing.

Side tie. A dock snubber brake can stop your boat before the bow hits the varnished stern of the powerboat at upper left. Your crew can then easily position your boat with markers on the docklines for the cleats.

Snubber brake holder. If your cockpit winch or deck cleat is 24 inches or more above the snubber dock cleat, position the snubber brake eye on the end of the pole as shown so the eye is easy to reach.

Rail marker/dock marker. A 67′ motorsailer made a perfect landing in a 70′ slip with no help on the dock. The owner said,"If I am in my normal wheelhouse steering position, and the marker on my boat railing and the dock line up...my boat is correctly positioned in its slip".

Sailboats and powerboats 40′ and longer need the combination dock marker/boat marker to make soft accurate landings...***PLUS a dock snubber brake*** when your landings don't work out as planned.

Mooring problems. Does your boat want to climb up on its mooring can with the banging damaging the hull finish and keeping you awake?Lash a temporary bowsprit or holdoff pole to the bow. Add a stout shock cord to the outer pole end with the other end secured to the mooring can. Pleasant dreams.

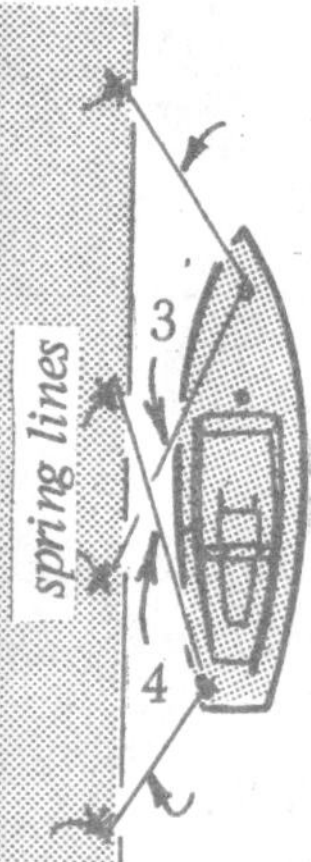

Long, lean, narrow beam, heavy meter sailboat designs usually dominated the racing scene until 1960. The first successful wide beam design to challenge the meter design was ***Finisterre.***

Spring lines. When current or other problems developed, an ***after bow spring,*** and/or ***forward bow spring*** were added. The spring lines reduced fore and aft movement without strapping the narrow beam sailboats to the dock.

Many large sailboats were in our local harbor in 1958 when we moved to Newport Beach. A few of them were the 161' top-masted schooners ***Goodwill*** and ***Pioneer,*** the 71'6" yawl ***Barlovento II,*** the 98' ***Evening Star,*** several 10, 12, and 14 meter sailboats, the 16 meter ***Pursuit,*** the ***Roland von Breeman,*** etc.

Fiberglass hulls. Around 1960 taxes began to skyrocket to subsidize the world and outer space with large sailboats and full-time crews disappearing. The trend changed to shorter, lighter , and beamier sailboats made of fiberglass.

Middle-class people,for the first time with a little money in the bank,could afford sailing. Professional deck hands disappeared with more owners doing their own maintenance.

Wide beam, lighter fiberglass sailboats. After operating and teaching on heavy, narrow meter craft with endless inertia for coming about, it proved hazardous on the new sailboats. ***Backing the jib*** became standard procedure for coming about with maneuverability becoming a pleasant surprise.

Docking. The bow and stern lines for narrow meter-type hulls made wide beam sailboats difficult to board except amidship.Our sailboat proved an excellent example, pg.63, for this new problem.

Midship cleats were added for ***midship dock lines (spring lines?)*** to pull the stern to the dock for boarding, or the bow to the dock for other reasons.

Three sets of docklines. Our little, wide beam, 24' sailboat often uses three sets of docklines, with the fore and stern dock lines staying on their boat cleats when leaving the dock, with the midship docklines usually removed. The six docklines helped our students learn to leave, and dock in many unusual situations, especially if their boats had awkward docks.

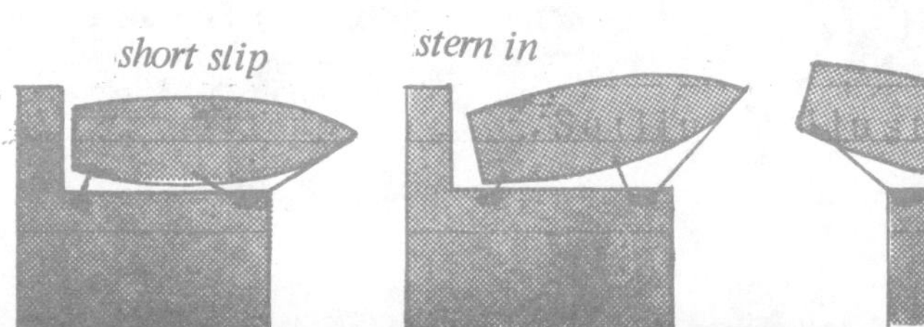

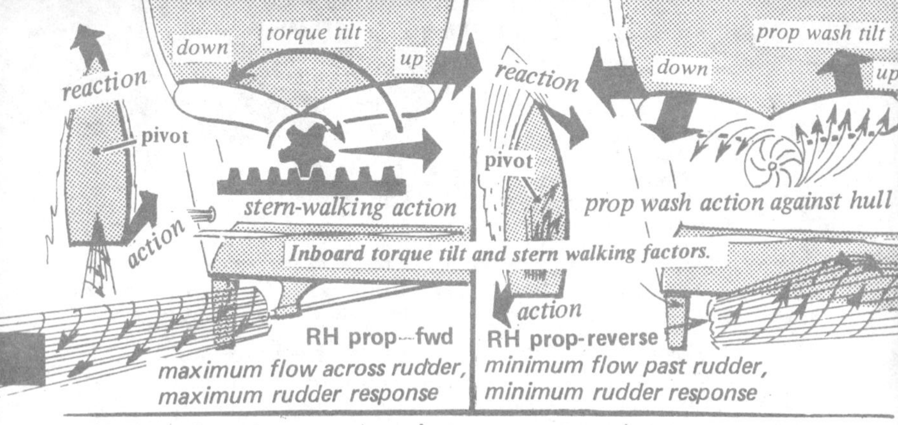

Single-engine powerboat. While an auto tracks straight ahead with the steering wheel straight ahead, powerboating steering factors are quite different, especially when accelerating.

Accelerating forward. Prop blast passes rudder flowing aft of transom. *Thrust action* is maximum, the difference between prop thrust and hull speed. *Stern walks to right.* Torque reaction lifts right or starboard side of boat... with the bow turning the other way to port.

Reverse acceleration. *Rudder neutralized.* Rotary prop thrust blasts upward against right side the *lifting hull action,* pushing port or left side down. The *depressed port hull reaction* pulls stern to port, bow to starboard.

Stern action is normally stressed. While it is the action, the *reaction* is just as important pulling the bow the opposite direction.

Sailboat steers with rudder. Outboard motor in our sailboat with RH prop, is locked in position so it won't turn. It follows stern-walking acceleration pattern shown above.

Single screw prop has maneuvering problems leaving dock in adverse conditions requiring spring, bow, or stern pivots.

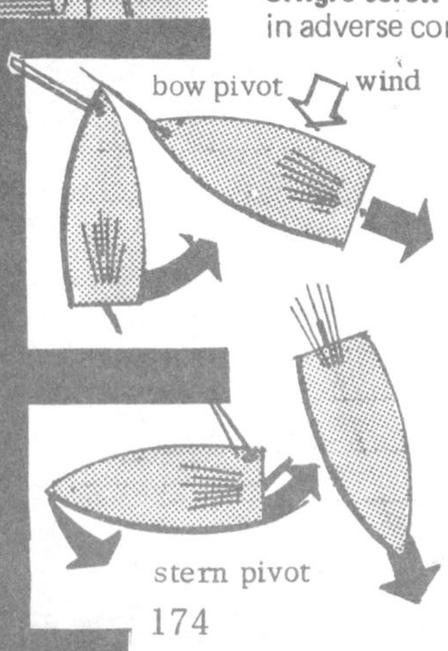

Bow pivot– *rudder over, prop reverse.* Boat pivots out from dock on bow line. When boat has steerage way far enough from dock, bow line is slipped and taken in. *Warning*– does bow line have a knot on the dock end to hang up on the cleat?

Off-center stern pivot– *rudder over, prop reverse.* Stern pivots around dock until clear, then pull in stern line without wrapping around prop. Forward spurts are used to clear dock. *With wind on beam*– let it blow bow out, slip stern line, apply throttle.

PROP TORQUE IDEAS

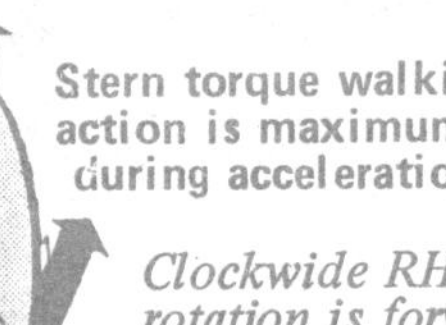
Stern torque walking action is maximum during acceleration.

Clockwide RH prop rotation is forward

Stern walking is shown during acceleration in fwd.

boat going forward
rudder in center
prop in reverse

Normal port side docking method.

boat is backing
rudder in center
prop in forward

Stern may swing to starboard if it isn't affected by wind or current.

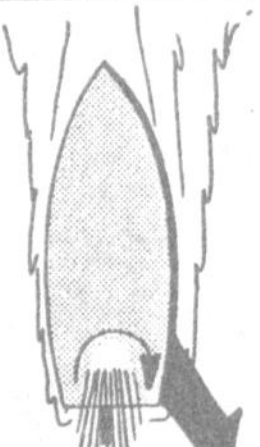

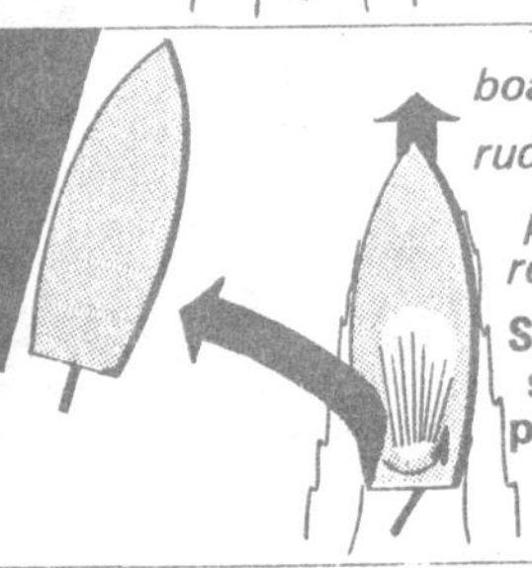
boat going fwd
rudder to port
prop in reverse

Stern pulls to stbd then pulls rapidly to port.

boat is backing
rudder to port
prop in forward

Stern swings to stbd rapidly bow may hit dock.

Approach slowly with less angle to dock.

boat going fwd
prop reverse

Stern to port, straighten out with short bursts of forward throttle.

boat is backing
prop in forward then reverse

Stern rapidly turns to port. Will bow hit the dock?

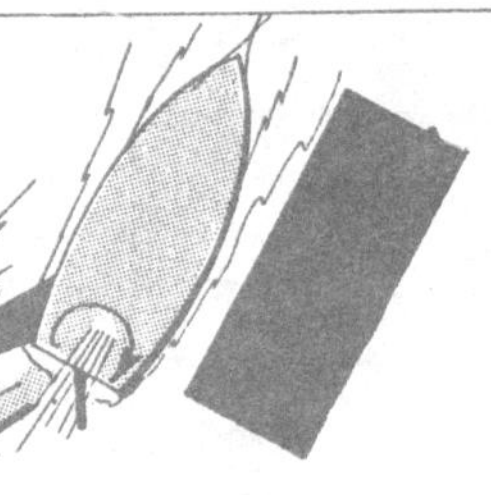

boat is backing
prop in reverse

Stern walks rapidly to port as bow swings rapidly to starboard.

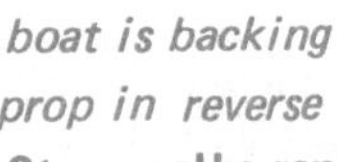

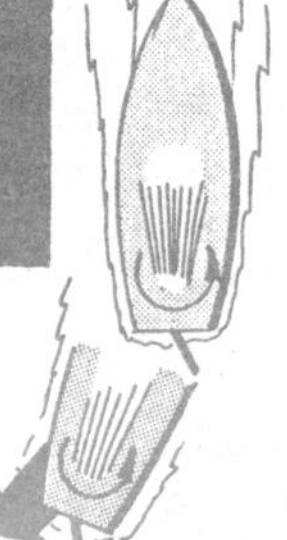

Powerboating Illustrated

boat is backing
rudder to starboard
prop in reverse

Stern turns slowly to port.

Examples are exaggerated to show the peculiar action of prop torque.

Sailing Illustrated

Also see page 266.

Over four years were needed to wear down the neurological complications, waking up depressed, the mind going one way, the body the other way. It was the miserable effects of the 30-40% COHb level, while a 40-50% COHb level of poisoning might cause irreversible changes.

Physicians today question the duration of the four year nervous system upset, indicating complex side problems may also have been involved that may be diagnosed today, but not in the mid 1960s.

100% oxygen CO poison treatment. Victim needs a tight-fitting, non-rebreathing mask to take the COHb level below 5% while monitoring heart patients closely.

AVOID smoking on gasoline-powered boats. It dulls your smelling sensitivity of smoker and nonsmokers nearby in the cockpit and below.

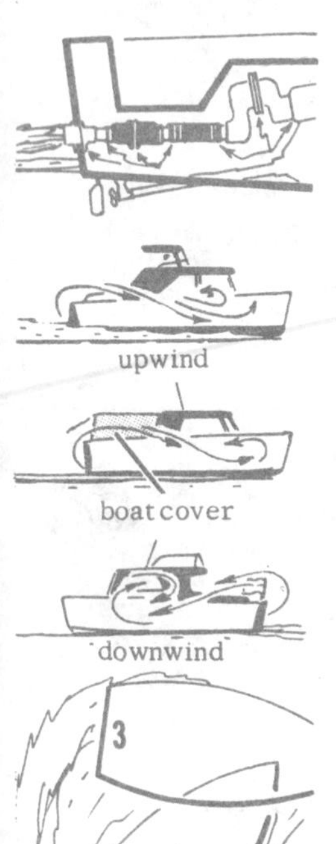

CO fumes may be found on most gasoline powered boats underway. Hull contours topside, below, and outside, can play all kinds of tricks. Avoid buying powerboats with inside controls, and stay topside in the cockpit when underway.

Develop an alertness to that ***sweet, sickly exhaust smell.*** Engine exhaust can be pulled over the transom into the cockpit, some more than others going upwind, and others downwind. Awareness is self protection as much of the time it may be weak, probably less than we face daily in our autos.

Reverse the flow. A new flying-bridge cruiser was sucking fumes into cabin below. I warned the owners wife of the problem that boat would always have. open a window or hatch below. The air flow would eliminate the CO trap potentials.

Periodic inspection is important. Check all exhaust system clamps, hoses, and manifolds. Replace any part showing potential failure before it fails.

Trolling downwind under power is an efficient way to pull CO fumes into the cockpit and cabin.

Boat covers? USCG boarded a pilotless boat going in circles with one of seven passengers still conscious. A boat cover pulled in and trapped exhaust fumes.

Mild to moderate CO poisoning contributes to accidents reducing the thinking process.A woman partially overcome on the boat at left with inside controls, fell overboard when a door opened.

The operator should have turned the bow towards her as shown. He turned the wrong way with his CO exposure. She was killed by the prop blades.

Lower hp gasoline and diesel inboard engines designed for sailboat displacement operation, may operate almost troublefree for many years if adequately maintained and understood.

The gasoline engine was standard on older sailboats, has been replaced by the diesel engine in recent years, also page 126 of our *Guide*.

- **Compression isn't critical** in 10 to 40 hp engines permitting them to operate on lower octane fuel than many autos. Most problems of diesel and gasoline engines are minimum and/or sporadic operation, then long periods of full throttle during the summer vacation.
- **The iron block develops a considerable heat buildup.** *Before putting under load,* idle the engine to begin heat buildup. .. then ***afterwards*** idle the engine to release excess heat.
- **Aluminum vs iron.** Aluminum outboard motors can be put under full throttle when cold. They can be turned off after full throttle operation without damage as aluminum releases heat 5 times more easily than iron. if this practice is followed with iron inboard engines, uneven heating can cause distortion of head and block with expensive repairs.
- **A Jaguar mechanic** was invited to examine his customers 40' sailboat. He replaced the 120 degree thermostat with a 180 degree thermostat, with the owner soon selling the boat. I was operating it when turning on the engine for heavy Long Beach commercial traffic. In less than a minute engine temperature zoomed, having to sail the boat into its dock. An expensive overhaul was required to remove the boiler scale.
- **A maximum 140 degree thermostat** is required to operate engines with outside cooling water. This provides sufficient heat for operation to permit minerals and salts to stay in suspension and be exhausted overboard to avoid boiler scale limestone deposits.
- **Lubricating oil changes are critical** for colder operating engines to remove sludge and sulfuric acid contaminants buildup from condensation and gasoline blow-by. Higher auto engine operating temperatures at freeway speeds burn off much of these contaminants.
- **Familiarity** is the best advice for owners of gasoline and diesel inboard engines by obtaining the operational manual, parts catalog, and any other information on your engine. Painting the names on the parts and adding direction arrows on hoses with nail polish is a good idea. Add tags to electrical leads for rapid identification. Keep the engine and its compartment clean as possible to avoid oil vapor deposit buildup.

housing

the stainless hose clamp

- **Stainless hose clamps** often have corrosion problems due to mixing of different stainless grades. Look for "300 all stainless" which includes the clamp, housing, and locking screw.
- **Use double hose clamps** on all hose ends in your boat as both clamps seldom fail at the same time– check clamps periodically.

Many more outboard motors are used on sailboats under 30′ long, than inboard engines...we've owned 15 or 16 of these 2 cycle lightweight powerplants. It is the little praised workhorse of the world from cold Arctic, to steaming jungle backwaters of the Nile and Amazon Rivers.

- **Transom mounting** with long shaft motors do a good job except for the noise...which won't work on sailboats with reverse transoms.

- **Brackets aft of the transom** for outboard motors may be excellent for protected water operation. If caught in an bad storm and the motor can't be removed, tremendous momentary forces develop on the motor and bracket from a breaking wave which also affects steering. When the stern comes down on a wave, water can be forced up into the powerhead with damaging corrosive salt spray.

- **Engine compartment.** Our 24′ sailboat has this type installation for our 7½ hp ''aluminum spinnaker''. It uses remote controls with adequate heavy weather protection which considerably reduces engine noise. The disadvantage, considerable effort is required for instllation.

  A form fitted plate bolted to the top of the motor well seals the engine compartment from the ocean. We wish outboard manufacturers could provide templates outlining this shape for lower hp motors at this intersection to help others wanting to make similar quieter installations.

- **Hand-cranked motors.** We prefer them for operation in closed compartments following USCG ventilation requirements. If a 12V battery was used, lower unit corrosion potentials would increase due to current leakage out the lower unit not able to tilt out of the water.

- **Lower unit protection.** Since the motor can't be tilted out of the water, it should come out of its compartment three times yearly for zinc paint then two coats of non-corrosive TBTO bottom paint to retard weed and barnacle growth. For environmentalists wanting to ban the paint from boats, oyster beds aren't grown in marinas. ***AVOID copper bottom paint on outboard lower units as the copper rapidly corrodes aluminum.***

- **Portable fuel tanks** require one or two coats yearly of paint with high zinc content for corrosion protection, especially on the lower lip.

- **Ventilation** is required for the tank bottom surface to minimize condensation corrosion potentials. The tanks must be fully restrained during a knockdown. They must be mounted in a wooden frame on all four sides, with a strong shock cord over the top.

- **Boiler scale is a hazard** for 2 cycle and 4 cycle engines operating in salt AND many fresh water areas ***if they use a continuous flow of outside cooling water.***

  We prefer cold operating outboard motors without thermostats. The reason, in over 30 years and 15 or more outboard motors we have never had boiler scale problems. ***P.S. Replace 2 cycle waterpumps yearly*** which also helps to eliminate boiler scale problems.

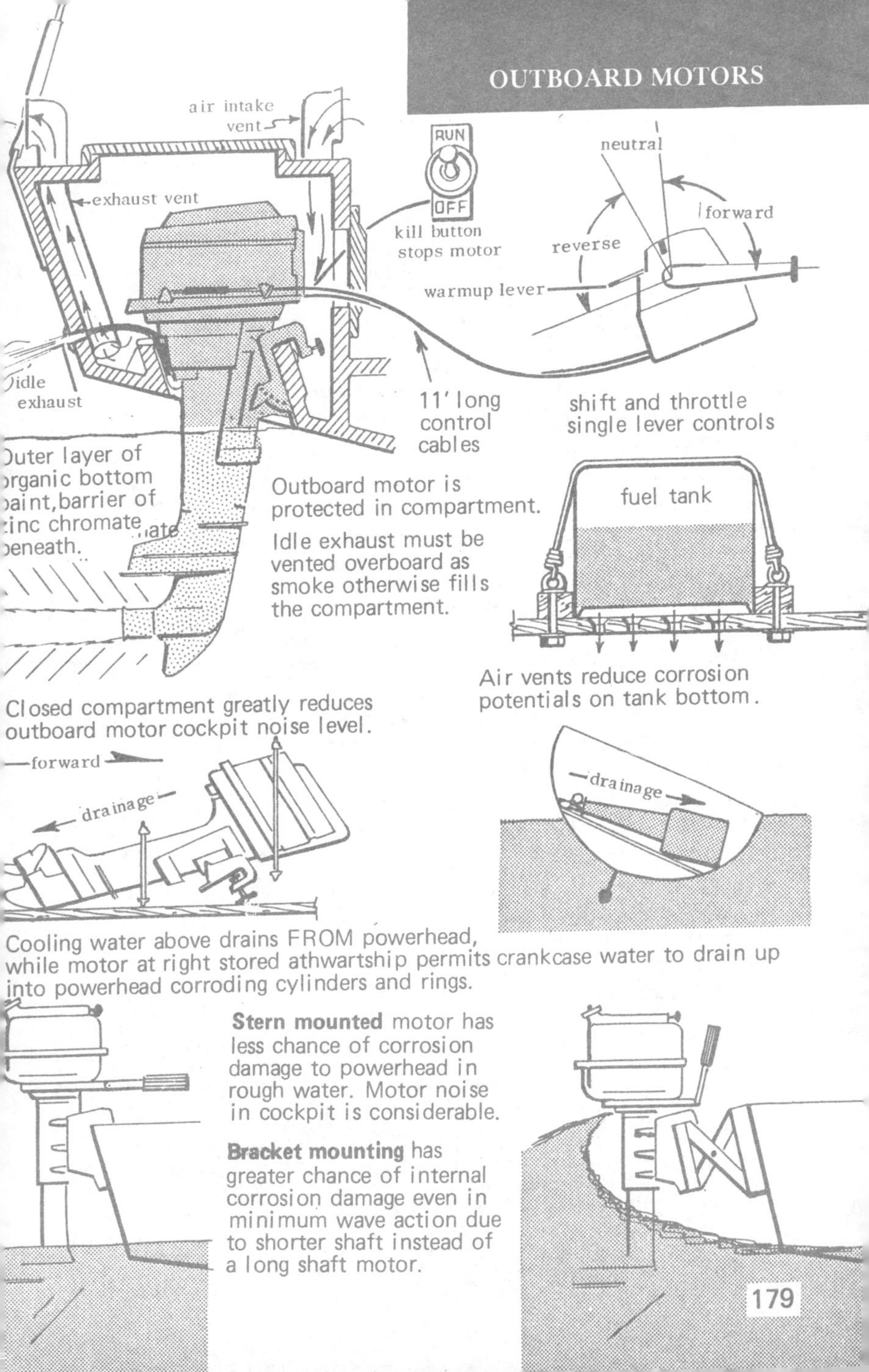

uter layer of rganic bottom aint,barrier of inc chromate eneath.

Outboard motor is protected in compartment.

Idle exhaust must be vented overboard as smoke otherwise fills the compartment.

Air vents reduce corrosion potentials on tank bottom.

Closed compartment greatly reduces outboard motor cockpit noise level.

Cooling water above drains FROM powerhead, while motor at right stored athwartship permits crankcase water to drain up into powerhead corroding cylinders and rings.

Stern mounted motor has less chance of corrosion damage to powerhead in rough water. Motor noise in cockpit is considerable.

Bracket mounting has greater chance of internal corrosion damage even in minimum wave action due to shorter shaft instead of a long shaft motor.

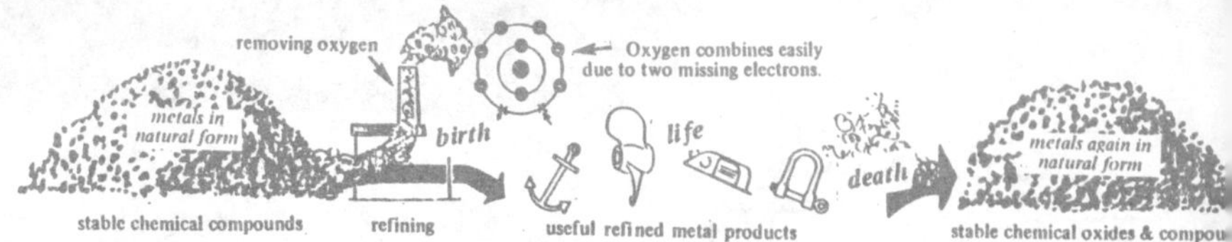

HEMATITE (red iron-oxide ore) ...becomes pig iron...changes to iron,steel compounds & alloys...corrodes to a brown powder (iron oxide)

BAUXITE is refined to Alumina (aluminum oxide)..to become aluminum compounds and alloys...corrodes to a white powder (aluminum oxide)

Seagoing metals have a complex, interesting history. They begin as stable oxides in nature then shipped to the smelter. They oxygen is removed or cooked out, the raw products then refined into temporary alloys or compounds for our seagoing use. Your responsibility is to choose stable, quite expensive refined metals having varied methods of corrosion protection to extend their useful ocean lifespan...before they corrode to more stable oxides no longer of use to sailors.

- **Wrought iron** has considerable protection with many centuries of use. This black metal is still used for large dock cleats, bollards, and large fittings for commercial vessesl, and earlier, for stagecoaches.
- **Carbon steel** is a product of molten iron with carbon added. It is a strong, hard, brittle metal excellent for endless varieties of tools such as drills, bits, screwdrivers, etc. ***They need continuous protection*** or rapid corriosion results in the salt water environment. ***AVOID*** carbon steel parts for sailboat use due to rapid corrosion. Bolts, screws, parts, etc., with rust stains rapidly expand against each other as they corrode.
- **Stainless steel** covers various steel alloys with minimum rust potentials. Stainless is a pretty topside metal ***requiring a continuous oxygen flow.*** This flow allows the protective chromium ions to surface and corrode at a programmed rate,protecting stainless with minimum rust stains.

  The advantage of stainless– failure potentials become obvious with stress cracks, while a broken wire strand on halyards, stays, or shrouds called **fish hooks,** reduce its breaking strength 10 to 20 %.
- **Shroud rollers** require a larger diameter than the shroud wire for a continuous, protective oxygen flow. If water pockets develop when taping stainless turnbuckles...or a small shroud area, chromium ions may panic flowing to the area,expediting local ***crevice corrosion.***
- **Stainless steel lifelines.** They are sealed in vinyl their full length. This pacifys and balances the chromium ions until a break occurs in the vinyl cover to which chromium ions flow to produce rapid ***crevice corrosion.***

  Distilled water is used to remove hygroscopic salts. Dry, then seal the break to stop corrosion by making the chromium ions happy again.
- **AVOID stainless underwater fittings in the water for extended periods as minimum oxygen content variables cause stainless corrosion.** Limit underwater fittings to the bronze family. If you inherited an oil well, consider titanium for such use. It is an element without an ion exchange which won't act nor react on itself nor surrounding metals. Salt water metal education is one that will last a lifteime for ocean sailors...with unexpected surprises, expected.

- **Bronze compounds** have a 5000 year history. They begin with copper and tin to which alloys are added for corrosion protection. *Oxygen is the enemy, and friend of bronze.* Bronze corrodes with dirty face oxides which are removed by polishing. Tape bronze turnbuckles to extend their useful life. Bronze is an excellent underwater metal due to minimum oxygen content in the water.

  The bronze family ranges from red to yellow/red color. The more expensive the bronze part...the more corrosion steps that are involved sometimes as much as seven, before metal fatigue or failure occurs.

- **Brass, a compound**— is a confusing term often used in marine hardware stores, which means the bronze family. English naval brass is a traditional term for an excellent, corrosion-resistant bronze compound.

- **Brass, a mixture** of copper and zinc, is a bright yellow metal excellent for the protected home environment sold in home improvement stores. The copper/zinc brass fitting topside *rapidly dezincs* leaving a weak, spongy, salmon-colored part due to ocean hygroscopic salts.

  You can fully seal a copper/zinc screw in a topside deck, or bulkhead below, which can rapidly dezinc and fail due to electrolytic action of resins in the wood, while a bronze screw in the same location may have an indefinite lifespan with full strength for a higher price. We face a brass/bronze terminology problem which needs more publicity.

- **Aluminum** is a product started by the aircraft industry with advantages and pitfalls. Bolts or parts designed for aircraft may corrode rapidly on a boat, an environment for which they weren't designed.

- **Anodizing** is an electrolytic process of controlled corrosion to develop a hard, outer oxide layer, to seal and protect the metal beneath. When a lightly anodized surface is exposed due to chafe, *the white powder rust corrosion* is often mistaken for ocean salts. **Heavy black anodizing** for aluminum masts, blocks, winches, etc., provides the best protection from chafe...the major enemy of our seagoing aluminum.

- **Zinc is our waster metal friend.** requiring understanding for maximum protection. Zinc corrodes or self destructs while protecting surrounding metals. If a zinc anode corrodes rapidly, *replace with a same size OR smaller zinc anode* until you find the problem. A larger zinc may reverse the process to corrode surrounding metals. *DON'T paint zinc anodes* as bottom paint seals and neutralizes any zinc protection.

- **An introduction to metals** is all we provide on these two pages of six metal families. Considerable differences occur with corrosion protection and resistance within each family, which can be improved or the corrosion rate escalated when mixing the various metal families...for which you have to become your own expert. More information in depth will be found on pages 128 to 134 of our *Homestudy Guide* which is probably the most complex and least reported field faced by sailors.

Sailors use a variety of organic and synthetic products which will be the best, or worst of both worlds...or a compromise between.

- **Canvas and flax sails are heavy.** They are made of organic materials requiring the best of care for a relatively short life. We use a variety of synthetic sailing cloth today having a different enemy.
- **UV ray cloth resistance?** Dacron sails never covered in the tropics for six or more months, will need replacement due to UV ray age hardening. If cared for and covered when not in use, they may provide two or more years continuous use in tropic areas with much sunlight. They may have ten years of weekend use if they have periodic restitching.

Stitching thread fails first, then the cloth becomes tired and easy to rip...**replace sails before you can stick a finger thru tired sail cloth.**

- **Fitted sail cover** is required for a mainsail not in use stored on the boom. An Acrilan cover may begin to fail in our area after 3 years of sun exposure. A fitted sail cover with an Acrylic sunscreen will be fade resistant, stronger, and shower proof. It has a longer life allowing the covered sail to breathe, a good way to resist mildew stains.
- **Furling jibs are prone to early UV failure.** Sew an Acrylic strip to the jib foot and leach to provide a wrap-around sunscreen to protect the furled jib...***will it have a locking device to avoid unfurling in a storm?***
- **Cruising sails**—chafe is a major factor to consider. Eliminate sail roaches and battens on new sails to avoid a major cause of sail failure. Vertical cut mainsails and jibs may have longer life expectancy.
- **Wood** was used for boatbuilding before recorded history. When a tree is cut down the 20% moisture is a hazard as it tries to decompose the wood to return its organic chemicals back to nature. *Air drying* is the method to stabilize the wood reducing moisture content to 15% so rot is minimized. Wood use and protection is a highly complex subject with many variables, read pages 137 to 143 in our ***Homestudy Guide.***
- **Battle of wood vs fiberglass.** Tempest, 5.5 meter, and Soling classes provided interesting moments in the 1960's...as wooden hulls were more competitive. Wood is lighter, has less flexing, and more strength; disadvantage; continuous air flow is required to prevent rot. Fiberglass hulls were heavier, and due to flexing weren't as competitive. Their advantage; organic deteoriation was eliminated reducing maintenance.
- **Lightning 8383** *Black Magic* was the first perfect boat I sailed. The hull was made of balsa blocks in a fiberglass sandwich combining the best of both worlds as it was light and rigid. Though it was my first time on a Lightning, I was ambushed by the Mission Bay Lightning fleet.

I started in the rear of the fleet. After beating a mile upwind to the first mark the west coast fleet champ in his heavier wooden boat was 4 lengths aft, and 3 to leeward. The secret, I didn't touch the tiller letting the boat head up in a puff and drop off as the force 4 wind eased. This quickness confused the other owners, and the harder they tried with a heavy hand, the farther they dropped behind. It was a crazy incident to prove the importance of a light tiller touch.

- **Hemp** was grown near early American and British shipyards. The organic rope was used for standing rigging, and two miles of running rigging on our *USS Constitution.* During periods of high humidity and rain... *the diameter of hemp rope increased and the length shortened* on standing and running rigging. Diameter of the hemp rope shrunk while it became longer in dry sunny weather requiring compensation with running rigging.
- **Manila**, an organic rope, was introduced to the U.S. around 1860, a relative of the banana tree. *Manila had half the stretch of hemp, with similar strength.* Our first sailboat in the late 1940's had manila sheets, halyards, and anchor line that chafed easily. As the oil in the rope disappeared, it became weak and limp, deteriorating rapidly.
- **Manila halyards** must be hardened in dry weather. They must be eased in rain and high humidity conditions to avoid strains on masts, winches, and cleats on older traditional sailboats found worldwide.
- **Manila anchor line** must be thoroughly dried, coiled, and stored in a locker with air flow after use in fresh water. After salt water use it had to be washed off with fresh water to remove the *hygroscopic* (water seeking) *salts* and dried to avoid moisture inside the yarns and strands to avoid rot. The advantage of manila rope today is to provide a salty decore for bars and restaurants.
- **Nylon rope vs UV rays.** Three-strand nylon anchor lines and dock lines will age harden and become brittle due to continuous exposure to the sun. While we've seen imported nylon rope fibers harden and begin breaking in three years, quality American and British nylon rope lasts much longer, and keeps improving. Nylon anchor line will last longer if the only part exposed is from the hull to the water using three-strand line, when at anchor.
- **Wool is our organic friend** according to survival expert George Siglar, pages 224-5. The greatest heat loss areas of the body are extremities such as head, hands, and feet in survival conditions. A woolen cap is the best way to protect the head. Use woolen socks and gloves.

  Even when wet wool fibers will retain 70% to 80% of your body heat. Wool dries more rapidly in open air than cotton or synthetics; it is more resistant to wear and doesn't deteriorate as fast as cotton.
- **Synthetic and cotton** fibers are excellent for sports clothing as they release body heat in competitive conditions...not survival conditions.
- **Sun screen** for sunburn protection found Zinc Oxide chosen for the nose and cheeks. Their beards grew rapidly with hats and sunglasses protecting all but the nose requiring continuous Zinc Oxide use.

The fascinating competition of synthetic and organic products, and their combinations are endless. Take time to understand their weaknesses and strengths, then help them do their jobs to the best of their abilities. It is amazing the endless numbers of excellent products that have been introduced to help the sailing public in the last 32 years.

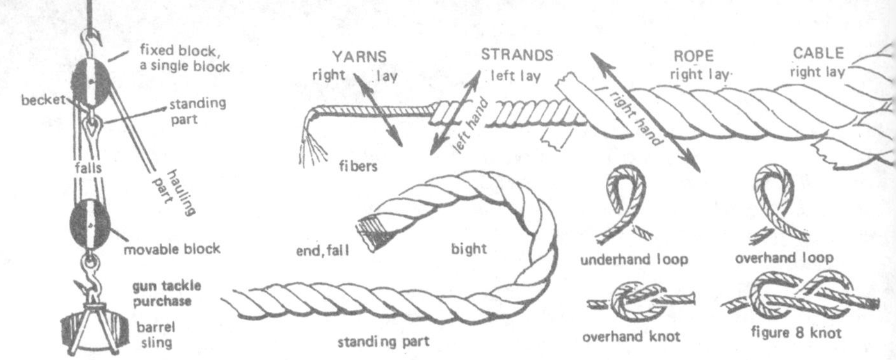

● **Rope vs line**—expect variables. Our USN seamen refer to **rope** as wire rope and **line** as fiber rope. It becomes more complex with the sailing fraternity defining rope as raw material...**which becomes line when cut for specific use in boat operation.** This includes anchor line, standing, and running rigging.

Rope used to secure an object, or the sail bolt rope is still called rope.The **traditional square rigger ropes** were foot ropes, yard ropes, bell ropes, bucket ropes, back ropes, top ropes, tiller ropes, and man ropes.

● **Three-strand twisted rope** is always under its own tension, use ***medium lay only.*** This tension results from the alternate twisting of the individual fibers, yarns, and strands shown above to increase the internal friction of the various elements of the rope working together.

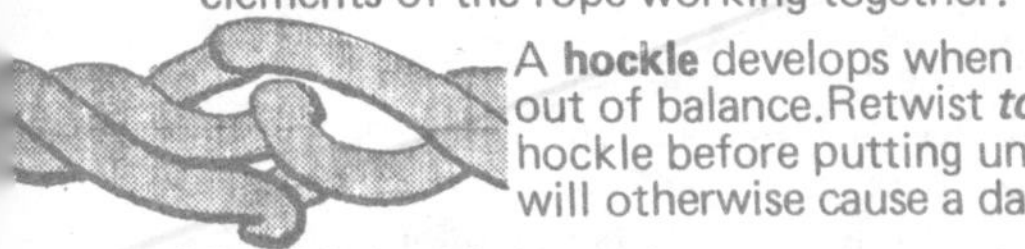

A **hockle** develops when the three rope strands are twisted out of balance.Retwist ***to unkink*** to eliminate the three-strand hockle before putting under load. The overstressed fibers will otherwise cause a dangerous defect in a sound line.

● **Double-braided rope** is not under tension with itself. It is a rope within a rope with a ***hollow-braided cover*** over a ***hollow-braided core.*** It is held together by the natural geometry of the interlocking cover and core sharing the load equally.

This interlocking method produces a softer and more flexible rope with less elongation and greater strength. Built-in variables can however result if the cover is made to provide extreme abrasion resistance...with the high strength core carrying 90% of the load.

Double-braided rope not under tension with itself ***does not have a memory.*** This lack of memory makes it excellent for heaving line use page 194, and for easy anchor line stowage free of kinks, page 186.

● **Lever's Young Sea Officers Sheet Anchor.** It is an exact reprint of the original 1819 book of knots, splicing, gaskets, blocks, how to make rope, plus how to fully rig and sail square riggers of that era. This book is excellently illustrated, that present for a special friend, or yourself. *Edward W. Sweetman Co., Box 1631, Valdosta, GA 31603.*

● **The Art of Knotting and Splicing**—Cyrus Day. It is an excellent, thorough photographic book of 3 strand knots and knotting. *Naval Institute Press*.*

● **The Junks & Sampans of the Yangtze**—G.R.G. Worcester. This is the only authoritative book of Chinese sailing technology requiring 30 years research and 7 years to produce. The 3000 year history covers evolution of their sailing craft, rope and sail making,etc., with references on our pages 17,278 to 281. Can you donate it to your public library or yacht club library? *Naval Institute Press, *United States Naval Institute, Annapolis, MD 21402. (301) 268-6110*

Breaking strength table is for new rope in laboratory test conditions.

diameter	mm-metric	traditional 3 strand manila	impact absorption—controlled stretch 3 strand nylon	impact absorption—controlled stretch braided Gold-N-Braid	minimum stretch—for control lines 3 strand Dacron & polypro	minimum stretch—for control lines braided Yacht Braid	galvanized chain
1/4	6	600	1850	2100	1750	2300	2700
5/16	8	1000	2850	3500	2650	3450	3700
3/8	9	1350	4000	4800	3600	4950	4600
7/16	10½	1750	5500	6500	4800	6600	6200
1/2	12	2650	7100	8300	6100	8600	8200
9/16	14	3400	8350	11200	7400	11700	10200
5/8	16	4400	10500	14500	9000	15200	12500
3/4	18	5400	14200	18000	12500	19100	17700
7/8	22	7700	19000	26500	16000	28300	24000
1	24	9000	24600	31300	20000	33600	31000

Braided rope specifications are provided by *Samson Ocean Systems, Inc.*
Expect many variables with 3-strand rope specifications.

- **Marine rope** is the term commonly used by dealers, while sailors use the term **marlinspike seamanship.** It is the mark of an able seaman to care for, handle, plus being able to splice a variety of kinds and sizes of ropes.

- **Rope strength tables** list new rope being tested under laboratory conditions. American tables list the ***average tension*** which rope may break at any given point exclusive of damage from chafe, sharp edges, etc. European tables list the rope **minimum tension** breaking strength. **Chain breaking strength** tables follow identical American and European reporting methods.

- **Safe working load.** It is computed with a safety factor of **20% or 5 to 1,** providing maximum security where life and property are involved. A rope for example with a normal working load of 2000 pounds without chafe, should require a ratio on the table above of 10,000 or more pounds.This large safety factor ratio is recommended for unusual conditions for your boat with extreme wind and wave action, sudden jerks and strains, etc.

Splices and knots reduce rope strength.

eye splice with thimble	*95%*
long splice	*90%*
short splice	*85%*
two half hitches	*65%*
fisherman's bend	*65%*
fisherman's knot	*65%*
bowline	*60%*
carrick bend	*55%*
sheet bend	*55%*
square knot	*50%*
figure-eight knot	*45%*
overhand knot	*45%*

- **Friction** between the fibers is the force holding a knot together.This decreases with slippery synthetic fibers...and increases with rougher, coarser manila organic fibers.

  Complex friction stresses are involved with rope knot strength, which will decrease rapidly when knots are used repeatedly in the same area.

- **Rope failure.** The standing part is the major culprit where maximum stress is put on rope fibers entering the knot.

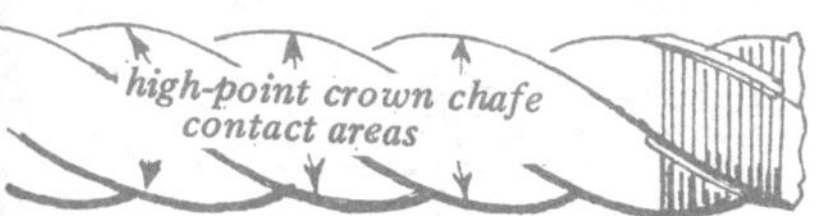

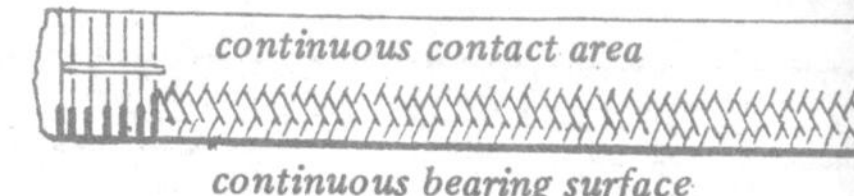

Enjoy the strong opinions for and against organic and synthetic rope variables. sailors gain thru experience. Some of our ideas are...

Three-strand rope is easier to splice, yet the energy absorption and elasticity may be excessive and questionable. While rapid chafe of three-strand anchor line crowns mean little for a weekend sailor...the active long-distance cruiser should only use chain where the anchor line touches the bottom.

- **Minimum bearing surface contact areas.** We tested the chafe resistance of three-strand, and braided anchor lines in 1965, fore and aft in a rough anchor anchorage with maximum tidal ranges.We had to leave on the 4th day as the boat movement was excessive. Rocks and barnacles had cut numerous high point crowns with a strength reduction on the three-strand anchor line.
- **Continuous bearing surface contact areas.** The same diameter braided line showed wear. No broken threads resulted as the impact area was spread out, rather than being concentrated in a few high point areas.
- **Three-strand nylon anchor line...will keep stretching under load.** After approx. 50% elongation, it may break and the ends snap back.We were in a poor anchorage having to leave when the wind reversed itself. The rubber band stretch in a vicious surge made the three-strand anchor line difficult to take in as I continually wondered...is it 20%, 30%, or 40% longer than normal?

  It takes more time to know if a three-strand anchor line has the anchor dug in properly. Up north a powerboat anchor was caught under a log, the anchor line was three-strand. Tremendous windlass pressure was applied.The anchor suddenly broke loose, flying up thru the window of a flying bridge cruiser, with the window approximately 30' above the water surface.
- **Double-braided tow lines only!** "During an attempt to refloat a grounded cruiser with a nylon towing line...the towing cleat on the cruiser suddenly pulled free and became a lethal projectile under the impetus of the violent recoiling line. The cleat struck a man...Death was instantaneous". This is from *Proceedings of the Merchant Marine Council, May, 1964.*
- **Sheets and halyards.** The continuous bearing surface of double-braided Dacron or polyester is preferred with a 50% better surface area contact with the winch, it is easier on the hands, with minimum elongation for crucial settings.

  After three sets of braided dock lines, we spliced a set of three-strand dock lines. Their performance seemed equal in our short slip.
- The **neutral lay** permits braided anchor lines to be stowed easily **without hitches and/or kinks.** They can be dropped into synthetic sail bags for stowage; add grommets for drainage and ventilation. They can be stored in easy to carry plastic buckets. All braided anchor lines stowed this way should pay out rapidly and easily without problems.

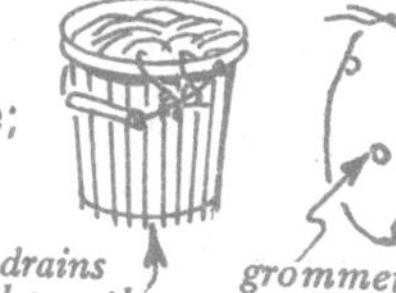

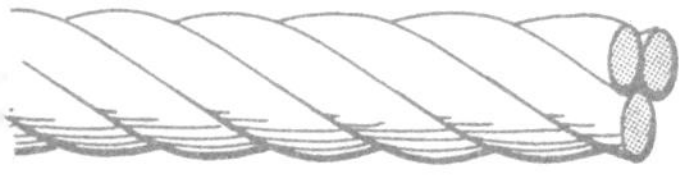

- **Twisted lay three-strand rope.** In the U.S. it has a ***right lay,*** is always under stress with itself, is rotational, and will unwind. Splicing methods using an endless variety of fibers are unchanged in 7000 years.

- **Solid-braided ropes** have small diameters. They aren't hollow as the strands cross and fill the center. They aren't spliceable, resist rotation, and can't hockle.

- **Hollow** or **single-braided ropes** don't have a hole in the center though they have a "void". They have a tendency to flatten in larger diameters as the number of strands increase. They resist rotation, and they can't be hockled.

- **Double-braided rope** consists of a *hollow* braided core inside a *hollow* braided cover, both equally sharing the load in a balanced construction. The result is higher strength and lower elongation than solid, and single-braided rope.
- **Woven construction.** Double-braided ropes are held together by the geometry of their woven, interlocking construction allowing a looser lay (longer helix angle).
- **Visual safety check** is easy with double-braided rope. The cover should wear evenly along its length, protecting the inner core.
- **Continuous bearing surface** with over 50% more surface grip than the same diameter three-strand, provides a better winch grip for youngsters and the first mate.
- **It is always flexible** whether double-braid rope is new,old, dry, or wet. And who enjoys cold weather frozen rope sailing?
- **Splicing is easy** though a new skill with 35 basic steps required in the correct sequence.

size	threads	circumference	diameter
3	6 fine	9/16"	3/16"
4	6	3/4"	1/4"
5	9	1"	5/16"
6	12	1 1/8"	3/8"
7	15	1 1/4"	7/16"
8	21	1 1/2"	1/2"
10	27	2"	5/8"
12	33	2 1/4"	3/4"
14	–	2 3/4"	7/8"

Rope diameters are actual size.

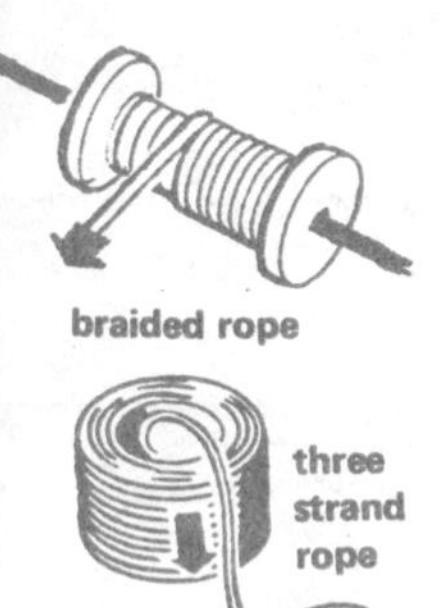

A full spool of rope may average 600' long.

Braided rope. It is taken from a freely moving spool letting it fall into a container, page 188, so it is able to *maintain its neutral lay* without kinks .

Three-strand, right-lay rope. It is removed from a coil by pulling the inside end, coiling it *counterclockwise.* If right-lay three-strand is coiled clockwise, it rapidly develops kinks and hockles, see hockle on page 187.

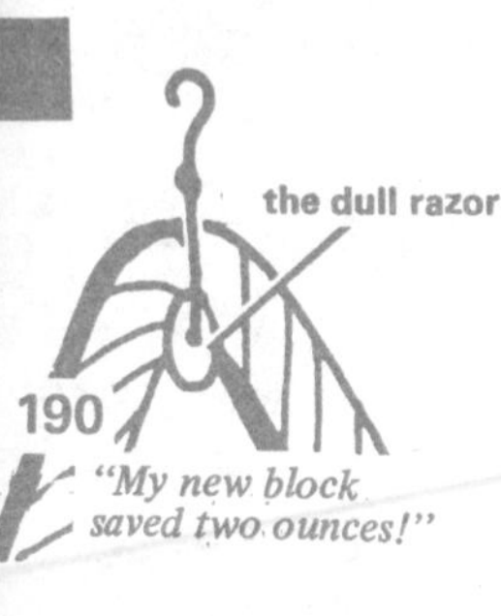

"My new block saved two ounces!"

- **When three-strand kinks develop**—after the ends are whipped or fused so they can't unlay, tow a larger dia. line behind a boat for a few minutes to stabilize itself, then coil. For smaller diameter short lengths,pull thru your hand while maintaining some tension on the line. You can watch it untwist and stabilize itself.
- **Good rope is expensive.** An understanding owner may have a long, useful, and productive life...or a short, expensive, and dangerous one with his rope investment.
- Hardware catalogs list **maximum line diameter for each block.** If a larger diameter line goes thru the block, the line begins to chafe on the outside...while the tight radius starts to crush and break the inner fibers.
- **Small straight chocks** with sharp cutting edges are members of the knife and razor family.Dock lines or anchor lines can chafe at the chock in wind or wave action cutting your boat adrift at the worst moment.

  Another disadvantage of the straight chock in wave action...your dock or anchor line may jump out of the chock to chafe on nearby sharp edges, screw heads,etc.

- **Adequate size locking skene chocks** should be installed of a larger size than first considered. This reduces anchor and dock line chances of jumping out of the chock in wave action. **Leather chafe guards** of correct size are in kit form with punched holes, needle, and thread to minimize dock line chafe when going thru chocks.
- **Manila rope chafes rapidly** due to its coarse, abrasive surface, occuring much faster when wet.

  We towed our 14' outboard boat *Blunder* behind a 40' ketch. The manila tow line of top quality chafed rapidly at the outboard bow chock, We had to resplice it twice in three days during the early part of our vacation.

  The third short splice was wrapped with a hard surface vinyl electricians tape. Little chafe was evident two weeks later at the end of the vacation with thanks to the tape.

locking skene chock

The **fisherman's knot** is used to join fishline, twine, and small rope.

The **sheet bemd** is used to join small and medium ropes.

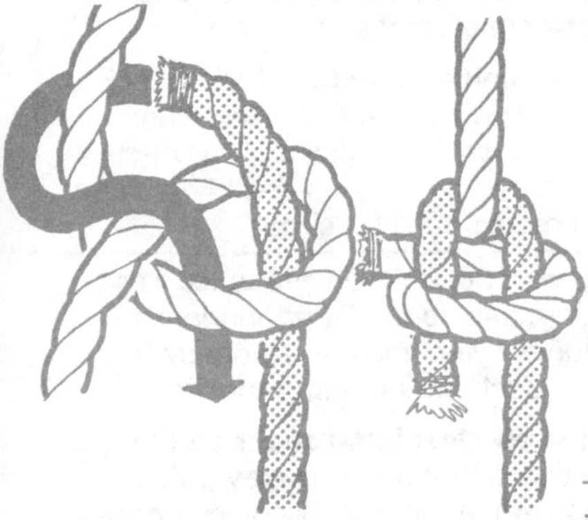

The **fisherman's bend** is used to secure a rope to a ring.

191

The **double sheet bend** is used to join small to medium size ropes.

The **carrick bend** is used to join heavy ropes, cables, and hawsers.

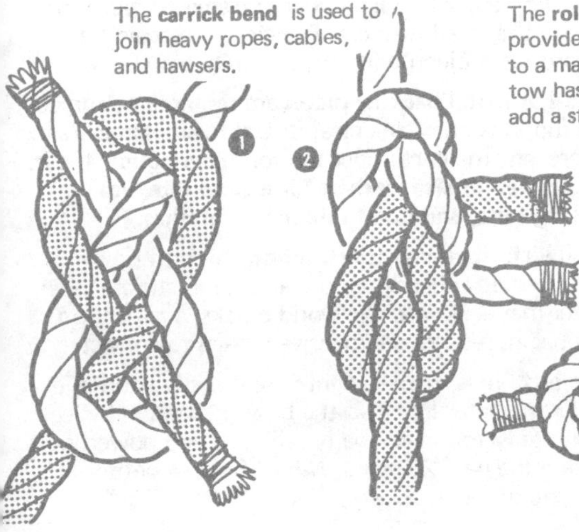

The **rolling hitch** is used to provide a lengthwise pull to a mast or spar. If the tow has a slippery surface, add a stopper knot.

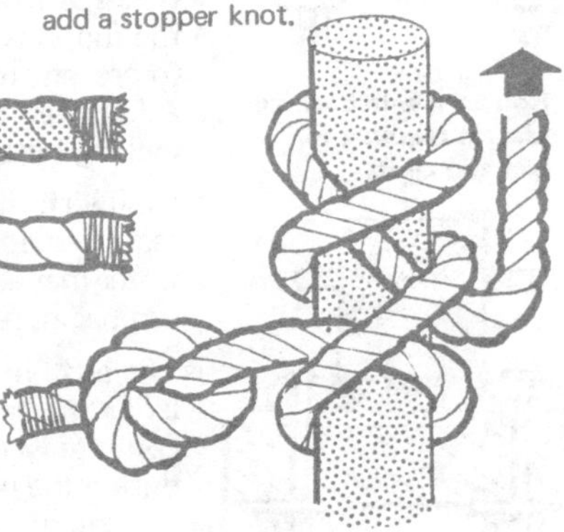

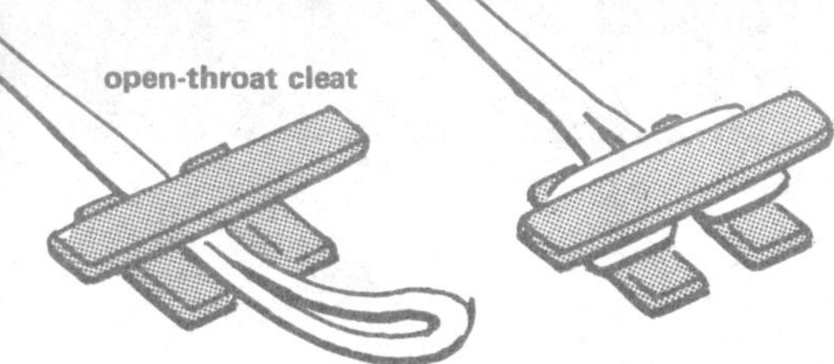

Loop splice thru eye...over top...and pull snug.

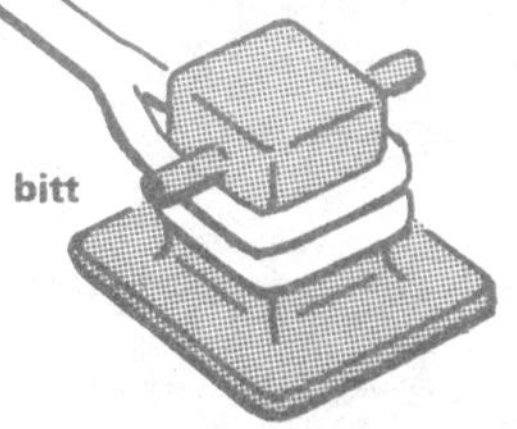

Use two loops...then pull tight.

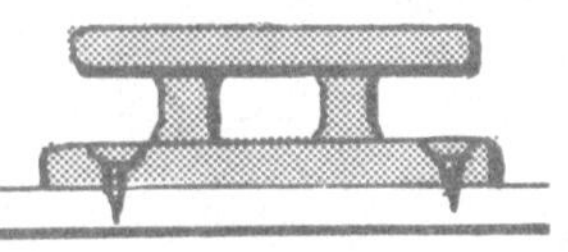

AVOID short wood screws!

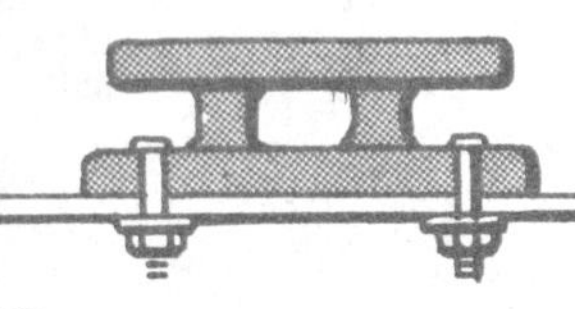

92 **Cleat may still pull out under extreme pressure.**

Bolt thru with backing plate is required for bitt and cleat.

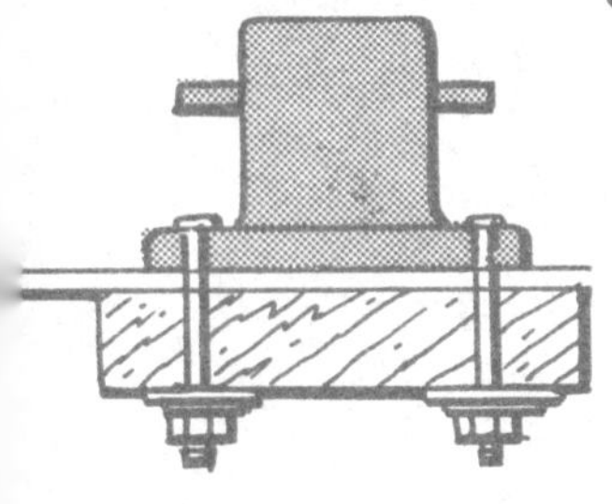

Organic vs synthetic dock lines.

Coarse surface friction. Large diameter manila dock lines with larger cleats were standard to 1960. Two locking hitches were usually sufficient.

Smooth surface, minimum friction. Nylon dock lines were stronger, with smaller diameter line ample for the purpose. Extra locking half hitches are required to prevent the nylon dock lines from slipping, and jumping off their cleats.

- **Open throat cleat.** It permits an eye splice to go thru the opening, then looped over and locked tight. Two locking loops overcome the tendency for small dia. nylon dock lines to jump the bitt.
- **AVOID wood screw cleat installations** on fiberglass AND wooden boats. Wood screws may pull out with minimum stress, while the cleat becomes a hazardous projectile, see page 188.
- **Bolts and washers are better, BUT** the fiberglass may momentarily open under extreme pressure to release the small washers. The cleat can again be a hazardous projectile for anyone in its path.
- **Wood or metal backing plates** are required to spread the full tension of the cleat or bitt over a large area to prevent the part under tension from pulling loose. **Add different size washers for a good bite, use locking nuts, and don't mix metal families.**
- **Sandwich fiberglass construction.** All bolt holes require special handling to seal out moisture. If water may leak into the wood blocks, a rot action can begin, requiring expensive repairs to correct.
- The **bitt.** *It* is smaller, lighter, and easily handles a larger diameter line than the bow anchor/dock cleat commonly found on many sailboats and powerboats during the past 20 years. Will a bitt do a better job for you on your boat?

Take the line **twice** around a cleat...add a half hitch...then as many as required. The line can then be released without taking up on the standing part.

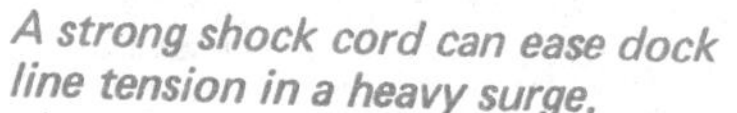

A strong shock cord can ease dock line tension in a heavy surge.

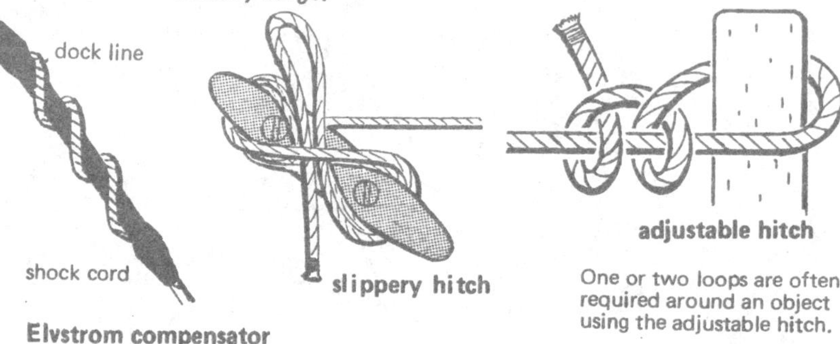

Elvstrom compensator

One or two loops are often required around an object using the adjustable hitch.

193

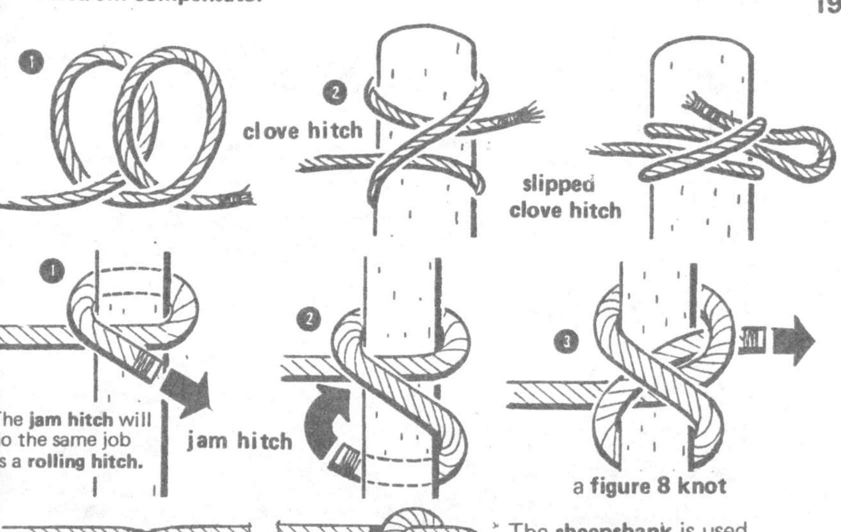

The **jam hitch** will do the same job as a **rolling hitch.**

The **sheepshank** is used to shorten a line. It must remain under tension to avoid slippage.

BOWLINE, SQUARE knots

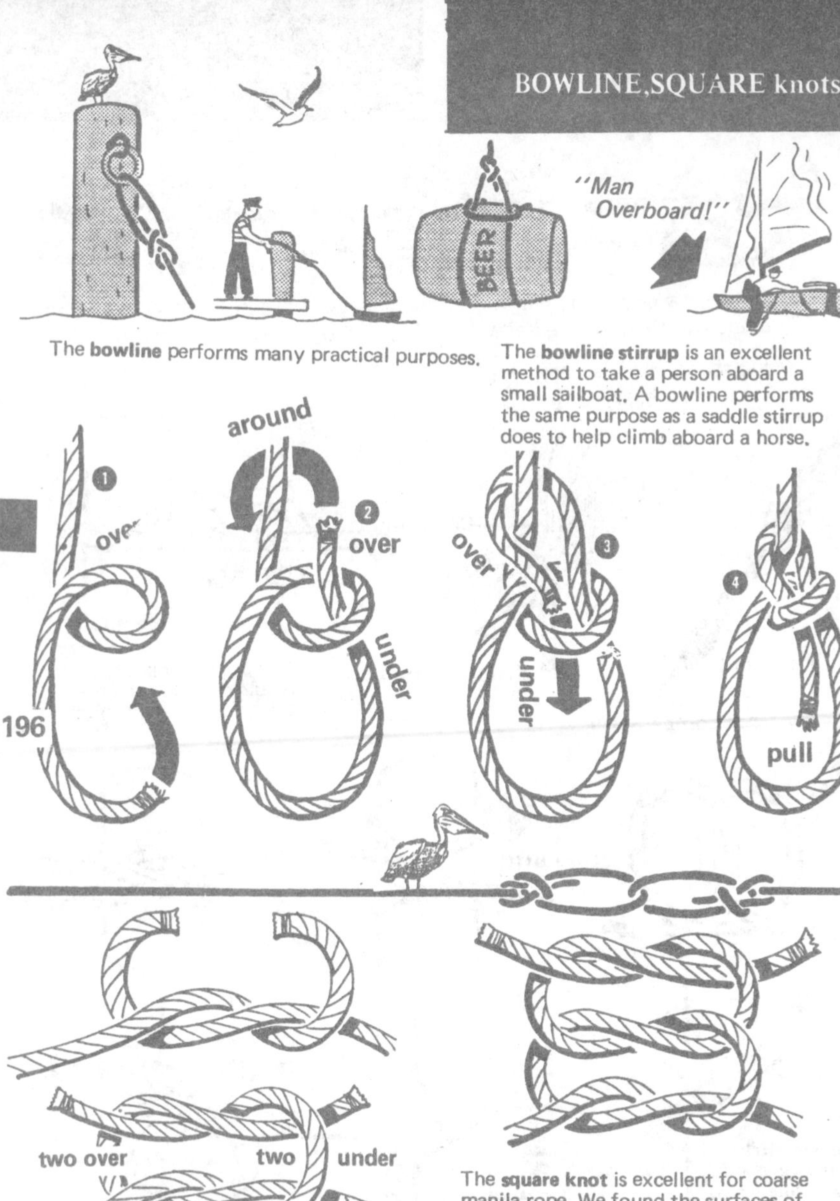

The **bowline** performs many practical purposes.

The **bowline stirrup** is an excellent method to take a person aboard a small sailboat. A bowline performs the same purpose as a saddle stirrup does to help climb aboard a horse.

The **square knot** was originally called a *reef knot.*

The **square knot** is excellent for coarse manila rope. We found the surfaces of polyethylene and sometimes nylon, so slippery we had to add a third half hitch called the **double-square knot** above which hasn't failed with synthetic rope.

Lever's Young Sea Officers Sheet Anchor— *Edward W. Sweetman Co., Box 1631, Valdosta, GA 31603. It is excellently illustrated reproduced exactly from its 1819 printing from making rope to rigging square rig sailing vessels.*

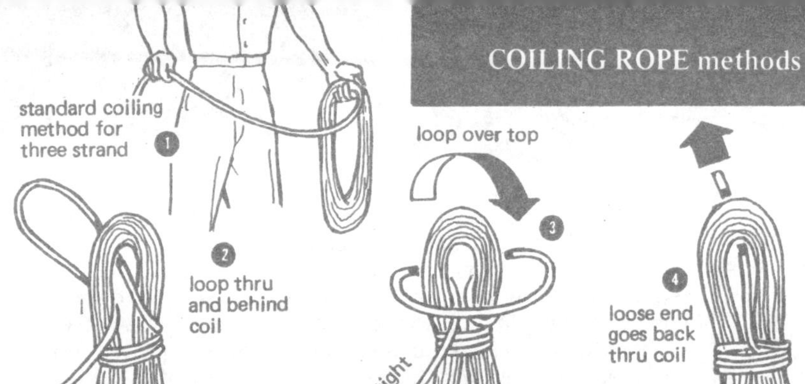

Coiling three strand line for storage.

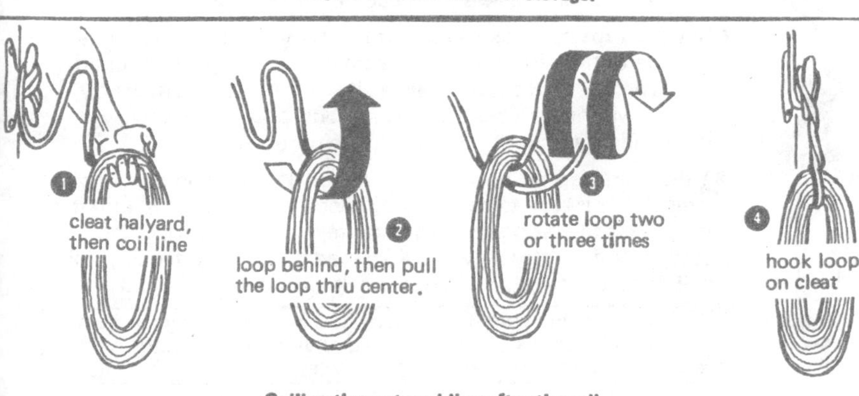

Coiling three-strand line after the sail is raised. The halyard should run freely when released to take the sail down.

add twist

Coiling braided halyards.

Neutral lay. New double-braided rope due to this will produce figure eight loops.

Thes loops can be avoided when coiling halyards by adding a little twist with each coil.

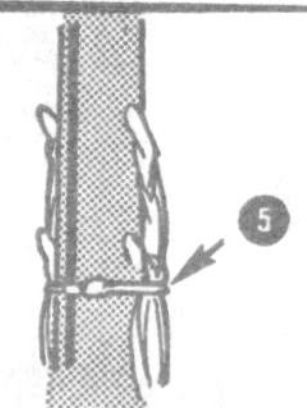

Add a **shock cord** around the halyards and mast in sloppy weather to keep the halyards from uncoiling.

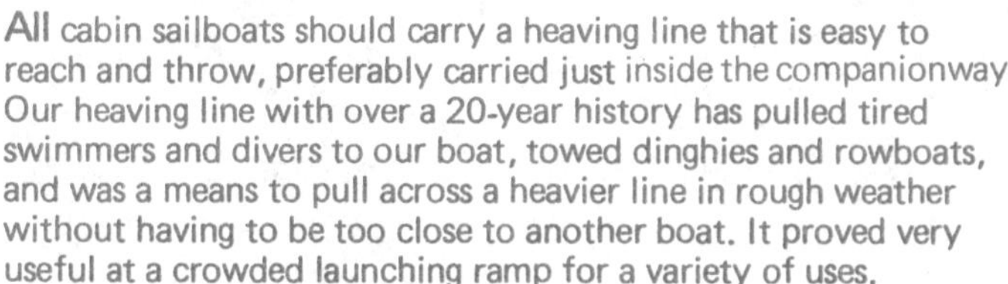

All cabin sailboats should carry a heaving line that is easy to reach and throw, preferably carried just inside the companionway. Our heaving line with over a 20-year history has pulled tired swimmers and divers to our boat, towed dinghies and rowboats, and was a means to pull across a heavier line in rough weather without having to be too close to another boat. It proved very useful at a crowded launching ramp for a variety of uses.

- **Three-strand heaving lines** are questionable. When used by professionals the heaving lines must be coiled in the morning. If they won't be used until the evening, they must be coiled again...to avoid hitches. If coiled by a right hander then given to a left hander or visa versa, expect endless hitches.
- **Braided rope** can make a practical heaving line for recreational use due to the ***neutral lay, or resistance to coiling.*** If the braided line is dropped into its container, it will stow itself efficiently for use without hitches for long periods, plus being used by left handers and right handers without problems.
- **Yellow braided ¼" polyethylene** has an 1100-pound breaking strength. It is easy to see, easy to handle, and since it is a **floater** it protects the propeller. Our favorite is the 50' heaving line using a "soft" softball, while a 75' one uses a small fender. Neither ball or fender can hurt a receiver as they are soft and light.

The best way to avoid most drownings is to stay on your boat. Whether you face a short vicious summer squall,or a storm of several days, rope yourself to and become part of your boat.

- **Shoulder harness.** While an excellent idea providing maximum protection for major storms especially during a night watch, they are clumsy and seldom worn in changing weather conditions.
- **Waist harness.** It is easy to use, and is less confining during hot summer weather in a short duration squall, but you will have to make your own. Use a 10' length of ½" three-strand nylon, and a size 3 bronze snap.Have the line go thru the bronze snap twice before starting the eye splice.

The waist harness is also a **belt.** When not being used, it is long enough to circle your waist a second time. It should be snug and out of the way when snapped onto itself when going below, though always ready for instant use. After adjusting to a snug, comfortable fit for you, cut the excess rope, burn to seal the end, then add whipping, page 200. Both harnesses are excellent for their intended purposes, to help you become a part of your sailboat.

splicing BRAIDED ROPE

Double-braided rope has been used for over 25 years...yet few sailors seem able to make a braided eye splice.

- Synthetic double-braided rope appeared in 1960. It provided a new splicing education for ALL sailors...while three-strand eye splices were found in Egyptian tombs reputed to be 7000 years old.

  Our first double-braided splices were less than satisfactory. To find the answer I made 47 braided splices during the following days until running out of things that could go wrong. While the basic theory is simple...the problem seemed to be oversimplified splicing instructions.

- We tested, then prepared our sequence of 35 simple steps shown on the following four pages. **Take these steps in exact numerical sequence without shortcuts** *until* the sequence involved in this new skill becomes easy and simple to use. ..then make several splices at the same time.

  We chose seven people at random to test our sequence who had never made a braided eye splice. All made a successful double-braided eye splice on the first attempt. All admitted total confusion in the final steps before the splices suddenly came together.

> **Make a braided eye splice soon as practical.** Order a splicing kit from *Samson Ocean Systems, Inc., Pleasure Boating Division, 99 High Street, Boston,MA 02110.* OR you can buy 18' of 3/8" double-braided rope, plus a pusher and a 3/8" fid. The rope can be cut into three 6' lengths for six eye splices. The ice pick at first may seem to be a good substitute pusher, 201
> though the sharp point under pressure can become dangerous.

- **New rope.** This is a major factor to consider since after a double-braided line has been put under tension, the diameter tends to shrink with the core and cover binding together. Wash the line to remove sand, lubricate between the core and cover, and **use a next smaller size fid.**

- **Fid MUST be correct size.** for steps (15) to (21). The next larger size fid will be almost impossible to pull or push thru the rope...while a smaller diameter fid will hardly provide sufficient opening to PULL the core thru the cover, or visa versa. Choose **metal fids** for smaller rope sizes, which doesn't seem to be as critical for larger diameter rope using plastic fids.

- **Pushing/holding angle step (18).** This is the most difficult part of the sequence for most sailors. ***A slight angle provides the best leverage*** to push, then pull the cover behind the fid and out thru the core. Women, dentists, and medical doctors with good hand dexterity and nimble fingers master it easily.

- **Reserve a full afternoon or evening without interruptions** when making your first braided eye splices...then teach other members of your family or crew to make braided eye splices. You will find numerous uses for your new splicing skill on your boat, in your home, and in the garage.

> **Jim McGrew** is our splicing expert. Request his catalog with unique splicing methods and tools. Order his economical **hour video**, listening to words of our expert while watching his hands perform all kinds of splicing as many times as desired, until you master 3 strand, braided, wire splicing. 8120 Rio Linda Blvd.,Elverta, CA 95626,(916) 991-1142

outer cover *double braided rope*

inner core

The double braided eye splice is quite simple **IF you follow the 35 simple steps in exact sequence.** Chances are excellent then that your first braided eye splice will be successful. The next splices will be faster and easier to make as *the splicing sequence starts to make sense*...while you pick up a new skill.

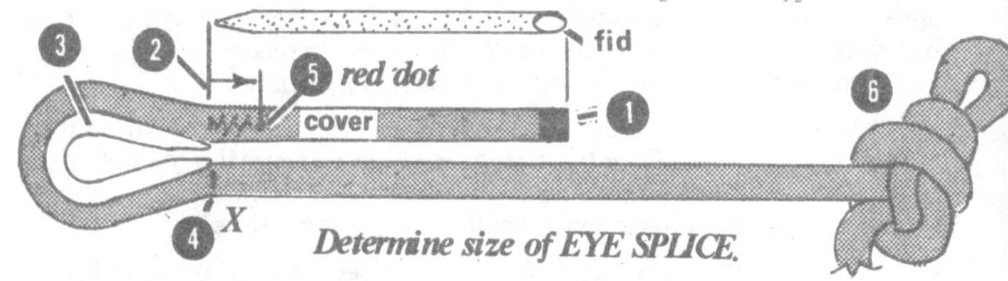

Determine size of EYE SPLICE.

❶ Tape end. ❷ Measure back fid length and add a mark. ❸ Add thimble to determine size of eye. ❹ Mark it *point X.* ❺ Count seven pairs of threads forward of mark 2 and make a *red dot* on cover. ❻ Tie SLIP KNOT 4 to 6 feet from eye.

202

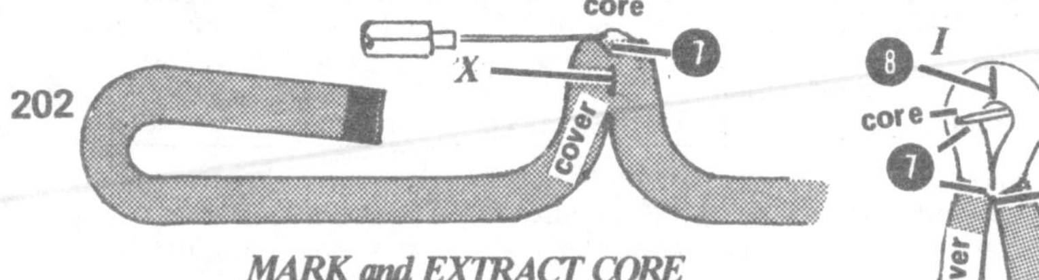

MARK and EXTRACT CORE

❼ Bend rope at *X*, see right. Separate strands with pusher, and pry out inner core. ❽ Mark inner core *I* at this point.

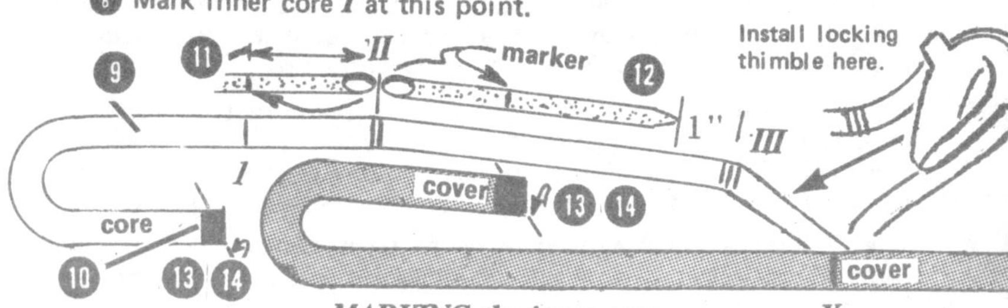

MARKING the inner core

❾ Pull out core. ❿ Tape core end. ⓫ Measure back from *I* amount of fid shown, then mark it *II*. ⓬ Measure a fid length from *II*, add an inch and marke it *III*. ⓭ Cut *to taper both ends* to fit eye in fid. ⓮ Retape with electrical tape, *cut excess tape.*

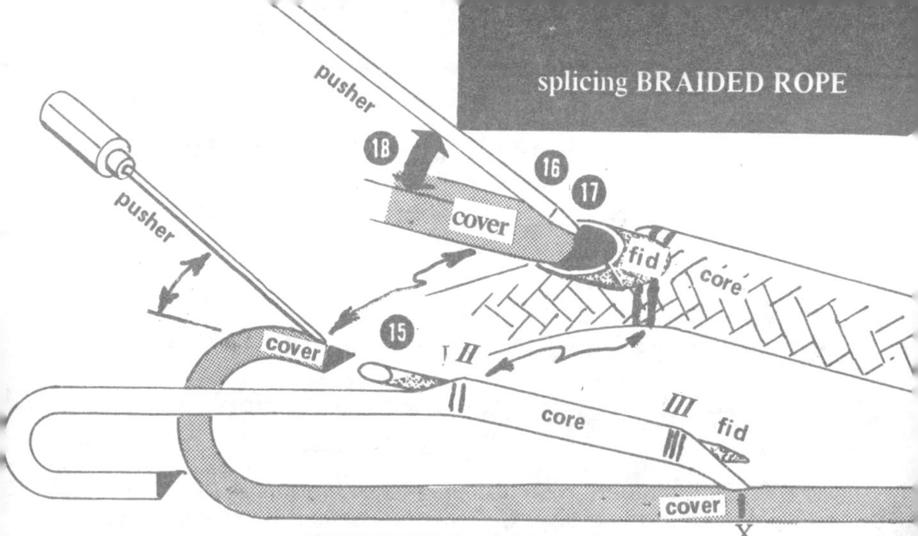

INSERTING the fid into the core.

(15) *Insert fid into core at II* and pull out at *III*. (16) Insert taped end of cover into eye of fid. (17) Angle taped end forward to lock cover into fid eye. **Push fid at slight angle BEHIND taped cover end** at (18) until the cover comes out of the core as you see below at step (19).

203

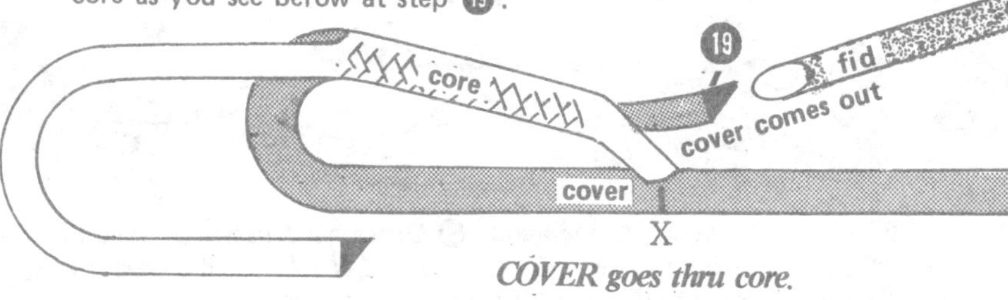

COVER goes thru core.

CORE enters cover.

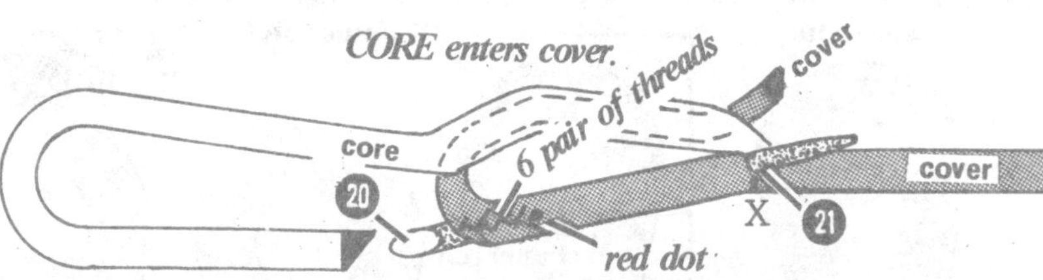

(20) Insert fid 6 pairs of threads *after red dot*, with fid coming out at point *X*. (21) Push core into fid so it comes out at point *X*. (16) (17) (18) Use the same holding/pushing method only this time it is to pull the *core thru the cover*.

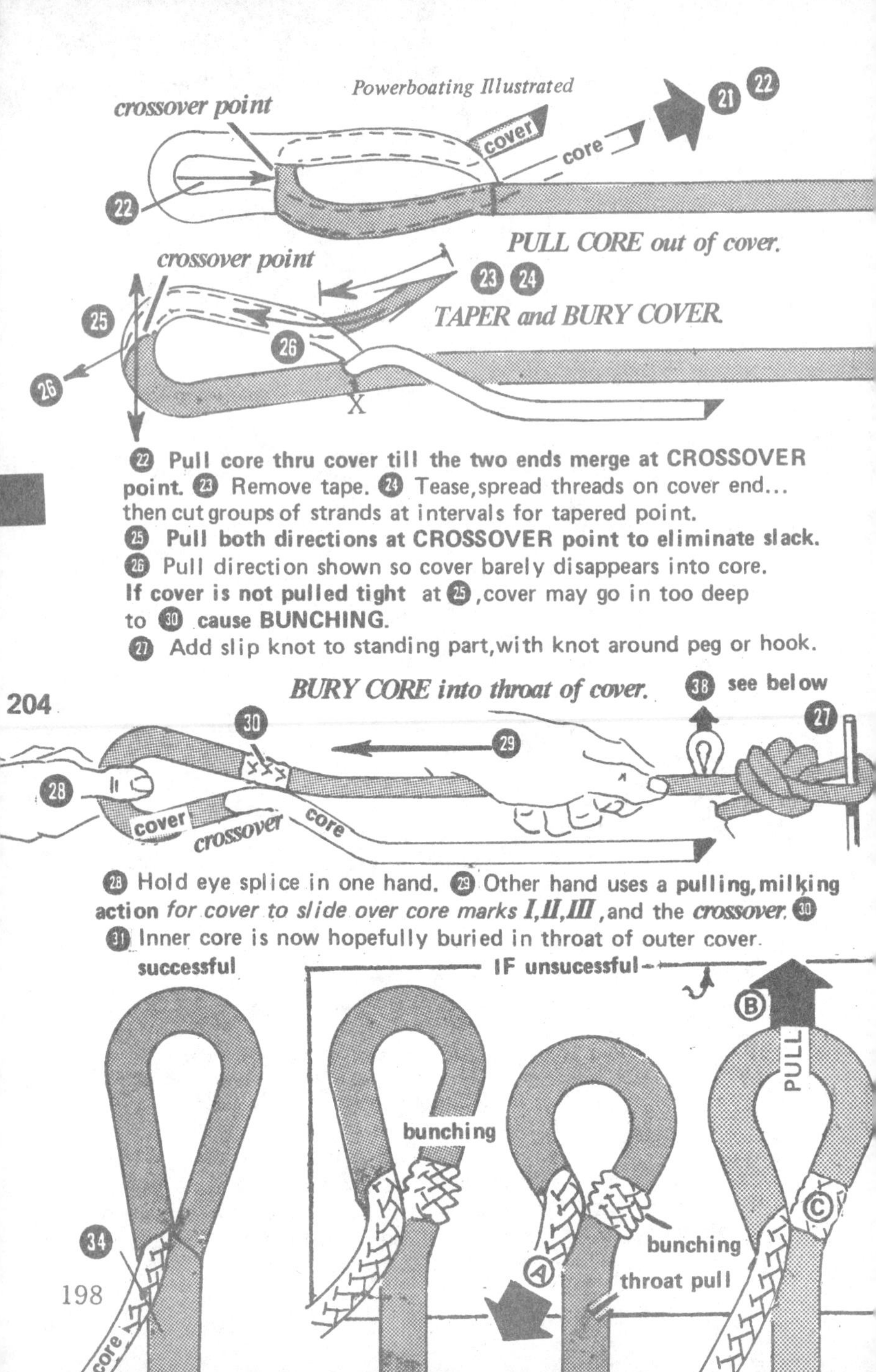

(22) Pull core thru cover till the two ends merge at CROSSOVER point. (23) Remove tape. (24) Tease, spread threads on cover end... then cut groups of strands at intervals for tapered point.

(25) **Pull both directions at CROSSOVER point to eliminate slack.**

(26) Pull direction shown so cover barely disappears into core. **If cover is not pulled tight** at (25), cover may go in too deep to (30) **cause BUNCHING.**

(27) Add slip knot to standing part, with knot around peg or hook.

(28) Hold eye splice in one hand. (29) Other hand uses a **pulling, milking action** *for cover to slide over core marks* ***I, II, III***, and the ***crossover.*** (30)

(31) Inner core is now hopefully buried in throat of outer cover.

204

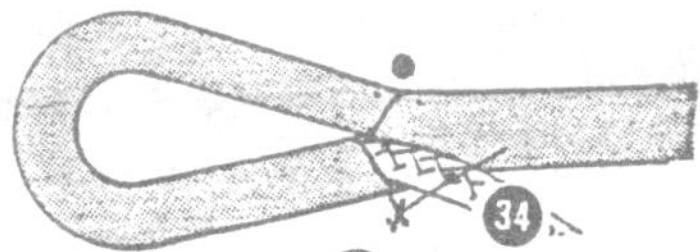

32 Open eye splice loop, add thimble.
33 Close eye with milking action to lock thimble.

34 **Rabbit tail.** Rigger practice is to cut core tail short enough to disappear just in cover. Author prefers it 3/8" or even a little longer before cutting... with the *rabbit tail* still showing under pressure outside of cover.

rabbit tail

34

Core tail cut too short. Breaking tests indicate double-braid splice usually fails at the ...*end of buried section,* USN term is called "necking down".

Buried section flat hollow core space can develop with only cover carrying load under pressure. USN states "These lines are potential killers and can fail without warning as much as 50% below breaking strength".

buried section end

35 **Stitch-lock throat.** this prevents crossover being pulled out under load. Add whipping thread thru throat with an equal length on both sides of throat. **Face up**— insert whipping 3 to 4 times pulling snug on each pass.

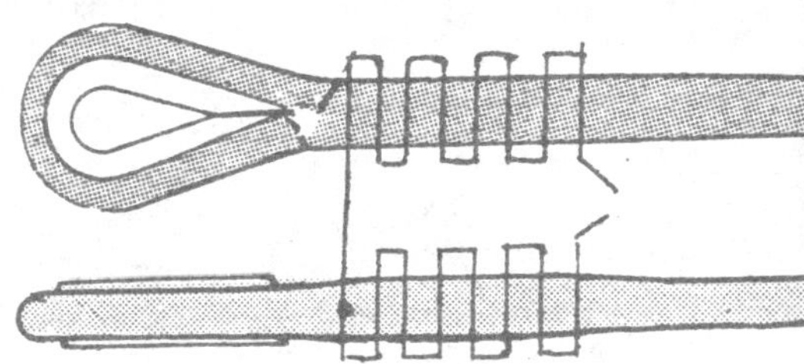

Rotate splice 90 degrees. Use whipping thread on other side 3 to 4 times pulling snug at each pass. Tie both whipping ends with a square knot. Bury knot in throat.

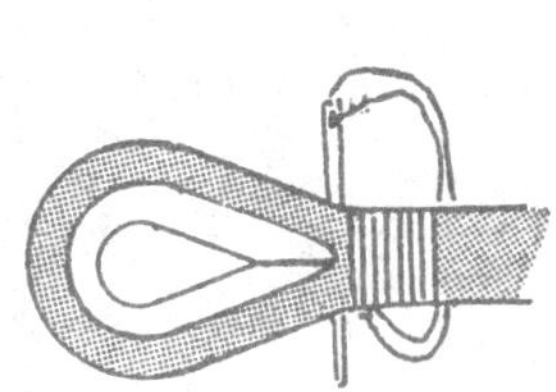

36 **Lock thimble.** Use nylon whipping for nylon dock lines, and Dacron or polyester for halyards and sheets.

37 **Anchor line chafe.** Sand chafes both external AND internal fibers of the line. Tape eye as shown, and at least two or more feet to protect throat and line. Use *duct tape* and retape when chafe begins to show on tape.

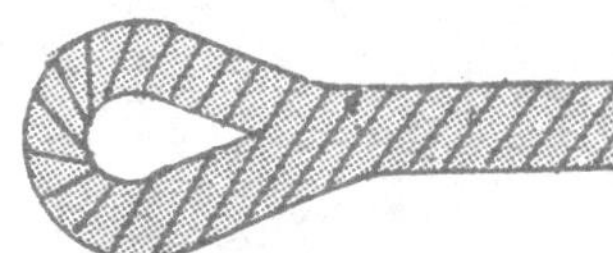

38 Recover with a martini or double *sarsaparilla.*

rope END WHIPPING

We have tested synthetic and organic whipping thread during the past 25 years under identical conditions.

Both kinds of thread seem to last a similar amount of time.

Permanent needle whipping is required for synthetic rope ends.

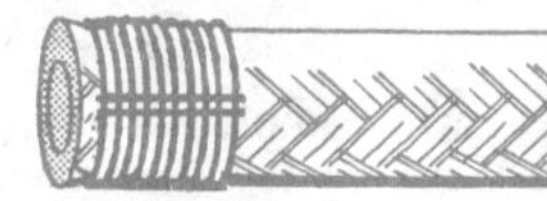

double-braided whipping.

Avoid short matches as they don't develop enough heat!

1 Add tape an inch from end.

2 Cut end ¼" from tape.

3 Fuse ends, rolling melted end to hold same diameter.

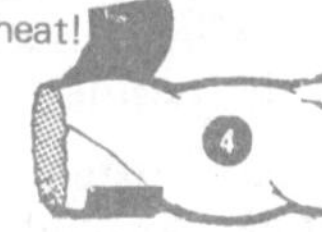

4 Remove tape after end cools.

A **soldering iron** is excellent to fuse synthetic rope strands, while 12" **fireplace matches** also provide enough fusing heat.

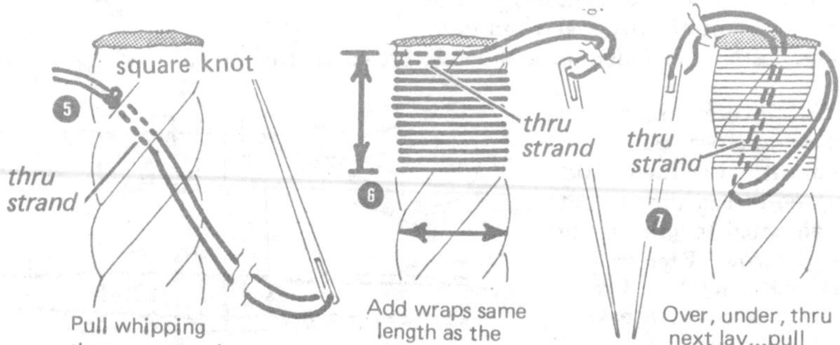

5 square knot / thru strand — Pull whipping thru one strand.

6 thru strand — Add wraps same length as the diameter.

7 thru strand — Over, under, thru next lay...pull tight 3 lays.

Pull end A out from lay.

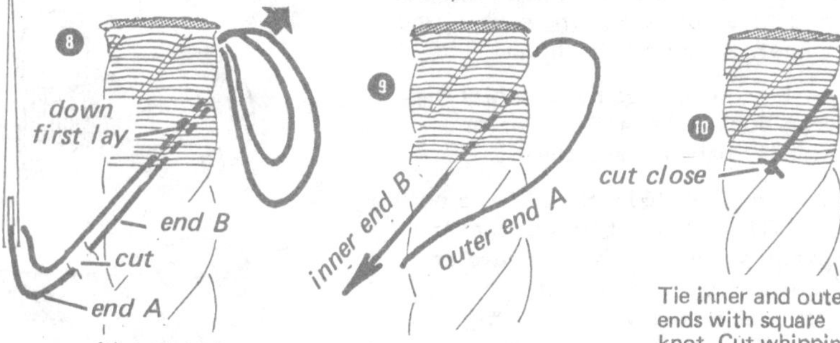

8 down first lay / end B / cut / end A — 4th tuck is thru first lay...then cut as shown.

9 inner end B / outer end A — Pull whipping end B tight.

10 cut close — Tie inner and outer ends with square knot. Cut whipping tails close to the square knot.

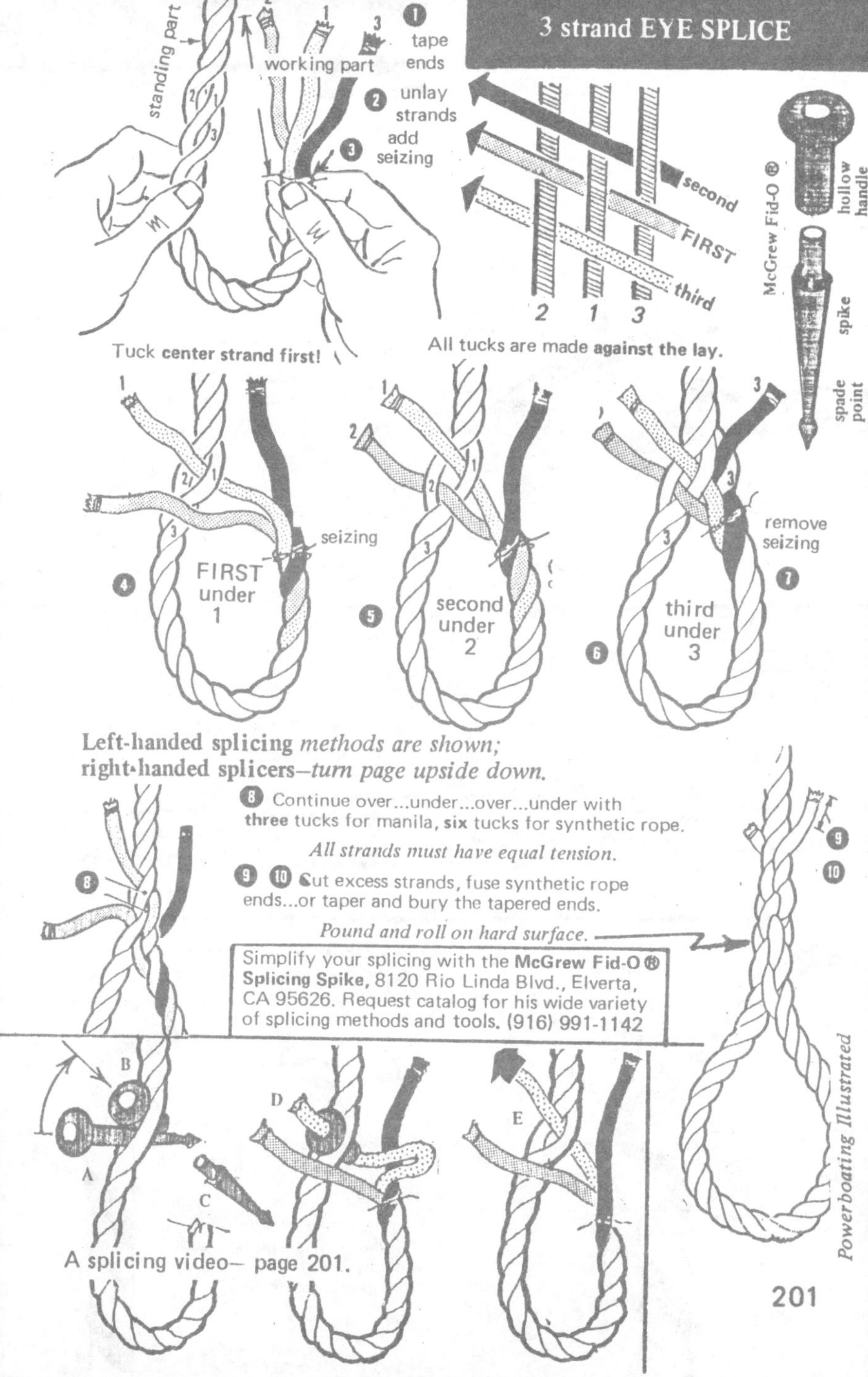
3 strand EYE SPLICE
standing part
working part
1 tape ends
2 unlay strands
3 add seizing
second
FIRST
third
2 1 3
McGrew Fid-O ®
hollow handle
spike
spade point
Tuck center strand first!
All tucks are made against the lay.
seizing
4 FIRST under 1
5 second under 2
6 third under 3
7 remove seizing
Left-handed splicing methods are shown;
right-handed splicers—turn page upside down.
8 Continue over...under...over...under with three tucks for manila, six tucks for synthetic rope.
All strands must have equal tension.
9 10 Cut excess strands, fuse synthetic rope ends...or taper and bury the tapered ends.
Pound and roll on hard surface.
Simplify your splicing with the McGrew Fid-O ® Splicing Spike, 8120 Rio Linda Blvd., Elverta, CA 95626. Request catalog for his wide variety of splicing methods and tools. (916) 991-1142
A
B
C
D
E
A splicing video— page 201.
Powerboating Illustrated

the SHORT SPLICE

1. Tape synthetic rope ends... then fuse the strand ends.
2. Unravel desired strands for manila...with twice as many strands for synthetic rope.
3. Add outer seizings to prevent further strand unwinding. 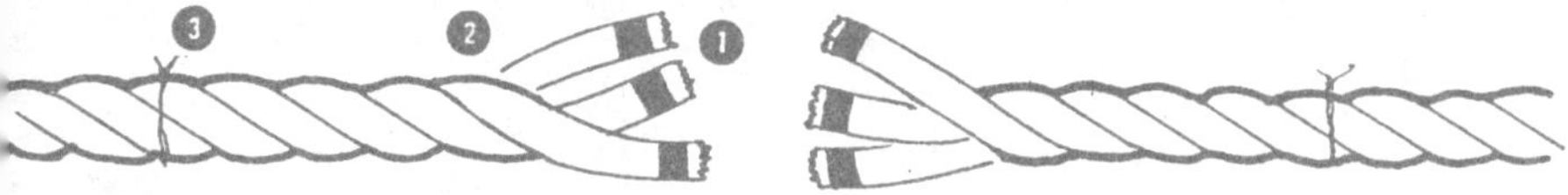 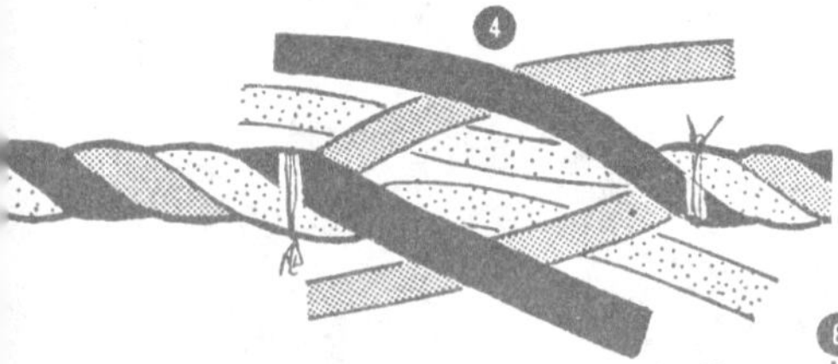
4. Pull all six strands together.
5. Tie center seizing around all six meeting strands.
6. Remove both outer seizings. 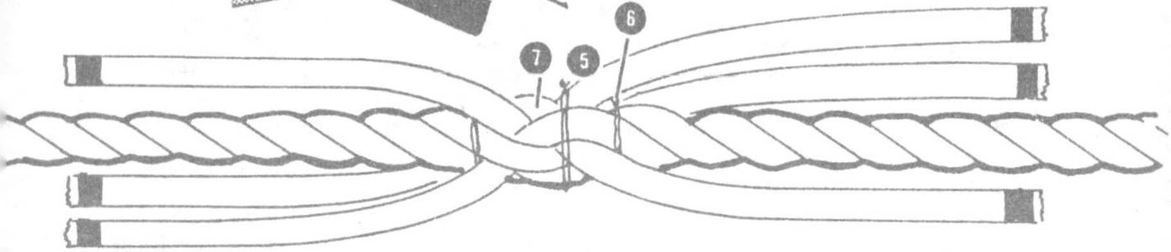
7. Continue over—under—over—under to end of strands...then remove center seizing.
8. If taper is desired cut back some threads and bury.
9. Add whipping.
10. If ends show, removed tape.
11. Roll and pound on hard surface.

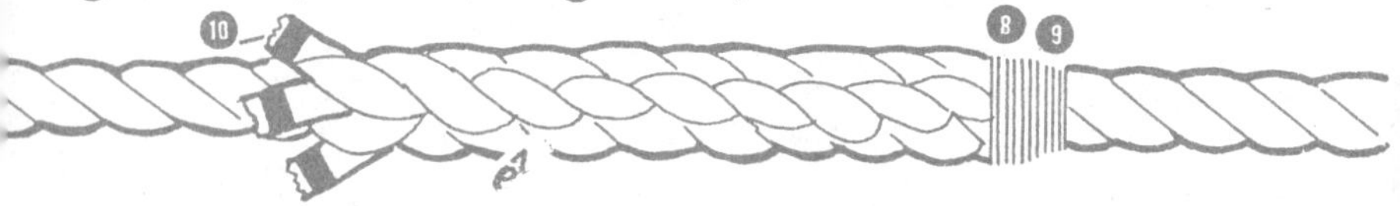

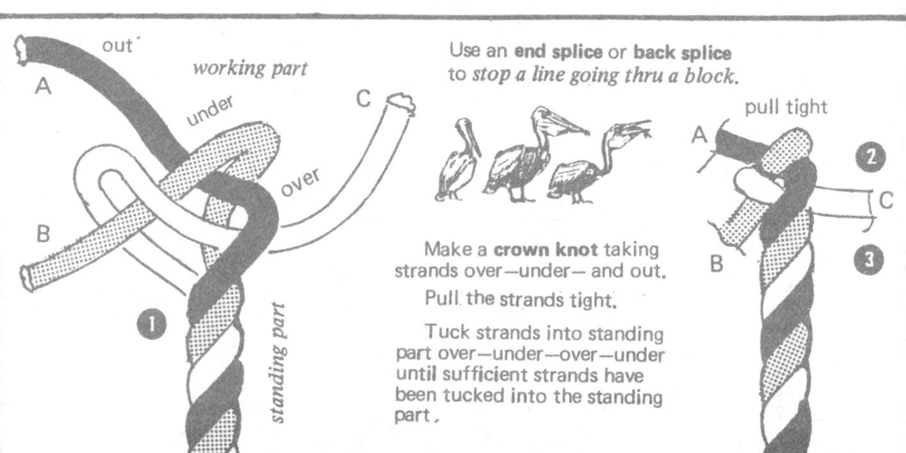

Use an **end splice** or **back splice** to *stop a line going thru a block.*

Make a **crown knot** taking strands over—under— and out.

Pull the strands tight.

Tuck strands into standing part over—under—over—under until sufficient strands have been tucked into the standing part.

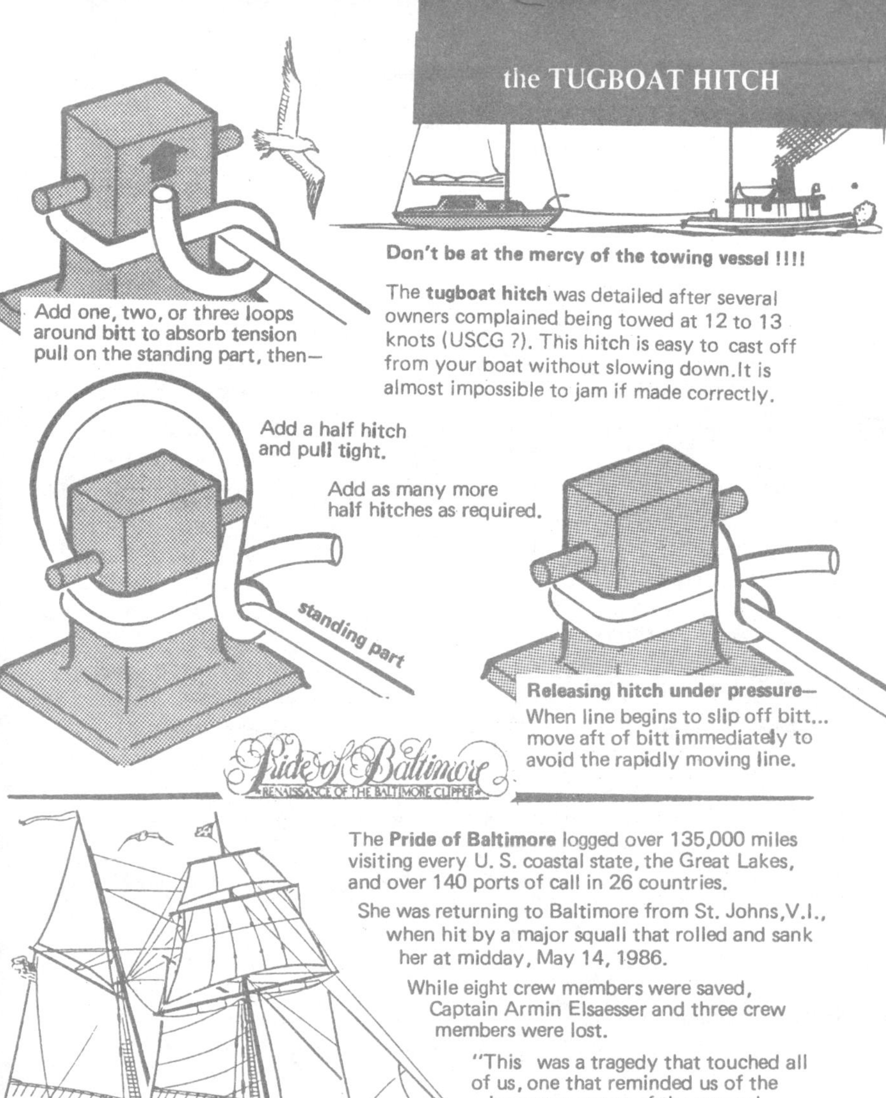

the TUGBOAT HITCH

Don't be at the mercy of the towing vessel !!!!

The **tugboat hitch** was detailed after several owners complained being towed at 12 to 13 knots (USCG ?). This hitch is easy to cast off from your boat without slowing down. It is almost impossible to jam if made correctly.

The **Pride of Baltimore** logged over 135,000 miles visiting every U. S. coastal state, the Great Lakes, and over 140 ports of call in 26 countries.

She was returning to Baltimore from St. Johns, V.I., when hit by a major squall that rolled and sank her at midday, May 14, 1986.

While eight crew members were saved, Captain Armin Elsaesser and three crew members were lost.

"This was a tragedy that touched all of us, one that reminded us of the immense power of the sea and the untold courage of those who sail on it.

"Let **Pride** sail on until sunset in our memory"– William Donald Schaefer, Mayor of Baltimore.

One of my happiest memories is a three hour discussion on a rainy afternoon with Captain Elsaesser. Ir began with rope, progressing thru many subjects for which we enjoyed endless disagreements. Several of his ideas are covered on page 50 of our *Homestudy Guide*...plus a photo of the huge bowsprit at the top of the page. Little did we realize till later how important the **Pride of Baltimore** is to the history of our young nation and our major revision of *Sailing Illustrated.*

The clouds above. Nature sends advance physical warnings of storms in the every changing world of clouds. While well known to most farmers, much effort is required by us city folks living in air-conditioned homes and offices to understand these storm patterns.

Most radio and TV forecasts are of secondary importance to sailors as they cover large areas. You have to become your own weather expert to predict wind patterns in your immediate area to power your sailboat. Will the water surface action be stronger, or weaker than predicted?

upper clouds — middle — low clouds

- **Cirrus**-- (ringlet) is thin, stringy Mares tails that make beautiful sunrises and sunsets due to light refraction thru ice crystals.
- **Cirrocumulus**-- (ringlet-heap) is called Mackerel sky as it resembles fish scales. It has no cloud shadows...indicating a weather change.
- **Cirrostratus**-- (ringlet-layer) is white, frozen, cobwebby fog which often predicts rain.
- **Ringlet?** These high clouds make a halo or ringlet around the sun and moon predicting a weather change in a day or two.
- **Altocumulus**-- (middle-heap) form lumpy patterns producing flattened globular masses as shown at right.
- **Altostratus**- (middle-flat) may thicken to nimbostratus. It does NOT produce a halo around the sun or moon.
- **Stratus**-- (layer) is low, indefinite, with a dry bottom giving water a hazy appearance...becoming **fog** down on the water surface.
- **Nimbostratus**-- (storm-layer) cloud is flat, gray, ragged, with a wet looking bottom. It usually indicates steady rain over a large area.
- **Cumulus**-- (heap) clouds are clean, fluffy, and dome shaped on the upper surface. If one grows tall enough to reach the high cloud ice crystal area where temperature is below freezing, it becomes the—
- **Cumulonimbus**— (heap storm) results when cumulus clouds develop into **clouds 2 to 5 miles tall.** When it reaches the freezing area, the cumulonimbus top flattens. *An anvil top* results with thin, wispy Mares tails indicating the direction of the thunderhead producing strong winds in a short duration storm.
- **Stratocumulus**-- (flat layer) may resemble altocumulus though they may appear darker, lower, and larger, sometimes covering most of the sky. They can develop from altostratus, or flattened cumulus clouds.

Weather proverb accuracy? Sailors went down to the sea long before recorded history, while weather forecasts are a few decades old. These seamen developed their own weather prediction methods in proverb form to drive their sailing vessels hundreds and thousands of miles, reported on page 56 of our *Homestudy Guide.*

I wish we made a tape of our discussion with Lin Pardey while testing the proverb page. Many held up, while a few were inconclusive. Word interpretation may be involved with some proverbs hundreds of years old such as ***when the sea hog jumps...stand by your pumps.*** Sea hogs?

from Sailing Illustrated

basic CLOUD FORMATIONS

ringlet

cirrus

high clouds are
ice particles

anvil top

cirrostratus

cirrocumulus

20,000 feet

medium clouds

altostratus

altocumulus

6,500 feet

low clouds

stratocumulus

cumulonimbus,
thunderstorm,
thunderhead

cumulus

roll cloud

stratus

nimbostratus

catspaw

Weather proverbs, rhymes, and reasons, may be of more use to ALL boat operators than they may realize.

Sailors have gone down to sea in small sailing vessels since before recorded history, before newspaper and TV weather reports, and way before the barometer. These seamen developed a primitive, practical weather wisdom to survive, while using the forces of nature to drive their vessels sometimes for weeks out of sight of land.

Ancient sailors had to be continually alert to changing weather applicable today in proverb form. It involved temperature changes, different colors of the sky with rising or setting sun, the moon with its halo, changing cloud patterns, plus the erratic action of porpoises, fish, and sea birds.

- *Mackerel sky and mare's tails, make lofty ships carry low sails.*
- *When wind shifts against the sun, trust it not, for back it will run.*
- *When clouds appear like rocks and towers, the earth is refreshed by frequent showers.*
- *If clouds look as though scratched by a hen, get ready to reef your tops'ls then!* Mare's tails develop, followed by a scratchy mackerel sky, with a white cirrostratus film produces a ***lunar halo,*** soon to follow is a **backing wind.** A storm is indicated in 12, 24, to 48 hours. As barometer drops, wind flowing from the W and SW may ease, then blow hard.
- *At sea with low and falling glass, the greenhorn sleeps like a careless jackass.*
- *But when the glass is high and rising, may soundly sleep the careful wise one.*
- *Short warning, soon past.* Shorter the warning and change, shorter will be the disturbance. It defines the 20 minute thunderstorm that may have winds of hurricane force, rapidly changing directions plus downdrafts.
- *Long foretold, long last!* Longer the warning, the longer the disturbance will last. Duration and intensity of bad weather depends on size and speed of the advancing low pressure cyclonic storm in our northwesterlies.

  A rapid barometer drop indicates rain and stormy weather. Severe N and NW gales often occur AFTER a barometer is very low, then begins to rise—

- *Quick rise after a low... foretells a stronger blow.*
- *While rise begins after a low... squalls expect and a clear blow.*

  If barometer is erratic or rises rapidly, it indicates unsettled weather. When a barometer rises slowly and steadily, it can indicate fair weather... but still be prepared for the few exceptions.

- *A red sky in the morning is a sailor's warning; but a red sky at night is a sailors delight.*
- *A light blue sky clap on all sails, yet think twice with a dark, gloomy blue sky.*

- *A pale yellow sky brings rain... while a bright yellow sky at sunset presages wind.*

  Light color tints with soft delicate cloud forms indicate light winds... while ragged, oily, to greasy looking clouds with hard edges and/or bright colors, indicate strong winds.

- *The moon, governess of the floods (high tides)... pale in her anger, washes all the air.*

  Positive ion behavior disturbances. Expect such occurances worldwide... also– *when the desert winds are howling.* As the positive ion moves into our bodies greatly restricting our analytical ability, unanticipated brawls and riots increase with intensity. .. while horses stumble, and cats trying to jump up on a high fence, miss and go over the top. When maximum tides and **devil winds** peak at the same time, avoid making decisions for at least 24 hours until the body recovers from the positive ion.

- ***Wooly fleeces deck the heavenly way... make sure no rain will mar a summer day (on the open ocean?).***

  Beware on land– if it is a hot, humid, inland afernoon. The wooly fleeces can grow skyward into unstable air masses. This provides short duration thunderstorms, with possible winds of hurricane intensity that also include strong downdrafts.

  Thunderstorms are predictable. with static from an inexpensive AM radio!

- ***Seagull, seagull, sit on the land........ it's never good weather when you are on the land (sand).***

  A low pressure grounds many birds, especially my favorite the heavy cormorant built like a heavy bomber, is barely able to take off and fly. It is fun chasing them perched on mooring cans, barely able to gain any altitude for 200 feet or more.

  Then we have other reasons such as no minnows are around. Civilization has also made its contribution in the last fifty years when we see rows of gulls sitting on our beaches in the mid afternoon. I soon found they had returned with a full stomach after their gourmet feast at the local garbage dump five miles away. So... expect variables.

- ***When the sea hog jumps... stand by your pumps.***

  While we've seen propoises and fish jumping before a few large storms, erratic bird behavior was more obvious. As Lin and Larry Pardee built their own 24'7" ***Seraffyn,*** spending ten years sailing it around the world without an outboard motor or engine, I asked Lin to review these proverbs.

  We were both stumped with the ***sea hog jumps.***

  Two years later I met a deliverly skipper who suddenly had the answer. He was taking a well-found sailboat from Hawaii to the U.S. He was caught in an **El Nino** with tremendous wind, wave action violence. Porpoises were jumping erratically, running into the sailboat, while birds were ramming into the rigging and hull. Glad I didn't do THAT research.

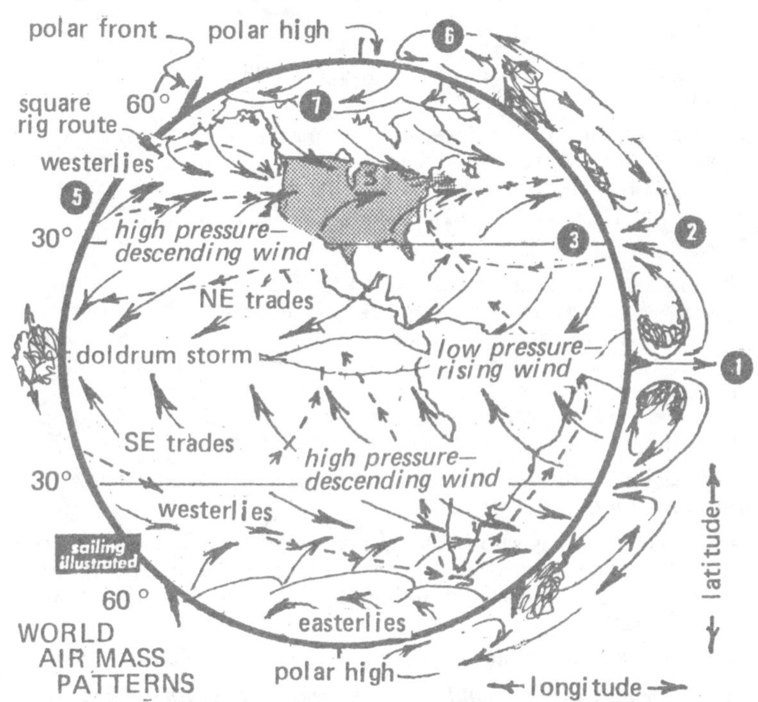

Our continually changing weather is a product of varying degrees of heat from the sun producing rising masses of warm air, and descending masses of cold air. To this we add rotation of the earth varying from a thousand miles an hour at the equator... to zero, at the poles.

The interaction of these factors produces complex tug-of-wars and collisions of worldwide air masses eternally on the move from the surface of the earth and ocean to the stratosphere.

Six surface wind patterns result with updraft and downdraft separation barriers caused by rising masses of warm air and descending cold air masses.

- **Doldrum barrier** at the equator has the most heat and high humidity. It has weak, changing surface winds due to rising masses of warm air.
- **30 degree north and south barriers,** *the horse latitudes,* result from the warm air doldrum masses bumping into cold polar air masses. Both mingle and descend producing a vertical barrier of weak surface winds. This separates the trades from the westerlies to the north influencing most U.S. weather.
- **Our prevailing westerlies** in the northern latitude belt of 30 to 60 degrees flowing from south, southwest, west, and northwest, produce the best and most varied climates in the world. They range from the dry, balmy latin weather conditions in our local buffer zone, to the rapidly changing seasonal conditions in our eastern wind funnel producing lush vegitation with ample moisture with more predictability than elsewhere in the world.

from Sailing Illustrated

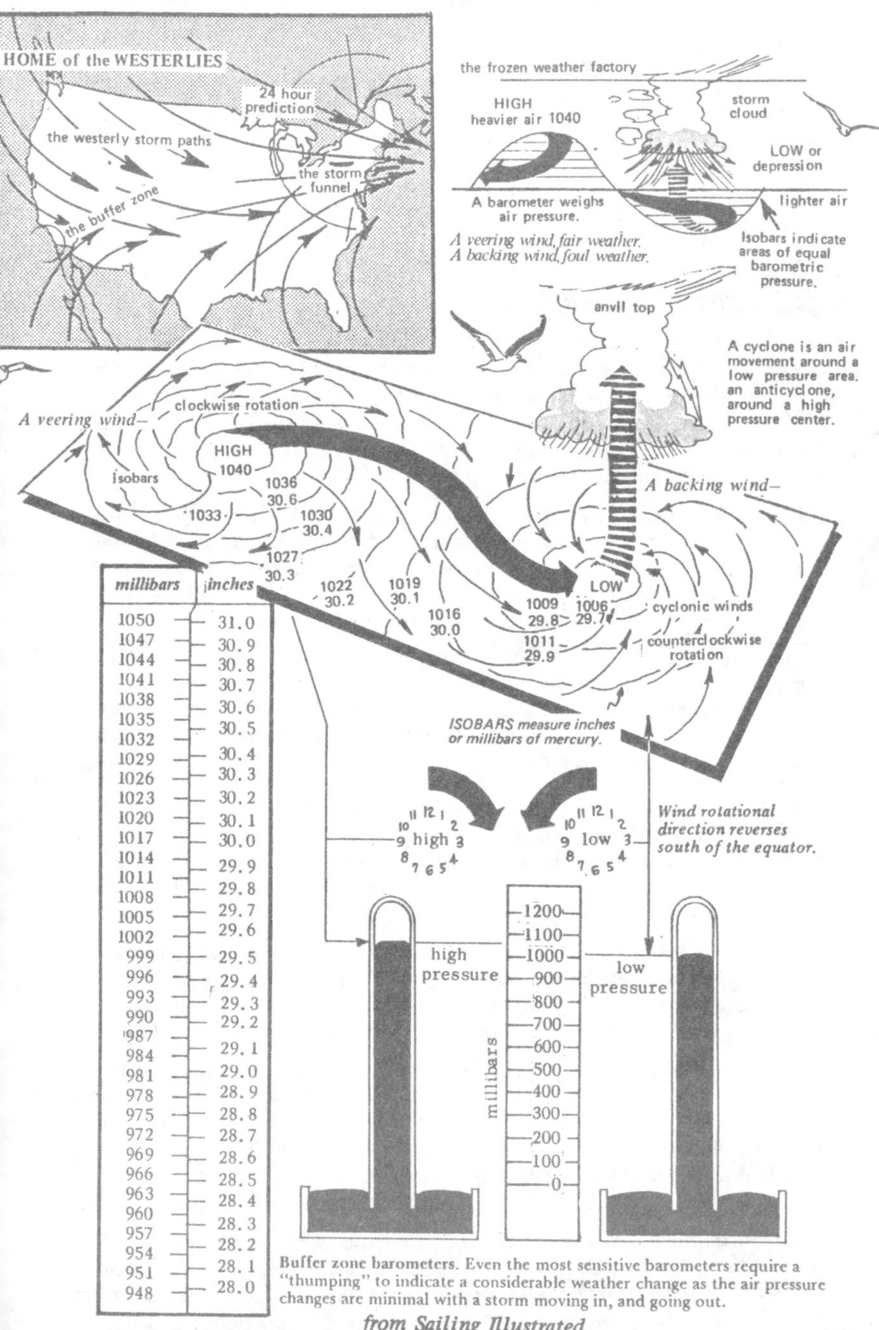

Buffer zone barometers. Even the most sensitive barometers require a "thumping" to indicate a considerable weather change as the air pressure changes are minimal with a storm moving in, and going out.

from Sailing Illustrated

Sovereign of the Seas 1852-1858

LOA 258′ 2″
beam 245′ 0″
draft 20′ 0″

disp. 2403 long tons
hold depth 23′
canvas 12,000 yards
crew—105 men & boys

- ***Sovereign of the Seas*** was loaded with casks of whale oil in Honolulu, the next destination, New York City. She was headed for the horn on a SE course in the Roaring 40's,sailing more than 400 sea miles in 24 hours. At 1000 hours, March 18, 1853, the mate reported she was holding 19 knots. The captain replied, "Now you can take the royals off her mister"....yet by 1100 hours she was still making 18 knots.*

Tea clipper boom. It lasted a scant ten years from 1848 to 1858. It was a period of sleek, square-rigged clippers with fine entrances forward, wide aft stern support, and maximum beam from midship aft. While competitive speed records to China and back received much publicity, similar records of involvement in the opium and slave trade seem nonexistant.

Square riggers sailed worldwide making the best use of available wind and currents to deliver cargo in minimum time. Slow, clumsy, plodding whalers followed the same worldwide paths to their varied whaling grounds. Up to 3 years were required to return to New England home ports with all casks full of whale oil,and after 1886 San Francisco became their new home port.

- **It is 1850.** You are on a square rigger with Manhattan to port on the North River on an outgoing ebb tide. After clearing Sandy Hook your vessel will make Rio the first stop. The shortest route recently required 55 days.while USN Lt. Maury in his new monthly ***Pilot Charts*** recommended a course three times the distance with the ***W.H.D.C. Wright*** making Rio in 38 days.

  Your vessel holds an easterly course to mid Atlantic. It slowly turns south to the **30N downdraft barrier** ***varying 2 to 3 degrees north or south,*** with NE trades taking you to the equator. After clearing the hot, high humid doldrums, the SE trades take your vessel to Rio on an easy beam reach.

- After provisioning, the vessel goes 100 miles to seaward, turning right to parallel the coast far enough out to avoid land disturbances. You clear the **30S downdraft barrier** into the sou'westerlies on a beam reach. It becomes very cold as your ship reefs down thru the roaring 40's into the screaming 50's. It is a square rigger graveyard with strong headwinds and huge waves circling the world without being slowed down by any land mass in its path.

- Cape Horn and the screaming 50's produce the most rugged sailing area in the world with a month sometimes required to turn NW. Some captains turned ENE with sou'westerlies on the stern thru the spice islands into the South Pacific.

Excerpts reprinted by permission of G.P.Putnam's Sons from* **Clipper Ships and Their Makers by Alexander Laing 1966.

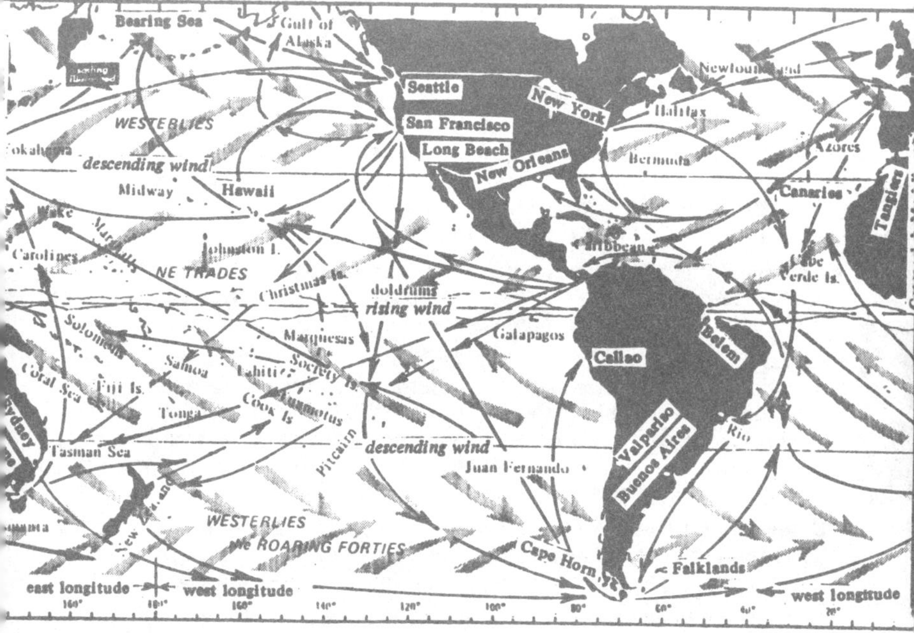

- **Southern Pacific.** Your vessel points high as possible on port tack to clear the horn. As the wind eases,your vessel on a reach to beam reach may hold a course roughly to Kodiak, Alaska plodding thru the 30S barrier, into the SE trades to the equator. After clearing the humid hot doldrums, the same course is held thru the NE trades.After 30N into the nor'westerlies, a slow turn to starboard hauls the wind aft for a downhill romp to San Francisco with a maximum 5.6 knot ebb tide, and 4.3 knot flood tide. Is your timing right for a flood tide...especially if the wind quits.

- **Return trip.** Hawaii is the next stop to pick up casks of whale oil. You sail on a reach to 30N for following trade winds, with another stop in Tahiti. After a reach to beam reach, the lush tropical islands disappear. You pass 30S into the sou'westerlies. The wind hauls aft increasing daily to the screaming 50's. You pass the horn to port with minimum storm canvas for steerage with strong following storm winds and high wave action.

  You head NE, then north, turning NW after the doldrums for a stop in the Carolina's. Your vessel passes the 30N barrier into the nor'westerlies on a broad reach for Sandy Hook. The captains concern is to meet an incoming flood tide up the North River to the Manhattan company dock.

- Such a trip under ideal conditions would have poor food, rationed water, and other discomforts. We hope you enjoyed our theoretical square rigger rocking chair cruise to analyze the complexity of worldwide sailing.

- **Worldwide weather patterns** are well defined today by scientists. Without such documentation, square rigger captains had to pick up parts of this information by trial and error. Columbus,with experience sailing the west coast of Africa,sailed south thru 30N to make his 28N westing with steady following winds. For the return he crossed 30N to 37N to make his return easting to pick up the Azores.
- **North Atlantic circle route.**Spanish conquestidores and colonists used it for over 200 years...and Benjamin Franklin knew about and tried to publicize the Gulf Stream. Why were Northern European captains past 1800 still sailing against the westerlies to reach the young United States?
- **Variables?** Prevailing winds don't always prevail. While Cape Horn is littered with square rigger wrecks, it was flat and windless as the ***Queen Mary*** passed it to starboard to her new home port of Long Beach, California.
- **El Nino** is a new term for an old phenomenon with trade winds reversing direction following an equator temperature rise in the eastern Pacific. It was fully documented for the first time in 1982-3 while raising havoc worldwide. Suppose you were a square rigger captain in the Pacific two centuries ago with trade winds suddenly reversing themselves. It was just one of many mysteries of the ocean they would face in their lifetime.
- **Columbus** left Palos in 1492 on an ebb tide down the river Rio Trinto then SSW thru 30N to the Canaries. He sailed down to 28N to make his westing for Japan, though raising land at 24N...it must be India. Surprise.

  The return trip began at the equator. His caravels with poor pointing ability had to beat across the NE trades to 30N to make his easting,with the following nor'westerlies aft across the North Atlantic trip to pick up the Azores.
- **1850 emigrant trade** was often on vessels carrying lumber back to Europe. Makeshift bunks were used on the outward run for emigrants crowded in the hold with primitive conditions. Many captains sailed down to stay between between latitudes 41N and 42N to make their westing between Long Island and Cape Cod against the westerlies, a long, wet, miserable trip.
- **Northern route.** Another course was found from Northern Scotland to almost the tip of Greenland. A SSW course with the Labrador Current could take fishing vessels to the Newfoundland Grand Banks, and cargo vessels to Halifax. Mileage and time were greatly reduced compared to the circle route. It was cold, stormy, and foggy...while dodging icebergs.
- **Dull food vs spices.** Food choice was minimal for cold northern European winters requiring spices, though caravans proved too costly to carry spices from the east. England colonized India and nearby areas for the tea and spices, while the spice islands were colonized by the Dutch. Vessels for the east indian trade were small, beamy, and heavily armed.

  For an examination, how would you sail one of these three masted vessels on the long voyage to the spice islands and return to make the . most of the prevailing weather patterns. As they were warships they carried a large crew. Bad food and a considerable loss of life was expected on these vessels in the early 1700's.

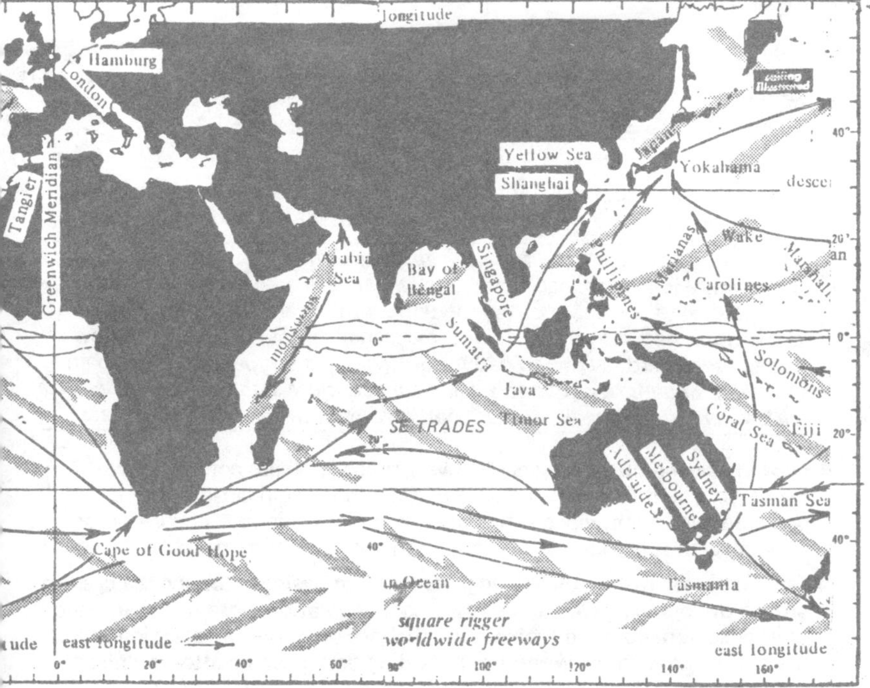

- **Yankee skippers.** Lax time for port to port requirements were common up to the tea clippers. They developed a new generation of hard working captains running tight ships continually performing to maximum potential. While following prevailing world wind patterns, they were pleased to do a better job with strong following winds if a storm passed thru.
- **Windjammers.** This discipline continued as cargo capacity increased requiring iron hulls, masts, yards, and rigging with ***Preussen*** the largest, page 282. The Big P Laeisz Line of Hamburg with hard driving masters never had one of their vessels dismasted rounding Cape Horn, which they passed regularly.
- **Engines** added weight, reducing cargo space.Hull masts, yards, and rigging windage proved impractical to make headway in a headwind, and discipline grew lax with engine power. The bark USCG ***Eagle*** with a 728 hp diesel is an exception, a training vessel not operated for profit.
- **Traps.** A square rigger was becalmed in a South Pacific high for two months with an island on the distant horizon. The last days of the captain's command were surrounded by empty wine bottles clanking against the hull.
- **Young Sea Officer's Sheet Anchor** by Darcy Lever, is a reprint of an 1819 manual in the same exact language used at the time to make rope, fully rig, and sail square riggers. It is an excellent, unusual present for an active sailor. Sweetman Pub. Co., pg. 184.
- **The Way of A Ship** by Alan Villers is excellent, covering global sailing conditions from clippers thru the growth to the end of the windjammer era. Charles Scribner's Sons.

early ketch

Thomas W. Lawson

Pride of Baltimore

America

European sailors joining us for an afternoon sail continually photograph schooners, the first they've seen. Why is it a unique American design?

Land and sea breezes develop in the absence of other patterns. When land temperature is greater than the nearby ocean, sea breezes flow onshore from noon to dusk, then disappear as the temperatures are equalized. The land temperature becomes cooler than the ocean after midnight when a flow of air begins seaward, lasting to early morning when temperatures are again equalized. ***Square rigged vessels had stronger, more stable winds on the west coast where prevailing westerlies combined with the coastal sea breezes.***

- **Westerly facing European coasts** have strong westerlies combining with sea breezes permitting normal square rigger operation close to shore. A parallel situation provided efficient square rigger operation on our west coast, except it is rocky and hostile with few natural harbors.
- **Our east coast** with weak shifting westerlies opposing incoming sea breezes, proved discouraging for early square rigger operation close to shore. Land breezes seldom go more than a mile offshore on our west coast, join on the east coast with the westerlies providing better sailing after midnight.
- **1700 east coast commerce.** Schooners began taking trade from square riggers with smaller crews, better maneuverability, and less time from port to port. Our only successful craft to equal the English in the Revolutionary War was a handful of privateer topsail schooners. Read ***Baltimore Clippers**** by Howard Chapelle, an excellent history of its evolution from pirates and slavers to the Baltimore clippers, influencing pilot schooners such as ***America,*** to the fishing and racing Glousterman schooners.Schooners captured by the British had their rigs cut down being "overhatted" for European waters.
- **West coast commerce.** Prevailing westerlies greatly increase the sea breeze flowing thru the San Francisco Bay and Sacramento Slough wind funnel spawning large fleets of lumber schooners and barkentines after 1850.

East coast boatbuilders lured by our gold rush, found the real gold in endless western forests. They built tiny maneuverable schooners to pick up lumber in small dog holes along rocky coasts. Lumber was transferred to large barkentines and schooners. The largest schooner was the 1,443 ton five masted ***Crescent*** launched 1904, abandoned at sea in 1918 after catching fire.

- **Wind funnels.** One coming up the Colorado River canyon is further squeezed as it rises up and over Hoover Dam into Lake Mead. Another funnel coming down a long converging canyon combines with it,tripling the overall speed of an undisturbed wind flow. These violent random winds are predictable by studying large area ***USGS Topographic Maps*** affecting mountain and canyon lakes and reservoirs.

from Sailing Illustrated

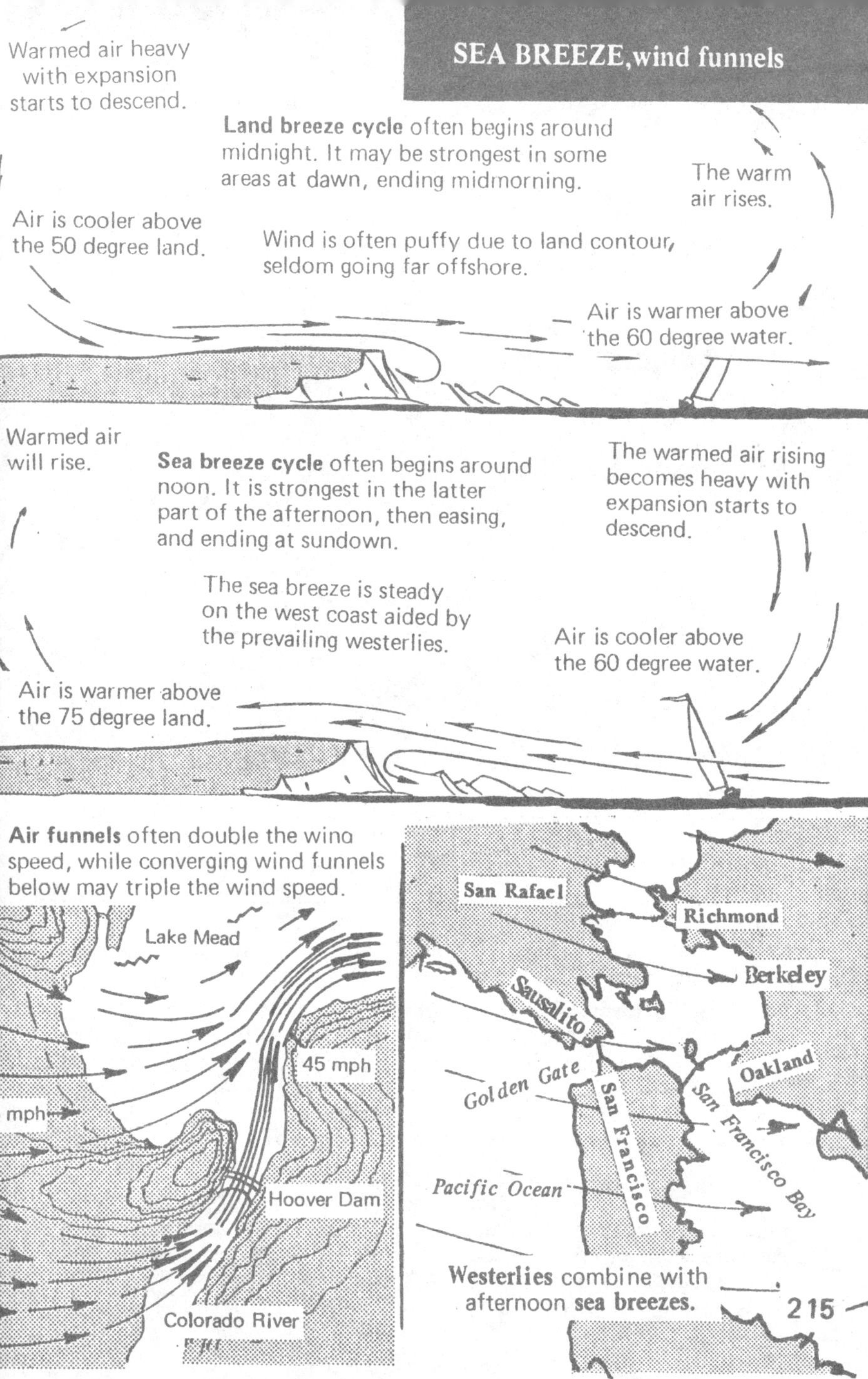
Warmed air heavy with expansion starts to descend.
Land breeze cycle often begins around midnight. It may be strongest in some areas at dawn, ending midmorning.
The warm air rises.
Air is cooler above the 50 degree land.
Wind is often puffy due to land contour, seldom going far offshore.
Air is warmer above the 60 degree water.
Warmed air will rise.
Sea breeze cycle often begins around noon. It is strongest in the latter part of the afternoon, then easing, and ending at sundown.
The warmed air rising becomes heavy with expansion starts to descend.
The sea breeze is steady on the west coast aided by the prevailing westerlies.
Air is cooler above the 60 degree water.
Air is warmer above the 75 degree land.
Air funnels often double the wino speed, while converging wind funnels below may triple the wind speed.
Lake Mead
45 mph
mph
Hoover Dam
Colorado River
San Rafael
Richmond
Berkeley
Sausalito
Oakland
Golden Gate
San Francisco
San Francisco Bay
Pacific Ocean
Westerlies combine with afternoon sea breezes.

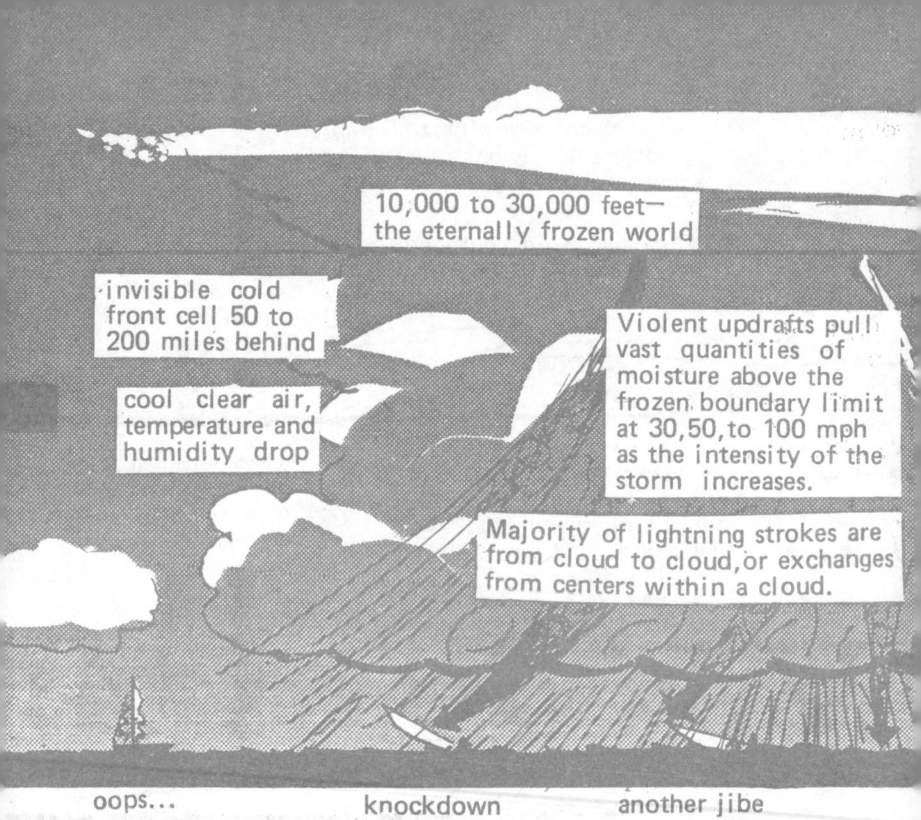

Highly complex thunderstorm lightning protection is covered on page 63 of our *Homestudy Guide.* Thunderstorms vary from one predicted yearly in our buffer zone, to 90 predicted for the west coast of Florida.

- **Hurricane.** It is a storm with winds force 12 and above, covering a large area of long duration. A thunderstorm may have violent, rapidly changing winds of hurricane strength averaging 20 minutes passing thru your area.
- **Low pressure storm areas** in our westerlies can be seen from the SW, W, to NW quadrants. They may be visible one to five hours before passing thru your area. **Dusters** occur in clear weather in our western and midwestern states which are just as violent, with dust clouds coming from the same direction. **AM radio static** which keeps increasing, ***is an excellent inexpensive method to predict, and be ready for a thunderstorm or duster moving in.***
- **Thunderstorms**—a cool updraft is the beginning. The wind momentarily stops and reverses direction with strong downdrafts requiring ALL sails down. When the center passes overhead, it is vertical with downdrafts slowly changing direction. As the thunderstorm moves out, wind direction will make a sudden reverse with a strong updraft. This is your final chance to enjoy a strong accidental jibe if any sails are still up. *Powerboating Illustrated*

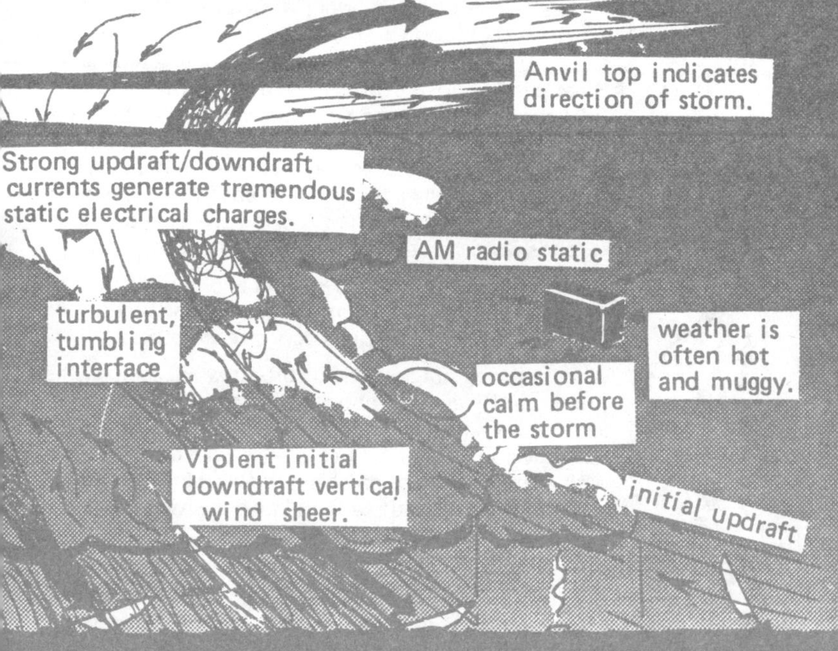

Cable requires a minimum turn angle...avoiding metal objects on sailboat.

- **Permanent lightning protection** is questionable for wooden and fiberglass boats relying on metal bonding systems. Whether the surge goes up or down the mast, ***vertical lightning surges require the straightest path which has the least resistance.***
- **Temporary protection.** Use a 1/16" thick sheet of copper a square foot or larger as a grounding plate. Use a copper grounding strap bolted temporarily to the mast...an aluminum strap will have 2/3 as much conductivity.
- **Sudden 25,000 degree heat** requires bolt on or crimp-on fittings as solder and insulation are instantly incinerated. Fore and aft insulated tiedowns will keep the grounding plate fully submerged in erratic wave action, as the strap must be isolated from aluminum fittings to avoid lightning flashovers.
- **Stainless has 1/50th the conductivity of copper.** An 18-8 stainless ground strap secured to stays or shrouds may cause unnecessary flashovers.

from Sailing Illustrated

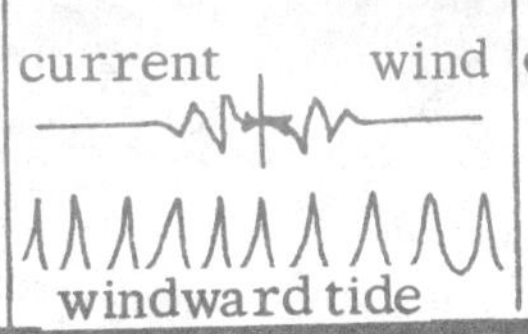

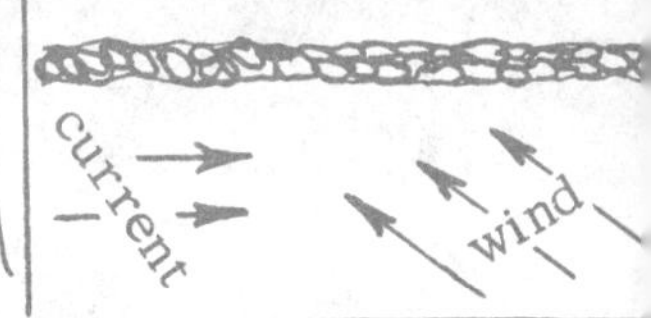

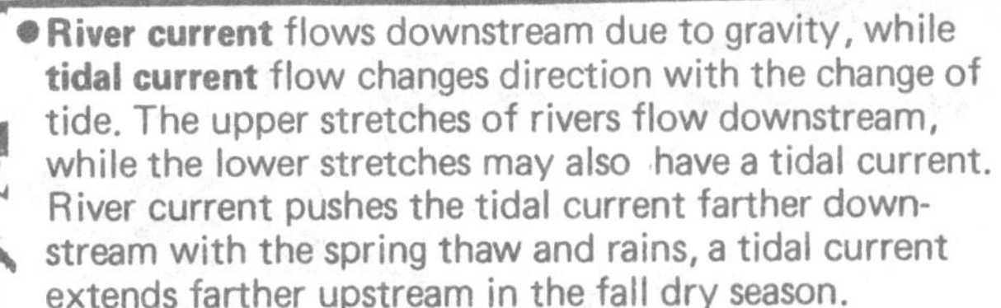

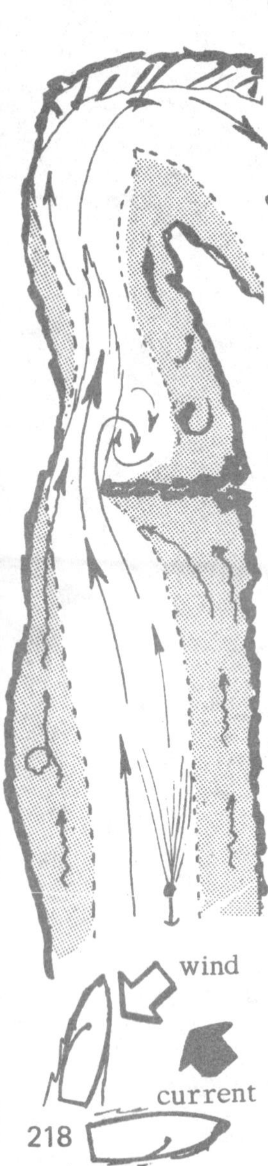

- **River current** flows downstream due to gravity, while **tidal current** flow changes direction with the change of tide. The upper stretches of rivers flow downstream, while the lower stretches may also have a tidal current. River current pushes the tidal current farther downstream with the spring thaw and rains, a tidal current extends farther upstream in the fall dry season.

- **Wave action** is minimal when wind and current flow the same direction, with maximum wave action when wind and current directions oppose each other.

  When a strong outgoing tidal current is opposed by the strong wind at an angle above fighting against a concrete jetty, vicious haystack random waves out of sequence may develop. If you sail in a similar tidal current area with a similar jetty, plan ahead to avoid losing steering control when these three elements fight each other.

- **Leebowing.** A sailboat makes better headway towards its destination with current on its lee bow. It will be making minimum headway towards its destination with wind on the windward bow, though going just as fast.

- **Manhattan tidal currents.** Our first craft was a Folbot kayak. It provided a rapid exposure to the Hudson River tidal currents. It was possible to drift upstream one weekend, and down towards the Battery the next weekend with little effort. A person can use the tidal currents to circumnavigate Manhattan with little effort.

- **Reading the river** is the term used to analyze and make the most of river currents. ***Current flow*** will be faster and smoother in the center, while slower and more disturbed in shallow water next to the bank. If a ***V points upstream,*** it indicates an underwater obstruction or funnel,A ***V pointing downstream*** in a straight stretch indicates the greatest depth.***The greatest depth in a bend*** is on the outside near the river bank. ***Eddies and whiri-pools*** on the downstream side at the end of a dike is a hazard to be avoided.

  Shooting the rapids in our Folboat in the spring when rivers peak provides thrills. A sharp bend with a strong current sent us charging into a herd of cows cooling off in the river causing a mass panic.To put it tastefully, we couldn't dodge the sudden bombardment as they ran tails high for the river bank. ***Sailing Illustrated***

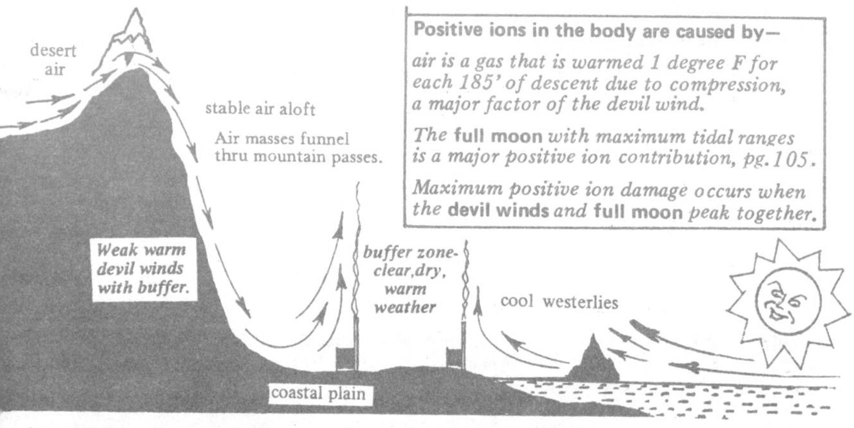

The least understood weather pattern found worldwide under a variety of names is called *Santa Ana* by our weather bureau and TV weather forecasters.

A better descriptive term was needed for worldwide recognition. We began with the term used by indians in the LA basin surrounded by high mountains.Their *santanta* was shortened to *santana* for *devil wind*. After 30 years research feeling its wrath on the land and ocean...we could find no better term than *devil wind*.

- **Warm devil winds** occur during spring, summer, and early fall with a high pressure area on the high Nevada plateau to the east, and a lower pressure on the ocean. The weak devil winds flow down the passes to be stopped by the cool incoming westerlies...with a warm, no wind **buffer area** between the opposing forces.
- **Cold devil winds** can become strong and vicious after Thanksgiving in our area as the storm tracks move south. While the winds may be weak on the high plateau, they gain speed as after going thru the passes they tumble down the slopes. This compresses and warms the air 20 to 30 degrees...while reducing the humidity. The *relative humidity averages 30%* as the cold devil winds move in...while the relative humidity in the warm devil wind buffer zone often registers *10 to 0 % relative humidity.*
- **Positive ion body charge** is developed as the devil winds move in. It blocks the analytical ability of the mind for 6 to 12 hours until the mind recovers its normal functions though the mind may produce normal mechanical operations. During this period you should avoid critical decisions. It is a time when auto collisions escalate,friendly arguments turn into dumb fights...and riots suddenly balloon out of control. Switzerland has well documented the escalating number of suicides as the devil winds move in.

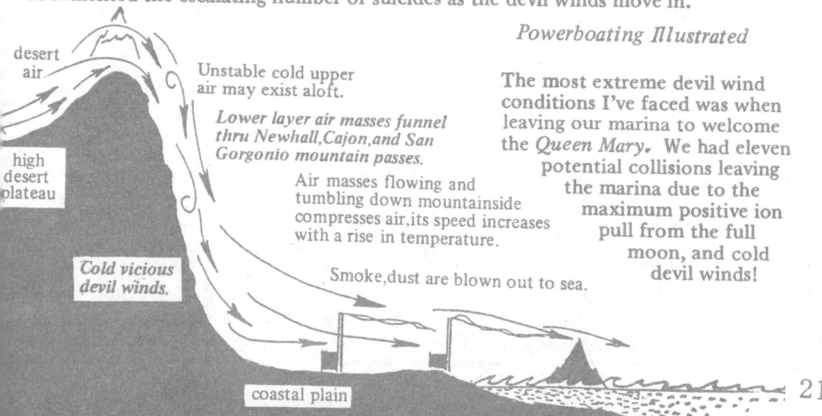

- **Our tidal day.** *The moon averages approximately 24 hours and 50 minutes to go around the earth. This corresponds to the two highs and lows on the facing page which complete a full tidal day.*
- **Tide** results on the ocean and in a glass of water, from the alternate vertical rise and fall of water caused by the gravitational pull of the moon and the sun, with a month required to go thru the four tidal stages.
- **Spring tide** has the greatest normal tide range occurring twice a month when the sun, moon, and earth work as a team to provide the maximum gravita-tational pull; while a **neap tide** occurs when moon and sun gravitational forces are in conflict and nullify each other.
- **Perigee and apogee.** Additional tide variables result due to the ***elliptical course*** of the moon with a maximum pull when it is closer to **perigee,** and a weak pull at **apogee** when it is farther away as shown on facing page.
- **Tidal surges occur during a hurricane** producing more extreme tidal ranges than found in spring tides. A large mushroom anchor is a pivot for the mooring chain, with the chain weight providing the holding power even in a storm with spring tides. During a hurricane tidal surge the scope may disappear with a direct pull on the mushroom anchor. This may pull the mushroom loose setting the boat adrift.

•

Depths listed on our navigational charts are charted on the east coast at **mean low tide**...while it is a **mean lower low tide** on our west coast.

As we sail farther south the tides begin to follow different rhythms.We recommend ***The Sea Around Us*** by Rachel Carson. While we find one type of rhythm in our area, the tides around Tahiti without the 50 minutes advance each day may find high tide at noon and midnight, plus low tide at 0600 and 1800.

- **Current** is a horizontal flow of water such as a river current gravity flow.
- **A tidal current** results when a tide change causes a directional change in flow in the current which reverses itself with the next tidal change. A good example is the Hudson or North River tidal current with the flow going farther north during the fall with minimal rain, and with the tidal current farther downstream with the spring snow thaw and rains with a much stronger outer ebb tidal river current.
- Tsunamis or **tidal waves** are caused by earthquake activity under the water making their own rules. They will pass on the open ocean surface with jet plane speed. Their wave peaks are so far apart they are seldom noticed.

As the tsunamis approaches the shore at right angles, the ocean can receed a half mile, then return a similar distance past the high tide mark with waves 60' to 100' high. Waves may have peaks to 200' high in narrow fiords.

When a tsunamis warning indicates one is coming straight into your harbor entrance in 3 to 4 hours, consider taking your boat out as far as practical into deep water for protection. If it is expected to pass at right angles to the harbor entrance, expect wild tidal surges without high,damaging wave action.

the WORLDWIDE TIDES

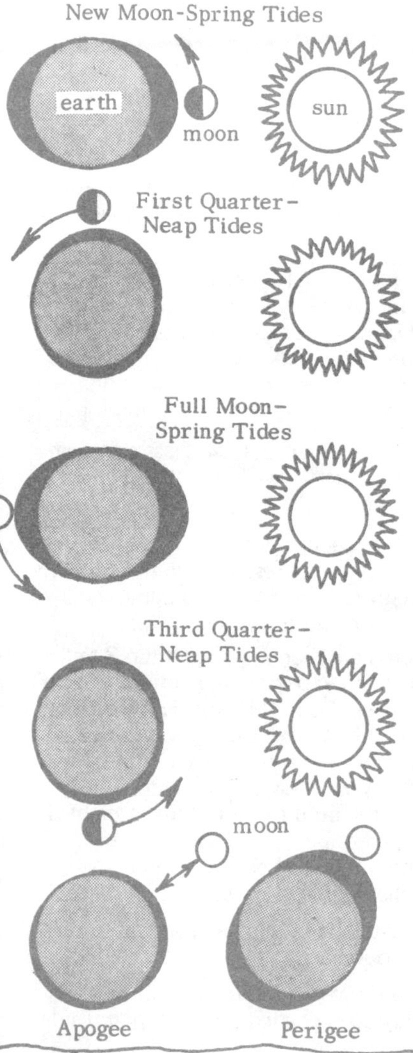
New Moon-Spring Tides
earth
moon
sun
First Quarter-
Neap Tides
Full Moon-
Spring Tides
Third Quarter-
Neap Tides
moon
Apogee
Perigee

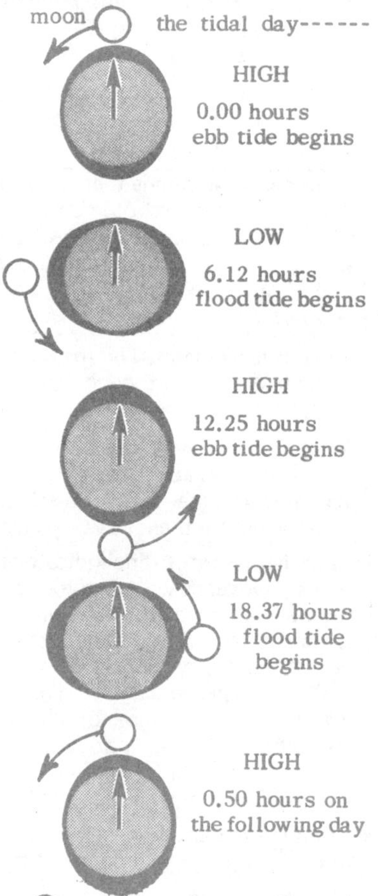
moon
the tidal day------
HIGH
0.00 hours
ebb tide begins
LOW
6.12 hours
flood tide begins
HIGH
12.25 hours
ebb tide begins
LOW
18.37 hours
flood tide
begins
HIGH
0.50 hours on
the following day

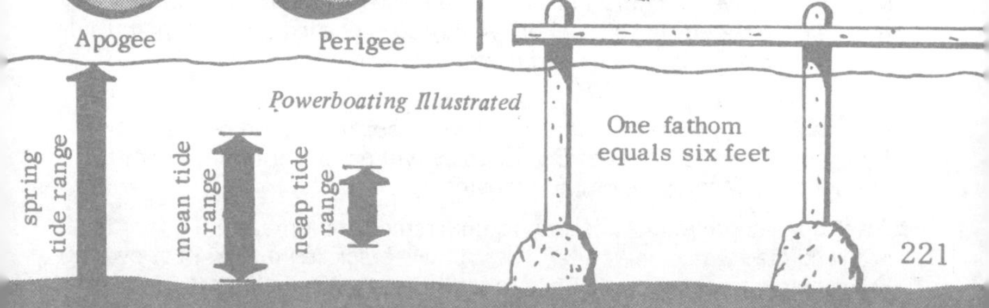
spring
tide range
mean tide
range
neap tide
range
One fathom
equals six feet

Powerboating Illustrated

- **Limited visibility.** *Fog signals must be given by all vessels underway, adrift, or at anchor, that need to be started before a vessel enters a fog bank, or area of restricted visibility including a sandstorm. Speed must be reduced so a vessel can theoretically stop in half the visibility distance. A lookout is required, especially in low visibility, with no other duties at the time.*

While the low visibility operational rules are well defined, their application may be poorly applied on recreational craft...though the rules are made to protect the same people.

Consider air a sponge that will soak up a lot of water vapor on a warm day. The air sponge volume is reduced during the evening when the temperature drops. ***Saturation begins*** as temperature drops, the sponge not able to hold the water vapor. The ***dew point is reached*** with fog potentials. The problem becomes finding an instrument which will indicate when the ***dew point*** is reached...with ample time to warn you of an incoming fog.

- **Sling psychrometer.** The theory sounds good in a protected classroom. How many boat owners though will swing one around their heads two or three times an hour to anticipate a fog moving in?

A better answer was required when we were caught out on the ocean with sailing students aboard as a thick fog moved in. We tested a **relative humidity indicator** for three years. The time lag required three years to understand its patterns before the idea was ready to recommend to readers..

- **Time lag patterns.** The indicator predicted approaching fogs often 3 to 5 hours hours in advance ...AND the two types of fog expected. A **medium to dense fog** was indicated with the humidity between 88 to 93% for daytime displacement operation, NOT for sailing at night. A **peasoup fog** was indicated during the day or night if visibility was clear, and the relative humidity 100% or above. If a light fog developed in your area, the peasouper was over the hill or a couple of miles away. A medium fog could lift at night. If visibility was suddenly above normal, a peasouper would soon move in, with the short visibility period nicknamed ***the kiss of death.*** Without the fog warning indicator it seemed an excellent time to go sailing.

- **Outgoing fog** also involves the time lag with the humidity dropping to 60% or 50%....though the fog may lift three hours later.

Mount a relative humidity indicator topside where it has a continuous air flow, easy to see from the cockpit. A shroud is needed on the top and sides to provide a more accurate reading when raining.

A new inexpensive humidity indicator designed for inside use has to be replaced yearly, preferably in the fall when our fog season begins. If used for a longer period, a loss of 5% accuracy will no longer be sufficient to predict a fog moving in, or a fog moving out.

- After 3 years preliminary testing to understand the time lag, the first fog not predicted was 6 years later when a huge black fog moved in at over 40 knots blanketing our area with zero visibility. A minute later the indicator needle jumped from 55% to over 100% then broke!

HUMIDITY vs FOG

Moisture particles in suspension

Air contains water vapor which is invisible below the saturation or dew point.

Much is written about fogs. The object is to predict a fog to avoid it, or keep your problems to a minimum by staying clear of shipping lanes.

temperature

relative humidity

Heavy falling moisture particles

A light fog results with an inflow of moist air, or a temperature drop. It will be indicated up to 5 hours in advance when humidity increases to 87-93%.

Light daytime fogs have sufficient visibility for sailboats to operate at displacement speeds...*but NOT enough visibility for night operation.*

fog signals are often required

light to medium fog

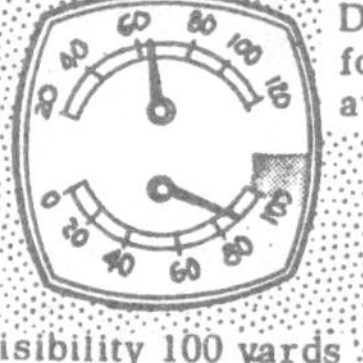

Displacement speeds for daytime operation, avoid nighttime operation.

visibility 100 yards to a quarter mile

Fog is visible moisture.

Heavy blanket of moisture particles

If a light fog exists and the humidity climbs to 100%, a peasouper can follow.

WARNING—a light fog can lift with excellent visibility as humidity increases, with a peasouper moving in.

Time lag proved confusing with early testing.,,before a fog moved out.

fog signals are mandatory

heavy fog or 'peasouper'

Any boat movement may be hazardous.

DEW POINT is 100% humidity

visibility 100' or less

Humidity can drop to 50% in a fog, lifting 3 to 5 hours later... be patient!

Boating safety is a term we have tried to understand for over 30 years.

We enjoy the challenges and thrills of sailing which requires the best equipment with continual maintenance. A parallel situation applies to flying to keep your airplane operating with minimum equipment problems. So who goes sailing or flying to be safe?

It is difficult to find any boating safety advances of consequence made by our appointed boating safety experts.

Advances seem to come from dedicated individuals such as Maurice O'Link of Stearns, who had to overcome considerable resistance from "safety" experts to produce practical Approved life preservers, page 227. Another was George Sigler, a USN fighter pilot, who was highly trained in the art of survival conditions from the desert to the jungle, the arctic, and on water.

When George and his wife Judy returned stateside, they bought a 22' sailboat. The more George checked into our "safety" standards, the more he questioned their shallowness for anyone facing a long time survival situation.

The only group listening was our navy, but the interest had to be unofficial. George sold his sailboat to buy a 15' Mark III inflatable, outfitting it with survival equipment. He was joined by another fighter pilot friend, Charlie Gore. Their ***Courageous*** was towed 20 miles from San Francisco, out past the Golden Gate Bridge and cast adrift July 4, 1974, destination Hawaii.

The worst moment occurred late the next morning in a force 7 upsetting their inflatable. It had to be dissasembled, righted, and reassembled requiring 1½ hours during which they lost much backup equipment. The cold water drained their body heat, requiring three days to recover from hypothermia.

The suspense grew in Hawaii as our navy didn't want to lose two highly trained carrier pilots. They were ordered to be picked up on the 56th day during which ***Courageous*** with a little sail covered 2700 miles downwind.

After three days of intensive testing by a team of service doctors, both were found in excellent health and discharged from the hospital. They lost approx. 45 pounds each in their self-caused high risk test.

George and Charlie fared quite well without food for 56 days with solar stills to make drinking water, plus other basic equipment. I wish those manufacturing survival equipment could take a similar interest to test their new equipment on the water in similar survival conditions before they are marketed. But...

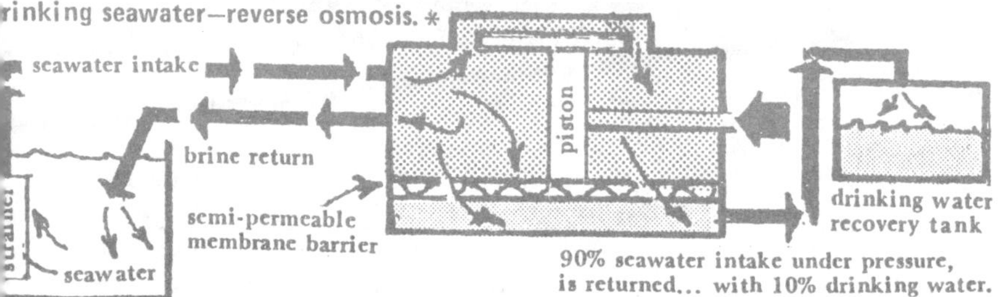

The vast Pacific— it didn't rain once during the 56 days underway on *Courageous,* providing the need for thorough planning with the fickle patterns of nature. George and Charlie used surplus USN solar stills to provide drinking water from sea water, no longer available.

Present answer— William and Simonne Butler spent 66 days in a liferaft when their 38' sloop was sunk 6/15/90 by whales in the Pacific... "Without the *Survivor 35* T.M., we would have not survived".

Sigler summarizes, "This system has been proven as you see, but it is expensive... cheap if you are on a life raft 1000 miles from nowhere".

While the manufacturer has various models, the one chosen by Butler was designed to USN specifications, producing 1.4 gallons of purified fresh water average per hour output. It weighs less than 7 pounds, is 22 inches long.

If life raft emergency equipment carries canned water, or a desalting kit producing hardly palatable water... *both are limited and not reusable, wasting much precious space aboard.*

A continuous supply of fresh water becomes the major need for survival conditions. **Three quarts of liquid daily** are used in normal conditions, average consumption for most people in one form or another.

A pint of fresh water is recommended minimum every 24 hours for survival when NOT eating. *Drinking water requirements are doubled* when air temperature increases from 70 to 90 degrees F.

Readers may have heard of half authenticated accounts of survivors living by drinking sea water... but how much, and for how long?

Dr. Alan Bombard, MD, was one of the first to test answers in 1952 as he drifted across the Atlantic from the Canaries to the Barbados on his raft *L'Heretique...* **drinking lots of rainwater.** He used a fruit press to squeeze juice from fish he caught containing some fresh water. In between he was reported to have drank sparingly of sea water.

"Do not drink sea water"— is summarized in U.S. Air Force Manual 64 carried in all Air Force survival kits, and on many commercial aircraft.

Drinking sea water. Dehydration begins with loss of weight. Thirst will increase as discomfort grows. It follows with loss of appetite, sleepiness, nausea, inability to walk develops as the senses fail. Victim becomes silent, his eyes are glassy, he has bad breath, followed by delirium. He may die quietly, become violent, and/or jump overboard to drown.

* Recovery Engineering, Inc., Minneapolis, MN phone 1-800-548 0406

Avoid becoming seasick.

Motion sickness. The small percentage of people who experience it in autos, trains, and airplanes, will also face it on boats requiring medication.

Seasickness potential is almost always a temporary situation with one in four sailing students facing the problem to some degree. Time and exposure are needed for the subconscious mind to accept a new type of motion.

The first symptom begins when a person looks down instead of out at the horizon. He has an uneasy feeling as his confused subconscious mind says, "Hey boss, something is wrong!" Disorientation begins as the victim looks down. His subconscious mind panics as a one foot wave grows to three, seven, then fifteen feet high. The disorientation process speeds up when going below. The mind panics with the stomach out of control.

Sailboat motion is easy to adjust to in normal conditions at displacement speed, operating with the normal motion of the ocean. The abnormal motion of powerboats, plus diesel exhaust, will require much more time for the subconscious mind to adapt to, especially on a fishing boat.

- **Fight back** without medication is the best answer while the subconscious mind analyzes, accepts, and adjusts to the new motion.Watch the horizon, keep busy, and enjoy a spirited discussion or argument to ignore the early stomach symptoms.

Medical doctors and their wives were the most seasickness prone students, as they are continually monitoring their body actions. While prescribing medication to patients, it is the first time many doctors have faced this new sensation. They unwittingly talk themselves into becoming seasick, a pattern repeating itself many times.

- Their minds had to be kept very busy to overlook the stomach symptoms for the adjustment period lasting up to an hour or so. After the minds have adjusted to the new sensation, I disclose my secret method to fight this monster with a good laugh as they know how to fight back.

It backfired twice with overmedicated medical doctors as their confused subconscious minds speeded the panic process. They were taken ashore to prescribe more drugs...with results worse than a 15 martini hangover!

- The best advice— **keep seasickness problems to a minimum.** Have ample sleep, then begin the day with a good breakfast even if you are on a diet. If you are on a race or cruise for a few days, avoid greasy foods such as sausage, pork chops, and fried chicken for the first day or so. *Seasickness will be assured for a person with little sleep,having donuts and coffee for breakfast,after a wine and pizza party the previous night.*

Our USN and USCG recruited many professional seamen at the beginning of WW II. A top secret conference was called as the majority had chronic seasick problems. Each person had to comment starting with a long list of admirals down to the lowest in rank, enlisted man Fred Kissner who said, "The answer is simple as they aren't accustomed to the slow roll of 300' to 400' vessels. Return them to the small rapidly moving craft they had been operating".The admirals groaned as the answer was so simple.

All sailboats and powerboats underway must carry at least one USCG Approved preserver for every person on board or the operator will be subject to a stiff fine.

Type 4

- **Before 1970.** If your boat was swamped or sunk and you had to rely on the Approved cushion, you would spend considerable time and effort to just hang onto it...instead of being able to have it become a part of your body as a swim aid to go to shore.
- **AK-1 Approved jacket.** The theory was to hold the head of an unconscious person above water, a rare occurrance. When exposed to spray and humidity the metals corroded rapidly, and the organic cloth was mildew prone. Due to the basic design theory, it proved almost impossible for use as a swim aid.
- **Ski belts** proved the most practical swim aid and on more than a a couple of occasions we used them to make rescues of persons drowning. Guess they were too practical for Approval.

Type 2

Four major life-preserver factors for you to consider–

- A comfortable swim aid with practical flotation that becomes a part of the body.
- Comfortable enough to wear for long periods without inner condensation.
- Tough synthetic cloth with corrosion-resistant metals.
- Storage–size is important and it must be ready for instant use. **123**

- **Stearns Mfg. Co.** was the pioneer in the new preserver field in the late 1960's, producing new jackets fitting the factors above before Approval. We put endless hours testing on two of them in four years, finding them practical, efficient swim aids.

We preferred the next smaller size to fit comfortably under jackets, windbreakers, and foul weather gear, providing protection by padding the body in a sloppy sea to protect it from sharp objects.

Type 3

- **Condensation** built up in other jackets we tested at the time. They became hot and uncomfortable in a half an hour in humid weather.On a cold winter night the condensation would soon drain body heat providing chills, As they interrupted your concentration span they became hazardous.

The Sterns inner mesh minimized condensation buildup on inner surfaces being comfortable to wear in a hot summer squall with high humidity. I wore one continually in a three day cold weather sail in heavy weather. It protected my body when below, and was warm to wear while sleeping.

The preserver picture is confusing to many new sailors due to regulations, price...and the purpose for which we have provided the history above.

- Swim with preservers at least 100 yards,then wear them topside and below to know their strengths and weaknesses. Do this under ideal conditions as you may have no more testing time when you and your friends suddenly have to use them as a last resort.

Swimming is an excellent exercise, the perfect way to cool off after a hot day, and/or strenuous sail. But how far can you normally swim?

The *Sea Temp indicator* is excellent to find warm spots in the ocean for snorkeling, swimming, and fishing, as a temperature drop of one degree finds fish losing their appetite...also to recognize hypothermia potentials with water below 70 degrees.

- **It is easy to fall overboard.** The nonswimmer will panic instantly while hollering for help underwater. Rescue must begin immediately which will always be hazardous. I've seen a 100 lb. weakling in a drowning trauma I rescued with the momentary strength of an angry professional wrestler.
- **Ski belt or horseshoe preserver.** Throw one to the victim to hang onto to stop the panic. My choice is usually a quality, correct size ski belt.
- **The heaving line,** page 194, with a boat fender tied onto the other end is excellent. Pull panicky victim slowly to the boat. Let nonswimmers come aboard on their own power as they are still dangerous.
- **Minimum swimming standards?** A medical survey listed ¾ of all drownings occur within 60' of shore. While many of these drownings occur on the beach...***it makes good sense for all sailors to easily swim 100' in normal conditions.*** During a fall overboard, or a sailboat capsize, they will be comfortable in the water and easy to rescue.
- **Take swimming lessons** if you can't easily swim this distance...yet what happens to the person who claims he can't be taught to swim? We took a new approach to help a few nonswimmers with this claim.

We took a different approach than swimming pool lessons. They used flippers and ski belts, joining us for an hour or so swim around the bay for ten days. Their reaction was laughter when I suddenly removed the ski belts in deep water. They knew they had positive flotation in ocean water as the mental hangups had disappeared, and the flippers gave them good propulsion.

Scuba diving instruction is the next major requirement so you can enjoy the additional benefits of snorkeling, tank, and free diving.

During the winter months take the time to invest in Scuba diving lessons. A warning is necessary as the pool has to be at least 13' to 15' deep to continually practice clearing your ears until it becomes second nature. Little did I realize I was a poor swimmer before taking these lessons in 1958. Though seldom using tanks afterwards, they taught me competency in the water to retrieve items dropped overboard, to check anchor holding, and snorkling to enjoy underwater scenery. While having positive flotation in salt water, I found many people also have negative buoyancy in fresh water, the author included.

- *Underwater Christmas?* The first televised underwater Christmas was held in Avalon Harbor at a depth of 30' in 1960. We found it difficult to have neutral buoyancy long enough to tie decorations on the Christmas tree, while schools of confused fish tried to fathom what the strange black land animals were doing.

Overboard

If you fall overboard--can you come back aboard under your own power without assistance under ideal...and under extreme conditions?

We recommend you try to climb aboard in a protected harbor under ideal conditions. You will learn enough variables to help a person come aboard under adverse conditions. Or suppose you are the victim?

The overboard drownings we checked into began to fall into predictable patterns. Though victims were alongside the boat, they couldn't climb aboard, and those on board couldn't help the victim.

After 15 to 20 minutes in water below 70 degrees the body heat is drained. As hypothermia moves in the victim falls into unconsciousness. The male or female victim often drowns in sight of their loved ones or friends.

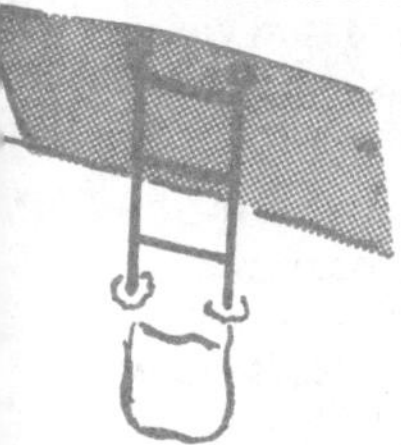

- **Boarding ladder.** With few exceptions these drownings could have been avoided IF the owners had taken the effort to install permanent, rigid boarding ladders, with the lower half dropping into the water to help a person coming aboard.

We are pleased to see many stern ladder installations on sailboats operated today...though wider teak steps should be added to the stainless rails.

The victim should always come aboard under his or her own power. An excited crew member under stress pulling a victim aboard...may pull the person across sharp screw heads, a sharp cleat, or other object that can cause unnecessary bodily harm.

- **Avoid rope ladders**— as they do almost everything wrong making it almost impossible to come aboard under ideal conditions. If you question this idea as several readers have, please test your rope ladder on your boat dockside in ideal conditions with help readily available.

- **Dinghy crew overboard.** Tippy outboard dinghies and sailing dinghies are a challenge to come aboard, with the stern being the least practical method.
- **Bowline stirrup.** Tie a bowline on one end of a short line, and secure the other end to a cleat or object in the dinghy. You can come aboard a tippy dinghy similar to climbing up on a horse under your own power.. The other person is on the opposite side of the dinghy to use their weight as a counterbalance to help the person coming aboard.

With all the popularity of ***National Safe Boating Week,*** according to USCG, 1986 had the lowest boating fatality in 25 years. Sailing is a sport which indicates a risk is involved. The sailor using reasonable preparation will enjoys his sailing thrills and have many wonderful memories.

Sailing risks rank far below major risks we face daily which are the bicycle, the auto, the shower...and the real crippler, the bathtub.

USCG NAVIGATION RULES International—Inland is the name of the official rulebook referred to. The official long name is COMDTINST M16672.2A. Buy from Superintendent of Documents, U.S. Gov't Printing Office, Washington, D.C. 20402.

Annex V— **88.05-Copy of Rules.** *After 1/1/83, the operator of each self-propelled vessel 12 meters (39.4 ft.) or more in length shall carry on board and maintain for ready reference a copy of the Inland Navigation Rules.*

While the rulebook is mandatory to be carried on sailboats 39.4' and longer, it is also an excellent idea to be carried aboard cabin sailboats and power-boats 20' to 25' and longer...for your own protection.

We have taught sailboat and powerboat operation going back to 1958 in Newport Harbor more as a personal test to understand problems faced by new boat owners, to develop methods to help them adapt to their new sailing and powerboating worlds.

Local boating traffic was heavy even in those early days, the reason we developed the sailboat and powerboat right-of-way rules, illustrating the basic regulations, with the rule numbers if further information was needed.

Powerboat rules are just as important to sailboat owners because if their sailboat operates with an outboard motor, or an inboard engine, it becomes a powerboat even if the sails are up. The operator then has to follow the powerboat rules, making it obvious so nearby powerboat operators know it is no longer following the sailboat rules.

We prepared laminated all-weather charts of the sailboat and powerboat rules that can be used for instant reference so you can show to family, crew, and visitors the unique world of Admiralty Law. It has a long history, being probably the first kind of international law to prevent collisions, with one vessel ordered to maintain course called the ***stand-on vessel,*** while the other ***give-way vessel*** must use methods to avoid the stand-on vessel.

Admiralty law is designed not only to prevent collisions,but the potential of collisions. When any potential collision may be in the developing stage, you are ordered ***to take appropiate action in time to maneuver out of a misunderstandin***

If an unusual situation develops where you have to break all the rules to prevent a collision, you begin to understand Admiralty Law, which is a unique world of its own. If you operate your sailboat in any high-density traffic area, take ample time to study the thinking of this type of law which is very strict that is designed for your self protection.

Deck-sweeper genoa jibs. This is a chronic problem we have faced for over 30 years as it blocks a large area of the operators visibility. When an owner uses this large size jib, he must take the responsibility to ***maintain a proper lookout by sight and hearing*** to prevent collision potentials. We recommend a jib to be raised at least 7" off the deck when not racing to provide much better visibility for the cabin sailboat owner.

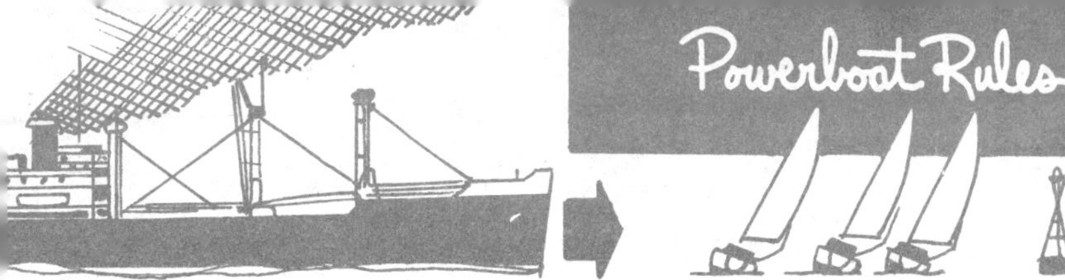

- **Sailboats and powerboats must give way to large vessels with highly limited maneuverability—**

▲*Rule 9 (b) A vessel of less than 20 meters in length (65.6') or a sailing vessel shall not impede the passage of a vessel that can safely navigate only within a narrow channel or fairway.*

▲*Rule 9 (c) A vessel engaged in fishing shall not impede the passage of any other vessel navigating within a narrow channel or fairway.*

▲*Rule 9 (d) A vessel shall not cross a narrow channel or fairway if such crossing impedes the passage of a vessel which can safely navigate only within that channel or fairway. The latter vessel may use the danger signal prescribed in Rule 34 (d) if in doubt as to the intention of the crossing vessel...*see right page.

- **River currents and tidal currents.** The rules governing a vessel under power are a vast improvement over the previous CG-169 rulebook, as the obligations of vessels operating in tidal currents are now defined. While not covered in the previous rules...they were still applied in little publicized court decisions.

- **Narrow channels.** *Rule 9 (a) (ii) Inland—...a powerdriven vessel operating in narrow channels...and proceeding downbound with a following current shall have the right-of-way over an upbound vessel, shall propose the manner and place of passage, and shall initiate the maneuvering signals...The vessel proceeding upbound against the current shall hold as necessary to permit safe passage.*

- **Crossing situation.** *Rule 15 (b) Inland— ...a vessel crossing a river shall keep out of the way of a power-driven vessel ascending or descending the river.*

- **Power and sails.** *International Rule 25 (e) A vessel proceeding under sail when also being propelled by machinery shall exhibit forward where it can best be seen a conical shape, apex downwards.*

  Rule 25 (e) Inland—...A vessel of less than 12 meters in length (39.4') is not required to exhibit this shape, but may do so.

  The first black cone I remember was more than 20 years after the rule was introduced that was torn and nailed to the spreader of an old motorsailer with the engine horribly out of tune. The boat was rolling miserably as it limped out our jetty belching a smoke cloud out the exhaust.

- **Sailboat engine controls should be mounted on the starboard side of the cockpit.** This permits the operator when his vessel is under power, to have better visibility of his danger zone to reduce chances of a collision. For night operation under power remember the idea, **red—STOP....green—go.**

ENJOY SAILING

It is cheaper to buy a sailor a friendly drink at the bar, than spend a week in court while the judge explains the term "port tack" to the newcomer. Can you think of a better reason to know the sailing regulations thoroughly?

"I suppose youse gentlemen know the rules regarding my sailboat right-of-way!"

Rule 12 (a). When two sailing vessels are approaching one another, so as to involve risk of collision, one of them shall keep out of the way of the other as follows:—

Sailboat **International AND Inland** *right-of-way* **Rules** *are identical.*

port tack ❶ starboard tack ❷ GREEN RED

WIND

Rule 12 (b)...the **windward side shall be...***the side* **opposite to...***which* **the mainsail is carried.**

port tack ❹ ❸ starboard tack

Rule 12 (a)(i) ***port tack KEEP clear***

When **each has the wind on a different side,** *the vessel which has the wind on the* **port side shall keep out of the way** *of the other.*

---

❻ ❺ leeward windward GREEN RED ❼ ❽ windward leeward RED GREEN ❾ windward port tack ❿ leeward port tack

Rule 1a (a)(ii)

windward KEEP clear

When both have the wind on the same side, the **vessel** *which is to* **windward shall keep out of the way** *of the vessel which is to leeward.*

Responsibilities Between Vessels—Rule 18 (a): **A power-driven vessel underway shall keep out of the way of:** *(iv)* **a sailing vessel.** *Exceptions are— Rule 9—Narrow Channels? Rule 10—Traffic Separation Schemes? Rule 13—Overtaking.*

Overtaking, Rule 13 (b). **A vessel shall be** *deemed* **to be overtaking when coming up...** *from a direction more than 22.5 degrees* **abaft her beam...to the vessel she is overtaking.**

Rule 13 (d)... **keeping clear** *of the overtaken vessel* **until she is finally past and clear.**

meeting ⓬ powerboat keep clear ⓫ overtaking vessel keep clear ⓭ overtaking sailboat OR powerboat 135° ⓮

Rule 9 (b), Large Vessels, Narrow Channels— A vessel of less than 20 meters in length (65.7 feet) **or a sailboat shall not impede the passage** *of a vessel that can safely navigate only within a narrow channel.*

Overtaking, Rule 13 (a). Nonwithstanding anything contained in the Rules... **any vessel overtaking... shall keep out of the way** *of the vessel being overtaken.*

Rule 2 (a)—**Nothing in these rules....shall exonerate any...master or crew... from the consequence of the neglect to comply with these Rules.** If your vessel is involved in a collision and you didn't know the rules, ignorance becomes a questionable defense. If your vessel has the right-of-way, and you want to be a nice guy giving the right-of-way to another vessel and a collision results...you are in trouble for breaking *Rule 2 (a).*

Admiralty law exists for a single purpose—to prevent collisions. You have strict regulations to follow to avoid collisions, yet when a collision is inevitable, you are ordered to break some or all the rules to prevent a collision. You then begin to realize the basic concept in an unclear situation, **is to initiate action so both vessels will have time to maneuver out of a misunderstanding.**

Less than 9% of collisions occur in open waters!

ENJOY POWERBOATING

Since a collision at sea can disturb one's whole afternoon, study, then follow the **International and Inland Rules** *closely.*

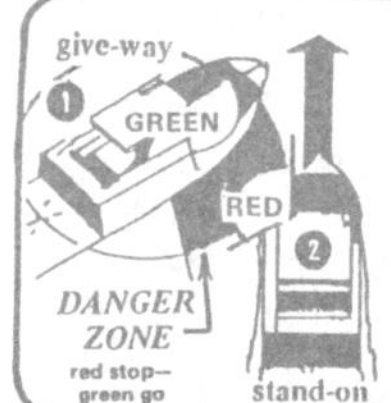

Crossing Situation, Rule 15 (a)—
When two power-driven vessels are crossing *so as* to involve risk of collision, the vessel which has the other on her starboard side shall keep out of the way and *shall*... avoid crossing ahead of the other vessel.

Rule 16. Give-Way Vessel..shall.. keep well clear..*R.17(a)(i) Stand on Vessel*—keep course and speed.

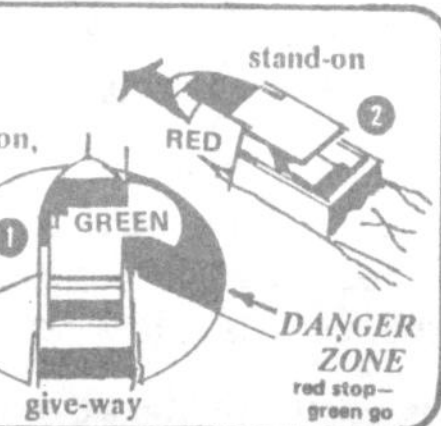

TOOT
RED
TURN to RIGHT
TOOT
RED

Head-on Situation, Rule 14 (a). When two power-driven vessels are meeting...*so as* to involve risk of collision, which shall alter her course to starboard *so that each shall pass on the port side of each other.*

River/Tidal CURRENTS

Exceptions *to above rule: Inland Rule 9 (a)(ii)— a* power-driven vessel...with a following current shall have the right-of-way over an upbound vessel, *shall...initate...the signals...It is applied under International with Rule 18 (a)(ii).*

*Inland Rule 15 (b)...*a vessel crossing a river shall keep out of the way of a power-driven vessel ascending or descending the river.

*Rule 32 (b)..*short blast..*about* 1 :second *duration. R.32 9c)..* prolonged blast..*4 to 6 second's duration.*

TOOT TOOT
GREEN
GREEN
TOOT TOOT

Maneuvering and Warning Signals— Rule 34 (g). When a power-driven vessel is leaving a dock *or berth, she shall sound* one prolonged blast.

TOOT

Narrow Channels, Rule 9 (a)(i)— A vessel proceeding along...a narrow channel...shall keep *as near* to the outer limit...*as is safe and practical. Sound Signal—Rule 34 (e).*

TOOT

Rule 34 (e). A vessel nearing a bend *or*...*a channel or fairway* where other vessels may be obscured...sound one prolonged blast.

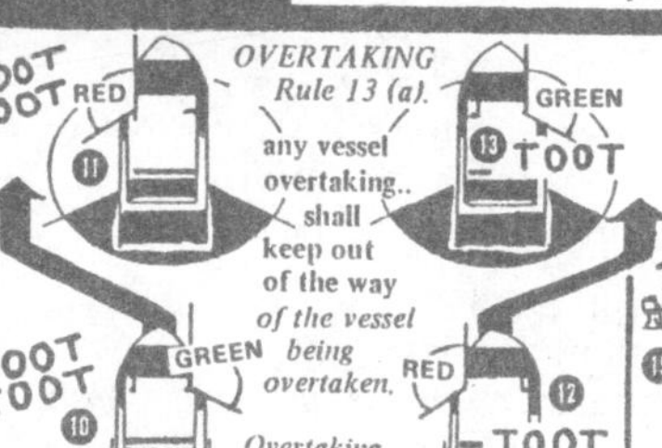

OVERTAKING Rule 13 (a).
any vessel overtaking.. shall keep out of the way *of the vessel being overtaken.*

Overtaking Signals—Rule 34 (c(i)(ii)

Rule 34 (a)(i)— three short blasts ..*"I am operating* astern propulsion".

TOOT TOOT TOOT

Warning Signals, Rule 34 (d). When vessels ...in doubt...to avoid collision...the vessel in doubt...giving at least five short *and* rapid blasts *on the whistle... may be supplemented by a* light signal *of at least five short and rapid blasts.*

Left-hand steering controls with limited visibility are hazardous because—

The powerboat on the right has the right-of-way in a crossing situation where risk of collision exists. The *stand-on* powerboat is ordered to hold course and speed....while the *give-way* powerboat takes evasive action. Powerboat should have an unobstructed view of the right side of their vessel with right side controls for visibility, while center steering controls provide excellent visibility for flying-bridge powerboats.

stand-on vessel holds course and speed
give-way vessel takes evasive action
mirror for over-taking vessels
Right side visibility can't be overstressed.

USCG NAVIGATION RULES International—Inland
Become THE expert by carrying the official 211 page rulebook aboard and refer to it continually. The official long number is COMDTINST M16672.2A.

Buy your copy from a marine dealer, GPO bookstore, or Superintendent of Documents, U.S. Government Printing Office, Washington, D. C. 20402.

A sailboat becomes a powerboat when its outboard or inboard engine is turned on requiring sailors to thoroughly know powerboat operating rules.

Rule 35– *Sound Signals...In or near an area of restricted visibility, whether by day or night...*will include sandstorms, fog, heavy rain or snow.

Freon horns are excellent for boating use, always carry a spare full tank aboard. AVOID weak, mouth-operated horn devices.

Use your autopilot as much as possible for a more predictable course in fog than steering by hand as the helmsman tends to under, then overcompensate. You must be able to disengage the pilot immediately if required for a course change to avoid a collision.

- **Most collisions occur on the edge of a fog.** We were underway at night from Catalina to San Pedro on a Newporter ketch. We entered a light fog that rapidly became a peasouper. One of the crew was on the bow making fog signals with a freon horn, with another lookout stationed between us as I could barely see the forward mast from the cockpit.

  I told the owner to call Long Beach USCG to find if their weather was clear. The answer,"That is restricted information", provoked my reply which was unprintable as we were close to the steamer lane. We suddenly broke out of the fog bank in clear visibility...on a collision course with a freighter 200 yards or so from us NOT in the fog and NOT making signals, breaking Rule 35–...*In or near an area of restricted visibility...*

- **Portable RDF.** We were returning to San Diego after a disasterous sea trial on the 97' schooner ***Estrilita*** when entering a fog bank. One of my crew had taken along his RDF, using it as a homing device standing next to me on the bow while I was operating an old hand pump fog signal. We tangled with a large outbound navy vessel we couldn't see, but we could hear the bow wave. We suddenly came out into bright sunshine to find we were missing the partially submerged south jetty by a few adequate feet.

- **17' outboard cruiser.** We were swallowed up in a fog bank in 1960 on the way to Catalina as we entered the steamer lane. The ocean was very flat and it was difficult to hold an adequate course at displacement speed. I cut the engine hearing a swissshing sound with a tow line dead ahead.

  Fog can play strange sound tricks. Neither of us heard fog signals, nor saw the towing or towed vessel, with the tow line too close for comfort. Even the traditional four-legged fog warning, a barking dog, would have helped.

- **My mistake.** I had a sailing lesson the next day in San Pedro with a thick fog outside our jetty. I waited for it to lift until midafternoon. I left under autopilot and power knowing that *if a collision occurred I would have a hard time defending my action.* I soon picked up the sounds of a very large vessel at anchor, getting my curiosity.

  Suddenly I saw the anchor chain and bow but not the deck line above which was lost in the fog. I turned 180 degrees heading back to the harbor using RDF and depth sounder, disoriented and horribly scared, to postpone the lesson. The large vessel was a USN transport that had just returned from Korea, anchoring probably an hour or so earlier. The crew was preparing it for an open house for local residents the next day.

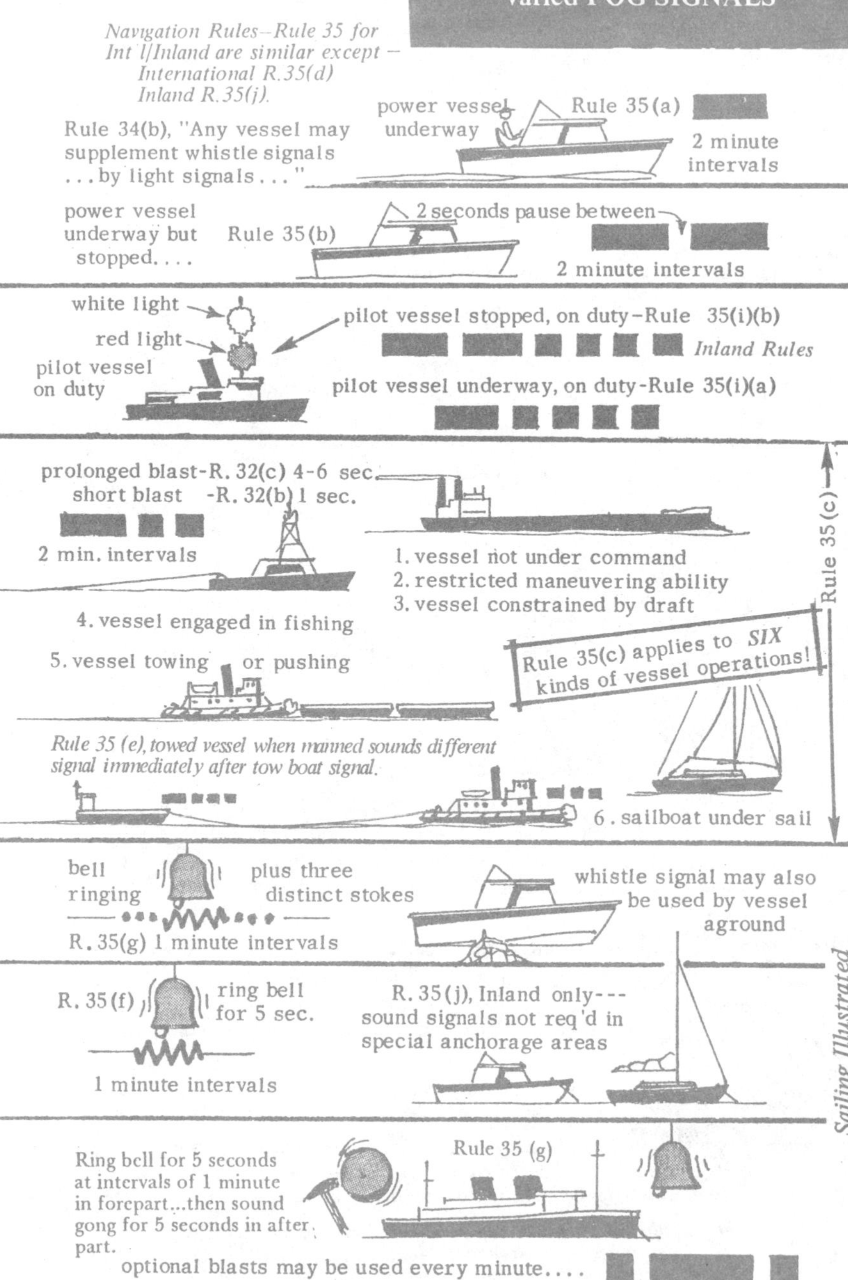
Navigation Rules–Rule 35 for Int'l/Inland are similar except – International R.35(d) Inland R.35(j).
Rule 34(b), "Any vessel may supplement whistle signals . . . by light signals . . . "
power vessel underway
Rule 35(a)
2 minute intervals
power vessel underway but stopped. . . .
Rule 35(b)
2 seconds pause between
2 minute intervals
white light
red light
pilot vessel on duty
pilot vessel stopped, on duty-Rule 35(i)(b)
Inland Rules
pilot vessel underway, on duty-Rule 35(i)(a)
prolonged blast-R. 32(c) 4-6 sec.
short blast -R. 32(b) 1 sec.
2 min. intervals
1. vessel not under command
2. restricted maneuvering ability
3. vessel constrained by draft
4. vessel engaged in fishing
5. vessel towing or pushing
Rule 35(c)
Rule 35(c) applies to *SIX* kinds of vessel operations!
Rule 35 (e), towed vessel when manned sounds different signal immediately after tow boat signal.
6. sailboat under sail
bell ringing
plus three distinct stokes
R. 35(g) 1 minute intervals
whistle signal may also be used by vessel aground
R. 35(f)
ring bell for 5 sec.
1 minute intervals
R. 35(j), Inland only--- sound signals not req'd in special anchorage areas
Ring bell for 5 seconds at intervals of 1 minute in forepart...then sound gong for 5 seconds in after part.
Rule 35 (g)
optional blasts may be used every minute. . . .

Sailing Vessel Underway

Rule 25(a)..shall exhibit (1)sidelights;(ii)sternlight.

Def.;Rule 21(b)sidelights .. green light on the starboard side,and red .. on the port side showing an unbroken light ... of 112.5° (each).

Int'l/Inland Rule 21(b)continues .. In a vessel of less than 20 meters (65.6')the side lights may be combined in one lantern carried *on* the fore and aft centerline of a vessel.

Inland only Rule 21(b)continues ... a vessel of less than 12 meters (39.4')... the sidelights when combined in one lantern shall be placed as ***nearly as practical*** to the fore and aft centerline of the vessel.

Int'l/Inland Rule 25(a)(ii) sternlight-Def. Rule 21(c)... a white light placed as nearly as practical at the stern showing an unbroken light over an arc ... of 135 degrees ...

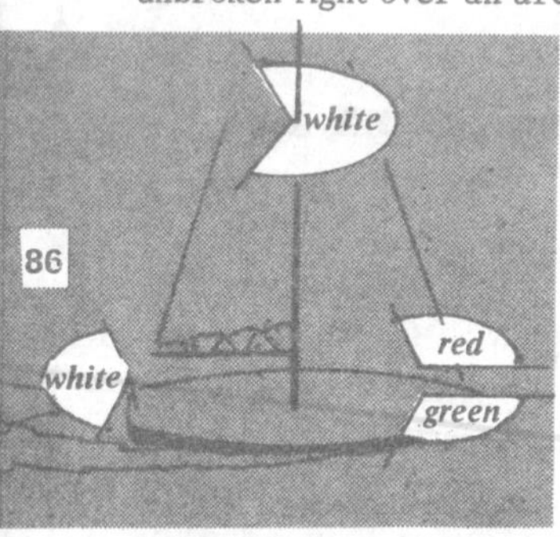

Power Driven Vessel Underway

Int'l/Inland Rule 23(a).. shall exhibit:

(i)a masthead (engine) light forward.. (iii) sidelights; and (iv)a sternlight.

Int'l/Inland Def.; Rule 21(a) "Masthead light" (engine light)..a white light ... showing ... over an arc ... of 225 degrees.

Sternlight variables Under Power-

Int'l Rule 21 (c) ... a white light ... of 135 degrees ...

Inland-Rule 23(c) A power-driven vessel of less than 12 meters (39.4').. may .. exhibit an all-round 360° white light and sidelights.

Int'l-Rule 23(c) A power-driven vessel of less than 7 meters (23') .. whose maximum speed does not exceed 7 knots may ... exhibit an all-round white light ... if practical, also exhibit sidelights.

Anchored Vessels and Vessels Aground

Int'l/Inland Rule 30 (a) ... shall exhibit.....
(i) in the fore part, an all-round white light ...
Def.;Rule 21(e).. an unbroken light.. of 360 degrees.

Inland (only) Rule 30 (g) A vessel of less than 20 meters (65.6').. when ... in a special anchorage area .. shall not be required to exhibit anchor lights ...

Inland (only) Rule 30(e) ... less than 7 meters (23') at anchor, not in or near a channel ... where other vessels normally navigate .. shall not be required to exhibit .. (an all-round white light).

NOTE: *the original 1977 (COLREGS) Navigation Rules list 20 meters as 65.7 feet... while the 1982 rules, list it as 65.6 feet. Did the meter expand, or did our foot measurement shrink?*

tricolor light — anchor light — strobe light

bird chaser

Sailing Vessel Underway-Sail ONLY

Several manufacturers combine the running, anchor, and strobe lights shown above into one unit (at left).

The 1983 USCG Navigation Rules are now identical for International and Inland Rules 25(b). . . sailboats less than 20 meters (65. 6'). . . the lights. . . may be combined in one lantern. . . at top of mast where it can best be seen.

Advantages of tricolor running light . . . visibility increases with height above water surface . . . while its visibility cannot be blocked with the jib.

Tricolor running light uses one bulb with less drain than pulpit mounted sidelights/stern light requiring two or three bulbs. A 10 watt bulb may have a mile visibility . . . while a 25 watt bulb may double its visibility, with an increased battery drain.

If your sailboat has both running light systems, pulpit mounted sidelights and sternlight at eye level are easier to see in close quarter harbor maneuvering situations.

When a sailboat becomes a powerboat, the tricolor MUST be turned off . . . replaced by the engine light, side lights, and the stern light.

KEEP CLEAR warning to a vessel on a collision course with our vessel. Inland Rule 27 states instead—*When a vessel is in distress and requires assistance she shall use or exhibit...* A high intensity white flashing light at regular intervals from 50 to 70 times per minute.

Tricolor light disadvantage . . does your mast have a tabernacle to lower your mast in order to replace a burned out tricolor bulb?

STROBE light (pg. 232) should only be turned on *when a vessel is in distress and requires assistance.*

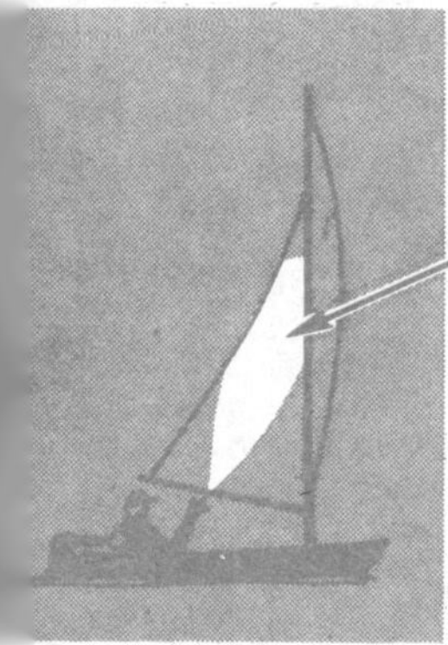

Int'l/Inland Rule 25(d)(i) A sailing vessel of less than 7 meters (23'). . (if she doesn't show other lights covered) . . shall have . . a white light which shall be exhibited in sufficient time to prevent collison (see left).

Marine Strobe Light— *for emergency use only.* We use it for vessels in distress requiring assistance. The original purpose in heavily traveled European waters was a warning in addition to the horn for large vessels underway to keep clear of each other.

International Rule numbers are listed.

72 Colregs

Rule 25(d)(ii). A vessel under OARS...show white light in... time to prevent collision.

lengths meters	feet
7	23
12	39.4
20	65.6
50	164
100	328
150	492
200	656

Rule 23(c), POWER-DRIVEN vessel less than 7 meters(23 feet)whose maximum speed(underway) doesn't exceed 7 knots (though it can go faster) may..exhibit all-round light...if practicable, also exhibit sidelights (shown on vessel under 39.4' long. Outboard powered rowboats and dinghies are included in this rule.)

Rule 22(b)(c)	less than 12 meters (to 39.4 feet)	12 to 20 meters (to 65.6 feet)	less than 50 meters (to 164 feet)	
R/G 112.5° each	comb. or separate 1 mile vis.	comb. or separate 2 mile vis.	separate 2 mile vis.	Rule 21(b)
masthead 225°	2 mile vis. 3.3' above R/G	3 mile vis. 8.2' above gunwale ←	5 mile vis. (Annex 1)	Rule 21(a)
stern light 135°	2 mile vis.	2 mile vis.	2 mile vis.	Rule 21(c)

A POWER-DRIVEN VESSEL THAT EXCEEDS 7 KNOTS—

navigation light definitions Rule 21 (a)(b)(c)
navigation light visibility Rule 22(b) 12 meters to under 50 meters; (c) vessels less than 12 meters (39.4 feet long)

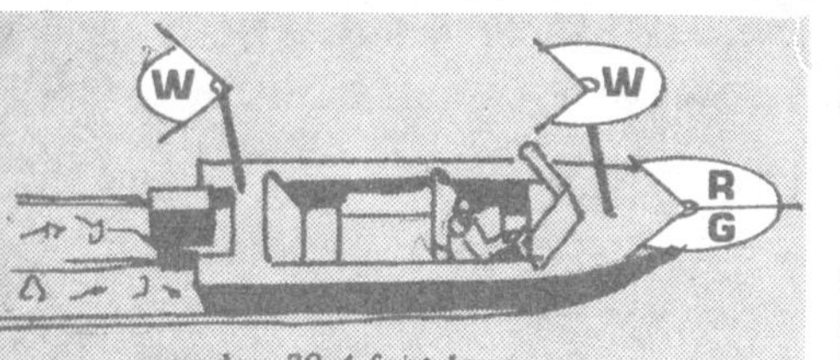

under 39.4 feet long

All powerboat lights are covered in Rule 23(a)----
(i) masthead light (225°)
(iii) sidelights (112.5° each)
(iv) sternlight (135°)

(International Rules require SEPARATE masthead and stern lights...they may NOT be combined as with Inland Rules).

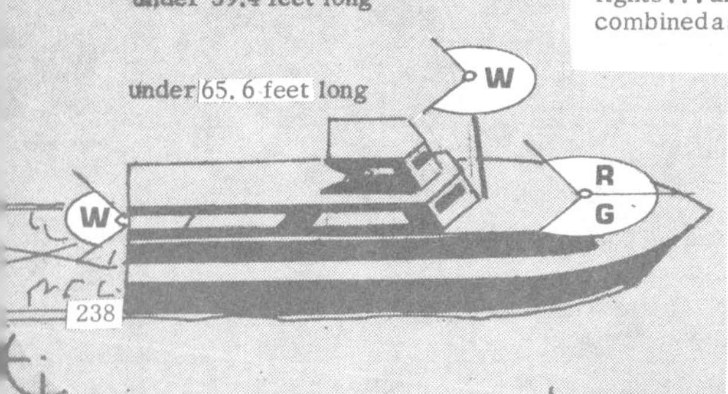

under 65.6 feet long

Int'l/Inland R.21(b) ..a vessel less than 20 meters(65.6 feet) ...sidelights may be combined into one lantern.

BOATING UNREACHABLES?

Capsize, **USCG 1972**– *613 vessels 432 fatalities*
Capsize, **USCG 1989**– *576 vessels 330 fatalities*

When USCG was trasferred to DOT in 1967, the new big boss demanded more tax revenues with boat operator licensing (sound familiar?). The new Commandant in 1972 demanded it before the Boating Industry Association. *"We are willing to give voluntary education one last chance".*

The statement by Admiral Wagner that 68 % of boats were 10' to 14' long came at the right time to make USCG licensing leaders uncomfortable. We prepared a 24 page booklet challenging USCG licensing, with over 370 copies hand delivered to Wash., D.C. Headquarters Dec. 7, 1972.

40% of Californian1972 statistics involved the high risk *accidental boater fisherman/ duck hunter* with 52 vessels, 41 fatalities, and 32 injuries. Our booklet well defined USCG was the problem. Their answer was the 1976 *Nationwide Boating Survey* proved the accidental boater hazard much higher than anticipated. The bottom line,.. *fishermen and duck hunters are licensed!*

Car top transportation boats must serve a purpose. Most are cheap, portable, hard or soft boats, minimum size, narrow, tippy, with little freeboard that are often department store 'weekend specials'.

Most fishermen have to stand up to cast (why?). They seldom check the weather, often wearing heavy, bulky clothing that rapidly soaks up water in a capsize. Many are *nonswimmers* as they panic immediately, hollering for help underwater... I have investigated several of these problems.

Pants fly unzipped? Many single occupant capsize drowning victims seem to answer the call of nature, probably standing up on the side of their tiny, tippy boat before capsize, especially after a couple of beers.

A plastic jug/ boat bailer (Approved?). It needs to be carried aboard all small tippy boats to eliminate the high-risk open zipper hazard.

After USCG licensing push came to a screeching halt in 1973, we were invited to a closed conference in Alameda with officers representing the retired Commandant. Was it to reduce drownings? Our comments–

"The troublemakers are licensed.. fishermen and duck hunters. They need to produce a certificate they could swim 100' under normal conditions, tested by Red Cross, YMCA, school systems, etc., *before being able to apply for their next license".* This would eliminate the major share of capsize, nonswimmer drownings in so shallow water they can walk ashore".

"Second, Approval of a quality ski belt, the most practical answer for this high-risk field". As their new tax source disappeared, their minimum interest dropped to zilch for an answer to help recreational boating.

Mandated Boating Course? USCG began a quiet end run in 1976 to again raise taxes with little in return for boat owners. It was a pleasure to stop it in 1977 in a 3 day USCG seminar. Present USCG plan in the works started by present USCG Commandant Admiral William Kime in 1981, is a yearly *$25 duck stamp user fee* for registered boats. Will it support their *no tolerance, no intelligence, no responsibility* boarding policy?

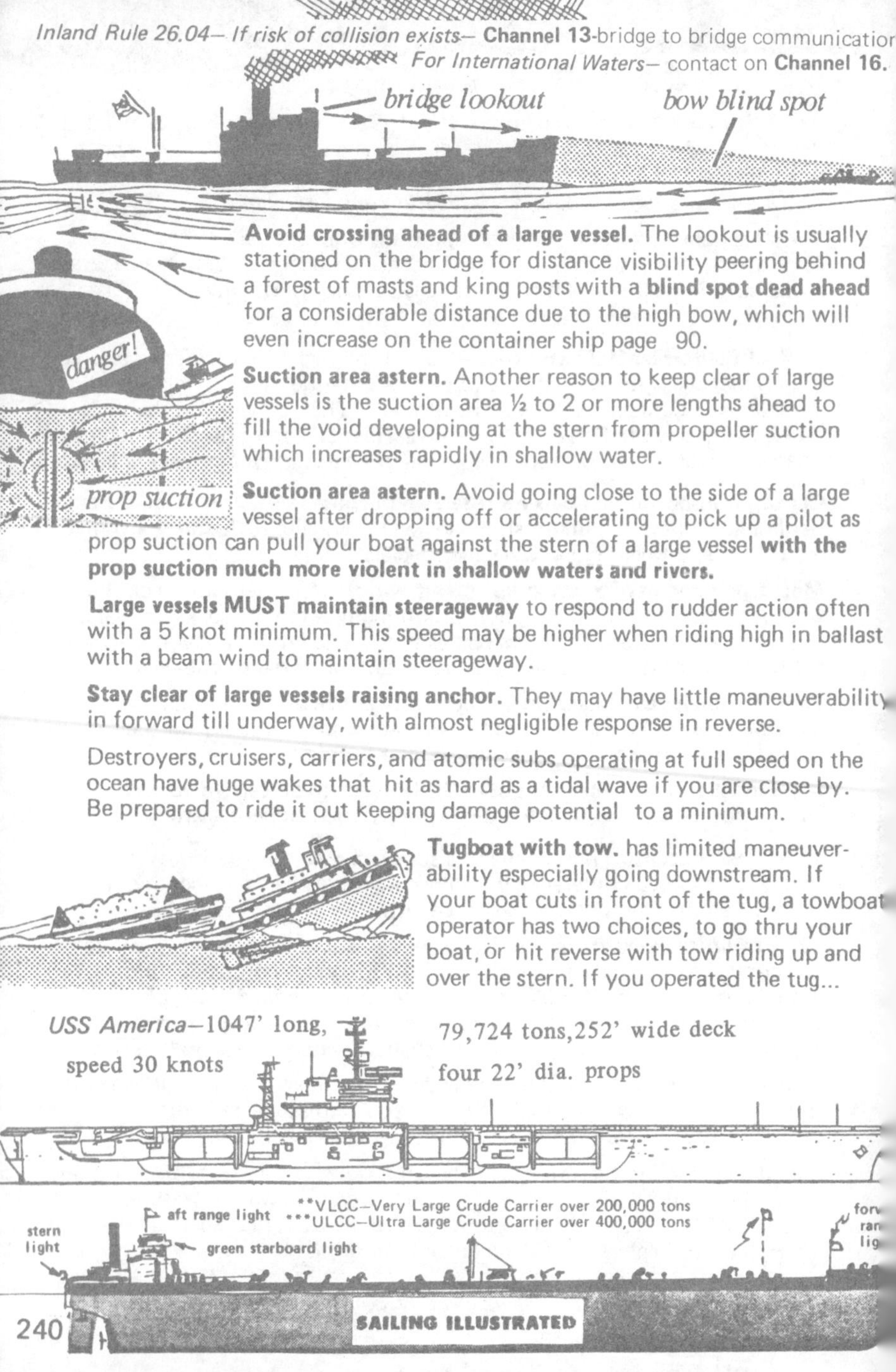

Inland Rule 26.04– If risk of collision exists– **Channel 13**-bridge to bridge communicatior

For International Waters– contact on **Channel 16.**

Avoid crossing ahead of a large vessel. The lookout is usually stationed on the bridge for distance visibility peering behind a forest of masts and king posts with a **blind spot dead ahead** for a considerable distance due to the high bow, which will even increase on the container ship page 90.

Suction area astern. Another reason to keep clear of large vessels is the suction area ½ to 2 or more lengths ahead to fill the void developing at the stern from propeller suction which increases rapidly in shallow water.

Suction area astern. Avoid going close to the side of a large vessel after dropping off or accelerating to pick up a pilot as prop suction can pull your boat against the stern of a large vessel **with the prop suction much more violent in shallow waters and rivers.**

Large vessels MUST maintain steerageway to respond to rudder action often with a 5 knot minimum. This speed may be higher when riding high in ballast with a beam wind to maintain steerageway.

Stay clear of large vessels raising anchor. They may have little maneuverability in forward till underway, with almost negligible response in reverse.

Destroyers, cruisers, carriers, and atomic subs operating at full speed on the ocean have huge wakes that hit as hard as a tidal wave if you are close by. Be prepared to ride it out keeping damage potential to a minimum.

Tugboat with tow. has limited maneuverability especially going downstream. If your boat cuts in front of the tug, a towboat operator has two choices, to go thru your boat, or hit reverse with tow riding up and over the stern. If you operated the tug...

USS America–1047' long, 79,724 tons,252' wide deck

speed 30 knots four 22' dia. props

**VLCC–Very Large Crude Carrier over 200,000 tons

***ULCC–Ultra Large Crude Carrier over 400,000 tons

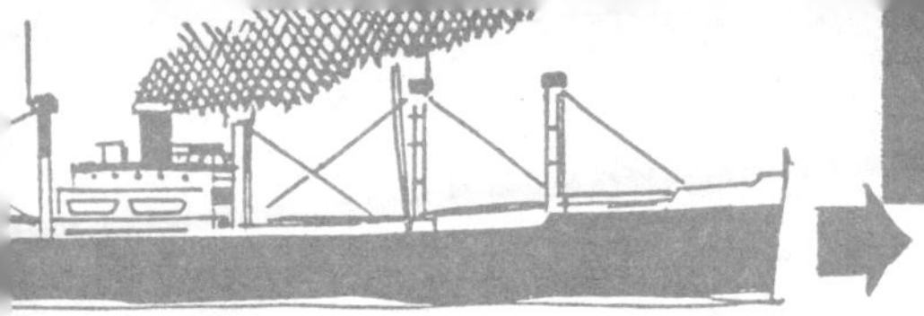

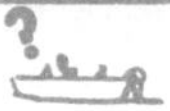

Do everything possible to avoid collision courses with large vessels on the ocean and in narrow channels as you are placing yourself in a difficult position, and you may not be around afterwards to argue your case.

The WW II T-2 **17,000 ton tanker** below, 523′ long, 68′ beam, requires ½ mile and 5 minutes to come to a ***crash stop*** from 15k cruising speed.

The **Very Large Crude Carrier 200,00 tonner** *Idemitsu Maru* requires from 10 to 15 ship lengths, or 2½ miles and 21 minutes for a ***crash stop.***

The **326,000 ton** *Universe Ireland below, **engines put on stop*** not full astern will take an hour to run her way off and come to a stop.

A **400,000 ton Ultra Large Crude Carrier** requires 4 to 5 miles and 30 minutes backing full to come to a ***crash stop.*** During this time she will be unable to respond to her rudder or regulate her speed.

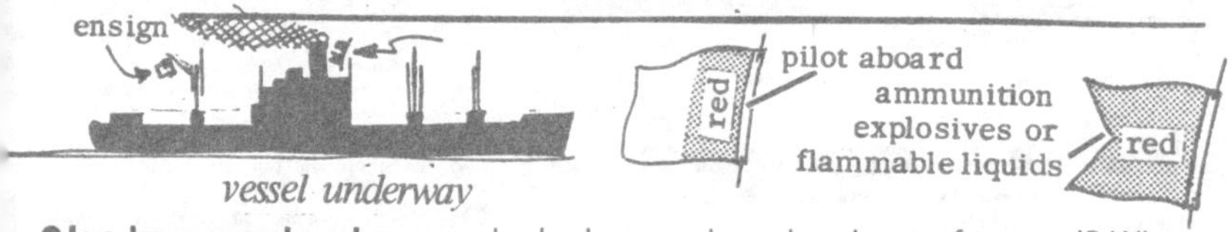

vessel underway

- **Is a large vessel underway...**docked, or anchored and out of control? When the black anchor ball forward, and the Union Jack (on U.S. military and other vessels under our government control) are coming down, and the national ensign is being removed from the stern staff...**Stay clear as the vessel is out of control while preparing to get underway.**

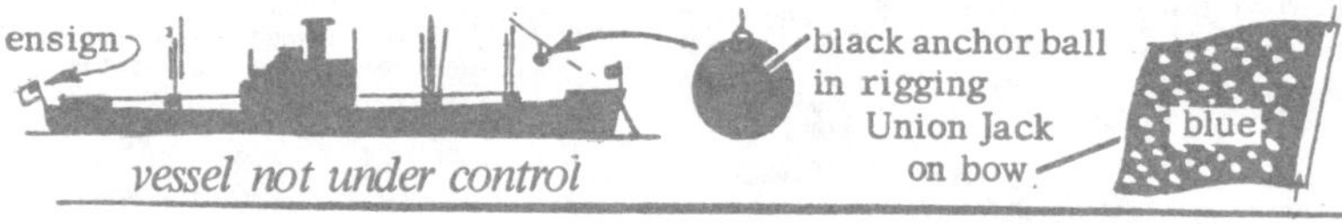

vessel not under control

- **How large is large?????** The carrier *J.F. Kennedy*, a **83,0[illegible]onner,** is 1050′ long, 270′ beam, with a crew of 5000, while the *Qu[illegible] Elizabeth II* is a **67,000 tonner** 963′ long and 13 stories high.

  The 1968 Bantry Bay Class tanker *Universe Ireland* is a **326,000 tonner** 1136′ long, 174′ beam, carrying 2,513,588 barrels of oil, with largest tankers **1,000,000 tonners** 2000′ long, with a 300′ beam.Our LA/ Long Beach Harbor is one of 20 ports in the world...with a maximum 65′ high tide draft,the only U.S. port able to handle smaller supertankers.

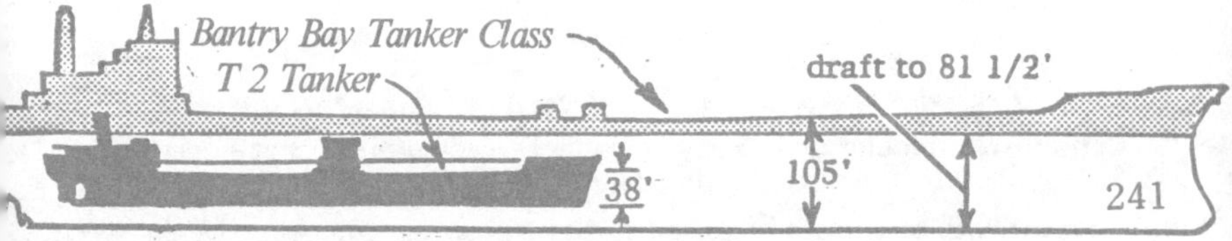

Do you know these warnings?

"Instead of taking the long way around the barge, the shortcut will save us thirty seconds".

A shortcut across a towing hawser may disturb more than just one's afternoon.

aft bridge lookout *blind spot dead ahead* Oops.

metric conversion		
1 m–3.3 ft	5 m–16.4 ft.	50 m–164.0 ft.
1.5 m–4.9 ft.	6 m–19.7 ft.	75 m–246.1 ft.
2.0 m–6.6 ft.	7 m–23.0 ft.	100 m–328.1 ft.
2.5 m–8.2 ft.	8 m–26.2 ft.	150 m–492.1 ft.
3.5 m–11.5 ft.	10 m–32.8 ft.	200 m–656.2 ft.
4.0 m–13.1 ft.	12 m–39.4 ft.	500 m–1640.4 ft.
4.5 m–14.8 ft.	20 m–65.6 ft.	1000 m–3280.8 ft.
	25 m–82.0 ft.	

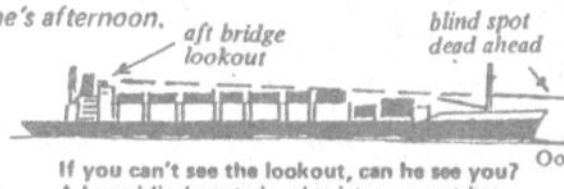

If you can't see the lookout, can he see you? A huge blind spot ahead exists on most large vessels, with the poorest lookout potentials on containerships averaging 20 to 25 knots.

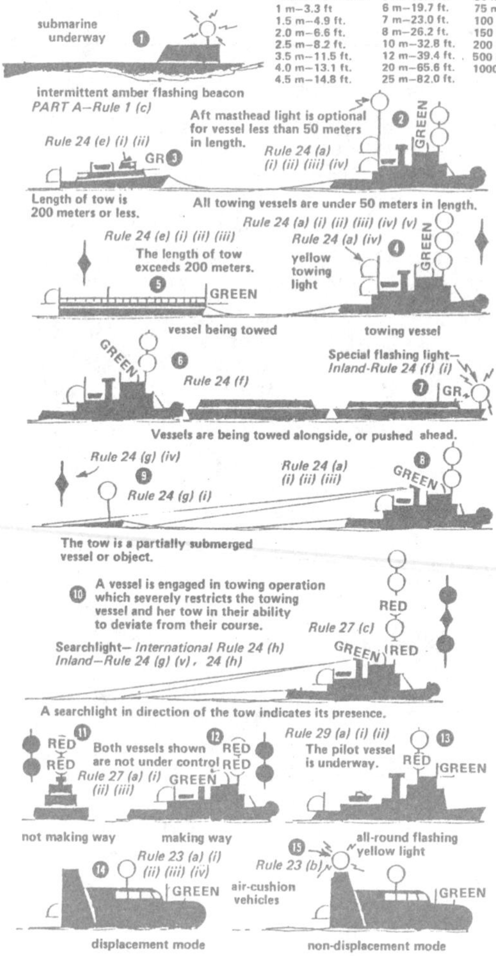

submarine underway ①

intermittent amber flashing beacon
PART A–Rule 1 (c)

Aft masthead light is optional for vessel less than 50 meters in length.

Rule 24 (e) (i) (ii) GR ③ *Rule 24 (a) (i) (ii) (iii) (iv)* ② GREEN

Length of tow is 200 meters or less.

All towing vessels are under 50 meters in length.

Rule 24 (e) (i) (ii) (iii) *Rule 24 (a) (i) (ii) (iii) (iv) (v)* *Rule 24 (a) (iv)* ④ GREEN

The length of tow exceeds 200 meters. ⑤ GREEN

yellow towing light

vessel being towed — towing vessel

GREEN ⑥ *Rule 24 (f)*

Special flashing light— *Inland-Rule 24 (f) (i)* ⑦ GR

Vessels are being towed alongside, or pushed ahead.

Rule 24 (g) (iv) ⑨ *Rule 24 (g) (i)* *Rule 24 (a) (i) (ii) (iii)* ⑧ GREEN

The tow is a partially submerged vessel or object.

⑩ A vessel is engaged in towing operation which severely restricts the towing vessel and her tow in their ability to deviate from their course.

RED *Rule 27 (c)* GREEN RED

Searchlight— *International Rule 24 (h)*
Inland—Rule 24 (g) (v), 24 (h)

A searchlight in direction of the tow indicates its presence.

⑪ RED RED Both vessels shown are not under control ⑫ RED RED *Rule 27 (a) (i) (ii) (iii)* GREEN

Rule 29 (a) (i) (ii) The pilot vessel is underway. ⑬ RED GREEN

not making way — making way

Rule 23 (a) (i) (ii) (iii) (iv) ⑭ GREEN air-cushion vehicles ⑮ *Rule 23 (b)* all-round flashing yellow light GREEN

displacement mode — non-displacement mode

Many thanks go to the Port of Los Angeles harbor pilots, and to Chief Pilot Jackson Pearson, for patience with the final review of this chart.

This chart was prepared for the author's personal use.

While teaching commercial vessel light recognition for over 30 years, after being wet, cold, and fatigued with too many operational hours on the water...the memory of red over white and white over red becomes fuzzy.

Commercial vessel operator friends grinned saying the chart could also help their judgment when fatigued for rapid identification...*in time to maneuver out of a misunderstanding* as the reason for Admiralty Law is to avoid collisions AND collision potentials.

These lights and signals are used worldwide. They are basic theories...which in application have variables that are endless. To this we add careless operators, plus tired or fatigued operators on the approaching vessel.

① Naval vessels due to unusual construction often find it difficult to display normal running lights. A **submarine** on the surface displays an intermittant flashing beacon with one flash each second for three seconds on, three seconds off.

Avoid taking a shortcut BETWEEN tugboats and tows. The lethal hawser can upset and sink many vessels going between tugboat and tow.

②③ The tug has **a tow 200 meters long or less.** Will the tow have strong running and stern lights, or will the last barge have a weak kerosene lamp?

④⑤ The tug has a tow that **exceeds a length of 200 meters.** The **yellow towing light** is an aid when helmsman is steering the towed vessel.

⑥⑦ The tugboat is pushing barges ahead. A special **flashing light** is added as a special warning on a long string of barges for Inland.

⑧⑨⑩ These are difficult towing situations. Can you see the light or diamond on a partially submerged object? Can you recognize a tug with a submerged tow which can't deviate from course?

⑪ The two vertical lights indicate a vessel **not under command** and not underway.

⑫ The vessel is underway though not able to respond to steering controls.

⑬ These lights show a pilot vessel on **pilotage duty underway** at night...with pilot vessel painted on the side for daytime identification.

⑭ A strange shaped vessel is operating at displacement speed.

⑮ The all-round **flashing yellow light** indicates an air-cushion vehicle operating above displacement speed. The light also provides a warning to avoid trying to follow the vehicle to port as it can operate in shallow water, and operate on dry land.

Inland – Annex V, Rule 88.05, the operator of each self-propelled vessel 12 meters or more...**shall carry on board** and maintain...a copy of the Inland Navigation Rules.

If you run into a submarine...please don't sink a friendly one.

Containership lookout visibility is highly restricted producing a major hazard for any vessel crossing under its bow in the blind spot dead ahead.

Tugboat with tow. Hazards of the tow line between cannot be overstressed by operators blundering across the lethal tow line.

These signals indicating NO maneuverability or LIMITED maneuverability provide the warning...KEEP CLEAR.

225 degree higher aft masthead light

GREEN

16

The 476,025 ton ULCC **Globtik Tokyo** in a panic stop backing full, may take 30 minutes and 4 to 5 miles to come to a full stop. During this time it cannot respond to the rudder...nor the speed regulated.

Rules 22, 23—recognition lights

225 degree forward lower masthead light

"Don't worry Henry. It is only a supertanker... and we are on starboard tack".

Ships are the largest moving monsters designed, built, and operated by men.

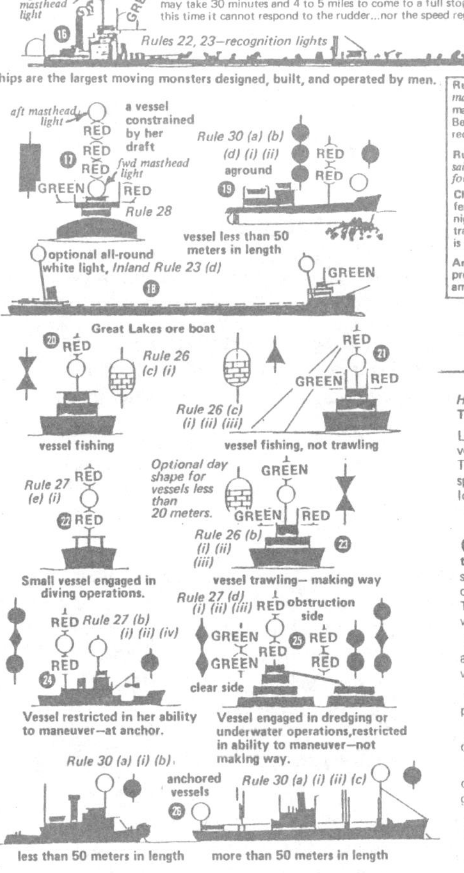

Rule 10 (b)—...*vessels of less than 20 meters in length and sailing vessels may under all circumstances use inshore traffic zones.* We have sailed many times in recent years near coastwise traffic lanes from Newport Beach to Oxnard. **Rule 5.** A trained **lookout** is required for early recognition of various kinds of vessels underway to estimate their speeds.

Rule 10 (e), and 10 (e) (i)—*A vessel of less than 20 meters in length or a sailing vessel shall not impede the safe passage of a power-driven vessel following a traffic lane.* **Rule 9 (b)— narrow channels** also applies.

Closing speed? This had to be anticipated correctly so as not to interfere with eight large vessels operating from 6 to 20 knots on a stormy night crossing the Santa Barbara Channel southbound coastwise traffic lane going to the Channel Islands. Early vessel type recognition is required to anticipate closing speeds to keep clear of those vessels.

Anticipating fog. We found quality relative humidity indicators may provide a 1 to 5 hour warning of an approaching fog. This provides ample time for your vessel to be well clear of coastwise traffic lanes.

USS Missouri—880' long
108' beam 36' draft
57,950 ton displacement when fully loaded

How large is large? The Ultra Large Crude Carrier **Globtik Tokyo** has eight times the tonnage of the **USS Missouri.**

Large crude carrier speeds vary from 12 to 15 knots, fishing vessels and containerships may average 20 knots or more. The 962' long, 66,581 ton **Queen Elizabeth 2** has a service speed of 28½ knots, and a top speed of 32 knots. The Iowa Class **USS Missouri** has a top speed of 33 knots.

17 *A vessel constrained by her draft* indicated at night by **three vertical red lights,** and a **cylinder** in the daytime— is severely restricted in her ability to deviate from her course due to available water depth, often a channel. The **Globtik Tokyo** can draw up to 92', and larger ULCC carriers to 100 with similar percentages to that of an iceberg underwater.,

18 A Great Lake ore boat averaging 618' long, 61' beam, and 24' draft, under Inland Rules can carry an all-round white light aft instead of aft range light and stern light.

19 The vessel is aground displaying these special lights, plus lights and signals for vessels at anchor.

20 The vessel is not underway engaged in fishing. Two cones or basket in the rigging are shown for daytime use.

21 The vessel is underway engaged in fishing. The single cone with apex upward in the rigging indicates outlying gear more than 150 meters horizontally from the vessel.

22 A small vessel engaged in diving operations. During the daytime it can fly the International Code flag "A".

23 The vessel is underway trawling, dragging a dredge net or other apparatus thru the water.

GREEN
GREEN GREEN
GREEN RED
27
Rule 27 (f)

vessels underway engaged in mineclearance operations

24 The buoy tender is restricted in her ability to maneuver shows these special signals, plus the regular signals showing she is also at anchor.

25 A vessel is engaged in dredging or underwater operations. The dredge has a barge alongside restricting her ability to maneuver. Signals indicate clear side and obstruction side.

26 Vessels are at anchor with one under 50 meters long, the other over 50 meters long.

27 The vessel engaged in minesweeping operations is dangerous for other vessels to approach closer than 1000 meters astern...or 500 meters to either side of the minesweeper.

For International Waters— contact on **Channel 16.**

Inland Rule 26.04— If risk of collision exists— **Channel 13**-bridge to bridge communication.

We have enjoyed operating near large vessels for over 30 years, requiring us to know the lights and signals to keep out of their way. We planned to have several pages in this major revision covering these lights and signals.

After considerable day and night testing on the water, the full size 8½ x 11 charts we were also testing proved more practical for your use. These facing pages show greatly reduced identical reproductions of this chart.

- **Coast Guard Ensign** is flown on USCG vessels in commission. It is recognized by the vertical orange and white stripes, with a blue eagle and white stars on a white background.
- **Coast Guard Auxiliary Ensign,** the *blue ensign,* is flown from a members vessel after passing inspection, with the owner having to be an active CGA member. It is dark blue with a white diagonal stripe.
- **U.S. Power Squadrons' Ensign** is flown on a vessel commanded by and operated by a USPS member in good standing. It has alternate blue and white stripes, with an anchor on a red square background.
- **International Divers Flag** is a recent addition, the Code Flag A which is blue with a white vertical stripe. It is rigid, not less than 1 meter in height.
- **U.S. Divers Flag** is red with a white diagonal stripe which was introduced in 1958. If flown on a vessel it indicates a diver below, or swimming in the vicinity of the vessel. Look for a second divers flag nearby on a divers float.
- **Racing Pennant????** Since 1960 we have recommended this pennant to be flown from the bow of a sailboat racing...after the start flag for the class is given. The pennant would be advantageous for jockeying in a large regatta in tight quarters with numerous classes to identify those who are starting, and those not yet starting. Though sailors we have contacted liked the idea for various reasons, the idea is still ignored over 25 years later.
- **U.S. National Ensign,** our ***Stars and Stripes,*** is flown from a sailboat stern staff under sail, power, and at anchor.Before 1971 protocol was to fly it on a gaff-rigged main hoist. When it was sewn to the leach of a marconi mainsail, it often tangled with the backstay.
- **Yacht Ensign** was originally restricted to documented vessels. It follows the same protocol today that is practiced with our ***Stars and Stripes.***
- **Union Jack** is flown on military and commercial vessels operated by our government, see page 241. It evolved from the ***Jack Tar Crew Flag*** indicating limited authority of crew members when a vessel was docked or at anchor. For recreational boating use, it is to be displayed on the jackstaff of a sailing vessel with two or more masts on Sundays and holidays, and when dressing ship.

U.S. FLAG ETIQUETTE

Flag Etiquette began with USN usage. Others such as New York Yacht Club and USYRU started the practices we follow today.

Traditional practice was to fly the U.S. Ensign on a flag halyard from the outer end of the boom up to the gaff.

As a marconi mainsail eliminated the gaff and flag hoist, the Ensign was sewn to the mainsail leach which was clumsy.

By 1971 those in charge of Flag Etiquette realized this was impractical, agreeing to the stern mounted use under sail, power, and at anchor.

U.S. Ensign, U.S. Yacht Ensign, USPS Ensign, CGA *blue* Ensign

blue-owner absent; *white*-meal flag; *blue/white strips*-guest flag

honoring a foreign ensign in another country

yacht club burgee

officers flag, or owners private signal

The yacht club burgee takes preference on a sloop instead of the officers flag, or private signal, flown from the masthead.

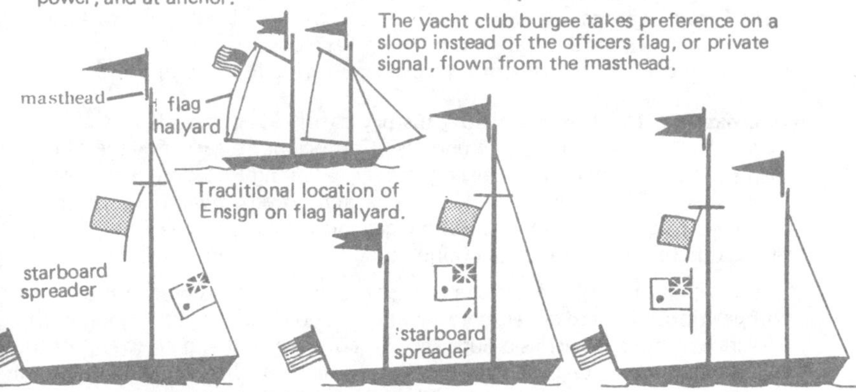

Traditional location of Ensign on flag halyard.

Flag locations are shown above for vessels at anchor or under power. Flag locations below are used when under sail.

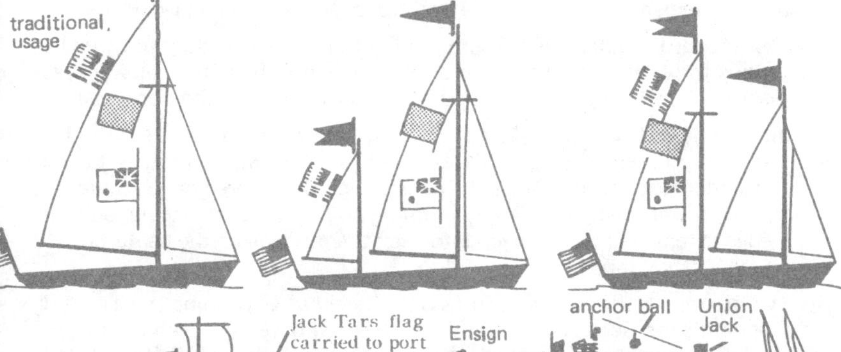

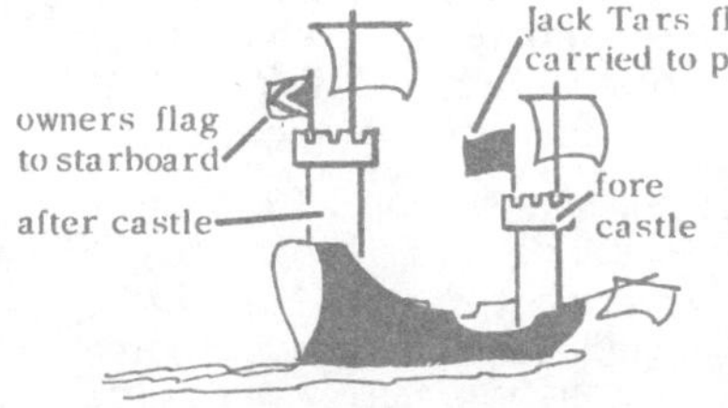

the *Jack Tar Crew Flag*

anchor ball Union Jack

Ensign

Military vessels moored or anchored–*KEEP CLEAR as they need room to get underway IF*–**forward,** black anchor ball and Union Jack are coming down, and **aft**–Ensign is being lowered on stern staff.

Commercial vessels follow same procedure while eliminating the Union Jack.

We have frozen two dinghies in time with distinct, highly competitive personalities to be avoided for sailors buying their first sailboat.

- **Finn.Class.** *Wild Turkey* was the 3rd Finn we detailed, a low production, super quality fiberglass dinghy. It was on our front lawn for a week while we detailed the rigging with all the neighborhood kids standing in it as they pretended to be pirates, when we weren't looking. *Wild Turkey* was to later place second in the 1970 Finn Worlds.

  We compared it with Finns prepared for the 1984 Olympics nearby. Since the only differences were the location of the cam cleat adjustment controls, *Wild Turkey* was way ahead of its time, built by Fred Cook, a teenager, and his dad. It takes little imagination to find Fred has been in charge of hardware testing and development for Schaefer Marine for several years.

- **International 14.** It has an official history dating back to 1887 as a gaff-rigged, clinker-built racer. The unofficial history dates earlier as the old man's pet carried aboard square riggers for gambling for open ocean racing. It was an open boat requiring skill to race and prevent swamping...which meant sinking. This was the spawning ground for a distinctive group of racing dinghies listed on page 40, including the International 14.

  The International 14 is a custom built, development class with tremendous competition. Chances are slim you will find two rigged exactly alike, with a variety of hulls. It carries a huge sail rig requiring skill and crew ability to attain maximum speed. Class numbers are small with little publicity compare to many production one-designs. The I-14 has outlived many similar size one designs, being in a continuous state of change with the latest in technolog and refinements, while the class traditions remain unchanged.

- **Centerboard saddle.** It is also used in FD to minimize rudder pressure by pulling the centerboard forward or aft to balance the helm. It minimizes leeway when sailing closehauled without raising the centerboard, page 17.

- **Jibing board.** It was introduced in the I-14 class, which is used in the Lido 14 and other classes. Is it legal for your class? A small wedge in the aft end of the centerboard trunk forces the board to point a degree or so higher into the wind, improving the dinghy pointing ability. When changing tack, the wedge is removed and wedged into the other aft side of the centerboard trunk for maximum pointing ability.

  Daring was detailed a few months old, shortly after winning the Yachting's One-of-a-Kind Series with a 1-1-1-1-1 record. I have only seen photos of *Daring* requiring considerable help from local I-14 racers. It is important for competitive racers to study this unusual dinghy for new ideas.

  Turnbuckles are eliminated with shroud and stay tension adjusted by a jack under the mast. The mast, weighing 9 pounds, was a 1½ diameter TV antenna with the top falling off sideways. It went well upwind. That flexibility saved the mast in a storm during the racing series when some of the standard masts went faster than the hulls. Will IOR racers ever consider super size TV antennas?

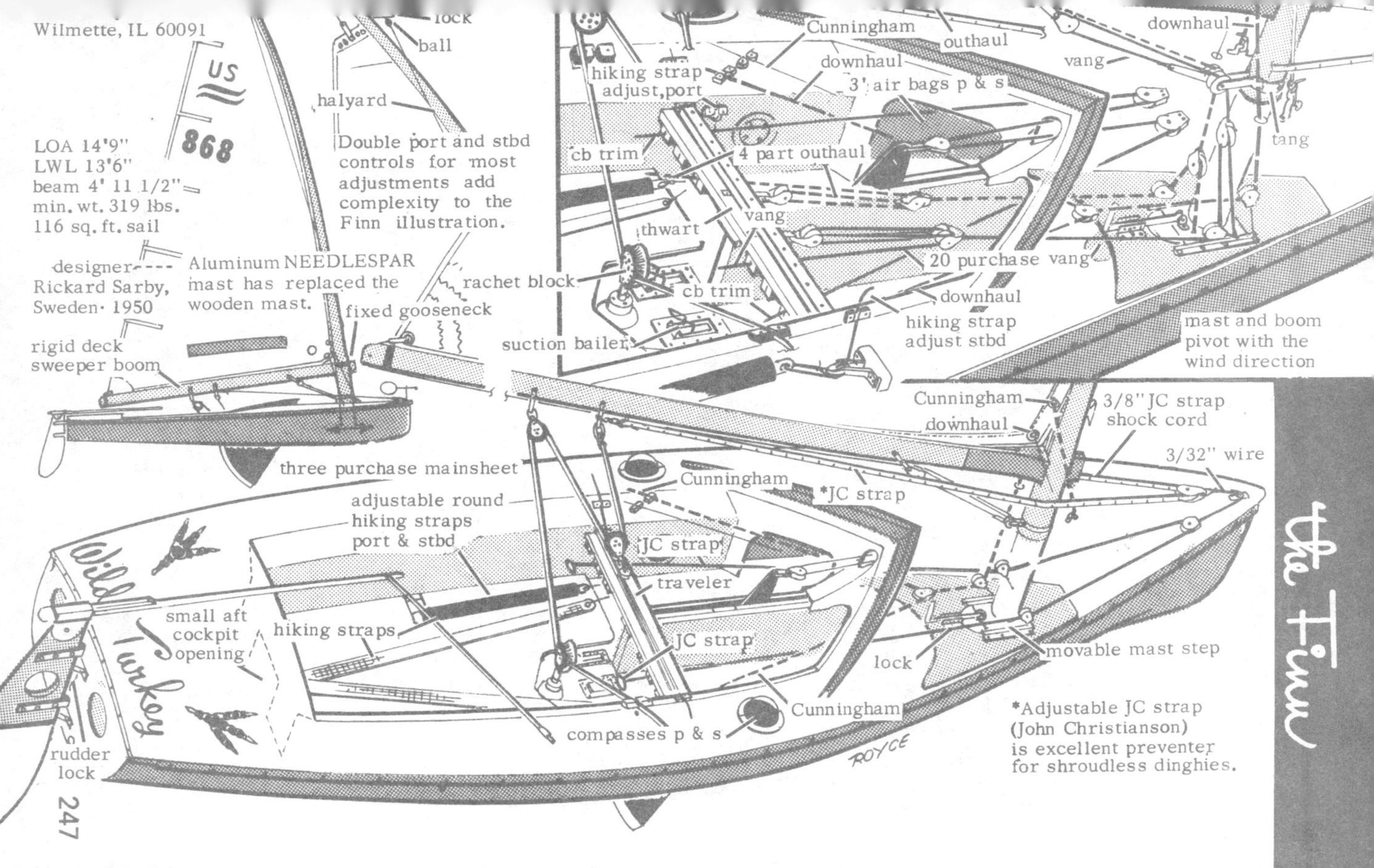
the Finn
Wilmette, IL 60091
US
868
LOA 14'9"
LWL 13'6"
beam 4' 11 1/2"
min. wt. 319 lbs.
116 sq. ft. sail
designer
Rickard Sarby,
Sweden· 1950
rigid deck
sweeper boom
lock
ball
halyard
Double port and stbd controls for most adjustments add complexity to the Finn illustration.
Aluminum NEEDLESPAR mast has replaced the wooden mast.
fixed gooseneck
rachet block
suction bailer
Cunningham
outhaul
downhaul
vang
tang
hiking strap adjust,port
downhaul
3' air bags p & s
cb trim
4 part outhaul
vang
thwart
20 purchase vang
cb trim
downhaul
hiking strap adjust stbd
mast and boom pivot with the wind direction
Cunningham
downhaul
3/8" JC strap shock cord
3/32" wire
three purchase mainsheet
Cunningham
*JC strap
adjustable round hiking straps port & stbd
JC strap
traveler
small aft cockpit opening
hiking straps
JC strap
lock
movable mast step
Cunningham
compasses p & s
Wild Turkey
rudder lock
ROYCE
*Adjustable JC strap (John Christianson) is excellent preventer for shroudless dinghies.

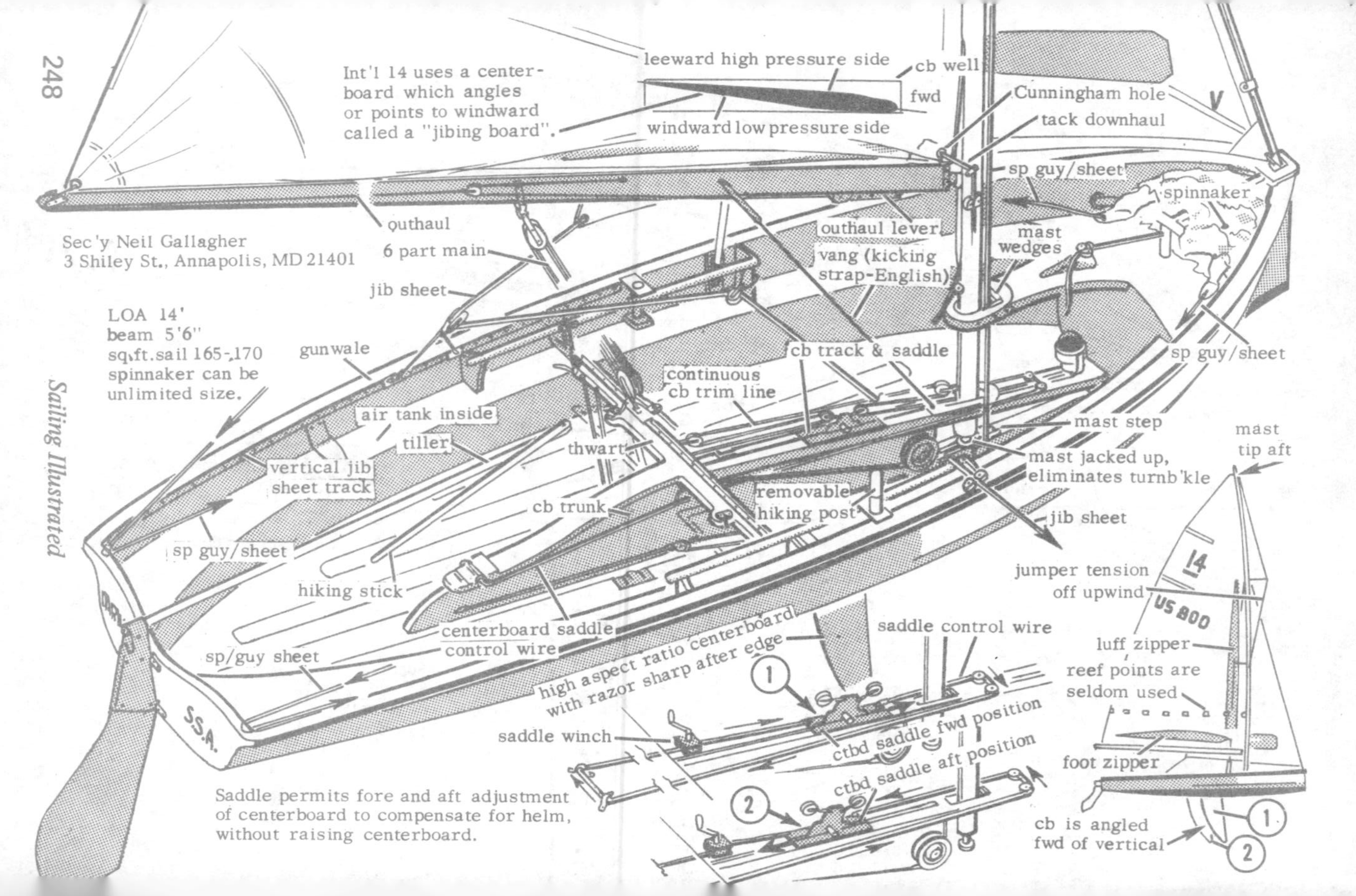

Sec'y Neil Gallagher
3 Shiley St., Annapolis, MD 21401

LOA 14'
beam 5'6"
sq.ft.sail 165-170
spinnaker can be
unlimited size.

Saddle permits fore and aft adjustment
of centerboard to compensate for helm,
without raising centerboard.

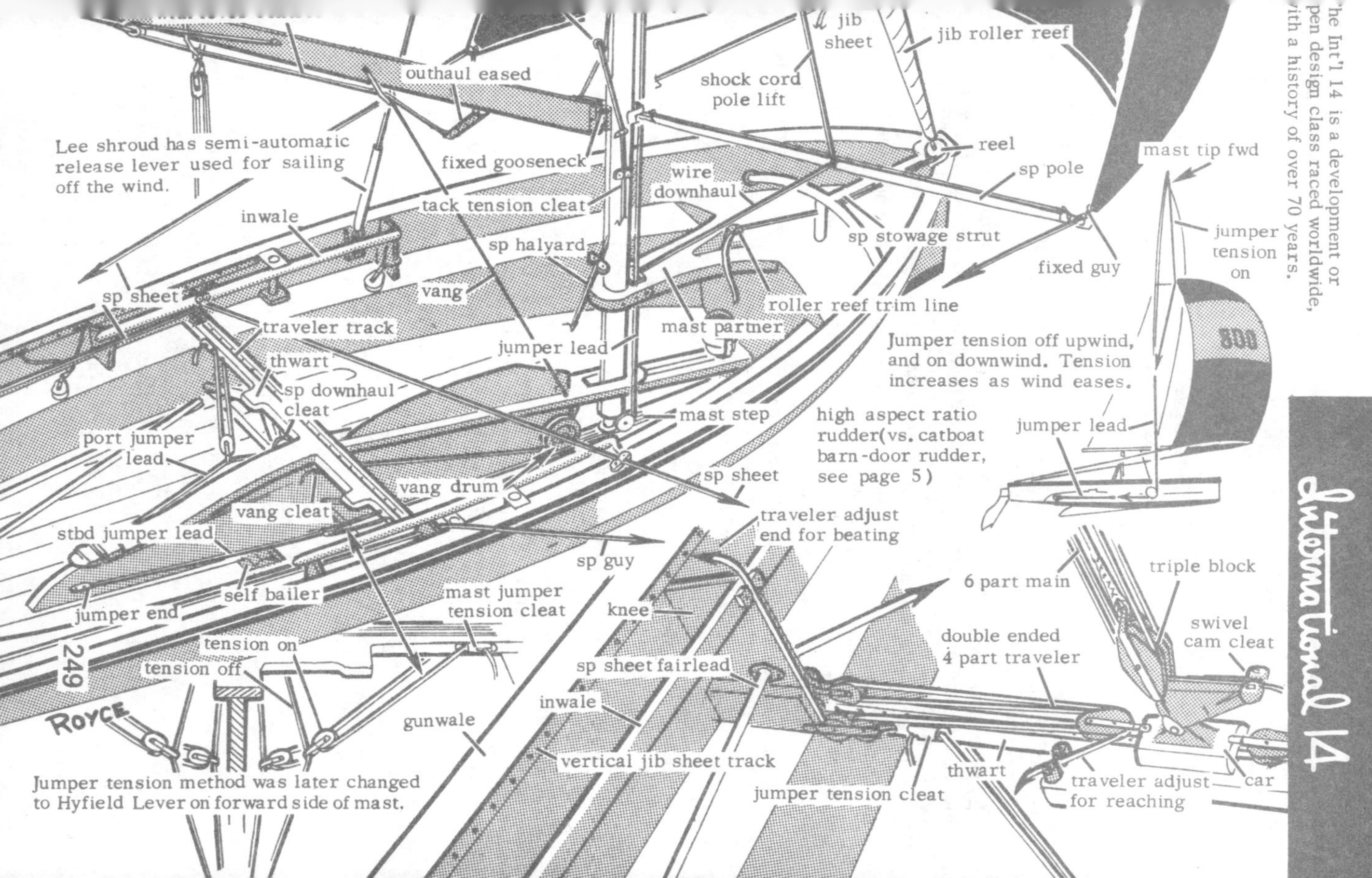
International 14
'he Int'l 14 is a development or
pen design class raced worldwide,
ith a history of over 70 years.
outhaul eased
jib sheet
jib roller reef
shock cord pole lift
Lee shroud has semi-automatic release lever used for sailing off the wind.
fixed gooseneck
reel
wire downhaul
sp pole
mast tip fwd
tack tension cleat
inwale
sp halyard
sp stowage strut
jumper tension on
fixed guy
vang
sp sheet
roller reef trim line
traveler track
mast partner
jumper lead
Jumper tension off upwind, and on downwind. Tension increases as wind eases.
thwart
sp downhaul cleat
mast step
high aspect ratio rudder(vs. catboat barn-door rudder, see page 5)
jumper lead
port jumper lead
vang drum
sp sheet
vang cleat
traveler adjust end for beating
stbd jumper lead
sp guy
triple block
6 part main
self bailer
mast jumper tension cleat
knee
jumper end
swivel cam cleat
double ended 4 part traveler
tension on
tension off
sp sheet fairlead
inwale
gunwale
ROYCE
vertical jib sheet track
thwart
jumper tension cleat
traveler adjust for reaching
car
Jumper tension method was later changed to Hyfield Lever on forward side of mast.

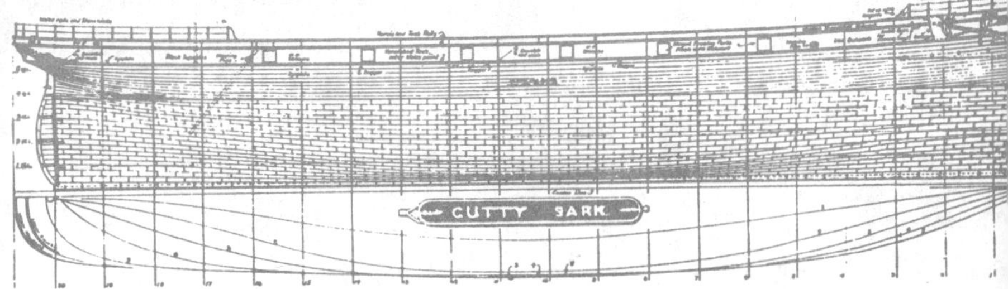

● **The end of an era.** *Americans had the largest fleet of sailing vessels in the world 100 years ago. Steam vessels with better predictability of cargo arrival time slowly, then rapidly replaced most commercial sailing vessels.*

When we were preparing our book in the late 1940's, and the early 1950's we had to rely on discussions with square rigger experts on the east coast and west coast as little printed information was then available. All stressed the need for our nautical sailing history chapter. Only one was alive by 1957.

Only a few sailing vessels of that period survived. They are maintained as inoperative sailing museums such as the whaler ***Charles W. Morgan,*** frigate ***U.S.S. Constitution,*** the **Balclutha** in San Francisco, the ***Star of India*** in San Diego...but to see and touch isn't enough.

● **Sailing exists in a unique world of its own.** After operating present day craft, sailors often want to know more of our vessels roaming the seas of the world just a hundred years ago, and their interesting sailing methods.

This chapter covers development of sailing craft from colonial days to the present. Forget straight-line patterns as you will find many interesting zigs, zags, and compromises. Our west coast and European waters favored square riggers with stronger, more predictable winds. Lighter, less predictable east coast weather patterns favored the development of fast lean hulls with the tall schooner rigs...and squrre rigs carrying tremendous sail areas.

● **Worldwide weather patterns** are evaluated on a 1850 square rigger leaving Manhattan on an ebb tide for Rio, then to San Francisco and return on pages 210-211, followed by Europeans sailing to their new American home.

Our thanks go to a handful of people who want to carry on our American sailing heritage for future generations. They spend endless hours raising money, and encouraging others to build and bring alive these traditional operating sailing vessels with crews fortunate to get berths aboard.

● **Pride of Baltimore II** is being launched today, 4/30/88 to replace their original ***Pride,*** launched 1977, lost in a 1986 Atlantic storm. We give thanks to the good people of Baltimore for making us aware of our sailing heritage.

● The Official Tallship of California, the **Californian,** launched May 1984, is a full-size replica of the 1849 Revenue Cutter **Lawrence.** She is a sailing classroom for those ages 16 to 21, continually on the move off our coast.

● The 180 ton brig **Pilgrim,** launched 1825, in Dana's ***Two Years Before the Mast,*** proved illusive to detail until finding a sail plan sketch by the author for his future wife. After studying various brigs of that period undergoing change, we chose a narrower bow entry, instead of the broad bow, beakhead bowsprit on the way out. The whaling bark ***Charles W. Morgan*** was in continuous operation for 80 years, the probable reason for the varied rigs in paintings and illustrations.

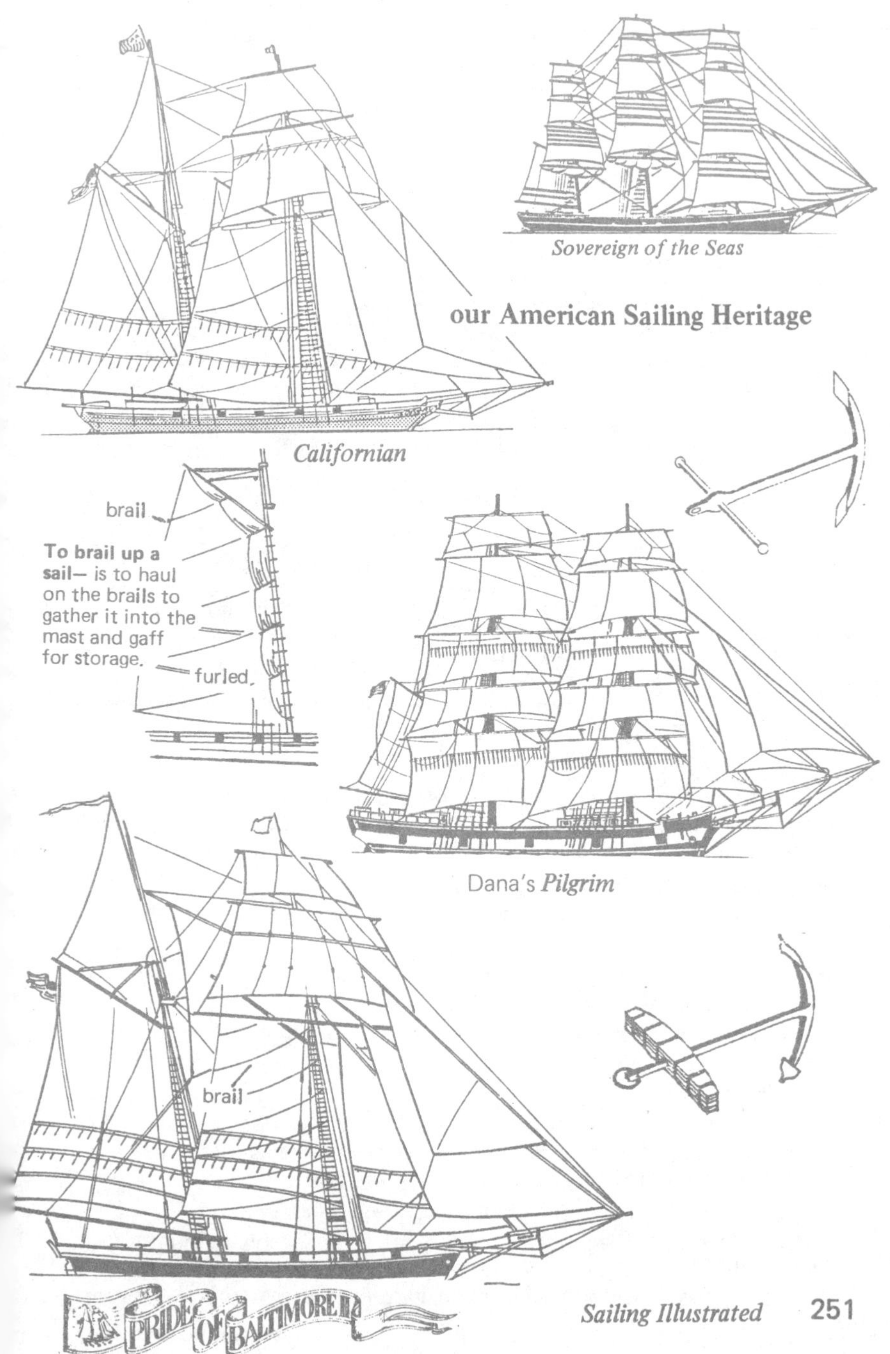

Sovereign of the Seas

our American Sailing Heritage

Californian

Dana's *Pilgrim*

Line plans of the *Iris,* pages 70-73 were chosen. You can see a painstakingly accurate model of the lovely *Iris* made by owner John Martucci This was the keynote piece for the 1930 Yachting exhibit at the Mystic Seaport Museum in Mystic, Connecticut.

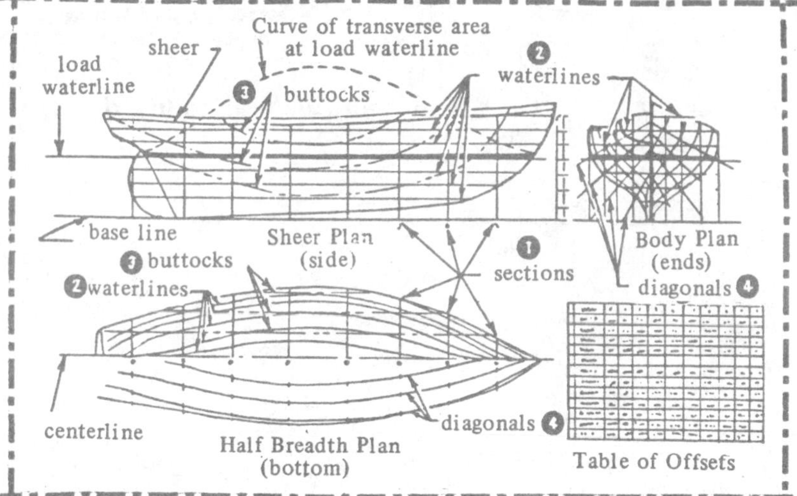

We show the flat plan drafting methods above used by naval architects to develop the lines and shape of a hull.

At right we have translated the flat plans into perspectives of the same hull detailing sections, waterlines, buttocks, and diagonals to help you analyze reviews of sailboat lines in sailing books and magazines.

- The **sheer plan** details the side view of a hull...will it be graceful, pudgy, long, or lean. This view also shows the freeboard and sheer of the deck, plus the rake of the bow and stern.
- The **half-breadth plan** shows the beam, how wide the hull is, and how the width is distributed along its length.
- The **body plan** or **end views** provide the exact shape with accurate *offset measurements* of the hull shape at each station...or each point in its width.

After the hull plan lines have been approved, the line plans are then laid out full size on the mold loft floor using measurements that have been provided in the **table of offsets.**

The line plans above and the line plans on the mold loft floor should be identical...except the lines on the floor are full size which should be within 1/8" of offset table measurements. Pages 102, 103, and 116 of our *Homestudy Guide* provide much additional information on development of the sailboat hull.

The sailboat lines are as important to build a sailboat as it is to make our perspective illustrations. The advantage I have...my mistakes are easy to correct with white paint.

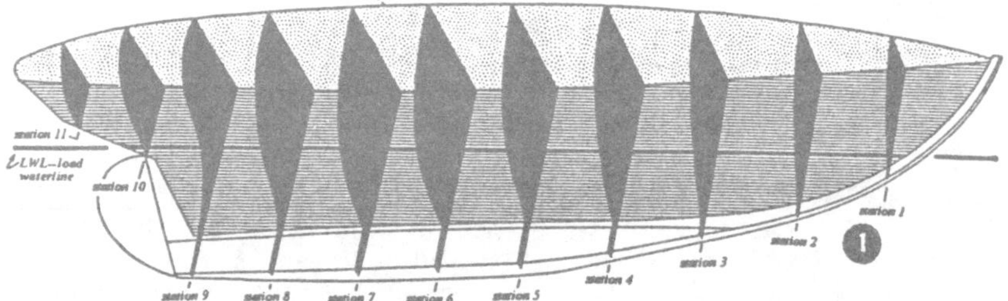

1 Sections, cross sections, and stations. The black areas above show the athwartship sections of the hull above.

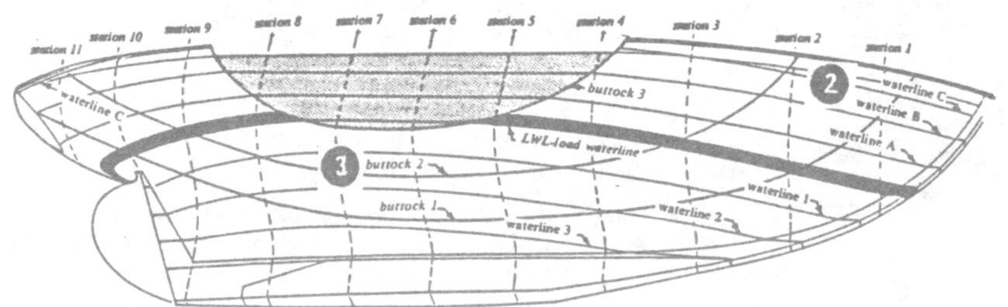

2 Waterlines are horizontal planes parallel to load waterlines given in inches.

3 Buttock lines represent vertical planes shown at regular intervals in the shaded area, which are parallel to the keel.

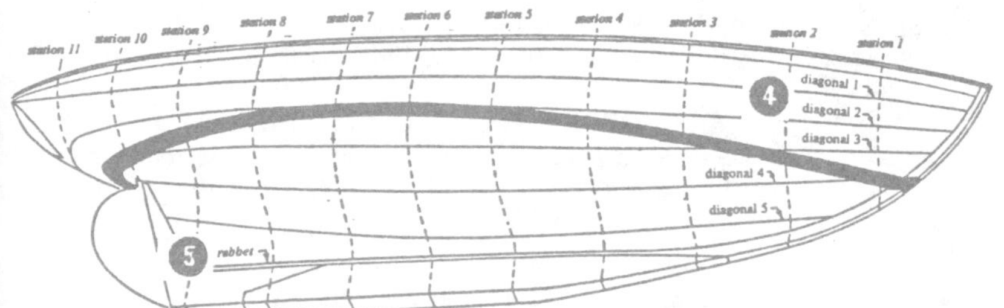

4 Diagonals are lines used to develop a hull form crossing the frames as close to right angles as possible.

5 A rabbet is a groove that is cut into the stern, keel, sternpost, etc., to receive the edges of planking.

Catalina 38

Our friend the clumsy albatross careens across his beach into the wind to be airborn. He can glide effortlessly for days or *weeks using wind off the wave tops for lift on his long lean wings with a span to 11'. When the wind stops he lands on the water waiting for the wind to return.*

Aspect ratio is the length to width ratio of the horizontal albatross wing airfoils, while sailboats use vertical airfoils and waterfoils for upwind sailing lift. Water and air are similar fluids with water density 800 times that of air.

Cascade

- **High aspect ratio mainsail flexible airfoils** with tall masts and short booms are shown on Pacific Cat, Catalina 38, and *Cascade.* Similar long, lean wings keep the albatross moving effortlessly with their high aspect ratio.
- **High aspect ratio rigid symmetrical waterfoils** are obvious on four sailboats at left with long, lean, narrow rudders. These rudders provide maximum leverage for turning, with minimum surface area parasitic drag.
- **Waterfoils** have a blunt, rounded entry. The leading edge is wider, tapering to a sharp narrow trailing edge for controlled waterflow lift with minimum turbulence. This pattern is shown on two fin keels, a centerboard, and a daggerboard.

Coronado 15

- **Medium aspect ratio airfoils and waterfoils** are used on cruising sailboats. Larger mainsails and smaller jibs require smaller crews for upwind and downwind sailing.
- **Low aspect ratio gaff mainsails** may have considerable square footage for waterline length. Short drive area limits windward performance, with upper part of the gaff sagging to leeward, spilling useful wind pressure.

The gaff mainsail becomes an excellent performer in a good breeze from a reach to a broad reach. Rolling tendencies may be experienced running downwind due to hull shape and narrow draft, with the catboat an example.

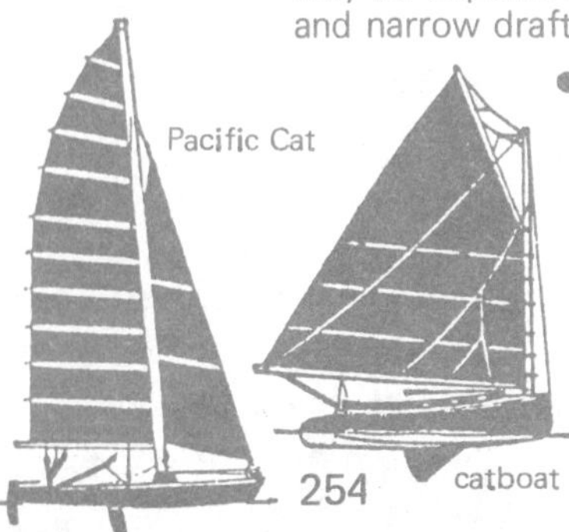

Pacific Cat

catboat

- **Low aspect ratio waterfoils.** The catboat has a shallow, long rudder. It doesn't have a waterfoil shape for lift.

The large surface area flat centerboard has considerable parasitic drag. Pointing ability is limited without a waterfoil shape. It stalls out at a shallow upwind angle with a turbulence growing on the upwind side of the centerboard producing leeway or sideway drift.

The 82' LOA bright red IOR maxi **Cote d'Or** *won second place in the 27,000 mile, 1985/6 Whitbread Round-the-World Race with 15 racers.*

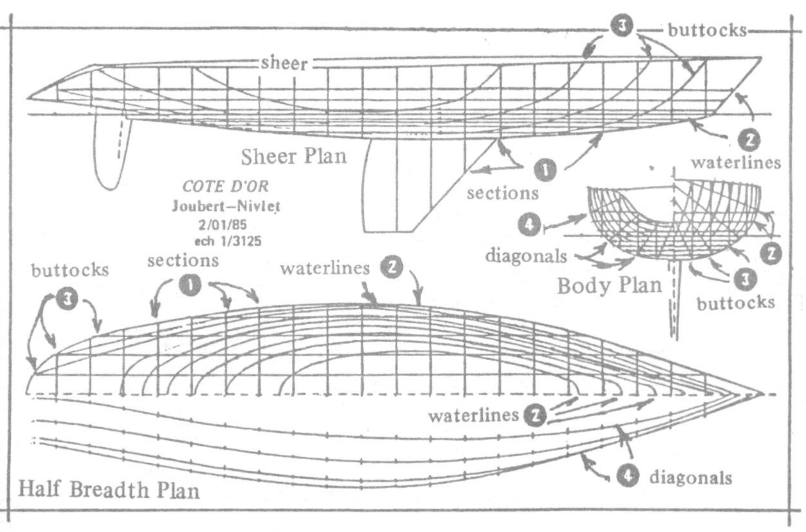

Fin keel/spade rudder combination provides two waterfoils for upwind lift efficiency. Parasitic drag is cut to minimum with long, lean, all muscle, high-aspect ratio blades, on a hull with minimum underwater surface area.

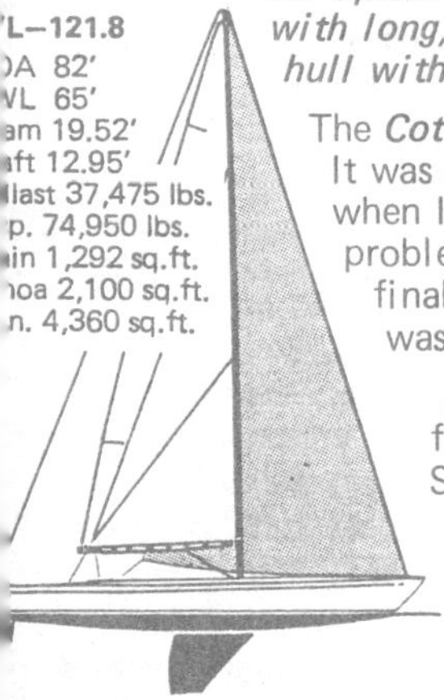

'L–121.8
)A 82'
VL 65'
am 19.52'
ıft 12.95'
llast 37,475 lbs.
p. 74,950 lbs.
ıin 1,292 sq.ft.
ıoa 2,100 sq.ft.
n. 4,360 sq.ft.

The *Cote d Or* was built in a 5 month rush in Belgium. It was 4 tons heavier than her designed displacement when launched July 1985. I hate to think of the varied problems with no shakedown races and her crew finalized 10 minutes before the starting gun. Skipper was French competitor Eric Tabarly.

A 96 hour penalty followed a keel change at the first stop in Cape Town, South Africa. Yet at the Solent finish she was reaching at 17 knots, the second home behind ***UBS Switzerland.***

We thank Joubert-Nivelt for permission to show the *Cote d'Or* sailboat lines for comparison with the 1938 *Iris* pages 70-73, 252, 253.

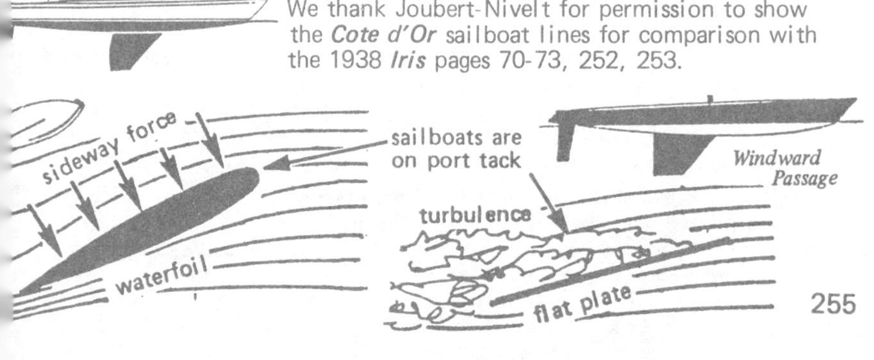

One-Design Handicap Racing

Different one-design classes may race against each other with the **Ports-Yardstick Ru[es,***a performance handicapping method,* Contact USYRU for details. Yachting's **One of a Kind Regatta** has developed its own complex *measurement rule.*

Corrected Time Offshore Handicap Racing

If all factors are equal in offshore racing the longer sailboat will win most races due to the longer waterline speed factor, pg. 140. A *handi-capping method* was developed so sailboats of differing lengths may race equally...to mathematically finish at the same time.

This method began by adopting the **1790 Custom House Rule** based on bulk, volume, or tonnage cubic content. It was updated in 1883 using the **Seawanhaka Rule** which combined the waterline length, added to the square root of the sail area based on measurement of spars with a divisor of two.

After this rule developed the huge 1903 Cup monsters, pg. 273, a change was needed to produce healthier racing craft. The **International Rule** was introduced in 1907 to tax long overhangs, and ease the penalty of the excessive draft of British cutters. The racers were to be measured by Lloyds scantling rules. From this grew the present 12 meter *measurement rules* with their simplicity...which produced so much complexity.

We finally abided by the **International Rule** in 1920 for the 13th Cup Challenge with Lipton racing his 110'4'' loa and 75' lwl *Shamrock IV* which won 3 out of 5 races, yet it lost the cup with a 7 minute, 1 second measurement time penalty.

It was replaced in 1929 by the **American Universal Rule** which allowed length flexibility without taxing sail area. This rule produced the 80' to 87' long J Classes in 1930, 1934, and 1937.

Social and economic changes from 1950 to 1970 eliminated most of the super rich, while some Americans had money in the bank for the first time. Sailing became a recreational pursuit as technological advances in fiberglass, Dacron, nylon, and electronics became a part of the everyday sailing scene. Will Americans ever be able to enjoy a little money in the bank in the future?

The first cup challenger after 1937 was in 1957 when the 12 meter sloops chosen for the competition were midgets compared to the J Class, pg. 273, as an example of the dollar shrinkage. If our government's debt continues to grow to subsidize the world and outer space... will the America's Cup competitors soon be racing used Snipes?

So goes the fun and gamesmanship of the *grand ould mug* soon to be 150 years young. It was also called the 100 Guinea Cup worth $300 when silver at 1851 prices was approximately $40. I just wish the little old mug maker who forgot to add a bottom to the cup, could see the commotion he started. Dream on—

Dual purpose racing/cruising sailboats.

Consider a dual purpose cabin sailboat for your your first boat with a compromise in either direction according to your personality. Avoid a single-purpose racer, though after some racing exposure when you know the complex and critical factors to look for, it may be your ideal dream boat. The single-purpose cruiser may be just as questionable for your first sailboat without sufficient sailing exposure to recognize the various compromises which will best fit your needs.

The racing rules you will be using are a combination of the **Cruising Club of America (CCA)** and the **Royal Ocean Racing Club (RORC)**, each of which has strong supporters and strong antagonists for philosophical, technical, and personal reasons.

- The **Performance Handicap Racing Fleet** (PHRF) provides a *time allowance* as compared to a hypothetical scratch boat. The PHRF can help encourage dual-purpose racer/cruisers by arbitrarily providing a smaller time allowance for a racing machine with a flexible formula which can sometimes be based on questionable data, that may be periodically adjusted as performance recommends.

The PHRF rating is compared to the scratch boat, the fastest, highest rated sailboat to provide a time allowance the scratch boat must give to each slower, lower-rated boat in the same fleet.

The PHRF *time allowance* is multiplied by the length of the course in miles, and subtracted from each boat's elapsed time over the course. This difference is the sailboats corrected time for the race...the sailboat with the lowest corrected time will become the winner.

- The **Midget Ocean Racing Club** (MORC) is for sailboats under 30'... and the **International Offshore Racing** (IOR) rules have similar *time allowances* for a given boat. They however require more complex rule measurements of beam, draft, and sail areas which have to be measured physically. These are plugged into a formula ratings which may encourage extreme design features such as the IOR beam and pinched sterns, and the MORC full sterns with naval architects having to tailor their designs to fit the rules hoping to produce consistant winning racers.

- The new **International Measurement System** (IMS) is a *handicapping system* based on a math model **Velocity Prediction Program** (VPP). It has to know a hull shape to calculate the speed the VPP thinks that shape can do, though the VPP can vary the handicap for specific conditions. The purpose is hopefully to eliminate extreme designs if the only purpose is to get around a specific rule.

- The **International Meter Rule** is a flexible formula *measurement rule.* Each 12 meter sloop is individually designed to be as competitive as possible with length and sail areas the major factors involved. If one factor is increased, the other must be decreased which is the reason they may be 64' to 70' long yet compete equally without a handicap.

The big dinghies.. how big is huge?

The 12 Meter Class IYRU Rule was introduced by 13 European countries in 1907, revised in 1920, with the final change in 1936 reducing sail area, while increasing the overall, and waterline lengths. Each meter sailboat is designed to win races following a flexible measurement rule, with tradeoffs in length, weight, and sail areas. 12 meter craft varied from 64′ to 75′ LOA with increases or decreases in weight and sail area.

The cube comparison. It is the easiest way to understand the various meter boat sizes, with the 6 and 12 meter ratios shown at right. The 12 meter was a heavy afternoon racer with a ***260 D/L*** and ample sail spread with a ***19.6 SA/D,*** pages 20, 21. Engineering improvements were slow and continuous until reaching maximum potentials.

12 meter racers were the darlings of the racing aristocracy. Some of the ideas trickled down to the recreational sailing fleets such as rod rigging, dip-pole jibe, triradial spinnakers, etc. As racing performance increased, stress factor variables became more critical on everything. *Practical limits* were passed in the 1988 Cup challenge. A dismasting could result with even a minor fiber or metal line failure with the U.S. catamarans and the New Zealand 120′ monohull *aircraft carrier*. **A new answer was needed.**

The International America's Cup Class developed by 20 designers in 1988 also used a flexible measurement rule. We show the 12 meter and new AC class with average dimensions, and proportional drawings.

Measurements for both racers are down-the-middle for comparison. The major AC Class goal is performance with D/L and SA/D ratios becoming the most important.

Grade school math is enough to show the new AC boats with a **100 D/L** are much lighter than the 12 meter **260 D/L,** with a tremendous sail area, **SA/D 42** for its length, compared to 12 meter **SA/D 19.6,** pages 20, 21.

Weight and draft differences. The shorter 12 meter boat weighs 20,000 pounds more than the AC boat. The AC boats are 10′ longer overall, and 10′ longer on the waterline, while 6′ wider. The much lighter AC boats carry 2000 square feet more of sail than the 12 meter craft.

Heeling factors. The 18′ beam with narrow waterline beam, plus well-flared topsides, keeps wetted surface drag to a minimum. They are tender upright, becoming very stiff with the topsides down in the water while heeling 15 to 18 degrees. **Crew weight is critical** with the 16 crew a ton of movable ballast for the huge overcanvassed AC dinghies, obvious in the light 1992 winds off San Diego. The crew moved to leeward in light winds, and to windward as the wind increased, with fore and aft weight equally as critical.

Titanium masts with five spreaders, 10½ stories tall, a cool million each, produced their share of ulcers with a $300,000 to $600,000 dismasting charge. Is this the afternoon racer you are looking for?

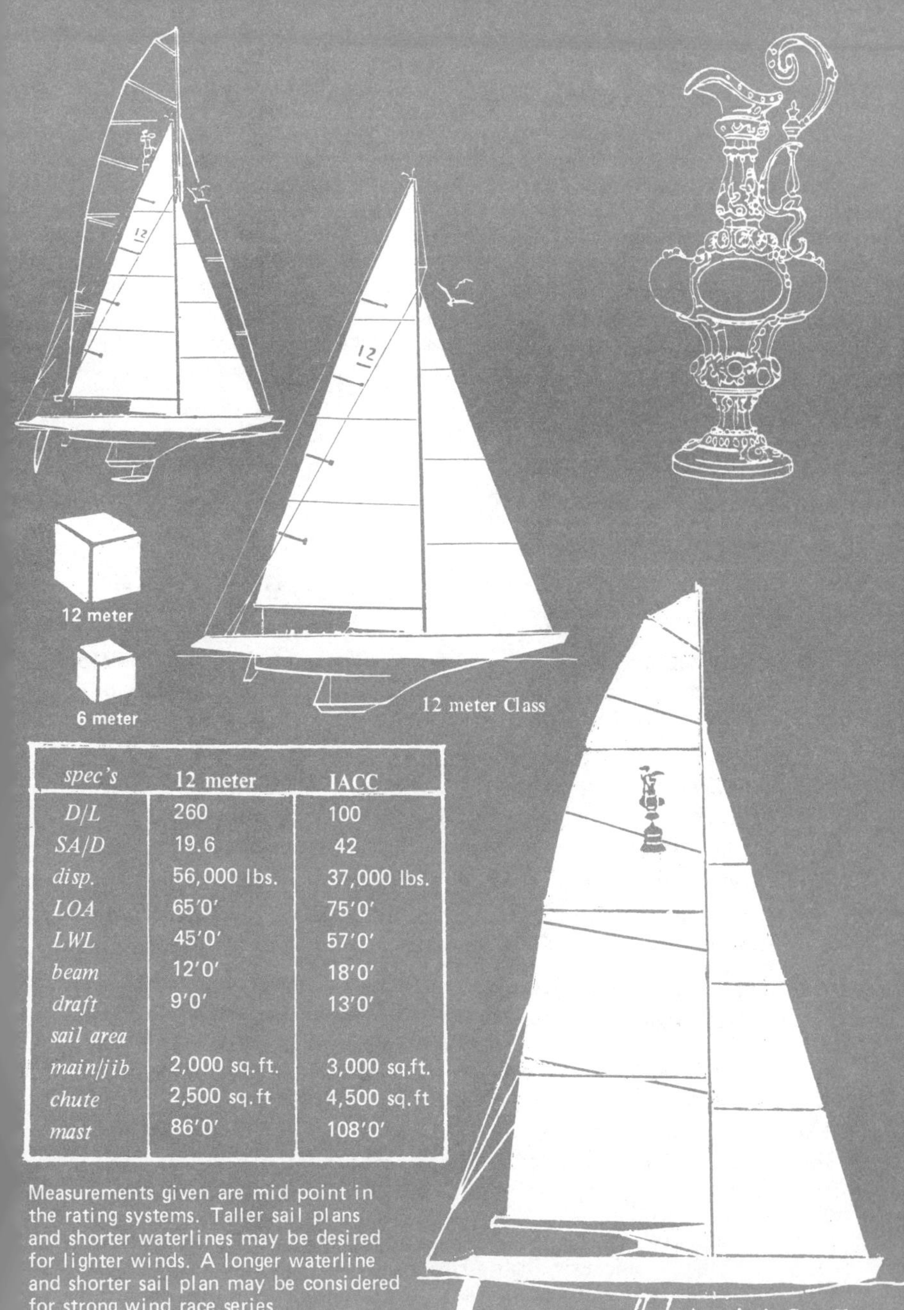

12 meter Class

America's Cup Class

spec's	12 meter	IACC
D/L	260	100
SA/D	19.6	42
disp.	56,000 lbs.	37,000 lbs.
LOA	65'0'	75'0'
LWL	45'0'	57'0'
beam	12'0'	18'0'
draft	9'0'	13'0'
sail area		
main/jib	2,000 sq.ft.	3,000 sq.ft.
chute	2,500 sq.ft	4,500 sq.ft
mast	86'0'	108'0'

Measurements given are mid point in the rating systems. Taller sail plans and shorter waterlines may be desired for lighter winds. A longer waterline and shorter sail plan may be considered for strong wind race series.

How tall are the lofty America's Cup rigs?

A ten story building with 10' per story is approximately 100' tall. Using this for comparison a 12 meter mast is 8 stories tall; the *Ranger* mast is 16 stories high; and the 1903 *Reliance* holds the record for the largest sail ever made, and the tallest mast which is close to 20 stories tall. The 212' LOA square-rigged *Cutty Sark* main mast was approx. 150' above the deck or 15 stories tall. The Chinese junk masts will range from 3½ to 9 stories tall.

The *America* was launched 5/3/1851 and outfitted,sailing to England on its own bottom in 21 days. Syndicate organizer James Steven's interest was gambling,his favorite was horse racing. After selling *America* in England for a small profit, they returned winning a small wager, and an ungainly cup open at both ends. Little did the promoters realize their cup would grow into the most coveted and expensive sporting prize in history...with at present over $100 million invested in a single event.

The schooner *America* had a long, active, and colorful life serving under a variety of flags. It came to an untimely end high and dry during WW II when its shed collapsed in a heavy snowstorm. An *America* replica was launched 5/3/67 116 years later on a date easy to remember as we share the same 5/3 birthday. Following are winners of the America's Cup Series—

- Schooner rigs—*America*-1851;*Magic*-1870;*Columbia* and *Sappho*-1871; and *Madeleine* in 1876.
- Gaff-rig topsail cutters—*Mischief*-1881:*Puritan*-1885;*Mayflower*-1886; *Volunteer-1887; Vigilant*-1893;*Defender*-1895;*Columbia*-1899,1901; *Reliance*-1903;*Resolute*-1920.
- Marconi rigged J Class cutters—*Enterprise-1930;Rainbow*-1934;and the *Ranger*-1937.While the 1893 *Vigilant* required a racing crew of 70 professionals for racing,The J Class in an economy move cost only a million dollars with professional crew members limited to 26 , and for the first time 4 nonprofessionals* in the afterguard.
- 12 meter sloop rigs—*Columbia*-1958;*Weatherly*-1962;*Constellation*-1964;*Intrepid*-1967,1970;*Courageous*-1974,1977;and *Freedom*-1980.
- Our *Liberty* lost the 26th America's Cup Series to *Australia II* in 1983. The **grand ould mug** moved to the new host club after 136 years, the Royal Perth Yacht Club in southwestern Australia. After a 1,227 day vacation it returned to the San Diego Yacht Club February 1987. The 27th Series score was Australia *Kookaburra III*—0, *Stars & Stripes*—4.

America's Cup history? It had been a ho-hum affair to this author until the 1983 loss. Though no other subject has been so thoroughly reported in sailing history, the answers I found made little sense with few patterns.

Then I began reading two extensive books on the subject* at the same time by Canadian and British authors. After studying comparisons of the same races by different reporters, the missing parts of the jigsaw puzzle began to fall together to provide fascinating reading...beginning with the proportions to scale at right of various competitors.

***Winning the America's Cup—Ian Dear, and The America's Cup—J.Julius Fanta**

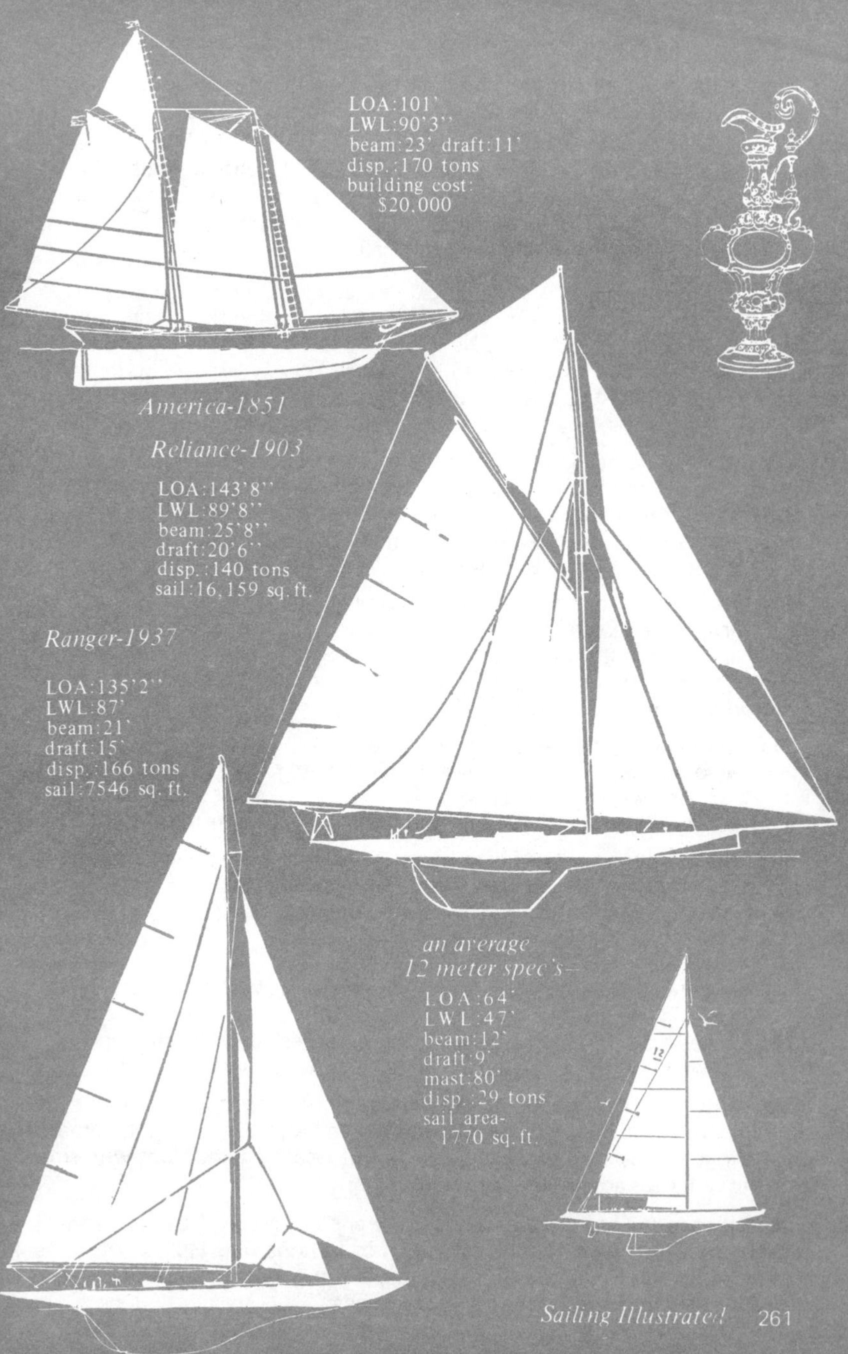

LOA:101'
LWL:90'3''
beam:23' draft:11'
disp.:170 tons
building cost:
$20,000
America-1851
Reliance-1903
LOA:143'8''
LWL:89'8''
beam:25'8''
draft:20'6''
disp.:140 tons
sail:16,159 sq.ft.
Ranger-1937
LOA:135'2''
LWL:87'
beam:21'
draft:15'
disp.:166 tons
sail:7546 sq. ft.
an average
12 meter spec's–
LOA:64'
LWL:47'
beam:12'
draft:9'
mast:80'
disp.:29 tons
sail area-
1770 sq.ft.
12

The term **jacht** *originated as a swift craft or hunter.*

The term **sloop** began with the Dutch **sloep** recorded as early as 1599. It was followed with the English **shallop**, a square-rigged **sloop of war**, and recently, a British Navy gunboat...and tomorrow, a space shuttle to Mars.

Small, swift 17th century Dutch sailing vessels called **jachts** were used as dispatch boats, for scouting, and to carry important persons. Lighter and more elegant craft eventually including small open sailboats with various rigs that were used for pleasure were also called **jachts.**

The Dutch inhabitants adapted their gaff-rigged **inland sloep** with topsail to the Hudson River called the **North River sloop.** As the first sloeps, due to their keels, couldn't sail above Newberg, shallow draft hulls were built which used centerboards or leeboards. The well-known cargo sloop replica ***Clearwater,*** 106' LOA, 25' beam, and 4305 square feet of sail is an excellent example of this type Dutch sloep sailing the Hudson today.

Our **marconi** or **jib-headed rig** called the *leg-of-mutton,* with an extreme mast rake, seems to have first appeared in Bermuda Britishers called it the **Bermudian sloop.** Americans adapted the term **marconi rig** due to a vague resemblance to shrouds and guys supporting tall Marconi radio transmitters. P.S., Marconi had no interest in sailing.

During the early part of this century larger single-masted sailboats with masts further forward than cutters, using bowsprits, were called **sloops,** while smaller ones without bowsprits were called **knockabouts.** When better engineering eliminated the need for most bowsprits in the 1950's, the term *knockabout* which could include the 12 meters, became obsolete.

The **fractional sloop** has the jibstay coming from the bow 3/4, 5/6, 7/8, 15/16 or so up the mast, not to masthead. Dinghies prefer the taller mast for inland areas with the wind several feet above the water's surface. IOR and ULDB racers prefer its flexibility for better mainsail trim upwind.

The **masthead sloop** has the jibstay going to masthead with the ability to use larger gennies and larger spinnakers. Since the rigging is less complex, this rig is more practical for cruising with a minimum crew.

Sloops, cutters, and divided rigs.

For basic generalities—the sloop to 36' has most advantages for weekend offshore racing and cruising in normal U.S. weather conditions. The cutter up to 40' has more flexibility for long cruises, especially in English and European waters with rapidly changing wind and weather conditions.

If your interest is a sailboat over 40' with a minor interest in racing, it is time to consider divided rigs such as yawls, ketches, and schooners. Larger divided rigs are easier to handle in a variety of weather conditions with small crews as sail areas are broken into smaller units.

Exceptions to the basic patterns above are endless. Much depends on the personality of the owner and local sailing conditions. The H 28 yawl seems a poor performer in our light local winds, is highly recommended by our Hawaiian sailing friends for their strong winds.

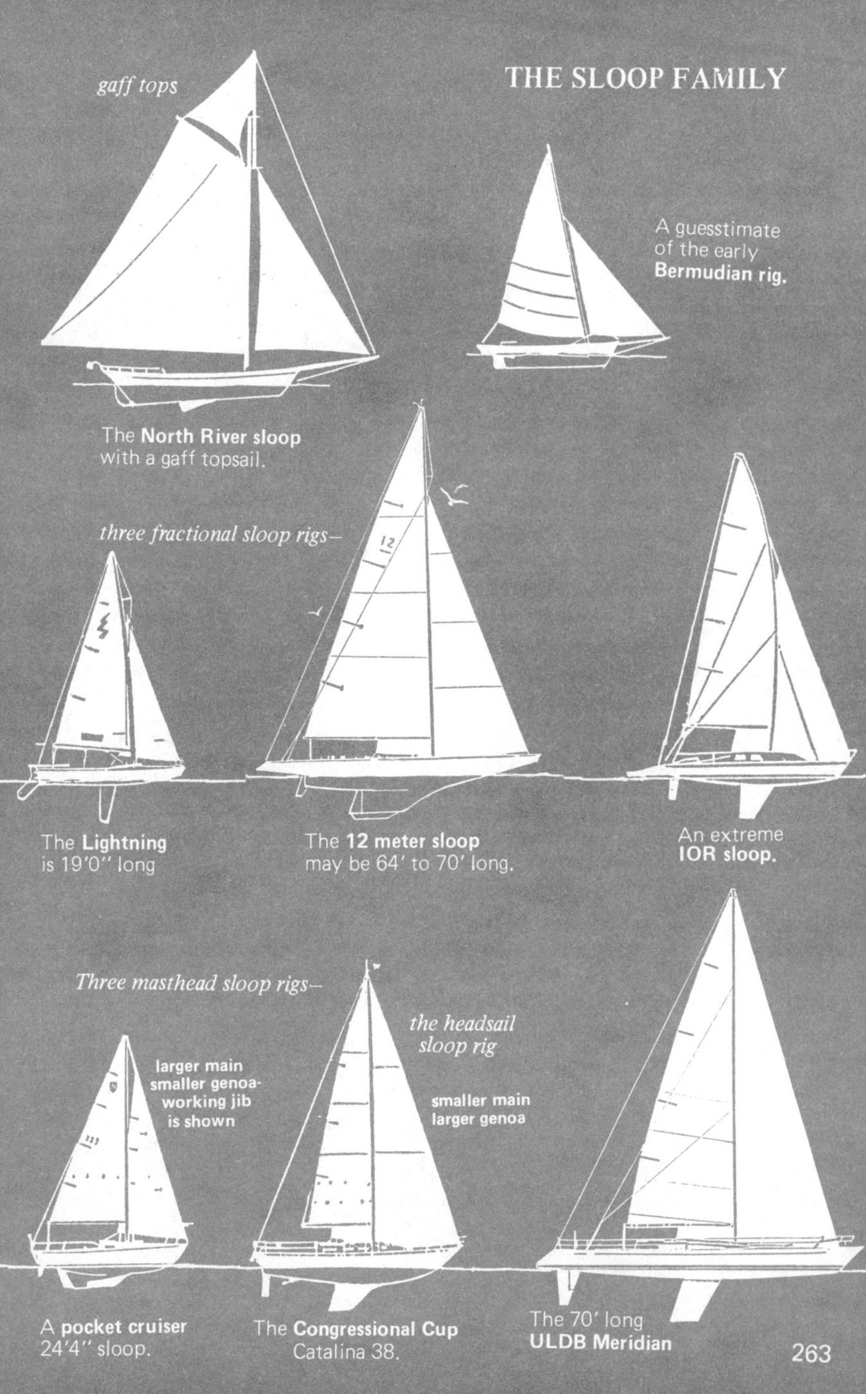
THE SLOOP FAMILY
gaff tops
The North River sloop
with a gaff topsail.
A guesstimate
of the early
Bermudian rig.
three fractional sloop rigs–
12
The Lightning
is 19'0" long
The 12 meter sloop
may be 64' to 70' long.
An extreme
IOR sloop.
Three masthead sloop rigs–
larger main
smaller genoa-
working jib
is shown
the headsail
sloop rig
smaller main
larger genoa
A pocket cruiser
24'4" sloop.
The Congressional Cup
Catalina 38.
The 70' long
ULDB Meridian

The heavy-weather cutter workboat.

The **sloop** is permanently rigged for one jib though a second temporary headsail may be added. The **cutter** will carry a smaller mainsail with rigging to normally carry two headsails or jibs. The mast is stepped further aft averaging 2/5 of the waterline length.

Our admiration goes to the English ***West County Pilot Cutter*** with a working rig that operated 12 months of the year. In stormy winter months it would be down to a tiny **spitfire jib,** while in good summer weather it could carry a loosefooted main,topmast and topsail, plus two headsails.

- **The cruising cutter.** Larry and Lynn Pardey sailed their 24'7" LOA engineless cutter ***Seraffyn*** around the world which is well documented in books and articles. Their present engineless 29'9" ***Taleisin*** with more cargo-carrying capacity looks identical to ***Seraffyn*** plus a porthole near the bow.

Larry summarizes,"***Seraffyn's*** designer, Lyle Hess, tried to combine the best of both worlds, the seakeeping ability of the long-keeled English cutters, with the room and stability of the beamy American bottom".*

- **The racing cutter.** ***Branta*** was launched in 1928, one of fifteen identical 10 meter cutters made in Germany. The hull was made of African mahogany or teak over steel frames. She was bought in 1956 by Dick Reineman, the present owner, an inventor and powerboat designer. This is a very active and competitive Southern California racer on which I've enjoyed a few good races in the past. It is designed for speed and comfort.

Dick had to rebuild ***Branta*** after major damage from an extinguisher explosion. Her performance improved considerably as the displacement dropped from 25 to 21 tons, and her 30 hp diesel increased the cruising speed to 7½ knots. Her wooden mast, 11 ton keel, and wrought iron frames remain unchanged. She was surveyed, insured, and registered as a new vessel in 1984.

The first Valiant cutter shown, was sailed by Dan Byrne in the initial BOAC singlehanded race around the world.

- **The 1893 America's Cup Series** was won by the cutter ***Vigilant.*** She required a working crew of 45...and a racing crew of 70 to put 4½ tons of movable ballast on the weather rail.

Equipment failure was common while racing with sprung or broken spars, sheaves crushed in blocks, etc. We were fortunate in those days to enjoy a home-court advantage as our English competitors had to be sailed across the Atlantic to compete with us up to 1937.

Wood vs metal hulls. The *Vigilant* hull was made of bronze to resist marine growth,with a metal centerboard weighing 4 tons. The decks were made of a combination nickel and silver.

The huge 1903 America's Cup winner ***Reliance,*** page 263, had a bronze hull, steel ribs, and an aluminum deck. Both of these huge monsters had tremendous corrosion problems.

- **Sloop vs cutter rigs.** If we choose two identical hulls with the same total sail area, the sloop with one large jib may have the windward advantage to force 5. In heavy weather with the sloop close to bare-pole operation,the cutter can still be operating and under control with the small inner staysail called the **spitfire jib.**

*from **Seraffyn's European Adventure,** W.W. Norton & Company

THE CUTTER FAMILY

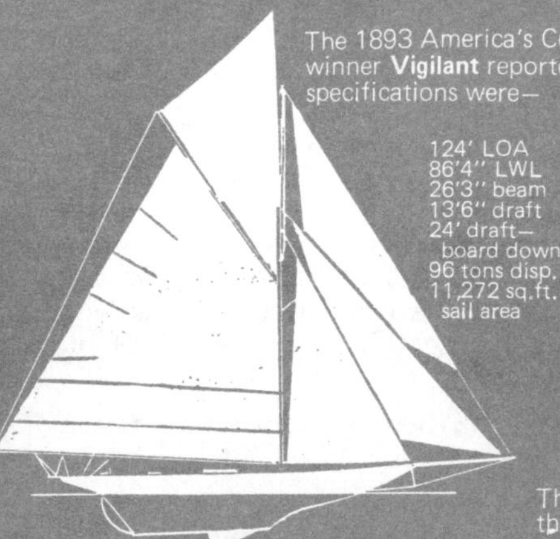

The 1893 America's Cup winner **Vigilant** reported specifications were—

124' LOA
86'4" LWL
26'3" beam
13'6" draft
24' draft—
board down
96 tons disp.
11,272 sq.ft.
sail area

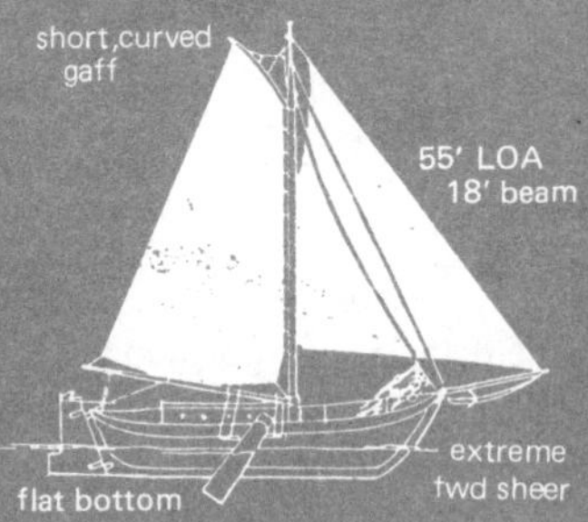

The **Groote Beer** was built on the lines of the traditional Dutch *Lemsteraak*. It came to Newport Beach in 1957 where it had various owners.

The engineless **Seraffyn** required ten years to circumnavigate the world.

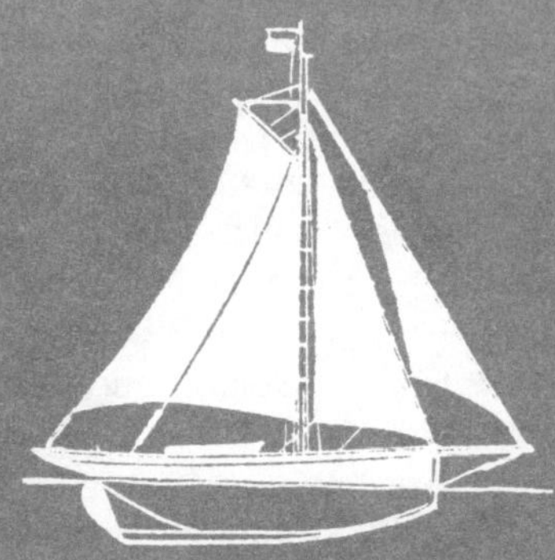

The English West County **Pilot Cutter** in the latter 1800's operated outside their harbors all-year long. It carried pilots who would take larger vessels into their harbors.

The lovely 10 meter 1928 classic **Branta** is even more competitive sixty years later.

59'0"
Length Over Deck
10'6" beam
7'6" draft
21 tons gross weight
11 ton lead keel
76'0" mast
30 hp diesel

The first cutter-rigged Valiant raced single-handed around the world.

"Is it a yawl...or a ketch?"

The yawl is easy to recognize in the distance having a tall main mast and a short jigger or mizzen mast...with the rudder post located between the masts. We include an exception, the 73' *Windward Passage* with a small mizzen mast in its original rig. As you move in closer you begin to realize the rudder post is aft of both masts...making it a ketch.

- **Vigilant.** We show the 124' gaff-rigged topsail cutter with its racing rig on page 265. We show it on the facing page as a "typical" cruising yawl taking 20 days to sail across the Atlantic on its own bottom. After arriving in England, she changed back to her cutter rig while racing with a crew of 49 professionals, who also bunked aboard. As for privacy...

- **Bermuda 40.** We show the first one built in 1959, the *Huntress* which was yawl rigged. In the first 25 years 187 Bermuda 40's were built, with the rest being sloop rigged.

- **The yawl is a sloop with added flexibility.** In a light wind while beating it will carry a mainsail and gennie, with the jigger acting more as a trim tab to balance the helm. The jigger is dropped at force 5, and the gennie changed to a working jib to balance the helm while beating to windward.

  The yawl rig racing downwind will drop the jigger to operate under main, spinnaker, and a huge mizzen staysail between the masts often resembling a *mizzen spinnaker.* We show a small mizzen staysail on *Finisterre* page 69, to help readers, as a larger one would block many important details.

- **Clara.** She is a rare, full-batten, 35' 4" cat yawl. It was built in 1887 by Nathaniel Herreshoff for his own use. Was it to prove a point?

- **1938 Iris.** She is one of our favorites, pages 70-73, and 254-5, with her model becoming the Mystic Museum example of 1930 Yachting.

- **Finisterre.** She was launched in 1964, a classic we have frozen in time, pages 67-69. She started an endless number of look-alike yawls to 60' long.

- **Spray.** We have an exclusive with an old acquaintenance who wanted to meet Slocum who had just pulled in after many days at sea. As he was walking towards *Spray* he realized it was sinking. He ran down the dock and jumped aboard to open the main hatch. Slocum was dressed formally for dining with water creeping up to his knees, totally ignoring his intruder. After leisurely finishing his candlelight dinner...Slocum began bailing.

- **Sea Dawn.** The 36' yawl which resembled *Finisterre* was built by the owner in his backyard and in the water for two weeks. She had no engine and gravel was used for ballast. She was an empty shell below without any creature comforts. All halyards and sheets were 3 strand nylon. The owner had a working jib, but no gennie, nor spinnaker.

  I "Liberated" a gennie from a Newporter charter I was supposed to skipper, tying a knot in the head of the jib as it was too long, to fake it as a chute. We took first place in Class C in the 1959 Ensenada Race...missing first overall by nine minutes.

  When meeting the Newporter owner while receiving our trophy, after assuring him he would only need his chute not the gennie...

the YAWL VARIABLES

The 124′ **Vigilant** is shown rigged as a cruising yawl.

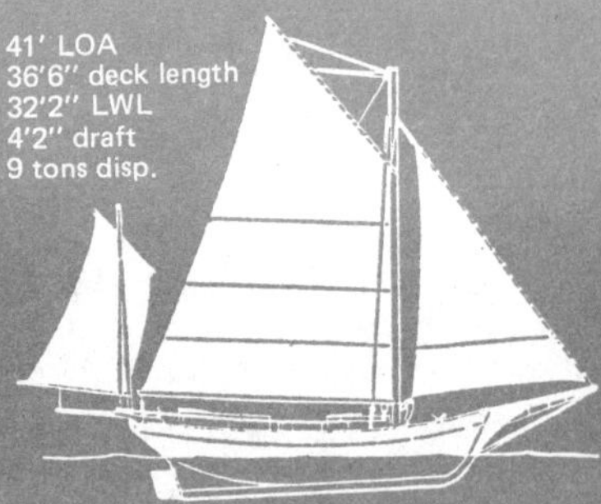

Slocum's **Spray**wwas a 100 year old lobster hull sloop he rebuilt and launched in 1895.He changed it to a yawl rig for self steering on his way around the world.

Clara—the 1887 cat-yawl designed by Herreshoff.

Iris is a traditional 1938 design with many excellent similar designs

The 1954 **Finisterre** challenged the the heavy, narrow-beam trend of that period. The wider-beam sailboats soon followed.

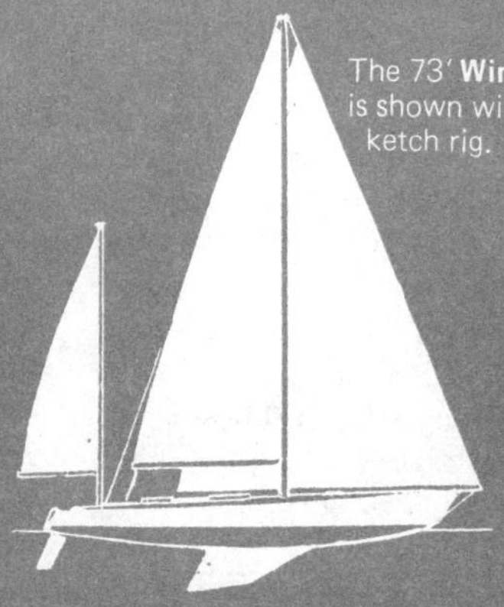

The 73′ **Windward Passage** is shown with its deceptive ketch rig.

The **Huntress,** the first Bermuda 40 was yawl rigged, while the rest were sloop rigged.

The flexible ketch rig.

The ketch rig under square sail dates back to Colonial times.The specialty was coastwise commerce using small crews. This trade was later taken over by larger, faster, and more maneuverable schooners with larger crews.

A temporary ketch? The J Class 135'9"*Endeavour II* with a sail area of 7561 sq.ft., was rigged as a ketch, plus a small square sail also added to the main mast. After sailing from England to the U.S. in 1937, it was changed to the cutter rig to compete for the America's Cup Races.

- **40' Newporter ketch.** It is a typical example of a ketch rig for leisurely long-distance cruising with the taller mast forward, and the rudder post aft of both masts. After winds reach mid-force 5, the large gennie is lowered, and the double-headsail rig shown at right is used.
- **40' Newporter cutter.** The *Black Swan* with full sail rig, competed equally in the 1960's with similar length sailboats. The Newporter motorsailer ketch rig with 85% sail area of similar length sailboats, was limited to downwind handicap racing such as the Ensenada race.
- **Tahiti ketch.** It could be owner built, and sailed away in the 1930's for $1000. The long keel provided good directional stability for long courses with little attention to the tiller. A light weather topsail was added that is common with British gaffers for light winds, which designer Hanna forgot.
- **Yankee.** It was a roomy 50' long cruising ketch with 4' draft. It was designed with considerable flexibility to cruise the inland waterways of Europe and Africa. Both masts have tabernacles to be lowered for going under bridges. Twin centerboards minimized weather helm for the shoal-draft hull.
- **Wishbone rig.** The 72' *Vamarie* in 1933 introduced a novel racing idea. She used a wishbone or twin-spar boom to set her mainsail high up in her rig, with the main sheet going to the top of the after mast, and down to the deck for trimming. The wishbone boom was raised and lowered with the mainsail, which others called a **trysail.**
- **Cat ketch.** A simplistic cruising rig was introduced in 1975. It used the wishbone boom or spar on both sails for easy upwind and downwind sail trim which eliminated vangs and travelers. Jibing is easy with the booms high above the passengers heads.
- **Cascade.** It is one of my favorites, a fascinating cat ketch that appeared in 1973. While asthetics are questionable, it proved a highly efficient rig within the IOR rules causing considerable anxiety with IOR rule makers.
- **Argus.** It is an underrigged 68' topsail ketch launched in 1908, and built for the North Sea trade. It was built in Denmark, and except for WW II, was owned by the same family up to 1970.

  The ***Argus*** moved to our local Sea Scout Base with its traditional running rigging, requiring considerable ***Svedish Steam*** or muscle power without winches. During the first 12 years it introduced over 20,000 boy and girl scouts to the ocean. She required considerable rebuilding in 1986. It is a busy vessel as reservations have to be made several months, to a year or two in advance by various scouting groups.

the FLEXIBLE KETCHES

A 1700 square rig ketch used in colonial coastal commerce.

The square rig would soon be replaced by the larger and more efficient schooner.

The 40′ **Newporter ketch** rig began in 1955.

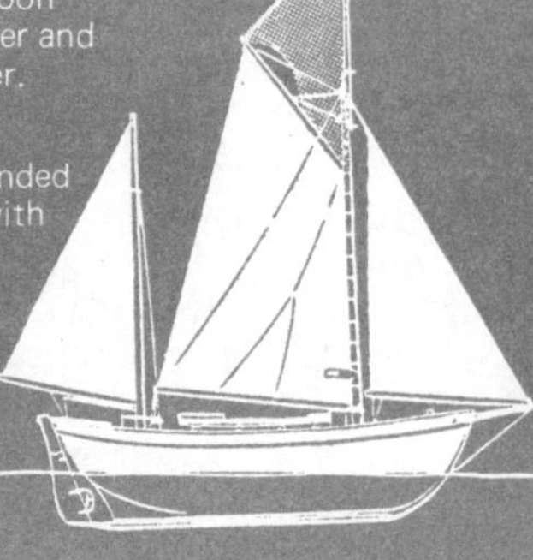

The 1923 30′ double-ended **tahiti ketch** is shown with a rare gaff topsail for light winds.

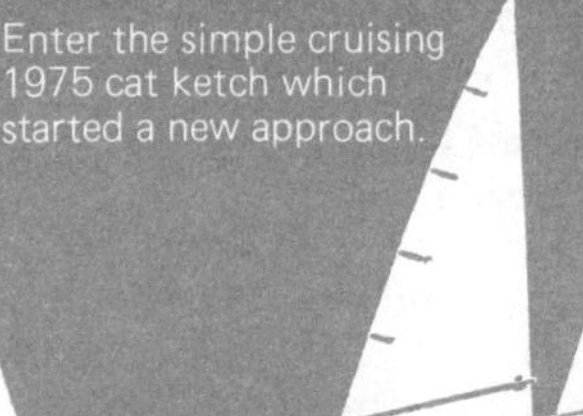

Enter the simple cruising 1975 cat ketch which started a new approach.

The shallow draft 50′ **Yankee.**

The 72′ **Vamarie** introduced the wishbone or twin-spar boom.

The Freedom 40 reintroduced the wishbone rig.

Cascade is a high performance 1973 cat ketch. What are the high-aspect ratio potentials for cruising?

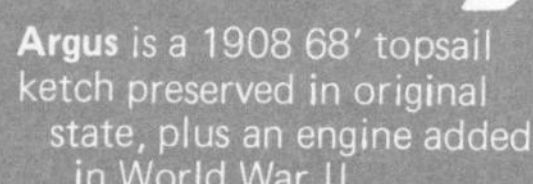

Argus is a 1908 68′ topsail ketch preserved in original state, plus an engine added in World War II.

The schooner has a unique American heritage.

The American schooner has a variety of rigs with both masts as tall, or the after mast is taller. When it has three masts it is called a tern schooner. The three-masted topsail schooner *Atlantic* has held the speed record since 1905 for the fastest monohull crossing of the Atlantic. For the 3014 mile distance from Sandy Hook to Lizard Point off the southern tip of England it averaged 10.32 knots, requiring 12 days, 4 hours, and 1 minute.

- **East coast schooners.** They began taking trade from square riggers as they could sail higher along the coast using sea breezes, and operate with smaller crews.Schooners could change tack easily, and raise their centerboards for narrow rivers and shallow harbors to deliver cargo.The topsail schooner *Pride of Baltimore* * was a replica of the early 1800's, launched in 1977.

Fishing schooners from the early 1800's enjoyed racing while returning from the Newfoundland Grand Banks to New England. While the race began for the best fish price to market, gambling soon became popular as owners began adding more canvas, as they also enjoyed betting on horse races. When nets drying between the upper masts had enough kelp to catch the wind,they were replaced with a new sail in that area aptly called ***the fisherman.***

One-topmast schooner. The *America* was launched in 1851, page 273, built along the lines of ***Maria,*** a 110' Sandy Hook centerboard cutter pilot boat. ***Maria*** was designed for speed in protected water, was the continual winner while racing against the heavier ***America*** which had to sail across the ocean.

- **West coast schooners.**** They began after the gold rush with over 500 little schooners called **outside porters,** were built to sail into tiny exposed niches along the rocky coast from San Francisco north called **dog holes** to pick up redwood, Oregon pine, and Douglas fir.The lumber was unloaded in San Francisco for loading on large lumber schooners. They included larger two-masters, over 125 three-masters, over 180 four masters, and around 100 five masters, plus brigantines and barkentines. They carried the lumber to Southern California, thru the South Pacific to Australia, and to China where 60 year old Oregon pine to 90' tall was the choice for junk masts.

The **standard schooner rig** has a gaff-headed foresail with a marconi-rigged main...becoming a **topsail schooner** when square sails are added to the foreward mast. A **bald-headed schooner** has no top masts. The **Staysail schooner** carries a staysail between the masts...becoming a **hermaphrodite brig** when square sails are added to the forward mast.

- **The seven mast** *Thomas W. Lawson* was launched in 1902, requiring a crew of 16. While Americans called the sails by the days of the week, British sailors preferred traditional terms. After conversion to an oil tanker it was sunk on 12/13/1907 on Hellweather Reef,Scilly Islands,South of England.You can see an excellent model of it in the Mariner's Museum,Newport News,Virginia.

***The Baltimore Clipper**— Howard Chapelle. An excellent, thorough history of these fast brigs and schooners contributing so much to our early colonies. Sweetman, pg. 184.

****Windjammers of the Pacific Rim**— Jim Gibbs. It covers schooners, barkentines,etc., made on Pacific Coast from 1850 to 1921. Appendix lists all these vessels with their specifications— Schiffer Pub. Ltd., 1469 Morstein Road, West Chester, PA 19830

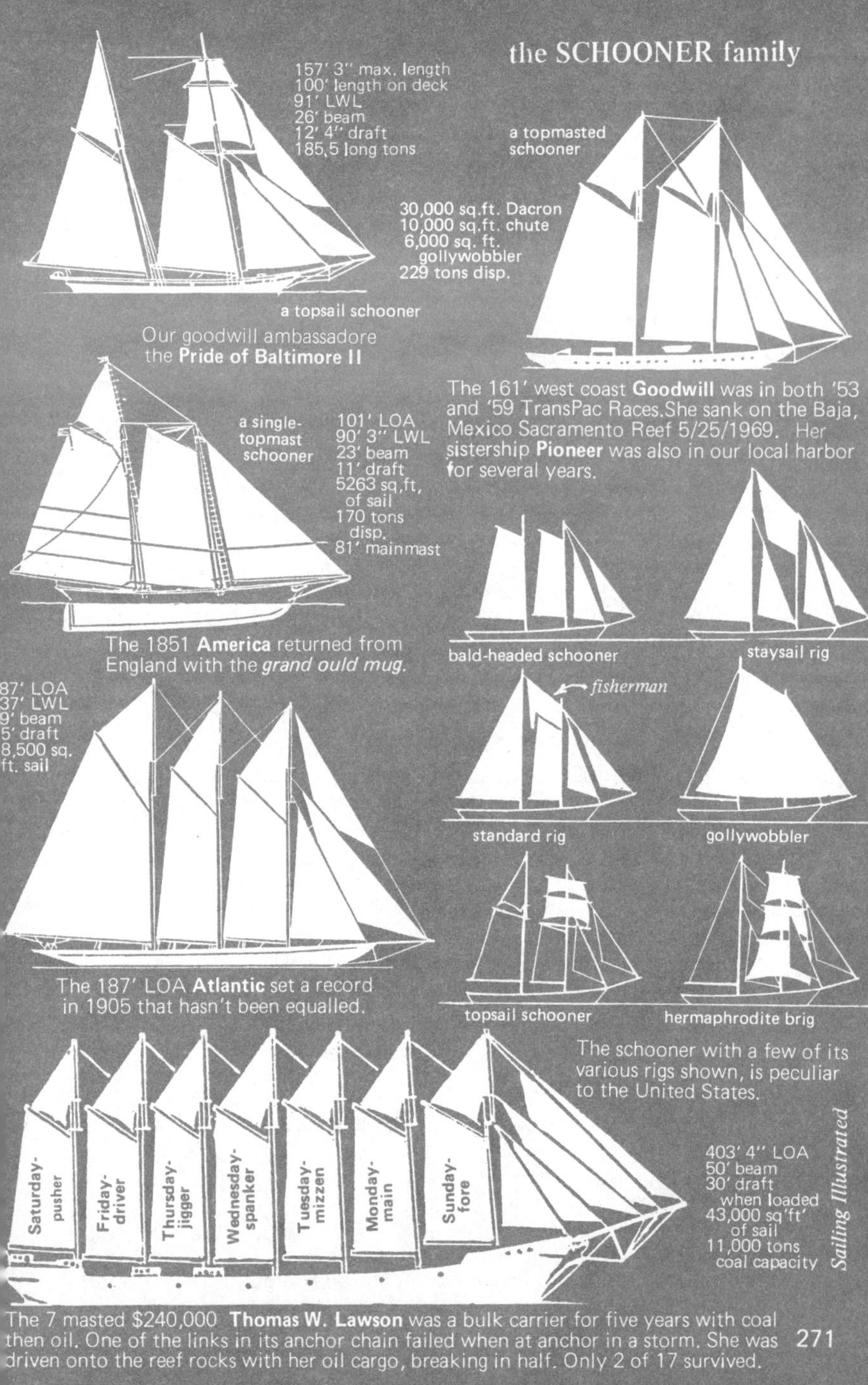

Our goodwill ambassadore the **Pride of Baltimore II**

The 161′ west coast **Goodwill** was in both '53 and '59 TransPac Races. She sank on the Baja, Mexico Sacramento Reef 5/25/1969. Her sistership **Pioneer** was also in our local harbor for several years.

The 1851 **America** returned from England with the *grand ould mug.*

The 187′ LOA **Atlantic** set a record in 1905 that hasn't been equalled.

The schooner with a few of its various rigs shown, is peculiar to the United States.

The 7 masted $240,000 **Thomas W. Lawson** was a bulk carrier for five years with coal then oil. One of the links in its anchor chain failed when at anchor in a storm. She was driven onto the reef rocks with her oil cargo, breaking in half. Only 2 of 17 survived.

The term motorsailer emerged 50 years ago when it was rare to find a sailboat with an auxiliary engine. It is obsolete today as most cabin sailboats use outboard, or inboard engines. The question is how much power today. Will the engine be limited just for docking, or be operated for long periods?

- Naval architects specify adequate engine hp for their sailboat designs such as 20 hp for the ***Minka.*** The owner specified a 32 hp diesel which moved us in a force upper 7 on a close reach with steadying sails up.

  Windward Passage is the other extreme having a small engine just able to maneuver her around the docks. The engine is fully retracted and the opening sealed as it becomes an all-out racing machine.

  The 40' Newporter ketch as a motorsailer has 85% of the normal sail area for a similar length sailboat, as it is designed to spend more time under power. While the original 40 hp diesel would power the ketch up to a force 6, the first Newporter was repowered with a 53 hp diesel for a force 7.

- **Quest** *(ex Califia)* was a 51' 8'' displacement speed powerboat built in Hong Kong. Her first owner John Herndahl took her westward thru the Mediterranean, Atlantic, and the Panama Cánal to Newport Beach.

  The next owners Charles and Vann Carter added the sail rig shown at right in San Diego. ***Quest*** became the family home for the next 8 years and 90,000 miles on their trip around the world.Their book,copyrighted 1987,* provides excellent information for anyone planning to sail around the world, in one of the most unusual motorsailers afloat.

- **Steadying sails** were used in the 1940's when we were on the east coast to provide a stable, predictable ride for clamming or fishing underway. A small aft **jigger** is used on workboats to take in trotlines and lobster pots.It weather cocks the bow into the wind long enough to eliminate anchoring.

- The **sliding gunther** is an adaptation of the gaff rig with the gaff locked into a vertical position. It is a British idea where all spars and sail are stowed in a dinghy, which is carried aboard a larger vessel.

- The **Ljungstrom** is a 1950 Swedish design to eliminate the potential of an accidental jibe. The mast had no stays, with the sail reefed by furling around a revolving mast. The sail area is doubled while sailing downwind.

- *Iwalani*, built in Singapore, has sailed one and a half times around the world. Owner Bill McNaughton combined his research with ours for pages 288-9 to show operational methods for those wanting to add square sails to their boats

- The **Thames barge** used its sprit as a derrick to load and unload cargo.The barge has a 500 year history on the estuary seaward from London up to the 1960's. It was a very maneuverable 100% sailing vessel which could move in light airs, and carry working sails in a force 6. At the turn of the century an average one was 85' long, 20' beam, and a 150 ton capacity.

- The **pinnace** ***Virginia,*** 30 tons, estimated 50' LOA, was built in Sagadohoc, Maine, and launched in 1607. It was built by English colonists who used the vessel for 20 years in regular transatlantic trade. The fore-and-aft spritsail rig,for operation with a small crew, was popular at the time for Dutch sailing craft. During the next 70 years similar Dutch sailing craft of similar size changed to a loose-footed mainsail and gaff rig so the main could be brailed up to the mast and gaff. But where is the bowsprit?

***A Family Goes to Sea**—Charles H. Carter, Western Marine Enterprises,Inc. 4051 Glencoe Ave.,Suite 14,Marina del Rey, CA 90292-5607

MOTORSAILER variables

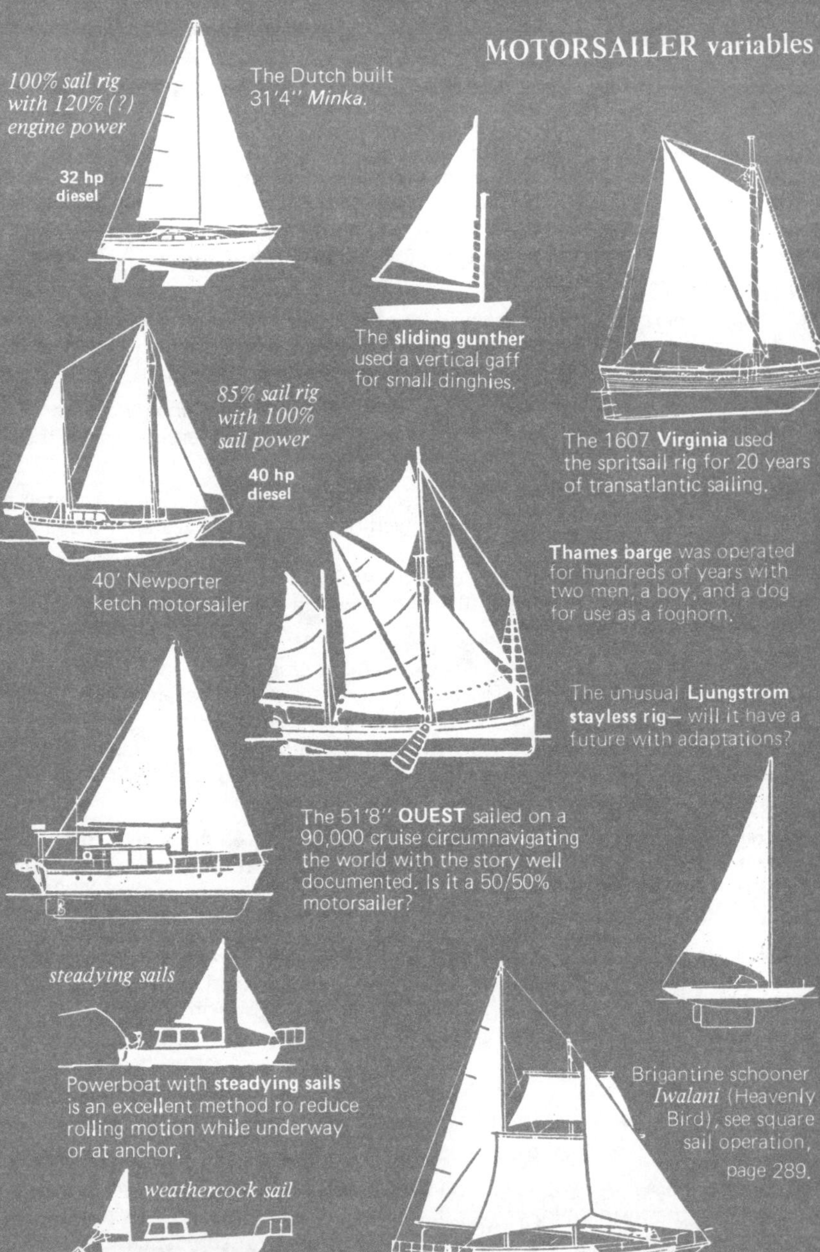

The Dutch built 31'4" *Minka.*

The **sliding gunther** used a vertical gaff for small dinghies.

The 1607 **Virginia** used the spritsail rig for 20 years of transatlantic sailing.

40' Newporter ketch motorsailer

Thames barge was operated for hundreds of years with two men, a boy, and a dog for use as a foghorn.

The unusual **Ljungstrom stayless rig**— will it have a future with adaptations?

The 51'8" **QUEST** sailed on a 90,000 cruise circumnavigating the world with the story well documented. Is it a 50/50% motorsailer?

Powerboat with **steadying sails** is an excellent method ro reduce rolling motion while underway or at anchor.

Brigantine schooner *Iwalani* (Heavenly Bird), see square sail operation, page 289.

The small **stern sail** on workboats holds the bow head to wind to reduce the need for anchoring.

Economic necessity developed unique American sailing rigs.

Our country produced several working sailboats beginning with the unique New England catboat. Many of these specialized rigs evolved while fishing and dredging for oysters in shallow, protected east coast areas. The areas ranged from Cape Hatteras to the Chesapeake Bay, and from the Long Island Sound north along the coast and bays of New England. *

Besides large fleets of lumber schooners on the west coast,we had large fleets of double-ended Monterey powerboats from 20' to well over 40' long. Many are in operation daily, some being 50 to 60 years old.

- **Block islander.** It had a ketch or schooner rig that was developed by Block Island fishermen, a rocky island east of Long Island.. These craft were launched from the beach and rocks were added for ballast. The rocks were dumped overboard on the return with the fish used for ballast.

- **Bugeye.** We show one with two raked masts, a single jib, and a pointed stern. The extreme main mast rake was useful for commercial craft as the main halyard block is over the main cargo hatch.

- **Skipjack.** Due to local rules it has been used to dredge oysters in the shallow Chesapeake Bay. While none have been built in over 30 years, of the last reported "jacks" at time of writing, probably 28 still exist with some of them 75 to 100 years young. It has a V-bottom with centerboard. The long raked mast is stepped well forward, with a large jib tacked to a long, well-hogged bowsprit.

- **Sharpie.** It was popular on the eastern end of Long Island in the late 1800's. This seemed a normal development to oystermen who became tired paddling their log canoes, to which they added sails. The sharpie was easy to build, a flat bottom craft with one or two centerboards, with some reported to be 60' long.The freestanding cat-ketch rig was fast and weatherly, easy to operate with a man and a boy.

- **Log canoe.** Early Chesapeake Bay aristocrats deplored physical effort. They bartered log canoes from natives for local transportation to which they added sails. It is difficult to call the present monsters that developed from 30' to 40' long with up to six sails a "log canoe"...yet the name remains.

  When the wind comes up the crews scramble out on ***hiking planks*** or springboards extending several feet over the weather side of the craft to prevent a capsize. The mainsheet tender meanwhile moves out on an aft ***outrigger*** to reduce the chance of the bow digging in. Masts weren't stayed in traditional designs, and extra masts were sometimes carried aboard. The mad scramble with the crew changing tack in a spirited wind, is a sailors dream.

- **Head?** The lavatory in 1700 naval vessels was a beak-head grating, page 279, or similar bow grating in the area with most privacy and washing action.

  Since the bow area was wet and uncomfortable in smaller vessels sailing upwind, the term **pink**, which referred to the sailboat stern, not the rig, seemed a better idea. As we advanced into the age of sophistication, the head moved downstairs...oops, below.

*Considerable information on these sailing craft may be found in most libraries.

Was the practical **pink stern** the final answer...or a temporary solution?

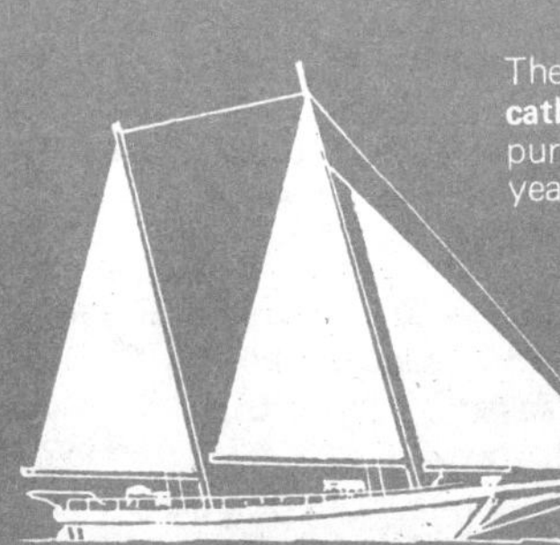

The **bugeye** *Little Jennie* was built in 1884. It still sails but for pleasure today.

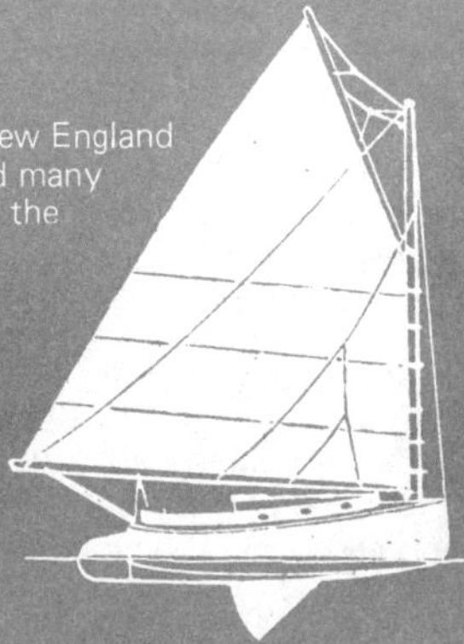

The unique New England **catboat** served many purposes thru the years.

The **Block Island schooner,** used rocks and fish for ballast.

The **skipjack** *Theodore J. Ford* built in 1880 is still working.

The **sharpie** began as a log canoe.

Is this a basic **log canoe????**

Does a large lug sail become a lateen sail?

Lateen yards 80' to 150' long are made of several tree trunks lashed together. Crew members must scramble up the yards maintaining a precarious foothold without rat lines or foot ropes to change sails instead of reefing in a strong wind. If you are invited to crew on a lateener, try climbing 100' palm trees in inky darkness with a strong wind... **is a start.**

- **The unrecorded beginning** of sail probably started with a square sail of hides for downwind use. When later cloth sails are tilted at an angle, which is the practice of some Chinese junks...it changes to a lug sail that permits junks to point higher or sail higher into the wind.
- The **Nile River current** in Egypt carried merchants with their cargo downstream to market. The lug rig was tested unsuccessfully for the upstream return. The sail or sails had to be increased in size with the **Nile gyassa** shown sailing wing and wing to catch the light prevailing winds coming over the high nearby hills. The lateen rig must change from one upwind tack to the other by changing the wind over the stern by **wearing.**
- **Lateeners** may have been developed by Phoenician traders, were adapted by Arab merchants with minimum changes thru the centuries. They often had to anchor at night until the 1920's when the compass came into use.
- **Arab dhows***followed the yearly monsoons for centuries from the Persian Gulf to Africa or India...then returned when the monsoons reversed direction. OPEC money changed the Arab lifestyle. Most labor-intensive lateeners disappeared, and their ***ship-of-the desert*** camel friend, ended in the stew pot.
- The **Mediterannean** has a history of the lateen rig more than a thousand years where the wind seemed to be too light...or too fresh for heavier European trading vessels. It proved excellent for small coasters, to larger, lighter Italian merchantmen. Galleys with rams used lateen rigs for warships up to 170' long. Auxiliary power (before outboard motors) was used for calms with up to 62 oars, using 7 galley slaves per oar.
- The square rig remained standard for Northern European nations, while luggers were often limited to harbor cargo-carrying lighters. Both the Dutch and the English began testing the lateen rig until the defeat of the Spanish Armada when it was phased out in favor of the square rig. For an example–

  On the first voyage of Columbus in 1492 his *Nina* carried lateen sails on all three masts which were good for upwind work. It had to be rerigged at Las Palmas in the Canary islands to a three-masted square rig 'that she might follow the other vessels with less danger and more tranquility'.

*The little recorded lateen sailing technology and philosophy of the Arab culture is well recorded by Alan Villers in his classic **Sons of Sinbad**, Charles Scribner's Sons. It is an excellent record of his 1934 year of sailing Arab dhows by one of our most outstanding sailing authors.

The Sinbad Voyage, G.P. Putnam's Sons, is by Oxford scholar Tim Severin who built an 80' lateener, then sailed it from Oman on the Persian Gulf to China, which provides many hours of excellent reading. It had an excellent TV coverage which we hope will be available in video cassette for home viewing. He also wrote **The Brendan Voyage**– Avon Publishers, of his crossing the Atlantic in a leather boat beginning May 16, 1976. It was 36' long with a five-man crew.

LATEENER RIGS

The **felucca** was a Turkish galley.

No Arab lateener was called a **dhow** ...it is a European term.

The **xebec** was used by Barbary corsairs.

a large **boom**

The flat stern **sambuk.**

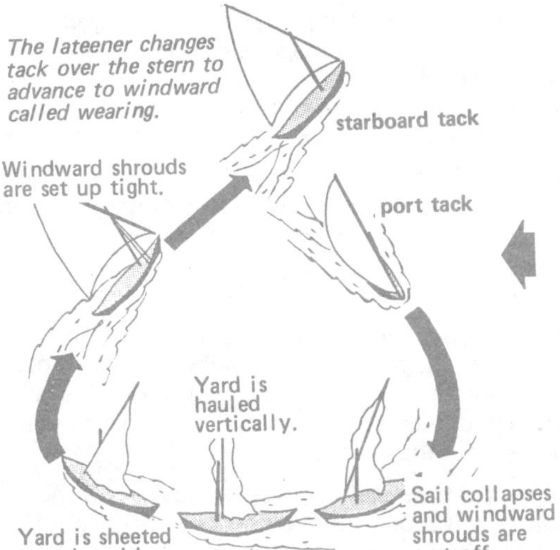

The lateener changes tack over the stern to advance to windward called wearing.

starboard tack

Windward shrouds are set up tight.

port tack

a Swiss barque

Yard is hauled vertically.

the Nile gyassa

Sail collapses and windward shrouds are cast off.

Yard is sheeted on other side of the mast.

Chinese junks (Dutch-*djong)* with full-length battens, balanced lug rigs, have changed little thru the centuries, though little known by outsiders.

Chinese historians have ignored their unique sailing craft.This responsibility was taken by G.R.G. Worcester in his **The Junks & Sampans of the Yangtze**, Naval Institute Press, see address below*. This book required a lifetime of dedication to complete. It provides a thorough, excellent coverage with a long history of the Chinese junkman culture and sailing craft. This book provides answers to questions we have been seeking for over 30 years.

Much information on junks, ours included,seems to come direct from this excellent book. The sail at right,for example, seems almost identical to the mizzen on page 62 of a photo of a Foochow pole-junk.

- **Masts.** Junkmen use a solid pole mast or a made mast (with several pieces joined together) with iron hoops. The mast partners have to work as a unit to bend as a tree in a monsoon,without supporting shrouds or stays. Oregon pine is preferred for these masts 3 to 9 stories tall which are often worth more than the hull. While we cure new wood by air drying...junkmen season their masts by burying them in damp earth.
- **Flat camber, full-batten lug sails** permit good pointing ability. Their organic cloth is weaker than our synthetic cloth for similar size sails. While our jibs and mainsails rip or tear when the cloth or seams can no longer take the full pressure of the wind...**wind pressure is spread evenly over the battens** with minimum pressure on the sail cloth.
- **Preservatives.** Their new organic sail cloth is soaked in a solution of mangrove bark curing for several hours with the tannin content being a preservative. The brown tanbark sails are then washed and dried.
- **Reefing?** After two years of constant use the lug sails become ragged and tattered developing small to large holes...yet the sails still draw efficiently as the battens take the stress. Though not as efficient in a light breeze, junkmen are enjoying their **broken-in sails.** The sails don't have to be reefed as early with some of the wind pressure leaking out the holes in the organic cloth. Can you imagine such a mind-boggling concept for American sailors?
- **Brown sails.** U.S. and European sailors cruising in the tropics prefer brown Dacron sails to reduce the glare of white sails in strong sunlight. While the brown sails provide earlier daytime visibility for approaching vessels, this becomes a disadvantage at night...except for smugglers.
- **Can you poke your fingers** thru your synthetic sail cloth? If you can, the sail replacement is overdue. In our high technology sailing world, our best Dacron cloth treated for ultra-violet rays under continuous exposure in tropical areas such as Florida with high sunlight ratios... also seems limited to two years use due to aging from the UV rays.

Was Hasler trying to combine the best of western technology, with the eastern tradition of full-batten sail support hundreds of years old?

 *United States Naval Institute, Annapolis, MD 21402 phone (301) 268-6110

Modern Lugger

Hasler—
1960 OSTAR

sail cover

boom crutch

The modern lug rig can be reefed in seconds by dropping as many panels as needed into the lazy-jack cradle with all the lines handled inside the cabin in bad weather...and topside in warm weather.

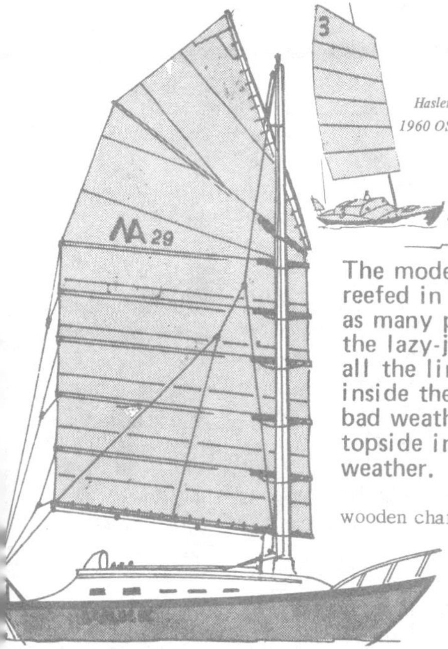

wooden chafe strips

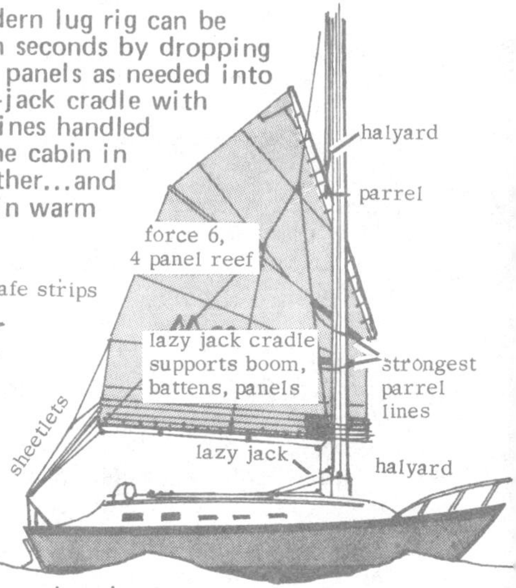

halyard

parrel

force 6,
4 panel reef

lazy jack cradle
supports boom,
battens, panels

strongest
parrel
lines

sheetlets

lazy jack

halyard

The North American 29',a 1970 design is by H.G.(Blondie) Hasler and Angus Primrose for singlehanding the North Atlantic,is an enlarged version of the 26' *Jester*.

Homestudy Guide pg. 122

The modern balanced lug rig was introduced by Hasler on his 26' Folkboat *Jester* for the first singlehanded 1960 OSTAR race,in which he also introduced the self-steering wind vane.

The laminated wooden mast without stays or shrouds,which is stepped on the keel,bends under load like a tree.*Jester* made 14 singlehanded transatlantic crossings by 1986*.

The **balanced lug rig** with 1/6 to 1/3 of the sail carried forward of the mast,eliminates the boom and gaff leverage with our type of sails when jibing or coming about in heavy winds.The lug sail bent to a yard,remains on one side blowing onto the mast on one tack...and away on the other tack with rope parrels on the battens securing the sail to the mast.

Hasler's 21' loa,6'11" beam,2'4" draft *Pilmer* is shown at right. It is a **mud duck** which settles upright high and dry into soft mud as the tide goes out.

Jester's* **ultimate storm—her 14th crossing, capsized, dismasted, and rescued. June 1987 *SAIL*.

Western lug rigs vs eastern lug rigs.

European luggers were used for harbor work though their fame came as *hot rods* for pirates, slavers, and smugglers...as luggers could outpoint square riggers in an upwind hot pursuit. English customs used luggers with the idea it takes a thief to catch a thief. They even made it a crime to build or operate a narrow-beam lugger.

- **Pirate luggers.** Clumsy, plunder-laden Spanish galleons returning from the new world to Spain sometimes had little wind when drifting past nearby Caribbean islands. Some were overtaken by agile, shallow-draft luggers hidden ashore. They were loaded to the gunwales with pirates who would plunder,and sink the evidence. As walking the plank was discouraging and few crew members could swim...they eagerly joined the pirates.

- **Want to build a junk?** Specify the number of compartments and forget the plans. The hull will resemble a shoot of bamboo split lengthwise with watertight compartments. Building will start with a flat bottom having a rocker, then bulkheads are added from the bluff bow to the high stern. Side planks are added and reinforced with **log stringers,then it is time to add** the deck. Northern junks have flatter bottoms and bluff pram bows for shallow river traffic plus beaching their craft to unload cargo...while southern junks may have deeper draft with narrow pram bows.

- **Upwind sailing**—due to flat junk bottoms, centerboards, leeboards, or daggerboards are required. Unique junk rudders are lowered by block and tackle to provide steering AND resistance to leeway. The rudders are raised out of the water when at anchor, or running ashore to unload cargo.

- **Ningpo iceboat.** They follow the widely spread estuary and ocean fishing fleets to buy their catch, then bring the fish to market between layers of ice. The iceboat, a recent junk design, sails long distances to serve markets from coastal Ningpo (Ninghsien) to Shanghai. When the bluff-bowed junk experiences pounding in a seaway, two **holes are opened in the bow to permit flooding** to reduce pounding action stresses in the forepeak. The junk can heave to in heavy weather using an 8′ diameter 1′ deep basket secured to a bridle. This **water parachute** keeps the junk head to wind.

- **Lorcha.** It is a southern hybrid junk using the Portugese influence for the hull and deck. To this was added the Chinese lug rig which proved an excellent warship to fight pirates with 180 lorcha's in the 1855 Portugese fleet,which also carried cargo.The last lorcha recorded by Worcester was 138′ long, while Siamese-built lorcha's were reported to be 200′ long.

- The **Kiangsu, Antung, or Pechili trader** was the largest of northern ocean-going junks, probably the type Marco Polo sailed on and reported in 1298 of these great fleets. The largest had four masts plus two auxiliary masts requiring a crew of up to 300 men. The largest had a single deck with up to 60 cabins below for merchants plus thousands of baskets of pepper.

  The largest junks had up to 13 watertight bulkheads. If a junk was hit by a whale, or the hull damaged in a grounding, the junk wouldn't sink as the flooded compartment was sealed from the rest of the vessel. If the designer of the 'unsinkable' *Titanic* 600 years later had exposure to junk design,woul it have been covered since 4/14/1912 with 13,000 feet of water?

TRADITIONAL LUGGERS

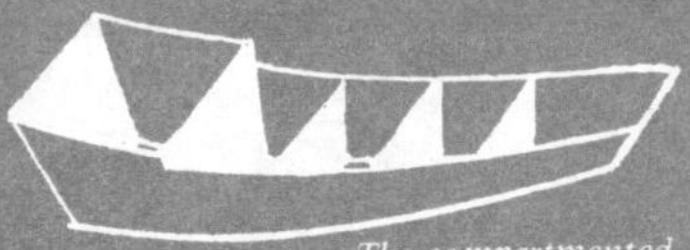

The high, wide weathercocking junk stern.

The compartmented junk hull.

the compartmented bamboo

Chinese vessels had extensive trade with Korea and Indo-China 2000 years ago, and 400 years later India, the east coast of Africa, and the Red Sea.

Arab vessels were arriving in China by 800 A.D. While the Arabs took some of these ideas to the Mediterranean,pg.17, the two highly-developed cultures seem to have little influence on each other.

"To catch a thief..."

the **dipping lug**

the **split lug**

the Ningpo iceboat

the hybrid **lorcha**

fiber matting sails

The huge **pechili trading junk** described by Marco Polo.

The Yiyang **sampan** with its unique pipe mud anchor.

The **full-rigged ship** has three or more masts all square rigged. The 212' *Cutty Sark,* still in existence, had a total of 32,000 sq.ft. of sail downwind. The *Preussen,* the largest windjammer and only five-masted square-rigged ship, had 47 sails carrying a total of 50,000 sq. ft. of sail.

- **Square riggers** are designed to follow the prevailing ocean winds and currents around the world, often facing adverse headwinds when they approach land. Sometimes they had to anchor to await a favorable wind, since even if they had a clean bottom they couldn't sail higher than 7 points from the eye of the wind, see page 99. After bottom growth started, many were limited to a beam reach, and a broad reach with more bottom growth.

- **Codfish head.** While Arab lateeners and Chinese junks for many centuries had sharper bow entries following the "duck waterplane" concept used today...European hull speeds were restricted due to the wide, blunt bow waterline entry, and the slim **mackerel tail** stern water exit. Most of these slow vessels Americans had were captured in the Revolutionary War.

- "Virginia-built" brigs and schooners fared much better. They evolved into the **Baltimore Clipper** with fine lines of swift, narrow beam that could be schooner rigged or square rigged.to help our struggling colonies in the early days, with more information on page 214.

The **Pride of Baltimore,** pages 203, & 271, was an excellent topsail schooner replica of this critical period. The quest for speed produced long, lean hulls, with deeper keels that could carry a much larger sail area. The bow had a sharper concave entry with the major beam from midship aft.

It also evolved into the square rig **tea clippers** from 1848 to 1858 with flax sails, wooden hulls, masts, and yards with hemp rigging. In this short period starting with ***Rainbow*** and ***Sea Witch*** both under 1000 tons, records were produced that haven't been equalled. Large **windjammers** followed with the largest being the ***Preussen.*** Windjammer hulls, masts, yards, and rigging were made of steel. They had a tremendous bulk-cargo carrying capacity.

- **Economy** became a major factor. Schooners with smaller crews and better windward ability, replaced clumsier square riggers requiring much larger crews, for coastal work. A compromise developed trying to find the best of both worlds with the **barkentine** and **hermaphrodite brig.**

The difference in English and American terms for the new emerging vessels was confusing. Terms on facing page are by our expert Gershom Bradford, Master of Sail and Steam in his *A Glossary of Sea Terms,* © 1927, 1942, published by Dodd, Mead, and Company, Inc.

- The **three masted bark** with two masts square rigged, the after fore-and-aft rigged, proved an excellent combination for the slower speeds of under-rigged whalers. We are fortunate to have the ***Charles W. Morgan,*** an active whaler for 80 years launched in 1841, on permanent display at the Mystic Seaport Museum in Connecticut.

the SQUARE RIG family

Most sailing vessels existed in their own time capsules, these from 1800 to 1930.

Square riggers have a long history. Our fore-and-aft rigs began developing after 1750 on our east coast, and 100 years later on the west coast.

Many large schooners and barkentines were launched on the west coast for the lumber trade... while the square rig was the European favorite up to the end of the sailing vessel era around 1930.

Sovereign of the Seas. A **ship** had to be fully square-rigged on three or more masts.

Pilgrim was a **brig** as it was square-rigged on both masts.

bowsprit with a jib-boom

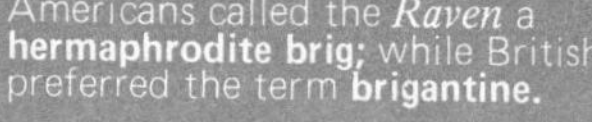

Americans called the *Raven* a **hermaphrodite brig;** while British preferred the term **brigantine.**

Americans called this rare two-masted vessel without a mainsail a **brigantine.**

A three-masted **barkentine** was square-rigged on the fore, fore-and-aft rigged on main and mizzen.

Sailing Illustrated

USCG Eagle is a three-masted **bark.**

A four-masted lumber **bark.**

The **bark** has three or more masts. It is fore-and-aft rigged on the aftermost mast, and fully square-rigged on the other masts.

square rig standardization

Square riggers had built-in complexity, plus variables, due to the wishes of the captains and mates. Two existing standards were the **language** and the location of **all lines going to the same belaying pins** on deck on American, English, Dutch, and Finnish square riggers.*

- **The reason**— two square riggers met in the Indian Ocean on a sunny afternoon in the early 1800's to exchange crew members wanting to go other directions. A few hours later at 0200, a vicious squall hit in inky darkness requiring all crew members aloft and on deck to understand the same commands to work as a team to reduce sail.

- **The spoken language.** Such was the reason for the international sailing language, and the standard location of lines going to the belaying pins on deck... *Eagle* has 154 lines on deck. Below in the fo'c's'le, the East Indiaman, the Upsala Swede, the County Cork Irishman, and others had difficulty talking to each other due to their homeland language barriers.

- **The written language.** The transition from the spoken to the written word is a difficulty facing all sailing writers. Readers will find spelling differences as we try to report a working language used by men with little schooling. I was fortunate in 1955 to have several square rig sailors help with these pages. It was the end of a passing era with only one alive a year later.

  *Edward Cunningham had 45 years of background preparing square rig sets and models for movie backgrounds who helped the preparation of pages 282-5. I still regret not having made recordings of his fluent use of the square rigger terms on these pages.

  After meeting him and discussing my book for a few moments, he asked of my background. He grinned, "Your daddy is responsible for my business. I had been adopted by the Hole in the Wall Gang and was 13 when your dad and his posse made the raid that finished our gang. Only two of us escaped. I headed for California to be as far from your sheriff dad as possible".

•

Basics of the complex square rigger standing and running rigging–

- **Masts** are supported by stays going forward, backstays going aft, and shrouds athwartship to support the masts, see *Cutty Sark* details in back of book.
- **Braces** leading aft control horizontal movement of the yards, except on aft mast where they lead to the mast ahead where adjustments are made.
- **Movable yards** page 288, are hoisted by halyards and supported by **lifts.** Their leads go to the deck where approximately 90% of square sail setting and furling is accomplished.
- **Downhaul tackles** page 288, haul the upper topsail yard down to just above the lower topsail yard. They also help support the lower fixed yard which doesn't have lifts.
- Squaresail **clews** are secured to and adjusted by **clewlines** on the yard beneath, pg.288. Lowest square rig sails-fore course, main course, crossjack, and jigger have **sheets** going aft, pg. 287, and **tacks** going forward to hold the clews dowr

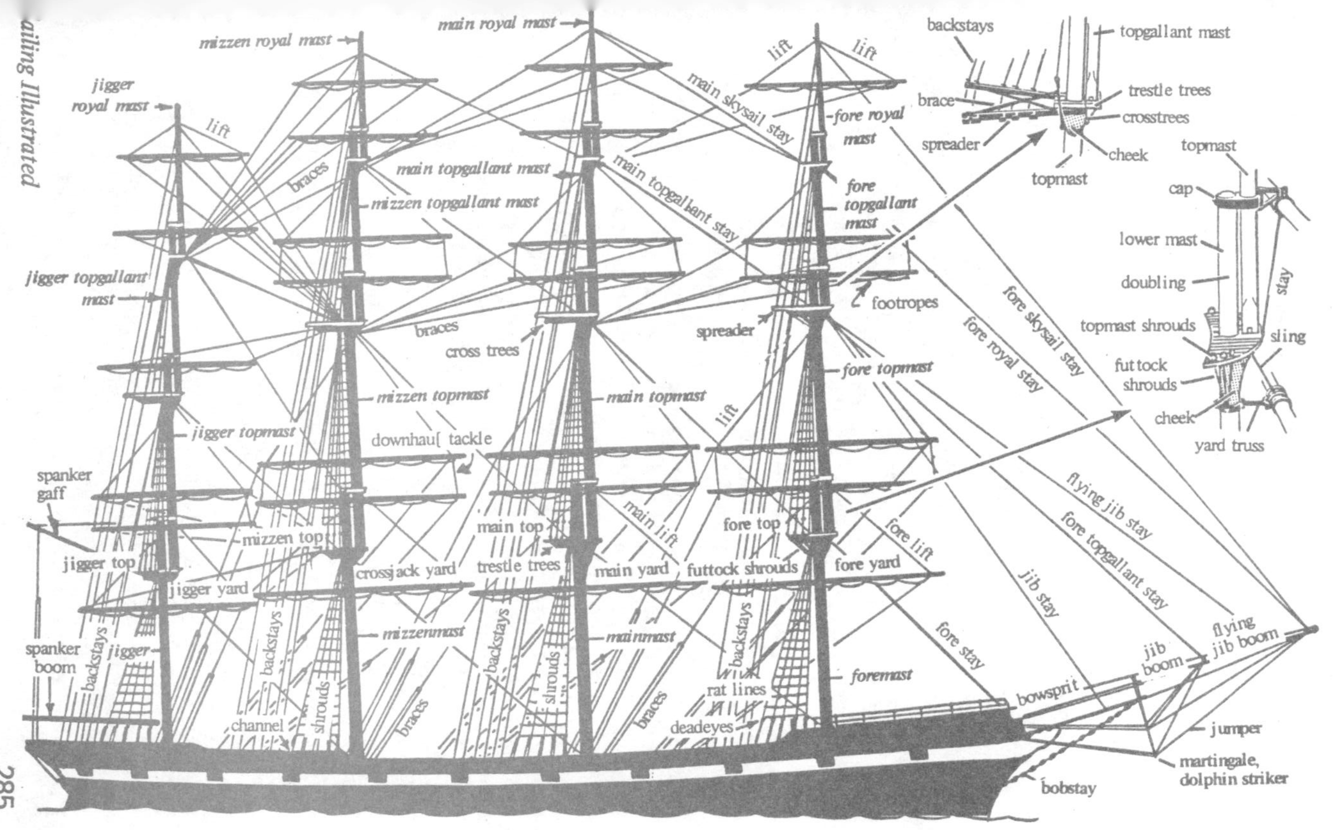
main royal mast
mizzen royal mast
jigger royal mast
lift
lift
lift
main skysail stay
fore royal mast
braces
main topgallant mast
mizzen topgallant mast
main topgallant stay
fore topgallant mast
jigger topgallant mast
footropes
braces
spreader
cross trees
fore skysail stay
fore royal stay
fore topmast
mizzen topmast
main topmast
lift
jigger topmast
downhaul tackle
spanker gaff
main top
fore top
flying jib stay
mizzen top
fore lift
main lift
fore topgallant stay
jigger top
crossjack yard
trestle trees
main yard
futtock shrouds
fore yard
jigger yard
jib stay
fore stay
backstays
mizzenmast
mainmast
backstays
backstays
flying jib boom
spanker boom
jigger
backstays
jib boom
foremast
shrouds
shrouds
rat lines
bowsprit
braces
braces
channel
deadeyes
jumper
martingale, dolphin striker
bobstay
backstays
topgallant mast
brace
trestle trees
crosstrees
spreader
cheek
topmast
topmast
cap
lower mast
doubling
stay
topmast shrouds
sling
futtock shrouds
cheek
yard truss

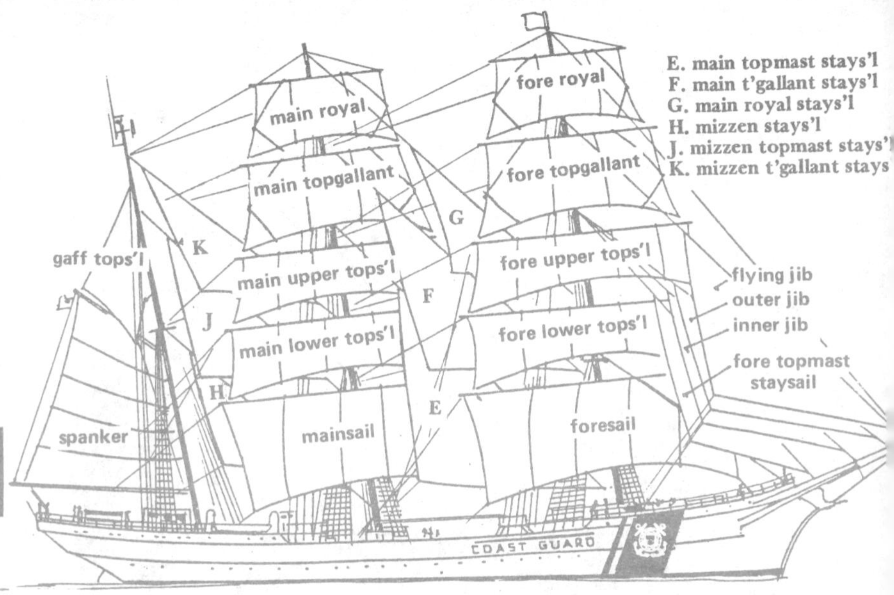

- **Masts.** As square riggers became larger the single *pole-mast* trees reached a limit. More masts were needed with the trees joined together between the *cheeks or hounds,* and the *mast caps,* their overlapping parts called *doublings.* 3 to 4 pole masts or trees added on top of each other made some tall masts with the *Cutty Sark* mainmast 150' above the deck.

  Sails. As the masts grew taller, sails had to be divided into two areas. The *topsail* became *upper* and *lower topsails.* This increased the number of lines while simplifying reefing, when even small sails in a storm were dangerous and backbreaking to take in.

- The **President,** a frigate, was captured by the British in 1815. It had a lofty rig with a 190' mainmast, with ***skysails*** carried above the ***royals*** on all three masts. ***Moonsails*** or ***moonrakers*** were rarely seen on even the largest square-rigged sailing vessels.

- The *poop deck* of the 1600's,page 288.which had been a full deck aft had too much windage. When the full deck disappeared, it became the deck area directly abaft the helmsman though a part of the ***quarter deck.***

- **The Windjammers**—Oliver E. Allen, 1978 copyright, Time-Life Books,Inc. It provides an excellent different coverage of square rigger operation, especially the *Preussen.*

- **The Way of a Ship**—Alan Villers, 1970 copyright, provides an excellent coverage of late square rigger history, rigging, and operation; Charles Scribners' Sons.

- **Lever's Young Sea Officer's Sheet Anchor**— an 1819 book without changes still in print, half of the pages are full size illustrations. It taught young British officers to completely rig, then sail a square rig ship of that period—Sweetman, page 184.

- **The Lore of Ships**— massive compilation of full-page illustrations from Santa Maria,to naval and cargo vessels to 4-masted barks with highly intricate rigging and hull details. Crown Publishers, Inc., 225 Park Ave. South, New York, NY 10003

- **Pacific Square Riggers**— Jim Gibbs. West coast square riggers from 1900 to end of the sailing ship era, plus the environment seamen faced—Schiffer Pub. Ltd., page 270.

This ship shows a variety of square sails, some which were rarely seen. Sails were often trimmed by, and the helmsman steered by the main royal.

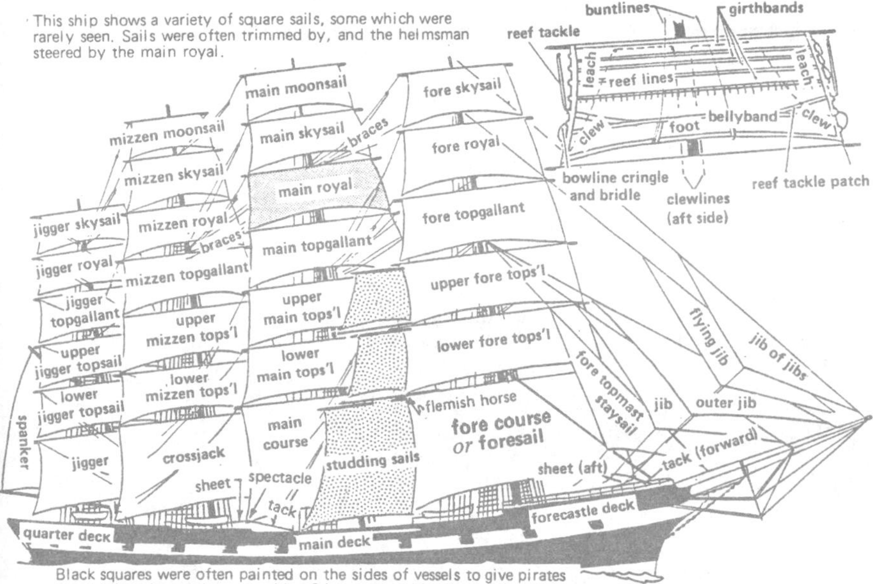

Black squares were often painted on the sides of vessels to give pirates second thoughts as they resembled 6th rater warships in the distance.

Early sailing vessels were built for fishing, to carry cargo, and for naval use. For a brief square rigger resume from 1500 to 1930–

- **High poop.** A high aftercastle was common from the 1492 carrack *Santa Maria,* and the 1570 galleon, page 290. These vessels could ride easier at anchor especially in a storm with bow weathercocked into the wind, while extra windage aft was clumsy for downwind sailing. High poop protection disappeared when naval cannon accuracy improved as it became a target.

- **Clippers** were the first hulls built primarily for speed with minimum cargo space. It began on our east coast with tall schooner rigs as blockade-runners. Square riggers with clipper hulls were built later to make excellent profits in the China tea trade, for which *Cutty Sark* launched in 1869, made eight trips. The Suez Canal opening in 1869, permitting steam vessels to save 4000 miles, eventually took over the European tea trade in the next decade.

  Cutty Sark entered the million ton yearly Australian wool trade, racing east around Cape Horn to England for the London exchange with wool action limited to January thru March. The last clipper leaving had the lowest wool price. If late, was the high warehouse storage penalty until next January.

- **Wooden hulls** have structural length limitations. The U.S. with an unlimited wood supply, kept building wooden sailing vessels with the largest the 350' long, six-masted schooner *Wyoming,* launched in 1910.

  European forests had been used up for shipbuilding with most wood having to be imported from the U.S. in the 1800's. Sailing vessels built to carry wood to Europe, had makeshift arrangements to carry immigrants back to the U.S.

- **Windjammers.** Europeans began building full-bodied square riggers for their stronger winds. The iron hulls without structural limits were much larger with huge cargo-carrying capacity, some making profits up to 1930 in the Australian grain trade.

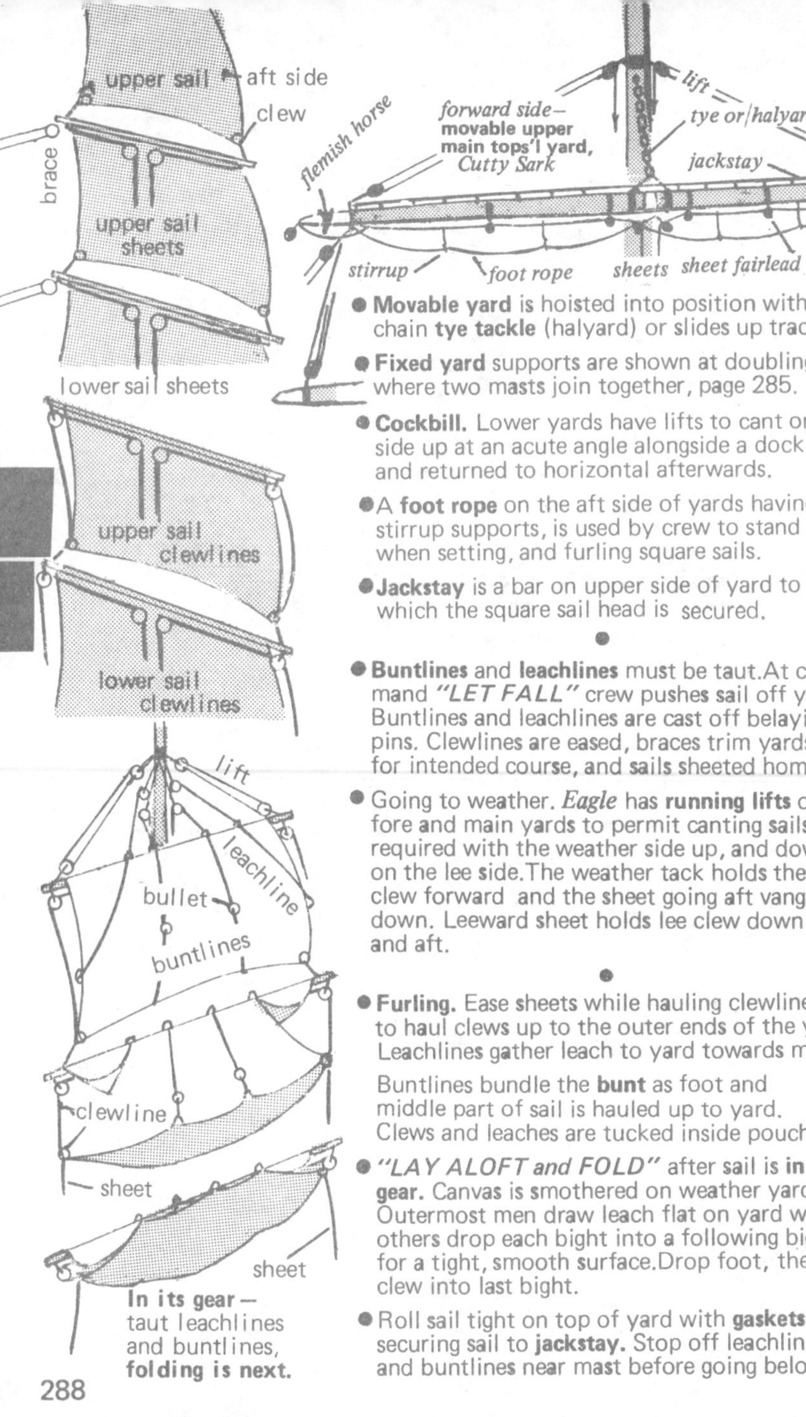

In its gear— taut leachlines and buntlines, **folding is next.**

- **Movable yard** is hoisted into position with a chain **tye tackle** (halyard) or slides up track.
- **Fixed yard** supports are shown at doublings where two masts join together, page 285.
- **Cockbill.** Lower yards have lifts to cant one side up at an acute angle alongside a dock, and returned to horizontal afterwards.
- A **foot rope** on the aft side of yards having stirrup supports, is used by crew to stand on when setting, and furling square sails.
- **Jackstay** is a bar on upper side of yard to which the square sail head is secured.

●

- **Buntlines** and **leachlines** must be taut.At command *"LET FALL"* crew pushes sail off yard. Buntlines and leachlines are cast off belaying pins. Clewlines are eased, braces trim yards for intended course, and sails sheeted home.
- Going to weather. *Eagle* has **running lifts** on fore and main yards to permit canting sails as required with the weather side up, and down on the lee side.The weather tack holds the clew forward and the sheet going aft vangs it down. Leeward sheet holds lee clew down and aft.

●

- **Furling.** Ease sheets while hauling clewlines, to haul clews up to the outer ends of the yard. Leachlines gather leach to yard towards mast.

  Buntlines bundle the **bunt** as foot and middle part of sail is hauled up to yard. Clews and leaches are tucked inside pouch.
- *"LAY ALOFT and FOLD"* after sail is **in its gear.** Canvas is smothered on weather yardarm. Outermost men draw leach flat on yard while others drop each bight into a following bight for a tight, smooth surface.Drop foot, then clew into last bight.
- Roll sail tight on top of yard with **gaskets** securing sail to **jackstay.** Stop off leachlines and buntlines near mast before going below.

USCG bark *Eagle* is 295' long, 1800 tons, with a sail area of 21,350 square feet, trains 200 recruits at a time. It has ten square sails set in the sequence shown at left, with 90% of setting and furling done on deck.

The 293' German *Gorch Fock,* 293' Portugese *Sagres II,* Mexican *Cuauhtemoc,* Norwegian *Statsradd Lehmkuhl,* resemble *Eagle.*

3000 year history. Square rigger setting and furling rigging has endless variations with their own complexity. Study rigging basics at left, then their operation below. This provides a foundation to study and analyze square sail handling methods for cargo vessels going back to almost 1000 B.C.

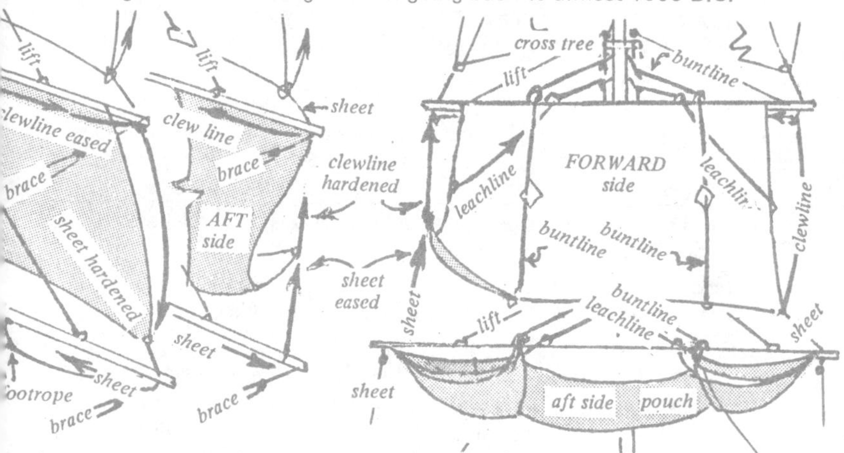

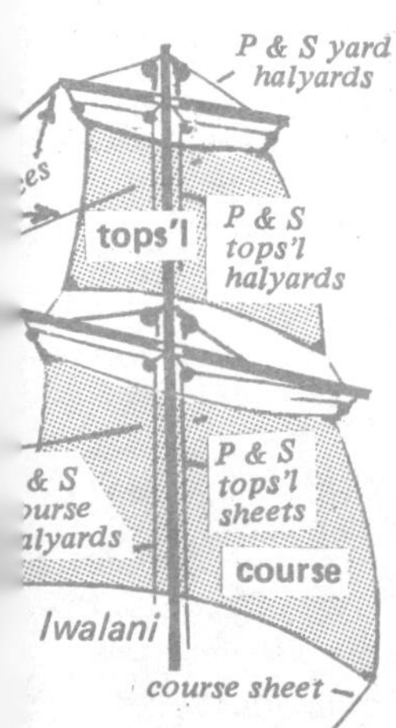

Do you want to add square sails to your sailboat?

Bill McNaughton rerigged his 42'5" staysail schooner *Iwalani* to a brigantine schooner by adding square sails to the forward mast, see page 273.

Raising. Yards are rigged on deck. The upper yard has three halyards, the center locking the yard in position, the outer ones acting as braces. The lower yard is raised on a track with two halyards as braces.

Sails are raised with their own halyards and cleated. The braces are trimmed, and the sheets sheeted to the sailboat course.

Taking down. Braces are released, then yard halyards are released, the tops'l requires a downhaul. Color-coded lines are removed and coiled. The sails are folded and stored below while the yards are stowed on deck lashed in their own saddles.

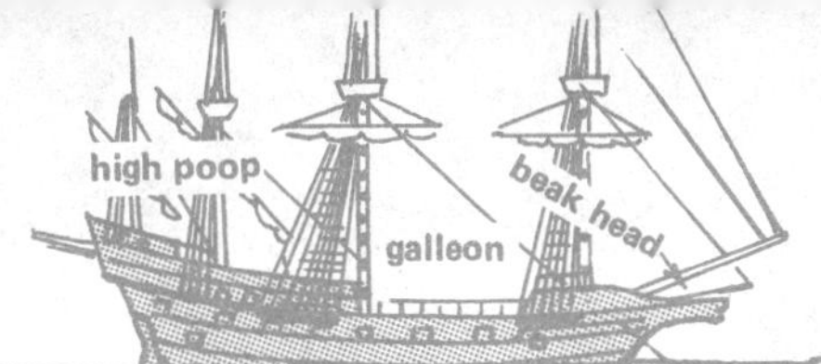

Lateeners to junks, plus early European trading vessels and warships, had high sterns to weathercock the bow into the wind to ride easier at anchor.

British 18th Century **warship terms applied to armament** not rigging.

- **Sixth rater**—a 125′ square-rigged sloop with less than 200 crew.
- **Fifth rater—a frigate** 130′ to 150′ long with 250 crew.
- **Fourth rater**—a two decker 150′ or longer with 350 crew.

These smaller vessels served a variety of purposes such as troop carriers, convoy escorts, colony guard vessels, storeships, etc. **Fifth-rate frigates** were fast, maneuverable, and far-ranging scouts to seek out and shadow the enemy for larger, lumbering raters, also to prey on merchant vessels.

- Our ***President*** and ***United States*** were listed as 44 gun frigates, while the ***Chesapeake, Constellation,*** and ***Congress*** were 36 gun frigates. Though our ***USS Constitution*** was listed as a 44 gun frigate, it carried 55 cannons with a range of 1200 yards when defeating ***Guerriere*** and ***Java.***

- "Old Ironsides" was commissioned 10/21/1797, After restoration it may be visited in the Boston Naval Shipyard. Her statistics—204′ LOA, 115′ LWL, 43′6″ beam, 1,576 tons displacement. She required 2 miles of hemp for running rigging to control an acre of cloth for 36 flax sails.Since it was a larger frigate it could carry up to 450 crew members.

- **Third rater**—from 64 gun two deckers, to 80 gun three deckers with 500 to 700 crew members.

- **Second rater**—approximately 190′ long, it carried 90 to 98 cannon on three gun decks with over 700 crew members.

- **First rater**—up to 206′ long, it carried 100 or more cannon. The fleet flagship ***H.M.S. Victory*** had 850 crew members.

- **First, second,** and **third raters** were **ships of the line** to sail in the **line of battle ships** (from where the term battleship originated) carrying 64 or more heavy cannon to fight in large fleet engagements. They were clumsy with tremendous windage and limited sailing maneuverability. When the opportunity came, their 12, 24, and 32 pound cannons could send a half ton of iron shot with a mile range, and still go thru two feet of solid oak in a single broadside. During an hour 30 tons of shot could come from a first rater...though these engagements often lasted several hours.

- The restored **first rater *H.M.S. Victory,*** Lord Nelson's 102 cannon flagship, is at the Portsmouth Dockyard, Hants, England. It was launched 5/7/1765 and commissioned 13 years later, being almost 30 years old at the battle of Trafalgar. Her statistics—226′6″ LOA, 152′3″ LWL, 51′10″ beam. She had 2162 tons burden, or3500 tons displacement.

  First raters were expensive requiring 60 acres each of prime oak trees with the ***H.M.S. Victory*** mainmast towering 205′ above the main deck. Can you think of any better reason to change to iron vessels?

- **Fighting Sail**—A.B.C. Whipple, 1978, Time-Life Books, Inc. It provides excellent reading and technical background of the life aboard British Navy vessels under sail.

P.S. It ain't an 8 to 5 job.

The British Navy began using the cutter rig after 1762 for carrying dispatches and hunting privateers, becoming Revenue Cutters around 1800.

They were the fastest craft at the time. Sizes ranged from 51' long of 82 tons, to 77' long of 140 tons, the larger craft operating with two officers and 20 crew members.

An 1800 14-gun English Revenue Cutter

The 1765 28 gun sixth rater could be 125' long. It could be a scout, courier, or guard ship with under 200 crew members.

a sixth-rater sloop-of-war

The major role of the frigates had been to prey on commerce. The American frigates were 20' longer and 3' wider than the 250 crew 44-gun British frigates.

The *President* had the tallest rig of our frigates with skysails on all 3 masts above her royals. She was captured in 1815, measured, then destroyed by the British.

a fifth-rater frigate

the first rater flagship
H.M.S. Victory

While a **ship of the line** may take to a half hour to change tack...when in position it could fire ½ ton of cannon balls in a single broadside.

Hemp ***was the sailors best friend for many centuries.***

Sailors lives depended on hemp from our early colonial days, and earlier, for British sailors. It was the best rope for standing rigging to support masts, and running rigging to raise, trim and control sails on small harbor vessels ferrying cargo, to fast clipper ships, and huge wndjammers. *Availability* was excellent as hemp could be grown next to rope mills and boatyards. Around 1860 imported manila rope began to replace hemp on sailing vessels for convenience, not strength.

Hemp and manila have similar strength. Hemp rigging would become slack in dry weather. Hemp rigging in high humidity shrank excessively, enlarging its diameter. Manila rope advantage–it shrank and stretched less.

1849 gold miners arrived in San Francisco to find the real gold was one of the largest forests. The lumber was soon used to build new homes and factories. It built large fleets of wooden ships delivering lumber thru out the Pacific as far as China and Australia This huge forest has shrunk to under 10% today, with replacement trees needing 40 to 50 years growth before becoming lumber.We must conserve these dwindling forests by beginning to manufacture newspapers from a fast growing weed called hemp, instead of destroying vast acres of forests weekly for newspapers.

- **Tobacco** . Congress found it easy to control and tax tobacco as it is a difficult product to grow in limited areas,
- **Hemp.** Congress tried to tax hemp smokers with over-the-counter sales. Congress soon found it a happy weed that could grow worldwide under a variety of conditions... beyond bureaucratic control. Frustration changed to vengeance with their 1937 act. Their logic as the new tax source was wiped out... *make hemp growing and smoking illegal!*

IF hemp growing and smoking were legalized tomorrow, with those behind bars released for only selling and smoking hemp, prison population would shrink to normal... and police could return to their main responsibility, helping the public. Hemp has many medicinal uses, plus replacing wood pulp for newspapers. Many people could relax with a hemp cigarette instead of three martinis.Our present bureaucratic hemp blunder cost is bankrupting the U.S.

P.S., the author is a nonsmoker, has never smoked tobacco nor 'hemp'. Good bourbon needs no substitute. *Sailing Illustrated*

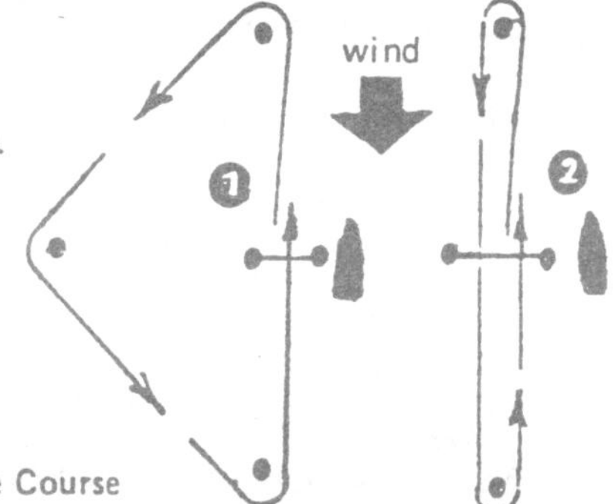

We provide a brief pictorial presentation to key *USYRU 1985-88 International Yacht Racing Rules* for exposure to racing, also for familiarization to help you locate rules involved in a protest.

51. Sailing the Course

51.1 (a) A yacht shall *start* and *finish* only as prescribed in the starting and finishing definitions.

51.2. A yacht shall sail the course so as to round or pass each *mark* on the required side in correct sequence, and so that a string representing her wake, from the time she *starts* until she *finishes*, would, when drawn tight, lie on the required side of each *mark*, touching each rounding *mark*.

1 **A fixed triangular course** shown usually has marks passed to port or counterclockwise. The first leg is a beat, then a reach, a run, and a beat to the finish.

2 **A windward leeward course** may be specified used either once or twice around.

The Olympic 12 meter course covering 24.3 nautical miles combines the fixed triangular course ending with a windward leeward course.

A selective course may be used in areas having a variety of markers. Just before the race the course to be sailed is given. Race instructions provide the sequence of markers to be followed.

4.2 SIGNALS FOR STARTING A RACE

(a) Unless otherwise prescribed in the sailing instructions, the signals for starting a race shall be made at five-minute intervals exactly, and shall be either:

System 1

Warning Signal—Class flag broken out or distinctive signal displayed.
Preparatory Signal—Code flag "P" broken out or distinctive signal displayed.
Starting Signal—Both warning and preparatory signals lowered.

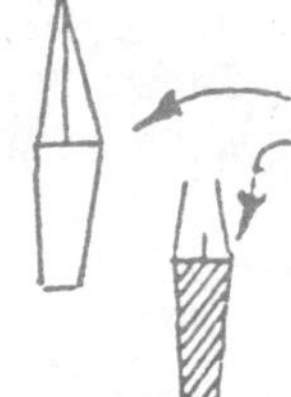

System 2

Warning Signal—White or yellow shape.
Preparatory Signal—Blue shape.
Starting Signal for first class to start —Red shape

44. Returning to Start

44.1 (a) After the starting signal is made, a premature starter returning to *start*, or a yacht working into position from the course side of the starting line or its extensions,

shall keep clear of all yachts that are *starting* or have *started* correctly, until she is wholly on the pre-start side of the starting line or its extensions.

(b) Thereafter, she shall be accorded the rights under the rules of Part IV of a yacht that is *starting* correctly; but when she thereby acquires right of way over another yacht that is *starting* correctly, she shall allow that yacht ample room and opportunity to keep clear.

44.2 A premature starter, while continuing to sail the course and until it is obvious that she is returning to *start*, shall be accorded the rights under the rules of Part IV of a yacht that has *started*.

wind

51.1 (b)...a yacht that either crosses prematurely or is on the course side...shall return and *start* ...

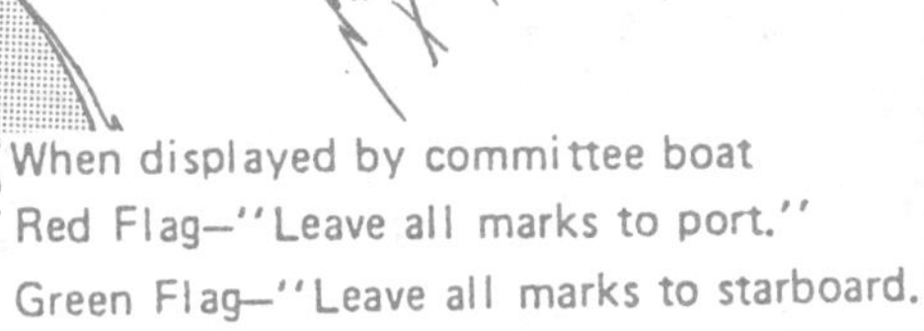

When displayed by committee boat

Red Flag—"Leave all marks to port."

Green Flag—"Leave all marks to starboard."

Blue Flag or Shape—Finishing Signal. "The committee boat is on station at the finishing line."

committee boat

"Anti-Barging" Rule

42.4. AT A STARTING MARK SURROUNDED BY NAVIGABLE WATER

When approaching the starting line to *start* and after *starting*, a *leeward yacht* shall be under no obligation to give any *windward yacht* room to pass to leeward of a starting *mark* surrounded by navigable water;

but, after the starting signal, a *leeward yacht* shall not deprive a *windward yacht* of room at such a *mark* by sailing either:

(a) above the compass bearing of the course to the first *mark*, or

(b) above *close-hauled*.

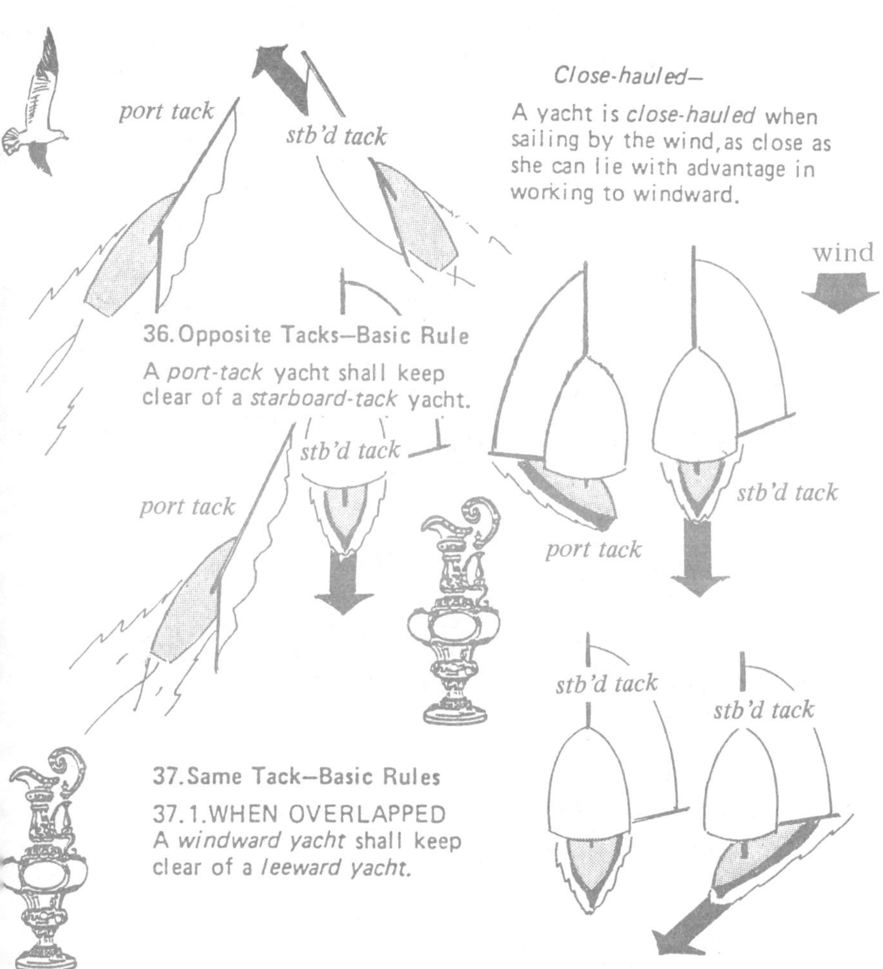

Close-hauled—

A yacht is *close-hauled* when sailing by the wind, as close as she can lie with advantage in working to windward.

36. Opposite Tacks—Basic Rule

A *port-tack* yacht shall keep clear of a *starboard-tack* yacht.

37. Same Tack—Basic Rules

37.1. WHEN OVERLAPPED

A *windward yacht* shall keep clear of a *leeward yacht*.

Thanks to the U.S. Yacht Racing Union for permission to reprint portions of the IYRU racing rules as adopted by the U.S. Yacht Racing Union.

Copies of the complete official racing rules may be obtained from the USYRU for their *1989-1992 International Yacht Racing Rules*, Box 209, Newport, RI 02840.

These regulations are very complex—***know them thoroughly and revue them continually***. The alternative is to be an also ran, and/or a collision and DSQ resulting with expensive damage claims.

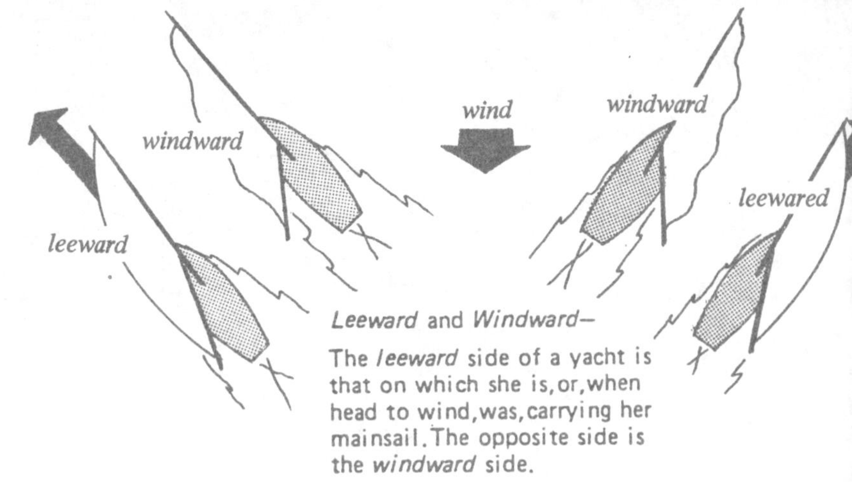

Leeward and *Windward*—

The *leeward* side of a yacht is that on which she is, or, when head to wind, was, carrying her mainsail. The opposite side is the *windward* side.

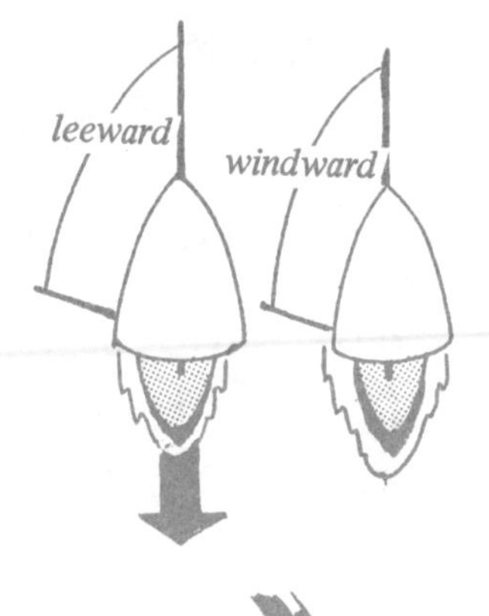

When neither of two yachts on the same tack is *clear astern,* the one on the *leeward* side of the other is the *leeward yacht.* The other is the *windward yacht.*

Luffing—Altering course towards the wind.

Bearing Away—Altering course away from the wind until a yacht begins to gybe.

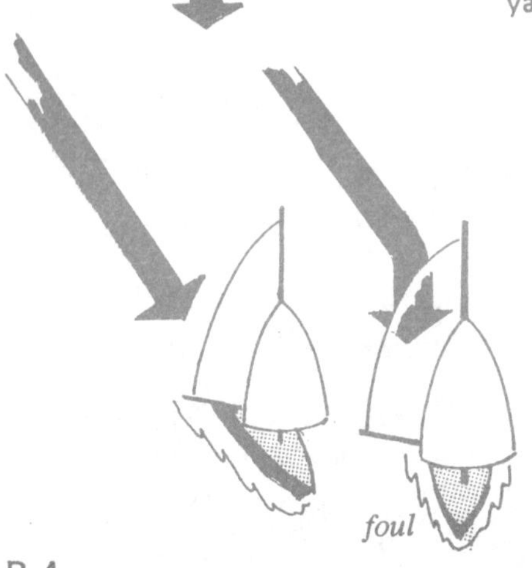

39. Same Tack—Sailing below a Proper Course after Starting—

A yacht that is on a free leg of the course shall not sail below her proper course when she is clearly within three of her overall lengths of either a *leeward yacht* or a yacht *clear astern* that is steering a course to pass to *leeward.*

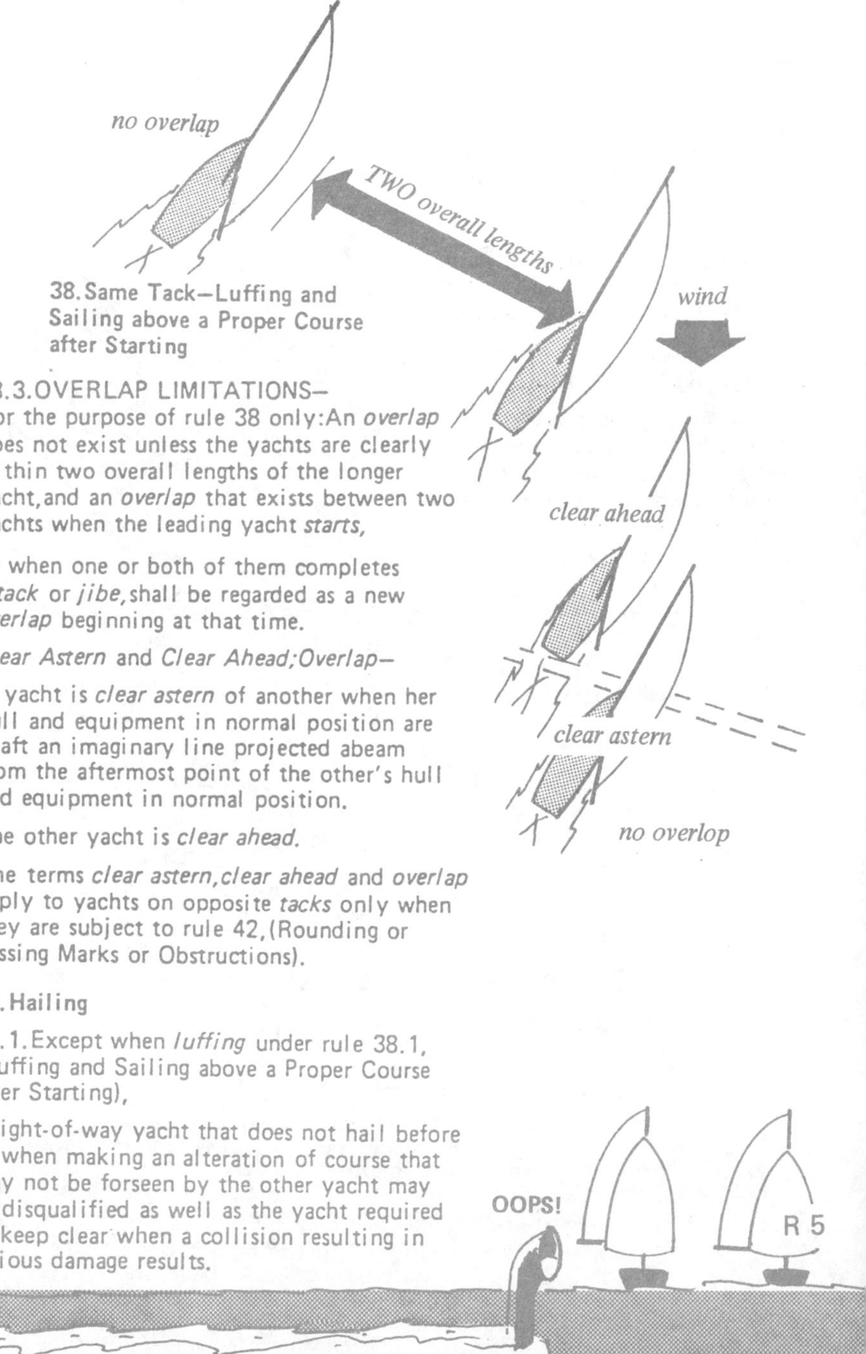

38. Same Tack—Luffing and Sailing above a Proper Course after Starting

38.3. OVERLAP LIMITATIONS—
For the purpose of rule 38 only: An *overlap* does not exist unless the yachts are clearly within two overall lengths of the longer yacht, and an *overlap* that exists between two yachts when the leading yacht *starts*,

or when one or both of them completes a *tack* or *jibe*, shall be regarded as a new *overlap* beginning at that time.

Clear Astern and *Clear Ahead; Overlap*—

A yacht is *clear astern* of another when her hull and equipment in normal position are abaft an imaginary line projected abeam from the aftermost point of the other's hull and equipment in normal position.

The other yacht is *clear ahead.*

The terms *clear astern, clear ahead* and *overlap* apply to yachts on opposite *tacks* only when they are subject to rule 42, (Rounding or Passing Marks or Obstructions).

34. Hailing

34.1. Except when *luffing* under rule 38.1, (Luffing and Sailing above a Proper Course after Starting),

a right-of-way yacht that does not hail before or when making an alteration of course that may not be forseen by the other yacht may be disqualified as well as the yacht required to keep clear when a collision resulting in serious damage results.

38.6. LUFFING TWO OR MORE YACHTS

A yacht shall not *luff* until she has the right to *luff* all yachts that would be affected by her *luff*, in which case they shall all respond, even when an intervening yacht or yachts would not otherwise have the right to *luff*.

38.5. CURTAILING A LUFF

The *windward yacht* shall not cause a *luff* to be curtailed because of her proximity to the *leeward yacht* unless an *obstruction*, a third yacht or other object restricts her ability to respond.

The yachts *overlap* when neither is *clear astern;* or when, although one is *clear astern*, an intervening yacht *overlaps* both of them.

37.3. TRANSITIONAL

A yacht that establishes an *overlap* to *leeward* from *clear astern* shall allow the *windward yacht* ample room and opportunity to keep clear.

38.1. LUFFING RIGHTS

After she has started and cleared the starting line a yacht *clear ahead* or a *leeward yacht* may *luff* as she pleases, subject to the *proper course* limitations of this rule.

40. Same Tack—Luffing before Starting

Before a right-of-way yacht has *started* and cleared the starting line, any *luff* on her part that causes another yacht to have to alter course to avoid a collision shall be carried out slowly and initially in such a way as to give a *windward yacht* room and opportunity to keep clear.

However the *leeward yacht* shall not so *luff* above a *close-hauled* course, unless the helmsman of the *windward yacht* (sighting abeam from his normal station) is abaft the mainmast of the *leeward yacht*.

38. Same Tack—Luffing and Sailing above a Proper Course after Starting

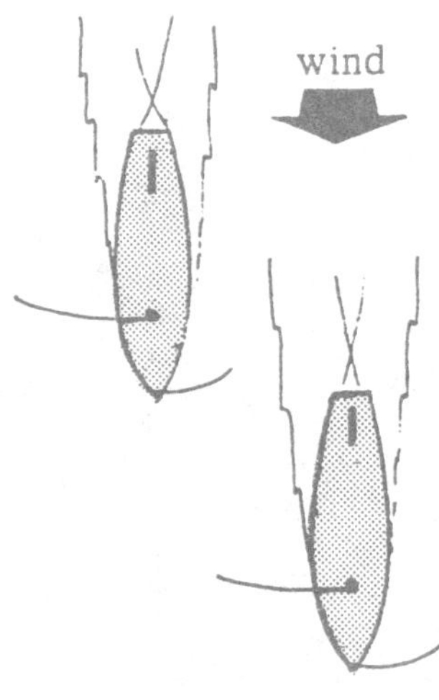

overlap starts

38.1 LUFFING RIGHTS After she has *started* and cleared the starting line, a yacht *clear ahead* or a *leeward yacht* may *luff* as she pleases, subject to the proper course limitations of this rule.

38.2. PROPER COURSE LIMITATIONS A *leeward yacht* shall not sail above her proper course while an *overlap* exists, if when the *overlap* began or at any time during its existence, the helmsman of the *windward yacht* (when sighting abeam from his normal station and sailing no higher than the *leeward yacht*) has been abreast or forward of the mainmast of the mainmast of the *leeward yacht.*

38.3. OVERLAP LIMITATIONS For the purpose of rule 38 only: An *overlap* does not exist unless the yachts are clearly within two overall lengths of the longer yacht and an *overlap* that exists between two yachts when the leading yacht *starts*, or when one or both of them completes a *tack* or *gybe*, shall be regarded as a new *overlap* beginning at that time.

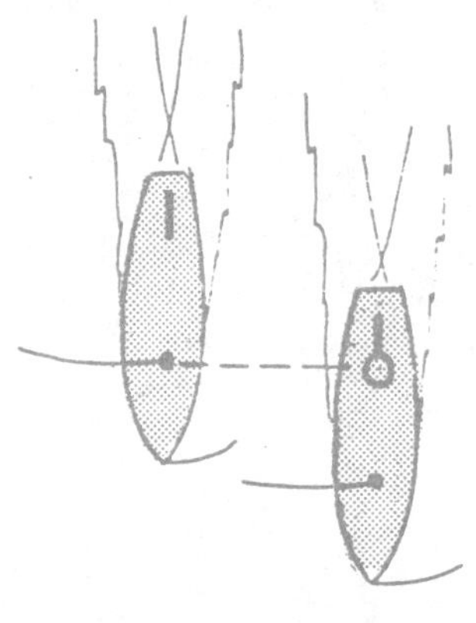

overlap completed

38.4. HAILING TO STOP OR PREVENT A LUFF When there is doubt, the *leeward yacht* may assume that she has the right to *luff* unless the helmsman of the *windward yacht* has hailed "Mast Abeam", or words to that effect. The *leeward yacht* shall be governed by such hail, and, when she deems it improper, her only remedy is to protest.

38.5. CURTAILING A LUFF. The *windward yacht* shall not cause a *luff* to be curtailed because of her proximity to the *leeward yacht* unless an *obstruction*, a third yacht or other object restricts her ability to respond.

38.6. LUFFING TWO OR MORE YACHTS ...see our page R 6.

Same Tack—Luffing and Sailing above a Proper Course after Starting

38.5.CURTAILING A LUFF The *windward yacht* shall not cause a *luff* to be curtailed because of her proximity to the *leeward yacht* unless an *obstruction*, a third yacht or other object restricts her ability to respond.

Obstruction—An *obstruction* is any object including a vessel under way, large enough to require a yacht, when more than one overall length away from it, to make a substantial alteration of course to pass on one side or the other, or any object that can be passed on one side only, including a buoy when the yacht in question cannot safely pass between it and the shoal or object that it marks. The sailing instructions may prescribe that certain defined areas shall rank as *obstructions*.

55.Aground or Foul of an Obstruction

A yacht, after grounding or fouling another vessel or other object, is subject to rule 57, (Manual and Stored Power), and may, in getting clear, use her own anchors, boats, ropes, spars and other gear, may send out an anchor in a boat; may be refloated by her own crew going overboard either to stand on the bottom or to go ashore to push off, but may receive outside assistance only from the crew of the vessel fouled. A yacht shall recover all her own gear used in getting clear before continuing in the race.

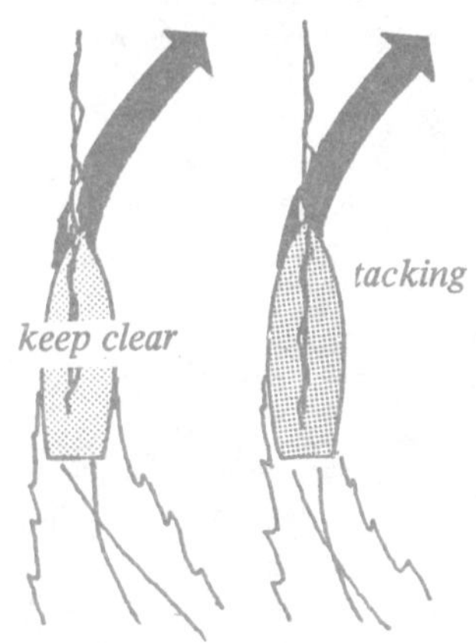

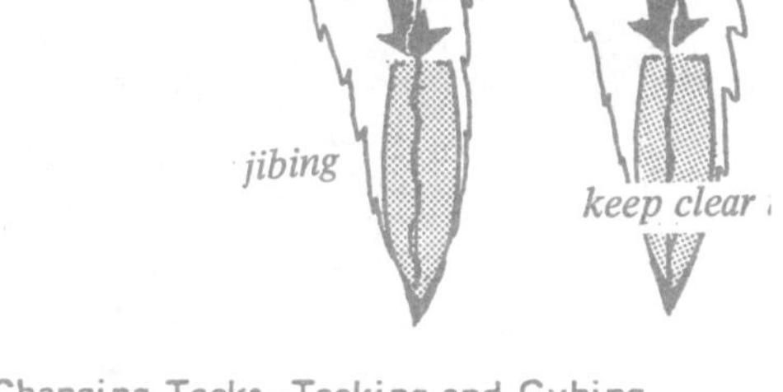

Changing Tacks—Tacking and Gybing

41.4.WHEN SIMULTANEOUS

When two yachts are both *tacking* or both *gybing* at the same time, the one on the other's port side shall keep clear.

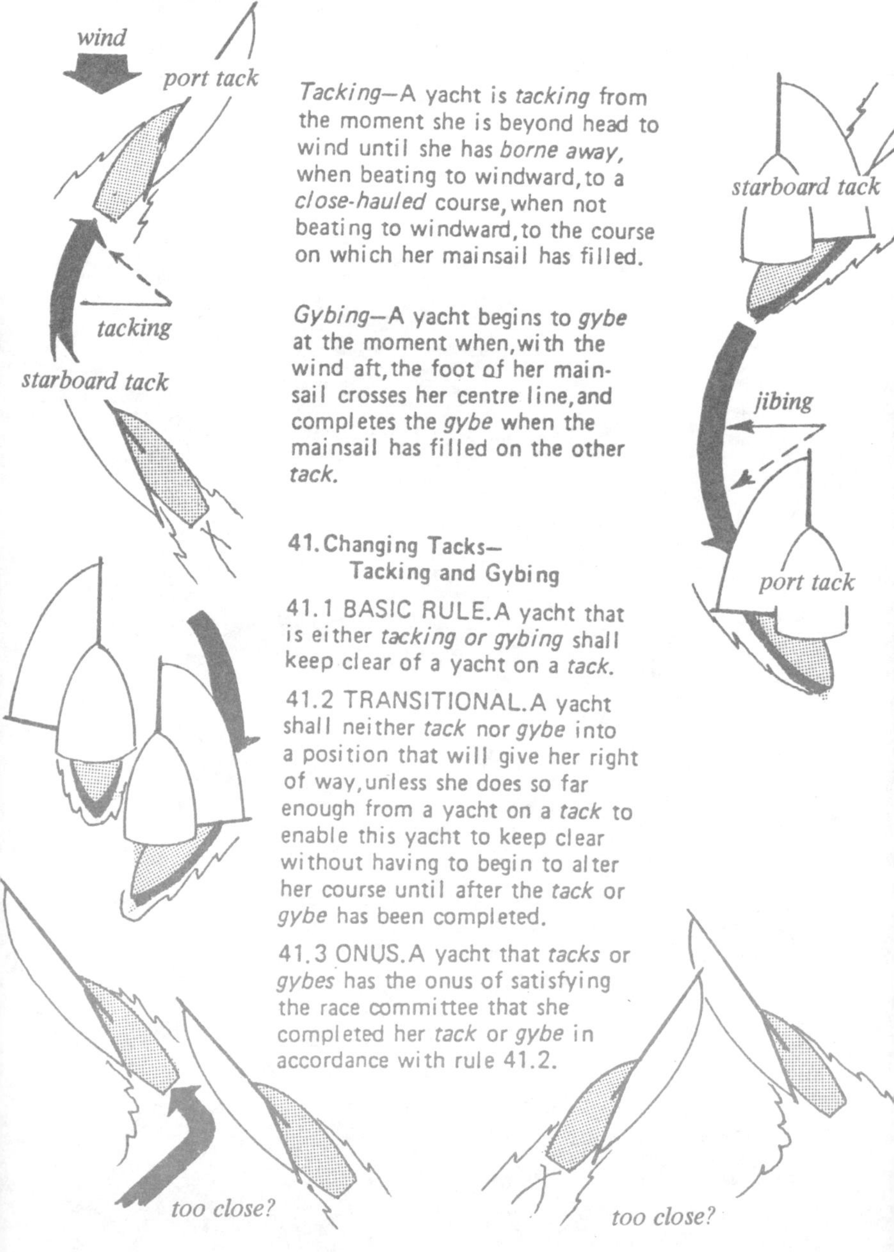

Tacking—A yacht is *tacking* from the moment she is beyond head to wind until she has *borne away*, when beating to windward, to a *close-hauled* course, when not beating to windward, to the course on which her mainsail has filled.

Gybing—A yacht begins to *gybe* at the moment when, with the wind aft, the foot of her mainsail crosses her centre line, and completes the *gybe* when the mainsail has filled on the other *tack*.

**41. Changing Tacks—
Tacking and Gybing**

41.1 BASIC RULE. A yacht that is either *tacking or gybing* shall keep clear of a yacht on a *tack*.

41.2 TRANSITIONAL. A yacht shall neither *tack* nor *gybe* into a position that will give her right of way, unless she does so far enough from a yacht on a *tack* to enable this yacht to keep clear without having to begin to alter her course until after the *tack* or *gybe* has been completed.

41.3 ONUS. A yacht that *tacks* or *gybes* has the onus of satisfying the race committee that she completed her *tack* or *gybe* in accordance with rule 41.2.

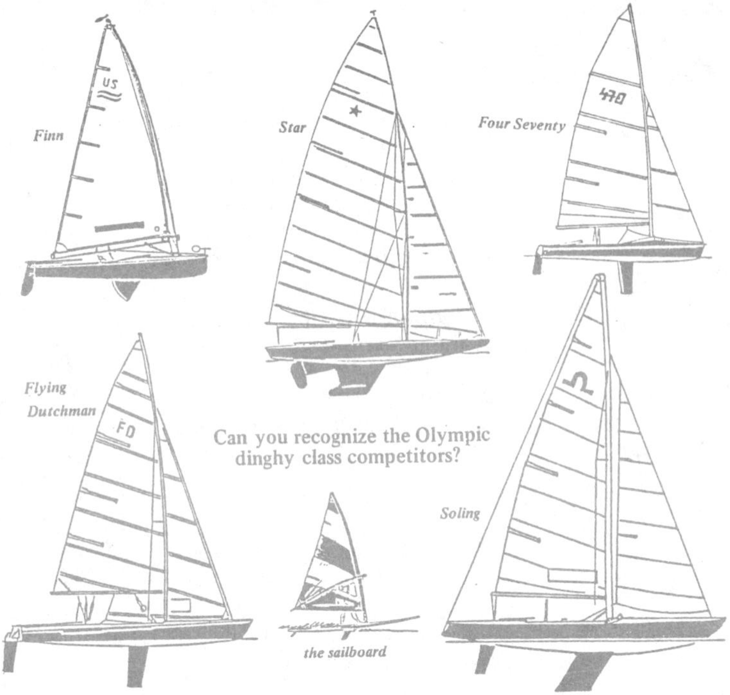

Finn

Star

Four Seventy

Flying Dutchman

Can you recognize the Olympic dinghy class competitors?

the sailboard

Soling

35. Limitations on Altering Course

When one yacht is required to keep clear of another, the right-of-way yacht shall not alter course so as to prevent the other yacht from keeping clear or so as to obstruct her while she is keeping clear, except:

(a) to the extent permitted by rule 38.1, (Same tack, Luffing and Sailing above a Proper Course after Starting), and

(b) when assuming a proper course either

(i) to *start*, unless subject to rule 40, (Same Tack, Luffing before Starting), or to the second part of rule 44.1 (b), (Returning to Start), or

(ii) when rounding a *mark*.

These rules apply except when over-ridden by a rule in Section C.

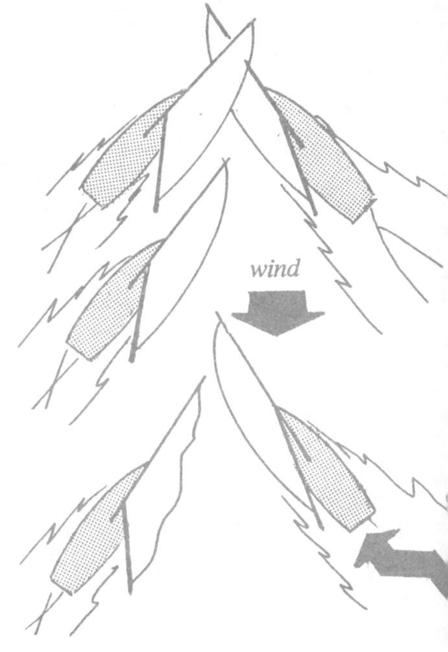

43. Close-Hauled, Hailing for Room to Tack at Obstruction

43.1. HAILING When two *close-hauled* yachts are on the same *tack* and safe pilotage requires the yacht *clear ahead* or the *leeward yacht* to make a substantial alteration of course to clear an *obstruction,* and when she intends to *tack,* but cannot *tack* without colliding with the other yacht, she shall hail the other yacht for room to *tack* and clear the other yacht, but she shall not hail and *tack* simultaneously.

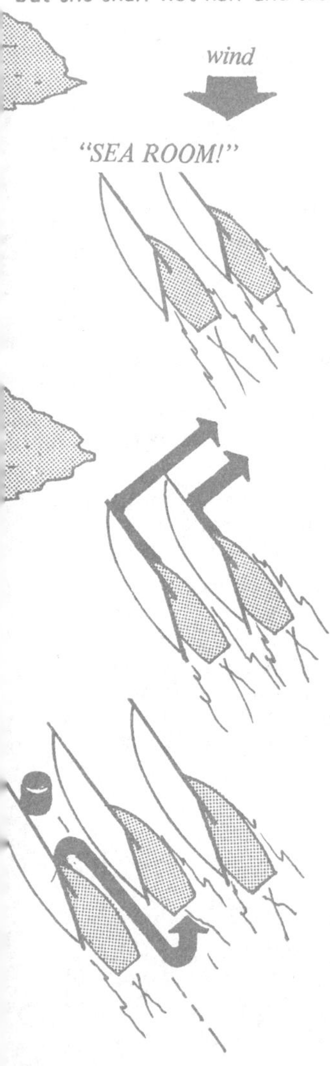

43.2. RESPONDING The hailed yacht at the earliest possible moment after the hail shall:

(a) *tack,* in which case the hailing yacht shall begin to *tack,* either:

(i) before the hailed yacht has completed her *tack,* or

(ii) when she cannot then *tack* without colliding with the hailed yacht, immediately she is able to *tack* and clear her;

or

(b) reply "You *tack*", or words to that effect, when in her opinion she can keep clear without *tacking* or after postponing her *tack.* In this case:

(i) the hailing yacht shall immediately *tack* and

(ii) the hailed yacht shall keep clear.

(iii) The onis of satisfying the race committee that she kept clear shall lie on the hailed yacht that replied "You *tack*".

43.3. LIMITATION RIGHT TO ROOM TO TACK WHEN THE OBSTRUCTION IS ALSO A MARK

(b) At other *obstructions* that are *marks,* when the hailed yacht can fetch the *obstruction,* the hailing yacht shall not be entitled to room to *tack* and clear the hailed yacht, and the hailed yacht shall immediately so inform the hailing yacht. When, thereafter, the hailing yacht again hails for room to *tack* and clear the hailed yacht, the hailed yacht shall, at the earliest possible moment after the hail, give the hailing yacht the required room. After receiving room, the hailing yacht shall either retire immediately or exonerate herself by accepting an alternative penalty when so prescribed in the sailing instructions.

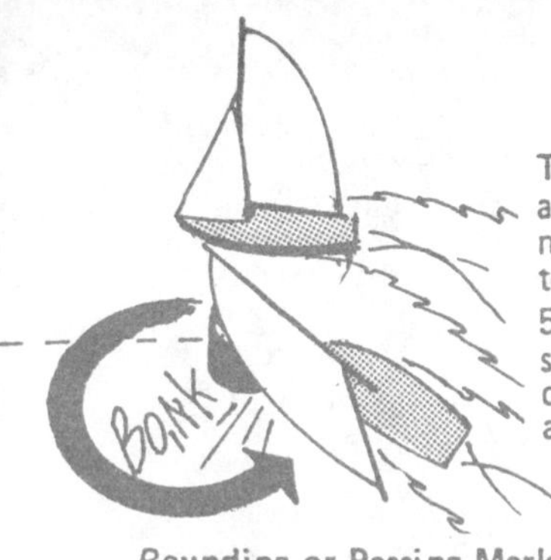

Touching a Mark 52.2(a)When a yacht touches a *mark* surrounded by navigable water,she may...re-rounding it or re-passing it without touching it...

52,2(c)When a yacht touches a *mark* not surrounded by navigable water,she may...by completing one 360 turn at the first reasonable opportunity.

Rounding or Passing Marks and Obstructions
42.1.WHEN OVERLAPPED-An outside Yacht

(a)An outside yacht shall give each inside *overlapping* yacht room to round or pass the *mark* or *obstruction,*except as provided in rule 42.3. Room is the space needed by an inside *overlapping* yacht...to pass in safety between an outside yacht and a *mark* or *obstruction,*and includes space to *tack* or *gybe* when either is an integral part of the rounding or passing manoeuvre.

(b)An outside yacht *overlapped* when she comes within two of her overall lengths of a *mark* or *obstruction* shall give room as required,even though the *overlap* may thereafter be broken.

(c)An outside yacht that claims to have broken an *overlap* has the onus of satisfying the race committee that she became *clear ahead* when she was more than two of her overall lengths from the *mark* or *obstruction.*

An Inside Yacht (d) A yacht that claims an inside *overlap* has the onus of satisfying the race committee that she established the *overlap* in accordance with rule 42.3.

(e)When an inside yacht of two or more *overlapped* yachts,either on opposite tacks or on the same *tack* without *luffing* rights,will have to *gybe* in order most directly to assume a proper course to the next *mark,*she shall *gybe* at the first reasonable opportunity.

Mark—A mark is any object specified in the sailing instructions that a yacht must round or pass on the required side.

Every ordinary part of a *mark* ranks as a part of it including a flag,flagpole,boom or hoisted boat,but excluding ground tackle and any object either accidentally or temporarily attached to the *mark.*

R 12

O.K.

DSQ

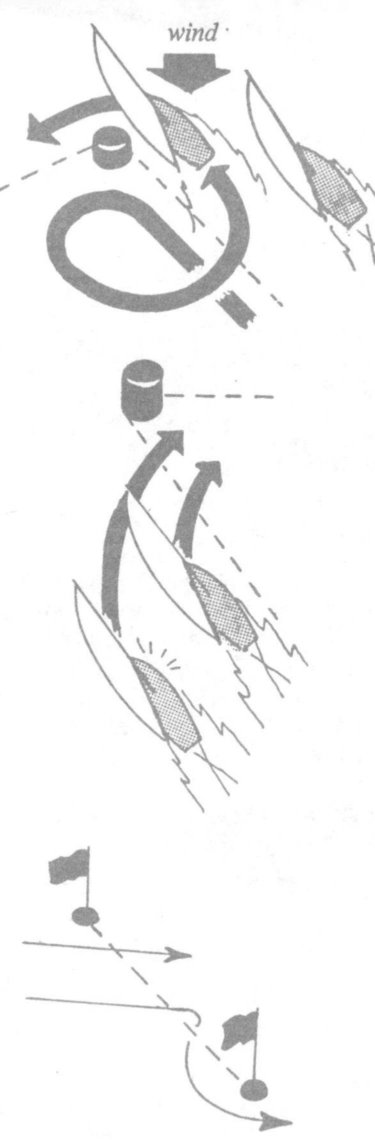

42.3 (c) Taking an Inside Yacht to the Wrong Side of a Mark. An outside *leeward yacht* with luffing rights may take an inside yacht to windward of a *mark* provided that she: (i) hails to that effect, and (ii) begins to *luff* before she is within two of her overall lengths of the mark, and (iii) also passes to windward of it.

Mark—A *mark* is any object specified in the sailing isstructions that a yacht must round or pass on a required side.

Every ordinary part of a *mark* ranks as part of it, including a flag, flagpole, boom or hoisted boat...

51. Sailing the Course

51.1 (a) A yacht shall *start* and *finish* only as prescribed in the starting and finishing definitions.

51.2. A yacht shall sail the course so as to round or pass each *mark* on the required side in correct sequence, and so that a string representing her wake, from the time she *starts* until she *finishes*, would, when drawn taut, lie on the required side of each mark, touching each rounding *mark*.

51.3. A *mark* has a required side for a yacht as long as she is on a leg that it begins, bounds or ends. A starting line *mark* has a required side for a yacht from the time she is approaching the starting line to *start* until she has left the *mark* astern on the first leg. A finishing line *mark* and a finishing limit *mark* cease to have a required side for a yacht as soon as she *finishes*.

51.4. A yacht that rounds or passes a *mark* on the wrong side may exonerate herself by making her course conform to the requirements of rule 51.2.

51.5. It is not necessary for a yacht to cross the finishing line completely after *finishing*, she may clear it in either direction.

P. S. Have you thanked the race committee for their time and effort?

Our first edition 1956 glossary raised many questions. We compared many American and British sailing books which seemed too specialized. While some stressed traditional terms, others chose present day terms.We decided on a multipurpose glossary should include a comfortable mix of both areas plus terms used in our favorite sea stories like the Hornblower Series. As the older terms came from numerous sources, we wondered how close they came to traditional terms used 150 years ago.

Many years later we found our answer for sailing scholars in an 1819 book still in print— **Lever's Young Sea Officer's Sheet Anchor** in his chapter, ***A Dictionary of Sea Terms.*** We use ***italic type*** for those wanting to check his traditional terms in a well-illustrated book published by Sweetman Company, see address on page 184. We took the liberty to print some of them close to modern thinking, and others only showing the term.

Our glossary is a technical dictionary of the sailing language. The terms grew from slang used in various cultures back to the Phoenicians. The **sounds** surviving the test of time were sharply concise, accurate, and extensive. They evolved into the international square rigger language all crew members had to understand and use, see pages 22 and 84. You are using the oldest technical language still in use developed by seamen with little schooling.

Some terms will only be found in nautical histories, and a few traditional vessels out of the past preserved for future generations such as the ***Cutty Sark, U.S.S. Constitution, Charles W. Morgan, H.M.S. Victory, Balclutha, Star of India,*** and new traditional craft such as the ***Californian,*** page 251.

ab *aback*— a square sail is aback with the wind on the forward side. The sails are pressed toward the mast forcing the vessel astern, page 100.

abaft— a shipboard object being further aft than another.

abaft the beam— aft of the beam; bearing of object between beam and stern.

abeam— on the side of a vessel, amidships, or at right angles.

ablock, two block— tackle taken in until both blocks come together.

aboard— in the ship— as the cargo is a-board.

about— a ship is said to be going about when in the art of tacking as it changes the wind over the bow to the other tack, pages 109, 170.

abox— a square rigger hove to while maintaining position, page 151.

abreast— opposite to; side by side, alongside, or abeam.

accommodation ladder— portable steps or ladder to climb aboard a vessel.

a-cockbill— square rigger yards dockside topped up at an angle to clear warehouses, etc., on the dock.

to go on the account— a sailor turned pilot.

Admiralty knot— is 6080 feet; the International Nautical Mile is 6076.10′.

adrift— broken loose from the moorings.

advance— distance a vessel maintains original course after rudder is put over.

 afloat— swimming— not touching the bottom.

af *afore*—forward, opposite of abaft.
afoul— tangled or fouled in any way.
aft— at, near, or towards the stern.
after body— stern section of a vessel.
after bow spring— bow spring leading aft on a vessel for docking.
after brow— an aft portable gangplank.
after quarter spring— spring leading aft from a vessels bow.
after waist spring— spring coming from amidship and going aft.
after yards— yards aft of the foremast.
aground— stranded, keel or vessel hull resting on the bottom.
ahead— toward the bow, in front of the bow.
ahoy— a greeting used in hailing a vessel or boat.
a-hull— a vessel hove to under bare poles with the helm alee.
air or flotation tank— sealed air tank for buoyancy in a capsize.
albatross— largest sea bird with wing span to 13′ in Southern Hemisphere.
alee— to the leeward side; helm is away from the wind.
all aback— when wind is pressing against the forward side of square sails.
all-a-taunt-O— ship shape, or all gear hauled in tight.
all hands— the entire crew.
all in the wind— pointing too high with all sails shaking.
all night in— maintaining no night watches.
all standing— fully equipped; brought up all standing is a rapid stop.
aloft— up above; up the mast or in the rigging.
alongside— side by side, by the side of a vessel or pier.
alow— below deck, or low in the rigging near the deck.
alow and aloft— all sails including stuns'ls are set, page 287.
altar— steps of a drydock. **amain**— on the run, all at once.
ambergris—sperm whale intestinal secretion used to blend perfume.
anchor— a hook which digs into the bottom to prevent drifting, page 163.
anchorage— a suitable place for anchoring.
anchor aweigh— anchor broken out of bottom, or coming to surface.
anchor hoy— lighter with derrick for handling heavy anchors.
anchor lights— anchor riding lights carried on anchored vessels.
anchor watch— crew deck detail to watch anchored vessel at night.
anemometer— wind velocity measuring instrument.
aneroid barometer— mechanical barometer without liquid.
anti-cyclone— spiral eddy of wind that is flowing out.
antifouling paint— poisonous boat bottom paint to retard underwater growth.
anvil top— cirrus top or peak of thunderhead— page 217.
apeak— anchor cable in vertical line with vessel over anchor; position of square rig yards, or oars when vertical or nearly so.
aport— to the left or port side of a vessel when looking forward.
apparent wind— wind direction felt on sailboat under way, page 100.
apron— timber behind lower part of stem above fore end of keel.
arm— lower part of sheet and kedge anchors, page 163.
ash breeze— flat calm requiring engine power or oars.
astern— in direction of stern or bearing behind a vessel.
athwartship— across the keel of a vessel.
atoll— a small circular coral island enclosing a lagoon.
atrip— the anchor has broken loose from the bottom.
a-try— sailboat in a gale riding without any sails set.
autopilot— mechanical helmsman steering to a compass heading.
auxiliary— an engine used as secondary propulsion in a sailboat.

aw *aweather*– to windward, towards the weather side.
awning– tarp covering boat or deck for protection from sun, rain, or snow.
aye– yes; reply that an officers orders are understood.

ba **backing**– the wind changes counterclockwise.
back the jib– hold it when coming about till wind is on lee side,page 109.
backstay– mast support leading aft to deck or to another mast.
running backstays– temporary or shifting backstays–page 109.
backwater– stop rowboat movement by reversing direction of oars.
back wind– a sail backwinds another with the wind funneling on wrong side.
bag– a sail bags when the leach is taut yet the center of the sail is slack.
baggy wrinkle– chafing gear made from old rope, page 75.
balanced rudder– part of rudder area is forward of rudder post.
baldheaded schooner– schooner without topsails, page 271.
ballast– heavy material stowed inside a sailing vessel to provide stability.
ballast tanks– double bottom water tanks pumped out or flooded at will.
bar– shoal or bank. **capstan bars**– heavy timbers that work the capstan.
bare poles– sailing vessel in a gale with no sails set, page 157.
sailing bare– sailing with the sheets set too tight.
barge– ship's boat used by flag officers.
Thames Barge– roomy, flat bottom English cargo vessel, pages 16, 273.
bark (barque)–3 masted, square rigged fore & main, page 283.
barkentine– 3 masted, square rigged only on foremast, page 283.
barnacle– small shell fish that enjoys camping on the bottom of your boat.
barney post– short Star class cockpit post with jam cleat for main sheet.
barometer– instrument that registers atmosphere pressure, page 209.
barratry– dishonest action such as unauthorized sail of a vessel.
barrier reef– exposed reef above the water along a coast.
batten– thin rigid strip in pocket on after edge of sail to keep its shape,pg.97.
batten the hatches– lashings to secure tarp over hatch coamings.
beachcomber– unemployed seaman on the beach.
beacon– navigation or danger recognition mark.
beak-head grating– was location of naval vessel lavatory, page 291.
beam– maximum width of a vessel.
beam ends– vessel hove over till beam is almost vertical to repair bottom.
beam reach, wind, sea– wind at right angles to keel, page 99.
bear– an object bears in the direction a person is looking.
bear down– to approach a vessel from windward.
bearing– direction of object as to vessels heading or compass course.
bear off– steer away from the wind, shore, or object.
bear up– steer up towards the eye of the wind, shore, or object.
beat– advancing to windward on alternate tacks, page 101.
becalmed– the vessels sails hang limp and lifeless without wind.
becket– eye or loop made with fiber or rope wire, page 184.
bees– pieces bolted to outer bowsprit end to reeve foretopmast stays thru.
belay– change order; make fast or secure line to cleat or pin.
belaying pin– iron or wooden pin fitted into railing to secure lines, pg. 73.
bell buoy– navigational buoy with bell warning actuated by wave action.
belly– fullness of sail when filled with the wind.
belly strap– rope beneath a boat when carrying out a kedge anchor.
below– beneath or under the deck (seldom called downstairs).
bench hook– hook with swivel in cloth counteracting pull of sailors needle.
bend– knot by which one rope is made fast to another,page 189.

be *to bend*– to make fast a sail to a spar or stay; **to bend a cable** is make it fast to an anchor; **a bending shackle** connects chain cable to anchor ring.

beneaped or neaped– boat aground at high tide following tides can't float.
bermudian sail– British term for marconi or jib-headed sail, pages 6,7.
berth– boat dock or anchorage; place a person sleeps on board.
berth deck– lower complete deck used for berthing near waterline.
between decks– space between decks.
bight– bend in a rope; bend in shore making a cove, bay, or inlet.
bilge– curve of hull between keel and gunwale; largest diameter of cask.
bilge blocks– blocks in dry dock upon which a ships bilge rests.
bilged– when the bilge is broken.
bilge keel– keels at turn of bilge to reduce vessel rolling motion.
bilge water– water draining into and collecting into a vessels bilge.
bilge ways– timbers bolted together and propped under keel for launching.
bill– point at the end of an anchor fluke, page 163.
bill board– inclined metal plate for anchor to rest on without marring deck.
bill of health– port health certificate obtained as a vessel clears port.
bill of lading– receipt from a vessel for cargo received.
binnacle– compass stand containing compensating magnets, page 75.
bite– an anchor to take hold.
bitter end– last inboard link of anchor chain; end of anchor line, page 167.
bitts– deck posts to secure mooring or towing lines, page 191.
black gang– engine crew when coal was the principle fuel.
blade– back side of anchor palm; flat part of oar or propeller.
blanket– a windward sailboat takes the wind out of the sails on a sailboat too leeward. A bridge, building, or headland can also blanket sails.
blocks– frames to support pulleys to increase rope pull or change line pull.
bluff– steep shore or a full-bowed vessel.
board– windward tack or leg when sailing closehauled, page 101.
boat boom– it swings out from a vessels side when at anchor to secure a dinghy.
boat hook– pole with hook to pick up a mooring buoy or ring.
bos'n's chair– canvas or wood seat sling to raise man working aloft.
boatswain's chest– a chest containing bos'n's gear.
boatswain– officer in charge of line, boats, rigging, etc.
bobstay– rod, chain, or wire from stem to cutwater securing bowsprit,285.
bollard– vertical posts on dock to secure hawsers, page 191.
bolsters– chafing gear for trestle tree rigging.
bolts– early round iron bolts without threads had to be peened over.
bolt rope– it is sewn around a sails edge giving cloth strength, page 11.
bone– spray at stem or cutwater of a vessel underway.
bonnet– additional sail area laced to bottom of square sails or jibs.
booby hatch– a small raised hatch.
boom– a horizontal spar to extend the foot of a sail.
boom– spars to extend and support studding sails, page 287.
boom cradle, boom crutch– support for boom with furled sail, page 75.
boom horse– metal traveler for sheet block, page 75.
boom irons– rings of yards for studdingsail booms to be rigged out.
boomkin– spar projecting from stern to secure backstay, page 71.
boot top– different color strip of paint at the waterline, page 71.
bottomry– marine law term for mortgaging ships.
wind bound– adverse headwind keeping a sailing vessel in port.
bow– the forward part of a vessel, page 84.
bow breast– forward mooring line used for docking.

bo *bowers*— two heavy anchors stored forward on square riggers, with the heavier one called the ***best bower,*** page 163.
bow line— docking or mooring line led forward thru bow chock, page 173.
bowline— a most useful knot with an eye in the end, page 192.
bow painter— bow line attached to mooring line, aage 89.
to bowse— to haul down and inward a sail tack with a tackle.
bowsprit— spar extending forward from bow to secure headstays, page 285.
bowspritting— sentence of sailor roped to bowsprit. His choice was starving to death with a small food and water allowance, or cut the ropes and drown.
box-hauling— wearing ship in a small area by backing the head yards for the bow to pay off quickly under sternway, running square before the wind, then tending all braces as the vessel comes to the new tack.
boxing off— backing the headsails to turn a vessels bow from the wind.
boxing the compass— calling the names of 32 compass points in order.
brace— lines controlling horizontal movement of square sail yards,pg. 287.
brackish– mixture of fresh and salt water.
brails— ropes applied to after leaches to draw them up to mast and gaff,251.
breaker— waves broken by shoals or ledges; small fresh water cask.
break ground— to break an anchor loose from the bottom.
break off— to stop. **break out**— to open or release.
breaks— a wave breaks when the top going faster curls forward into the surf.
break shear— a vessel that is restless at anchor or on a mooring, see **bull rope.**
breakwater—small splash board forward so spray won't come into cockpit. Also a sea wall to break the force of the waves.
breast line— a dock line that doesn't lead forward nor aft.
breast band— rope or canvas band across leadsmans chest lashed to the chains.
breast hooks— knees or timber supports in forward part of wooden hull,73.
bridle—the Lightning uses a mainsheet rope bridle, page 35.
brig— the ship's prison; a two-masted square rigger, page 283.
brigantine— American and British terms differed, see page 283.
brigantine schooner— see the *Iwalani,* pages 273 and 289.
brightwork— highly-polished brass or varnished woodwork.
bring to— a square rigger **heaving to** to hold position, page 151.
broach to— the bow of a sailing vessel running digs in. The bow stops to become a pivot for the stern to slew around up into the wind,pgs.153-5.
broadside—side of vessel above waterline. All guns can fire a broadside salvo on one side of a naval warship.
broken back— a vessel is hogged if it droops at both ends.
brow landing— platform on vessels side to support a portable gang plank.
bucklers— plugs fitted into hawse-pipe holes when at sea.
buckling— bending or working. **Bugeye**—see page 275.
building slip— location of ways where a ship is built.
bulb keel— Star has a keel with a cigar-shaped weight on the bottom, pg.19.
bulkhead— below-deck partitions in a vessel.
bull rope— shock cord leading from bowsprit end to mooring buoy to keep buoy from bumping into the boat when wind and tide are opposed,pg.172.
bullseye— round wooden thimble to change the lead of a line.
bulwarks— deck railing to prevent men and gear from going overboard.
bumboat— small craft alongside a vessel in port with articles for sale.
bumkin, boomkin— stern spar providing backstay support, page70. square riggers had a short boom forward to haul down the fore tack to.
bunk— sleeping berth. **bunting**— thin woolen fabric for flags.
 bunt— middle of square sail; surplus reefed sail area, page 148.

bu *buntlines*— lines used to haul up the body of a square sail, page 288.
burgee— triangular flag indicating boat owners yacht club, page 245.
burton— a variety of tackle purchases for many uses.
buoy— floating navigational marker, pg.169; permanent mooring marker.
buoyancy tanks— airtight buoyancy tanks to help upset boat,page 41.
butt— where two wooden planks touch end to end.
scuttle butt— crew gossip while drinking from water cask kept on deck.
buttock— rounding part of stern from waterline totransom.
by the board— overboard. **by the head**— bow lower than stern.
by the lee— running with wind on same side as the boom, page 122.
by the run— let go altogether. **by the stern**— stern lower than bow.
by the wind— square rigger term for sailing high as possible, page 99.

ca *cabin*— enclosed space of decked-over boat hull.
cable— a large dia. anchor line generally 120 fathoms long. *USS Constitution* anchor cable in wartime had a 22" circumference, page 163.
cable— as a measurement term is 200 yards or 1/10th of a nautical mile.by the early Greeks.Modern British Navy cable term is a unit of 608 feet, while it is 720 feet in the U.S. Navy.
caboose— the place where the Victuals are dressed in merchant-men which we called a deckhouse for cooking. I love his traditional definition.
Call— bos'n's pipe. **Calm**— wind under one knot, page 137.
camber—athwartship curve of sailing vessel deck to drain water overboard.
camel— floating wooden fender to keep a vessel off a dock or wharf.
can buoy— cylindrical odd numbered buoy to port side when entering, 169.
cap—a support securing a lower mast to an upper mast, page 285.
capstan— cylindrical device to take in anchors, to hoist yards and other parts.
capstan bar— a horizontal bar used to crank the capstan by 'Svedish Steam'.
cardinal points— four main points of a compass.
carline— wood stringer supports for cabin or hatches, page 73.
carrick bend— a knot used to join two lines, page 189.
carry away— to part a rope, break a spar, to break or tear loose.
carry on— carry all sails possible. **Carvel**— smooth planked hull, page 14.
cast off— let go. *To cast*— backing the headsails when taking up the anchor so the bow will pay off to the desired tack (backing the jib).
cat—tackle used to raise the anchor to cathead to secure it for sea.
catamaran— twin-hulled sailboat, pages155, 47-49, 82-3.
catboat, cat rig— boat with one sail, the mast stepped well forward, page 5.
cat harpins— ropes under the tops bracing lower ends of futtock shrouds,285.
cathead— timbers projecting from bows of sailing ships to secure anchors.
catenary— curve of anchor cable between boat and anchor, page 165.
cat's paw— small ruffled patch of water with stronger puff at that spot,205.
cat the anchor— secure the anchor for sea.
to caulk— fill wooden boat seams with oakum or cotton making seams tight.
centerboard— vertical hinged plate to reduce leeway sailing upwind,pg.17.
centerboard trunk— watertight well or housing for centerboard, page 17.
center of effort— center of sail area, page 133.
center of lateral resistance— center of underwater hull profile, page 133.
chafe— damage by rubbing...**chafing gear** is anything used to prevent chafe.
chain locker— compartment forward for storing anchor chain.
chain plates— metal straps bolted to a sailboats sides to secure shrouds.If square rigger chain plates project out to a narrow platform it is called the *chains or channels.*The leadsman was lashed to these chains.When bad weather made the head untenable, the chains were used instead.

chain stopper— short chain used as a quick release for the anchor.
channel buoy— buoy markers showing extreme limits of channel, page 160.
charley noble— galley smokestack named after a meticulous admiral, 75.
check— ease off cable gradually to ease it from breaking.
cheeks—sides of blocks; timbers supporting trestle trees, page 285.
chine— sharp edge of hull where side and bottom intersect, page 15.
chip log— an early device to measure square rigger sailing speed.
chips— the ship carpenter.
chock— metal fittings on sailboats to lead docklines, page 188.
chock-a-block— upper and lower tackle blocks run together, two blocked.
chronometer— accurate clock used for navigation.
chow— food. **clamp down**— swab down the deck.
cirrus— high frozen clouds made of ice crystals, pages 204-5, 217.
clamps— planks forming ceiling upon which deck beams rest, page 73.
to clap on—make fast; add more sail; haul away on a rope.
clapper— tumbler or tongue, movable fitting in gaff jaws prevents jamming.
claw off— to beat to windward from a lee shore.
clear— work clear of bar or shoal; untangle lines, gear, or rigging; land is cleared as vessel sails away; leaving port with all formalities transacted.
clear for running— ready to run without fouling.
clearing papers— all regulations are approved by port authorities for leaving.
cleat— wood or metal fittings to secure the ends of lines or act as a stopper.
clews,clues— lower corners of square sails; after corner of fore and aft sails; for spinnakers, the side to which the sheet is secured.
clewlines— they haul up the lower corners of square sails, page 288.
clinker, clinker built— overlapping fore and aft hull planking, page 14.
clinometer— device measuring degree of roll or heel, page 134.
clipper or schooner bow— has a graceful incurving bow entry,pgs.70, 271.
close-hauled— ***Lever,"As near the Wind as the Ship can lie".*** To us it is sailing as close to the wind, with sheets hauled as tight as efficiency permits.
closing— a vessel closes with the shore or with another vessel.
clove hitch— two half hitches around a spar or coiled line, page 191.
club jib— spar on bottom of self-tending jib or jib boom, page 71.
clubbing— drifting downstream, or with tidal current with an anchor out.
club topsail— replaces a gaff topsail, see ***Reliance,*** page 261,as it is larger.
clump block— small oval block with single sheaveffor square rigger headsails.
coaming— splashboard above a hatchway to prevent water coming below.
cockbilled— lower yards canted at extreme angle dockside, page 288.
cockpit— small well opening aft for crew on modern sailboats.
cofferdam— heavy bulkhead in modern ships for water or oil ballast.
coil— to lay a line in circular terms, see various methods on page 193.
coir— weak, buoyant rope from coconut fibers often used on lateeners.
cold wall— current of cold water flowing southward inside Gulf Stream.
collar— eye in shroud or stay end or bight to go over the mast-head.
collier— sail or powered vessel that carries coal.
come home— square rigger anchor broken loose and being taken in.
come up— slack away so gear may be belayed after hauling.
coming about, going about— changing course for bow to swing thru the eye of the wind and pay off on the other tack, pages 101, 109.
commissioning pennant— naval vessel pennant flown at the main truck.
companion— wooden covering over the cabin hatchway.
companionway— steps from the deck to the cabin below.
company— entire vessel crew including officers and ratings.

CO **mariner's compass**— it has a card graduated to points and degrees floating in distilled water and alcohol. A bundle of wires that are magnetized keeps the compass card on a north/south heading for navigation.
compass point— is 1/32nd part of a full circle or 11¼ degrees. Older compasses used the point system while we prefer them in degrees today.
compass rose— graduated circle on the card showing points of the compass.
composite built— vessel with wooden planking and metal frames.
cone— signal shown on sailboat using sails and engine power, page 231.
conning— to direct helmsman steering in congested or narrow waters.
controlling depth— minimum depth of channel or anchorage.
cordage— term for all diameters of rope though seldom used.
corinthian— amateur sailor interested in the sport without compensation.
corvette— the U.S. called it a sloop-of-war, page 291.
counter— part of stern from rudder post above the water to the transom.
course— foresail, mainsail, and mizzen are called courses. It can be the compass heading, or the angle a vessel is sailing into, or away from the wind.
courses—they include the foresail, mainsail, and mizzen, sails which are set from the lower yards.
cowl— sailboat ventilators have various shapes, page 160.
cow's tail, fag, irish pennant— untidy frayed rope end.
coxswain— petty officer in charge of a small boat.
cradle— the frame a vessel rests on when hauled out of the water.
crank, cranky, tender— top heavy sailing vessel that heels too easily.
cranse iron— metal cap at bowsprit end securing bowsprit to jib-boom, support for the martingale, plus an attach point for the bobstay.
cringle— metal thimble wrapped in a rope eye on the outside of a bolt rope. Mainsail tacks and clews often use cringles.
crojik(cross jack)— lowest sail or course on mizzen mast, page 287.
cross pawls— timbers bracing vessel frames during construction.
cross spales— temporary supports across a vessel nailed to frames. They keep the sides together until the knees are bolted.
cross trees— athwartship supports laid across the upper end of a mast to increase the span or width of the shrouds, pg.285, we call spreaders.
crowd on— use all sail possible.
crowfoot halyards— a bridle of several small ropes to suspend an awning.
crown— athwartship camber of deck so water and spray drain overboard.
anchor crown— the part where the arms are welded to the shank, page 163.
crown or wall knot— is used to stop a line going thru a block, page 202.
crow's nest— lookout area or platform high on foremast for lookout. Lookouts on whalers stood on wooden platforms inside a waist high metal hoop for their protection.
Crutch— support for boom when sails are furled, page 75.
cuddy— small shelter cabin.
cut of the jib— general appearance of a vessel or person.
cutter— single masted sailboat, see variations on pages 264-5.
cut-water— the Knee of the Head (lever). Our definition— the foremost part of the bow which is above the waterline.
cyclone— an air movement around a low-pressure area, while an anticyclone is movement around a high pressure area. While we use the term hurricane, a cyclone is the term used in the Indian Ocean, Bay of Bengal,& Arabian Sea.

da **daggerboard**— plate raised and lowered vertically to reduce leeway, pg. 16.
danforth anchor— see page 162. **danger, hazard buoy**— see page 168.
dasher block— small ensign halyard block at peak of gaff.
*davit— **wooden crane used to fish for anchors.*** We use the term for metal cranes projecting over the side of a vessel to hoist up small boats.
Davey Jones' Locker— bottom of the sea, collector of expensive anchors.
day's work— square rigger dead reckoning was from noon to noon, with morning and afternoon times sights for longitude, and a meridian altitude for latitude. See *Sovereign of the Seas* day's work, page 210.
dead ahead— directly ahead of a vessels course.
*deadeye— **a block with three holes to receive the laniard of a shroud or stay.***
dead light— thick glass fitted into deck providing natural light below.
dead reckoning— calculation for the log of a vessel's course and distance.
deadrise— vertical distance between the turn of the bilge and the keel.
dead rope— is used for hauling without using a block.
dead water— water pulled along with a vessel especially in the after part.
deadwood— strengthening members securing keel to stem and stern,pg.72
deck— decks of a vessel are similar to floors of a building, page 72.
deck beam— athwartship support for deck, page 73.
deck horse— metal rod for mainsheet traveler, see Newporter, page 75.
deck light— glass fitted flush to deck providing natural light below.
declination— angle distance measured from earths center thru a celestial body.
deep sea lead— was 50 pounds used in 120 fathoms or deeper.
deep six— articles thrown overboard are "deep sixed".
degree— is 1/360th of a circumference.
departure— bearing of coast object after which vessel begins dead reckoning.
derelict— a vessel abandoned at sea.
deviation— compass error due to metal objects that varies with vessel heading.
dew point— air saturation point causing a peasouper, page 223.
dhow— a European term for Arab lateeners, page 277.
diagonals— lines crossing the hull form at right angles to the frames, page 253.
dinghy— an open boat, or partially decked over without a cabin.
dismasted— the masts of a sailing vessel are carried away in a storm.
displacement— weight of water displaced by a vessel.
displacement length ratio— *page* 78 discusses various D/L ratios.
dog— metal fittings used to lock watertight doors, hatch covers, etc.
doghouse— shelter or enclosure built over companionway, page 75.
dog vane— was a masthead telltale resembling a wind sock used by helicopters.
dog watch— half watches from 1600 to 1800, and 1800 to 2000 hours.
doldrums— updraft barrier with little wind at equator,pages 206, 210-213.
*dolphin—**a wreath of rope placed round a mast to support the pudding.*** the term *pudden* was used for rope fenders when we started sailing, also for large protective rope mats used on tugboats.
dolphin striker, martingale—vertical spar under bowsprit to counteract the strains of the head stays.
dory— flat-bottomed boat with narrow stern and hard chines, page 15.
double block— block with two sheaves.
double ender— boat or vessel with pointed bow and stern.
double-sheet bend— joins small to medium size ropes, page 189.
doubling— overlap section between top of lower mast and bottom of upper one...the area between the trestle trees and cap, page 285.
*to douse— **let fly halyard topsail—to lower away briskly;*** lower and take in sail; put out light; cover with water.

do **downdraft—** vertical wind flow off tall buildings, cliffs, headlands,etc.

down-haul— ***rope to pull down staysails, topmast studding sails, etc.***

jib downhaul— it hauls down jib so it can't fill in wave action, page 59.

downhaul tackle— used on square riggers, page 286.

down helm— bring the vessel into the wind.

draft— water depth required to float a vessel, page 158.

airfoil draft— is required to sail upwind, page 103.

drag— anchor failing to hold a vessel; various designs of surface anchors to hold the bow or stern into the wind in a storm, page 157.

dredge— vessel used to dig a channel.

drift— ***driving to leeward-driving with the tide.*** A vessel's leeway.

drift lead— weight over anchored vessel's side indicates dragging anchor.

to drift— to move with the tidal current.

drive— to push a sailboat at maximum speed.

driver— ***a large sail suspended to the mizzen gaff.*** Sixth sail of the seven-masted *Thomas W. Lawson,* page 271.

drogue— a surface anchor to hold bow or stern to wind, see drag.

drop— distance from head to foot of a square sail.

drumhead— top of a capstan with holes for the push bars.

dry sailing— sailboat kept on trailer when not being used.

duck— cloth lighter than canvas for small sails.

dry dock— basin or cradle that can be pumped dry to repair vessels.

duff— flour and water mixture. **dumb compass—** see peloris.

dunnage— ***wood, etc., laid at the bottom of a ship to keep the cargo dry.*** Sailor's personal effects; loose material stowed in a boat.

dutch courage— artificial courage caused by drinking alcoholic beverages.

a *earings—* ***small ropes to make fast the upper corners of square sails, etc.***

ease— to slack; momentarily luff a sailing vessel with too much wind pressure.

ease off— ***to slacken.*** **ease out—** to slack out.

ease up— to slowly let up or work out. **easy—** slowly, carefully.

ebb tide— tide change from high to low with tidal current ebbing out to sea.

eddy— circular movement in air or water with meeting of opposing currents.

embark— go aboard a vessel preparatory to beginning a voyage.

end on— head on, page 233.

end for end— ***let a rope or cable run out;*** reversing ends of a rope.

ensign— flag showing vessel's nationality and/or owners organization, 245. Lowest commissioned USN or USCG commissioned rank.

entrance— a vessel's bow that cleaves the water just above the waterline.

equinox— March 21st and September 22 when the sun crosses the equator.

even keel— vessel is floating level on its lines.

eye bolt— an iron bar on a vessel's deck or side with an eye to hook a tackle. on large vessels. For small vessels it is a bolt with an eye on the end.

eyelets— grommet holes in a sail for reef points, outhaul, downhaul, halyard.

eye of the wind— into the center of the wind, page 99.

eye splice— spliced loop in the end of a rope, pages 196-199, 201.

eyes of a vessel— forward portion of the weather deck or bow. It is my guess the term originated with eyes painted forward on the bulwarks of Chinese junks...so the junks couldn't get lost.If you were a true believer it was supposed to work.Grotesque masks were painted on the bows to scare pirates away. Flowers and designs were sometimes painted on the sides and quarters. Foochow junks had beautifully painted sterns. The dominant figure was the phoenix,their symbol of immortality in a frame of dragons.

fa *fag end—untwisted end of a rope,* **fagged—** ragged, untwisted rope end.
fairlead— block or fitting to change the lead direction of a line such as a jib sheet. Page 59 shows various fairleads for single-handed operation.
fair tide— current running with vessel.**fair wind—** favorable wind.
fairway— navigational channel,pg. 169.
fake— a single turn of a rope in a coil.
fake down— coil 3 strand rope so it will run freely without hitches.
fall— hauling part of tackle to which power is applied.
falling glass— barometer pressure is dropping,page 209.
falling home, tumble home— side of a vessel inclining inboard above the waterline on cargo and naval sailing vessels to repel boaders or pirates.
fall off— to sail farther from the eye of the wind.
false keel— timbers added to fill the space at the after end of the metal or ballast keel, page 72. It can also be timbers added to the main keel to protect the keel and increase the draft.
fancy line— gaff downhaul; line to cross-haul the lee topping lift.
fanning— sailing vessel moving slowly in light wind.
fashion board, bin board— three planks slide into grooves to prevent water coming into companionway of ***Pink Cloud, page*** 65.
fashion pieces— aftermost timbers shaping the stern.
fast— is to make fast is to secure a line to a cleat.
fathom— a depth measurement of six feet. It may have been started by early seamen as a measurement of outstretched arms.
fathometer, depth sounder— it records water depth, page 158.
favor— to reduce a load on an old sail or weak spar.
feather— turn oar blade at end of stroke to reduce splashing.
felucca— large Mediterranean lateeners that were also rowed, page 277.
fenders— cushions to reduce the chafe between a boat and its dock.
fenderboard— a board with two or more fenders to protect a hull.
fender spars— float next to a wharf to keep the vessel off it.
to fetch— sailboat can pass a windward mark without changing tack, 106.
fiber rope— rope made of organic instead of synthetic materials.
fid— a tapered piece of wood or iron to splice ropes with, page 201.
fidded— a short iron bar goes thru a hole in the heel of a topmast or bowsprit to hold it in place.A topmast is said to be fidded, fixed, or locked, when a square section pin goes thru a hole of the topmast into the trestle trees.
fiddle head— ornamental timber on a clipper bow instead of a figure head.
fiddler's green— a sailor's dreamland with dance halls and other amusements.
fiddle block— has a smaller and a larger sheave in one block.
field day— the dreaded day of scrubbing and washing down a vessel.
fife rail, pin rail— a rail around a mast with openings to insert belaying pins.
figure-eight knot— stopper knot for end of line, page 184.
figurehead— ornamental head, butt, or figure mounted under the bowsprit.
to fill— brace the yards so wind will strike square sails on their after surfaces.
Sails filling as a sailing vessel gains headway after changing tack, page 109.
fin keel— rudder and keel are separate with space between, page 19.
fish— a broken spar has splints or 'fishes' wedged and lashed over broken are
fish block— heavy—duty block used for fishing an anchor.
fit out— overhauling period before trip, or before vessel goes into water.
fix— finding vessel's position by land or celestial observations.
flare— upward outward curve of side or bow, opposite of tumble home.
flare up— a blazing warning or signal light.
 flat— a sail that is empty without wind pressure in a calm.

fl **flat aback**— wind on the wrong side of square rigger sails.
flat bottom— see page 15. **flat calm**— no wind pressure.
flat cut spinnaker— page 125. **flatten in**— haul in the sheets.
flaw or catspaw— wind gust stronger than prevailing breeze, page 205.
fleet— a group of vessels sailing together.
flemish coil— three strand rope coiled correctly to run free.
flemish horse— short foot rope at the end of a yard, page 288.
flood— incoming tidal current, page 220.
floor— structural members under floorboards uniting hull's planking to the keel, page 73, upon which the **sole** or **floorboards** rest.
flotation tanks— air tanks prevent swamped boat from sinking, page 41.
flotsam— floating wreckage or goods. **jetsum**— goods thrown overboard to lighten a vessel. **lagan**— a heavy object thrown overboard and buoyed.
flowing sheet— sailing vessel is running downwind with eased sheets.
***flukes**— the broad parts or palms of the anchors,* pages 262, 263.
fluky winds— they are puffy and irregular.
fly— horizontal length of a flag, the **hoist** is the vertical length of a flag.
flying moor— first anchor is dropped as vessel keeps sailing twice the length of the chain it wants out. The bow anchor is dropped, then half of the length of the stern line is taken in. The vessel is anchored bow and stern.
foghorn warnings— pages 234-5. **foot**— lower edge of sails.
foot rope— is a rope support under the yards for crews to stand on, pg. 288. Bowsprit and jib-boom also had foot ropes for crew protection. Schooners often had foot ropes beneath the overhang of all its booms.
***fore**— part of a ship nearest to the head.* The foremast; opposite to aft.
***fore and aft**— the length-way of a ship, or in the direction of the keel.*
***fore castle**— a short deck in the fore part of the ship.* The crews quarters were forward under the fo'c'sle deck, page 287.
forefoot— bow area between keel and load waterline, page 73.
fore and aft rig— uses vertical masts instead of horizontal yards sailing higher and requiring less crew than square riggers, page 214. The Dutch may have started it removing the sail part forward of the mast which was the beginning of the gaff rig, page 55.
foremast—forward most mast of schooner or square rigger, pgs. 271,285, 287.
fore peak— extreme bow space forward, often an anchor locker, page 65.
fore reaching— earlier term of sailboat we call **shooting,** page 171, when head to wind for short periods to clear mooring or anchor lines.
fore sail— is set on the foremast of a schooner...and set on the fore yard of a square rigger, pages 271 and 287.
forestaysail, headsail— terms for what more sailors are calling a jib on a sloop showing our sailing language is in a slow but steady change.
fore topmast staysail— a jib on square riggers setting from fore topmast stay.
***forging a-head**— forced ahead by the wind.*
forge— is to shoot ahead bow into wind to go into stays to stop and anchor.
forward— in front of the bow.
fother, fodder— draw a sail filled with oakum under a bottom to stop a leak.
foul— jammed, stuck, opposite of clear or clean. The bottom of a vessel will be foulded with sea growth. An anchor is fouled and breaks loose if the line wraps around a fluke, page 165.
***fouled hawse**— when cables are twisted.* English naval sailing vessels in 1819 were subject to continual wind changes, and slack water between tidal currents, with the vessels often changing direction. This could wrap the port and starboard anchor lines around each other.

fo *to founder— to sink.* Lever tells it all.
frame— skeleton of a wooden vessel,in the early stages.After ribs and bulkheads are installed, the frames are removed, no longer needed.
frap— bind a sail, awning, or other object,with rope so it won't blow loose.
free— running free with the wind well aft.
freeboard— vertical distance amidship of a vessel from waterline to the deck.
freshens— an increasing wind freshens.
freshen the nip— change anchor line contact going thru chock,to reduce chafe
frigate— a fifth rater warship, see page 291.
full and by— closehauled, as near the wind as the ship can lie.
full spread—all sails set.
furling— making fast the sails to the yards by the gaskets. For us it is to roll or flake a sail snugly on top of the boom, then secure with gaskets, 97.
futtock plate— is the platform on the lower top, page 285, with deadeyes on the edge of the plate...which belong to the **futtock shrouds** beneath which terminate below at the **futtock band.**
futtock timbers— several pieces or timbers that are scarphed together to form a large rib that can't be made of just one timber.

ga **gadget—** landlubber term before he learns the new/old sailing language.
gaff— spar for the head of a gaff sail, page 5. **Scandalizing** a gaff sail in a strong wind is to harden topping lift and release the peak halyard, pg.148.
gaff jaws— inboard end fitting of the gaff that slides on a mast, page 5.
gaff sail— quadrilateral sail fitted with a gaff spar at the head.
gaff topsail— triangular sail above the gaff, pages 70,261, 263, 265, 271.
gaff vang— vang on aft end of gaff to prevent it from sagging to leeward.
gage— position of one vessel to another, one having the ***weather gage*** while the other has the ***lee gage.***
gain the wind— to work to windward of another sailing vessel.
gale— to force 9, pages 137, 139. **galley—** floating kitchen— see ***caboose.***
gallows— permanent frame to rest end of boom, after sail is lowered.
galleon— most were warships in the 1500's and 1600's recognized on page 290 by her high poop deck with a long slim beak forward.
gallows bitts or frames— frame above main or spar deck to stow spars, etc.
gamming— two square riggers hove to exchanging information, page 151.
gammoning— the *H.M.S. Victory,* page 291, had many rope lashings to hold down the inboard end of the bowsprit, against the upward pull of the forestay. The ***Iris,*** page 73, has a metal strap serving the same purpose.
gang plank— boards used as a walkway from a vessel to the dock.
gangway— platform from the quarter deck to each side of the fore-castle? also the place where persons enter the ship.
gantline— a rope going thru a block aloft to hoist sails, is also a clothesline.
garboard strake— planks on both sides of keel—***Iris,*** page 73.
garland— a rope or strap to hoist spars.
garnet— purchase on mainstay usually to hoist cargo.
gasket— cloth straps to secure square sails to yards, our sails to the boom.
gather way— pick up momentum.
gear— a general term for various kinds of spars and sails.
genoa jib— the largest size jib, page 12.
ghosting— sailing vessel making little way in a light breeze.
gimbals— method use to hold compasses, lamps, and stoves level regardless of the motion of a vessel.
 gimleting— turning an anchor by its stock to stow on its anchor bed.

gi *girt— a ship is girted when her cables are too tight preventing her swinging.*
girtline— another spelling for gantline.
girt the sail— line leading across lee side of sail making a hard edge.
glass— a spy glass; mariner's term for barometer, page 209.
glory hole— lazarette, stern compartment for storage; also an isolated area for patients with contagious diseases when a vessel is in quarantine.
gob line— a pair of supports from the end of the dolphin striker going back to the sides of the bow. The counteract the pull of the forward and upward pull of the jib-boom and flying jib-boom.
go about— change tack with wind over bow. **go adrift—** break loose.
go free, go large— vessel is running downwind.
gollywobbler— large sail peculiar to a schooner, page 271.
good full— square rigger course between close reach and close hauled.
gooseneck— an iron hook at the end of a boom. To us it is a universal joint that secures the boom to the mast.
goose wings— outer ends of main or foresail when loose, the rest is furled.
goosewing jibe— an accidental or flying jibe with the boom going vertical,110.
goosewinged— two masted vessels with main and mizzen on opposite sides.
goring— cutting a sail obliquely.
grafting— after a long splice is completed, yarns and whipping are used to make a woven cover over the length of the splice.
grapnel, grappling iron— small anchor with several claws, page 163.
grating— open lattice work frame to let in air/ and or light.Sailing vessels also used gratings in some areas to drain water. It is often used today as cockpit floor covers for decoration and/or drainage.
graving dock— a dry dock for graving to burn off the weeds and barnacles before retarring. It can also be performed by **careening** a vessel.
green sea— large volume of water breaking aboard without foam.
grip— an anchor when it bites and holds.
gripe— timber joining keel and cutwater. Vessel with excess weather helm.
gripes— webbing straps to hold boats in davits or chocks in a seaway.
grommet— a rope ring made of a single strand wrapped around three times. Two part grommet pieces are punched together to make eyelets in sails.
gross tonnage— measurement of all spaces below upper deck. **Net tonnage** is gross tonnange with deductions for areas not carrying cargo. **Registered tonnage** is the vessel cubical content divided by 100, an estimate for port charges and taxes for commercial craft.
grounding— running ashore. **ground swell—** large waves crossing shoal or bar.
ground tackle— general term for anchor and anchor gear, page 165.
gudgeon— eye supports for rudder pintles, page 31.
gunkholing— shallow water sailing.
gun-tackle purchase— two block tackle usually used for horizontal pulling.
gunter, sliding gunther— vertical gaff in small dinghy, page 272-3.
gunnel— upper part of a ship's side.
gunwale— upper railing of a dinghy or vessel. It is a dinghy rub rail.
gust— sudden wind puff.
guy— a steadying rope for various purposes.
after guy and fore guy — are used for spinnaker operation, page 128.
Nile gyassa— tall Egyptian lateen rig for river sailing, page 277.
gybe— British term, also used by some American writers for jibing.We have stressed the spelling of jibing as sailing developed as a spoken language...the spelling should be as close to the spoken sound as possible.
P.S.- **grog—** British Navy daily ration of rum diluted with water.

ha ***to hail— to call out to another ship.*** We use it to call to men in another part of the vessel, or to another ship.

half mast— a flag hoisted half way, a mark of respect for the dead.

half deck— after part of a naval vessel gun deck. The high poop deck of the galleon, page 290, aft of the main mast.

half seas over— walking unsteadily after too much grog or liquor.

halliards— tackles or ropes to hoist up the sails.

halyards— (from haul yards) lines used to raise sails, flags or gaff, pgs. 5, 7.

hand— a crew member with one hand 'for the ship', the other to hang on.

handicap ratings— pages 2, 78-9, 256-7.

to hand— the same as to furl.

hand lead— sounding lead—that is small.

hand rail— steadying rail on or next to ladder.

handsomely— smoothly and moderately, opposite of hasty.

handspike— lever to lift heavy weights, or set up rigging. One end has to be squared if used on a capstan or windlass.

hand, reef, and steer— traditional requirements of a seaman.

handy billy— hand pump; small tackle for miscellaneous jobs.

hanks— clips or rings to **hank on** jibs or staysails to their stays, page 13.

hard-a-lee— put helm hard over away from the wind to come about.

hard-a-weather— put helm over towards the wind to sail downwind or jibe.

harden in— haul in on a sheet to flatten a sail.

hard over— shove tiller far as possible to windward, or to leeward.

hard tack— ship's biscuits; general use, below average food.

hatch-way— square hole in deck which communicates with hold or other deck.

hatch— opening in deck with a sliding or hinged cover, pages 72-3.

hauls or veers— a clockwise wind change, **backing,** is counterclockwise.

haul her wind— a vessel changing course to sail higher upwind.

hauling part— part of a tackle upon which power is applied.

hawse— the vessel's bow where the **hawse pipes** are located. When two bower anchors are out the vessel can be riding with a clear **open hawse,** or with a **fouled hawse** with crossed lines due to a wind or tidal current change.

hawse block— wooden plug fitting into hawse hole for vessel going to sea.

hawser— heavy line used for warping, springs, etc. ***hawser— small cable.***

hawser-laid rope—is right-hand lay, or with the sun... while cable-laid rope is left-hand lay, or against the sun. See page 184.

head— the lavatory in naval ships, page 291, was a beak-head or similar bow grating forward with most privacy, officers had choice side. The leeward shrouds were preferred in sloppy weather; see **pink stern,** pg. 275.

head of a sail— is the upper side or upper corner of a sail.

headsails or jibs— are fore and aft sails forward of the mast.

headstay— jibstay, page 7. New Englanders prefer it called the forestay.

head wind— is from dead ahead of intended course. It will be necessary to sail closehauled making several tacks to reach your objective.

headway— a vessel moving ahead thru the water.

heave— the fall and rise of a vessel in a seaway. **heave away** is an order to haul on a line while **heave around** is to push on a capstan bar.

heave down— is to heel or **careen** a vessel to examine or repair its bottom.

heave short— take in anchor line until it is almost vertical.

heave taut— put a strain on a line or chain.

heave to— bring a vessel's bow to windward and hold it there.

to heave— to haul or throw; a vessel rising and falling in a seaway.

 heaving line— a small line used for heaving, see pages194.

he *to heel— to incline on one side.* A monohull heels on an upwind course to bring the balance factors together, pages 100,134, and 147. It is also the term for the lower end of a spar or the after end of a keel.
the helm— a wooden bar put thru the head of a rudder—also called the tiller.
hermaphrodite brig— see page 283.Their owners don't like that name.
high and dry— vessel aground above high water mark, page221
hike— moving weight to windward to reduce heel, pages 34 and 115.
hiking stick or ladies aid— see page 248, a hiking post.
to hitch— to make fast. **hitch—** combination of turns to make a rope fast to a spar, pages 189, and 191; also a **slippery hitch** on a cleat.
helm— the tiller. **port your helm—** tiller to port turns bow to starboard, or turn the wheel to starboard...confusion? **right rudder—** wheel turns to right as the bow turns to starboard. **helm up—** helm's aweather to go downwind, **helm down towards boom—** helm's alee to come about. Now I'm confused.
hogged, hog backed— shrouds too tight with vessel drooping at both ends.
hogging moment— a vessel with a wave under the middle, both ends out of water.
hogging— cleaning the bottom with stiff brushes called hogs.
hogwash— nonsense. It reminds me of the many facts coming from Wash. D.C.
hoist— raise a sail, spar, or cargo. Length of sail between boom and gaff jaws. Vertical edge of a flag along the staff.
the hold—lower compartment were provisions and goods are stowed. It is also the area where inboard ballast was carried on sailing vessels.
to hold— is anchor digging in so that it won't drag?
holystone— similar to flat grave stones to polish and clean a wooden deck.
home— the correct place for anything at sea...or on the land.
hooker— a term of love or hate for a vessel; an old vessel. It ain't obsolete.
horns— arms of cleat; ends of cross trees; projection to rudder end to secure chain.
hornpipe— seaman's dance to Celtic hornpipe replaced by the accordian.
horny, onry— hard working seaman with rough hands and character to match.
horse, deck horse— metal or rope traveler to sheet a sail.
hounds— was wooden shoulders at masthead on which trestle trees or shrouds rest. On the British ***Tempest one design*** it was jibstay attach area to mast.
house— to secure or stow in a safe place; also see home. also deck house.
house flag— private flag of owner, shipping line, or company.
housing— part of mast below deck; inboard end of bowsprit.
hove down—careening— vessel heaved down to have the bottom scraped.
Hudson River Sloop— it is my favorite after 3 years sailing the Hudson,263.
hulk— tired old vessel without spars, serves as storeship or lighter.
hull— body of a vessel without masts and gear. .
hull down— sailing vessel with only sails visible in the distance.
hull speed— limit of displacement hull speed, pages 140-1.
hurricane— long duration storm over force 12 or 65 knots, page 137, named after Caribbean natives with similar name called a **big wind.**

p.s.— **hen frigate—** owner or captains wife interferes with running of ship.

idlers— ***cooks, stewards, etc., without night deck watches at sea;***
in board— towards fore and aft vessel centerline. **In ballast—** sailing vessel without cargo using rocks or other means of temporary ballast.

in irons— a sailing vessel head to wind with no way on either tack.
initial stability— basic resistance of a dinghy relying on centerboard or leeboard to resist heeling potentials, pages 16- 17.
inner jib— is often called forestaysail, page 264.

in **in sail**— order to take in sail. **inshore**— in direction of shore.
in stays, in irons— head to wind with all sails shaking, pages 99, 104.
in the wind— pointing too high or pinching, page 104.

ja **jack tar**— British navy sailor. **union jack**— see page 244.
jacks or lazy jacks— lines on both sides to gather sail being lowered, page 5.
jackstay— see page 70. It is also a rod on top of a square sail yard, og. 288.
jackass— applied to unusual sailing rigs. The **mule**, page 269, was called a jackass when the first one was made. Mule seemed a kinder term.
jack ladder, jacob's ladder— has rope sides to climb aboard or aloft.
jack rope— laces gaff sail to boom and gaff, page 5.
jetty— breakwater protecting a harbor entrance or river mouth.
jewel blocks—are at topsail yard arms for topmast studding sail halyards.
jew's harp— anchor shackle. **jib**— triangular sails forward of foremast.
jibe or gybe— changing wind and tack over stern of sailing vessel, page 111.
jib boom— spar extension beyond bowsprit, page 285. **jib headed**— same as marconi or bermudian, first called leg-of-mutton, page 3.
jib topsail—light-weather jib on headstay or topmast stay, page 70.
jigger or mizzen— aft sail on ketch or yawl, page 135. After mast on a square rigged ship carrying a spanker, page 285.
jolly boat— work boat carried on stern of coastal sailing vessel.
Jolly roger— pirate flag from the 1500's, roger is corruption of rogue.
jumbo— a large inner forestaysail often used on schooners.
jumper— also called martingale to brace the dolphin striker, page 285.
jumper stay, jumper strut— bracing to keep upper part of mast straight,pg.7.
jump ship— leaving without authorized permission.
junk— pieces of old cable to make mats, gaskets, etc.
junks— pages 278 to 281 discuss various lug rigs, traditonal and modern.
jury rig— temporary or makeshift rig to take damaged vessel back to port.

ka **kapok**— buoyant vegetable fiber used in cushions, jackets, etc.
keawl— part yawl and part ketch. I'm still trying to find one.
keckling— old rope used as chafing gear on a cable.
kedging— moving a vessel by hauling on a kedge rope secured to a kedge anchor that was carried out on a small boat, and the anchor released. If a vessel drifts with the current with anchor just touching bottom, the traditional term was called **clubbing** or **dredging.**
keel— fore and aft backbone of a vessel, page 73.
keel block— line of blocks supporting a vessel's keel in dry dock.
keel haul— ancient punishment for a sailor who is hauled under the keel of a vessel and up the other side by ropes or whips from yardarms.
keelson— timber running fore and aft between keel and floor.
keep her full— an order to keep the sails full; **keep her off**— order to sail farther from the wind; **keep her so**— an order of steady on her course.
keep your luff— sailing closehauled without flutter in the sails luff.
kentledge— permanent iron ballast laid along the keelson.
ketch— two masted vessel with tiller aft of both masts, pages 9, 269.
kick— movement of a vessel's stern when turning.
killick— primitive anchor, page 163. **kink**— twist in a rope, page 188.
king plank— main deck plank other planks feed into, page 73.
king post— a short mast to support cargo booms for loading cargo, pg. 240.
king spoke— marked upper spoke of wheel when rudder is amidship.
knee— an angle support connecting a vessel's deck beams to hull, page 73.

kn **knightheads**— two vertical timbers with the bowsprit inner end between.
knockabout— obsolete term of sloop without a bowsprit.
knocked down— sailboat heeled so far it doesn't recover.
knot— one minute of latitude;, one nautical mile per hour, or 6076' to 6080'.

la *to labour— to pitch and roll heavily.*
lacing— lines used to secure a gaff sail to the boom and gaff, page 5.
laid up— a sailboat dry docked during the winter months.
land breeze— night breeze from land to the ocean, page 215.
land fall— discovering the land. A good landfall is the intended one.
land ho!— the hail when land is first sighted.
landlocked— entirely surrounded by land.**landmark**— distinct shore object.
lanyard— a lashing; ropes for setting up rigging, rove thru deadeyes.
larboard— the left side. The term was later changed to port for port side.
lash— secure or bind with rope. **lateen rig**— see pages 276, 277.
latitude— distance north or south of equator measured in degrees.
launch— the long boat. **to launch**— to set afloat.
lay or laid— the direction rope or hawsers are twisted, page 184. To come or go such as **lay forward, lay aft, lay aloft.**
to lay or fetch— sailboat lays a mark without changing tack, page 106.
layup— hauling out a vessel for the winter.
lazarette— stern storage compartment; isolation area for contagious diseases.
lazy guy— also preventer, rigging to steady boom to prevent jibe in wave action.
lazy jacks, jacks— lines on both sides of sails to gather sail being lowered,pg. 5.
leach or leech— after edge of fore and aft sail, pages 5,7, Square sail, pg.287.
leach line— line in leach to tighten sail leach, pages 115-119.
leads— the hand lead was used for shallow water weighing up to 15 lbs., while the deep sea lead weighed up to 100 lbs., obsoleted by depth sounder.
leading edge— forward part of sail. **leading wind**— beam or quarter wind.
lead line— line secured to lead weight marked at intervals to test depth.
leadsman— sailor detailed to the **fore chains or chain plates** to which the shrouds are secured or bolted to the hull.
league— the British and American marine league is three nautical miles.
leave— permission granting leave from a station or ship.
lee- wind blows onto a lee shore; wind flows from windward to leeward side of a vessel, and from windward rigging to rigging on leeward side.
leeboard— pivoted board secured to the side of a sailing vessel, page 16.
lee helm— sailboat out of balance wanting to turn down to a beam reach.
lee helmsman— assistant helmsman on lee side of steering wheel.
by the lee, running by the lee—running with wind on same side, page 122.
lee-oh— helm has been put down for sailing vessel to come about.
lee tide— tidal current running with the wind, page 218.
under the lee— object or another vessel between you and the wind.
leeward— that point towards which the wind blows.
leg— length of tack or board, page 101.
leg-of-mutton— traditional term for marconi, bermudian, and jib-headed sail.
let draw— fill sail on desired tack. **let fly**— release the sheets.
let her off— head farther from the wind. **let her ride**— sailboat is on course.
let her up— point higher to windward. **let go**— drop anchor.
lie to— square rigger slowing down to make little or no progress by bracing the yards to counterbalance each other, also **hove to,** page 151.
lifeboat— boat for emergency use. **life buoy**— life saving ring buoy.
life preserver— buoyant aid to keep a person afloat, page 227.

li **lifeline**— fore and aft lines along the deck to prevent crew going overboard.
waist lifeline— is secured to sailor's waist for heavy weather protectiong, 194.
topping lift— takes weight of boom while raising or lowering sails, pg. 65.
square rigger lift— supports the yardarms, page 288.
light— illuminated aid to navigation or lighthouse. A vessel with cargo discharged high in the water capsizing some square riggers dockside.
lighter— harbor craft carrying merchandise to load or unload vessels.
lightning— sailboat class, pages 34-7. Damage prevention, page 217.
lignum vitae— a hard wood used for blocks with its own lubricant.
limber holes— drain holes cut into wooden frames for drainage, page 73.
lime juicer— nickname for British vessel and British sailor with ratio of lime juice to prevent scurvey we now know as vitamin C started by Sir Francis Drake. A **limey** is also a lime juicer. Do you have vitamin C aboard??????
line— rope becomes line when used in operation of a sailing vessel, page 184.
the lines— are drawings of a vessel made of three separate plans which are used to show the shape and build the hull, pages 252 to 255.
heaving line— light line with weight on end for heaving, page 194.
list— an inclination of a vessel to one side and/or end due to greater weight.
*lizard— **a small piece of rope with a thimble, spliced into a larger one.***
ljungstrom— sailboat without a boom to minimize jibing danger, pg. 273.
L.O.A.— is the length over all of a hull, page 255. **L.W.L.** is the load waterline or allowed loading line of a vessel, see Plimsoll mark.
lock— canal compartment used to bring a vessel to a different water level.
locker— chest, box, or clothes wardrobe to stow items away. Every ship had a ***paint locker, a boatswain's locker*** for rigging, and ***two chain lockers.***
log— instrument to estimate a vessel's speed, see chip log.
log book— vessel's diary containing daily record of course,distance,weather. shipboard activity, and other items of importance.
Chesapeake log canoe — an unusual sailboat, see aage 275.
long board— a long tack, page 101. **long boat**— largest boat aboard.
long in the jaw— a rope that has stretched considerably.
longitude— distance in degrees east or west of Greenwich, England.
longitudinal— fore and aft structural part of a vessel.
longshoreman— laborer who loads and unloads cargo.
long splice— joining two ropes so dia. isn't increased at splice.
lookout— observer on vessel to report objects seen.
*looming— **appearance of a distant object, such as a ship, the land, &c.***
loose-footed—fore and aft sail not secured along full length of boom,265.
low— area of low pressure, page 209. **lubber**— a beginner.
lubber's line— mark in compass bowl to represent the bow of the vessel.
*luff— **a direction to the steer's-man to put the helm to leeward.*** This will bring the vessel higher into the wind.
the luff— forward or leading area of fore and aft sails, pages 5 and 7.
luff her— order to bring sailing vessel into the wind with sails luffing.
lugger, lug rig— see pages 278 to 281. **lurch**— sudden roll of vessel.
L.W.L., load waterline—waterline reached with the vessel trimmed to float to the designers specifications, page 255.

ma **mackerel sky**— resembles fish scales, pg.205.
magazine— space provided in a naval ship to store explosives.
main deck— principal structural deck running full length of the hull, 287.
main mast— second mast from the bow on square riggers, pages 285-7. The taller of the masts on ketches, yawls, and two-masted schooners.

ma **mainsail**— is the fore and aft set on the after side of the main mast, page 7, while it is called the **main course** set on the lower yard of the main mast on a square rigger, pages 286-7.
make sail— to set sail. **make fast**— secure or belay a rope or line.
make sternboard— vessel caught in irons going astern under sail.
make water— to leak. **mallet**— serving or caulking mallet.
make land— a landfall. **manila**— organic fiber rope, page 183.
manger— low coaming abaft hawse holes to prevent water running aft.
man rope— a steadying rope handhold for going up an accommodation ladder.
marconi rig— triangular sail rig with luff secured to a vertical, or nearly so mast. **P.S.**—the irony of it, Marconi wasn't even interested in sailing.
mare's tails— thin high clouds resembling a horse's tail, page 205.
mark— lead line markings to record water depth visually or by feel.
marlinespike seamanship— is the mark of an able seaman to handle many kind of knots, care for, plus being able to splice a variety of kinds and sizes of ropes.The **marlinespike fid** is used to splice rope, page 201.The term **marline** is small stuff such as used for whipping, page 200.The square-rigger expert in this field was a **marline-spike sailor.**
maroon— abandon a person by putting him ashore.
marry— sewing rope ends together to thread a rope thru a block.
martingale— rope or chain from the outer end of the jib boom, to the dolphin striker, then to the bow counteracting upward pull of the jib and jib stay. The **martingale boom** is an alternative name for **dolphin striker.**
mast— **vertical spar to support rigging**
mast— vertical spar to support rigging, yards, and sails.
master— captain of the vessel. **masthead light**— pages 236-9, 242-3.
mast tabernacle— a deck structure pivot to raise and lower a mast, 56-7.
mast step— frame or slot the secure lower end of mast, page 73.
mate— officer ranking next to the captain...or wife on a **hen frigate.**
matthew walker knot— a stopper knot on the end of a rope.
meal pennant— white rectangular flag flown on pleasure craft.
mast hoop— wooden luff hoops used on traditional gaff rig, aage 5.
meridian— em imaginary line of longitude passing north and south around the world corssing the equator at right angles.
messenger— rope attached to the cable to heave up the anchor by. We call it a light line used to haul over a heavier line or cable.
midshipman— a Naval Academy student. In the early days of our American Navy midshipmen learned his profession by serving on shipboard.
midships, amidships— widest part of a vessel; order to center rudder.
mildew— fungus growth on organic products, pages 182-3.
nautical mile— 6080', Int'l Nautical Mile is 6070.10'; one min.of latitude.
mirage— seeing an object not there. I question that as I'm positive Lever is standing next to me as we argue each definition in this glossary. **OOPS.....** here comes the gents again with my sports straight jacket, where can I hide????
to miss stays— a sailing vessel failing to change tack.
miter cut jib— has a seam where cloths meet at right angles, page 13.
mizen— the aftermost sail in a ship. We refer to the **mizzen** being on the after mast in a 2 and 3 masted vessel with the schooner the exception.
mizzen staysail— we show a small one set from the mizzen mast, page 69, though we've seen some large enough to be **mizzen spinnakers.**
mole— a stone pier or breakwater offering protection to a harbor.
monkey fist— a complicated knot used on the end of a heaving line.
monkey block— a small single block with a swivel.

mo **monsoon**— seasonal winds blowing the Persian **lateeners** south to Africa for several months, then reversing for several months blowing them home.
moonsail, moonraker— small, fair-weather sails above skysails, page 287.
moorings—the place where a vessel is moored. Also anchors with chains and bridles laid in rivers for Men of War to ride by. We refer to it as a permanent anchorage or dock space for a sailboat or powerboat.
mother carey's chickens— stormy petrels dark in color with a white spot on the rump that follow vessels continuously, they are about 6 inches long.
mold or mould loft— large room to prepare full size boatbuilding templates. **The templates** are assembled into a skeleton framework to which ribs, bulkheads, and other members are added, and the skeleton discarded.
motorsailer— is a term needing to be redefined, pages 272-3.
mouse— to close the mouth of a hook with several turns of a lashing.
muffled oars— chafing gear is added to kill noise in oarlocks.
mule— page 268. It is a kinder term than its original name, see jackass.
mushroom— heavy permanent mooring anchor, page 163.

na **nautical almanac or calendar**— comprehensive book of tides, tidal currents, navigational stars for the time period, sunrise and sunset, and other information.
naval architect— his vessel design starts with ***the lines,*** pages 252-255.
navigable— an area with sufficient water depth to permit passage of vessels.
navigation— we define it as the art of conducting a vessel from port to port out of sight of land with celestial observations. **piloting** is the art of navigating a vessel along a coastline using visual landmarks and **dead reckoning** by estimating vessel speed, estimated leeway, and course steered.
neap tides— tides which happen when the moon is in her quarters, and are not as high as the spring tides.
neaped— a ship is said to be neaped when she is left on shore by these tides, and must wait for the next spring tides. See pages 220-1.
Neptune— a mythical god of the sea new hands meet as they cross the equator
nesting— New England fishing schooners carried many dories.After thwarts were removed,up to ten dories could be stacked in a nest.
net tonnage— vessel measurement of cargo-carrying capacity only.
nimbus— thick dark rain clouds without ragged edges, page 205.
nip— sharp bend in an anchor line. **change the nip** periodically in a storm so any chafe going thru the chock will not be in just one location.
no higher— order to helmsman to point no higher into the wind.
norman— a preventer pin with many adaptations.
north river sloop— a tall rig sloop peculiar to the Hudson River, page 263.
northers— strong violent winds in the western Caribbean and Gulf of Mexico.
nun buoy— red tapered navigational buoy when entering from seaward, 169.

oakum— caulking material for seams, planks, etc., made from bits of old rope.
off and on— upwind coastwise sailing toward land and off again. See Lever.
offing— out to sea— with a safe distance from shore.
offshore wind— wind blowing from the shore.
offsets— naval architect measurements to lay a vessel's lines in a mold loft,252
off the wind— sailing downwind in square riggers and fore and afters.
oil bag— oil container to calm rough seas, page 157.
oilskins— waterproof organic clothing with many coats of linseed oil, which was tarred clothing before.Synthetic, light raingear is far superior.
old-fashioned kedge— small anchor used to warp out without steam in a tight channel, or holding steady a required position, page 163.
 old man— the captain. **on the wind**— closehauled. **off the wind**—downwind.

on **on the bow**— object bearing from abeam to the bow.
on the quarter— object bearing from between beam and stern.
on the wind, in a wind— racing sailor for term sailing closehauled.
one design— sailboat classes built to same spec's with variables, page 2.
open— a dinghy without decking; an open exposed anchorage.
open hawse— riding to two anchors that are clear of each others.
open up— hull leaking as seams open up or planks start to shrink.
orlop deck—lowest warship deck where cables are coiled and other stores kept. Another definition— deck aft of mainmast serving as a dressing station and hospital during action, the definition used by Hornblower.
outboard— beyond a vessel's side; a portable propulsion unit, page 179.
outfoot— to sail faster than another vessel.
outhaul— clew outhaul hauls OUT the sail clew, pages 88, 288-9.
out of trim— improperly ballasted vessel, page 131.
out point— sail closer to the wind than another sailing vessel, pages 98-9.
outrigger— the best known was the *Malibu Outrigger* on page 44. Also a small spar athwartship used in tops and crosstrees to spread backstays.
outsail— a sailing vessel that can sail higher and outpoint another.
length over all, LOA— is measured from fore part of stem to after part of stern with the *Pride of Baltimore* listed as 90' on deck, and 89'9" in another place... while her maximum length including bowsprit was 137' long.
overfalls— breaking waves caused by confliciting currents or a shoal.
overhang— amount a vessel extends beyond the waterline at bow and stern.
overhatted— a sailing vessel that is oversparred, see the Aussie 18, page 44.
overhauling— examining a ship; to haul a fall of rope thru a block till it is slack; to gain on another vessel.
over rigged— heavier gear than necessary.**over sparred**— spars too heavy.

pa **packet**— vessel with a regular schedule carrying freight, mail, and passengers.
pad— metal eye permanently bolted to deck or bulkhead.
painter— short piece of rope by which a boat is made fast, page 91.
palm— see fluke; a sailor's leather fitting over the hand to push a needle.
para-anchor— parachute surface anchor for deep water, pages 156-7.
parachute spinnaker—the first lifting spinnaker appeared in 1927, page 124.
parbuckle— was a purchase of two ropes for raising a barrel up a plank into a vessel, also used to similarily raise other cylindrical objects up the side.
parcel— to wrap canvas strips tightly around a rope with its lay.
parrel— a fitting to keep the jaws of a gaff next to the mast. An iron or rope collar in the center of a yard so the yard can slide up or down a mast.
parrel trucks— wooden or plastic balls threaded onto a parrel reducing friction.
part— a tackle has a hauling and a standing part.
partners— framework support where a mast goes thru the deck., page 73.
to pass— place a rope or lashing round a yard.
passage sails— downwind cruising sails, pages 123, and 289.
pass a line— reeve and secure a line. **pass a stopper**—reeve and secure stopper.
patent anchor— an early term for the stockless anchor, page 163.
patent log— was a taffrail log seldom seen today. See chip log.
paunch mat— thick mat of woven rope strands to reduce chafe used in the yards and rigging.
pawl— short metal pin to prevent the capstan barrel from turning backwards.
to pay— to rub tar, pitch &c. on any thing with a brush.
pay off— *to swing bow* away from wind.
pay out— to slacken out on a chain, rope, or line.

 pazaree, passaree— line used to haul out the clew of a studding sail on a studding sail boom. **pavisses** – protection against an enemy coming aboard. named after the Viking shields lining the rails of their long boats or ships.
pea coat— blue coat worn by USN enlisted men.
peak— outer end of gaff; upper aft corner of a gaff sail, page 5.
to peak up— to raise upper end of a gaff with a peak halyard, page 5.
pelorus— a sighting vane on a dumb compass to take bearings and azimuths.
pendant— a short line with many square rigger applications aloft with an eye, thimble, or block at the lower end which more writers prefer. Some of us use the term **pennant** instead such as the **jib tack pennant,** pages 65,67. There are answering, commission, meal, and homeward bound pennants.
permanent backstay— a fixed stay leading aft from masthead, page 7.
pierhead leap— wild jump a deserter makes as a vessel approaches a dock.
pigs— warships had iron ballast stowed first with 3' long iron pigs laid fore and aft on both sides of the keelson, each weighing about 300 lbs. Gravel ballast was added,then leveled on top of the pigs. **pigs and chickens** could take weather changes easily often provided fresh food aboard.
piling— spar with lower end driven firmly into the bottom to support piers and floating docks that rise and fall with the tide.
pillow— a block supporting the inner end or heel of a bowsprit.
pilot boat— it delivers pilots to vessels coming into port, and takes them off outgoing vessels after leaving the harbor; see ***pilot cutter,*** page 265.
pilot charts— are needed for coastwise piloting and navigation, page 168.
pilot rules— are changed to USCG NAVIGATION RULES— page 230.
piloting—is operating vessels inside harbors and along a coast using visual bearings while navigation is used out of sight of land with celestial observations.
dead reckoning— calculation for the log of a vessel's course and distance.
belaying pin— is a removable pin to belay ropes in a fife or pin rail, pg. 73.
pinch— higher than closehauled with sails starting to luff or shiver, pg.99.
pink stern— high, narrow, pointed stern. For the reason see page 274.
pin or fife rail— railing with holes around mast for belaying pins, page 73.
pinnace— seldom used.It was a tender used by larger vessels of Royal Navy.
pintle— metal pin used as a swinging support of a rudder, page 31.
pitch— fore and aft plunging and rising of a vessel. **pine tree product** used to fill the seams of a wooden hull in traditional sailing vessels.
pitch poling or cartwheeling— bow digs in and stops with the stern using the bow as a pivot point turns end over end, pages 152 to 155.
pivoting point— turning center a vessel pivots on when answering the helm.
plain sail— normal or regular working sails, page 9.
platform— naval vessels from the ***U.S.S. Missouri,*** page 141, and going back in history are movable, floating gun platforms.
plimsoll mark or line— is a mark on the side of merchant vessels indicating a depth a vessel can be loaded for different trades. or zones of risk named after Samule Plimsoll for his victory in 1929 to protect seamen.
plow, plough— of British background resembling a plow, page 162.
plug— a tapered pin for the drain hole in the stern of a dinghy.A long tapered plug should be carried on all sailing and power vessels to stop a sudden leak.
point— 11 ¼ degrees or a 1/32nd part of a circumference.
to point a rope— is to taper the strands of a rope to a point, see Lever.
pointing— sailing closehauled. One sailboat can **point higher** than another.
cardinal points— of a compass are north, east, south, west.
reef points— are lashings to tie in the bunt of a reefed sail, page 149.

po **pole**— part of mast between highest rigging and truck.
pole mast— a mast with one spar from keel to truck, page 284.
poop deck— is the high after deck on the galleon, page 290.It later became a partial deck aft of the helmsman. If the wheel is on the main deck, it is the deck portion aft of the helmsman, page 286.
pooping— a ship is pooped when struck by a heavy sea on stern or quarter.
poppets— timbers fixed to fore and aft part of bilgeways for launching.
porcupine— fraying strands of wire rope. **fish hook** is the term used when a strand frays and breaks on our stainless shrouds and stays.
port— to the left side. This term is used to toe helm's-man to put the helm to the left, instead of the word **"larboard"**— *to make a distinction from the affinity of the sound in the word* **starboard.**
port— is the left side of a vessel when you look forward.
port vs larboard— the loading port on 17th century vessels was on the left side with the loading side called the **ladeboard,** and later to **larboard.** The full coverage on page 84 is with thanks to Karl Freudenstein.
port captain— official in charge of berthing, etc.
port tack— wind coming over port bow, beam, or stern pages 98-9.
port of refuge— any temporary anchorage from storms or heavy seas.
port of entry— a port having custom authorities.
portuguese man of war— a large jellyfish, I've only seen one.
pram— we call it a dinghy with a bow and stern transom, pages 23 and 29, while Chinese junks have a pram bow except for the hybrid lorcha,pg. 281.
pratique— quarantine release after regulations are complied with to permit the landing of passengers, goods, and crew.
prayer book— is a small holystone used to scrub tight corners while larger ones are called **bibles.** English tombstones are made of the same type rock.
press of sail— all sail a vessel can carry.
press gang— authorized naval group who shanghaied British merchant seamen and others for navy service; Americans used unofficial press gangs.
preventer—*any thing for temporary security.* We show a ***preventer*** and a **prevang** to prevent a boom from jibing, page 121.
pricker— small fid, page 201. **pride of the morning**— early mist or shower.
privileged vessel— with right-of-way must maintain course, pages 230-233.
profile— side view or **side v plan** of a vessel, page 252.
prolonged blast— is 4 to 6 seconds long, page 235, Rule 32 (c).
pudden, pudding— chafing material on square rigger; rope fenders.
privateer— sailing vessel with a Letter of Marque. It is a government commission allowing a vessel to prey on enemy commerce for private gain.
punt— small, flat-bottom boat to clean boot top or paint the hull.
purchase— a block and tackle arrangement to increase hauling power.
pusser, purser— paymaster in naval vessel for storing and issue of the government stores. The purser in merchant ships and liners is in charge of passenger accommodations, welfare, and money transactions.
put to sea— leave port and lash down loose objects not properly stowed.

Q **Q-ship**— World War 1 decoy vessel looking helpless with concealed guns for surprise attack sometimes carrying lumber so they couldn't sink.
quadrant— simple navigational instrument replaced by sextant; rudder fitting to secure lines for wheel steering.
In Quarantine— when square riggers carrying immigrants to the U.S. in the late 1800's had infectious diseases aboard, they often had to put back to sea for Halifax, Nova Scotia, with little water or food still aboard. Vessels display a **yellow flag** if they are in quarantine and restricted.

qu *quarter— that part of a ship's side between the main chains and the stern.*
quarter deck— upper deck abaft the mainmast which is officer territory,287.
quarter master— petty officer attending to helm, binnacle, signals, etc.
quartering sea— wind and waves on a vessel's quarter.
quay— loading and unloading place for vessels common in Europe.
quilting— woven rope covering on the outside of a water container.
quoin— a wooden part used to elevate cannons.

ra **rabbet—** a groove cut near the keel to receive the edges of planking,pg. 253.
race— a rapid current with tide rips from conflicting currents.
rack— seizing two ropes together with cross turns of spun yarn.
rack block— has several sheaves or pulleys to change running rigging leads.
raffee— triangular sail set above a square sail, page 123.
rail cap— top of bulwark on outer edge of a deck, page 73.
raise— to bring an object over the horizon into view,"We raised Cape Horn".
raked— inclination of a mast forward or aft from a vertical line., page 135.
range— two objects in line in piloting. Tide raise is amount of rise and fall.
range alongside— come close abeam of another vessel.
range lights— white lights forward indicating direction of a power vessel.
range of cable—*enough length hauled up for anchor to drop to bottom.*
rate— naval sailing vessels had various ratings, page 290.
ratlines— horizontal rope rungs clove-hitched and seized to the shrouds on square riggers to go aloft. **rattle down—** work on ratlines.
rat tail— bolt rope worked down to a small point, page 88.
to rattle down the shrouds— to fix ratlings on them.
reach— all courses between running free and closehauled, page 99.
reaching jib— page 13.
ready about— preparatory order to coming about, page 109.
to reef— to reduce sail by tying it round the yard with points. We use the term to reduce sail area with various methods, pages 146- 155.
reef band— strengthening band across a sail with reef points on the gaff rig, page 5; square sails use **bellybands** and **girthbands,** page 287.
reef points— short lines thru a reefband to secure the foot of a sail, 149.
reef tackle— see 1938 version on *Iris,* page 71, square sails page287.
to reeve— to put a rope thru a block, &c. ..no change.
rat guard— (almost missed it), An enlisted man was explaining the function of the shields on hawsers to prevent the rats climbing aboard. When he asked,"Any questions?", I asked, "How do they leave a ship?"
register, registry— customs document permitting a vessel to engage in foreign trade. It includes measurements, characteristics, and name of master.
relieving tackle— emergency tackle for many uses.
render— a line running freely thru a block.
rhumb line— while it may be straight on a Mercator chart for shortest distance, it instead becomes a curve on the earth which is a sphere. The best example is the **great circle sailing route** from Europe to America.
Rib— permanent hull frame, pg. 73. **ride—** to lie at anchor, page 165.
ride out— to weather a storm safely underway or at anchor.*It will "ride easy" if it doesn't labour much and "ride hard" pitching violently.*
riding down the rigging— a seaman tarring down the rigging as he works his way in a boastwain's chair down the stays.
riding light— white anchor light displayed in the rigging, page 236.
to rig— to fit the rigging to the masts. **standing rigging** supports masts with shrouds and stays while **running rigging** sets, trims, and furls the sails.
 right— a vessel after being laid down in a squall returns to upright position.

ri **right-lay rope**— see page 184. If you can normally put your right hand where the arrow is when horizontal, it is a right lay. The left hand will fit easily in the direction of the arrow for the strands.
ring tail— small sail set abaft spanker in light winds; also page 44.
tide rip— water disturbance caused by conflicting currents or winds.
rise and shine— waking call on a man-of-war.
rising glass— a rising barometer.
roach— outward curve on mainsail leach supported by battens, page 7.
roadstead— an exposed anchorage along the coast or island.
rocker—upward aft curve of a vessel's bottom, pages 28-9.
roaring forties— strong prevailing westerlies 40 to 50 degrees south, 210.
rogue's yarn— colored yarn in a rope added for identification.
roll— side to side motion of a vessel, page 166.
roller reefing— sail is shortened by rolling around a revolving boom,149.
rolling tackle— was used to steady square rigger yards in heavy seas.
rope— yarns and strands of fiber or wire twisted or braided together, 184. Ropes used in the operation of a sailboat become **lines.** Those still called ropes average nine—**foot ropes, yard ropes, bell ropes, bucket ropes, tiller ropes, bolt ropes, back ropes, top ropes, and man ropes.**
round up, round to— change heading from run to reach.
round in, rouse in— are similar, to haul tighter.
royals— sails set above topgallants, page 287.
royal poop— a small, highest, aftermost poop deck, see galleon, page 290.
rubbing strake, rubber, rubbing piece— wooden molding on outside of gunwale to reduce chafe when alongside another vessel, or a wharf.
rudder— a flat plate hinged to the after end of a keel and connected to a rudder post on the forward end with tiller at the upper end of the stock.
spade rudder— is separated from the keel, may have a **skeg,** pages 20-1.
ruffles— drum rolls saluted high ranking officers while the **boatswain's whistle** piped the departure, or a high-ranking officer coming aboard.
rules of the road— has been replaced by USCG Navigation Rules, page 230.
run— upward sweep of a vessel's bottom from maximum beam to the stern as shown on the **buttock lines** of the sheer plan, pages 252-3.
running, to run— sailing before the wind, page 99.
run down— run down the trades; sail north or south on a given parallel of latitude; sail east or west on a given parallel of longitude, page 212.
to run down– when one ship sinks another by running over her.
runners, running backstays— temporary backstays, page 109. The windward one is set up when coming about, as the leeward one is slacked off.
running by the lee— sailing with wind on same quarter as the boom,122.
running lights— are displayed on vessels underway from dusk to dawn,236-9.
running rigging— is used to raise, set, and trim sails.

sa **to sag**— the jib luff sags to leeward if the jibstay is too slack.
sag away— a vessel with too much leeway...does it have a fouled bottom?
sailing free— is running with the wind aft, page 99.
sail ho!— the cry used by a lookout when a sail was sighted at sea.
sailing on her own bottom— the vessel that has paid for itself.
sailing trim— a sailing vessel with the most efficient sail trim.
sails— flexible vertical airfoils on fore-and-aft rigged sailing vessels, and square sails on square riggers using wind pressure to propel the vessels.
salvage— pay for saving a cargo or vessel from danger. The amount is based on the amount of labor and hazard involved. If a crew saves its own cargo or vessel, no salvage claim is involved.

 samson or sampson post— mooring bitt on bow or stern, page 190.
sand bagger— late 1800 racing shell using gravel bags for ballast, page 44.
save all, water sail— small sail under lower studding sail or driver boom.
scandalize— temporary reef by dropping gaff rig peak halyard, page 148.
scantlings— dimensions of members used to build a vessel, page 252.
scarf— joining timbers by beveling each other to look as one timber.
schooner— pages 9, 270-1. **schooner bow**— clipper bow, page 70.
scope— length of mooring line or cable let out, page 165.
score— groove in outer surface of a block or deadeye.
scotchman— grommet at luff of topsail to use as a purchase, page 70.
scow— has a flat bow, page 44. **Thames Barge**— a cargo carrier,pgs. 18, 273.
screen— sidelight boards limiting horizontal arc of red add green sidelights.
scrowl— ornamental carved timber piece, a substitute for a figurehead.
scrimshaw— sailor carvings on jaw bone or teeth of a whale or shark. Also etchings on shells, ivory, or bone that are polised with wax or canvas.
to scud— to sail before the wind in a storm.
scull— a short oar for dinghies and a long one for junks used at the stern for propulsion in a figure 8 movement.The **crooked-stern salt junk** a little over 80' long uses a **sweep** to scull it, is as long or longer than the junk.
scullery— a vessel's pantry for washing and stowing dishes.
scuppers— overboard drain holes on deck, page 71.
scurvy— a shipboard disease caused by salted beef, no vegetables or fruit. A seaman loses energy, the flesh becomes spongy, see **lime juicer.**
to scuttle a ship— to make holes in her bottom to sink her.
scuttle butt— crew gossip while meeting at their fresh water drinking cask.
sea or ocean— covers a little over 70% of our earth. The volume of all land above sea level is only an 18th as much as the cubic volume of ocean water. It has enough salt to cover all land with a salt layer 500 feet thick.
sea anchor— is a surface anchor. See various kinds on page 157.
sea breeze— applies to a cooling afternoon breeze from the ocean, page215.
sea chest— **trunk owned by a seaman** with ornaments and fancy rope work.
sea cock— valve with opening below the waterline for various purposes.
sea dog— the first fog horn had four legs.
sea going— a vessel designed for, and prepared to go to sea,
sea kindly— a vessel riding comfortably in rough weather, page 152.
sea ladder— portable ladder over the side of a ship as to take up a pilot.
sea lawyer— belligerant seaman who enjoys arguments with authority.
seam— space between planks; stitching holding two cloths together.
sea room— enough room to maneuver a vessel without risk of collision or grounding. See super tanker limitations on page 241.
seaworthy— a vessel in good condition, properly designed, constructed, equipped, manned, and prepared to go to sea.
section— vessel shape at right angles to keel, pages 73,252-3.
secure for sea— order for extra lashings on all movable objects.
to seize— to make fast, or bind. **seizings**— small stuff for binding.
selvagee strop—is made of small stuff marled together.
sennet,, sennit— braided rope yarn. **sentinel**— anchor rode weight, pg. 165.
to serve— bindings around a cable or rope to prevent chafe.
serving— after worming and parcelling a rope with small stuff to wind a rope keeping turns close together, tar is added to seal out the water.
serving boards and mallets— furnish leverage to make a serving.
set— is direction of current flow while **drift** is amount of sailboat leeway.

se **set flying**— page 127 shows sequence to set a spinnaker flying.
to set— to hoist or make sail. **settle**— a vessel is slowly sinking.
set course— give helmsman course. **set watch**— divide crew into watches.
set up rigging— use purchases to take up slack in shrouds and stays.
sextant— navigational instrument measuring altitude of sun and stars.
shackle— a 'U' shaped bar with a pin or bolt in one end: 15 fathoms of chain.
shake— sailboat pointing too high with sails luffing, page 99.
shakedown cruise— first cruise for vessel and crew to become a team.
shake out— let out a reef or hoist the sails.
shank— anchor arm, pg. 162.**shank painter**— secures anchor fluke to billboard.
shape a course— plot proper course to reach a specific point or port.
shanghied— taken aboard outward bound vessel against a persons will.
sharpie— a log canoe with sails for oystering, page 275.
sharp up— yards braced as close to fore and aft as possible.
sheers— ***Lever page 17,*** spars lashed together to raise heavy objects.
to sheer, sheer about— a vessel ranges from side to side when at anchor.
shear hulk— old vessel with sheer legs for shipping tall masts into others.
shearwater— 20 inch sea bird commonly seen on Nova Scotia's Grand Banks.
sheathing— copper plates on a vessel's bottom to keep out marine borers.
sheave— pulley in a block, the **sheave hole**— space between the cheeks.
sheepshank— a bend or hitch temporarily used to shorten a rope, page 191.
sheer off— bear away. **sheer plan**— **sailboat profile shape**— page—252.
sheer pole— the first ratline, the iron bar above the dead eyes on the shrouds.
sheer strake— topmost plank on a vessel's side, page 73.
sheets— trimming lines used to control sails on boom or clews.
sheet anchor— largest anchor on sailing vessels carried in waist, page 163.
sheet bend— joins rope ends, page 189. **shell**— outer casing of a block.
ship— a sailing vessel square-rigged on all masts from three or more. USN version is 75' long or longer capable of taking passengers and/ or cargo for long seagoing voyages...while carrying smaller boats aboard; expect variables.
to ship a sea— when the sea breaks aboard a ship; put any thing on board.
shellback— an old sailor who goes to sea for a living.
shipshape— everything is in place, and everthing has its own place.
ship chandler— a dealer in ship supplies.
ship of the line— naval vessels, first, second, and third raters, page 290.
shipping articles— contract between officers and crew with wages, etc.
ship's bells— occur once every 30 minutes to record sailing vessel watches,etc. Every oceangoing sailboat needs a clock with ship's bells today to accurately record the course every 30 minutes, and the sound is pleasant in your den.
ship's papers— are legal documents with ship's registry, manifest, clearance papers, charter party, and bill of health.
shoal— shallow water with breakers to look for in heavy weather.
shoe— timber used for an anchor bill to rest upon. Lower support for rudder, page 72; also **false keel** providing more draft protecting the keel.
shoot, shooting— momentum or distance a heavy narrow sailboat will keep going pointing head to wind in crowded moorings, page 171.
shore, shore up— to protect a sailboat hard aground, page 159.
short board— is a short tack; a **long board** is a long tack, page 101.
short handed— not enough crew members. Rig for single handing, page 59.
shorten sail— reduce sail area by dropping sail or reefing, pages 146-155.
short scope— anchor scope almost vertical when taking anchor in.
short splice— joins to pieces of rope, oops 3 strand, page 202.
shot— 15 fathoms of chain cable. My preference is a shot of bourbon.

sh **shoulder-of-mutton**— early version of gaff sail with short gaff, page 3.
shroud-laid— rope made of four strands with a right-hand lay.
shrouds— they provide athwartship support to a mast, pages 5, 7, 285.
side boys— crew at side of gangway on naval ship saluting visiting officers.
side lights— red and green running lights, pages 236-239.
single sticker— a sloop or cutter with one mast.
sister ships— are built on the same lines. Congress authorized funds to resume construction of six frigates. *U.S.S. Constitution* was one of the sister ships.
skeg— metal shoe or socket supporting bottom of rudder, page 72, attached to bottom of keel. Sailboats 6 and 7, have separate **spade rudders** supported by skegs that are aft of and not secured to the rudder, page 19.
skipjack— is a Chesapeake Bay sailing vessel used to dredge oysters, pg. 275.
skipper— usually the captain of a sailboat used for pleasure.
skysails— are set above royals, pg. 287. **skysails**— trinagular sails set above skysails; if a square sail is used it becomes a **moonsail** or **moonraker.**
skylight— glass hatch protected by metal rods to admit air and light.
slack water— period between flood and ebb tide when tidal current stops.
the slack of a rope— the part which hangs loose.
sleeper— is similar to **deadhead,** timbers almost waterlogged, difficult to see.
sliding gunter, gunther— sailing dinghy with vertical gaff to stow all spars in dink
slings— chain support for a fixed or non-lowering mast; also a tackle.
slip— is a dock with fingers to tie up pleasure craft while a **slipway** in a boatyard can haul out vessels for repair in a mobile cradle, and launch it again. A dock **slip line** is used as a pivot, then one end is released, page 174.
slip the mooring— cast off from mooring, pg. 91. **slippery hitch**— page-191.
sloop— one masted sailboat designed for one jib, page 263. **knockabout**— is obsolete term for sloop if it didn't have a bowsprit.**sloop of war**— was a sixth rater with 18 to 32 guns on one deck, 125' LOA, with crew of 200, 291.
slough— swampy river inlet area where fresh and salt water mix. The best known is the delta area east of San Francisco called the Sacramento slough.
smack— Dutch small sailing vessel for fishing with a well to keep fish alive.
smiting line— a furled sail has several rope yarn stops that are secured to the smiting line requiring one pull to rapidly break open the sail on old vessels.
snorter— metal eye to which topping lifts are secured to a light yard, pg. 288.
sprit rig snotter— rope or metal loop around mast supporting sprit jaws,pg. 3.
snow— a brig with another mast abaft,close to mainmast carrying spanker.
snub— to suddenly stop a chain or line going out.
snug down— prepare vessel for storm. **snugged down**— small sail area.
soldier's wind— advantageous only to other vessel sailing in opposite direction.
soft eye— eye splice at end of line without a thimble in the eye.
sole,shole— protective timber under rudder to line up with **false keel** beneath, reinforcing main keel... to protect rudder and keel if vessel goes aground.
to sound— to find the bottom by a leaden plummet. Before the depth sounder, page 158, depth was measured with a tapered lead cylinder on a **lead line.** A **hand lead** weighed up to 15 pounds, a **deep-sea lead,** up to 100 pounds.
soundings— depth of water is shown on chart plus nature of the bottom.
sou'wester— rainproof hat with a broad stern, oop's, rear brim.
span— rope or chain sling with both ends attached to a yard or similar object with a purchase hooked to its bight, see topping lifts, page 288.
spanker— fore and aft sail set on aft mast of square riggers, pages 286-7.
spanking breeze— a good wind coming over the stern or quarter.
 spar— basic term for masts, yards, gaffs, and booms.

spectacle— two or three rings at the clews of square sail courses, page 287.

to take a spell— to be in turn on duty at the lead, the pump, &c.

spencer— gaff sail on any mast of a square-rigged ship except the mizzen.

spider— metal outrigger to keep a block clear of a vessel's sides.

spider band— band around mast to secure futtock shroud shackles, pg. 285. It can also be a metal band around a lower mast with sockets for belaying pins.

to spill— to take wind out of sails by braces, &c, to reef or hand them.

spilling line— while the **buntline** is secured to the footrope of a square sail to pull the bottom up to spill the wind, page 288, the **spilling line** continues up the after side also to spill the wind before **furling begins.**

spinnaker— a large triangular racing sail, pages 124-7, the "emotional sail".

spitfire jib— small heavy weather jib, page 264.U. S. sailmakers have tried to corrupt the term for various sails, fortunately with little success.

to splice— to join two ropes together by uniting the strands...page 201.

splice the main brace— it is March 17th Saint Paddy's Day this writer is looking forward to. I hope he wasn't a teetotaller.

spoon drift, spindrift— spray blown from top of cresting waves in bad weather.

*spoondrift— **continued flying of spray and waves over the surface of the sea.***

spreader— athwartship strut to spread shrouds to keep the mast "in column". Square riggers used spreaders at the cross trees to spread the backstays, 285.

spring— a pivot line used for docking, undocking, and to prevent a vessel moving ahead or astern while docked, pages 173-4.

spring stay— horizontal stay between mastheads of a schooner, page 271.

spring tides— the highest tides at the full and change of the moon.

spritsail rig— quadrilateral sail, pages 1 and 273, with the peak extended by the **sprit spar** with the lower jaw end secured to the mast. An earlier term— Columbus carried a **spritsail or watersail** under the *Santa Maria* bowsprit.

spun yarn— various terms from coarse marlin, to small line with yarns twisted from old rope , knotted and tarred for various purposes.

spurling line— is a light line from tiller or wheel to an indicator showing the rudder position, plus the amount of lee or weather helm.

spur— timbers bolted to bilgeways to support the bilge of a vessel under construction or in for repairs.Also curved timbers serving as half beams to support decks where whole beams cannot be used.

spy glass— a short telescope used at sea which was replaced by binoculars.

squall— often a sudden violent wind in a small area such as a thunderstorm.

microburst— is a new term in a storm with an overall force 7 with a small area 2 to 4 miles across with an intense force 12 or more, the best reason for sinking the *Pride of Baltimore.* After experiencing the hell of two microbursts... a **warning!** Listen for **static on an inexpensive AM radio** . The louder the static, the greater the static due to upper level disturbances, the greater are the chances for cyclones and microbursts in your area.

square a yard— bring it square with the braces, then they are **squared by the lifts** to become horizontal with whipping markers on the lift lines.

square riggers— carry square sails set from yards slung athwartship on the forward side of the mast, using retangular sails, pages 282 to 291.

stability— a vessel which wants to return to an upright position after heeling over. A **tender sailboat** has little stability, a **stiff sailboat** has excess stability.

stanchions— upright supports for lifelines, page 67.

square mark— running rigging markers to show various correct settings.

stand by— preparatory order to wake up for an order to execute a maneuver.

stand of tide— low and high extremes when no vertical motion is detected.

st *to stand on—to hold course. to stand by— to be ready.*
standing part— part of tackle made fast to block or object that does not move.
standing rigging— supports masts and spars such as shrouds and stays.
starboard— the right side of a vessel when looking forward, page 84.
starboard tack— sailing with wind over starboard bow, beam, or stern, 99.
station bill— posted list of crew stations to abandon ship, fire drills, etc.
staunch— able, stiff, steady, seaworthy. **stave in—** to crush.
stays— provide fore and aft support for a mast, pages 7, 112-3.
in stays— caught in irons; the dinghy **big splash,** page 145.
staysail— triangular fore and aft sail named according to its stay which is a jib on a modern sloop, to the *Eagle* main royal tops'l, page 286.
staysail schooner rig— has a staysail and fisherman between masts, page 271.
steady— an order to maintain the present course.
steerage— lower portion of vessel occupied by passengers paying lowest fare, see 1850 emigrant trade, page 212.Whaling ship quarters for the steerers.
steeve, steeving— angle of a bowsprit from the horizontal.
stem— bow timber between keel and bowsprit into which the forward ends of a vessel's planking are rabbeted, page 73. **stem head—** top of stem.
stem the current or tide— sailing against it yet still making some way.
stemming— maintaining position yet not making headway in a tidal current.
mast step— a frame support for the mast heel, page 73.
stern— after end of a vessel or boat. **sternboard—** a vessel in irons gaining enough sternway to answer the helm to pay off on either tack.
sternsheets— aft part of an open boat for passengers abaft the rowers.
stevedore— is in charge of cargo stowage with longshoremen the laborers.
stiff— a sailing vessel that doesn't heel easily or normally; opposite of tender.
stirrups— short ropes supporting foot ropes under yards, page 288.
bowline stirrup— is a foot pivot to take a person aboard a dinghy, page 229.
stock— anchor crosspiece, page 162. **stocks—** framework on which a vessel and its launching crade rests. The stocks must slope down towards the water.
stopper knot— a knot on the end of a line to stop it going thru a block, 202.
stops— weak twine which is easily broken when a spinnaker is raised, 126.
stopwater— wooden dowel or **treenail** into a hole bored across a joint that can't be caulked. It swells after a vessel is in the water making a tight fitting.
storm sails— small heavy-weather sails, pg 147. **storm warnings—** page 139.
stowaway— person illegally aboard. **strakes—** hull planking— page 73.
strand— a number of rope yarns woven together, page 184.
stranded— a vessel driven ashore. **strap—** binding around a block.
stream anchor— medium size sailing vessel anchor, page 163.
strike— to lower a sail, yard, mast, or the colors.
stringer— fore and aft longitudinal inside a wooden hull, page 73.
strop— is synonymous for strap; Lever uses strap instead of the older strop.
studding sails, stun'sa'ls— light weather sails with portable boom extensions which extend beyond square sail yards, page 287.
sun over the foreyard— it is time for a drink. I like the idea.
superstructure— any permanent structure built on the upper deck such as a raised quarterdeck, wheel house, etc.
supporters— knee timber supports under the **cat heads.**
swells— storm waves caused by a storm elsewhere that haven't flattened out. The **windless storm** with huge swells that have fallen out of sequence is a major square rigger hazard which can cause dismastings and split decsk . It is fortunately a rare phenomenon I have only been involved in twice. A sailing vessel with swells and no wind becomes a bucking bronco.

sw **swells**— large waves caused by a storm elsewhere that haven't flattened out. A major square rigger hazard was a **windless storm** with huge swells that have fallen out of sequence. Without wind vessels act like a bucking bronco splitting decks and causing dismastings. It is a rare phenomenon.
to sway—hoist up yards and topmasts. **swedish jib**— genoa jib, pg. 125.
sweeps—are long oars. The Chinese **crooked-stern salt junk** is used on the Crow River above Fowchow. While it is a little over 80' long, the single sweep to scull it is longer than the junk, reported by Worcester, page 278.
swifter— aftermost shrouds on fore and main mast, the last to be tightened.
swinging— a vessel at anchor or on a mooring swings with the tide or wind.
to swing ship— is to take it thru all points of the compass to find deviation.
swivel— a fully rotating part on a cable with a constant turning action.
swivel block— can easily rotate to face any direction.

ta **tabernacle**— a fitting permitting a mast to be lowered and raised, pgs. 56-7.
tabling—a hem sewn around a sail to which a bolt-rope is sewed, page 11.
tack— sailing course, page 98; lower forward corner of a sail, pages 5, 7, 11.
change tack— to change wind and boom to other side of sailboat, 109, 111.
to tack— to turn a ship by the sails and rudder against the wind.
tackle— a purchase made of ropes and blocks to increase power or leverage to move heavy objects, supporting masts, and working sails and rigging, 184.
tackline, tack downhaul— is used to hold down tack of gaff tops'l, pg. 70.
taffrail— wooden railing around stern, page 75.
taffrail log— is mounted on the taffrail to measure speed and distance by rotation of a spinner on a line towed astern has been replaced by better instruments that sharks won't swallow.
taken aback— caught unprepared with wind on forward side of square sail, 100.
take off— remove sails; tides changing from springs to neaps, page 221.
take up— tighten or shorten rigging; a wooden boat going into the water in the spring will leak until the planks take up or swell up to stop the leaks.
tall ships— with lofty rigs paraded past our Statue of Liberty and up the Hudson for **OPSAIL'86,** on July 4, coming from all over the world that was led by the *Eagle.*
tangs— fittings on a mast to secure shrouds and stays, page 68-9.
tan, tanbark— soak sails in an extract of oak bark as a preservative which makes the redish-brown sails on Thames barges. Chinese use a mangrove bark curing solution with a tannin content as a preservative, page 278.
tar— black pine tree gum used to seal and protect rigging and yards against corrosion and weather. A vessel's bottom was cleaned by burning off the weeds and barnacles before being **re-tarred.** My bottom paint expert told me the British Admiralty has bottom paint records going back 500 years.
tarp, tarpaulin— canvas painted, treated, or tarred to protect hatches. It also applied to a sailor's hat that was tarred. Dana tarred his jacket to make it waterproof and warmer in his first job as a seaman.
taunt— tall-sparred vessel. **taut**— streched tight and snug.
telltale, telltail— cloth, yarn, or other wind indicators, page 101.
tending— caring for an anchored boat especially at a tidal current change.
tender— sailboat or dinghy with too much sail area and poor stability.
teredo— sea worm gourmet that enjoys eating into your unprotected wood bottom planks with a 5' one found in a minesweeper keel in WW II.
thimble— a round or heart-shaped metal ring that can be used with an eye splice. The thimble adds tremendous strength to the eye splice while it protects the eye splice from chafe, page 199.

th **thole pins**— are on the gunwale of a boat on both sides of an oar when rowing, the worst answer for use on a rowboat.
three sheets in the wind— unsteady gait due to too much imbibing.
throat— inner end of gaff where it fits the mast, page 5.
thrum mats— were chafing gear used to muffle noise of oarlocks.
throat brails— pull up and gather a sail for storage on the mast and gaff.
thumb cleats— are small with one horn.
thwart— is a rowboat seat for an oarsman; see dinghies pages 28-9.
tide— page 221, the alternate rise and fall of ocean water even exists in a glass of water but don't try to measure its range.
tidal current— the inflow and outflow of currents caused by changing tides with both the lower Hudson River and San Francisco bay for examples.
tide race or rip— is easy to see in the San Francisco bay where tidal currents pass over an irregular bottom producing a surface disturbance. **Overfalls** are violent tide rips with breaking waves.
tide rode— an anchored or moored vessels swings to the tidal current, while **a wind rose** vessel swings to meet the force of the wind.
tideway— where the tidal currents are strong.
tie, tye— a single part halyard which hoists a yard thru a mast sheave, 288.
tier— row of mooring buoys to which several vessels are moored close to each other, all pointing the same direction with Avalon harbor an example.
tier— the place where cables are stowed.
tight— a wooden vessel that doesn't leak.Painting a wooden hull black may make it too tight squeezing out the caulking between the planks on hot days.
tiller— a bar secured to the rudder post to steer a vessel.The rudder **quadrant** used for a steering wheel may also be classed as a tiller.The **whipstaff** was a long lever at the rudder post toggled onto it with a gooseneck for a helmsman on an upper deck to move the tiller below with a limited swinging radius in the15th to 17th centuries.It was replaced by a **steering wheel** in the early 18th century. The *H.M.S. Victory* uses two steering wheels with a drum between. A **tiller rope** around the barrel drum is connected to the rudder post Early **autos** were steered with tillers. When steering wheels were added a major battle started whether the wheel should turn as it does today... or as sailing vessel wheels which **turned opposite** at that time than they do today. Before steering an 80 year old sailboat, check wheel rotation first!
timbers— large pieces of wood that were often long used in shipbuilding. They usually had to be steamed before bending into the desired shape.
timber heads— are timbers above deck level for a bitt to belay ropes.
toggle— a wooden or metal pin thru the eye of a rope for a quick release.
to leeward— away from the wind sounds simple and basic. The various uses of leeward become very confusing to me.
tompion, tompkin— a muzzle plug in a cannon to keep away moisture.
ton— a long ton is 2240 pounds, a short ton is 2000 pounds. A cargo ton is 100 cubic feet, a measurement ton is 40 cubic feet.While **tonnage** begins as a weight measurement, it evolved into volume equivalents for cargo vessels. Sailboat **tonnage** has its own complexity, page 256.
tongue— is a vertical wood piece in the gaff jaws to slide it up and down masts
top— a platform on the mast supported by trestletrees, page 285.
to top a yard— on square riggers next to a wharf was to cockbill it.To top a gaff or boom is to raise the after end.
top hamper— rigging and spars above the deck.
 top rope— is used to hoist topmasts.

to **topping lift**– tops up the after end of a boom while raising and lowering sails to avoid stretching the sail cloth, page 91.
gaff topsail– is set above a gaff, pages 70, 261-267.
topsail schooner– the schooner *Californian* is square rigged on foremast, 251.
topsides– sides of a sailing vessel from the waterline to the upper deck; also on deck. You come up from below to go topside.
touch and go– is to teach docking a sailboat by stopping at the dock many times without using dock lines.
trade winds– steady wind areas from 30 degrees south to 30 degrees north of the equator. Study pages 210 to 213.
island traders– are vessels that barter one cargo for another while going from one port to another.
train tackle– was used to run guns in and out on naval sailing vessels.
transom– stern planking on a square sterned dinghy, sailboat, or large vessel.
traveler, traveller– track to adjust mainsheet, pages 28, 65,75, 77, 116-121.
treenails, trunnels– are sylindrical wooden pins or pegs averaging an inch in diameter for a vessel 100' long. They swell with moisture making a good fitting after a vessel is in the water with a history going back thousands of years.
trestle-trees– two short fore and aft timbers at the head of the mast resting on the **cheeks** at the head of the mast. They support the heel of the next higher mast while supporting the **cross trees** we call spreaders today.
triatic stay– is a horizontal stay running between the mast caps.
trice– to haul up. **trick**– a period of duty at the helm.
trim– fore and aft balance of a vessel trim; the trim of the sails.
trip line– is used to capsize sea and storm anchors, page 157.
trochoidal wave– deep sea waves with orderly shape and movement that coincide with the wave length/hull speed of displacement hulls, pages 140-141.
truck– wooden cap at masthead, may have sheaves for a flag halyard.
true wind– direction it blows on dock differing from apparent wind underway.
trunk– a vertical shaft for daggerboard and centerboard trunks, pgs.16,17.
trunk cabin– is raised above the deck for headroom below, page 62.
trunnion– arms of a cannon that rests on the carriage is the axis it can be elevated or depressed.
truss– an iron bracket supporting a lower yard. It is hinged to allow the yard to move in both horizontal and vertical planes.
trysail– usually a storm trysail, page 147.
tumble home– inward curve of a vessel's side above the waterline was used on cargo and naval ships to 1800 making it difficult for pirates to board.
turnbuckle– a metal cylinder with internal right hand threads on one end, and left hand threads on the other to pull two standing rigging eyes together to set up standing rigging, pages 69 and 113.
take a turn– take a turn once or twice around an object. **turn turtle**–upset.
to turn in– to rest in a hammock or bunk; **to turn out**– to get up and rise and shine! **turn up!**– send the rascals topside!
tye, tie– single part halyard to hoist a yard thru a mast sheave, page 288.
typhoon– is comparable to our hurricanes for the China Seas and western areas of the North Pacific. **twin spinnakers**– twin jibs, page 123.

un **una rig**– named after *Una* the first catboat shipped to England, pages 4,5.
to unbend– to cast loose; to cast off; to remove sails from spars.
under bare poles– vessel with no sails set in a force 12, page 137.
under foot– anchor is directly under the hawse hole.

un **under manned**— short handed, not enough crew members.
under the lee— to leewar of a sailing vessel, headland, or building.
undertow— strong confused reverse current in the surf with water teying to level itself between two basins in the surf with different water capacities.
underway— a vessel not aground,at anchor,or made fast to a shore or dock.
the union jack— has prompted more letters from readers knowing little more about it than yachting protocal. The **boatswain's pipe** on English vessels can be traced back to the Crusades around 1250 A.D., and the Union Jack probably began in that era. My early reference material is misplaced, but—

The Union Jack today is flown on the bow of merchant vessels and naval, and USCG vessels in commission when anchored, moored, dockside, or when hauled out for repairs. The traditional purpose was to show limited authority the crew had when a vessel was not underway.

If my ancient memory serves correct, it was used on pirate vessels which when underway the captain had all authority. As they were operating for profit, when at anchor or dockside with a captain that was weak or cowardly, the crew could vote in a new captain.***Can any readers help me?***
to unmoor— leave one anchor down and heave up on the other.
to unreeve— to pull a rope out of a block.
to unrig— to deprive a vessel of her rigging.
to unship— to take anything from the place in which it is fixed.
up anchor— an order to raise or weigh anchor. **up and down**— the anchor cable is vertical, further hauling will break the anchor out.
up helm— putting tiller to windward so a sailing vessel can bear downwind.
upper deck— the highest uninterrupted deck from bow to stern... while the **quarterdeck** became the part of the upper deck from the mainmast to the poop. Earlier vessels had high **fore castles** and high **after castles** to pour tar and other nasty things on boarders between the castles, page 245.These castles became excellent targets with cannons as they and **poops** disappeared. The professional sailing language has a history of possibly 1000 years. The more you understand this history, the more you will enjoy sailing.
upper works— all parts of a vessel for sailing balanced for an ocean voyage.
upstream— into the tidal stream or river current.

V **V-bottom**—it provides an excellent dinghy hull with hard chines to resist an upset while dinghies with rounded chines are quite tippy,page 15.
vane— a masthead vane showing wind direction.
vang— a steadying line to prevent the peak of a gaff falling off to leeward.
boom vang— prevents the boom from lifting while sailing downwind, 121.
vast, avast— stop or pause such as 'avast heaving'.
veer— wind change in a clockwise direction. The wind **backs** when the change is counterclockwise.**veer and haul**— alternately slack and haul.
veer and haul— to alternately slack up and haul away.
very signal— red, green, and white star signals fired from a pistol.
vessel— is a term used in our glossary covering a variety of sailing craft from Viking ships, to square riggers, to present day fiberglass sailboats.
viol block— a large double block for heaving up the anchor.
visible horizon— is the line in the distance where sky and water meet. While limited on deck, a lookout stationed high aloft on the foremast had much better distance visibility. Lookouts during the day were posted at the bow and at masthead when danger of fog and/or ice existed.
voyage— an outward and homeward passage or trip.

wa **waist**— portion of the upper deck between the quarter deck and f'c'sle.
waist anchor— the **sheet anchor,** the heaviest anchor was carried at the waist for emergency use weighing 5,443 lbs. on *U.S.S. Constitution,* 163.
waister— a green hand, incompetent, tired, or worn out sailor.
wake— the track left by the ship on the water she has passed over.
wales— strong planks running fore and aft the entire length of a vessel to reinforce the decks forming the curves of the hull; also **rubbing strake.**
wall sided— vessel with vertical sides (compare it with **tumble home**).
ward room— commissioned officers' mess room; others call it officers' quarters on a naval vessel.
to warp— to move a ship by hawsers, &c. It was a combination of skill and art to turn around, and/or move a large sailing vessel by hauling on dock lines and/or anchor lines...plus making the most of wind and tidal currents. It was the only method used before the days of steam tugs.
wash— the waves or wake left by a passing vessel.
watch— working shifts aboard ship. Lever calls one a ***starboard watch,*** the other a ***larboard watch*** though using term **port** elsewhere.
a watch— is usually four hours long changing at 12, 4, and 8 o'clock. The **dog watch** from 4 to 8 p.m. is two hours each so no sailor has the same watch the next day. **The bells** on a shipboard striking clock is every half hour with eight bells indicating the end of the watch.
watch cap— a blue woolen cap used by Navy enlisted men.
watch ho watch, watch there watch!— warning the lead will be heaved.
waterline— the boot top indicates the load waterline, page 252, indicating proper trim of vessel not underway.
waterlogged—a leaky ship so full of water to be heavy and unmanageable.
waterway— navigable channel: gutter water drain on deck going to scuppers.
way of a ship— her progress thru the water. A vessel drifting is underway making **headway** if going forward, **sternway** if going backwards, and making **leeway** if drifting sideways.
shipyard ways— vessels in the water come into a cradle on a marine railway. The movable cradle is hauled out for the vessel to be examined, repaired, and new bottom paint added. The cradle returns to the water for the vessel to float off and be underway again.
wear, *to ware— to turn a ship round from the wind* (square riggers),pg.101. A complexity of the lateener, page 277,it also has *to ware.*
weather— the side towards the wind is the windward side. **weather bound**— sailing vessel staying in port due to storm or wrong wind direction.
keep weather eye open— be on the alert. **weather gage**— a vessel that is to windward of another. **weather helm**— heeling sailboat wants to come head to wind, page 135. **weatherly roll**— vessel rolling when going to windward.
to weather a ship— to get to windward of her. **weatherly ship**— one that makes little leeway when working to windward. ***a weather tide— a tide or stream that runs to windward.*** **to weather**— to safely pass to windward of a vessel or object without changing tack. **weather deck** — uppermost deck without overhead protection.
to weigh— to heave the anchor out of the ground.
well— order meaning sufficient. **centerboard, daggerboard wells**— pgs. 16,17.
well found— a well equipped vessel with all gear in good condition.
westerlies— the prevailing wind patterns across the U.S., pages 206,211,214.
whale back, turtle back— sailboat with a high deck crown so a person can walk on a horizontal part of the deck when the sailboat is heeling.
whaleboat— double-ended utility boat and lifeboat 24' to 30' long.

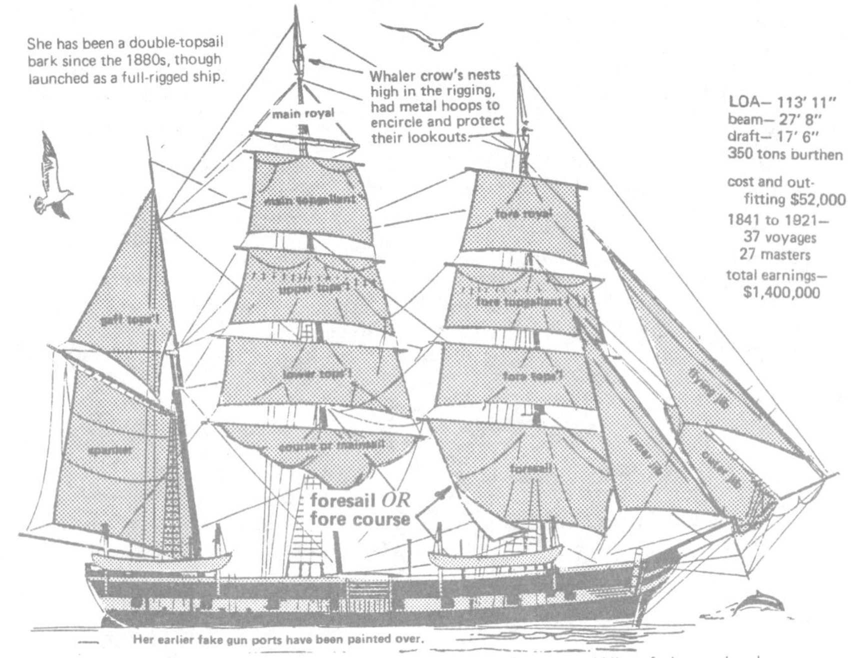

Visit the *Charles W. Morgan* at her Mystic Seaport Wharf, launched in 1841, the only surviving 19th century wooden whaling ship.

This is just one of her rigs used in eighty years of operation.

wh **steering wheel–** see tiller definition for its history.
to whip– to bind the end of a rope with yarn to prevent its untwisting. To hoist anything by a rope which is reeved thru a single block.
whisker pole– is used to hold out jib clew running wing and wing,pg. 121. A woman student of mine continually called it her "whiskey pole".
whiskers– horizontal spars on bow to spread out the jib-boom guys. See page 73;the *Iris* uses whisker stays without whisker booms.
whistle buoy– has a whistle actuated by wave movement,page 169.
whitecaps– are breaking wave crests beginning at force 5, page 137.
white squall– sudden furious storm with minimum visibility.
winch– a mechanical device to increase hauling power of running rigging, and to take in anchors.Chinese junks introduced the first windlass, the forerunner of the capstan with the same results as a winch.
wind bound– adverse winds trapping a sailing vessel in a channel or port.
wind funnel– narrowing hills or canyon conditions that compresses and accelerates the wind speed in that localized area, page 215.
windlass– a large winch to haul in cable, see winch.
windjammer– a windy politician. Sailing vessels kept growing in size in the 1800's with the Clipper Ship era from 1850 to 1860. Following them were much larger for cargo carrying capacity called windjammers, pg. 282.

WIND FORCE SCALE– page 137, with our thanks to Admiral Beaufort.

wind rode– when a ship is kept astern of her anchor solely by the wind.
windsail– cloth air scoop funneling air into a vessel.
 to windward– towards that point from whence the wind blows.

wing and wing— running before the wind with sails on opposite sides,pg. 99.
withe, wythe, boom iron— band on yardarm with a fitting for the studding-sail boom, holding the heel of the boom when rigged out, page 287.
wishbone gaff or twin-spar boom— see *Vamarie*, page 269.
woolding— repairing a broken spar by winding several tight rope lashings close together. **working sails**— are those used under normal conditions.
working to windward— sailing closehauled upwind on opposite tacks, 101.
works— old sailing vessels such as the *Santa Maria* with the mackerel tail and cod head with squaresail had continuous and endless noises as the parts of the hull worked and complained together with much flexing.
worming— filling in the lay of a rope with small stuff to make a smoother surface for parcelling and serving square rigger rigging.
wring— to strain and distort the hull and/or rigging with too much strain.
wring bolts— are used to bend a strake into position while building a wooden vessel until it has been permanently fastened.

X **xebec**— a lateener, often three masted with long bow and stern overhang,277.

ya **yacht**— is a vessel designed for pleasure or state. This includes a presidential yacht and your dinghy, except the rowboat by legal definition is a rowboat.
yankee— is a gaff topsail on *Iris*, page 70, and *Reliance*, page 261.
yard— is a spar on which square sails, lateen sails, and lugger sails are bent.
yardarm— outer part of yard between tip and lift attach. "Hang the rascals from the yardarms", was the cry. Would you nominate any politicians?
yardarm to yardarm— square riggers alongside with yardarms touching.
yard slings— fixed non-lowering masts had a metal truss and a short chain sling in the center for support. **lifts** went from masthead to outer ends of the yards to square or change the angle of the yards., page 288.
yarns— are fibers twisted into yarns to make rope, page 184.
ya **yare**— prepared, prompt, eager, lively.
yawl— two-masted sailboat with after mast stepped behind rudder post,267.
to yaw—overpowered sailboat having a hard time steering a steady course in a rough sea with high swells on quarter or stern, pages 153-5.
yellow flag— signifies a vessel is in quarantine— keep clear.
yeoman— naval vessel rating, assistant to storekeeper or navigation officer.
yeoman— midshipman in the Royal Navy.

Z **Z**- international code flag, "I require a tug".
zulu— a double-ended, two-masted Scottish fishing lugger with a long bowsprit and a long boomkin of 1880 period. It may just be a dusty museum model but I'll be darned to finish a 38 page glossary without a letter Z .

Numerous times while producing this glossary I remembered the term **mirage**— ***seeing something that wasn't there.*** It was necessary to have continuous spirited discussions with Lever, Freudenstein, and other sailing language experts as we tried to sift and choose the best of present working sailing terms, with those of Lever over 160 years ago.

We let our glossary grow on its own to provide operational sailing terms in our book for modern sailing craft. When readers begin to wonder about sailing in the past, they can also learn more of our proud sailing heritage.

FINIS

An old Chinese proverb states, *"A picture is worth a thousand words".*

Modern sailing terms. The best way to learn our strange foreign language used today, is with illustrations listed below.

The largest of northern ocean-going junks a thousand years ago was the **pechili trading junk** requiring a crew of 300.

• HULL TERMS

• KEELS and BOARDS

• the MAINSAIL

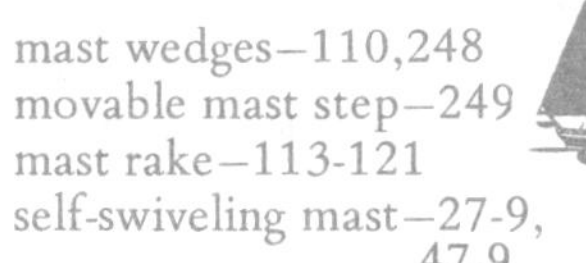

the JIB

the MAST

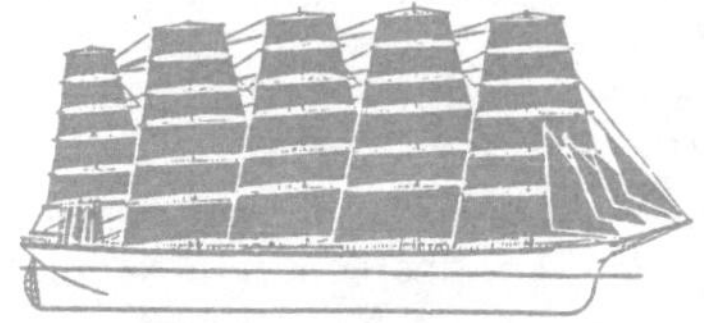

the SPINNAKER

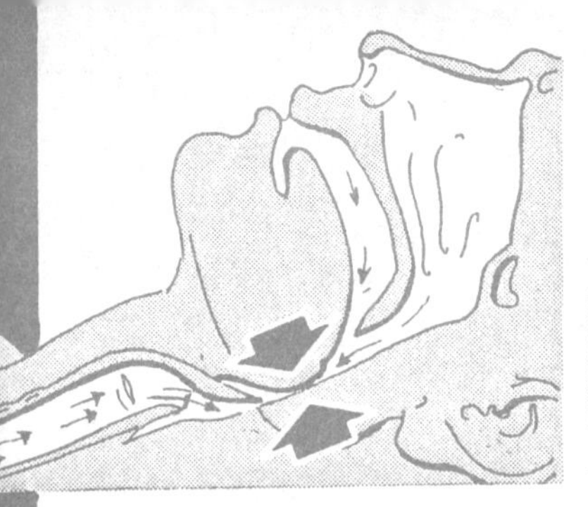

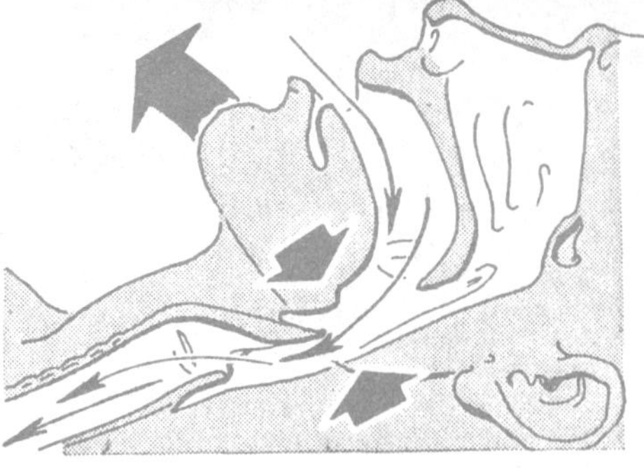

Drowning is the third major cause of accidental U.S. fatalities with nonswimmers who fall overboard, a major boating contribution. Panic is immediate followed by trying to holler for help underwater.

- **The throat is a one-way valve** with the back of the tongue pressing against and blocking the upper air passageway involved in suffocation, drownings, and heart attacks. Many auto deaths are caused by an airway obstruction,shock, or respiratory arrest, NOT primary injuries.
- **The throat must be opened immediately** by pulling or pushing the jaw so air can be inhaled...and exhaled from the lungs.
- **Air must be forced into the lungs** by mouth to mouth, or mouth to nose.

Few people seem interested in artificial respiration which is simple to understand and apply. Then with startling swiftness a drowning victim's life is in your hands, or the situation reversed with you the victim. Will your sailing friends or family be able to help you?

- The **timing cycle is critical.** Adults may have irreversible brain damage in 4 to 6 minutes from oxygen starvation, while damage occurs much more rapidly with small children and infants with smaller lungs.
- **Before you start**— clear victims mouth and air passage, then force air into an adults lungs. Give an adult victim **four quick breaths** without an interruption. Take a deep breath (twice normal), then open the victim's mouth and begin forcing air into his lungs.
- **If the heart has stopped**— which is determined after the artificial respiration procedure has started, CPR is required.
- **CPR** (cardiopulmonary resuscitation) **training?** Are CPR classes offered by hospitals or other organizations in your area? Please take a course which will not require much time so you are able to act immediately if required to help a heart attack, or drowning victim.

Emergency Care— Robert J. Brady Company, Bowie, MD 20715. It is used to teach police, firemen, and rescue units. A copy protected in a zip-lock bag should be aboard sailboats and powerboats going offshore, and a second in the home library as you never know when it is needed.

Artificial Respiration

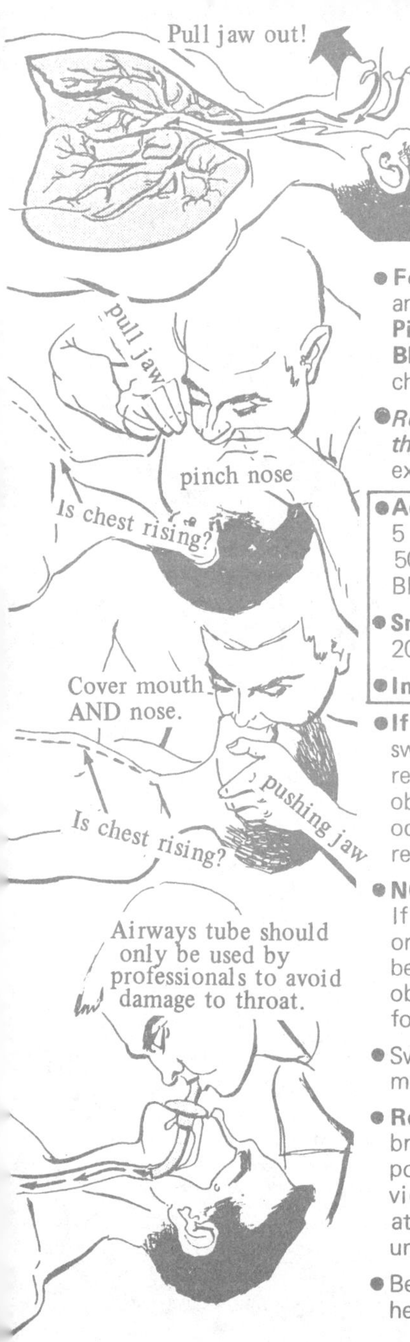

- **Tilt head to break the air block** so chin points 45 degrees upward.
- **Push/pull jaw** to lift tongue from back of throat to open throat.
- **Force air in** by opening your mouth and place it tightly over victims mouth. **Pinch adult's nose** to make a tight seal. **Blow forcefully** to make the victim's chest rise.
- *Remove your mouth, turn your head to the side.* Can you hear or feel an air exchange with an **outward rush of air?**
- **Adult breathing cycle**– is once every 5 seconds (count 1000 2000 3000 4000 5000) or approximately 12 per minute. Blow forcefully and vigorously.
- **Small child**– use normal breath pressure 20 times per minute or every 3 seconds.
- **Infant**--use small puffs from your cheeks.
- **If obstruction exists**– drowning victim swallows some **water** and if **food** is regurgitated from the stomach, it will obstruct the air passage. If vomiting occurs, turn victim on side, wipe mouth, reposition victim, continue blowing.
- **NO air exchange?** Check head and jaw. If not successful—turn victim quickly on his side. Hit several sharp blows between shoulder blades to dislodge obstruction, reposition, and continue forced air cycle. Occasionally—
- Sweep your fingers through victim's mouth to remove any foreign matter.
- **Recovery**– continue **cycle** till victim breathes freely. Keep him quiet as possible till breathing regularly. Cover victim with blanket so body temperature doesn't go down. Treat for shock until medical help arrives.
- Beach drownings also occur from heart attacks and sun strokes.

Sailing Illustrated

Powerboating Illustrated

Contents

INDEX to 97 VESSELS

☛ *Clipper ship wind force reefing sequence, page 137.*

Yankee clipper ship building boom though only lasting from 1848 to 1858, had much publicity. Also see pages 210-3, 282, and 287.

Clippers were the first sailing vessels having to pay their way with speed by operating their wooden hulls, flax sails, and hemp rigging for long periods to maximum limits. They carried bulky but light cargo such as tea or wool with limited storage area. When passengers were added they became ***packets.***

Sailing vessels had to pay for their operation, crew, and maintenance, plus making enough profit for an owner to build a similar vessel ten years later.

Sailors had a risky life with a quarter of clippers lost in their first ten years. Some sank on reefs, and some were pounded to pieces on rocky coasts. Others just vanished after the cargo caught on fire... or being rolled in heavy weather when caught aback and/ or the cargo shifted.

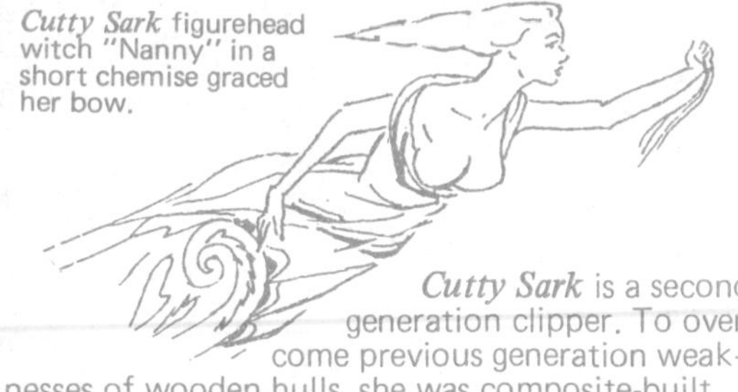

Cutty Sark figurehead witch "Nanny" in a short chemise graced her bow.

Cutty Sark is a second generation clipper. To overcome previous generation weaknesses of wooden hulls, she was composite-built with diagonal plates added in stress areas across the iron frames, beams, and stringers..

Cutty Sark, one of eleven clippers launched 1869, had her share of groundings and hurricane damage. Her coal cargo shifted in 1915 with decks awash in heavy weather. Topgallant masts were cut away, and when on beams end and almost submerged, the mainmast was cut down to save her. She righted, the wreckage was cleared, and she was towed to Capetown. She was rerigged as a barkentine due to wartime lumber shortage for her yards.

She was opened to the public in 1957. Only the *Cutty Sark* remains of her high-performance racing sisters to show the grace, beauty, and fullness of her glory in the golden age of sail when the beautiful clippers roamed the seven seas.

We were sorry to learn of the passing of George Campbell in June 1988. It was his excellent detailing that required thousands of hours to complete, which helped guide me thru the maze and complexity of *his Cutty Sark* we show on these pages.

Sailing Illustrated

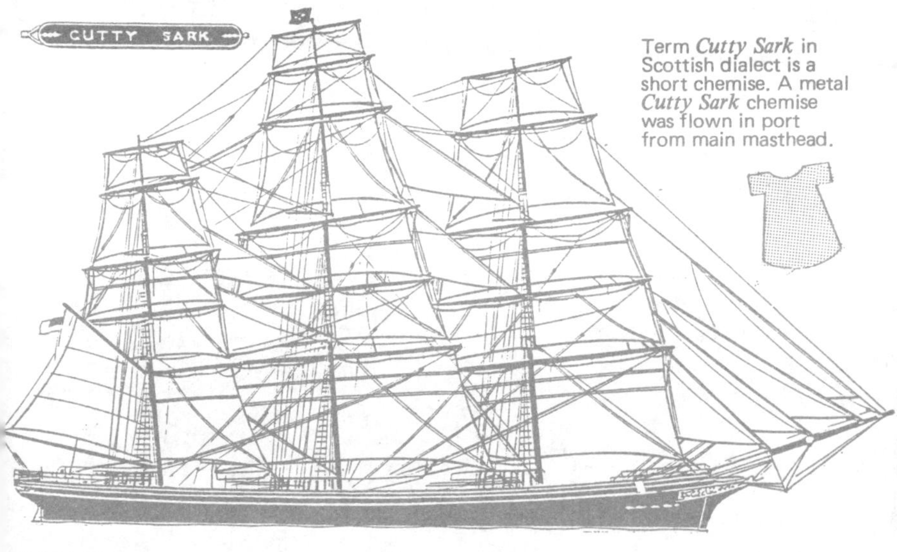

Term *Cutty Sark* in Scottish dialect is a short chemise. A metal *Cutty Sark* chemise was flown in port from main masthead.

Cutty Sark, *the only surviving clipper ship, is shown with her witch figurehead holding the remnant of a horse's tail, was 120 years old in 1989. She is preserved by* **the Cutty Sark society**, *a group of individuals contributing time and money to preserve their sailing heritage for future generations.*

We added more pages to our book to expand information on square riggers, as a personal goal since a young teenager, was to make illustrations of the **Cutty Sark**. *Their approval was given, sending beautiful illustrations of her in the return mail we list, which may be desired by many readers.*

- **Max Millar**– produced a magnificent 30″ x 22″ line illustration of her which you often see reproduced in various sailing books.
- **David Ditcher**– made a beautiful 23″ x 17″ perspective illustration of the **Cutty Sark** underway. Many sails are reefed to show her rigging.
- **George F. Campbell, M.R.I.N.A.**– produced three excellent details with his Sail Plan, Rigging Plan, and General Arrangement Plan. Each is approximately 30″ x 25½″, products of a master marine draftsman.

All are collector items for framing to display in offices, yacht clubs, your nautical den at home ...plus the special occasion or birthday gift. They may be obtained on board the **Cutty Sark**, *or by post on application to–*
The Master, The **Cutty Sark**, *Greenwich, London, S.E.10., England.*

Our thanks to **the Cutty Sark society** *for preserving this unique, extreme clipper ship, the last of a sailing era a century ago, and for their help to us. Expect differences among details by draftsmen detailing a clipper ship that sailed for 50 years, and those of artists, all trying to show the* **Cutty Sark** *to the best of their ability... including this author.*

Sailing Illustrated

CUTTY SARK

Cutty Sark was launched in 1869 in Scotland, at Dumbarton on the Clyde. She is composite-built with a strong iron skeleton of ribs, beams, diagonal plates, and supports, with strong 6″ thick teak

Cutty Sark— hard on the wind— force 5, port tack, all plain sails.

LOA— 280 feet

registered length, length between perpendiculars— 212′ 5″

beam— 36 feet
tea cargo draft— 17′ 6″
wool cargo draft— 20 feet
2,100 tons—21′ draft displacement
hold depth—21 feet
registered net tonnage— 921 tons
gross tonnage— 963 tons

sail area with 29 sails set, ¾ acre or approx. 32,000 sq. ft.

max. crew including officers was 28, minimum crew of 19 in the wool trade

maximum speed— 17 to 17½ knots

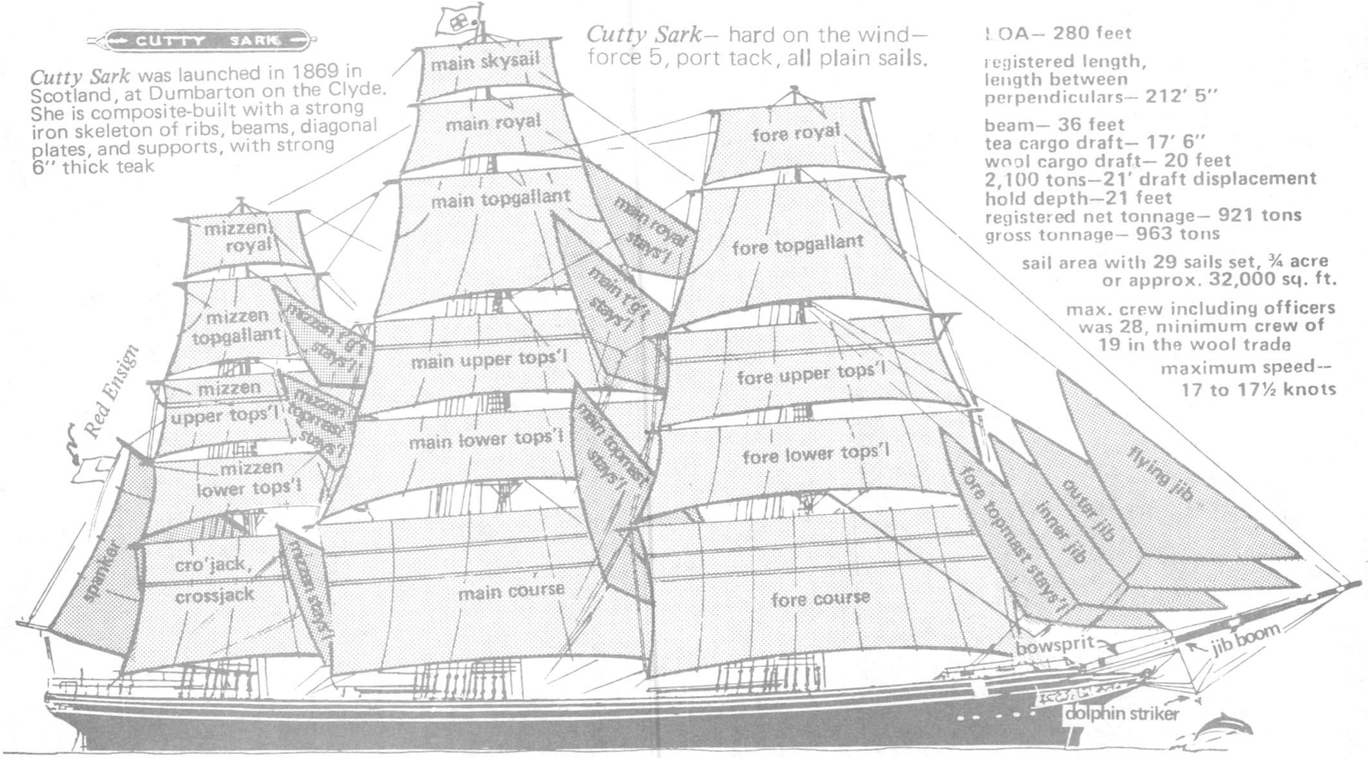

Cutty Sark was an excellent compromise for the tea clipper trade. Visitors see her today as she was in her early years in her home port of London between voyages in her tall rig to set records. All standing rigging is set up taut, her running rigging still rove, her sails unbent and stowed.

Her sail plan was reduced in 1880 to become a worldwide cargo carrier. She was driven hard for 50 years as she roamed the oceans of the world to make a profit by delivering cargo. She made fifteen wool

main yard— 78′ long
spanker boom— 52′ long

main mast from deck to truck— 145′ 9″

We show *Cutty Sark* not as a model nor museum, but in modern sailing approach as though she were alive and able to reach her full sailing potentials today.

Cutty Sark— hard on the wind, force 5 (17-21 knots), starb'd tack, all plain sails.

Copper bottom sheets prevented barnacle and weed growth. Wood planking is an insulator. This protected the iron framework by eliminating the corrosive action of copper bottom sheets.

Her nickname while operating for 27 years under the Portugese flag was— *El Pequina Camisola* (short chemise).

We show *Cutty Sark* moving in a force 5 from both forward, and aft side of her sails for your analysis.

She was an extreme clipper (with narrower hull requiring deeper draft for stability), a powerful hull that could drive well to windward. She was at her best standing hard driving downwind in heavy following seas with speeds up to 17½ knots. This provides a speed-length ratio of $1.2\sqrt{WL}$ for her 212′ Load Waterline Length, formula page 140.

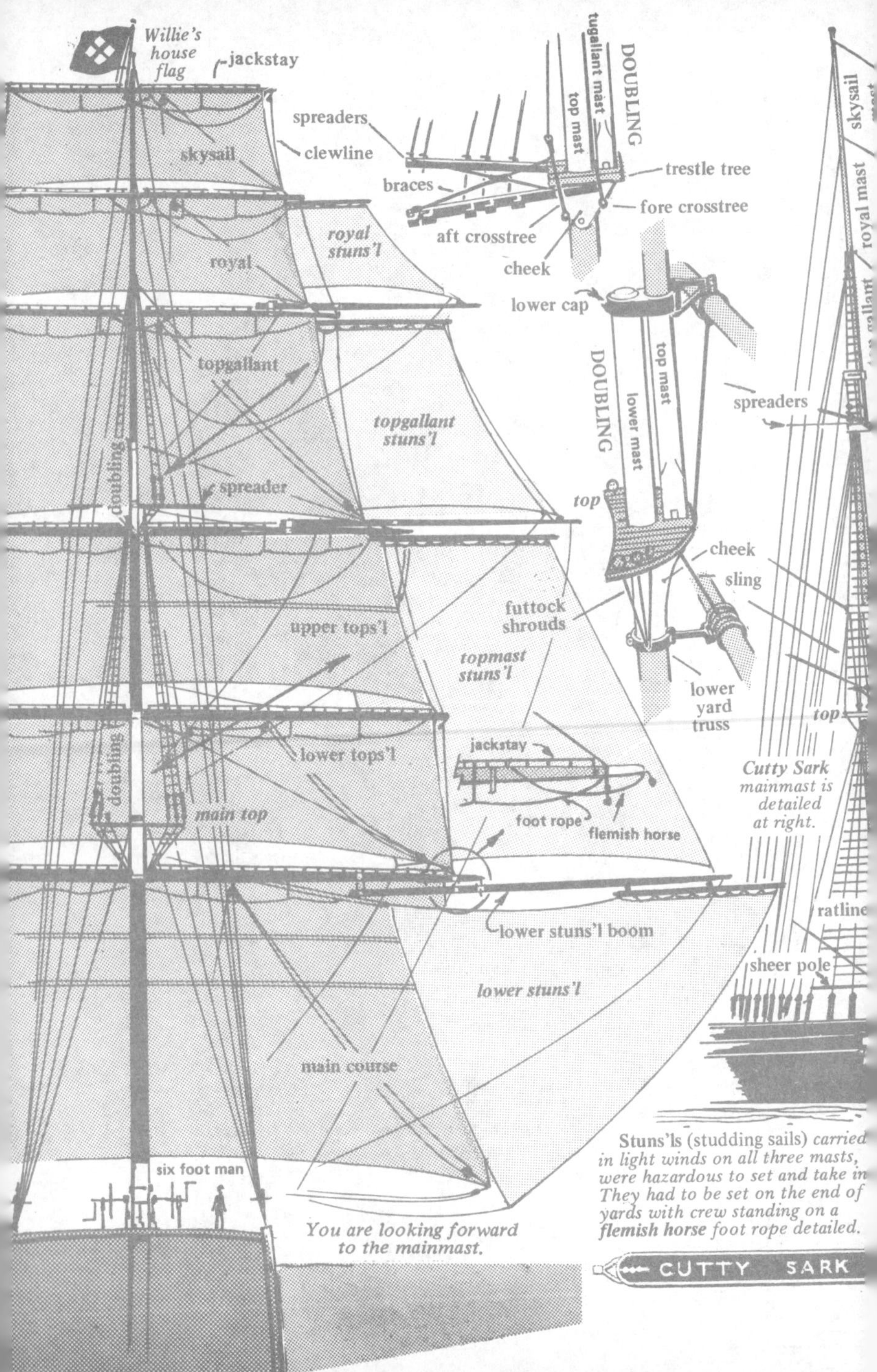

You are looking forward to the mainmast.

Stuns'ls (studding sails) *carried in light winds on all three masts, were hazardous to set and take in. They had to be set on the end of yards with crew standing on a* **flemish horse** *foot rope detailed.*

pg. 232	pg. 233
sailboat right-of-way	powerboat right-of-way

pg. 242	pg. 243
commercial vessels signals daytcme and nighttime underway and anchored	

Right-of Way Chart, 8 ½ x 11 Commercial Vessel Chart, 8½ x 11

Diamond Coated protection for much handling, 3 hole punch-- $4.00 each. We intended to laminate our charts. When we found they would have to retail around $10.00, we realized it was more practical for owners to laminate their charts if desired as lamination potentials are rapidly increasing nationwide. We are very sorry the non-lamination decision was made after printing our **Sail Course**, a mistake to help most readers.

Since a collision at sea can upset the captain's entire afternoon, carry BOTH charts aboard for quick reference in busy waterways and harbors... **"to take appropiate action in time to maneuver out of a collision"**. The practice of Admiralty Law in its basic form, is to AVOID collisions, and ALL potentials of collisions.

- **Right-of-Way Chart** covers powerboat operation on one side, and sailboat operation on the other for day and night reference. International and Inland Rules define the **give way** and **hold course** vessels, easy for crew and friends to use when operating your vessel.

- **Commercial Vessel Warnings,** all 27 situations have one meaning, Keep Clear. Day and night warnings are for commercial craft to avoid **as they have minimum or NO manuverability** underway, adrift, aground, or at anchor.

- FIRE-- **Cause and Prevention.** 8½ x 11. Diamond Coated. $4.00 each.

This chart was started to help boat operators, then this chart decided to go many directions as the foundation has endless applications.

The Fire Chart has equal applications in homes, kitchens, garages, shops, your auto, electrical, and electronic equipment fires. Spare time for five months dragged on to research and report what we thought would be simple answers... such as the **self-ignition temperatures** of 16 basic items.

With TV fires involved in over 15% of home fires, ask your friends how they would put out a TV fire... then a butane or LPG fire.

ROYCE'S
sailing
illustrated
course
sailors helping sailors

Royce's Sailing Illustrated

368 pages $12.00

ISBN 0-911284-00-1

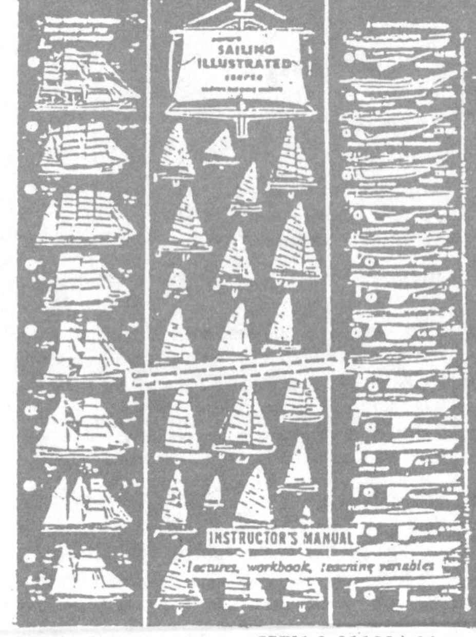

100 pages

ISBN 0-911284-01-X

Learn the full spectrum of sailing from square riggers to modern sailboats with our new 100 page *Sailing Illustrated Course.* The course can be taught by any organization, with seven 2½ hour lectures plus ample homework, as well as on-the-water public and private sailing lessons. Individuals can learn sailing on their own at their own speed, living hundreds of miles from the ocean as word for word lecture material is included. Reference text is the latest edition of Royce's *Sailing Illustrated.*

30 year testing began in 1960 with the Long Beach Coast Guard Auxiliary. They taught evening c[asses for ten years using large charts provided by the author. Similar evening sail classes open to the public, began at the same time in Newport Beach lasting over ten years. Local sailors handled our lectures adding variety, as well as sailboat designers, sail makers, marine surveyors, and many other sailing experts.

The final version was expanded by the author adding more charts to cover nationwide standards, plus your sailing heritage. Ample charts now provide flexibility for coastal instructors teaching cruising and racing, to inland dinghy sailing on lakes and rivers The sail course would be excellent for Sea Scout use anywhere in the U.S.

Sailboat charter companies can assign potential customers homework with our sail course reducing time and training costs. Their customers will have a better standardized background to be prepared to become their own skipper in considerably less time.

Sailing Illustrated

The Best of All Sailing Worlds

Our Sail Course offered to readers after endless testing covers dinghies, cabin sailboats and square riggers. It provides an equal coverage to help active sailors... and heritage sailors.

Workbook pages—

1. 22 dinghies
2.-3. 39 sail rigs
4. 24 hull terms
5. sail, rigging terms
6. Sabot, Penguin
7. Lido 14, Snipe
8. Lightning
9. U.S. buoyage
10. tacks, courses
11. sailing rules
12. sail trim
13. sail trim variables
14. sailing closehauled
15. controlled mast bend
16. marlinspike
17. coming about, jibing
18. tide, current, fog
19. corrosion basics
20-23. marine hardware
24. pocket cruisers
25. raise/lower sails
26-27. docking methods
28-29. *Finisterre*
30. Catalina 30
31. Catalina 38
32. spinnakers
33. gaff/lug rigs
34. disp. hull speed ratios
35. wind force
36. U.S. westerlies, thunderstorms, dusters
37. capsize, recovery
38. sailing worldwide
39. *Cutty Sark*
40. 9 square rigs
41. *USCG Eagle*
42. commercial vessels
43. power Right-of-Way
44-45. commercial vessel signals and lights
46. clouds, proverbs
47. sailboat balance
48. workbook index and lecture sequence

An all-purpose adult sail course. Factors required are concentration to listen to lecturers, taking notes, and finishing homework. Our testing found age 15 to be the minimum limit.

Evening classroom testing, was continuous for ten years open to the public in Newport Beach and Long Beach. Continuous input came from instructors and students with periodic additions and revisions.

When tight docking questions developed, instructors helped us develop 30 tight situations on workbook pages 27 and 28. Students afterwards will have a better chance to handle tight docking problems.

On-the-water testing was with full-day lessons by the author with over 1600 students to test the same course materials on one, two, and three hulls. Almost anything that could go wrong... did.

The final testing version began leisurely after 1986 working with new sailors owning or chartering a variety of sailboats 26' to 36' long.

The 100 page Sail Course is required by all instructors, and those wanting to learn sailing on their own, plus the reference text *Sailing Illustrated*, latest edition.

A separate 48 page workbook with self cover, can be ordered in volume by various organizations. Their own additional cover can be added if desired.

The 100 page Sail Course includes the 48 page workbook, the remaining pages cover a variety of information for instructors with most of the seven 2½ hour lectures word for word. Also— starting sail classes in your area or organization, age groups, developing sail instructors, publicity ideas, industry members to contact to help you, plus ways to help Sea Scouts in your area.

16 hour weekend seminars with the Sail Course is an excellent method to develop instructor staffs.

Private sailing lessons— instructors have flexibility to assign homework before lessons on the water for dinghies to a variety of cabin sailboats.

Homework assignments are essential to cover the large number of sailing terms and ideas in 7 short weeks. Eleven full pages include standing and running rigging terms to be added to five dinghies, six cabin sailboats from 22' to 38', plus the famous square riggers *Cutty Sark* and the *USCG Eagle*.

Welcor
of basi
with o

Sailing Illustrated